ROWND ⊙ ROWND

yn dathlu'r

30

Diolch i

Dafydd Nant (ffotoNant)

Siôn Land a Ffion Elin Davies

Cedron a Lefi yn Y Lolfa

Y cyfranwyr i gyd

Y ffans triw

Pob aelod o gast a chriw *Rownd a Rownd* dros y blynyddoedd, gan gofio'n annwyl a hiraethus am y rhai 'dan ni wedi eu colli ar hyd y daith.

ROWND A ROWND

yn dathlu'r

30

Llio Non (gol.)

Argraffiad cyntaf: 2025
© Hawlfraint S4C, Rondo Media a'r Lolfa Cyf., 2025

Dymuna'r cyhoeddwyr gydnabod cymorth ariannol
Cyngor Llyfrau Cymru

Cynllun y clawr: Siôn Eifion Land

Lluniau: Archif S4C a Dafydd Nant (ffotoNant)

Rhif Llyfr Rhyngwladol: 978 1 80099 762 2

Cyhoeddwyd, rhwymwyd ac argraffwyd yng Nghymru gan
Y Lolfa Cyf., Talybont, Ceredigion SY24 5HE
gwefan www.ylolfa.com
e-bost ylolfa@ylolfa.com
ffôn 01970 832 304

Rhagair

Geraint Evans
(Prif Weithredwr S4C)

Wrth sgwrsio â gwylwyr S4C, lle bynnag fydda i, dwi'n aml yn clywed pobl yn dweud cymaint maen nhw'n mwynhau gwylio *Rownd a Rownd*. Mae hi'n gyfres i'w thrysori, gan ei bod yn cynnig rhywbeth i gynulleidfa o bob oed, a'r cymeriadau a'r straeon doniol a dwys yn denu gwylwyr ffyddlon.

Mae'n anodd credu bod 30 mlynedd ers i *Rownd a Rownd* ddod i'r sgrin fel cyfres sebon i bobl ifanc, gyda phenodau deuddeg munud o hyd oedd yn canolbwyntio ar helyntion pobl ifanc ar rownd bapur.

Dri degawd yn ddiweddarach, mae hi wedi prifio ac aeddfedu, ac erbyn hyn yn un o gonglfeini amserlen oriau brig S4C. Tra bo rhai'n darogan bod dyddiau operâu sebon yn prysur ddiflannu wrth i arferion gwylio newid, mae *Rownd a Rownd* yn parhau i fod yn un o gyfresi mwyaf poblogaidd S4C ar blatfformau digidol.

Y nod gwreiddiol oedd apelio at gynulleidfaoedd ifanc, ac mae hi'n gyfres sy'n dal i ddenu cyfraddau gwylio uwch na'r arfer ymysg plant, pobl ifanc rhwng 16 a 24 oed, a'r rhai llai hyderus eu Cymraeg.

Beth sydd mor arbennig amdani? Wel mae hi'n fwy na chyfres deledu.

Mae hi'n cynnig portread o fywyd bob dydd – y profiadau, yr iaith a'r cymeriadau sy'n adlewyrchu cymaint o gymunedau Cymraeg gogledd Cymru. Dros y blynyddoedd mae ei straeon wedi trafod themâu dwys – iechyd meddwl, colled, cyfeillgarwch – mewn ffordd sensitif a realistig, ochr yn ochr â straeon a chymeriadau llawn hiwmor, a hynny oll mewn Cymraeg naturiol, agos-atoch.

Mae cenhedlaeth gyfan o wylwyr wedi tyfu i fyny gyda'r gyfres, ac mae hi wedi bod yn feithrinfa ar gyfer actorion, ysgrifenwyr, cynhyrchwyr a thechnegwyr yng ngogledd Cymru; a gwych oedd gweld y doniau hynny yn trosglwyddo eu sgiliau o sebon i fyd tywyll carchar, gyda chyfres bwerus *Bariau* yn denu cynulleidfaoedd newydd i S4C.

Mae cwmni Rondo wedi sefydlu cartre arbennig yn Sir Fôn. Mae'n fusnes sy'n cefnogi amcan S4C i fod yn fwy na sianel deledu, i ddatblygu sgiliau, swyddi a budd economaidd ar draws Cymru.

Wrth nodi carreg filltir mor bwysig â 30 mlynedd, rydym yn dathlu cyfraniad diwylliannol *Rownd a Rownd*, a chyfres arbennig iawn sy'n tynnu teuluoedd at ei gilydd ar y soffa i fwynhau drama ac adloniant yn y Gymraeg.

Rownd a Rownd (yn 30 oed)

I blant, â hithau'n blentyn – *Rownd a Rownd*
    Oedd yn driw o'r cychwyn;
   Heno hi sydd tipyn hŷn,
   Yn aelwyd i'r oedolyn.

Robin Evans
(Cyd-sylfaenydd y Gyfres)

2 – Sue Waters
(Cyd-sylfaenydd y Gyfres)
6 Mis yn Troi'n 30 Mlynedd

Roedd Robin Evans a finnau wedi bod yn cynhyrchu *Gemau Heb Ffiniau*, gyda nifer o wledydd eraill Ewrop, ers 1990; ond pan benodwyd prif weithredwr newydd yn S4C, ym 1994, fe ddaeth hefyd newid yn strategaeth y Sianel. Doedd dim mwy o gyd-gynhyrchu'r *Gemau* i fod, er i'r gyfres barhau yn llwyddiannus am nifer o flynyddoedd wedyn, ar y cyfandir.

Roedd yr 'year planner' ar wal ein swyddfa yn Ffilmiau'r Nant, o ganlyniad, yn wag ym Medi '94.

Tua'r un pryd, fodd bynnag, dyma dendr yn ymddangos gan Adran Blant S4C. Roedd y Sianel eisiau cyfres ddrama "sebon i blant."

Fe gynigiodd 13 o gwmnïau am y gwaith, ni yn Nant yn eu plith. Ar ôl ystyried y ceisiadau, fe wahoddwyd tri chwmni i gynhyrchu rhaglen beilot – ac roedd *Rownd a Rownd* yn un o'r rheiny.

Roedd Phil Redmond (cynhyrchydd *Grange Hill*, *Brookside* a *Hollyoaks*) ar y panel dewis, a'i eiriau ef wrth gynghori S4C oedd, "You've only been offered one soap." *Rownd a Rownd* oedd honno.

Fe ddaeth y syniad o sebon am bobl ifanc ar rownd bapur yn sgil siarad gyda lot o blant a phobl ifanc. Roedd pob un ohonyn nhw yn gofyn i ni beidio â chreu drama mewn ysgol yn unig, nac ychwaith, yn ymwneud â chyffuriau yn ormodol. Wrth greu sebon oedd yn seiliedig ar rowndiau papur, roedd y bobl ifanc yn gweithio ac yn ennill eu harian eu hunain – ac roedd yn ein galluogi i fynd o gwmpas y dref a'r cyffiniau. Oedd, roedd potensial y straeon yn ddiddiwedd. Gallai fynd ymlaen am byth, sef prif hanfod opera sebon!

Aethpwyd ati, felly, i recordio rhaglen beilot 1/4 awr mewn penwythnos. Yn ogystal, roedd yn ofynnol i ni greu sgerbwd stori ar gyfer 26 pennod

1/4 awr i'w dilyn. Cefin Roberts, Robin a finnau fu'n gweithio ar y "stori-leins" hynny – llosgi dau ben y gannwyll efo lot fawr o goffi yn hen festri Moreia Caernarfon, swyddfa Ffilmiau'r Nant ar y pryd. Y diweddar Gareth F Williams oedd awdur y peilot a ddaeth wedyn yn bennod gyntaf, gydag ychydig o newidiadau i'r sgript. Roedd y rhaglen beilot yn rhy fyr! Bu newidiadau i'r cast hefyd, ar ôl y peilot, am amryw resymau.

Ionawr y 10fed 1995 – diwrnod fy mhenblwydd, digwydd bod: dyna'r dyddiad y cawson ni wybod fod *Rownd a Rownd* yn mynd i weld golau dydd. Wedi hynny, bu chwe mis gwyllt-wallgo o sgwennu, castio, criwio ac adeiladu set yng nghanol tref Porthaethwy. Ac,

F
F
I
L
M
I
A
U'
R

N
A
N
T

Swyddfa Ffilmiau'r Nant yn hen festri Capel Moreia, Caernarfon

yn wyrthiol, fe ddarlledwyd y bennod gyntaf ddechrau Medi.

Dewiswyd Porthaethwy fel 'cartref' y gyfres nid yn unig am fod lleoliad addas gwag ar werth, ond am fod y dref yn cynnig cymaint – yn siopau, caffis, gwesty, tafarndai, garej, ysgolion… pob math o leoliadau a fyddai'n cynnig eu hunain i ffilmio cyfres deledu. Heb anghofio Pont y Borth a'r Fenai! Londrét oedd yr unig le y bu'n rhaid i ni ei adeiladu yn ei grynswth. A chan fod gan Borthaethwy dai cyngor, tai hynod o foethus, drud, a thai rhent (i fyfyrwyr Bangor yn bennaf), roedd yn rhoi'r cyfle i'n straeon ni ddangos pob haen o gymdeithas.

Ar ôl ennill y tendr, aeth Robin a finnau i dreulio diwrnod gyda Phil Redmond a'i wraig Alexis yn eu pencadlys yn Sir Gaer lle'r oedden nhw'n cynhyrchu *Brookside* a *Hollyoaks*. Fe gawson ni sawl tip amhrisiadwy gan y Redmonds. Un gwerthfawr oedd bod angen trin y gymdeithas leol gyda pharch, bob amser: cynnal boreau coffi / diwrnodau agored, fel bod y cymdogion yn teimlo eu bod yn rhan o'r holl beth.

Adeilad set Glanrafon cyn ei drawsnewid

Set Glanrafon wedi'i thrawsnewid

Côt dda o baent!

Siop Bob Beics ar ei newydd wedd

"I don't think you realise the monster you've created. But you soon will!" oedd geiriau – a rhybudd – Phil Redmond. Mor wir y llefarodd! Roedd Phil ac Alexis hefyd yn meddwl mai syniad gwallgof oedd creu set ynghanol tref, er i ni'n dau geisio eu darbwyllo y byddai'r cast a'r criw yn cael llonydd gennym ni yng Nghymru. Diolch i'r drefn, ni oedd yn iawn, ac fe aeth bywyd Porthaethwy yn ei flaen heb gymryd lot o sylw ohonom ni'n creu a chynhyrchu *Rownd a Rownd*.

Mae'n diolch ni'n fawr i Meirion Davies, comisiynydd plant S4C, ar y pryd, am gredu ynom ni a'n cefnogi dros y blynyddoedd. Ei weledigaeth ef oedd creu sebon i blant ar S4C. Wedi hynny, mae ein diolch i Deryk Williams (y pennaeth rhaglenni) a Phil Redmond am ddewis ein cynnig ni!

Dennis Pritchard Jones oedd cyfarwyddwr y bennod gyntaf oll gan Gareth F. Daeth y rhan fwyaf o'r actorion oed ysgol o Ysgol Glanaethwy, a mawr yw ein diolch i Cefin a Rhian yn fanno – a'r Adran Addysg, ar y pryd – am ein cefnogi 100%. Nid felly pob athro ysgol, fodd bynnag!

Criw yn dathlu

Criw ysgrifennu
Cefn (chwith i'r dde):
Lowri Hughes,
Tony Llewelyn,
Kristy Roberts,
Merfyn Pierce Jones,
Llio Non a
Graham Jones

Blaen:
Sue Waters
a Robin Evans

Dim ond chwe mis ac un gyfres oedd y cytundeb gwreiddiol, ond er gwaetha'r holl "amheuwyr" ar ddechrau'r daith – ac wedi hynny (ac roedd 'na nifer fawr ohonyn nhw) – mae *Rownd a Rownd* yn dal yma, ddeng mlynedd ar hugain yn ddiweddarach.

Mae bwystfil Borth yn dal i ruo!

SGANIWCH!
Teitlau Agoriadol RaR dros y blynyddoedd…

11

3 – Cefin Roberts
(Awdur Gwreiddiol)

Cig ar yr Asgwrn

Roedd Ysgol Glanaethwy yn dathlu ei phen-blwydd yn bump oed pan ges wahoddiad gan Robin Evans a Sue Waters, nôl ym 1995 i fynd draw i swyddfa Ffilmiau'r Nant i weithio ar ryw egin syniad am opera sebon newydd i S4C. O fy mlaen yr oedd sgerbwd o stori am siop bapur newydd a phedwar o blant yn gwneud rownd bapur foreol; eu hynt a'u helynt hwy fyddai llinyn arian y gyfres. "Fedri di roi cig ar

asgwrn honna?" oedd y frawddeg a roddodd wyth mlynedd o gydweithio hyfryd gyda'r ddau gynhyrchydd ar y gyfres *Rownd a Rownd*.

Bu cryn ddathlu draw yng Nghaernarfon y noson y clywson ni ein bod wedi ennill y tendr. Ond fel pob dathliad o'r fath, byrhoedlog iawn barodd y miri. Roedd angen rhoi trwyn ar y maen yn syth bìn gan greu lleoliadau, cymeriadau, sefyllfaoedd, straeon a mwy i gyfres a ddatblygodd yn un o raglenni mwyaf poblogaidd S4C erbyn heddiw.

Gan mai cast o blant a phobl ifanc oedd canolbwynt y gyfres yn wreiddiol, roedd yn her aruthrol i greu peiriant i gynhyrchu cymeriadau i actorion ifanc oedd yn mynd a dod o'r gyfres yn gyson. Natur y rhan fwyaf o operâu sebon yw fod y sêr, sef y prif gymeriadau, yn aros yn y cyfresi hynny am flynyddoedd lawer. Ond buan iawn y tyfai'r actorion ifanc gan symud ymlaen i golegau neu yrfaoedd eraill. Roedd yn rhaid cael 'bugeiliaid newydd' yn gyson iawn i neidio ar eu beics a pharhau i'w rowndio hi o gwmpas Glanrafon a strydoedd Porthaethwy.

Contract Pennod 1, Cyfres 1
a'r cast gwreiddiol

Ond dwi ddim yn meddwl y caech chi well lleoliad ar gyfer cyfres o'i bath yn unman. Roedd ganddon ni'n môr a'r mynydd, y dref a'r wlad, y bont a'r rheilffordd i gyd at ein gwasanaeth. Ac fe gawson ni gnwd ar ôl cnwd o dalent ifanc i ddiwallu pob galw am gast a ymddangosai'n flynyddol fel mwyar ar wrychoedd y straeon.

Braf yw gwbod fod y gyfres yn dal i ddod 'rownd' bob blwyddyn. Braf hefyd i ryw hen begor o sgriptiwr yw gweld fod rhai o'r 'hen' fugeiliaid a greais ac a flodeuodd dros y blynyddoedd yn dal i grwydro hen strydoedd y Borth. Ambell un ohonyn nhw wedi cychwyn yn y gyfres fel plant (bach iawn) ond sydd bellach â'u teuluoedd eu hunain yn y gyfres ac sy'n cadw'r hen olwynion yna i droi o hyd. Dwi wir yn teimlo fel hen daid yn gwylio'i wyrion yn tyfu ac yn symud yn 'u blaena.

Ond os mai fi ydi un o hen deidiau'r gyfres, yn sicr Dewi Pws oedd tad y gyfres, heb os. Fe gadwodd Dewi ysbryd hwyliog y rhaglen i fynd am flynyddoedd lawer. Dychmygwch fod yn blentyn ar set a chael gweithio am flynyddoedd efo creadur mor unigryw.

Dymunaf ben-blwydd hapus iawn i gyfres a roddodd imi'r hyder a'r profiad fel sgwennwr i fentro 'mhellach i fyd sgriptio a dyfeisio ar gyfer teledu, ac am fod yn feithrinfa i gymaint o actorion ifanc sy'n dal i'n hadlonni flynyddoedd ar ôl iddyn nhw neidio oddi ar eu beics a dechrau hedfan yn eu gyrfaoedd. Hip-ip! Hwrê!

4 – Angharad Llwyd
(Sophie Phillips/Barclay/Roberts…!)

Dysgu gan y Gorau

Mae stori Sophie yn dechrau ym 1997, pan o'n i yn y chweched dosbarth – ar fin gorffen lefel A. Roedd Nain wedi gweld hysbyseb yn *Golwg* yn chwilio am actorion ar gyfer *Rownd a Rownd*, felly es i amdani, a chael clyweliad llwyddiannus! Ro'n i wrth fy modd yn cael ymuno efo'r gyfres boblogaidd, fel Sophie Phillips.

Yr atgof cyntaf sydd gen i ydi golygfa yn hwfro'r siop, a Dennis Pritchard Jones, y cyfarwyddwr, yn tynnu 'nghoes i – gan ei bod yn amlwg nad oeddwn i wedi arfer helpu rhyw lawer rownd y tŷ, adra. Ro'n i'n hollol ddi-glem efo'r hwfyr, ac yn methu canolbwyntio ar gofio 'ngeiriau a hwfro 'run pryd… ac ro'n i'n mynd adra'r diwrnod hwnnw yn siŵr na faswn i'n para'n hir yn y gyfres!

Mi wnes setlo dipyn, wedi hynny, a dod yn ffrindiau mawr efo gweddill y cast a'r criw. Ac er bod sawl un wedi mynd a dod dros y blynyddoedd, maen nhw i gyd yn bobol sy'n agos iawn at fy nghalon.

Roedd y blynyddoedd cynnar yn rhai melys iawn, yn ffilmio ac yn dysgu llawer gan Elliw Haf (Glenda) a John Glyn (Terry) sy'n actio rhieni Sophie. Gyda'u cymorth nhw, mi wnes ddatblygu 'nghrefft o actio teledu, gan iddyn nhw gael cymaint o ddylanwad arna i ar y set – yn fy rhoi ar ben ffordd wrth feddwl am ystyr a deinameg golygfeydd. Maen nhw'n actorion profiadol a thrylwyr, yn hollol naturiol ac yn meddwl am bob manylyn, ac

Y chwiorydd… Manon, Sophie, Menna a Lucy
(Fflur Davies, Angharad, Sara Davies a Nerys Lewis)

felly ro'n i'n dysgu gan y gorau. Mae 'na natur chwareus yn John Glyn, ac mae chwerthiniad Elliw yn heintus; ond unwaith y byddai'r camera'n troi, fe fyddai'r ddau'n rhoi perfformiad perffaith, bob tro!

'Nôl yn y nawdegau, roedd chwiorydd Sophie yn amlwg yn y gyfres – sef Lucy (Nerys Lewis), Manon (Fflur Davies) a Menna (Sara Davies), ac roedd hi'n bleser cael actio efo nhw. Fe gawson ni straeon difyr tu hwnt, yn ffraeo a chymodi, ac roedd ein golygfeydd dros frecwast yn rhai digri iawn efo'r pedair ohonom ni'n tynnu'n groes, a Terry yn anwybyddu'r stŵr ac yn sglaffio ffrei-yp yn y cefndir trwy'r cwbl.

Doedd hi ddim yn hir nes i Sophie ddechrau cyboli efo cariadon – ac mae 'na sawl un wedi bod dros y blynyddoedd! Dwi'n meddwl mai Martin (Rhys ap Trefor) a'i feic modur oedd y cariad cyntaf, ond barodd y berthynas ddim yn hir iawn, a buan wedyn roedd llygaid Sophie ar Eifion (Martin Thomas)... oedd, yn anffodus, yn briod efo Gwenllïan (Bethan Hughes) – merch y gweinidog, ar y pryd! Roedd y rheini'n olygfeydd cyffrous, wrth i Sophie sleifio ei ffordd i galon Eifion a thorri calon Gwenllïan.

Roedd Eifion yn plesio Glenda, hefyd, a chyn hir roedden nhw'n trefnu priodas. Dwi'n cofio i'r stori honno fod yn un afaelgar tu hwnt, gan fod cymeriad Elfyn (Hefin Rees) wedi cyrraedd i fod yn was priodas i Eifion. Roedd 'na sbarc rhwng Sophie ac Elfyn o'r dechrau, ac fe ddaeth y stori i uchafbwynt wrth i Sophie ildio i'w theimladau a chael ffling efo'r gwas... noson cyn y briodas! Wna i fyth anghofio ffilmio pennod y briodas honno. Yn gynnar ar fore Mawrth oer ym mis Rhagfyr, roedd John Glyn a minnau yn teithio yn ein dillad priodas ar gart a cheffyl drwy Borthaethwy. Tra roedd pobol y pentref yn teithio heibio i'w gwaith, roedd John a fi yn rhewi'n gorn yn y cart, yn gweddïo y byddai'r ceffyl yn cyrraedd y capel yn reit handi!

Yn fuan wedi'r briodas, roedd Sophie yn disgwyl babi. Ond pwy oedd y tad?! Y gŵr newydd ynta'r gwas priodas?! Roedd hon yn stori fawr i mi, ac fe wnes i wir fwynhau'r ddrama a'r twyll a'r holl lanast ddaeth wedyn!

Mae gen i gof o ffilmio'r olygfa pan oedd Eifion yn ffeindio fod Sophie wedi bod yn anffyddlon. Roedd hyn yn y cyfnod ble roedden ni'n dechrau defnyddio ffonau symudol – a thrwy glywed neges ffôn gan Elfyn, daeth Eifion i wybod y cyfan. Roedd amseru'r neges ar gamera yn ddigon cymhleth bryd hynny – ac fe gymrodd sbel i'w gael yn gywir – ond, erbyn hyn, rydan ni'n defnyddio ffonau ymhob pennod, bron!

Ar fore Mawrth oer ym mis Rhagfyr...

Fel y disgwyl, nid Eifion oedd y dyn i Sophie, na chwaith Elfyn. Vince (Huw Llŷr) oedd y nesa ar y sîn – eto ar foto-beic! Dwi'n cofio diwrnod priodas Vince a Sophie ym Miwmares yn dda, gan 'mod i newydd ddarganfod 'mod i'n disgwyl babi ac yn teimlo'n reit sâl drwy'r dydd! Yn rhyfedd iawn, dyma ddeall wedyn fod Sophie, hefyd, yn mynd i gael babi 'run pryd! A dyna sut y daeth fy merch go iawn, Gwenno, i actio babi Sophie – Mair!

Fe fu'n rhaid i mi actio golygfa genedigaeth Mair, pan oeddwn i'n wyth mis yn feichiog. Wna i byth anghofio'r nerfusrwydd ar wynebau'r

Mam a merch (Angharad a Gwenno / Sophie a Mair)

holl griw ffilmio ar y set, yn poeni y baswn i'n dechrau geni go iawn!!

Roedd yn gyfnod braf iawn cael dod â Gwenno fach yn fabi i'r gwaith efo fi. Doedd hi ddim cweit mor hawdd pan ddechreuodd hi siarad ar draws pawb yn yr olygfa pan oedd hi tua dwyflwydd oed! Ond wrth gwrs, mae Gwenno wrth ei bodd yn cael bod yn rhan o deulu *Rownd a Rownd*, ac wedi dysgu'r grefft o actio teledu ers yn ddim o beth.

Ers iddi fynd i'r ysgol uwchradd, rydan ni wedi cael sawl golygfa ddifyr a chyffrous: Mair yn mynd ar goll, yn camymddwyn yn yr ysgol, yn dianc i ffwrdd o gartref ac yn yfed dan oed… ac mae'r ddwy ohonom ni'n mwynhau portreadu mam a merch eithaf gwahanol i ni ein hunain!

Wedi i briodas Sophie a Vince chwalu, daeth Mathew (Robin Ceiriog) i'w byd. Ond un o'r golygfeydd dwi wedi ei mwynhau fwya oedd pan chwalodd perthynas Sophie a Mathew, drachefn. Roedd hi wedi gweld y gwyllt, go iawn, a phenderfynodd falu bonet a ffenest flaen ei gar smart efo rhaw fawr! Roedd angen bôn braich i roi tolc iawn yn y car, ac roeddwn i'n stiff am ddyddiau wedyn! Fe ddefnyddiwyd yr olygfa mewn clip fideo yn ddiweddarach yn y stori, wedi addasu'r rhaw i fod yn lightsaber!

Erbyn hyn, mae Sophie wedi dod o hyd i ŵr sy'n gallu delio gyda'i natur wyllt, sef Dylan 'Goggles' Roberts (Dafydd Evans)! Fo sydd wedi gorfod delio efo cam anodd nesa bywyd Sophie, sef golygfeydd y stori menopos. Ro'n i'n falch iawn o gael cyfleu'r stori hon, gan ei fod yn rhywbeth mae pob merch yn gorfod ei brofi, ond sy'n anaml yn cael ei drafod mewn drama deledu. Fe gafwyd golygfeydd anodd, wrth i Sophie bryderu am ei hiechyd, ochr yn ochr â rhywfaint o ysgafnder – pan ddreifiodd car drwy bwll dŵr a'i gwlychu wrth iddi drio cadw'n ffit. Ro'n i'n cael llawer o ferched yn cysylltu â mi yn diolch i mi a *Rownd a Rownd* am amlygu'r menopos ar y rhaglen, ac felly ro'n i'n falch iawn o'r stori.

Tybed be ddaw nesa i Sophie? Mae wedi bod yn fraint cael chwarae ei rhan dros y blynyddoedd, a dwi'n dal i fwynhau derbyn sgriptiau newydd i weld beth fydd ei hantur nesa!

Bôn braich!

5 – Dafydd Charles
(Cynllunydd Gwreiddiol)

1-30, a Dal i Gyfrif...

1. Swydd:

Cynllunydd gwreiddiol *Rownd a Rownd*, ac yn dal yma ers y peilot. Gwnaethpwyd y gwaith cynllunio cychwynnol yn swyddfa Ffilmiau'r Nant yng Nghaernarfon, nôl ym 1994, cyn dechrau addasu'r lleoliad ym Mhorthaethwy. Adeiladu, paentio, addurno'r setiau, sortio'r props...

Dafydd wrth ei waith

2. Cyn *Rownd a Rownd*?

Coleg Celf yn Wrecsam ac yna Abertawe. Cwrs Hyfforddi Cyfle am ddwy flynedd, yna bob math o raglenni – o *C'mon Midffîld* i *Noson Lawen*, *Penblwydd Hapus* i *Celf ac Ati*.

3. Cyrraedd *Rownd a Rownd*?

Mewn cyfarfod dros ginio yn y Ship & Castle, Caernarfon efo Robin Evans a Sue Waters ges i'r cynnig i ddod i gynllunio peilot, a gobeithio wedyn, cyfres o *Rownd a Rownd* dros gyfnod o flwyddyn i gyd. Y penderfyniad gorau wnes i oedd derbyn, gan 'mod i'n dal yma 30 mlynedd yn ddiweddarach!

4. Hoff Set?

Does gen i ddim hoff set fel y cyfryw, dim ond balchder fod ein cynlluniau cychwynnol – neu layout safle prif setiau *Rownd a Rownd* – yr un fath ers y diwrnod cyntaf, sy'n profi ein bod wedi'u cael yn

Y chwedlonol Qs

19

gywir. Roedd yn drafodaeth eang rhwng y cynhyrchwyr, cyfarwyddwyr a finna. 'Sa hi'n amhosib i mi roi rhif ar sawl gwaith mae lliw paent waliau a decor tai wedi newid dros y blynyddoedd, cofiwch!

5. Hoff driciau set?

Mae waliau sy'n symud yn handi ofnadwy ar unrhyw set deledu, a hynny er mwyn creu mwy o le, a gallu saethu o fwy o ddyfnder a gwahanol onglau ac ati. Yr un yw diben 'camera traps', sy'n gallu bod yn ddrych ar y wal sy'n cuddio twll i'r camera, er enghraifft. Fel y gallwch ddychmygu, mae sawl eitem ffug mewn set caffi a siop, fel cacennau a

Caban rhentu fideos Roger (Arwel Roberts), cyn ei droi'n Grib Goch

bara wedi'u gwneud o blastig i'w harddangos, paent gwyn tu mewn i boteli llefrith, tomen o bapurau newydd wedi dyddio, a bwydydd yn y siop lle 'dan ni'n rhoi'n labeli ein hunain arnyn nhw fel nad oes gormod o hysbysebu cwmnïau penodol.

Cyn damwain Mal (Tirion Roberts)

6. Hoff stynt?

Oherwydd yr holl waith cynllunio ac adeiladu ar ei gyfer, mae'n rhaid i mi ddweud: cymeriad Mal (Tirion Roberts) yn disgyn oddi ar ysgol trwy do conservatory tra'n gweithio efo Terry (John Glyn). Cafodd y conservatory ei adeiladu'n arbennig, a'r gwydr i gyd wedi'i wneud o sugar glass – sy'n dipyn llai peryg na gwydr go iawn,

20

wrth gwrs! Mi aeth y stynt rhagddo'n wych, diolch i waith cydlynu Richard Hammet, ac fe laniodd y dyn stynt ar y smotyn perffaith.

7. Stynt aeth o'i le?

Gan ein bod wedi gweithio gydag amryw o gydlynwyr stynt profiadol dros y blynyddoedd, mae popeth wedi gweithio'n reit dda. Efallai na rowliodd ambell i gar i'r union le roeddan ni isio, ond tydi hynna'n fai ar neb, wrth gwrs. Mae'n benbleth i mi, hyd heddiw, sut y cawson ni ganiatâd i chwythu fan fwyd o flaen y setiau yng nghanol Porthaethwy (K-Babs!)... ond, yn ddiweddar iawn, gawson ni ganiatâd i gau'r lôn gyhoeddus er mwyn ffilmio stynt. Dwi'n cofio flynyddoedd maith yn ôl, bu i ni gau'r lôn er mwyn i gar yrru trwy ffenest y siop, a'r cynhyrchydd Robin Evans yn mynnu bod yn rhan o'r digwydd – yn gyrru'r ail gar oedd yn achosi'r ddamwain! Mae'n rhaid i mi ddweud

"Chei di'm parcio yn fanna, mêt!"

bod ceir o ddiddordeb mawr i mi'n gyffredinol, felly bosib mai'r rhan fwyaf o'r rheiny dwi'n eu cofio orau!

8. Straeon anifeiliaid anwes?

Dwi wrth fy modd yn gweithio efo anifeiliaid – anwes, ac fel arall – oherwydd 'dan ni wedi cael tomen dros y blynyddoedd: cŵn di-ri, byji, pysgod, defaid, ieir, mul... ond mae'n rhaid i mi ddweud bod y cyfnod pan oedd Kelvin Walsh (Kevin Williams) yn cadw llygod mawr yn un reit lletchwith a thrafferthus ar brydiau! Roedd angen person arbenigol i'w trin ac ati, a hyd yn oed mwy o waith pan benderfynodd fynd â nhw i'r ysgol yn y stori!

Kelvin Walsh a'i lygod!

21

9. Sut mae *Rownd a Rownd* wedi newid dros y blynyddoedd?

Mae technoleg wedi newid cymaint dros y blynyddoedd, fel mae pawb yn gwybod, sydd wedi rhoi'r cyfle i greu straeon gwahanol wrth i'r blynyddoedd fynd yn eu blaenau – efo ffonau symudol, y we, ac ati. O ran cynllunio, mae'r gwaith ymchwil yn haws; mae'n haws gwneud props a phrynu props, gan fod (bron â bod!) popeth ar gael ar-lein. 30 mlynedd yn ôl, pe baen ni angen creu tudalen flaen papur newydd ar gyfer stori benodol, byddai'n rhaid tynnu llun ar gamera analog, datblygu'r ffilm mewn siop, cael sgriptiwr i sgwennu'r

Prop papur newydd

erthygl – yna mynd â honno, efo'r llun, i Gyffordd Llandudno yn y car er mwyn iddyn nhw argraffu tudalen flaen i ni. Heddiw? Tynnu llun ar y ffôn, rhoi popeth at ei gilydd ar y cyfrifiadur, a gwasgu 'print'!

10. Peth gorau am y swydd?
Cyfarfod Catherine (Adran Golur), a'i phriodi.

11. Peth gwaethaf am y swydd?
Cyfarfod Cather... (!!)

Retro... salon Grib Goch

12. Beth sy'n gwneud *Rownd a Rownd* yn unigryw, ac yn gwneud i chi aros?

Oherwydd bod cymaint yn digwydd o fewn y sgripts, mae pob diwrnod ffilmio yn wahanol; ac o'r diwrnod cyntaf un ym 1994, mae o fel un teulu – a thros y blynyddoedd, wrth reswm, mae'r teulu wedi tyfu'n enfawr!

K-Bŵm!

SGANIWCH!
Angharad Llwyd yn dangos y triciau set

GOLYGFA 1   **19:20**

MEWN – TŶ'R K'S (LLOFFT KYNAN) – NOS

KEN, KAY, MEL, KYNAN

KYNAN YN GWINGO YN EI GOT, TRA BOD MEL A KEN AR EU GLINIAU YN PWYSO AR ERCHWYN Y COT YN CEISIO EI SUO I GYSGU DAN GANU. KAY YN SEFYLL UWCH EU PENNAU.

KEN/MEL
Nos da, cysga dy ooora, nos da, wela i di'n bora, ma pawb...

KAY
(TORRI AR EU TRAWS)
Neith yr 'ogyn byth gysgu efo chi'ch dau'n udo fel'a, siŵr.

KEN
G'neith siŵr! Fi oedd yn canu i Kelvin, Klaire a Kylie pan o'ddan nhw oed Kynan bach...

MEL
Ia? Oo, ciwt, Ken!

KAY
'Swn i'm yn alw fo'n ganu.

MEL
Yn y stafall yma 'fyd?!

KEN
Kylie, ia. Ond ddim y ddau hyna'. Sawl blwyddyn sy 'na ers i ni symud i fa'ma, Kay?

KAY

Dau ddeg saith.

MEL

Waw. Pwy oedd yn byw yma o' flaen chi?

KEN

Prynu'r tŷ gin Anna Parry a Bob Beics naethon ni.

KAY YN RHAGWELD CWESTIWN MEL.

KAY

Siop feics oedd yn lle ma Copa 'sdalwm. Bob o'dd bia hi.

MEL

Ia? O'n i'n meddwl na lle chwara pŵl udodd Kelv?

KAY

Cyn iddo fo droi'n Q's.

MEL

Oo, reit. Felly 'mond yr Anna a'r Bob Beics 'ma oedd yn byw 'ma cyn chi 'lly?

KEN

Na, o'dd gin Anna ddau o blant. Dylan a Ffion.

MEL

Gin dai gymaint o hanas, does?

KAY

Ma gin y pentra 'ma gymaint o hanas!

KEN

O'dd lawr grisia, y stafall fyta a'r lownj yn ddwy stafall ar wahân pan symudon ni mewn.

KAY

Ond cyn i'r fan removals orffan llwytho, jest, ro'th Ken a Meical 'y mrawd forthwl yn y wal. Am lanast!

MEL

Ond werth o! Gymaint brafiach, dwi'n siŵr. Meical o'dd yn llnau ffenestri rownd ffor'ma cyn Kelv, ia?

KAY

Ia, o'dd o'n g'neud rownd lefrith 'sdalwm, 'fyd.

KEN

Chwith heb honno, dydy.

KAY

Di o'm fath â bo' ni'n byw yn bell o siop Philip nadi, Ken!

KEN

'Igon gwir.

MEL

Pwy oedd yn rhedag y siop cyn Phil ta?

KEN

Islwyn, 'chan. A Liz 'i wraig o, a Roger y mab. O'dd o'n rhentu fidios yn lle ma'r salon rŵan, adag hynny.

KAY

Gwynt teg ar ôl rheiny.

KEN

Hei! O'dd Islwyn yn foi iawn! 'Dwn i'm be 'di'u hanas nhw rŵan, chwaith. Na Nia, o'dd yn rhedag y caffi.

KAY

Siŵr bo' gin ti hiraeth ar ôl honno.

KEN

Sawl gwaith dwi angan deud?! Ddigwyddodd na'm byd rhwng Nia a fi!

KAY

Deud ti. Ond mi na'th 'na rwbath ddigwydd efo Jo, do. Ath'i o gysgu ar y stryd i gysgu efo chdi!

MEL YN ANGHYFFORDDUS.

MEL

Dim o flaen Kynan, plis.

KEN

(ANWYBYDDU MEL)

O's raid i ni sôn am hynna?! Os oes, be amdana chdi a'r darlithiwr Gareth posh 'na, pan es di i wastio pres ac amsar yn g'neud ryw wersi nos?! O'dd Klaire bach yn crio'n ffenast llofft yn sbio arna chdi'n gadael ni...

KAY

Dŵr dan bont, i gyd, dydi.

KEN

(WEDI MYND I HWYLIAU)

A Vince, wedyn! Yn ffrind gora fi!

KAY

Wel o leia dwi'm 'di gadael 'y nheulu i fynd am holides i jêl am ddwyn stolen goods, naddo Ken?!

MEL

Newch chi stopio?! Neu neith Kyni bach byth gysgu!

KEN

(TAWELU)

Ia, wel. Dŵr dan bont – fel ti'n ddeud.

KAY

A be am dy syniad di o brynu fan fwyd K-Babs a'i rhedag hi o flaen K-Kabs ta, Ken? 'I gadael hi'n unattended i Klaire fynd yno i chwara yng nghanol gas a saim poeth?!

MEL
(WEDI DYCHRYN)
Na?!

KEN

Doedd Klaire ddim yn y fan pan nath'i ffrwydro, nagoedd!

KAY

Do'n i'm yn gwbod ar y pryd, nagon!

KEN YN OEDI WRTH FEDDWL YN ÔL YN SOMBR.

KEN

Mi oedd 'na bobl tu mewn pan a'th yn garij ni ar dân, doedd...

KAY YN FUD AC YN GWYRO EI PHEN. MEL WEDI CLYWED AM Y STORI HON.

MEL
(TAWEL)
Chris?

KEN

Ia... mab Rhys y postman, a Jackie. 'Di menthyg y garej i ymarfer band o'dd gynno fo, Osian Pŵal, Justin ac Arfon Bach.

KAY

Trydan a rhyw hen dunia paent a farnish a ballu o'dd hynny, de... Dychmyga farw fel'a, llosgi'n ulw... cradur.

MEL

Mor ifanc... mor drist...

SAIB.

KEN
Ond doedd 'na neb yn K-Wash pan nath fanno ffrwydro, diolch i'r drefn.

KAY
Garantîd bod yr explosion hwnnw yn fai ar Meical neu Michelle, dwi dal i goelio hynny.

KEN
Nhw o'dd yn gweithio yna, ond ty'd 'laen Kay, fedri di'm dal i weld bai hyd heddiw, naf'dri?

KAY
O gallaf!

KEN
Be am y 'Dolig 'na lle na'th y ddau yn hachub ni, chwara teg?

KAY
Michelle na'th yn hachub ni, Ken! Ro i hynny iddi. Chdi a Meical ddoth nôl i tŷ ni 'di meddwi'n gaib Christmas Eve a byta'n tyrci 'Dolig ni!

MEL
O, Ken! 'Swn i 'di mynd yn wallgo efo chi'ch dau!

KAY
O, mi nesh i, Mel bach, coelia di fi.

KEN
Ia wel, gafon ni rannu 'u twrci nhw drannoeth, do?!

KAY
Euogrwydd Meical, de.

KEN
Sôn am 'Ddolig, o'dd y goedan nes di i Kylie 'chydig flynyddoedd yn ôl yn ddel, Mel.

MEL

Yr un efo trimings lliwia'r enfys?

KEN

Ia, 'na chdi. O'dd hi'n ddigon o sioe!

KAY

Dwn i'm pam o'dd isio'r holl ffys a gwario ar dinsel bob lliw. 'Mond deud bod hi'n hoyw nath'i! Kylie ni 'di Kylie ni, de.

MEL

Ia, bechod.

KEN

Benderfynodd ddod i'r byd yn y caffi, o bob man!

KAY

Y ddwy o'nan ni 'di geni babi mewn lle cyhoeddus, Kay!

KEN

Chwip o ddiwrnod. Y ddau ohonyn nhw! Er, 'dwn i'm os o'dd yr un cystal â pan briododd Kelv a Mari yn Goodison, chwaith. Dwi 'rioed 'di bod mor prowd.

KAY

Prowd fod y briodas heb bara 'fyd? Na'i ail briodas o efo Lowri. Mae o'n hel mwy o wragedd na ma Arthur yn hel o drêns!

MEL

Sgiws mi?! Dwi'n fa'ma, 'chi?!

KEN

O leia bod gynno fo Kate a Mia i ddangos am y ddwy.

MEL

A Kynan bach, erbyn hyn, de!

KAY

Ti'n meddwl newch chi'ch dau bara 'ŵan, Mel?

KEN

Kay!

KAY

O, be?!

KEN

Siŵr iawn y gwnawn nhw! G'newch, Mel?

MEL

Dwi'n meddwl 'nawn ni. Kel a Mel. 'Dan ni'n mêd i'n gilydd, 'chi.

KEN

Ooo... fath â ni'n dau! Sa'm yn bosib cael Kay heb Ken na'sa? Na Ken heb Kay.

KAY

Achos 'sa chdi'n para dim hebdda fi, Ken bach. Para dim.

Y TRI YN GWENU, CYN I'W GOLYGON DROI AT KYNAN BACH YN Y KRUD, SYDD BELLACH YN KYSGU'N SOWND.

Y Kwpl: Ken a Kay
(Idris Morris Jones a Buddug Povey)

Evertoniaid ffyddlonaf Glanrafon!

Hiraeth am Kylie (Leisa Gwenllian)

Y Kapteiniaid Kelvin a Klaire
(Kevin Williams a Ffion Llwyd)

7 – Rhian Mair
(Cyfarwyddo)
Steilio Stynts

Mae'r awyrgylch ar y set, bob tro, yn wahanol ar ddiwrnod stynt. Cynnwrf a thensiwn yn yr aer, a phob un yn canolbwyntio gymaint â hynny'n galetach. Nid oherwydd bod pryder am ddiogelwch yr actorion a'r criw – gan bod wythnosau o baratoi manwl wedi digwydd o flaen llaw i osgoi hynny – na, mae'r nerfusrwydd yn codi o ffilmio rhywbeth sydd mor aruthrol o gostus, heb sicrwydd 100% y gwnaiff weithio i fod yn foment gofiadwy. Ond, mae'n saff dweud bod nifer o stynts cofiadwy wedi bod ar *Rownd a Rownd* dros y blynyddoedd – y ffrwydriad yn y londrét, marwolaeth David, y tân yn y garej, a sawl car sydd wedi mynd ben i

Rhian yn ei chap cyfarwyddo

waered ar lonydd Ynys Môn? Yn y dyddie cynnar, Dennis Pritchard Jones a Dafydd Arthur oedd yn cyfarwyddo'r stynts mawr. Rwy'n cofio'r stori am Dennis yn siomedig gyda'r ffrwydriad yn y londrét, ac yn holi'r trefnydd stynts ai dyna'r gorau fedre fe wneud? "Nage," oedd yr ateb... Mi ddyblodd e'r bil, a chafwyd andros o ffrwydriad cofiadwy – i gyd ynghanol pentre Porthaethwy! Mi briododd Dafydd a fi ym 1995; felly petai Daf wedi cael byw, bydden ni'n dathlu'r 30 eleni, hefyd. Yn anffodus, cafodd drawiad yn 2007, ac er mwyn sicrhau cyflog cyson i mi a'r plant – oedd yn ifanc, ar y pryd – wnes i gymryd ei le yn cyfarwyddo *Rownd a Rownd*.

Fel cyfarwyddwr, fy rôl i ydi dehongli'r hyn sydd yn y sgript yn y modd mwyaf diddorol, ac annisgwyl, efallai, ond hefyd yn y modd mwyaf cost-effeithiol. Y balans rhwng y ddau ydi'r peth anoddaf yn fy swydd. I sicrhau gwerth am arian, bydd cryn drafod wedi digwydd gyda'r rheolwr cynhyrchiad a'r trefnydd styntiau, o flaen llaw, a syniadau dirifedi yn cael eu cynnig cyn hoelio'r union drefn. Creu bwrdd stori wedyn, sef cyfres o ddarlunie syml (syml iawn yn fy achos i!) sy'n dangos yn union ble mae'r actor/person stynt a ble fydd y camerâu. Mae stynt dda yn medru rhoi'r argraff bod rhywbeth yn llawer mwy peryglus nag ydy o go iawn. Ceir ffi ychwanegol i bob person stynt, sy'n ddibynnol ar lefel risg y stynt. Wrth syrthio i lawr grisiau, maent yn cael eu talu fesul gris; ac os yn cael eu taro gan gar, mae ffioedd gwahanol e.e. mae glanio ar y bonet yn £XXX ychwanegol, ac yn y blaen.

Roedd cynllunio sut y byddai Lea (Mali Grigg) yn syrthio i lawr grisiau'r selar yng nghyfres 29 yn andros o her, oherwydd y risg i Christina y ferch stynts. Roeddwn yn ddibynnol ar Owain y Rheolwr Lleoliadau i ffeindio'r grisiau addas, ac wedyn ar yr Adran Gelf i addurno'r lleoliad i fod yn debyg i weddill y bwthyn gwreiddiol. Yn y pendraw, daethpwyd o hyd i hen risiau carreg oedd y lled a'r ongl cywir mewn ffermdy ymhell o'r bwthyn, felly bu'n rhaid i Math Morris y Cynllunydd adeiladu ffrâm a drws ynddo, cyn ei addurno. Gyda goleuo celfydd Dyl Wyn ar gamera, roedd bob dim yn barod. Yna, gosododd Andy y trefnydd stynts bâr o welingtons melyn hanner ffordd i lawr y grisiau i arbed pen Christina wrth iddi redeg ffwl sbîd a thaflu ei hun dwmbwl-dambal i lawr y grisiau carreg. Dyna chi ffordd od iawn o ennill bywoliaeth!

Weithiau, wrth gwrs, mae pethau yn medru mynd o'i le. Efallai y gwnewch chi gofio rhai o fechgyn Glanrafon yn penderfynu mynd â speedboat am sbin ar y Fenai liw nos? Doedd gen i ddim trefnydd styntiau ar gyfer y stynt honno, dim ond tîm o nofwyr tanddwr i guddio yn y dŵr ac achub yr actorion fesul un wrth iddynt syrthio i'r culfor oer. Yn ffilmio ym mis Hydref, dim ond am 8-10 munud oedd bob actor yn gallu bod yn y dŵr cyn iddynt ddiodde o hypothermia, felly roedd rhaid gweithio'n gyflym. Rydym wedi hen arfer cydweithio gyda'r cwmni cychod ym Mhorthaethwy, gan taw nhw sydd yn cyflenwi'r cychod ar gyfer Yr Iard yn y stori, ond roedd cychwyn o Borth y noson honno mewn un fflyd yn olygfa ryfeddol. Yn y tu blaen roedd y cwch cyflym, yna'r RIB gyda'r criw ffilmio, wedyn dau gwch diogelwch yn y cefn. Er 'mod i wedi cael rhybudd, dyna pryd nes i sylweddoli go iawn pa mor dywyll ydi'r môr gyda'r nos... a does dim headlamps ar gwch!

Doeddwn i ddim yn poeni'n ormodol, oherwydd ro'n i'n gwybod bod craen anferth wedi cael ei logi i godi lampau mawr – i efelychu golau lleuad – a

David a Rhys eiliadau cyn y ddamwain angheuol (Iestyn Arwel a Meilir Rhys)

Damwain Jonathan a Wyn

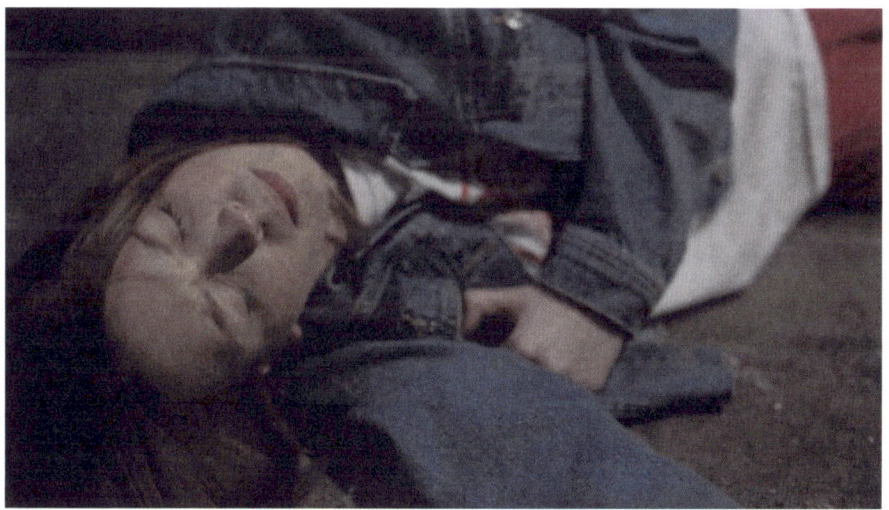

Damwain grisiau Lea (Mali Grigg)

bod hwnnw yn ein disgwyl i fyny'r afon yn y lleoliad ger Ynys Faelog. Wrth i'r fflyd o gychod nesáu, doedd dim golwg o'r lleuad ffug... yna daeth neges ar y walkie-talkie bod gyrrwr newydd ar y craen, a doedd e ddim yn hapus i yrru lawr y lôn gul at y dŵr. Mewn ymdrech i achub y sefyllfa, roedd ein trydanwr wedi gosod y lampau ar y lan, ond roedd rheiny yn rhy isel, ac os rhywbeth, yn ein dallu! Penderfynais i ac Iwan Môn, y Cynorthwyydd 1af, gario 'mlaen gyda'r stynt ac addasu pob un siot – oedd wedi'i gynllunio mor ofalus – gyda'r hyn roedd Aled ar y camera yn medru ei gyflawni gydag ond ychydig o olau. Chwarae teg, wnaeth e job fendigedig, ond roedd fy nghalon yn fy ngwddf am y rhan fwyaf o'r noson! Roedd yr actorion yn wych, gyda Robin Ceiriog (Mathew), Tudur Evans (Iolo) ac Iwan Fôn (Jason) yn hynod o ddewr yn plymio i'r dŵr rhynllyd, du y noson honno – dim stynt-dybls iddyn nhw.

Fedrwch chi ddim cael stynt-dybl wrth eni babi. Wrth eni Kynan yn y bws mini, roedd tipyn mwy o reolaeth ar y sefyllfa – yn wir, roedd rheolaeth Buddug Povey (Kay) ac Elain Llwyd (Mel) yn rhyfeddol, ac yn tanlinellu crefft actor da. Gyda'r cast a'r rhan fwyaf o'r criw yn fenywod, roedd yn bleser cael bod yn rhan o ddathliad Diwrnod Rhyngwladol y Merched. Dros y blynyddoedd, rwyf wedi "geni" sawl babi, ond efallai mai genedigaeth Wyn, babi Dani (Ffion Medi) – gyda John (Huw Garmon) yn canu 'Yma o Hyd' – oedd yr un mwyaf doniol! Eto, roeddwn yn ddyledus iawn i Huw a Ffion am eu perfformiadau campus, tra 'mod i a'r criw i gyd yn rholio chwerthin rownd y gornel.

Elfen hynod bwysig o bob stynt yw'r effeithiau sain a'r gerddoriaeth. Mae dewis y sŵn cywir i'r slap neu yr hyd cywir i'r sgid car yn y stafell ddybio yn medru trawsnewid golygfa. Mae'n rhyfeddol sut mae'r glust yn medru twyllo'r llygad i gredu unrhyw beth. Yn y stafell olygu, wrth wrando ar Mel yn bloeddio mewn poen wrth eni heb boenladdwr, gwyddwn bod angen cerddoriaeth bwerus i bontio'r golygfeydd. Creodd Non y cymathydd sain seinwedd hudol drwy'r cyfan i blethu'r golygfeydd a chreu undod. Pan gafodd John druan ei ladd yn dilyn damwain car hit and run erchyll yng nghyfres 28, roedd hi'n stynt dda; ond efallai taw'r golygfeydd ar ôl y stynt sy'n aros yn y cof, fwyaf. Dewiswyd y gerddoriaeth yn ofalus iawn i gyfleu difrifoldeb y sefyllfa a chyfleu sut mae un eiliad wan yn medru trawsnewid bywydau.

Hogiau Glanrafon yn mynd i drafferthion ar y Fenai

Mel wedi geni Kynan

John a'i stynt-dybl!

Meredydd Rhisiart (Efan) ac Ian Rowlands

Nid fi wnaeth gyfarwyddo pennod marw John; Ian Rowlands oedd hwnnw, ac roedd y golygfeydd dirdynnol rhwng Llyr (Llew Davies) ac Efan (Meredydd Rhisiart) – a pherfformiadau gwych yr actorion ar ôl y ddamwain – yn dangos taw'r stori sy'n bwysig yn y pen draw. Dim ond am eiliadau mae stynt yn para ar y sgrin, ond gyda sgwennu da, mae'r ôl-effeithiau'n para'n hir iawn.

8 – **Catrin Mara**
(Dona / Elen Edwards)

Fel Déjà Vu

I997 oedd hi, ac yn ystafell 6ed Ysgol Berwyn y Bala, rhoddodd Lois fy ffrind hysbyseb roedd ei mam wedi ei dorri allan o gylchgrawn *Golwg* i mi:

'Ydych chi rhwng 16 ac 19 oed? Oes gennych chi ddiddordeb mewn actio? Dewch am glyweliad!'

"Ydw, oes, a IAWN!" medda fi!

Catrin fel Dona

Doedd y ferch 17 oed yna ddim yn breuddwydio am eiliad y byddai'n CAEL rhan yn y drydedd gyfres o *Rownd a Rownd*, ond aeth ati'n ddiwyd i lunio CV (gan ychwanegu ychydig o liw) cyn dechrau panicio am ddreifio yr holl ffordd i Sir Fôn.

Ond cael rhan wnes i, yn ogystal â merch arall 17 oed o'r enw Angharad Llwyd!

Roedden ni'n dwy yn ymuno â chast arbennig o actorion oedd eisoes wedi bod yn y ddwy gyfres flaenorol. Rhai ohonyn nhw'n gewri ro'n i wedi eu hedmygu ers i mi fod yn blentyn bach.

Yn y stori, roedd fy nghymeriad i (Dona) yn rhannu tŷ gydag Emma (Lisa Jên Brown), Mei (Owen Arwyn) a Mal (Tirion Roberts). Fel rhan o un o'r straeon cyntaf i mi gael fy nghynnwys ynddi, roedd pawb i fod i gael sioc o ddarganfod bod Mal wedi cuddio'r ffaith ei fod yn gallu chware'r drymiau i safon aruthrol. Ond yn anffodus, cafodd Tirion ddamwain – gan anafu ei lygad yn ddrwg – felly doedd dim amdani ond rhoi ei stori i gymeriad arall, rhywun oedd wedi nodi ar ei CV ei bod yn gallu chware'r drymiau...

Y peth rhesymol i'w wneud fyddai cyfadde'n syth 'mod i wedi rhoi ychydig o gig ar asgwrn fy CV, ymddiheuro a chadw fy mhen i lawr am sbelan, ond na. Dim o'r fath beth. *Fake it till you make it* oedd fy agwedd flinderus i, a mynd amdani yn llawn argyhoeddiad ar ôl gwers fach gudd gan Tirion. Does gen i ddim cof o'r cyfryw olygfa orffenedig, sy'n awgrymu ei bod hi wedi'i ffeilio yn y rhan o'r ymennydd sy'n blocio cywilydd ac embaras.

Catrin fel Elen

Bu Dona 'Drygs' druan farw ar ôl cymryd tabled ecstasi ym 1998, a dyna ddiwedd ar fy nghyfnod hwyliog a gwerthfawr yng Nglanrafon. Neu dyna i mi ei feddwl ar y pryd...

Un mlynedd ar hugain yn ddiweddarach, ces alwad gan fy asiant i fynd am glyweliad am ran yn *Rownd a Rownd*. Eglurais (â'm calon fel y plwm) fy mod eisoes wedi marw yn y gyfres, a bod camgymeriad wedi bod – rhyw Catrin arall lwcus oedd am gael rhoi cynnig ar y rhan.

Ond na, ym mis Mawrth 2019, ces ddychwelyd – a hynny i olynu Jim Gym (Iestyn Garlick) fel pennaeth newydd Ysgol Glanrafon: Ms Elen Edwards. Gweddw a mam i Mali (Luned Elfyn) ac Anna (Gwenlli Dafydd), ac yn fwy diweddar, gwarcheidwad i Ioan (Macsen Stevens), hefyd.

Ro'n i'n eithaf ofnus i fynd yn ôl a chamu i mewn i'r cynhyrchiad, er bod gen i ffrindiau yno ar ddwy ochr y camera, ond buan iawn y diflannodd yr ofn gan fod y ferch ddwy ar bymtheg gychwynnodd yn y gyfres ar yr un diwrnod â fi, nôl ym 1997, yn dal i fod yno! Da 'di Sophie (Angharad Llwyd). Mae ambell un arall yn dal i fod yno hefyd, yn rhan o dimoedd colur, gwisg, cyfarwyddo a chriw.

Mae'r caffi a'r siop yn strwythurol yr un fath, ond mae Siop Bob Beics wedi newid i fod yn Q's, yna Copa; siop rhentu fideos wedi newid i salon Grib Goch, yna Nikki's, Dani's, a bellach, Dal i Dorri; ac, ar un adeg, roedd y Tŷ Pizza yn weithdy crochenwaith i gymeriad Anna (Bethan Dwyfor). Erbyn hyn, mae gynnon ni ddau safle parhaol ychwanegol i'r setiau ym Mhorthaethwy, sef setiau Cibyn, Caernarfon, a stiwdio newydd Aria lle mae setiau y rhan fwyaf o'r tai, bellach.

Yn wahanol i'r drefn saethu wreiddiol, ac oherwydd bod y "bwystfil" wedi tyfu gymaint ers y cyfresi cynnar, mae dau griw bellach yn ffilmio ar yr un pryd – sy'n golygu tua un golygfa ar bymtheg yn y can bob diwrnod.

Un prif gymeriad sydd yno yn dawel ers y cychwyn, wrth gwrs, ydy Porthaethwy.

Does dim un diwrnod yn mynd heibio nad ydw i'n cael fy atgoffa, wrth yrru dros un o'r pontydd anhygoel 'na, o ba mor wirioneddol lwcus ydw i o fod wedi cael bod yn rhan o'r teulu yma cyhyd.

Felly, diolch. Diolch i Dilys a Lois am roi'r hysbyseb o *Golwg* i fi. Diolch, Robin a Sue. Diolch, *Rownd a Rownd*. Ymlaen i'r 30 mlynedd nesaf, y bwystfil hyfryd.

9 – Gwenlli Dafydd
(Anna Edwards)
Jyglio Bywyd, Ysgol a *Rownd a Rownd*

Ers yn beth bach, dwi 'di mwynhau perfformio. Byddaf yn edrych yn ôl ar fideos ohona i yn actio yn yr ystafell fyw, yn yr ysgol, Ysgol Sul, llwyfan yr Urdd, Adran Bro Alaw ac yn Theatr Fach, Llangefni – wrth fy modd o flaen cynulleidfa! Sian Miriam, y tiwtor drama yn Theatr Fach, gynigiodd i fi (ac eraill) fynychu clyweliad efo *Rownd a Rownd*. Nes i ddim meddwl llawer am y peth a bod yn onest, am fod tua 80 o blant yn y clyweliad cyntaf. Feddyliais i ddim erioed y baswn i'n cael y rhan, ond dwi'n cofio

mwynhau y clyweliad yn ofnadwy yn ferch wyth oed, yn actio bod yn flin, a mynd i'r siop a ballu!

Roedd hi'n ddiwrnod Eisteddfod Sir Ynys Môn pan ges i wybod 'mod i wedi cael y rhan. Roedd Mam wedi peidio dweud wrtha i nes ein bod ni yn y car yn barod i adael, a dwi'n cofio cael blodau ganddi am y tro cyntaf erioed, a chardyn a bar o siocled, a nes i ffonio Gwenno Beech (Mair) yn syth bìn, am ein bod ni'n ffrindiau ers cael ein geni!

Dwi ddim yn cofio actio y golygfeydd cyntaf un, ond dwi yn cofio cymryd at Luned (Mali) oedd yn actio fy chwaer fawr ar y sgrin. Roedd hi'n hŷn na fi, ac yn glên. Nes i gymryd at Catrin Mara (Elen) yn syth, hefyd, sef fy mam ar y sgrin. Doeddwn i ddim wedi "hygio" fawr o neb heblaw am fy mam fy hun cyn cychwyn efo *Rownd a Rownd*, ond roedd caredigrwydd Catrin Mara yn gwneud pethau fel'na yn haws.

Eleni dwi wedi dechrau TGAU, a dwi'n trio jyglio gwaith ysgol, Ffermwyr Ifanc, treinings rygbi a dysgu geiriau *Rownd a Rownd*. Croesi bysedd fydd dim un yn dioddef yn sgil y llall!

Mae bod ar y set yn hwyl, ond weithiau 'dan ni'n cael gormod o hwyl! Dwi'n cofio unwaith ynghanol ffilmio, dyma'r botel sôs coch yn gwneud sŵn rhech ynghanol golygfa ble roedd sgwrs ddwys wrth y bwrdd bwyd efo Llyr (Llew Davies) ac Efan (Meredydd Rhisiart), a doedd dim modd i neb ddal yn ôl rhag chwerthin! Bu rhaid ailddechra ffilmio yr olygfa eto, ond heb y botel sôs coch! Weithiau ma bol Catrin Mara yn gwneud sŵn ar y set, yn enwedig os ydi bron yn amser cinio, ac ar yr adegau hynny, bydd rhaid ail-gymryd y "têc" os ydi'r bŵm wedi codi sŵn y rymbls!

Mae Anna wedi datblygu lot ers cyrraedd Glanrafon saith mlynedd yn ôl, ond mae hi'n ferch annwyl iawn – a dwi'n ei hoffi hi. Ges i stori'n ddiweddar, yng nghyfres 30, lle'r oedd Anna yn profi blacmel rhywiol gan fachgen oedd yn galw ei hun yn Miles. Daeth i adnabod 'Miles' wrth chwarae gemau ar-lein, cyn i'r siarad symud i apiau cymdeithasol personol. Arweiniodd y berthynas at Anna yn tynnu llun ohoni hi ei hun a'i yrru i 'Miles', ac yntau'n troi'n syth arni, yn mynnu arian i beidio â gyrru'r llun at ei theulu a'i ffrindiau i gyd. Roedd y stori yma yn brofiad newydd, lle ges i gyfle i arbrofi mwy efo fy actio a bod ar ben fy hun ar y sgrin eithaf dipyn. Er ei fod yn bwnc anodd, roedd y criw camera a phawb arall mor glên, ac roedd Lisa Jên

Anna yn cyd-chwarae efo Miles

Brown efo fi fel cydlynydd agosatrwydd yn gofalu 'mod i'n gyfforddus o fewn fy nghylch personol, ac wrth gwrs, Sian Evans, y chaperone sydd mor ofnadwy o annwyl a chefnogol. Roedd Sian rhyw ddwy fedr o bellter oddi wrtha i bob tro ro'n i'n ffilmio'r darnau anoddaf, a doedd hi'n methu â dal ei dagrau yn ôl pan roedd Anna druan yn tynnu ei llun i Miles. Dyna sut mae pethau ar y set yn *Rownd a Rownd*, mae pawb yn agos ac yn glên, ac yn hynod ofalus o'i gilydd.

Ges i'r dewis gan y cynhyrchwyr i wneud y stori am Anna a Miles, neu i beidio, gan ei fod yn destun a phwnc mor anodd ac anghyfforddus. Yn amlwg, nes i gytuno, achos os medra i helpu dim ond un person rhag gwneud beth wnaeth Anna, yna mae o yn sicr wedi bod yn werth ei wneud.

Diolch i bawb yn *Rownd a Rownd* am y profiad a'r hwyl, dwi'n gwerthfawrogi!

Anna a Mair (Gwenlli a Gwenno)

10 – Dewi Rhys
(Wyn Humphries)
Dyn ar Daith

A r fy niwrnod cyntaf o ffilmio *Rownd a Rownd* 'nôl yng nghyfres 12, cyrhaeddais Porthaethwy yn blygeiniol o gynnar gyda bag anferth o ddillad, gwahanol esgidiau ac eli haul!

Cerddais heibio'r dderbynfa ac mi ddois ar draws un o aelodau'r criw ffilmio.

"Wel, wel," meddai. "Ti prin yma bum munud a ti'n galifantio i Sbaen!"

Yn wir, ro'n i off i Sitges ger Barcelona i ffilmio fy ngolygfeydd cyntaf fel Wyn Humphries, y dyn mawr cefnog oedd yn dad i Dani (a phedwar plentyn arall 'fyd, i'r rheiny sy'n cofio'n well na fi!)

Fanno oedd tŷ haf Wyn, a buom ddigon ffodus i ymweld â'r dref rhyw deirgwaith cyn i Wyn werthu ei fusnes dramor a chanolbwyntio ar dreulio ei holl amser yng Nglanrafon.

Cawsom ffilmio mewn tŷ modern moethus gyda phwll nofio anferth. Tŷ oedd yn cael ei rentu ar gyfer cwmnïau ffilmio a theledu yn benodol. Roedd gan Rondo gysylltiad gyda chwpwl oedd wedi bod yn gweithio ar 'movies' o amgylch y byd, gan gynnwys ffilmiau *James Bond*. Bu eu cymorth drwy gyfnodau ffilmio *Rownd a Rownd* yno yn amhrisiadwy, gan iddynt gynnig eu hunain i weithio gyda'r Adran Gelf a'r Adran Lleoliadau.

Wrth gwrs, nid mynd yno i galifantio oedd y bwriad, ond i greu golygfeydd difyr a gwahanol ar gyfer y gyfres. Mae cael cyferbyniad mewn golygfeydd

Wyn y dyn busnes, a'i nai Sion (Sion Emyr) yn mynd am ryn

yn ychwanegu at awyrgylch y bennod ac yn dod â phethau 'yn fyw', fel tae. Er enghraifft, roedd golygfa gyda Wyn a'i deulu yn gwledda wrth y traeth yn Sitges yn cael ei dilyn gan Arthur druan yn newid olwyn ei fan yn y glaw yn Llannerchymedd!

Roedd yr ardal lle'r oedd tŷ haf Wyn yn cael ei galw'n 'Rhes y Miliwnydd' gan y bobl leol. Ar y rhes, roedd sawl cyn chwaraewr pêl-droed Barcelona a Sbaen yn byw. Ac i'r rheiny sydd â diddordeb mewn pêl-droed, yno mae Hotel Melia wrth y môr a'r creigiau, sef y gwesty y gwnaeth tîm Manchester United aros ynddo ar ôl ennill y 'Treble' ym 1999!

Ar nodyn personol, mi ddewisais fynd i Sitges sawl gwaith fel lleoliad am wyliau neu benwythnos. Ewch draw os cewch gyfle, a mynd ar y trên ar hyd yr arfordir i Barcelona – bythgofiadwy!

Y criw a'r cast yn Sitges

Ffilmio ger y pwll

11 – Gwyn Vaughan
(Arthur Thomas)
'Ma bywyd fath â trên...'

Mae hi'n fwy o hwyl chwarae cymeriad drwg na chymeriad da. Yn sicr, mae Yncl Arthur wedi cyflawni hynny yn fy achos i!

Pan ymddangosodd Arthur Thomas ar *Rownd a Rownd* am y tro cyntaf yn ôl yn 2007, rhyw gymeriad digon amheus oedd o, a doeddwn i fel actor – na'r awduron, dybia i – yn siŵr iawn be oedd dyfodol y cymeriad yn y gyfres.

Mi ddechreuodd fel dreifar bysus, dipyn yn 'cheeky' ac yn sicr yn deud a gneud pethau cynllwyngar, dan din, ac yn fodlon troi'r dŵr i'w

Arthur y Cowboi!

felin ei hun bob cyfle bosib. Ac yn dipyn o un am y merched, hefyd, wrth gwrs! O fewn dim, roedd o wedi cael ei lygaid ar Iris Hardy (Karen Wynne) – hogan fywiog, naïf, a gonest. Yr union deip y byddai Arthur yn medru ei throi rownd ei fys bach. Mam i dri o hogia – Barry, Jason, a Dale – ac o'r dechra, roedd Barry (Gwion Tegid) ac Arthur fel ci a chath.

Mewn chwinciad, roedd Arthur wedi symud mewn at y teulu bach... Ac mi ddechreuodd ddangos ei wir liwiau mewn dim o amser, gan roi amser caled i'r hogiau – gan eu bod nhw, yn nhyb Arthur, wir angen trefn a disgyblaeth. Haws plygu brigyn na choeden oedd meddylfryd Arthur, ond roedd ei agwedd yn troi yr hogiau yn ei erbyn, a datblygodd Arthur i fod yn gymeriad roedd pawb yn ei gasáu. Roedd o yn cael affêrs tu ôl i gefn Iris, a chafodd berthynas ddirdynnol efo Julie (Tammy Gwyn); ond fe drodd petha'n chwithig, gan ei bod hithau, hefyd, yn ei ddefnyddio fo. Dau ddrwg efo'i gilydd oedd Arthur a Julie. Hi eisiau cael gwared ar Iris a chael symud mewn i dŷ Arthur, yn lle byw mewn carafán efo'i phlant. Ond daeth Barry i glywed am yr affêr, ac mewn pennod ymfflamychol – yn llythrennol – fe chwythodd Barry y garafán i fyny, a bron â lladd y ddau.

Arthur a Barry: Ci a Chath

Bwli oedd Arthur bryd hynny, ond fel llawer o fwlis, yn hen fabi hefyd. Ei sgams di-ddiwedd byth yn gweithio, a'i ymdrechion amheus i wneud ceiniog neu ddwy wastad yn methu.

Dros y blynyddoedd mae'r cymeriad wedi datblygu ac esblygu, wedi newid gyrfa sawl gwaith – gyrrwr bysiau, gyrrwr tacsi, a rŵan, yn danfon parseli – a wastad ar ruth! Mae'r elfen gomedi wedi dŵad yn fwyfwy pwysig yn ei gymeriad; deud pethau heb feddwl a deud pethau fyddai eraill byth yn ei feiddio. Dyna i mi ydi un o gryfderau'r gyfres – y cymysgedd o'r llon a'r lleddf. Y comedi a'r trasiedi!

Ac, yn sicr, daeth trasiedi at ddrws 'rhen Arthur rhyw dair blynedd yn ôl, pan fu Iris farw – neu gael ei lladd, yn hytrach – yn nhŷ Barry, ar drothwy ei phriodas ag Arthur. Roedd y penodau rheiny yn rhai hynod drist, yn enwedig gan fod y ddau wedi ffeindio rhyw gydbwysedd yn y berthynas – a'r ddau yn

meddwl y byd o'i gilydd. Cafodd Arthur sioc fawr yn y cyfnod yma, a bu iddo fynd trwy amser tywyll ac unig. Mi galliodd dros nos, fel petai. Closiodd Arthur a Jason (Iwan Fôn) yn eu galar am Iris, y ddau yn ceisio dod i

Dau ddrwg: Julie ac Arthur

*Ffion, Mei, Dylan ac Arwel "Ari" Stiffs
(Fflur Medi Owen, Owen Arwyn,
Emyr Prys Davies a Dyfrig Evans)*

*Osian a Kelvin
(Iddon Jones a Kevin Williams)*

*Osian, Dylan [criw], Justin, Tom, Klaire a Gemma
(Iddon Jones, Arwyn Jones, Dyfan Dwyfor,
Ffion Llwyd a Heledd Anna Roberts)*

*Jim Gym, Dylan ac Anna
(Iestyn Garlick, Emyr Prys Davies a Bethan Dwyfor)*

Beca Powell (Lois Jones)

Klaire a Haf (Ffion Llwyd a Heledd Lewis)

Y pêl-droedwyr cynnar!

Awel, Mei a Lowri Mai
(Sian Arfon, Owen Arwyn
a Bethan Ellis Owen)

Caryl, Lucy a Cadi
(Ann Roberts, Nerys Lewis a
Mirain Haf Roberts)

Bob Beics ac Anna
(Dafydd Emyr a Bethan Dwyfor)

Sneips a Mal
(Tudur Roberts a Tirion Roberts)

Elfyn (Hefin Rees)

Martin (Rhys ap Trefor)

Nia "Caffi" Carter
(Nia Williams)

Teulu gwreiddiol y siop:
Islwyn, Roger ac Elizabeth Morgan
(Dewi 'Pws' Morris, Arwel Roberts a Betsan Llwyd)

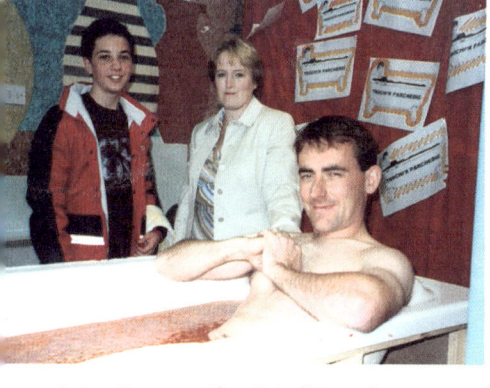

Osian, Nesta ac Alun "Pŵal" Powell
(Iddon Jones, Sera Cracroft a
Merfyn Pierce Jones)

Nesta, Eifion, Gwenllian ac Alun
(Sera Cracroft, Martin Thomas,
Bethan Hughes a Merfyn Pierce Jones)

Y Stevens: Jen, Jackie, Liam, Chris a Rhys
(Llio Non, Mari Emlyn, Sion Eifion,
Llŷr Gwyn Lewis a Robin Eiddior)

Sophie ac Eifion
(Angharad Llwyd a Martin Thomas)

Barry Hardy (Gwion Tegid)

Y Keegans: Dani, Jonathan, Nain "Madam Serena",
Sheree, Michelle a Britney
(Ffion Medi, Rhydian Lewis, Iola Gregory,
Llinos Hughes, Manon Elis a Ffion Owen)

Kay, Kylie, Klaire, Ken, Kelvin, Mari, Sioned,
Dilys, Arwel a Dyfan
(Buddug Povey, Awel Môn, Ffion Llwyd,
Idris Morris Jones, Kevin Williams,
Manon Medi Pari, Mari Rowland Hughes,
Emlyn Gomer ac Owen Alun)

Britney, Dani, Michelle, Meical a Jonathan
(Ffion Owen, Ffion Medi, Manon Elis,
Emyr Gibson a Rhydian Lewis)

Dalen flaen arbennig!

*Glenda, Alun, Ken, Kay, Meical, Michelle, Dani, Gareth "Sbecs",
Philip, Siôn, Kylie, Klaire, Huw, Sara, Elin ac Alwena
(Elliw Haf, Merfyn Pierce Jones, Idris Morris Jones,
Buddug Povey, Emyr Gibson, Manon Elis, Ffion Medi, Gruffydd
Owen, Maldwyn John, Sion Emyr, Awel Môn,
Ffion Llwyd, Lara Catrin, Lois Meleri Jones a Ffion Dafis)*

*Ail deulu'r siop: Dewi, Alwena,
Siôn a Philip Parry
(Cedron Sion, Ffion Dafis,
Sion Emyr a Maldwyn John)*

*Iwan Môn a Dyfan Roberts
efo criw Ambiwlans Awyr Cymru*

*Dale a Jason Hardy
(Harri Wyn a Dewi Erwan Humphreys)*

Ras Sion Corn!!

Alwena a Philip
(Ffion Dafis a Maldwyn John)

Llefrith marchnata!

Iwan Llywelyn
(Tomos Wyn Williams)

Siôn Parry
(Sion Emyr)

Lisa ac Adam
(Gwen Elin Jones a Jona Elis Owen)

Arwel a Dilys
(Emlyn Gomer a
Mari Rowland Hughes)

Jason, Hari a Dyfan
(Dewi Erwan Humphreys,
Anna Wyn Jones
ac Owen Alun)

Dewi a Jason
(Cedron Sion a Dewi Erwan Humphreys)

Morgan
(Emyr Lloyd Jones)

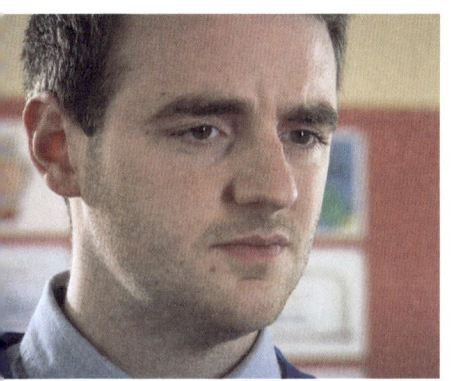

Paul
(Tom Blumberg)

Dafydd a Gemma
(Gwilym Bowen Rhys a Heledd Anna Roberts)

Alwyn, Mr Lloyd, Cathryn, Megan a Gemma
(Llŷr Ifans, Phylip Hughes, Sian Beca, Lowri Grug a
Heledd Anna Roberts)

Kelvin a Lowri a Mia fach
(Kevin Williams a Lowri Gwynne)

Iolo a Llio
(Tudur Lloyd Evans ac Elen Morgan)

Cathryn
(Sian Beca)

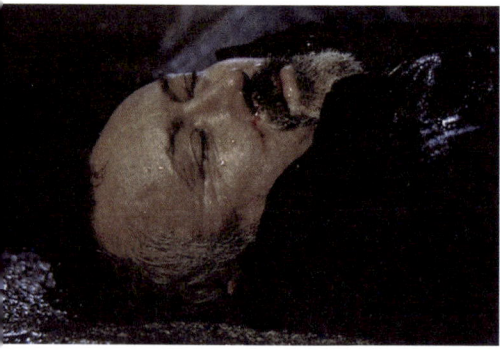

Terry
(John Glyn Owen)

Glenda ac Iris
(Elliw Haf a Karen Wynne)

Beth
(Catherine Ayers)

Nikki
(Tara Bethan)

Elin
(Lois Jones)

Gruff a Sioned
(Robyn Lloyd Piercy a Manon Dewi)

Sara (Lara Catrin)

Dathlu ffilmio'r 1000fed bennod!
(Sioned Wyn, Rheinallt Davies, Gwion Aled, Owen Alun, Tudur Lloyd Evans, Elliw Haf, Anna Wyn, Karen Wynne, Elen Morgan, Dewi Rhys a Kevin Williams)

Wil, Arthur a Jac
(Joseff Owen, Gwyn Vaughan a Jay Worley)

Meilir Rhys, Ceri Lloyd ac Iestyn Arwel

Rhian Mair yn cyfarwyddo Gwion Aled

Dewi Rhys, Jay Worley,
Ffion Medi a Fflur Davies

*Y Richards: Wil, Erin, John a Rhys
(Joseff Owen, Leri Ann Roberts,
Huw Garmon a Meilir Rhys)*

*Efan a Llyr Hopkins
(Meredydd Rhisiart a Llew Davies)*

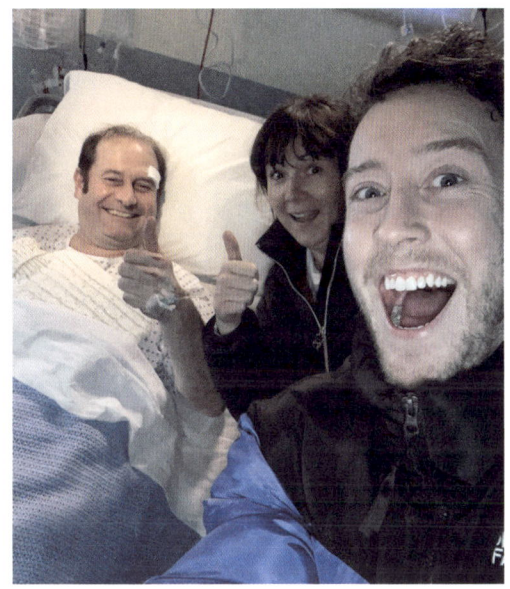

*John, Sian a Rhys
(Huw Garmon, Mari Wyn a Meilir Rhys)*

*Iolo Davies
(Tudur Lloyd Evans)*

*Teulu'r Iard: Iestyn, Anest, Gwenno a Carwyn
(Josh Morgan, Heledd Roberts,
Elen Gwynne a Meilyr Siôn)*

Kylie, Britney, Dani a Rhys
(Leisa Gwenllian, Fflur Davies,
Ffion Medi a Meilir Rhys)

Dani, Ben, Jason ac Arthur
(Ffion Medi, Geraint Morgan,
Iwan Fôn a Gwyn Vaughan)

Fflur, Llew a Dylan
(Ceri Elen Morris, Gwion Llwyd
a Dafydd Rhys Evans)

Mali Edwards
(Luned Elfyn)

Ioan Hopkins
(Macsen Stevens)

Lea a Mathew
(Mali Grigg a Robin Ceiriog)

Set Yr Iard

Trystan Armando Morgan-Richards
(Gethin Bickerton)

Britney, Cai ac Elliw
(Fflur Davies, Noel Davies a Poppy Burns)

Y Storfa Brops

Glanrafon heddiw

Dylan "Dyl" Wyn

*Catherine "Cath Colur" Hughes
(gwraig Dafydd Charles!)*

Siôn Land a Ffion Elin Davies (Adran Ddigidol)

Guto Howells ac Aled Ellis

*Celine Roberts yn coluro Manw Robin
(Caitlin)*

Owain Rowlands ar y ffôn!
Iwan Sion a Cian Wyn

Noel Davies, Rhian Mair
a Manw Robin ar set

Lowri, Robbie, Philip a Mia
(Lowri Gwynne, Tomi Llywelyn,
Maldwyn John ac Erin Fflur Owen)

Yr Adran Wisgoedd

Y Stafell Werdd binc!
(Buddug Povey, Maldwyn John,
Lowri Gwynne a Mali Grigg)

Gwion Tegid, Huw Llŷr, Elliw Haf a
John Glyn Owen

Ben a Tammy
(Geraint Morgan a Lois Elenid)

Cian Wyn, Kevin Morgan,
Dyl Wyn ac Ellis Jones

Vince, Gwenno ac Iestyn
(Huw Llŷr, Elen Gwynne a Josh Morgan)

Stiwdios Aria

Elen Edwards a Huw
(Catrin Mara a Siôn Dafydd)

Y clepiwr aur… ymlaen i'r 30 nesaf!

Ellis a'r clepiwr

dermau efo'u colled, a'r ffaith bod Barry wedi mynd i'r carchar a thu ôl i'r Bariau.

Fel actor, mae portreadu Arthur wedi bod yn bleser pur dros y blynyddoedd. Ydy, mae o wedi bod yn ddyn drwg a direidus, ac wedi bod yn wirion iawn ar brydiau, ond mae yna gymaint mwy i gymeriad Arthur. Mae o

Iris ar drothwy ei phriodas

wedi aeddfedu rhywfaint, erbyn hyn, ac yn rhoi cyngor i eraill, yn rhannu ei brofiad o bethau'r byd, gan gadw'r gomedi heb fod byth yn bell iawn o'r wyneb!

Roeddwn i yn rhaglen beilot *Rownd a Rownd* a wnaethpwyd 30 o flynyddoedd yn ôl, ond yn chwarae ymgymerwr o'r enw Dai Death (aeth wedyn yn Bryn Stiffs). Diolch i'r drefn na fedrwn wneud y gyfres pan gynigiwyd i mi rai wythnosau yn ddiweddarach, achos bu farw Dai Death (a chwaraewyd gan Ifan Huw Dafydd) ar ôl rhyw ddwy flynedd. A wedyn yn 2007 fe gefais gynnig rhan Arthur, a deunaw mlynedd wedyn dwi'n dal yn y gyfres ac yn dathlu pen-blwydd *Rownd a Rownd* yn 30 oed. Fedra i ddim ond diolch 'mod i wedi cael y cyfle i chwarae Yncl Arthur, ac wedi cael bod yn rhan o gast a chriw mor dalentog ac anhygoel dros y blynyddoedd. Ymlaen i'r 50!

12 – Cliff a Manon
(Cynhyrchwyr)
Cysgod COVID

*G*waith cynhyrchydd ydy gwneud yn siŵr fod olwynion y tancer yn troi'n esmwyth o ran beth wêl y gwylwyr ar wyneb y dyfroedd, a'r hyn sy'n digwydd ym mol y llong lle mae'r criw yn gweithio'n ddyfal yn y 'boiler-room'. Dau fu'n cynhyrchu *Rownd a Rownd* am flynyddoedd maith oedd Cliff Jones a Manon Lewis Owen. Y ddau wedi gwneud swyddi eraill fel rhan o'r gyfres cyn hynny, ond her fawr iddyn nhw oedd cynhyrchu yn ystod cyfnod cythryblus COVID-19 yn 2020/21...

Manon a Cliff yn y swyddfa

Cliff: Fe ddes i mewn i *Rownd a Rownd* yng nghyfres 3, fel cyfarwyddwr. Wedi bod yn gyfarwyddwr a chynhyrchydd ar *Pobol y Cwm* am bron i 10 mlynedd, roedd dod i mewn i *RaR* yn dipyn o sialens ac yn chwa o awyr iach ar yr un amser. Roedd medru gweithio yn gyfan gwbwl trwy'r Gymraeg yn rhywbeth doeddwn i ddim wedi'i wneud o'r blaen.

Roedd yn sialens creu penodau yn steil *Rownd a Rownd*. Roedd cyfarwyddwyr profiadol fel Dennis Pritchard Jones, Dafydd Arthur a Robin Evans wedi creu steil, ac roedd ffitio i mewn i'r steil hwnnw yn hanfodol – doeddech chi ddim ishe i'r gynulleidfa deimlo fod yna rywbeth gwahanol yn nheimlad ambell bennod. Mae fel rhedeg ras gyfnewid a phasio baton ymlaen i'r rhedwr nesa – gan drio gwneud hynny mewn ffordd esmwyth sy ddim yn tarfu ar lif y stori.

Yng nghyfres 8, cynigiwyd i mi gynhyrchu'r gyfres – ac roedd hyn yn dipyn o anrhydedd. Roedd Sue Waters a Robin Evans, sylfaenwyr y gyfres ers y dechrau'n deg, wedi gofalu'n annwyl iawn amdani ac wedi gosod sylfaeni cadarn iawn o ran safon iaith a hygrededd stori. Roedd eu hegwyddorion wrth greu a chynhyrchu'r gyfres yn gryf, ac roedden nhw bellach yn awyddus i greu a chynhyrchu dramâu eraill gyda Rondo, ond gan ddal i gadw llygaid arnom ni fel uwch-gynhyrchwyr! Fy job i oedd cadw'r olwynion yna i droi, ac un o'r pethau cyntaf wnes i oedd apwyntio tiwtor i'r plant/actorion ifanc o'r enw Manon Lewis. Bu bron i ni ei cholli achos, yn fy mhrysurdeb, fe anghofies i gysylltu i ddweud ei bod wedi cael y swydd… Lwcus iddi fy ffonio i ofyn a oedd penderfyniad wedi'i wneud, gan ei bod wedi cael cynnig swydd arall, fel athrawes.

Manon: Cefais flynyddoedd hynod ddifyr yn gwisgo het arall yn *Rownd a Rownd*, a hynny yn fy rôl fel tiwtor i'r cast iau. Pleser pur oedd dod i adnabod y cast iau a'u teuluoedd. Roeddwn yn rhyfeddu'n ddyddiol at eu dawn naturiol, eu gallu i gofio deialog a derbyn cyfarwyddyd, ond yn fwy na hynny, i gael y cydbwysedd cywir rhwng bywyd, ysgol a'u gwaith yn *Rownd a Rownd*.

Cofiaf un achlysur, yn nyddiau cynnar fy swydd, i'r ffair flynyddol ddod i Borth. Am gyffro! Roedd y ffair tipyn mwy bryd hynny, gydag un reid reit o flaen setiau *Rownd a Rownd*. Yn amlwg, toedd dim modd ffilmio ar setiau Borth y diwrnod hwnnw oherwydd y sŵn a'r hwrlibwrli. Cofiaf i ni deithio ar fws mini K-Kabs i leoliad arall, a'r plant yn tristáu eu bod yn colli allan ar hwyl y ffair. Dyma felly wneud cytuneb: os y gwnâi pawb fwyta eu cinio'n sydyn a gaddo gwrando(!), mi faswn yn mynd â nhw i'r ffair yn ystod yr awr ginio. Cadwyd at yr addewid a chafwyd yr hwyl rhyfedda yn y ffair, yn chwerthin a sgrechian ar y reids swnllyd… tan i ni ddod yn ein holau, bum munud cyn gorfod mynd nôl ar y set. Toeddwn i'm wedi cysidro bod yr holl gyffro wedi difetha gwalltiau a cholur y plant, yn enwedig y genod ifanc – a hynny, wrth gwrs, wedyn wedi difetha dilyniant (continuity) y bennod. Bu'n rhaid i bob un gael ei ail-goluro, a olygodd eu bod yn hwyr yn ôl ar y set. Toeddwn i ddim yn boblogaidd iawn ymysg yr oedolion y diwrnod hwnnw, ond dwi'n amau i'r plant faddau i mi!

Cliff: Mae sawl un wedi gofyn i mi be'n union mae cynhyrchydd yn ei wneud. Fe fyddai ambell un negyddol yn dweud taw sefyll o flaen ffan tra bod eraill yn taflu baw ati yw'r gwaith… Ond agweddau positif ydy cysylltu â'r criw a'r cast, a chadw'u hysbryd yn uchel; gwneud swydd pawb mor rhwydd ag sy bosib ac mor bleserus â phosib, a cheisio cynnal safon uchel ym mhob agwedd ar y rhaglen – o'r camau storïol cyntaf, i'r ffilmio, i'r ôl-gynhyrchu; a chreu momentwm sy'n sicrhau bod y penodau yn cyrraedd y darlledwr ar amser, ac o fewn y gyllideb.

Gadewais y gyfres ar ddiwedd cyfres 11, ond dod yn ôl wedyn ar ddechrau cyfres 16 lle roedd Manon, bellach, yn cynhyrchu gyda Bedwyr Rees. Roedd Bedwyr yntau am fynd i gynhyrchu cyfresi eraill i Rondo, felly am y 12 mlynedd nesaf, cefais gyfle i gydweithio gyda Manon fel cyd-gynhyrchydd a Bedwyr yn gofalu fel uwch-gynhyrchydd. Roedd natur y gwaith wedi newid cryn dipyn ers cyfres 3. Roedden ni'n cynhyrchu un bennod 15 munud mewn pum diwrnod o saethu bryd hynny; erbyn hyn, roedd hi'n un bennod o hanner awr mewn tridie. Wrth gwrs, roedd y dechnoleg wedi symud yn ei blaen, ond roedd rhaid gofalu am bwysau gwaith a lles criw a chast. A'r adeg y daeth hynny yn amlwg ac i'r wyneb, yn fwy nag erioed o'r blaen, oedd pan darwyd y wlad gan COVID.

Cliff a Manon: Nôl yn 2020 – am y tro cyntaf erioed yn hanes *Rownd a Rownd* – amhosib oedd cadw'r olwynion i droi, a hynny am resymau y tu hwnt i'n rheolaeth: COVID-19. Roedd datblygiadau cyson yn y wasg, a nerfusrwydd mawr yn dechrau cronni wrth i bawb ddeall bod 'na ryw aflwydd dieithr yn nesáu. O ddiwrnod i ddiwrnod, roedd rhaid addasu: tynnu actorion o olygfeydd, fel nad oedd gormod o bobl ar y set; peidio â defnyddio actorion cefndirol; newid lleoliadau – a'r cyfan yn esgor ar newidiadau golygyddol. Hyn oll nes i'r cyfan ddod i stop, 17 Mawrth, 2020. Er yr ofn tawel am beth oedd i ddod, roedd yna rhyw gysur tawel hefyd y basen ni – mwy na thebyg – yn ein holau ymhen rhyw bythefnos wedi i'r cyfan ostegu. Nid felly y bu, wrth gwrs.

Bu'r misoedd nesaf yn heriol tu hwnt ac yn rhai a fydd yn aros yn y cof am byth.

Mae *Rownd a Rownd* yn gynhyrchiad mawr, gydag oddeutu cant o bobl ynghlwm â'r gyfres, felly nid tasg fechan oedd dod â chynhyrchiad fel hyn i stop. Fel cynhyrchwyr, roedden ni'n poeni am ddiogelwch pawb; goblygiadau terfynu cytundebau; ac, yn dawel fach, dyfodol y gyfres. Rhaid dweud bod

S4C wedi bod yn gefnogol tu hwnt i ni fel cynhyrchwyr a chwmni ar yr adeg yma.

Yn yr un modd, nid tasg fechan oedd codi'r cyfan yn ôl ar ei draed. Daeth yn gwbl glir nad oedd setiau Porthaethwy, fel ag yr oedden nhw, yn addas. Roedden nhw'n gyfyng dan amodau arferol, felly roedd rhaid ailgynllunio ac addasu. Codwyd canopis y tu allan i setiau'r caffi, y siop a'r salon er mwyn gallu ffilmio mwy o olygfeydd y tu allan ymhob tywydd; crëwyd galeri gwylio pwrpasol gyda lle i bawb fod ar wasgar; symudwyd ein hardal wisgoedd, ac yn fwy na hynny, symudwyd ac adeiladwyd setiau mewn warws fawr fodern a adnabyddir bellach fel Stiwdios Aria yn Llangefni.

Wrth ailolygu sgriptiau a chydweithio gyda'r tîm storïo ar benodau newydd, penderfynodd Bedwyr Rees, yr uwch-gynhyrchydd – yn wahanol iawn i ddramâu a sebonau eraill, ar y pryd – na fuasai COVID yn bodoli yn ein pentref bach ni. Roedden ni wedi cael digon arno, erbyn hyn, felly siawns fod pawb arall? Roedd yn braf cael dihangfa! Ond, ar lefel mwy ymarferol, rydyn ni'n ffilmio cymaint ymlaen llaw, ac roedd canllawiau COVID yn newid mor gyson – byddai peryg i olygfeydd ddyddio'n hawdd.

Y setiau y tu mewn i Stiwdios Aria

Bu colli cwsg a gwaith di-flino i sawl un wrth geisio codi'r gyfres yn ôl ar ei thraed. Roedd cyfarfodydd dros Zoom yn ail natur bellach, a chofiwn ein cyfarfod torfol cyntaf gyda'r holl gast a chriw yn disgwyl yn bryderus eiddgar am y trefniadau ffilmio newydd. Cofiwn hefyd pa mor falch oedd pawb o weld ei gilydd wedi'r holl wythnosau. Diogelu pawb oedd y flaenoriaeth a pherswadio pawb ein bod am weithredu mor ddiogel â phosib.

Cofiwn y diwrnod cyntaf yn ôl ar y set, fel ddoe. Roedd aelodau o'r criw cynhyrchu eisoes wedi bod 'nôl a blaen yn paratoi ac yn ymgyfarwyddo â'r drefn newydd, a rhaid diolch am eu cydweithrediad parod a'u cefnogaeth bryd hynny. Daeth y cast i mewn fesul un gan ddilyn y

system unffordd at yr ardal wisgoedd, dadbacio eu gwisg o orchudd plastig pwrpasol a newid, cyn mynd i'r Adran Golur i gael cyfarwyddiadau ar sut i roi eu colur eu hunain – achos, wrth gwrs, roedd rhaid cadw pellter. Teg

Sws drwy'r sgrin: Carys ac Aled (Ceri Lloyd a Dan Lloyd)

*Dylan a Sophie yn nyddiau COVID
(Dafydd Rhys Evans
ac Angharad Llwyd)*

dweud bod colur sawl un wedi symleiddio yn ystod y cyfnod hwn, gan gynnwys tatŵs Ken (Idris Morris Jones)!

Er y cadw pellter cywir, y di-heintio rhwng 'têcs', a sicrhau fod pawb yn gwisgo eu mygydau – a bod y mygydau ddim yn difetha colur actorion – llwyddwyd i saethu nifer digon parchus o olygfeydd. Dyna ryddhad.

Ac fel yna y bu am fisoedd lawer. Petaech yn edrych ar benodau a ddarlledwyd yng nghyfnod cynnar COVID-19, fe sylwech fod merched y caffi yn gyson brysur, ond 'taech chi'n syllu'n fanwl, toedd 'na byth actorion cefndirol! Bu cyfarwyddwyr yn greadigol iawn yn eich twyllo, a'r Adran Ddybio yn yr un modd – drwy ychwanegu seiniau cynnil oedd yn awgrymu bod 'na bobl a bwrlwm yno, fel yr arfer.

Yn amlwg, roedd sawl stori yn ei hanterth cyn COVID, ac roedden ni'n awyddus iawn i anrhydeddu'r straeon hynny hyd orau ein gallu. Cofiwn drafod golygfa yn ein cyfarfod storïo wythnosol ar Zoom, ble roedd angen i gymeriadau gusanu. A oedd posib ei dwyllo? A fasa'r cyfan yn edrych yn hurt? Penderfynwyd y basen ni'n cadw at y gusan, a dod o hyd i ffordd o'i chwmpas hi.

Dyna brofiad rhyfedd oedd bod ar set y diwrnod hwnnw gyda Ceri Lloyd (Carys) a Daniel Lloyd (Aled) yn cusanu gyda sgrin fawr bersbecs rhyngddyn nhw. Bu'r actorion, y cyfarwyddwr a'r criw technegol yn ddychmygus a chrefftus iawn y diwrnod hwnnw.

Pan oedd angen i gymeriadau Vince (Huw Llŷr) a Kay (Buddug Povey) fynd am gusan, dyma feddwl am opsiwn gwahanol iawn. I'r rhai ohonoch sydd

*Dybl denims… Gwenno fel Kay
(Buddug Povey, Elen Gwynne
a Huw Llŷr)*

ddim yn ymwybodol, mae cymeriadau Vince a Gwenno yn briod yn y byd go iawn. Dyma felly feddwl… tybed a allai Gwenno fod yn 'ddybl' i Kay? Yn wir i chi, rhoddwyd wig melyn a denims fel Kay ar Gwenno (Elen Gwynne), a llwyddwyd i dwyllo'r cyfan… gobeithio!

Wrth edrych yn ôl, yn sicr, mi newidiodd COVID lawer ar y gyfres; ond drwy gydol y cyfan, roedd teulu triw a gofalus *Rownd a Rownd* yn ceisio sicrhau nad oedd profiad y gwyliwr o wylio *Rownd a Rownd* yn teimlo'n ddieithr. Roedd angen y cyfarwydd ar bawb a hiwmor, bryd hynny, yn fwy nag erioed – felly diolch byth am Arthur (Gwyn Vaughan)!

Er holl heriau COVID, edrych ymlaen oedd y nod a dal ati hyd orau ein gallu – a dyna wnaeth pob un o flaen a thu ôl y camera. O waelod calon, diolch i bawb a fu'n rhan o'r tîm bryd hynny.

Pen-blwydd hapus iawn i *Rownd a Rownd*! Diolch am gael bod yn rhan o'r cyfan.

Ffrindiau

13 – Holiaduron Ddoe (1996)!

Petaech chi'n cael siawns i gyf-weld rhai o sêr **Rownd a Rownd**, beth fyddech chi'n ei ofyn? Mae swyddfa **Rownd a Rownd** yn derbyn nifer o lythyrau bob mis yn gofyn am wybodaeth am yr actorion, felly dyma atebion i'r cwestiynau mwyaf cyffredin.

Enw:	**FFLUR MEDI OWEN**
Enw Cymeriad:	Ffion Parri
Cartref:	Llandudno
Man Geni:	Ysbyty Dewi Sant, Bangor
Dyddiad Geni:	9 Medi 1983
Arwydd Seryddol:	Firgo
Brodyr/Chwiorydd:	Un chwaer iau, Mari (sy'n dipyn o seren deledu hefyd)
Diddordebau:	Actio, canu, dawnsio, darllen, nofio a chanu'r delyn
Addysg:	Cyn-ddisgybl o Ysgol Morfa Rhianedd, Llandudno, ond erbyn hyn yn Ysgol y Creuddyn
Dechrau Actio:	Yn yr ysgol gynradd ac wedyn gydag Ysgol Berfformio Glanaethwy
Gyrfa Hyd Yma:	Hon ydy'r rhaglen deledu gyntaf i mi, ond rydw i wedi perfformio ar lwyfan sawl tro gyda'r ysgol

Hoff Fwyd:	Pizza *pepperoni*, tatws trwy'u crwyn a salad
Hoff Ddiod:	Leim a soda, a sudd oren ffres
Hoff Gerddoriaeth:	Oasis – pob un cân!
Hoff Lyfr:	Llyfrau **Point Horror** a'r awdur R. L. Stine
Hoff Ffilm:	**Fried Green Tomatoes** a **Forrest Gump**
Diwrnod Delfrydol:	Siopa am ddillad efo ffrindiau
Profiad Gwaethaf:	Unwaith, ar wyliau ym Mhortiwgal, defnyddio camera i dynnu llu o luniau ac wedyn sylweddoli nad fy nghamera i oedd o!
Cas Bethau:	Pobl yn taflu sbwriel ar lawr, cam-drin anifeiliaid a sŵn y cloc larwm yn y bore
*Ai ti **ydy** Ffion?*	Rwy'n benderfynol iawn wedi i mi roi fy meddwl ar rywbeth, a dwi'n barod i ddweud fy meddwl – ond dwi ddim cweit mor *cheeky* â Ffion!
Pum mlynedd o rŵan?	Paratoi i fynd i goleg
Uchelgais Bywyd:	Bod yn actores fydenwog!

❀

Enw:	**OWAIN EDWARDS**
Enw Cymeriad:	Aled Shaw
Cartref:	Rhiwlas
Man Geni:	Bangor
Dyddiad Geni:	Mawrth 5, 1983
Arwydd Seryddol:	Pisces
Brodyr/Chwiorydd:	Un chwaer
Diddordebau:	Chwaraeon, arlunio a pherfformio
Addysg:	Ysgol Dyffryn Ogwen
Dechrau Actio:	Cael fy newis tra oeddwn yn fy mlwyddyn olaf yn yr ysgol gynradd i gymryd rhan mewn fideo ar gyfer ysgolion Cymru gyda Cefin a Rhian Roberts
Gyrfa Hyd Yma:	**William Jones** (Cwmni Theatr Gwynedd) a **Giamocs**
Hoff Fwyd:	Sosej a *chips*
Hoff Ddiod:	Ysgytlaeth mefus
Hoff Gerddoriaeth:	**Wonderwall** gan Oasis
Hoff Lyfr:	**Boy** gan Roald Dahl

Hoff Ffilm:	**Forrest Gump**
Diwrnod Delfrydol:	Mynd i go-kartio
Profiad Gwaethaf:	Mae'n llawer rhy *embarrassing*!
Cas Bethau:	Nadroedd a phryfaid cop mawr!
*Ai ti **ydy** Aled?*	Mewn rhai ffyrdd; fel Aled, rydw i'n hoff iawn o anifeiliaid
Rownd a Rownd – *Y Da?*	Cymdeithasu gyda phawb
Rownd a Rownd – *Y Drwg?*	Sefyllian yn yr oerni wrth aros i ffilmio golygfa
Pa un peth na allet fod hebddo?	Pêl-droed
Pum mlynedd o rŵan?	Parhau o fewn y byd actio a chael fy nerbyn i goleg
Uchelgais Bywyd:	Actio yn un o ffilmiau Hollywood!

13 – Holiaduron Heddiw (2025)!

Enw: Fflur Medi Owen

Enw cymeriad: Ffion Parry

Pwt bach am dy gymeriad: Wedi tyfu i fyny yn nyddiau cynharaf y gyfres. Sonia Jackson Ynys Môn – efo bag papur a chi bach gwyn yn lle trwmped. Wedi cael chwarae sawl archetype: chwaer fach niwsans Dylan (Emyr Prys Davies), ffrind gora Sam (Gethin Rhys Williams), dan draed Roger siop (Arwel Roberts), mêt ysgol efo Cadi (Mirain Haf), cariad Aled (Owain Arthur) erbyn diwadd(!) – cyn ei miglo hi o adra am Loegar, heb sbio 'nôl.

Cartref: Caernarfon

Dyddiad geni: 20 Medi 1983 (cofio bod yn tshyffd bod y [llyfr *RaR*] gwreiddiol wedi cael teipo a 'ngneud i bythefnos gyfa yn hŷn – ddim yn gymaint o 'hell yes' ar yr ochr yma i 40!).

Diddordebau: Theoleg, diwinyddiaeth, hen weddïau a'u hystyron yn eu hieithoedd gwreiddiol, astroleg hynafol, hen ddefodau Celtaidd…

Dechrau actio: *Rownd a Rownd* ar ôl yr ysgol gynradd, ac Ysgol berfformio Glanaethwy.

Dylan, Ffion a Nia
(Emyr Prys Davies,
Fflur a Nia Williams)

Gyrfa hyd yma: Wedi ymdrafod â môr-ladrata a cholli babanod. Wedi'i 'Ribidirew!'-io hi, a'i grîn-sgrinio hi. Wedi chwarae rhan o ddychymyg rhywun, ac wedi cael fy nghroeshoelio gan rywun arall. Wedi ei sit-comio hi a'i myrdyr-mystereiddio hi. Wedi ei throsleisio hi, ei dawnsio hi a'i gorstumio hi. Ar wahân i hyn, wedi gweithio gydag elusen atal digartrefedd ac elusen sy'n rhoi cefnogaeth gorddibyniaeth. Wedi gweithio yn cefnogi pobl gydag anabledd dysgu a dementia. Ar hyn o bryd yn gweithio ym maes cadwraeth fel gwarcheidwad yn Nhŷ Mawr Wybrnant, ac yn ystyried ffyrdd newydd i adrodd hen hanes.

Hoff fwyd: Cyri Thai massaman hefo tofu.

Hoff ddiod: Sudd oren ffres (yn dal i fod!).

Hoff gerddoriaeth: Nick Cave (dim pob un cân).

Hoff lyfr: Ar hyn o bryd, *Call Me By Your Name*, gan André Aciman.

Hoff ffilm: Ar hyn o bryd, *The Dig*.

Diwrnod delfrydol: Crwydro i rywle dwi heb fod o'r blaen. Mi fasa'n grêt tasa 'na eglwysi hynafol, haul, traeth a tapas.

Profiad gwaethaf: Cael jaman am ateb 1996... O, na byddai'n haf o hyd! Gormod i'w rhestru, ond yn teimlo'n lwcus 'mod i'n gallu deud yr un peth am brofiadau da.

Cas Bethau: Anonestrwydd

Rownd a Rownd – y da? Cael dy dalu i chwarae.

Ffion ac Aled, y ddau gariad o'r diwedd!
(Fflur ac Owain Arthur)

Rownd a Rownd – y drwg? Bod yr iaith yn gorfod bod mor berffaith yn y dyddiau cynnar. Dim Saesneg, dim cam-dreigs, a dim llafareiddio. Dwi'n cofio un bennod pan oedd Ffion wedi bod adra yn sâl efo dolur gwddw, ac Aled yn dŵad i chwilio amdani ar ôl ysgol. Roedd hyn cyn dyddiau ffôns ('Lle t?' / 'Sâl' / 'K'), a lein Aled oedd, "Be sydd?", a dwi'n cofio fi'n gofyn am gael atab yn ôl yn ein ffordd 'teenage' arbennig – "Ma gwddw fi'n lladd" – a chael "NA" fflat. Roedd rhaid deud y lein fel oedd hi wedi cael ei sgwennu. Felly, "Be sydd?"… Wel…(deep breath)… "Ma 'ngwddw fi fel tasa 'na rywun wedi tynnu sgrafell gaws drosti…" Dwi'n cofio gwylio'r bennod hefyd, a gweld y 'resistance' yn fy nghorff a 'nannadd cefn, a fflach o isio chwerthin yn llgada Owain Edwards. Roedd o'n rhyw deimlad cyfatebol i gael dy riant yn tynnu i fyny reit o flaen drws ffrynt yr ysgol yn y car i nôl chdi ar ddiwadd y dydd pan o'ch chdi'n 14, dwi'n meddwl… #omg #parciarowndgongol

Pa un peth na allet ti fyw hebddo? Ga i ddau? Twm a Nyfain.

Pum mlynedd o rŵan? Pwy a ŵyr. Low key. Dim byd sy'n gofyn i fi siarad iaith rhy gywir (new addition).

Uchelgais bywyd: Gallu'i fyw o mewn ffordd sy'n gneud sens (i fi).

* * *

Enw: Owain Arthur

Enw Cymeriad: Aled Shaw

Pwt bach am dy gymeriad: Hogyn direidus, clên a gweithgar.

Cartref: Llundain

Dyddiad geni: Mawrth 5ed, 1983

Brodyr/chwiorydd: Mêt gora fi, Sioned.

Diddordebau: Chwerthin.

Addysg: Dal i ddysgu.

Gyrfa hyd yma: Lwcus.

Hoff fwyd: Bancwet. Unrhyw fancwet!

Hoff ddiod: Guinness.

Hoff gerddoriaeth: Rwbath heblaw am heavy-heavy-heavy metal.

Hoff lyfr: *Llyfr Mawr y Plant*.

Hoff ffilm: *Forrest Gump*.

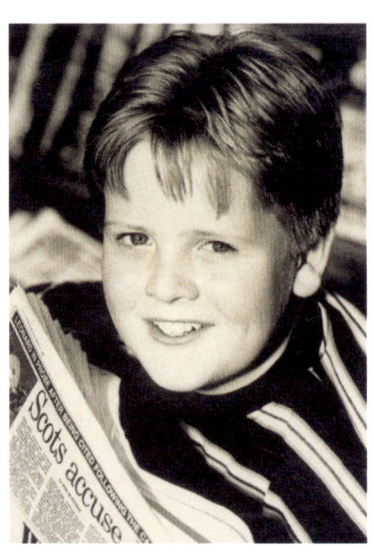

Diwrnod delfrydol? Efo ffrindia yn dathlu achlysur arbennig.

Profiad gwaethaf: Mynd ar goll ar draeth Pwllheli pan yn bump oed.

Cas bethau: Troi'r clociau yn ôl mis Hydref.

Rownd a Rownd **– y da?** Cyfarfod ffrindiau am byth.

Egin cariad...

Rownd a Rownd – y drwg? Gorfod gadael.

Pa un peth na allet ti fyw hebddo? Apple crumble Mam.

Pum mlynedd o rŵan? Bod yn iach a hapus, gobeithio.

Uchelgais bywyd: Adeiladu car efo fy nhad.

* * *

Enw: Ffion Medi

Enw cymeriad: Danielle "Dani" Keegan-Williams

Pwt am dy gymeriad: Mae Dani'n gymeriad cryf ofnadwy, yn enwedig ers colli ei thad. Mae hi wedi camu i mewn i'w hesgidiau o fel person caled busnes, ond wedi cadw'r ochr feddal i'w chymeriad er gwaethaf hyn. Ar ôl bod trwy gymaint yn ei bywyd, mae ei thraed hi'n dal ar y ddaear, ac wastad yn barod i helpu rhywun sydd mewn angen... Ond peidiwch, da chi, â'i chroesi hi de!

Cartref: Pen Llŷn.

Man geni: Y Felinheli.

Arwydd seryddol: Firgo/Libra.

Brodyr/chwiorydd: Dwy chwaer.

Diddordebau: Cerdded, coginio, chwerthin.

Addysg: Bywyd.

Dechrau actio: *Rownd a Rownd* yn saith mlwydd oed.

Gyrfa hyd yma: 25 mlynadd.

Hoff fwyd: Cinio dydd Sul.

Hoff ddiod: Blackcurrant a soda, efo lot o rew.

Hoff gerddoriaeth: Cerddoriaeth Soul.

Hoff lyfr: *Gone Girl*.

Hoff ffilm: *Titanic*.

Diwrnod delfrydol: Cerdded efo'r ci ar ddiwrnod braf.

Profiad gwaethaf: Baglu (bob achlysur)…

Y Dywysoges Dani yn cael ei choroni gan neb llai na Margaret Williams ei hun!

Cas bethau: Madarch.

Rownd a Rownd – **y da?** Gigyls ar set.

Rownd a Rownd – **y drwg?** Gigyls ar set.

Pa un peth na allet ti fyw hebddo? Panad o de (a'r tri o hogia bach anhygoel sy'n galw fi'n Anti!)

Pum mlynedd o rŵan? Hapusrwydd.

Uchelgais bywyd: Hapusrwydd i barhau.

* * *

Enw: Iwan Fôn

Enw cymeriad: Jason Hardy

Pwt bach am dy gymeriad: Mab i'r diweddar Iris, ac i Ben, yn frawd mawr i Dale a brawd bach i'r enwog Barry Hardy, Barry Ddrwg! Ma Jason yn berson annwyl, hael a ffyddlon i'w ffrindia a'i deulu, ond weithiau'n rhy naïf, sy'n golygu ei fod yn cael ei dynnu i mewn i sefyllfaoedd anodd. Mae o'n berson poblogaidd yn y pentref, ac yn ceisio gwneud ei orau i bawb o'i gwmpas – er bod hynny'n gallu rhoi pwysau arno, weithiau. Gyda'i fusnes yn ffynnu a'i berthynas gref efo Dani, mae'r dyfodol yn edrych yn addawol... ond, fel y gwyddom ni i gyd, does byth fawr o lonyddwch yng Nglanrafon!

Cartref: Llanwnda, unwaith fydda i wedi darfod adnewyddu'r tŷ newydd. Dwi'n wreiddiol o bentref Carmel yn Nyffryn Nantlle.

Man geni: Bangor.

Arwydd seryddol: Scorpio.

Brodyr/chwiorydd: Unig blentyn, ond yn lwcus bod gen i gefndryd a chyfnitherod sydd fel brodyr a chwiorydd i fi.

Diddordebau: Gwrando ar gerddoriaeth a chyfansoddi, pêl-droed, sboncen, pŵl, snwcer a choginio.

Addysg: Ysgol Gynradd Carmel, Ysgol Dyffryn Nantlle a Phrifysgol Glyndŵr Wrecsam.

Dechrau actio: Dechreuodd y cyfan wrth i fi ddynwared Syr Wynff a Plwmsan o gwmpas y tŷ pan o'n i'n blentyn bach. Rhai blynyddoedd yn ddiweddarach – tra yn y chweched dosbarth – nes i sgwennu a pherfformio sgets, o fath, yn eisteddfod yr ysgol. Ar y pryd, do'n i ddim yn siŵr be o'n i isio 'i neud fel gyrfa, ond dyma'r prifathro – Mr Emyr Hughes – yn fy annog i fynd i ysgol ddrama. Mae fy nyled yn enfawr iddo fo!

Gyrfa hyd yma: Dyma i chi restr o'r swyddi dwi 'di'u gwneud dros y blynyddoedd...
- Fy swydd gyntaf oedd dyn glo yn iard lo fy nheulu (yncyl)
- Siop jips Dinas Dinlle
- Siop jips J&C's, Caernarfon
- Cash and Carry R&I
- Theatr Clwyd (fy swydd actio gyntaf)
- *Mrs Reynolds a'r Cena Bach* (Theatr Genedlaethol)
- *Raslas Bach a Mawr* (Theatr Bara Caws)
- *Rownd a Rownd*
- *Dennis a Dannedd*
- Lleisio *Ysgol Ni*
- *Dyffryn Mwmin*

Hoff fwyd: Lamb tshops.

Hoff ddiod: Guinness.

Hoff gerddoriaeth: Oasis ac LCD Soundsystem.

Hoff lyfr: *King Solomon's Mines* (H. Rider Haggard)

Hoff ffilm: *The Shawshank Redemption*

Diwrnod delfrydol: Deffro mewn tent ar ben Mynydd Mawr efo Tracy fy nghariad. Helicopter o fanno i maes awyr Dinas Dinlle, a wedyn fflio mewn jet breifat efo fy nheulu a ffrindia i gael cinio a gwin neis yn Perpignan. Hedfan i Glastonbury wedyn, i hedleinio y Pyramid Stage – awr o Kim Hon ac awr o Y Reu. Gorffen y noson mewn parti efo Paul McCartney, Noel a Liam Gallagher, Eric Cantona a'm holl deulu a ffrindia.

Profiad gwaethaf: Colli fy nhaid, fo oedd fy arwr i!

Cas bethau: Pobol anghwrtais, traffic wardens a chaffis sy'n stopio g'neud ffrei-yps ar ôl hanner dydd.

Rownd a Rownd – **y da?** Cael actio, bron bob dydd, efo cast a chriw anhygoel.

Rownd a Rownd – **y drwg?** Boreau cynnar.

Pa un peth na allet ti fyw hebddo? Tracy.

Pum mlynedd o rŵan? Gobeithio fydda i'n briod â Tracy, ac yn ei chanol hi'n magu teulu bach hapus. A hefyd, gobeithio fydda i'n ddigon lwcus i gael parhau i chwarae Jason ar *Rownd a Rownd*!

Uchelgais bywyd: Rhyddhau albym Kim Hon.

14 – Merfyn Pierce Jones
(Alun Powell/Awdur yn y Tîm Cyfredol)
Conffeti a Chôt Ddu: Cofio'r 30

Diwedd 90au'r ganrif ddwaetha, gesh i wahoddiad i ymuno â theulu hyfryd *Rownd a Rownd*. Dydw i ddim yn siŵr pam fush i mor ffodus ond, hyd heddiw, mawr yw fy nyled a 'niolch. Y gweinidog – Alun "Pŵal" Powell – oedd y rhan a gynigiwyd i mi, a'r orchwyl wreiddiol oedd dod i mewn i arwain gwasanaeth priodas Nia "Caffi" (Nia Williams) efo Jac (Emyr Penlan). Dwi'n

cofio'r nesa peth i ddim am y diwrnod hwnnw, ond dwi yn cofio cael dod yn ôl y gyfres ganlynol, a hynny efo teulu cyflawn o Bŵals. Nesta fy ngwraig (Sera Cracroft), a thri o blant, Gwenllian (Bethan Hughes), Beca (Lois Jones) ac Osian (Iddon Jones). Wedi hynny, mi gesh i flynyddoedd o greu atgofion melys sy'n parhau hyd heddiw, ac er ein bod wedi cael straeon fel teulu cyfan ar un oes, bellach mae'r ymddangosiadau wedi'u cyfyngu i "weddings and funerals"! O, ac mi fuo 'na un bedydd hefyd! Wrth edrych yn ôl dros y gwasanaethau hynny, mae o wedi 'nharo fi faint o gymeriadau'r gyfres sydd wedi profi hapusrwydd cwlwm cariad, a phrofi tristwch y pegwn arall.

"Noson y Mileniwm", mi gawsom briodas fawr! Terry (John Glyn) a Glenda (Elliw Haf) oedd y ddau hapus, a'r parti'n cael ei gynnal ar gwch oedd wedi'i angori ger pier Porthaethwy. Dwi'n cofio'r gwisgoedd anhygoel (roedd pawb wedi'u gwisgo fel cymeriadau o'r 1930au), dwi'n cofio Kelvin (Kevin Williams) a Klaire (Ffion Llwyd) – fel rhan o'r chwarae – yn cuddio o dan y bwrdd gwledda, a dwi'n cofio un aelod o'r cast – dim fel rhan o'r chwarae

Priodas Terry a Glenda ar y cwch (Elliw Haf a John Glyn Owen)

– yn cael sawl ffrae gan yr Adran Gelf am fwyta'r bwyd a fwriadwyd ar gyfer y ffilmio. Fyswn i ddim yn meiddio, yn enwedig mewn print, cyhoeddi enw'r dihiryn, ond dwi yn fodlon rhoi cliw bach i chi... roedd ei enw'n dechrau efo Mr ac yn gorffen efo Lloyd (Phylip Hughes)!

Un briodas dwi'n diolch o galon nad oedd Mr Pŵal yn gorfod ei harwain oedd priodas Kelvin a Mari (Manon Medi). Pam, meddach chi? Wel, fel Sgowsar coch (yn hytrach nag un glas), fuo dim rhaid i mi osod yr un o 'nhraed ym Mharc Goodison. Gwell byth, ar gyfer ffilmio'r wledd, mi oeddan ni'n twyllo tu mewn y stadiwm fel gwesty'r Seiont Manor yn Llanrug – a dwi'n licio Llanrug yn iawn!

Yng Nghapel Mawr, Porthaethwy... Wrth baratoi ar gyfer ei phriodas efo

Mathew a Sian, eiliad cyn y slap... (Robin Ceiriog a Mari Wyn Roberts)

Mathew (Robin Ceiriog), mi glywodd Sian (Mari Wyn) bod ei darpar ŵr wedi bod yn chwarae o gwmpas tu ôl i'w chefn efo Llio (Elen Morgan); ond yn hytrach na deu'tho fo ei bod yn gwybod hynny cyn y diwrnod mawr, mi arhosodd tan oedd pawb wedi cyrraedd y capel ac, yn y sêt fawr o bob man, rhoi slap i Mathew – un y byddai Muhammad Ali ei hun wedi bod yn falch ohoni. Gallwch fentro i ni gael dipyn o hwyl yn ffilmio honno. Roedd yna ddigon o hwyl ym mhriodas Meical a Michelle (Emyr Gibson a Manon Elis) hefyd, efo rhyw thema a ymdebygai i rwbath allan o *Footballers' Wives*. Rhywbeth i'r unigolyn ydy chwaeth! Y briodas ddiweddara, wrth i'r pwt hwn fynd i brint, oedd priodas hyfryd Rhys a Trystan (Meilir Rhys Williams a Gethin Bickerton), ond dwi'n siŵr y bydd sawl un arall yn y dyfodol – pwy fydd nesa, 'sgwn i?!

*Priodas Meical a Michelle
(Manon Elis ac Emyr Gibson)*

Rhywbryd ar hyd y daith – tua dechrau cyfres 9, os dwi'n cofio'n iawn – pan oedd Bethan, Lois ac Iddon yn barod i adael y nyth a throedio eu ffyrdd eu hunain *Rownd a Rownd* y byd, roeddwn i'n gwbod bod fy nyfodol yng Nglanrafon y tu ôl imi! Ond, diolch unwaith eto i'r cynhyrchwyr, gesh i'r gwahoddiad i ymuno â thîm storïo a sgriptio'r gyfres, a dyna ddechrau pennod ddifyr a phleserus arall yn fy mywyd. Am gyfnod byr, roedd y ffilmio a'r sgwennu'n cyd-redeg. Roedd hynny'n cyflwyno sialensau amrywiol bob tro o'n i ar y set, pan y byddwn i'n cael cwestiynau di-ri am y straeon, fel, "Pam bod 'y nghymeriad i'n gneud peth fel'a?"; "Fyswn i ddim yn gneud hynna"; neu, "Be tasa 'nghymeriad i'n gneud hyn…?". Ond, mae yna un enghraifft o dynnu coes o'r cyfnod hwnnw sydd wastad yn gwneud imi chwerthin. Mi o'n i wedi bod yn sgwennu yn y bore ac wedi cael galwad i ddod i ffilmio jesd cyn cinio, felly mi ddoish i mewn ar gyfer gwisgoedd a cholur drwy ddrws cefn yr adeilad, heibio'r fan arlwyo oedd yno ar y pryd. Pan gerddish i mewn, pwy oedd yn eistedd yn y cantîn ond y cyfaill annwyl Mr Lloyd. Mi gododd ei ben, ac efo'r wên ddireidus-annwyl arferol, dyma fo'n gofyn: "A be w't ti'n neud yma heddiw… y *catering*?!".

Ym mhob opera sebon gwerth ei halen, fel yn ein bywydau ni i gyd, ni cheir y melys heb y chwerw. Felly i gyd-bwyso â'r priodasau, cafwyd sawl angladd. Y cynta i mi roi'r fendith ola iddo oedd Chris (neb llai na'r prifardd Llŷr Gwyn Lewis) a fu farw mewn tân. Wedyn, mi ddaeth angladd Nel, ac i mi roedd hwnnw'n brofiad braidd yn od gan mai Alis, fy merch yn y byd go iawn oedd yn chwarae rhan Nel; byd rhyfedd ydy'r byd ffilmio 'ma! Dros y blynyddoedd, mi gollon ni David (Iestyn Arwel), Wyn Humphries (Dewi Rhys) a Fflur (Ceri Elen), ond angladd gafodd effaith annisgwyl arna i oedd un Iris (Karen Wynne). Roedd hi'n amser y 'cyfnod clo' felltith, a phethau'n simsan-ddychwelyd i ryw fath o drefn. Yn angladd ei fam, roedd Barry (Gwion Tegid) druan yn cael trafferth i gelu'r ffaith ei fod yn rhannol-gyfrifol am ei marwolaeth. Wrth ffilmio'r te c'nebrwn gesh i drafferthion. Mi ddoish oddi yno efo anrheg annisgwyl… COVID-19! Fyswn i ddim yn meiddio, yn enwedig mewn print, cyhoeddi pwy oedd y sawl oedd mor awyddus i'm heintio, ond dwi'n fodlon rhoi cliw bach i chi… mae o'n dechrau efo Kelvin ac yn gorffen efo Walsh!

Nel (Alis merch Merfyn) efo Mr Lloyd ac Alwyn (Phylip Hughes a Llŷr Ifans)

Priodas Callum a Cherry (Lynwen Haf Roberts a Rheinallt Davies)

Dwi'n cofio mynd i angladd flynyddoedd yn ôl (mewn bywyd go iawn dwi'n ei olygu rŵan… neu farwolaeth go iawn, i fod yn fanwl gywir) lle, heb air o gelwydd, mi ddudodd y sawl oedd yn rhoi'r deyrnged ei fod yn cofio am y tair 'B' – "y blodau, y bêl-droed a'r blant"! Mi liciwn felly – efo'r un llacrwydd treigladol – ddiolch am flynyddoedd o hapusrwydd a hwyl yng nghwmni pobol dda, drwy ddeud y byddaf innau, wrth edrych yn ôl dros fy mywyd *Rownd a Rownd*aidd, yn diolch am y tair 'B' – "y brawdgarwch, y bants a'r Borthaethwy"! Gan ddiolch i Sue Waters a Robin Evans am eu hymddiriedaeth, a'u canmol ar eu gweledigaeth yn geni, magu a meithrin babi sydd bellach wedi prifio'n oedolyn 30 oed, hoffwn ddymuno Penblwydd Hapus i bawb fu'n gysylltiedig â'r gyfres ers 1995. Er budd y to sy'n codi boed iddi hi, fel yr heniaith, barhau.

15 – Non Llywelyn
(Dybio)

Dyb: Addurno'r Gacen

Yn aml dwi'n cael y cwestiwn, "Dybio? Oo? …a be'n union wyt ti'n 'i neud, felly?"

Sawl un yn meddwl 'mod i'n lleisio rhaglenni mewn iaith arall neu'n trio ffitio geiriau Cymraeg dros gegau'n symud mewn ffilmiau tramor. Yn wir, mae hynny yn berthnasol i waith dybio ar draws y byd, ond nid dyna mae criw bach dybio *Rownd a Rownd* yn ei wneud o ddydd i ddydd.

Creu'r trac sain terfynol gora bosib ydi'n nod ni ar gyfer bob rhaglen. Drwy gyfuno sain gafodd ei recordio ar leoliad gyda recordiadau newydd, effeithiau sain a cherddoriaeth mae'r dyb yn mynd â'r rhaglen gam ymhellach. Byddai'r cyfarwyddwr Dennis Pritchard Jones yn dweud mai'r dyb ydi'r "geiriosen ar ben y gacen", ond yn fy marn i mae'r dyb dipyn bach dyfnach na hynny. Os ydi'r sbwnj yn cracio, ma'r dyb yn ychwanegu cynhwysion cyfrinachol a'u smentio gydag eisin melys! Gora oll os ydi'r sbwnj yn berffaith yn barod, yna gall y dyb addurno ac ychwanegu sawl ceiriosen, sbrincyls a siocled moethus!

Mae dybio yn waith rhannol dechnegol a rhannol artistig. Ni sy'n gyfrifol am lefelau sain rhaglenni ac am sicrhau bod popeth i'w glywed mor glir a chywir â phosib. Rydan ni hefyd yn adeiladu byd sain, haen wrth haen, i'w wneud mor realistig ag y bo modd. Caiff *Rownd a Rownd* ei recordio ar leoliad ac ar set. Weithia bydd y tu allan i dŷ yng nghanol tref Porthaethwy

Y ddesg gymysgu

a'r tu mewn i'r tŷ yn stiwdio Aria yn Llangefni. Gall y dyb helpu i ddod â'r ddau at ei gilydd drwy gysoni cefndiroedd sain. Haws credu bod y ddau yr un lle os y byddwch yn dal i glywed y ci sydd tu allan i'r tŷ yn cyfarth yn y pellter o'r tu mewn. Efallai bydd yna wythnosau rhwng saethu'r ddau leoliad hefyd, wrth gwrs. Llawer o dwyll i helpu i greu ein gwir ni!

O'r gerddoriaeth agoriadol i radios a ffonau symudol, mae'r dyb yn ychwanegu seiniau di-ri ar ben y ddeialog i gyfoethogi'r byd sain ac i helpu i ddweud y stori yn y pen draw. Mae cerddoriaeth Gymraeg yn arbennig yn chwarae rhan amlwg iawn yn *Rownd a Rownd*. Dros y blynyddoedd mae wedi dod yn rhan o steil y gyfres ac mae artistiaid a chyhoeddwyr yn anfon eu traciau newydd atom ni yn gyson. Rydw i'n hynod falch o'r ffordd rydan ni'n plethu ystod eang o draciau Cymraeg i mewn i'r gyfres. O themâu cynnil i eiriau perthnasol ac alawon grymus, mae cerddoriaeth Gymraeg yn ennyn lefel arall o ymateb yn ein cynulleidfa. Yn ychwanegu cynnwrf, yn ein tynnu i mewn i gydymdeimlo â chymeriad, neu i fod yn llinyn sy'n cysylltu storïau ar draws nifer o benodau, mae cerddoriaeth yn elfen bwerus iawn o'r dyb. Mae'r berthynas rhwng y llun a'r sain, y tempo a'r curiad sy'n eu cloi at ei gilydd yn rhywbeth arbennig sy'n ein cyffwrdd drwy'r isymwybod.

Pen-blwydd hapus iawn, *Rownd a Rownd*! Dwi'n hynod prowd o fod yn rhan o'r tîm ôl-gynhyrchu ers dros ugain mlynedd!

Mor Ffôl

'Nôl yng nghyfres 21, bu i un o hoelion wyth Glanrafon brofi gwewyr mawr. Wedi colli ei ddiweddar wraig, Lena, mi fu i Mr Lloyd ddisgyn mewn cariad unwaith yn rhagor gyda gwraig o'r enw Megan, neu Megan yr oedd yn galw ei hun yng ngŵydd pawb yn ein pentref bach ni... Dyma bwt gan yr annwyl Mr Lloyd yn hel atgofion o'r cyfnod cythryblus hwnnw yn ei fywyd.

Lena annwyl (Olwen Rees)

Bu colli fy ngwraig annwyl, Lena yn ergyd drom, ond trwy drugaredd, bu f'ymroddiad i fywyd y capel – fel ysgrifennydd ac organydd, ynghyd â'm gwaith fel cynghorydd – yn gaffaeliad o'r mwyaf i mi.

Ni feddyliais am eiliad y buaswn, yn f'oed a'm hamser, yn cwympo mewn cariad unwaith yn rhagor, a hynny dros fy mhen a'm clustiau. Fe ddylaswn fod wedi gwybod yn well.

Mr Lloyd a Megan ddrwg (Gaynor Morgan Rees)

77

Megan oedd ei henw, menyw ddeniadol a chanddi wên ddireidus. Cymaint oedd ei diddordeb ynof, a minnau ynddi hithau, nes i mi ei gwahodd ar sawl achlysur i'r tŷ (gyda chryn anogaeth gan Michelle Keegan-Williams, oedd yn glanhau i mi ar y pryd), ac yno y gafaelodd yn frwdfrydig iawn yng ngorchwylion y tŷ, i'r fath raddau fel yr oeddwn yn ymddiried ynddi yn llwyr – hyd yn oed efo fy materion ariannol. Cymaint oedd fy ffydd ynddi fel i mi rannu cyfrinachau fy nghynilion yn y banc efo hi. Mor ffôl yr oeddwn.

Ei hawgrym hi oedd y buasai'n hyfryd cael byw efo'n gilydd gan ein bod yng nghwmni ein gilydd mor aml. Fe gytunais gyda brwdfrydedd. Onid oedd Megan yn gwmni ac yn gymorth hawdd ei gael mewn cyfyngder, yn enwedig a minnau'n 'tynnu 'mlaen'? Rhaid felly oedd gwneud yr hyn oedd yn iawn, sef priodi, a dyna a benderfynwyd.

Yr oeddwn mor sicr i mi wneud y penderfyniad cywir nes i mi rannu perchnogaeth y tŷ efo hi. Penderfynwyd ar ddyddiad ein priodas, a mawr fu'r llawenydd wrth ei baratoi.

Treuliasom oriau yng nghwmni ein gilydd yn trafod y dillad, y blodau, y gwahoddedigion a'r neithior. Cafodd Megan ryddid llwyr i ddefnyddio fy ngherdyn banc i hwyluso'r trefniadau.

Y noson cyn y briodas aeth Megan, yn ôl yr arfer, i dreulio'r nos mewn man arall. Nis gwn i ble yr aeth. Ni wyddwn ar y pryd, wrth ffarwelio, mai dyna'r tro olaf y byddwn yn ei gweld.

Wedi gwisgo ar gyfer yr achlysur hapus, euthum gyda fy nghyfaill Keneth, yn ei gar i'r swyddfa gofrestru priodasau i ddisgwyl ymddangosiad fy narpar wraig.

Wrth i'r amser agosáu at amser cofrestru, dechreuais anesmwytho gan nad oedd golwg o Megan. Cysurais fy hun mai un o ddefodau priodas oedd i'r briodferch fod yn hwyr. Wedi dros ugain munud o ddisgwyl cynhyrfus, roeddwn yn bendant fod rhywbeth wedi digwydd i'w hatal rhag dod – a rhaid oedd mynd i chwilio amdani.

Nid anghofiaf fyth y braw o weld ystafelloedd y tŷ yn wag heb unrhyw ddodrefnyn i'm cyfarch. Nid anghofiaf chwaith yr eiliad y bu i mi sylweddoli fy mod wedi cael fy nhwyllo'n llwyr, a'm cynilion i gyd wedi mynd. Yn rhyfedd ddigon, daeth geiriau'r gân y bûm yn eu canu fel bachgen yn eisteddfod y capel i'm cof… 'Dod dy law, on'd wyt yn coelio, dan fy mron, a gwylia 'mrifo; ti gei glywed, os gwrandewi, sŵn y galon fach yn torri.'

17 – Phylip Hughes
(Mr Lloyd)

Fy Llwybr i Lanrafon

Hap a damwain oedd i mi gychwyn fel actor i ennill fy mara menyn. Wedi cyfnod oddi cartref yn canu efo cwmnïau opera Cymru a Lloegr, cefais ddwy swydd ran amser – a llawer agosach at y teulu – a hynny efo Cantorion y BBC Manceinion, ac fel athro cerdd mewn ysgol fonedd o'r enw Lowther College ym Modelwyddan. Ar ôl dwy flynedd yn yr ysgol, cawsom wybod ei bod ar fin cau yn gyfan

Mr Lloyd a'i Gyfeillion

gwbl oherwydd nifer isel o ddisgyblion. Heb oedi, fe ysgrifennais lythyr at hen gyfaill, Rhydderch Jones a oedd, ar y pryd, yn gyfarwyddwr yn Adran Ddrama'r BBC yng Nghaerdydd… A oedd unrhyw waith actio y medrwn ei wneud, tybed? Atebodd gyda throad y post, a'm gwahodd i Gaerdydd i'w gyfarfod. Y canlyniad oedd i mi gael rhan mewn drama o'r enw *Bois y Bledren*. Ychydig wythnosau'n ddiweddarach, cefais alwad ffôn gyffrous yn cynnig rhan 'Stan Bevan' yn *Pobol y Cwm*. Yr unig anfantais, unwaith yn rhagor, oedd bod y gwaith ymhell oddi wrth y teulu.

Er hynny, fe'i derbyniais yn llawen.

Wedi deng mlynedd fel 'Stan Bevan', fe rois y gorau i'r gyfres; ond cyn hir, daeth cyfresi eraill i'm rhan fel *Hafod Henri*, *Con Passionate*, ac eraill.

A minnau'n bum deg a naw oed, penderfynais na fyddwn byth eto yn mynd oddi cartref am gyfnodau hir. Pleser annisgwyl iawn felly oedd derbyn galwad gan Robin Evans y cynhyrchydd yn cynnig dwy neu dair pennod i mi fel 'Mr Edwin Lloyd' yn y gyfres *Rownd a Rownd*. Deng mlynedd ar hugain yn ddiweddarach, mae Mr Lloyd a'i ffon addurnedig yn parhau yn y gyfres, a minnau'n cael mynd adref ar ddiwedd diwrnod hapus a dedwydd yng nghwmni teulu hen ac ifanc *Rownd a Rownd*. Hen ac ifanc. Dyna, mae'n debyg, y gwahaniaeth mwyaf rhwng *Rownd a Rownd* a'r cynyrchiadau eraill y bûm yn rhan

Meistr yr organ

ohonynt – y plant a'r bobl ifanc yn rhoi cymaint o hwb i hen ddyn sy'n gwneud ei orau i gadw'n ifanc!

Do, bûm yn filwr anfrwdfrydig am ddwy flynedd yn ystod cyfnod fy ieuenctid. Yr hyn sy'n glynu yn y cof yw'r gwmnïaeth a'r gyfeillach. Dyna hefyd a gefais ac a deimlais wrth fod yn rhan o deulu *Rownd a Rownd* cyhyd. Do, bûm yn athro cerddoriaeth am gyfnod sylweddol yn cydweithio efo plant a phobl ifanc mewn cynyrchiadau theatr a chyngherddau. Ond yma yn *Rownd a Rownd*, mae'r fraint o gydweithio efo plant a phobol ifanc yn gwneud i mi sylwi ar eu doniau a'u hyder yn prifio o flwyddyn i flwyddyn, ac o ddegawd i ddegawd.

Nid yw'n ormodedd dweud mai braint yw cael chwarae fy rhan yn *Rownd a Rownd*. Bu, ac mae'n amser i'w drysori.

SGANIWCH! *Taith Set efo Iwan Fôn*

Hoelen wyth Glanrafon

18 – Annes Wyn a Lleucu Gruffydd
(Cynhyrchwyr Cyfredol)

Rownd a Rownd o Ddydd i Ddydd

Be allwn ni'i ddweud sy'n wahanol i'r cynhyrchwyr blaenorol? Yr un problemau sy'n codi bob blwyddyn ers deng mlynedd ar hugain! Tywydd, criwio, amserlennu, storïo, castio, cyllidebu, hyrwyddo… Mae 'na gyfrifoldeb mawr i gadw'r injan fawr i fynd yn wyneb y ffactorau yma, i gynnal gwaith cyson i dros gant o bobl ac i greu arlwy y mae'r gynulleidfa'n ei fwynhau bob wythnos. Ond er gwaetha'r heriau, 'dan ni'n dwy yn ymwybodol iawn mai braint ydi cynhyrchu *Rownd a Rownd*. Braint ydy cael y cyfle i gamu i mewn i esgidiau'r cynhyrchwyr sydd wedi bod o'n blaenau, y rhai sydd wedi braenaru'r tir a gosod sylfeini mor gadarn er mwyn i ni barhau gyda llwyddiant y gyfres.

Wrth gyrraedd ein gwaith bob bore, does gennym ni ddim syniad beth fydd yn ein hwynebu'r diwrnod hwnnw. Os oes gwaeledd annisgwyl yn taro aelod o'r cast, mae'n rhaid cynnig datrysiadau er mwyn ei gwneud hi'n bosibl i ni barhau i ffilmio. Gyda chymorth cadarn Llio Non, sydd wedi bod yn golygu sgriptiau *Rownd a Rownd* ers blynyddoedd maith bellach, oes modd i

Annes a Lleucu wrth eu gwaith

ni ailsgwennu'r golygfeydd heb y cymeriad penodol hwnnw? Neu oes angen i'r amserlennydd ad-drefnu'r amserlen er mwyn ceisio ffilmio'r golygfeydd rywbryd eto? Mae nifer o ffactorau eraill all orfodi newidiadau funud olaf, ac rydyn ni'n cydweithio gyda chriw'r swyddfa gynhyrchu, a'r criw ffilmio er mwyn eu datrys yn ddyddiol. Er y gall yr elfen hon o'r gwaith brofi'n heriol, dyma'r elfen o'r swydd sy'n ein cadw ar flaenau ein traed, ac mae datrys problemau annisgwyl yn llwyddiannus yn dod â llawer o fwynhad.

Mae'r dyddiau hefyd yn llawn o gyfrifoldebau eraill sy'n dod â'r gyfres at ei gilydd – rhai sydd wedi bodoli ers y cychwyn cyntaf – megis darllen a thrafod y straeon mae'r storïwyr yn eu creu fisoedd o flaen llaw, darllen pob sgript, gwylio pob pennod cyn i'r Adran Ôl-gynhyrchu eu cyfleu i'r sianel, unrhyw ohebiaeth gyda chyrff allanol yn ogystal ag amryw drafodaethau gyda chast a chriw. Ac mae cyfrifoldebau eraill sy'n weddol newydd i gynhyrchwyr y gyfres, sef trafod syniadau a threfnu deunydd aml-blatfform gyda'r Adran Ddigidol. Yn yr oes ddigidol sydd ohoni mae 'na bwysau ar lwyddiant *likes*, *shares* a *views* ac mae'n rhaid i *Rownd a Rownd* ddal ei thir a llwyddo ar y cyfryngau cymdeithasol yn ogystal ag ar y sgrin erbyn hyn. Rydyn ni'n eithriadol o ffodus o'r tîm digidol dygn sy'n gweithio'n ddiflino i rannu clipiau o'r gyfres, creu deunydd newydd, ac sy'n llwyddo i gynyddu ein ffigyrau ar y platfformau digidol bob un flwyddyn.

Er y gall gweithio ar gyfres fel hon fod yn heriol o ddydd i ddydd, mae hi'n bleser pur cydweithio gyda chynifer o unigolion profiadol, yn ogystal â rhai sy'n gwbl newydd i'r diwydiant. Gwaith tîm ydi llwyddiant cyfres fel hon, ac mae tîm *Rownd a Rownd* yn un sy'n tynnu at ei gilydd i sicrhau bod pob golygfa, pob llinell o ddeialog, pob ymateb ac edrychiad gan bob cymeriad yn cyrraedd y "can" ar ddiwedd pob dydd. Does yr un diwydiant arall yn debyg i'r diwydiant teledu, ble mae teimlad cryf o gydweithio fel un teulu mawr. Ar un llaw, mae hi'n anodd credu bod y gyfres wedi cyrraedd ei degfed cyfres ar hugain. Ond ar y llaw arall, mae'n hawdd iawn gweld sut mae'n teulu ni wedi'i gyrru ymlaen cyhyd.

Ymlaen at y deg ar hugain nesaf!

19 – Gwion Tegid
(Barry Hardy/Cyfarwyddo/Awdur Achlysurol)

Barry: 58% o 'mywyd!

Dechreuodd fy nhaith efo *Rownd a Rownd* cyn i Barry Hardy fodoli, deud y gwir. Dim ond chwech oed o'n i pan ges i fy nghastio mewn drama o'r enw *Amdani* fel Eilir, mab y prif gymeriad Llinos – sef Ffion Dafis. Ffilmiau'r Nant oedd cwmni cynhyrchu'r ddwy ddrama ar y pryd, felly pan dda'th *Amdani* i ben wedi pum mlynedd, a *Rownd a Rownd* digwydd bod yn chwilio am hogyn drwg 12 oed, o'n i'n y lle

Dechrau a diwedd y daith yng Nglanrafon...

iawn, ar yr amser iawn – eisoes wedi datblygu perthynas efo'r tîm cynhyrchu a'r cyfarwyddwyr. Ches i'm clyweliad, dim ond "sgwrs" efo Robin, Sue a Cliff; ac wrth edrych yn ôl, roedd hon yn sgwrs hynod o bwysig i drywydd fy mywyd!

Roedd fy niwrnod cyntaf ar *Rownd a Rownd* yn fythgofiadwy – yn ffilmio yn Blackpool, dim Porthaethwy. Digwydd bod, o'dd hi'n ben-blwydd arna fi'r penwythnos hwnnw 'fyd, a ddudis i'm gair wrth neb. Do'n i'm isio sylw na ffys. Ges i fy nghroesawu gan yr anhygoel Karen Wynne (Iris, mam Barry); 'naeth hi edrych ar fy ôl i'n iawn y diwrnod cynta hwnnw, a byth ers hynny. Gytunon ni'n dau, y diwrnod hwnnw, mai'r frechdan ora oedd brechdan ffish-ffingyrs ar fara gwyn rhad efo llwyth o salad crîm – pwnc sy'n dal i godi hyd heddiw dros beint yn Y Felinheli.

Roeddan ni'n colli eitha dipyn o'r ysgol ar gyfer ffilmio, ond ro'n i wrth fy modd. Diolch i athrawon cefnogol yn yr ysgol a'r famol Manon Lewis, y tiwtor oedd yn ein cadw ar y trywydd iawn yn y gweithle. Mi oedd o'n od bod ar y teledu a chael eich adnabod yn y byd go iawn, ond fe sicrhaodd hogia Bangor bod fy nhraed i'n aros yn gadarn ar y ddaear!

Mae'n rhyfedd meddwl faint o 'mywyd i sydd wedi'i siapio gan y cymeriad ffuglennol yma. Dwi wastad wedi dweud na ches i draffarth yn gwahaniaethu rhwng Gwion a Barry… er, ella basa Mam yn anghytuno. Dwi'n eitha sicr y basa hi'n dweud bod 'na gyfnod yn fy arddegau lle nad oedd llawer o wahaniaeth rhwng Barry a Gwion!

Wrth i fi fynd yn hŷn, dwi'n sylwi faint o'n i a gweddill y cast ifanc yn jest amsugno bob dim. Doedden ni'm yn poeni am ddatblygiad cymeriad, na phoeni gormod am "fod yn actorion". Oedd o'n fwy fel hobi od, mi o'n i'n mwynhau mynd i'r gwaith. Ges i fy amgylchynu gan bobl dda, mentoriaid gwych, ac awyrgylch a oedd yn caniatáu i actorion ifanc fel fi dyfu i fyny heb or-feddwl.

Yn naturiol, wrth actio hogyn drwg, ga'th Barry lwyth o straeon boncyrs! Mae'n debyg mai dwyn a chrasho Seat Ibiza lime green Ifan sydd ar frig y rhestr. Diwrnod bythgofiadwy! Gweithio efo stuntmen oedd newydd orffen ffilmio *James Bond*, police chase ar A-frame, damwain ddramatig – y math o ddiwrnod lle 'dach chi'n meddwl, "Ie, ma hyn dipyn mwy cŵl na bod yn 'rysgol."

Ond yr hyn dwi'n ei gofio'n iawn ydi'r criw. Y rhedwyr oedd yn fy nôl i o'r ysgol; y chwerthin efo'r Adran Wisgoedd a Cholur; y tynnu coes efo'r criw sain a goleuo; a doethineb tawel y dynion camera a'r cyfarwyddwyr, a oedd – p'un a oedden nhw'n gwybod hynny ai peidio – yn llywio'r ffordd i fi fod yn wneuthurwr ffilmiau fy hun, erbyn hyn.

Pan ddois i'n ôl i'r gyfres yn 21 oed, ro'n i'n teimlo 'mod i'n cael fy nghyflogi'n iawn – fel actor y tro hwn, nid fel y plentyn oedd wedi tyfu i fyny ar set. Roedd y teimlad yn wahanol. Roedd disgwyliadau, rŵan – gan gyfarwyddwyr, cyd-actorion, hyd yn oed fi fy hun. Ro'n i wrth fy modd. Ro'n i'n benderfynol o brofi bod gen i rywbeth i'w gynnig, mai dod â fi yn ôl oedd y penderfyniad cywir.

Y stori amlwg o'r cyfnod hwnnw, heb amheuaeth, oedd y stori pan gafodd Barry ganser y ceilliau. Hwn oedd y tro cyntaf i fi wir ymchwilio i rôl; colli

Cariad Mam: Barry yn ystod ei driniaeth ganser (Karen Wynne, Gwion a Ceri Lloyd)

pwysau amdani, shafio 'mhen – i gyd i wneud cyfiawnder â'r sgript. Hwn oedd y tro cyntaf i fi wir deimlo fel actor yn yr ystyr cyflawn, rhywsut. Ond yn bwysicach fyth, ro'n i'n gobeithio y gallai helpu rhywun oedd yn gwylio.

Dros y blynyddoedd, ges i gyfle i weld beth oedd yn digwydd y tu ôl i'r lens. Nes i ddechra fel rhedwr pan o'n i'n dal yn yr ysgol, ond dros y gwyliau haf. Yna'n hwyrach ymlaen, daeth fy nghyfle cyntaf – diolch i Bedwyr Rees, uwch-gynhyrchydd presennol y gyfres, a pherson sydd wedi cael dylanwad enfawr ar fy nhaith broffesiynol. Ro'n i wedi ysgrifennu drama gomedi a'i rhoi i Bedwyr. Diolch byth, mi welodd rywbeth ynddi – a chyn pen dim, ro'n i'n ysgrifennu sgriptiau *Rownd a Rownd* tra'n dal i actio ar *Rownd a Rownd*.

O'n i'n dueddol o roi llai o linellau i fi fy hun... clyfar de?!

Gwion yn cyfarwyddo

O'r fan honno, es i'n rhan o'r tîm storïo – rhywbeth dwi'n dal i'w wneud o bryd i'w gilydd – ac yna fe ges i'r cyfle i gyfarwyddo *Copsan*, spin-off o *Rownd a Rownd*. Dyna oedd un o brofiadau mwyaf gwerth chweil fy ngyrfa. Roedden ni yn griw profiadol, ond roedd llawer ohonom ni'n camu i roliau newydd am y tro cyntaf. Bu'n ymdrech tîm go iawn. Dyddiau hir

ac uchelgeisiol – ond y teimlad cyffredin o bwrpas rhwng pawb a'i gwnaeth yn joban fythgofiadwy. Un o fy eiliadau balchaf yn ystod saethu *Copsan* oedd cyfarwyddo siot saith munud o

hyd o amgylch Plas Menai. Trosglwyddo'r camera ddwy waith dros far, coreograffi cywrain – roedd yn feiddgar (efallai braidd yn wallgo), ond mi lwyddon ni!

Pan adawodd Barry *Rownd a Rownd* am yr eildro, a hynny i fynd ar ei ben i jêl, ro'n i'n meddwl mai dyna ni. Ond doedd Bedwyr heb orffen efo'r cymeriad, eto. "Ma gynnon ni gynllunia," meddai. Ac ychydig fisoedd yn ddiweddarach, daeth *Bariau*. Drama dywyll yn dilyn yr un Barry Hardy yn y carchar, tu ôl i'r bariau… Er mai'r un cymeriad dwi'n ei bortreadu, mae o'n 'Barry' gwahanol i'r un oedd yn Glanrafon. Egni gwahanol, arddull perfformio gwahanol – cyd-destun cwbl newydd. Nes i weithio yn agos efo'r cyfarwyddwr, Griff Rowland i greu fersiwn o Barry a oedd yn adlewyrchu ei orffennol a'i bresennol. Dwi'n cyfaddef, mi o'n i'n nerfus ofnadwy. Roedd y darlleniad cyntaf yn frawychus. Actorion arbennig o'm hamgylch i, a finna'n arwain yr ensemble! Ond unwaith eto, nes i ffeindio'n hun wedi

cael fy amgylchynu gan dîm gwych, pawb yn cyd-dynnu. Roedd y dyddiau'n hir a chaled, ond roedd y llawenydd o fod yn rhan o rywbeth mor ffres, mor bwerus, yn gwneud y cyfan yn werth chweil.

Heddiw, dwi'n rhedeg fy nghwmni cynhyrchu fy hun, Docshed, gan arbenigo mewn rhaglenni dogfen. Dwi hefyd yn gweithio'n llawrydd fel cyfarwyddwr – gan gynnwys i *Rownd a Rownd*. Ni fyddai hyn wedi digwydd heb y platfform, y fentoriaeth, y cyfleon a'r teulu nes i ei ddarganfod yn *Rownd a Rownd*. Pe bawn i'n gallu siarad â'r Gwion 12 oed yna, y plentyn oedd rhy swil i ddweud wrth unrhyw un ei bod hi'n ben-blwydd arno fo, 'swn i'n dweud wrtho fo, "Ti yn y lle gora fedri di fod." Achos nid dim ond dysgu i fi sut i actio wnaeth *Rownd a Rownd*. Dysgodd i fi sut i gydweithio, sut i wrando, sut i arwain. Rhoddodd ffrindiau oes i mi, atgofion anhygoel, a'r hyder i wneud gyrfa yn y diwydiant gwyllt a rhyfeddol hwn.

'Dwn i'm lle y baswn i heb *Rownd a Rownd*. Dau ddeg a dau o flynyddoedd yn ddiweddarach, dwi'n dal i fod yn ffrindiau agos efo Barry Hardy; anodd peidio â bod, a f'ynta wedi bodoli am 58% o 'mywyd i! Tydw i ddim eisiau dychmygu fersiwn o 'mywyd 'naeth ddim cychwyn efo taith fŷs i Blackpool yn mwydro am frechdan ffish-ffingyrs efo Karen Wynne!

Felly, diolch – i bob aelod o'r criw a'r tîm cynhyrchu, pob cyfarwyddwr, pob aelod o'r cast, a phob person a helpodd i siapio 'mywyd i dros y blynyddoedd. I'r bennod nesaf, *Rownd a Rownd*. Diolch o galon.

20 – Wyn Williams
(Cyfarwyddo)
Rownd a Rownd a Fi

1996. Gwanwyn. Cerdded yn ymyl Stryd y Porth Mawr, Caernarfon a tharo ar Robin Evans a Susan Waters, cynhyrchwyr a chrewyr *Rownd a Rownd* oedd ar waith ers ryw flwyddyn. Minnau ar y pryd yn weithiwr theatr di-waith gyda theulu ifanc.

Robin: W't ti'n gweithio ar hyn o bryd?

Fi: Na.

Sue: Fydde ti'n lico dod i witho gyda ni ar *Rownd a Ro*...

Fi: Baswn!!

Fe ddes i'r setiau ym Mhorthaethwy i drefnu'r amserlen saethu a'r lleoliadau ffilmio, a'r job gyntaf oedd chwilio am gartref i Bryn Stiffs (Ifan Huw Dafydd) ac Edwina (Rhian Cadwaladr), eu mab Ari (Dyfrig Evans) a'r babi newydd (aelod cyfredol o'r band Fleur de Lys – ond, pa un?!).

Ers hynny, a hyd heddiw, mi ydw i wedi amserlennu, trefnu, rheoli lleoliadau, rheoli llawr, cynhyrchu a chyfarwyddo, ac wedi gweithio ar o leia rhan o bob cyfres (oni bai am y gyntaf un) – ac wedi cael braint a phleser, a lot o foddhad o wneud hynny.

Atgofion? Uchafbwyntiau? Isafbwyntiau? Gormod i'w rhestru, ond dyma flas:

- Hedfan i ffilmio ar ynys Jersey (pan redodd Dylan (Emyr Prys Davies) i ffwrdd i chwilio am Bob Beics (Dafydd Emyr)). Glanio yn St Helier a Gorey i'r sylweddoliad nad oedd 'run lleoliad na chaniatâd wedi'i drefnu gan y fficsar lleol. Plagio a pherswadio perchennog a staff y gwesty lle ro'n i'n aros… a ffindio fflat, tŷ bwyta, pwll nofio, ac amryw o leoliadau eraill cyn i'r criw ffilmio gyrraedd y bore wedyn.

- Gyrru John Parrott (pencampwr snwcer y byd yn 1991) o gwmpas Borth a Chaernarfon pan ddaeth yn ŵr gwadd i agor Q's, yr hafan i chwarae pŵl – sydd bellach yn 'Copa'.

- Trefnu dilyniant ffilmio yng nghanol Llundain pan oedd Cadi (Mirain Haf) yn chwilio am Greg (Dafydd Gwynne). Saethu yn yr Amgueddfa Wyddoniaeth, Covent Garden, ar diwb Charing Cross, ac ar Sgwâr Trafalgar – a hynny gydag actores oedd â ffobia o adar! Daethpwyd o hyd i Greg yn bysgio gyda'i sacsoffon ar y Strand.

- Gorfod saethu carnifal i'r gyfres ym Mhorthaethwy ar fore Sul stormus ym mis Ionawr; fflôts lliwgar, gwisg ffansi, majorettes a Band Pres Porthaethwy yno'n perfformio 'Gwŷr Harlech' dros y lle, cyn sylweddoli 'mod i wedi anghofio rhybuddio aelodaeth y capel gerllaw oedd ar ganol gweddi dawel eu gwasanaeth boreol… wps.

Cael cyfarwyddo stynts amrywiol:

- Terry (John Glyn Owen) yn disgyn oddi ar sgaffold uchel ar noson lawog. A gafodd ei wthio? Barry (Gwion Tegid) wnaeth.

- Carafán Julie (Tammi Gwyn) yn ffrwydro'n wenfflam ar ôl i Arthur (Gwyn Vaughan Jones) fod yno'n lapswchan. Barry wnaeth? Ŵyr neb, ond mi oedd o yno yn y cysgodion…

- Ken (Idris Morris Jones) yn taro Philip (Maldwyn John) oddi ar ei feic yn ystod ras gyda Mathew (Robin Ceiriog) a chwalu'r tacsi'n rhacs. Dim byd i wneud â Barry, tro yma.

Mi ydw i wedi bod yma trwy ddau Robbie, dwy Kylie, tri Jason a thair Britney – ond dim ond un Dani (Ffion Medi) ac un Kelvin (Kevin Williams), wrth gwrs.

Ond, uwchlaw popeth, mi ydw i wedi ca'l lot fawr o hwyl a chwmnïaeth ac wedi bod yn dyst i grefft a dawn ac ymroddiad degau o actorion, pobl camera, pobl sain, cynllunwyr, pobl colur a gwisgoedd a chriw cynhyrchu. Mae'r gyfres wedi creu a chynnal corff o weithwyr teledu o safon a phrofiad yng Ngogledd Cymru, ac mae hynny'n deyrnged i Robin a Sue am ddangos ffydd a theyrngarwch i gynifer o gast a chriw llawrydd sydd wedi gallu aros yn eu cymunedau i fyw a gweithio.

Mae diolch aruthrol yn ddyledus, hefyd, i bobl a chymuned Porthaethwy am ein croesawu a'n goddef cyhyd – cymaint o gartrefi a busnesau y buom yn ffilmio ynddynt, a llwyth o gymorth a chymwynasau gan gynifer dros y blynyddoedd.

Y pleser mwyaf? Cael cydweithio i adrodd straeon difyr, a phwysig yn aml, trwy gyfrwng y Gymraeg a bod yn rhan o gyfres unigryw; am hynny, rwy'n ddiolchgar – a diolch i Robin a Sue am y job ym 1996!

21 – Bedwyr Rees
(Uwch-gynhyrchydd)
Gwarchod dros Dro

Dwi'n cofio hyd heddiw y bennod gyntaf o *Rownd a Rownd* i mi fod ynghlwm â hi erioed. Cyfres 9, Pennod 13 – dyma'r bennod gyntaf i mi fod yn rhan o'r tîm storïo iddi, ac yn hon wnaeth Aled (Owain Arthur) a Ffion (Fflur Medi Owen) sylweddoli eu bod yn caru ei gilydd, ond hynny yn rhy hwyr gan fod car yn disgwyl tu allan i Q's i gludo Ffion i Morecambe, yn bell, bell o Lanrafon. Felly pennod olaf Fflur Medi Owen oedd fy mhennod gyntaf i, ac er fy mod wedi gadael am rai blynyddoedd i wneud pethau eraill, rydw i yma o hyd, a hynny gyda'r fraint o fod yn Uwch-gynhyrchydd wrth i'r gyfres arbennig hon gyrraedd y garreg filltir o fod yn 30 oed.

Dod i mewn fel aelod o dîm ysgrifennu wnes i i ddechrau – gyda Graham Jones, Merfyn Pierce Jones a Rhiannon Wyn. Ro'n i'n ffrindiau efo Rhiannon yn barod, ond dyma gyfle i wneud dau ffrind newydd arall, hynod werthfawr, hynod ddoniol. Mae'n rhyfeddol sut mae oriau, dyddiau ac wythnosau bwygilydd o eistedd mewn ystafell yn trafod bywydau cymeriadau ffuglennol yn tynnu pobl at ei gilydd! Mae gen i feddwl mawr o'r tri. 'Dan ni'n dal yn cydweithio, ac ydan – yn rhyfeddol efallai – dal yn ffrindiau!

Mae nifer o bethau wedi newid yn y byd, ac yn y maes darlledu, ers i *RaR* ymddangos yn gyntaf yn ein cartrefi. Yn y cyfresi cyntaf er enghraifft, mae'r cymeriadau ifanc, "drwg" yn ysmygu – byddai canllawiau darlledu a chyfraith gwlad o amgylch ysmygu yn y gweithle yn peri i hynny fod yn anghyfreithlon i ni ei wneud erbyn heddiw! Prin fod yna y ffasiwn beth â phlant yn gwneud rownd bapur erbyn hyn – mae hyd yn oed papurau newydd bron â bod yn amherthnasol bellach. Ond mae cymuned wastad wedi bod yn bwysicach i *Rownd a Rownd* nag unrhyw rownd bapur, ac mae'r gyfres ar hyd yr amser wedi ymateb ac esblygu i ateb gofynion pob cyfnod. Mae hi yma o hyd ac mae hynny diolch i wytnwch a chreadigrwydd pawb – yn gast a chriw – sydd wedi bod ynghlwm â hi dros y blynyddoedd.

Yn fy nghyfnod cyntaf i ar yr ochr gynhyrchu, wedi symud o'r ochr ysgrifennu, fe wnaethon ni sefydlu gwefan i'r gyfres am y tro cyntaf. Roedd ganddon ni hefyd broffiliau cymeriadau ar safleoedd sy'n angof erbyn hyn, fel Myspace a Bebo, lle'r oeddan ni fel cynhyrchwyr yn ymateb i geisiadau y gwylwyr yn "llais" y cymeriadau. Go brin y basan ni'n gwneud hynny heddiw! Wedi rhyw ddegawd i ffwrdd, fe wnes i ddychwelyd i weithio ar y gyfres fel Uwch-gynhyrchydd. Un o'r prif bethau rydyn ni wedi ceisio canolbwyntio arno yn ystod y cyfnod yna ydy ymateb i'r newidiadau aruthrol ar draws y llwyfannau digidol. Yn hynny o beth, 'dan ni bellach yn meddwl am *Rownd a Rownd* nid fel cyfres deledu, ond fel brand sydd yn byw ar draws sawl platfform digidol gwahanol, ar alw i'r gynulleidfa ar unrhyw awr o'r dydd, ac sy'n gallu tyfu brandiau eraill, fel *Copsan* a *Bariau*, yn ei sgil.

Rydw i'n falch iawn o *Bariau*. Dwi'n cofio flynyddoedd yn ôl trafod fel tîm storïo, a gyda'r cynhyrchwyr ar y pryd, ein bod isio teulu newydd o blant drygionus yn y gyfres. Wedi'r drafodaeth, fi wedyn ddigwyddodd sgwennu y 'biog' gwreiddiol ar gyfer cymeriad Barry, a'i enwi ar ôl Baz, fy ffrind gorau pan roeddwn i'n blentyn, ac sydd bellach wedi'n gadael ni (roedd Jason a Dale hefyd yn blant roeddwn i'n eu hadnabod o 'mhlentyndod!). Mae gen i feddwl mawr o gymeriad Barry, ac o Gwion Tegid, ac mae gweld llwyddiant *Bariau* – yn cael ei werthu i America, Seland Newydd ac Awstralia, hyd yma – yn foddhad mawr i mi. Ac mae'r cyfan oherwydd bod *Rownd a Rownd* wedi rhoi'r sylfaen i ni allu adeiladu arni.

Mae *Rownd a Rownd* hefyd wedi bod yn sylfaen gwbl hanfodol i'r diwydiant creadigol yng ngogledd Cymru ac wedi bod yn hwb eithriadol i'r economi leol. Mae wedi bod yn feithrinle i nifer dirifedi o actorion a chriwiau technegol a chynhyrchu. Mae'r ethos yna o hyfforddi a meithrin yn naturiol efallai mewn cyfres sydd wedi esblygu o'r gwreiddyn o fod yn rhaglen blant. Pan mae yna rywbeth mawr – priodas, stynt, neu debyg – mae gwylio'r criw yn gweithio (yn aelodau profiadol a newydd-ddyfodiaid fel ei gilydd) yn

Robin, Sue a Bedwyr â Gwobr BAFTA Cymru

creu argraff amlwg ar rywun; pawb yn gwybod beth maen nhw'n ei wneud, y gwaith paratoi wedi bod yn drylwyr eithriadol a phawb yn cyd-dynnu i greu'r deunydd gorau bosib i'r gynulleidfa. Ar ddyddiau felly, mae Glanrafon yn gallu bod yn lle arbennig iawn i fod.

Mae'r englyn hyfryd gan Robin Evans ar ddechrau'r gyfrol hon yn sôn am esblygiad *Rownd a Rownd* o fod yn rhaglen i blant i fod yn gyfres llawer ehangach. Fy nghred i ydy mai'r ymlyniad drwy'r cyfan at elfen o ddiniweidrwydd a chynhesrwydd plentynnaidd ydy hud *Rownd a Rownd* – dyma ydy'r allwedd a'r glud a dyma sy'n gwneud y cyfan mor hynod o arbennig. 'Dan ni'n dweud yn aml nad ydan ni'n gallu mynegi yn union beth ydy'r peth arbennig am *Rownd a Rownd*, ond mi ydan ni'n gwybod beth ydy o – yn gallu ei deimlo fo, bron â bod!

Petaech chi'n gofyn i mi am dri pheth sydd wedi'u serio ar fy nghof wrth ddathlu'r 30, dyma dwi'n credu y basan nhw:

1) COVID. Gweithio oriau dirifedi bob dydd mewn carafán yn ceisio dygymod â'r holl beth. Cydweithio ac ymroddiad aruthrol gan nifer o bobol i gadw'r gyfres nid yn unig ar ei thraed, ond gyda'r gallu i gyfleu dwy bennod yr wythnos yn ddi-dor i S4C. Treulio misoedd gydag un o'n cynllunwyr, Dafydd Charles yn cynllunio a chodi stiwdio newydd i'r gyfres yn Llangefni er mwyn gallu cario 'mlaen o dan ganllawiau COVID.

Yng nghanol y cyfan, colli Huw Geth – ein golygydd amryddawn, annwyl a ffrind i bawb. Y sioc a'r galar eithriadol o golli un mor ifanc.

2) Y gemau pêl-droed. Cyn i faterion blinderus yswiriant a iechyd a diogelwch ein trechu, roedd hi'n arfer i dîm pêl-droed *Rownd a Rownd* chwarae sawl gêm y flwyddyn. Fel arfer, ar gyfer codi pres tuag at rywbeth cymunedol roedd hyn yn digwydd, ac weithiau, fe fyddai wynebau adnabyddus fel Bryn Fôn a Neil Maffia yn ymuno â ni hefyd.

Rownd a Rownd Rênjyrs

Roedd aelodau o'r criw yn chwarae – Robin a Cliff o'r ochr gynhyrchu yn aml – a dwi'n cofio Phylip Hughes yn chwarae ar yr asgell ac yntau yn ei 70au ar y pryd! Llawer iawn o hwyl a chael teithio yma ac acw. Mwynhau ein hunain, ond ar yr un pryd, sylweddoli a gwerthfawrogi gymaint oedd y gyfres yn ei olygu i wahanol bobl ledled y wlad. A finnau bellach ddim yn gallu chwarae pêl-droed oherwydd fy nghluniau, mae'n braf meddwl am gyfnod pan roeddwn i dipyn bach yn fwy sionc!

3) Robin a Sue, sylfaenwyr y gyfres. Eu gweledigaeth, mentergarwch, creadigrwydd, hyder ac ymddiriedaeth mewn ieuenctid. Doedd dim byd yn rhy "fawr" i *Rownd a Rownd* allu ei handlo – achub cymeriad oddi ar ddibyn gyda hofrennydd; cannoedd o redwyr wedi'u gwisgo fel Sion Corn yn rasio dros Bont Borth; gorchuddio'r brif set i gyd mewn eira; crashio ceir a chychod mewn amryw ffyrdd; ffrwydro pob un dim i ebargofiant – a'r cyfan yn cael ei drin gyda'r difrifoldeb mwyaf ar y naill law, a hiwmor a phinsiad o halen ar y llall. Mae dyled cymaint ohonom i rym ewyllys a phenderfyniad y ddau ohonyn nhw. Y ddau, heb os, sydd wedi cael y dylanwad mwyaf ar fy mywyd proffesiynol; ond ar lefel bersonol hefyd, mi fydda i'n cofio am byth y cyfnodau hwyliog yn y Liverpool Arms efo'r ddau. Teimlad o gael fy edrych ar fy ôl – fy nghefnogi a'm hannog. Peth hynod brin mi dybiaf yn y maes yma. Diolch o galon i'r ddau ohonoch.

Rydw i'n gobeithio mai gwarchod dros dro mae pob un ohonom sydd yn gweithio ar *Rownd a Rownd* – ateb gofynion ein cyfnod ni, ond y bydd eraill yn dod ar ein holau i ateb gofynion y dyfodol, yn ddigidol, yn Ddeallusrwydd Artiffisial neu'n beth bynnag arall sydd ar y gorwel. Pen-blwydd hapus iawn i *Rownd a Rownd*, sy'n ddeg-ar-hugain oed, ond yn teimlo'n newydd-anedig. Ymlaen – ni thâl hi byth i *Rownd a Rownd* sefyll yn stond!

Introduction

Samuel Kalman and Sean Kennedy

Even casual observers of contemporary French politics will recognize that to speak of the French Right in the singular is profoundly misleading. France's modern Right has always been multifaceted in outlook, divided between moderates and radicals, pious Catholics and secularists, establishment elites and angry populists. While the lines between these various tendencies is often blurred, and short and even longer-term alliances are frequent, so is fierce rivalry and even outright political warfare. Focusing on the interwar period, the present volume seeks both to recapture the complexity and fluidity of the French Right, and contribute to a historiography marked by fierce controversies but more recently shifting priorities as well.

Since its formation in the 1870s, the French Third Republic had often faced powerful opposition from the Right.[1] By the early twentieth century, sharp criticisms of the regime were articulated by influential figures such as Maurice Barrès and Charles Maurras, rooted in strident nationalism, hostility to democratic principles, and animosity toward supposedly manipulative "outsiders" such as Protestants, Freemasons, and, above all, Jews. Populist movements, some enduring, most short lived, were another recurring feature of the French Right. In times of crisis—for instance in the 1880s and again after 1894 during the Dreyfus affair—organizations such as the Boulangists, and nationalist formations such as the Ligue des patriotes, the Ligue antisémitique de France, the Ligue de la patrie française, and the monarchist Action française (AF) took shape, assailing the republican system, its political establishment and the Left, to the point of advocating and even seeking the overthrow of the regime. Then in the years following the exoneration of Dreyfus, the separation of Church and state led to deepened political mobilization on the part of French Catholics, in both political and pressure group form. Throughout these years, emerging conservative parlia-

mentary formations, such as the secular and pro-business Alliance républicaine démocratique (ARD) and the nationalist and Catholic Fédération républicaine (FR), struggled to adapt to changing conditions while continuing to promote their vision of an orderly society.

The First World War transformed French political culture in complex ways. Memories of the wartime experience, defined in terms of an unquestioned nationalist unity and profound sacrifice, shaped the rhetoric and outlook of right-wing militants for decades to come. In some ways, the Republic came to enjoy greater acceptance in the eyes of hitherto hostile Rightists, on account of its wartime triumph: but the success of the Bolshevik Revolution and the spread of social unrest during and after the conflict engendered new fears among many conservatives and ultranationalists. The electoral victory of the Bloc National, whose candidates ranged from moderate republicans to Léon Daudet of the AF, in 1919 can be regarded as both an expression of nationalist triumphalism but also a reaction against the possibility of social revolution in France itself. In the years that followed, this right-wing coalition weakened as it was beset by economic troubles, social unrest, controversial political and religious reforms, and divisions over foreign affairs. By contrast, the French Left, itself multifaceted and often fragmented, nevertheless formed an electoral alliance (excepting the Communists) known as the Cartel des Gauches to win the 1924 elections.

The emergence and victory of the Cartel sparked a mass mobilization on the Right, leading to the creation and expansion of several new formations, many of them enjoying support from veterans. They included Antoine Rédier's Légion and Pierre Taittinger's Jeunesses patriotes (JP), both established in 1924, as well as the Faisceau, which was launched by AF dissident Georges Valois the following year. Relations between these movements were turbulent; the Légion was soon absorbed by the JP, while the creation of the Faisceau provoked bitter struggles with the JP and the AF over membership.[2] Serious as these internecine conflicts were, and despite distinct features in each group's platform, they shared a strident nationalism and bitter antipathy toward the parliamentary system. They demanded a stronger executive, called for more forceful measures against Communists and other dissidents, and decried "foreign" elements that supposedly manipulated France's economy and undermined its international prestige. They also attracted considerable, if volatile support: the JP had an estimated 65,000 members by 1926, the Faisceau around 60,000.[3]

Catholic political engagement also intensified at this time. The Parti démocrate populaire (PDP), established in 1924, promoted Social Catholic values in conjunction with an acceptance of republican institutions. However, its relatively moderate stance and limited success must be contrasted with rise of the Fédération nationale catholique (FNC), established by conservative Catholics in response to the anti-clerical rhetoric and agenda of the Cartel des Gauches. The FNC soon enjoyed spectacular growth, claiming 1.8 million supporters within

two years.[4] Catholic women's organizations such as the Ligue patriotique des françaises (LPF), which dated back to the early twentieth century, also gained renewed support as they mobilized against the Cartel.[5] Increased Catholic activism should not simply be conflated with the rise of the nationalist leagues, but it would be misleading to overlook the links and parallels between them. For instance, the FNC's attacks on the Cartel, and its calls for a spiritual and national revival, paralleled those of the leagues in some ways: in addition, these organizations often shared members.

Many older formations remained active during this period as well. The AF was weakened by a papal condemnation in 1926, but its newspaper remained influential and its authoritarian nationalist message helped shape the outlook of future generations of right-wing militants, even if they often moved on to other, newer organizations. Nor were the formations of the parliamentary Right inactive: stung by their defeat at the hands of the Cartel and impressed by the appeal of the leagues, conservatives tried to strengthen their party organizations. The Centre de propaganda des Républicains nationaux in 1926, spearheaded by the conservative politicians Henri de Kerillis and Paul Reynaud, was an important initiative in this regard.[6] But if on one level the parties were part of a system decried by the leagues, the links between individual conservative politicians and the new extra-parliamentary formations were sometimes extensive. The career of Xavier Vallat, who went on to become the first commissioner for Jewish affairs under the Vichy regime, is instructive. A sympathizer of the AF and militant for the FNC, Vallat went on to join the FR and also became a member of François de La Rocque's Croix de Feu for several years.[7]

The right-wing surge of the 1920s proved to be short lived, however. Generated in large measure by the election of the Cartel des Gauches, as the latter faltered and then fell from power in 1926, much of the impetus behind the mobilization of its foes also faded. The conservative Raymond Poincaré returned to office as prime minister and presided over the stabilization of the franc and a period of economic expansion: the Right's hold on power was cemented by victory in the 1928 national elections. However, despite the relative calm of the late 1920s, intellectual critiques of the Republic still appeared and conservative political parties sought to further consolidate their dominance of national politics even as they debated how best to achieve this goal. As for the extra-parliamentary organizations, it would only take another crisis to revive them.

That crisis soon came, and it proved to be notably more severe than its predecessor. The Great Depression did not strike France as quickly or as harshly as Germany or the United States, but its effects were debilitating enough. The impact of the economic downturn was magnified by a growing crisis of legitimacy for the republican system, which was intensified by the victory of a center-left coalition in 1932 and the ensuing failure of a string of administrations to address the country's problems. Already deep divisions between left and right were now

exacerbated, and remained so for the rest of the decade. The fact that one of Europe's leading democracies had entered a period of protracted crisis at a time when dictatorial solutions seemed to be vindicated in countries such as the Soviet Union, Italy, and above all Germany, ensured that French international and domestic politics converged in an extremely volatile way. Over the course of the 1930s, the country's political contestation was conditioned by growing debates over how best to confront Fascist and especially Nazi expansion, and to what extent the Soviet Union could serve as a partner. While it would be misleading to suggest that France's internal troubles made the shattering defeat of 1940 inevitable, the fevered political climate of the 1930s powerfully conditioned the subsequent years of Vichy rule and German domination.[8] For all these reasons, the activities of the Right (and Left) in the 1930s have been a source of perennial fascination and debate, as they were of profound significance.

A constellation of right-wing forces emerged to challenge the republican system in the 1930s. Well-entrenched intellectual and political foes of democracy such as Charles Maurras remained intensely active, and over the course of the decade were joined by new writers and polemicists. Some, such as the individuals associated with the Ordre nouveau group and the Catholic thinker Emmanuel Mounier, distanced themselves from conventional political labels but their denunciations of the liberal democratic state and corrupt bourgeois society converged with those of the far Right on key points. Others, like Robert Brasillach and Pierre Drieu La Rochelle, openly admired the dictatorships of Italy and Germany.

As for the nationalist leagues, the AF and JP reemerged as influential players, and were joined by new formations such as the Francistes and the Solidarité française (SF), both of which were established in 1933. For a brief time, they seemed to attract substantial numbers of supporters—the SF alone claimed 180,000 within a period of months—as they called for an authoritarian remaking of the political system. In the countryside, hit hard by the Depression, Henry Dorgères launched his Comités de défense paysanne, better known as the Greenshirts, which also attracted a significant following. Most successful of all was the Croix de Feu. Established as a veterans' movement in 1927, under the leadership of Lieutenant-Colonel François de La Rocque it developed into a mass organization, going on to attract perhaps half a million supporters by 1936. Nor were these movements alone: many of the roughly 800,000 members of the Union nationale des combattants (UNC), a nationalist veterans' group, were profoundly disaffected, as were supporters of the Fédération nationale des contribuables.[9]

Matters came to a head with the explosive events of 6 February 1934. Thousands of rioters, with the right-wing leagues and nationalist veterans playing a prominent role, marched on the Chamber of Deputies. The demonstrations only ended after considerable violence, and precipitated the resignation of the Radical-led government of Édouard Daladier. Though historians continue to de-

bate what the rioters intended at the time, there were widespread fears that an attempted fascist coup was imminent.[10] Thereafter, the Radicals gradually formed a coalition with the Socialist and Communist parties that became known as the Popular Front. This alliance mobilized against the Right in the streets, and won the 1936 legislative elections. Its victory, however, took place amidst a growing left–right polarization that only intensified after Léon Blum, France's first Socialist and Jewish prime minister, took office. In response, some right-leaning formations, such as the ARD and PDP, proposed a "centrist" solution whereby the Radicals would break with the Socialists and Communists and form a new coalition with conservatives. But on the far Right, Maurras and others unleashed a torrent of anti-Semitic hatred and wild accusations against Blum, evoking fears of an impending Bolshevik-style revolution. Most extreme of all were the group of nationalist conspirators who formed the secretive Cagoule, which sought to undermine the regime by terrorist means, wreaking havoc in the process.

As part of its platform, the Popular Front had dissolved the nationalist leagues, some of which transformed themselves into political parties. By far the most imposing of these was the successor to the Croix de Feu, the Parti social français (PSF), which likely attracted over a million members by the end of the 1930s. The creation of the PSF posed a serious challenge to established conservative parliamentarians. Before 1936, some members of the ARD and especially the FR had deemed the nationalist leagues potentially useful allies, but in their new guise they were competitors, and it did not take long for tensions to emerge.[11] The situation was further complicated by the creation of the Parti populaire français (PPF) by the former Communist Jacques Doriot. Initially, it seemed that the PPF might pose a major threat to the PSF, but by early 1937, the latter was clearly outdistancing it in the race for members. In May, Doriot tried to regain the initiative by proposing a coalition of anti-Marxist forces in the Front de la liberté, a strategy likely aimed in part at containing the PSF, but La Rocque quickly refused a formal alliance, as did the ARD and PDP. Nevertheless, the Front de la liberté did gain support from the FR and several smaller organizations, indicating how the crises of the 1930s and the challenge of the Popular Front were often met with growing cooperation between various conservatives and the far Right.

Despite claims that it was a stalking horse for Communist revolution, the Popular Front coalition was in fact riven with internal divisions, and proved fragile. By 1938 it had collapsed as the Radical Party moved to the right and Édouard Daladier formed a new ministry, in which conservatives occupied key positions. Mass demonstrations by the Right also waned as fears of a left-wing revolution subsided, and the focus shifted to how to confront Nazi expansion. But this did not mean an end to bitter partisan divisions, especially when it came to foreign affairs. There remained sharp differences between those who were advocating a more conciliatory approach in dealing with Hitler and the growing number of partisans of greater firmness: sometimes this led to a sundering of ties, such

as when Paul Reynaud left the AD. Nor had the bitter hatreds of the Popular Front years simply evaporated: fears of a left-wing revival endured among many nationalists. The chasm between Left and Right, and the conflicts within the Right, would shape French political life during the years of war and occupation that followed.

Historiographical Overview

What exactly the interwar French Right sought to achieve, and the implications of its activities, are issues that have attracted considerable scholarly attention and debate. Until recently, much of the relevant literature has focused heavily, though not solely, on the question of how the various components of the interwar Right should be labeled, a matter which in turn has profound implications for characterizing their significance. The foundational work in this regard is René Rémond's *Les droites en France*, which first appeared in 1954. Surveying the history of the French right since 1815, Rémond argued that the many movements that took shape over the following decades could usefully be understood as manifestations of three tendencies in French politics dating back to the revolutionary era: Legitimism, Orleanism, and Bonapartism. In his discussion of the 1920s and 1930s, Rémond identified the various nationalist leagues as examples of the Bonapartist tradition, stressing the virtues of stronger executive authority but also seeking popular endorsement in the form of mass mobilization. Rémond was aware that other labels, in particular that of fascism, had been applied to the leagues, but it was a category that in his view described only a small proportion of them. The largest movement, the CF/PSF was, he argued, too conservative and legalistic to be identified with fascism: the fact that La Rocque had accepted the dissolution of his movement in 1936 and transformed it into a political party was most revealing. Rémond did believe that a few formations, notably Doriot's PPF, merited the fascist label by virtue of their greater radicalism and unabashed emulation of foreign movements. Ultimately, however, he concluded that while Bonapartism in France was potent, fascism had remained essentially marginal.[12] Rémond also tended to stress distinctions between traditional conservatives and extremists, though he conceded that there were disturbing cases of formerly mainstream conservative politicians, such as Philippe Henriot and André Tardieu, who migrated to the far Right during this period.

Rémond's interpretation has proven tremendously influential, but it does have challengers, especially with respect to the significance of fascism in France.[13] Arguably the most controversial critic is the Israeli historian Zeev Sternhell, who in the 1970s published studies of the nationalist Right prior to World War I, and then turned his attention to the interwar years with *Ni droite ni gauche: l'idéologie fasciste en France*, published in 1983.[14] In many ways, Sternhell turned Rémond's

interpretation on its head. Rather than being simply a more extreme version of conservatism, as contended by some scholars, Sternhell argued that fascism had both a Leftist and Rightist heritage, in which an anti-materialist revision of Marxism melded with a nationalist critique of democracy. That ideology retained its purity in France, relatively uncompromised by association with established institutions in contrast to its Italian counterpart. Moreover, rather than being marginal in French politics, Sternhell concluded that the country was the "cradle" of fascist thought, and that by the 1930s fascist ideas permeated its political culture. The calls of dissident Leftists, such as the "neo-socialist" Marcel Déat, for an authoritarian, nationally minded brand of socialism converged in key ways with the right-wing nationalist views of writers like Thierry Maulnier, as well as the condemnation of materialist, bourgeois democracy emanating from non-conformist Catholics like Emmanuel Mounier. The growing purchase of these ideas gravely undermined the Third Republic, explaining the initial widespread acceptance of the Vichy regime after the defeat of 1940.[15]

Sternhell's interpretation evoked considerable debate in the years that followed.[16] In 1983, Serge Berstein contended that, while certainly faced with serious challenges during the 1920s and especially the 1930s, French democracy demonstrated notable "impermeability" to the fascist temptation.[17] Other scholars conceded some ground to Sternhell, but only to an extent. In his 1986 study *La dérive fasciste*, Swiss historian Philippe Burrin asserted that fascism appealed to a wide range of opinion in France, including dissident Leftists. However, he carefully distinguished between his position and Sternhell's, suggesting that the latter paid too little attention to the international context or to "fascistization" as a process. In later publications, Burrin, while noting that it was wrong to exaggerate France's "allergy" to fascism, also stressed that the latter's significance should not be overstated.[18] Similarly, in his 1987 survey, Pierre Milza discerned that fascism had appeal for various groups in France, ranging from radicalized conservatives to disillusioned Leftists. Nevertheless, he saw Sternhell's thesis as too sweeping and concluded that in terms of generating mass support, French fascists trailed conservatives and reactionaries.[19]

Sternhell was not alone in contesting the idea that fascism had limited appeal in interwar France. Another influential challenge came from the American historian Robert Soucy, who in two books and several articles detailed the activities of various formations and contended that many of these movements, notably the JP and CF/PSF, were indeed fascist.[20] However, in contrast to Sternhell, Soucy underscored the affinities between fascism and right-wing conservatism. In this regard, his work reinforced the conclusions of William Irvine, whose 1979 study of the FR noted how various members of a party supposedly committed to the democratic order also joined the JP and/or CF, and that cooperation with the nationalist leagues only really broke down when La Rocque created the PSF, thus challenging the FR's electoral position. Irvine also argued, in a later article, that

there were considerable parallels between the Croix de Feu/PSF and the Italian Fascists and Nazis.[21] Another major critic of the Rémond-inspired consensus is the French political scientist Michel Dobry, who in 1989, advanced a broad critique of what he termed the "immunity thesis."[22] For Dobry, the study of the interwar French Right has become distorted by a tendency to read backward from outcomes; hence, the fact that the Third Republic had not succumbed to fascism during the 1930s has led many scholars to conclude wrongly that French democracy was never seriously threatened at that time.

Regional studies of the Right have added depth and nuance to these interpretations. Kevin Passmore's 1997 study of the Rhône traced the evolution of the interwar Right as a whole in that department. Examining the various intra-Right divisions over attitudes toward democracy, economics, and religion, and assessing a range of movements, Passmore concluded that the rise of the CF was a response to the failure of local, established conservative elites: he also contended that the league's drive to attain power through paramilitary means placed it within the fascist camp. However, the dissolution of 1936 and resulting transformation into the PSF led the movement down a different path, still authoritarian but more constitutionalist in outlook.[23] Where Passmore stressed the mutability of far-Right movements, Samuel Goodfellow stressed their variety; in his 1999 study of the borderland region of Alsace, he concluded that fascist movements of various stripes gained considerable support there.[24]

Yet despite various challenges to the view that fascism was only a marginal player in interwar French politics, no consensus has emerged, certainly not as far as the CF/PSF is concerned. Jacques Nobécourt's extensively researched biography of La Rocque, published in 1996, repeatedly defended him against charges of being a fascist, instead characterizing him as a "Christian nationalist."[25] Albert Kéchichian's detailed study of the CF conceded that the movement evinced an authoritarian outlook, but the author also stressed its traditionalist ethos.[26] Jean-Paul Thomas has completely dismissed claims that the PSF was fascist, or indeed anti-democratic, instead emphasizing the continuities in its membership and outlook with General Charles de Gaulle's postwar Rassemblement du Peuple Français (RPF).[27] Prominent scholars such as Michel Winock have also reaffirmed their previous interpretations, conceding that the CF/PSF and other elements of the Right displayed worrisome features, but ultimately concluding that France was not fertile ground for movements akin to Italian Fascism or Nazism.[28]

Yet even as the debate continued, calls for moving beyond it emerged. In his 1991 article on the CF/PSF, Irvine suggested that the most important thing scholars could do regarding these formations—still relatively neglected at that time—was to give them the attention they deserved.[29] Kevin Passmore's study of the Rhône pays attention to classification, but also to the relationships between the various movements of the Right. Robert Paxton's study of the Greenshirts, published in 1997, also stresses the importance of studying context and processes

rather than applying rigid labels. Paxton argues that Dorgères did display elements of a fascist outlook, but that the real value of studying the Greenshirts was to show why it was that in France the far Right never succeeded in taking power. Among the factors he invokes are the fact that the French state remained more capable of ensuring order than did its Italian or German counterparts in times of crisis, thus reassuring frightened elites, many of whom thus did not feel sufficiently threatened to turn to a firebrand like Dorgères.[30]

By the 2000s, this desire to take the study of the interwar Right in new directions, beyond classification, was becoming increasingly apparent. A 2003 collection of essays edited by Michel Dobry challenges the tenets of the immunity thesis, but also seeks to break with an emphasis upon classification. Instead, Dobry stresses the need to study the ideas, structures, and actions of movements in a relational perspective, appreciating that nationalist organizations constantly responded to each other and adapted to a changing political climate.[31] Brian Jenkins, editor of the 2005 volume *France in the Era of Fascism*, assesses various critiques of the immunity thesis and concludes that they amount to a compelling challenge, but also closes the volume with a suggestion that the debate was growing stale and that new perspectives were needed.[32] Sean Kennedy's *Reconciling France against Democracy* attempted to situate the CF and PSF along the political spectrum but also sought to assess these movements' social presence.[33] Samuel Kalman's study of the programs of the Faisceau and the Croix de Feu, *The Extreme Right in Interwar France*, highlights the fluidity of far-Right doctrine and the significance of tensions within as well as between movements.[34] Laurent Kestel's 2012 study of the PPF concentrates on how a movement founded by ex-communists and non-conformist intellectuals moved to the far Right as a result of various agendas playing out on an ever-shifting field of political competition. He focuses on how the fascist label came to be applied to the PPF at the time, rather than whether scholars should use it.[35]

Evidently, much recent work has tried to heed the call for fresh perspectives. While this brief overview cannot discuss all recent publications, it does highlight some trends. One of these is the deepening interest in women's activism, and in applying gender analysis to the interwar French Right. There is a growing appreciation of the extent to which women played a key role in Catholic and nationalist organizations, and of the need to assess the visions of femininity and masculinity promoted by different movements. Scholars such as Cheryl Koos, Daniella Sarnoff, and Magali Della Sudda have explored women's presence in a variety of formations.[36] Works by Kevin Passmore, Caroline Campbell, and Laura Lee Downs focus on the CF/PSF, showing how these movements' mission of social pacification, in which women played a leading role, was at the heart of their vision of a future France.[37] Geoff Read demonstrates that the CF/PSF's vision of masculinity was crucial to grasping its sociopolitical objectives; Paul Schue shows that this was also the case for the PPF.[38]

A second trend is the enduring appeal and growing diversity of intellectual and cultural approaches, as demonstrated in recent works by John Hellman, Paul Mazgaj, Gisèle Sapiro, and Jeannine Verdès-Leroux.[39] Many of the new publications in these fields strike out in fresh directions, often transcending the issue of categorization. Thus Bruno Goyet's biography of Charles Maurras confirms the radical, even fascistic character of its subject's opposition to republican democracy, but also tries to understand Maurras's activities in light of his intellectual interests and professional aspirations.[40] Similarly, in his article about Bertrand de Jouvenel's activities as a member of the PPF, Laurent Kestel is less concerned whether or not his subject was a fascist than with detailing the various forces that shaped his complex intellectual and political itinerary.[41] Nimrod Amzalak's study of the convergence between non-conformist intellectuals, and professional groups such as engineers, around the goal of promoting technocratic government also eschews definitions in favor of tracing shifting alignments.[42] David Carroll and Mark Antliff have underscored the significance of aesthetic concerns to various right-wing authors and activists; this theme has also been explored by Sandrine Sanos, who considers the neglected connection between far-right conceptions of gender and racism of both the anti-Semitic and colonial varieties.[43] Other historians have examined neglected modes of popular mobilization, paying careful attention to distinctions but also parallels between different movements. Thus Jessica Wardhaugh explains how the cultures of the Right and Left related to one another as both deployed film, music, and celebrations to attract mass support, appropriate popular symbols, and promote their vision of "the people."[44] Having previously explored the role of commemoration in far-right discourse, Joan Tumblety has recently analyzed the significance of physical culture for interwar French politics, demonstrating its profound significance for a wide range of right-wing formations.[45]

Thirdly, organizations and areas that have been somewhat neglected are now receiving renewed attention. A 2008 collection of essays, *Les deux France du Front populaire*, provides new perspectives on the Right as well as the Left. Some contributors such as Gilles Le Béguec adopt a social perspective, focusing on the networks that helped to generate the emergence of a new generation of right-wing parliamentarians. Others revisit the programs and tactics of influential formations such as the ARD; Arnaud Chomette argues, for example, that during the 1930s Pierre-Étienne Flandin blended an ongoing commitment to liberalism with a growing admiration for authoritarian political systems and commitment to appeasing Nazi Germany.[46] Though the significance of the AF has been long affirmed, it has also been the subject of new work that revisits its evolving ideology, social bases, and political tactics.[47] The FNC, and its relations with other nationalist movements, is now the subject of a detailed study by Corinne Bonafoux-Verax.[48] Gayle Brunelle and Annette Finley-Croswhite have recently made a strong case for paying more attention to the threat that the terrorist Cagoule

posed to the Republic in the 1930s.[49] Extending the geographical scope of recent historiography, Samuel Kalman has drawn renewed attention to the extent and intensity of popular support for the far Right among the European population of colonial Algeria.[50]

Finally, there is evidence of a stronger interest in understanding better the relations between the different formations of the Right. David Bensoussan's 2006 book, *Combats pour une Bretagne catholique et rurale*, traces the evolution of multiple right-wing groups, as traditional Catholic elites and clergy confronted a changing society and the emergence of dynamic mass movements such as the Greenshirts and PSF.[51] Commenting on recent French-language scholarship on the Right in *Les deux France du Front populaire*, Gilles Richard sees the restructuring of the Right, prompted in particular by the emergence of the PSF, as a key feature of the 1930s. At the same time, he acknowledges that despite the rise of a potentially hegemonic movement the nationalist response to the Popular Front was in fact very diverse; notwithstanding shrill rhetoric about the need for unity, it provided unattainable.[52] Writing in the journal *History Compass*, Brian Jenkins has called for further examination of the relationship between right-wing parties and the leagues, arguing that in particular the rivalry between different formations, notably the PSF and the FR, is critical to comprehending the obstacles that La Rocque and his followers confronted in their quest to remake France. Tracing such rivalries, and the evolving outlook of various formations, is critical for grasping the dynamics of the late Third Republic.[53]

As this discussion indicates, it would be quite misleading to claim that a consensus has emerged in the study of the interwar Right. Though it has perhaps lost some of its intensity, the debate over whether fascism was a significant feature of French political life in that era continues, and scholars who have explored hitherto neglected themes such as gender remain engaged in debates over classification. Nor do those who share a desire to transcend longstanding controversies necessarily agree on key issues. For example, significant differences between scholars as to the role of women in nationalist movements have emerged, with some historians focusing upon the extent to which women were pressed to conform to conservative gender norms, while others highlight the opportunities and relative degree of independence that some individual women enjoyed.[54] This is hardly worrisome, however, as controversy is the lifeblood of good history. What does stand out is the extent to which the interwar French Right remains a subject of enduring historical interest and vibrant historical scholarship.

Chapter Overview

The present volume aims to contribute to the renewed debate on the nature and organization of the French interwar Right, highlighting current historiographi-

cal trends. Contributors provide a critical reassessment of the methodology and interpretation of French right-wing movements from traditional conservative figures to fascist leagues, eschewing the struggle for a plausible definition of fascism or attempts to categorize various figures and movements. Although not denying the scholarly value of such efforts, the authors nonetheless wish to move beyond the political labeling of groups, individuals, and political parties, instead seeking to broaden the characterization and historicization of the movements themselves. For this reason, the collection probes the Right in all of its forms, rather than confining itself to French fascism.

The contributors further seek to examine the French Right in situ, relating intellectuals, parties, and leagues to a variety of political, social, and cultural trends in the 1920s and 1930s, while engaging with the broader outlines of the historical experience of the late Third Republic. This implies a contextualization of their actions, programs, and memberships, an effort to avoid treating the Right as a historical actor detached from the events and debates of the interwar era, but rather as one participant in an ongoing quotidian negotiation between various actors, factions, and events, whose words and deeds were shaped by (and responded to) the lived reality of interwar France.

Thus certain authors seek to examine the traditional and extreme Right within the boundaries of diverse strands of historical inquiry, focusing upon the impact of gender/feminism, empire, and memory, or invoking collective psychology, satire, or pacifism in attempting to explain the relative success or failure, relevance or diminution, of various groups and movements. Such readings wish to transcend the positioning of the right-wing experience in the realm of masculine, metropolitan, and/or standard political discourse, attempting to move beyond the traditional analytical tools used by scholars of conservatism and the extreme Right. Others invoke previously peripheral movements or periodicals—the Union nationale des combattants, the Alliance nationale, the Ligue patriotique des françaises, and political science / law journals—in order to revise the political and juridical topography of the interwar French Right. Redrawing the boundaries of conservatism and fascism, they attempt to broaden the parameters of inclusion. Finally, certain contributors wish to modify the entire conceptual apparatus for investigating *les droites*, either reexamining the doctrinal foundations of prominent movements (the PSF, for example), or rethinking the political spectrum itself and the scholarly categorization of left and right altogether.

The collection is organized in four parts, each reflecting one facet of this collective effort. The first section proposes new methodological avenues for the study of the extreme Right, new interpretive directions for investigation from veterans associations to the Ligue des droits de l'homme, anti-southern prejudice to imperialism. Kevin Passmore makes this agenda clear in the opening chapter, providing a new explanation for the Right's nascent anti-republicanism in the 1930s. Using the functionalist sociology of Émile Durkheim and Max Weber

in combination with collective psychology, Passmore argues that the 6 February 1934 riot was not a simple reaction to political and economic crisis or a manifestation of public anger at various scandals. Rather, the demand for regime change traced to longstanding prejudices against Masons, Jews, and southerners, a demagogic "counter-elite" that had purportedly seized control of French politics by effectively swaying the masses. From detective fiction through the popular press and the discourse of conservative politicians, Passmore traces the impact of conservative anti-southern sentiments, which peaked with the Stavisky Affair and its epicenter in the town of Bayonne, and intimations of gangsterism, unbridled sexuality, and alcoholism. These accusations were habitually linked with anti-Semitism (the corrupt money-grubbing bankers of fiction and the popular press) and anti-Masonic rhetoric (the lodges as anti-Catholic and deeply republican) in a vast conspiracy theory that drove events like the 6 February riot.

The *évenements* of 6 February are equally central to Chris Millington's work on the Union nationale des combattants and the veteran's movement's ties to the French extreme Right in the 1930s. In contrast to previous historians such as Antoine Prost, Millington places the group squarely on the anti-republican extreme Right, a fact clearly visible in their central role on 6 February. Attempting to copy the organization and style of fellow veteran's movement and extreme Rightist league the Croix de Feu, the UNC left behind lobbying for politics, as leader Jean Goy authorized the formation of an Action combattante wing for civilians, complete with newspapers and mass meetings. Although highly controversial within the membership due to its embrace of non-veterans, the plan faltered due to the UNC's inability to compete with established rival leagues, and many members ultimately joined the CF, Jeunesses patriotes, and Action française. Although Millington notes that "a veteran may have joined the CF as he believed it was a genuine veterans' association," he effectively demonstrates that, by 1934, this was increasingly unlikely, and hence the UNC's later support for the Vichy regime.

A revision of previous historiography is equally at work in Norman Ingram's investigation of pacifism, the Ligue des droits de l'homme, and fascism during the interwar and Vichy eras. His piece simultaneously explains the evolution of certain non-communist Marxists toward collaboration while debunking the myth that the Ligue (and France as a whole) proved allergic to fascism. Many members condemned French militarism on pacifist grounds, a non-negotiable stance that led them to support Vichy and excuse Nazism in order to avoid conflict. Beyond Jacques Doriot, Robert Brasillach, or Pierre Drieu La Rochelle, the collaborationist extreme Right counted figures like the Ligue's Lyon section president Léon Emery, a Jacobin anti-fascist who nonetheless slid to the right due to his anti-communism and aversion to war. Ingram relates that Emery et al. (and their postwar supporters) ignored the ideological nature of World War II altogether, and "could not or would not see was that the advent of Hitler in 1933 changed

everything." Thus he effectively challenges the definitions of pacifism and fascism, asking where to place an anti-war/parliamentarian/Semite who nonetheless seemingly rejected the French extreme Right.

Such ambiguity could also result from geography, particularly in the French empire, where the extreme Right found fertile ground during the interwar era. As Samuel Kalman relates in surveying the department of Oran in French Algeria, the municipal police and *gendarmerie*—supposedly the defenders of republican order—engaged in a campaign of violence against Leftists, Jews, and Muslims at the behest of local authorities. The latter were frequently on the extreme Right, led by Oran mayor Gabriel Lambert, in a rabidly anti-Semitic department where the population consistently opposed the Left, and in a territory where the population viewed Muslims as dangerous religious fanatics subject to legal inferiority through the *indigénat*. Algeria became a repository for colonial fascism, which proved very attractive to police and soldiers trained by ultraconservatives, facing hostile local communities, and enduring poor pay and working conditions. Unsurprisingly, Kalman writes, violence against Leftists, Jews, and Muslims was commonplace, as officers and *gendarmes* assaulted Muslim and Jewish demonstrators and joined extreme-Rightist attacks against communists, in a display of colonial violence that foreshadowed the campaign of torture and murder perpetrated by security services during the 1954–1962 Algerian War.

Although traditionally highlighted in works on the French Right, race is only one component of conservative or fascist doctrine. The collection's second section focuses upon the centrality of gender in interwar right-wing discourse, in an attempt to move beyond the standard depiction of masculine-dominated movements. To Geoff Read, fascist groups in particular viewed women in contradictory terms, both as potential leaders and as housewives and mothers. Read rejects the notion that the extreme Right proved uniquely misogynist, reminding the reader that hegemonic femininity permeated the Left, Center, and Right in interwar France. If anything, fascist movements actually prioritized women, on one hand evincing the pronatalism of the day in the form of the image of the nurturing mother who ensured a proper moral and patriotic formation for her children, yet often providing employment and responsibilities outside the *foyer familial* at the same time. Thus the Croix de Feu women's auxiliaries had 100,000 members performing home visits, organizing charity sales, and advising the group's male leadership, despite its avowedly traditional rhetoric concerning gender roles. Yet in the final analysis, despite being remarkably innovative in organizational terms, the leagues did not truly support feminism, Read concludes, insisting that women first and foremost remained in the home and raised children.

Right-wing pronatalism was equally apparent outside of the leagues, where the Alliance nationale indefatigably harnessed masculine archetypes to define gender roles and national characteristics. Although heralded by politicians across the political spectrum, the AN regularly displayed a penchant for authoritarianism and

fascism, supporting Italian and German efforts to replace republican sterility with virile youth and large families. As Cheryl Koos demonstrates in her contribution, the group's gendered critique aided preparations for the Vichy regime, viewing women primarily as childbearers, and as weapons against demographically superior Nazi Germany. AN leaders Ferdinand Boverat and Paul Haury led the interwar chorus of voices against the *femme moderne*, Koos notes, accusing women of moral failings and encouraging *dénatalité*, while lauding Mussolini's bachelor tax and pronatalist speeches, the Soviet Komsomol, and the Hitler Youth in equal measure as antidotes to corrupt, lazy, and weak democracy. By 1934, the Nazi "new man" became AN policy in a critique of French obsessions with marketing and consumerism over sacrifice and discipline, combined with the Italian Fascist emphasis on family as the key to national renewal.

Yet as Daniella Sarnoff counters in her overview of women and gender in French fascism, "in many ways women would be simultaneously exalted and subjugated within fascist ideology." In a panoramic survey of gender and French fascism, Sarnoff probes attempts to recruit women and families to renovate the nation, attempting to restore gendered order but also enabling female agency. Various historians have overlooked the fascist portrayal of women as workers and voters, she claims, and if the leagues did not jettison the image of the nurturing mother saving the nation alongside the proud father, they nonetheless encouraged female militancy in the quest for national health and virility. Her chapter portrays women in various leagues as public figures in uniform, even policing events, unthinkable in Leftist, Centrist, or conservative movements. If anything, the extreme-Rightist obsession with femininity often diverted attention from their more sordid discussion of anti-Semitism and violence: using cooking tips and fashion pages, for example. Family also functioned as an antidote to the republic, which supposedly encouraged individualism, birth control propaganda, and prostitution.

However, the question of gender is not merely confined to studies of the extreme Right. Magali Della Sudda shifts the discussion toward conservatism, examining the Ligue patriotique des Françaises and the Fédération nationale des femmes, Catholic "feminist" organizations dedicated to preserving the "natural order" of fathers, mothers, and family as the primary social unit. With 800,000 members by 1919, the LPF engaged in "civic training" in order to obtain female suffrage, believing that conservative women could provide conjugalism through the ballot box. Della Sudda aptly observes that the group's agenda was far removed from struggles for women's rights or gender equality, with the LPF eventually moving away from suffrage altogether toward more traditional social work. The FNF filled the void after 1925, countering republican and secular feminist groups and eventually becoming the women's branch of the conservative Fédération républicaine. Both organizations were enabled by a postwar *ralliment*, in which the Church perceived an opportunity to use democratic means to spiritual

ends, while conservative parties granted women a political role in order to obtain their votes.

Much like gender, historians of the French Right frequently ignore the cultural dimension of their subject—the topic of the third section. Jessica Wardhaugh examines efforts by the leagues to attract mass support through cultural production, part of a continent-wide effort during the interwar era to provide state legitimacy through control of the arts, from the Soviet Union to Fascist Italy. Much has been made of the Popular Front's experiments with the aestheticization of politics, and mobilization of art as a conduit for politics in everyday life. Wardhaugh extends this argument to the Action française and Croix de Feu; if neither league took power, they nevertheless used newsreels, summer camps, film, and theatrical performance as "a means to develop images of political salvation, to satirize political events, and finally to promote an associative life." Both the AF's anti-republican plays lampooning a variety of enemies and the CF's counter society fulfilled this need, with the latter incorporating everything from collaborations with the *Ballets fantastiques* to the *Groupe photo-ciné* in order to showcase the group as an alternative to communism, the Popular Front, and rampant individualism.

Furthermore, as Sean Kennedy notes in his chapter concerning the PSF and Christian civilization, even after its 1936 transformation into a political party, the CF prioritized cultural means of transmitting anti-pluralism, albeit couched in the rhetoric of Christian reconciliation. However, there were strict limits to Christian tolerance, and PSF leaders and members rejected a variety of enemies, including Leftists, members of the Jewish community who supported the Popular Front, and those deemed incapable of embracing authentically French values— notably, Algerian Muslims. Furthermore, the group tended to view international relations through the prism of Christian civilization, lauding Franco in the Spanish Civil War as a staunch defender of Western civilization, and championing any authoritarian regime of the same cloth (albeit not the pagan and anti-Gallic Nazis). Hence, Kennedy concludes, the PSF social Catholic agenda was "primarily cultural and political, a weapon of ideological and rhetorical combat."

Yet as Laurent Kestel observes in his contribution, discussions of authoritarian political culture equally pervaded the French conservative press, which published leading academics, jurists, and political voices on the Right. The authors ignored unpalatable programmatic elements while praising various far-right regimes for bringing unions and communists to heel, improving economy and society, and eliminating decadence. Thus the same personnel who concocted Vichy's anti-Semitic laws claimed that anti-Semitism was not Nazi, but rather traced to a longstanding German tradition. The three journals in Kestel's study—The *Revue politique et parlémentaire*, *Revue du droit et de science politique*, and *Sciences politiques*—could barely contain their enthusiasm for Franco, Mussolini, and Hitler. They concomitantly portray the Third Republic as weak and corrupt, led by

the Popular Front's slaves to Moscow, and desire a "sanitization" of government, culminating in projects like the Plan Tardieu to strengthen the executive and minimize parliament, and calls to imitate the Nazi support of the strong over the weak.

Racial strength and national regeneration are more closely examined in Caroline Campbell's chapter concerning the CF/PSF's efforts at transforming French physical culture along gendered and racial lines. The league's program was sui generis, Campbell writes, not least because it included women on an equal footing in sports and training programs influenced by positive eugenics and social Darwinist theory. Group leaders wished to eradicate ugliness and flab, believing (pace Jean Ruffier and Margaret Mead) that physical and sexual traits were culturally formed. In this regard, Antoinette de Préval's Women's Section and Gaëtan Maire's Société de préparation et d'éducation sportive founded thousands of physical education centers across France, where instructors taught the natural method of Georges Hébert, using physical exertion and conditioning exercises on men, women, and children. Furthermore, in defiance of the stereotypical delicate female commonly portrayed by the Left and Right in interwar France, the SPES offered girls the chance to play basketball and soccer, while partaking in a similar regimen to their male confreres.

These subversions of the standard historiographical portrait of the French Right push William Irvine to challenge normative portrayals of Left and Right altogether in the concluding chapter. Irvine questions the value of political categorization *en-soi* in modern French history, adroitly demonstrating that attempts by historians to compartmentalize political movements through the formulation of a defined set of unique traits inevitably falter in the face of historical evidence. Both the Left and Right claimed to be progressive at various times, staking a claim as the inheritors of the French revolutionary tradition. Worse still, the Left formally advocated various positions often ascribed to the Right: anti-German nationalism, anti-feminism, anti-Semitism (in both metropolitan France and Algeria), and even philo-Nazism—a significant number of French fascists moved from Left to Right, after all. The Right, meanwhile, championed supposedly Leftist initiatives, from support for *Munichois* pacifism and female suffrage to the Parti démocrate populaire's ambivalence toward the Catholic Church, while many clerical conservatives actually dismissed anti-Semitism. To be sure, Irvine concludes, the extreme Right was authoritarian and xenophobic, and most on the Left consistently promoted anti-clericalism and defended Jews during the Dreyfus affair and again in the 1930s. Yet the ambiguity present in the discourse and platforms of the French Left and Right demand further debate concerning the characterization of Gallic politics.

Irvine's call for a new interpretive framework echoes the modus operandi of this collection: to reinvigorate the study of the French Right, harnessing new methodological perspectives and thematic investigations. Although far from an

encyclopedic overview of the topic or a "state of the field" manifesto, the authors and editors nonetheless collectively present a variety of new perspectives, simultaneously building upon older arguments and controversies while positing new modes of engagement. Most importantly, the emphasis is placed squarely upon a continuing dialogue between various historiographical opinions, methods of inquiry, and scholarly visions. If the contributors often disagree with established ideas concerning the French Right, and just as often with one another, this represents a sure sign of the vitality of the topic as an object of academic inquiry. Clearly there remains a vibrant intellectual desire to understand one of the most important actors in Gallic politics, society, and culture from 1789 onward.

Notes

1. Appearing as the present volume was in the final stages of preparation, Kevin Passmore's *The Right in France: From the Third Republic to Vichy* (Oxford, 2013) provides a comprehensive analysis from the regime's inception.

2. These complex struggles can be followed in Robert Soucy, *French Fascism: The First Wave, 1924–1933* (New Haven, 1986); see especially 174–184.

3. Soucy, *First Wave*, xi.

4. On the FNC, see Corinne Bonafoux-Verax, *À la droite de Dieu: la Fédération nationale catholique 1924–1944* (Paris, 2004).

5. On the LPF, see Odile Sarti, *The Ligue Patriotique des Françaises, 1902–1933: A Feminine Response to the Secularization of French Society* (New York, 1992); for an overview of women and Catholic activism, see Evélyne Diébolt, "Les femmes catholiques: entre église et société," in *Catholicism, Politics and Society in Twentieth-Century France*, ed. Kay Chadwick (Liverpool, 2000), 219–243.

6. Both of these figures are the subjects of biographies: see Jean-Yves Boulic and Anne Lavaure, *Henri de Kerillis 1889–1958: l'absolu patriote* (Rennes, 1997), and Tellier Thibault, *Paul Reynaud (1878–1966): un indépendant en politique* (Paris, 2005).

7. See Laurent Joly, *Xavier Vallat (1891–1972): du nationalisme chrétien à l'antisémitisme d'état* (Paris, 2001).

8. For an overview, see Julian Jackson, "1940 and the Crisis of Democracy in Interwar France," in *French History since Napoleon*, ed. Martin Alexander (London, 1999), 222–243.

9. For surveys of the Right during this period from contrasting points of view, see Pierre Milza, "L'ultra-droite des années trente," in *Histoire de l'extrême droite en France*, ed. Michel Winock (Paris, 1993), 157–171, and Robert Soucy, *French Fascism: The Second Wave, 1933–1939* (New Haven, 1995), 26–36.

10. Recent studies of the 6 February 1934 riots include Pierre Pellissier, *6 février 1934: la république en flames* (Paris, 2000); Brian Jenkins, "The Paris Riots of February 1934: The Crisis of the Third French Republic," *French History* 20, no. 3 (2006): 333–351; and Chris Millington, "February 6, 1934: The Veterans' Riot," *French Historical Studies* 33, no. 4 (2010): 545–572.

11. On the activities of the ARD and FR, see Donald Wileman, "P.-É. Flandin and the Alliance Démocratique, 1929–1939," *French History* 4, no. 1 (1990): 139–173; William Irvine, *French Conservatism in Crisis: The Republican Federation of France in the 1930s* (Baton Rouge, 1979); and Mathias Bernard, *La dérive des modérés: la Fédération républicaine du Rhône sous la Troisième République* (Paris, 1998).

12. René Rémond, *Les droites en France*, revised edition (Paris, 1982), 195–220.

13. See, for example, Robert Soucy, "The Nature of Fascism in France," *Journal of Contemporary History* 1, no. 1 (1966): 27–55; and William Irvine, "René Rémond's French Right: The Interwar Years," *Proceedings of the Western Society for French History* 5 (1977): 301–309; for a thorough review of the earlier historiography, see John Bingham, "Defining French Fascism, Finding Fascists in France," *Canadian Journal of History* 29, no. 3 (1994): 525–543.

14. Zeev Sternhell, *Ni droite ni gauche: L'idéologie fasciste en France*, 3rd ed. (Brussels, 2000).

15. Sternhell, *Ni droite ni gauche*, 142–144.

16. Commentaries include Antonio Costa Pinto, "Fascist Ideology Revisited: Zeev Sternhell and His Critics," *European History Quarterly* 16, no. 4 (1986): 465–483; and Robert Wohl, "French Fascism, both Right and Left: Reflections on the Sternhell Controversy," *Journal of Modern History* 63, no. 1 (1991): 91–98.

17. Serge Berstein, "La France des années trente allergique au fascisme: à propos d'un livre de Zeev Sternhell," *Vingtième siècle* 2 (1984): 83–94.

18. Philippe Burrin, *La dérive fasciste: Doriot, Déat, Bergery 1933–1945* (Paris, 1986), 19–21, 25–27; for his later views, see Burrin, *Fascisme, nazisme, autoritarisme* (Paris, 2000), 256–259.

19. Pierre Milza, *Fascisme français: passé et present* (Paris, 1987), chapters 2 and 3; The *Histoire des droites en France*, ed. Jean-François Sirinelli, 3 vols. (Paris, 1992), encapsulates the state of French-language historiography by the early 1990s.

20. Soucy, *First Wave*, which appeared in 1986, and *Second Wave*, published in 1995.

21. Irvine, *French Conservatism in Crisis*, and "Fascism in France and the Strange Case of the Croix de Feu," *Journal of Modern History* 63, no. 2 (1991): 271–295.

22. Michel Dobry, "Février 1934 et la découverte de l'allergie de la société française au fascisme," *Revue française de sociologie* 30, nos. 3–4 (1989): 511–533.

23. Kevin Passmore, *From Liberalism to Fascism: The Right in a French Province, 1928–1939* (Cambridge, 1997).

24. Samuel Goodfellow, *Between the Swastika and the Cross of Lorraine: Fascisms in Interwar Alsace* (DeKalb, 1999).

25. Jacques Nobécourt, *Le colonel de La Rocque 1885–1946, ou les pièges du nationalisme chrétien* (Paris, 1996).

26. Albert Kéchichian, *Les Croix-de-Feu à l'âge des fascismes* (Seyssel, 2006).

27. Jean-Paul Thomas's publications include: "Le Parti social français," *Cahiers de la Fondation Charles de Gaulle* 4 (1997): 39–77; "Les effectifs du Parti social français," *Vingtième siècle* 62 (1999): 61–83; "Le Parti social français (1936–1945): Une expérience de parti des masses et la préparation d'une relève," *Annales de Bretagne et des Pays de l'Ouest* 109, no. 3 (2002): 109–119; and "Fascisme français: faut-il rouvrir un débat?" in *Un professeur en République: mélanges en l'honneur de Serge Berstein*, ed. Rémi Badouï et al. (Paris, 2006), 289–297.

28. See Michel Winock, "Retour sur le fascisme français: La Rocque et les Croix-de-Feu," *Vingtième siècle* 90 (2006): 3–27.

29. Irvine, "Fascism in France," 294.

30. Robert Paxton, *French Peasant Fascism: Henry Dorgères's Greenshirts and the Crises of French Agriculture, 1929–1939* (New York, 1997), 154–164.

31. Michel Dobry, "La thèse immunitaire face aux fascismes: pour une critique de la logique classificatoire," in *Le mythe de l'allergie française au fascisme*, ed. Michel Dobry (Paris, 2003), 17–67.

32. Brian Jenkins, "Conclusion: Beyond the 'Fascism' Debate," in *France in the Era of Fascism: Essays on the French Authoritarian Right*, ed. Brian Jenkins (New York, 2005), 209–215.

33. Sean Kennedy, *Reconciling France against Democracy: The Croix de Feu and the Parti Social Français, 1927–1945* (Montreal, 2007).

34. Samuel Kalman, *The Extreme Right in Interwar France: The Faisceau and the Croix de Feu* (Aldershot, 2008).

35. Laurent Kestel, *La conversion politique: Doriot, le PPF et la question du fascisme français* (Paris, 2012).

36. Cheryl Koos, "Fascism, Fatherland, and the Family in Interwar France: The Case of Antoine Rédier and the Légion," *Journal of Family History* 24, no. 3 (1999): 317–329; Cheryl Koos and Daniella Sarnoff, "France," in *Women, Gender and Fascism in Europe, 1919–1945*, ed. Kevin Passmore (New Brunswick, 2003), 168–188; Magali Della Sudda, "Gender, Fascism and the Right-Wing in France between the Wars: The Catholic Matrix," *Politics, Religion & Ideology* 13, no. 2 (2012): 179–195.

37. Kevin Passmore, "'Planting the Tricolor in the Citadels of Communism': Women's Social Action in the Croix de Feu and Parti Social Français," *Journal of Modern History* 71, no. 4 (1999): 814–851; Caroline Campbell, "Women and Gender in the Croix de Feu and the Parti Social Français: Creating a Nationalist Youth Culture, 1927–1939," *Proceedings of the Western Society for French History* 36 (2008): 249–264; Campbell, "Building a Movement, Dismantling the Republic: Women, Gender, and Political Extremism in the Croix de Feu/Parti Social Français, 1927–1940," *French Historical Studies* 35, no.4 (2012): 691–726; Laura Lee Downs, "'Each and Every One of You Must Become a *Chef*': Toward a Social Politics of Working-Class Childhood on the Extreme Right in 1930s France," *Journal of Modern History* 81, no. 1 (2009): 1–44; Downs, "'Nous plantions les trois couleurs': Action sociale feminine et recomposition des politiques de la droite française: Le Mouvement Croix-de-Feu et le Parti social français, 1934–1947," *Revue d'histoire moderne et contemporaine* 58, no. 3 (2011): 118–163.

38. Geoff Read, "He Is Depending on You: Militarism, Martyrdom, and the Appeal to Manliness in the Case of France's 'Croix de Feu,' 1931–1940," *Journal of the Canadian Historical Association* 16 (2005): 261–291; Paul Schue, "The Prodigal Sons of Communism: Parti populaire français Narratives of Communist Recruitment for the Spanish Civil War and the Everyday Functioning of Party Ideology," *French Historical Studies* 24, no. 1 (2001): 87–111.

39. John Hellman, *The Communitarian Third Way: Alexandre Marc's Ordre Nouveau, 1930–2000* (Montreal, 2002); Paul Mazgaj, *Imagining Fascism: The Cultural Politics of the French Young Right, 1930–1945* (Newark, 2007); Gisèle Sapiro, "Figures d'écrivains fascistes," in *Mythe de l'allergie française*, ed. Dobry, 195–236; and Jeannine Verdès-Leroux, *Refus et violences: politique et littérature à l'extrême droite des années trente aux retombées de la Libération* (Paris, 1996).

40. Bruno Goyet, *Charles Maurras* (Paris, 2000).

41. Laurent Kestel, "L'engagement de Bertrand de Jouvenel au PPF, 1936–1938: intellectuel de parti et entrepreneur politique," *French Historical Studies* 30, no. 1 (2007): 105–125.

42. Nimrod Amzalak, *Fascists and Honourable Men: Contingency and Choice in French Politics, 1918–1945* (Basingstoke, 2011).

43. David Carroll, *French Literary Fascism: Nationalism, Anti-Semitism, and the Ideology of Culture* (Princeton, 1995); Mark Antliff, *Avant-Garde Fascism: The Mobilization of Myth, Art, and Culture in France, 1909–1939* (Durham, 2007); Sandrine Sanos, *The Aesthetics of Hate: Far-Right Intellectuals, Antisemitism, and Gender in 1930s France* (Stanford, 2013); see also Sanos, "Fascist Fantasies of Perversion and Abjection: Race, Gender, and Sexuality in the Interwar Far-Right," *Proceedings of the Western Society for French History* 37 (2009): 249–265.

44. Jessica Wardhaugh, *In Pursuit of the People: Political Culture in France, 1934–1939* (Basingstoke, 2009).

45. Joan Tumblety, "Civil Wars of the Mind: The Commemoration of the 1789 Revolution in the Parisian press of the Radical Right, 1939," *European History Quarterly* 30, no. 3 (2000): 389–429; Tumblety, *Remaking the Male Body: Masculinity and the Uses of Physical Culture in Interwar and Vichy France* (Oxford, 2012), especially chapters 4 and 5.

46. Gilles Le Béguec, "La nouvelle génération parlementaire modérée," and Arnaud Chomette, "Sauver une France libérale: Pierre-Étienne Flandin entre stratégie centriste et attraction autoritaire," in *Les deux France du Front populaire*, ed. Gilles Morin and Gilles Richard (Paris, 2008), 107–115 and 117–125 respectively.

47. See Brian Jenkins, "L'Action française à l'ère du fascisme: une perspective contextuelle," in *Mythe de l'allgerie française au fascisme*, ed. Dobry 107–154; and *L'Action française: culture, société, politique*, ed. Michel Leymarie and Jacques Prévotat (Villeneuve d'Ascq, 2008).

48. Bonafoux-Verax, *À la droite de Dieu*.

49. Gayle Brunelle and Annette Finley-Croswhite, *Murder in the Métro: Laetitia Toureaux and the Cagoule in 1930s France* (Baton Rouge, 2010); previous studies of the Cagoule include Joel Blatt, "The Cagoule Plot, 1936–1937," in *Crisis and Renewal in France, 1918–1962*, ed. Kenneth Mouré and Martin Alexander (New York, 2002), 86–104; and D. L. L. Parry, "Counter Revolution by Conspiracy, 1935–1937," in *The Right in France: From Revolution to Le Pen*, 2nd ed., ed. Nicholas Atkin and Frank Tallett (London, 2003), 161–181.

50. Samuel Kalman, "*Le Combat par Tous les Moyens*: Colonial Violence and the Extreme Right in 1930s Oran," *French Historical Studies* 34, no. 1 (2011): 125–153. See also the discussion of Algeria in Laurent Kestel, "The Emergence of Anti-Semitism within the Parti Populaire Français: Party Intellectuals, Peripheral Leaders, and National Figures," *French History* 19, no. 3 (2005): 364–384.

51. David Bensoussan, *Combats pour une Bretagne catholique et rurale: les droites bretonnes dans l'entre-deux-guerres* (Paris, 2006).

52. Gilles Richard, "Les droites contre le Front populaire: essai de bilan des recherches depuis dix ans," in *Les deux France du Front populaire*, 63–72.

53. Brian Jenkins, "The Right-Wing Leagues and Electoral Politics in Interwar France," *History Compass* 5, no. 4 (2007): 1358–1381.

54. Compare, for example, Passmore, "Planting the Tricolor," with Mary Jean Green, "The Bouboule Novels: Constructing a French Fascist Woman," in *Gender and Fascism in Modern France*, ed. Melanie Hawthorne and Richard Goslan (Hanover, 1997), 49–68.

PART I

POLITICAL MOVEMENTS

CROWD PSYCHOLOGY, ANTI-SOUTHERN PREJUDICE, AND CONSTITUTIONAL REFORM IN 1930S FRANCE

The Stavisky Affair and the Riots of 6 February 1934

Kevin Passmore

On 6 February 1934, several tens of thousands of members of right-wing leagues and veterans associations converged on the Place de La Concorde in central Paris.[1] They were protesting against the installation in the Chambre des députés on the other side of the Seine of a center-Left government under the Radical-Socialist Édouard Daladier. The most determined demonstrators attempted to force their way across the Pont de la Concorde and into the Chamber, some of them hoping to ignite a "national revolution." In the ensuing riots, fourteen demonstrators and one policeman died, and two more of the former succumbed some months later. The next day, Daladier tendered his resignation, frightened by the reluctance of the judiciary and forces of order to defend him. His party switched its support to a government dominated by the Right, under the elderly ex-President Gaston Doumergue, which promised to reform the constitution and implement budget cuts. On 12 February, fearful that France was about to fall to fascism, the trade unions organized a general strike. The Communist and Socialist parties formed the alliance that would become the Popular Front. Years of violent Franco-French conflict began.

The Right justified the riots on two grounds. First, it accused Daladier of sacking the anti-communist Paris prefect of police, Jean Chiappe, in order to secure

left-wing support for his new government. Secondly, it charged Daladier's Radical-Socialist predecessor, Camille Chautemps, with covering up a financial fraud, orchestrated by Alexandre Stavisky.[2] The latter had sold bonds of the Crédit municipal de Bayonne against overvalued or non-existent security. The fraud was discovered before Stavisky could reimburse investors with the proceeds of another scam involving Hungarian bonds. Joseph Garat, Bayonne mayor, Radical-Socialist deputy, and Freemason, was arrested for his part in the affair. On 9 January 1934, another Radical-Socialist, Colonial Minister André Dalimier, resigned because back in 1932 he had advised official social welfare funds to invest in the bonds. On the same day, the police "discovered" Stavisky's body in his Alpine chalet. Skeptics claimed that Chautemps had ordered Stavisky's death, and that his brother-in-law, Public Prosecutor Georges Pressard, had prevented a junior colleague, Albert Prince, from prosecuting Stavisky. That both Chautemps and Pressard were Freemasons brought more grist to the conspiracy theory mill, as did the discovery of Prince's dead body on a railway line on 24 February.

By previous standards, the Stavisky Affair was not especially serious.[3] Yet the Right, from the royalist Action française to the moderate republican Alliance démocratique, saw it as evidence of a deep crisis. The latter claimed that the bloodstains would never be washed from Daladier's hands, and demanded prosecution of mysterious *grands responsables*.[4] The Right agreed that the Stavisky Affair was more than a judicial matter, and that only constitutional reform and strengthening of the executive could solve the Republic's problems, not least through budget cuts.

For decades, the conviction persisted in the historiography that the Republic was intrinsically incapable of dealing with economic and international difficulties and scandals seemingly confirmed this impression. We may still glimpse the assumption in works that casually list economic problems, parliamentary instability, and social conflict as if they automatically explained calls for reform of the Republic and the emergence of the leagues. More importantly, until recently, historians such as Michel Winock and François Monnet unwittingly recycled the protagonists' own notions of "progress" and "modernization" to understand the "defects" of the regime, and used crowd psychology, with its elite/mass distinction, to make sense of 6 February itself.

Implicitly, these historians divide the protagonists of 6 February into three categories, according to their degree of awareness of the problems of the regime. First an elite, including right-wing politicians such as André Tardieu, understood the nature of the crisis and its solution. Such figures battled against the grain, suffered for contesting "common sense," and ended their careers as heroic failures—at least until Charles de Gaulle, after his own period in the wilderness, solved the problems of French history. By association, Winock and Monnet belong to this elite, for they possess historiographical understanding of the course of history and the national interest. Secondly, ordinary French people, possessed of the good

sense of the crowd, were vaguely aware of the regime's failures, without possessing the elite's capacity for detached analysis. Indeed, the "mass" was vulnerable to passions that "demagogic" politicians could exploit. Demagogues constituted the third category. They included the dwindling band of hereditary opponents of the regime, who exploited the anger of the normally sensible mass. Demagogues of a different kind led the Left.

Historians use these categories differently. Serge Berstein believed that the Republic's faults were exaggerated, and attributed the riots to a "mass" that suffered from real problems in daily life, and so was "available" to (demagogic) parties that proposed simplistic solutions.[5] Whereas Berstein's interpretation resembles that of the 1930s moderate Left, Winock's is closer to the moderate Right's. He contends that the 6 February riots brought together elite reformers with a reasonable majority that wanted to correct the Republic's real defects. Insofar as the riots expressed anti-republicanism, it was the work of a clique of right-wing demagogues who had exploited the Stavisky Affair.[6] Nevertheless, Winock argues, the demagogues ultimately won. He contends that for the Left the "trauma" of 6 February reactivated outdated myths of conflicts between republicans and their enemies, and installed "the demonology of civil war in *the collective psychology*, and provoked rumors of fascism and communism." Extremists "exasperated the passions" and provoked the victory of the Popular Front.[7]

Winock and Monnet assume that the Stavisky Affair and 6 February riots expressed an objective crisis of the Republic, to which the solutions were technical rather than ideological. Indeed, in *La fièvre héxagonale*, Winock combined positivism and crowd psychology to diagnose the ills of French society—Dr. Gustave Le Bon had the same ambition. Winock sought the "laws" underlying the successive crises of French history, and argued that however prone the French were to "fevers" and simplistic antiparliamentarianism, the riots of 6 February stemmed from a half-conscious recognition on the part of a "profoundly moderate" country of real defects in the Republic.[8]

Certainly, events since the Left's victory in the elections of May 1932 alarmed the Right. In 1932, they had experienced a stinging electoral defeat. Subsequently, four left-wing governments had come to grief on financial issues and another fell on the related US debts question. The Right accused the majority of failing to implement budget cuts, which it believed to be necessary to counter the effects of the world economic crisis in France. Meanwhile, in October 1933, Hitler's departure from the Disarmament Conference portended another war.

It is not self-evident that the government should have been held accountable for the aforementioned difficulties. It is even less obvious that conservatives should have believed that confronting economic and international dangers required a change of constitution, or even regime, rather than a change of government. Nor does it go without saying that the Stavisky Affair signified the corruption of the regime rather than the criminality of individuals. To under-

stand how contemporaries understood crisis we must distinguish their ideas and purposes from academic conceptualizations of evolving social structures, even though these changes were an important part of the context in which contemporaries operated. So far as contemporaries are concerned, we must ask "crisis of what" and "crisis for whom?" On the one hand, the Right was so convinced that the parliamentary regime endangered the nation that it was prepared to endorse the overthrow of an elected government through street violence. On the other hand, the Left saw a crisis of capitalism, but after 6 February denied that the Republic was in crisis, and took to the streets to defend it.

Indeed, much research nuances the view that the Third Republic was flawed. Ministerial instability was as much apparent as real,[9] the interchangeability of parliamentary majorities may have permitted flexible responses to new problems,[10] and the Right was wrong to believe that the Republic was ruled by over-promoted provincial nobodies.[11] It is an open question as to how much influence governments in the 1930s had on the economy, given the available knowledge and machinery. The Republic's response to the economic crisis was not obviously worse than that of any other regime, and plausibly parliamentary opposition spared France the extreme deflation that damaged other economies. The question of the Republic's response to the rise of Hitler is equally complex. One cannot read French history backward from the defeat of June 1940,[12] and anyway war was not necessarily the supreme test of the "fitness" of a political system.[13] Paul Jankowski argues convincingly that responses to the scandals of the Third Republic owed more to their cultural and social context than to their actual gravity.[14]

In fact, none of these revisionist accounts prove that the Third Republic was, after all, "effective" or "modern." My point is rather that expectations of the Republic were historically constructed, and evaluation of its effectiveness depended on perspective. Thus, state intervention during the Great War had encouraged the belief that government policy was decisive in orienting the economy, and André Tardieu's governments of 1929–1930 had explicitly staked their future on prosperity. Likewise, the Right's (often underestimated) Darwinist assumptions engendered the fear that Republic's alleged unfitness for war condemned it.

My purpose in this essay is to understand the logic that led the Right to see the Stavisky Affair as a symptom of constitutional dysfunction that rendered the nation vulnerable to invasion and communism. I shall therefore focus upon what for Winock were the "excesses" of 6 February, not least because they were actually widely shared in elite and popular culture. Of course, to demonstrate the importance of prejudices about Freemasons and Jews hardly counts as a historiographical discovery, but others, concerning southerners and criminality, are less well known, as is their relation to crowd psychology or their precise position in political debates.

The ideas that I discuss were not used unreflecting in the sense that they had been "internalized" or represented a pre-conscious "habitus." They were too contradictory for that; their meaning varied according to context, and confronted with the right sort of "falsification," or when they conflicted with other priorities, protagonists could modify them or drop them altogether. I focus on the political uses of historically constructed categories, used more or less consciously in proportions that varied according to context. My discussion of the meanings of 6 February complements a historiographical shift away from the use of transhistorical abstract models to detect the presence or absence of fascism or republicanism in the riot, models in which objectivist assumptions about the nature and ends of society also play a part. New approaches focus on the use and transformation of available ways of seeing the world as they were used for new purposes in political struggles. I examine the inherited intellectual and cultural resources that competing elements of the Right used to make sense of the circumstances of February 1934, to evaluate the goals of their opponents, and to pursue their own interests both against the Left and against rival conservatives. I do not argue that the ideas I discuss explain responses to the Stavisky Affair or the 6 February riots. Ideas on their own can do nothing—practice matters more.[15]

Conservative Political Culture

I have already stressed contemporary historians' unwitting debt to Le Bon's crowd psychology. Mark Meyers shows that both Left and Right used its categories.[16] However, they did so differently. The Left felt that the state (the elite) could nurture the rationality of the mass through education and by removing the influence of the obscurantist, demagogic Church from society. Moderate conservatives were less optimistic about the rationality of ordinary people, but believed that they possessed an innate conservative good sense. To govern effectively, the elite must know the mass through the study of history and experience of life, and thus govern in accordance with the "realities" of the national psychology. The extreme Right was more likely to stress an intuitive, elemental relationship between leader and mass, often discovered in the trenches of the Western Front. Both Left and Right saw their opponents as demagogic counter-elites.

The assumptions of crowd psychology pervaded the political culture of the Right. The discipline posited an unequal dialogue between two naturalized concepts, the "elite" and the "mass," conceived organically and hierarchically as a thinking head and body, and as a gendered, classed and racialized dichotomy. The mass was irrational, vulnerable to extremism and to exploitation by demagogues. It learned through the repetition of slogans and images, which may be incarnated in a leader. The elite shared the crowd's patriotism, but through the accumulation of reason over generations, it had learned to control its irrational impulses.

The elite would draw inspiration from the mass's idealism and channel it into purposeful activity.[17]

Crowd psychology was related to four key terms in contemporary political discourse: realism, experience, competence, and generalism. The elite's pursuit of "realistic" policies required knowledge of the psychology of the mass and the country. That in turn required "experience" of life, which could be gained through military, professional or academic careers, business, or involvement in provincial affairs. Experience also provided the "competence" necessary for government. Furthermore, a politician who brought experience to government would be a "generalist," a rounded man who was in contact with reality, capable of treating problems on their merits, and free from dogma. Generalism also transferred into the intellectual sphere. The Right largely rejected the specialized academic knowledge of the emergent human sciences in the universities—the history of Marc Bloch or the sociology of the Durkheimians. The elite used race science, social biology, social Darwinism, and Lamarckianism to understand national psychology. Thus, doctors could diagnose the ills of a polity by applying germ theory and Lamarckianism; the Facultés de droit dispensed a generalist education designed as much to equip graduates for government as to practice the law.

Crowd psychology remained influential in the 1930s and beyond. Le Bon died in 1931, bitter that the University had not recognized his talents. Yet the leaders of both main conservative parties, Pierre-Étienne Flandin of the secular Alliance démocratique and Louis Marin of the Catholic Fédération républicaine, were devotees.[18] In the 1930s, crowd psychology was given a new lease of life by the supposed success of Fascists, Nazis, and Communists in the "age of the masses." In France, crowd psychology was especially visible in the belief in the need for a "mystique," capable of rivaling that of the totalitarians. A mystique supposedly derived from the depths of the people, the elite would shape it and thus guide the mass. Contending political groups sought to elaborate a true mystique and to ensure that demagogues did not propagate false ones.[19]

Conservatives differed sharply among themselves over what the elite looked like, and their disputes were entangled with class, religious, and historic divisions. Royalists idealized the Catholic landed gentry and sometimes condemned lawyers as a category, while republican conservatives located competence in the "elite" of the professions and the administration. Such disputes hardly threatened crowd psychology because its categories were unfalsifiable and empty. They were vaguely enough formulated both to excuse imperfection in friends and to identify character flaws in political opponents.

Right-wing political culture disqualified the Left from government on two counts. First, left-wing politicians had chosen to become *professional* politicians precisely because they had failed in their careers. They lacked experience and could not be competent. They were lawyers without clients, doctors without patients, or bankrupt businessmen. For the Right, the Stavisky Affair confirmed

these failings. The *Journal des débats* attributed the Affair to the fact that politics was a salaried trade, and lamented the days when "the parliamentarian was a man who had decided to divert from his own work in order to serve the public."[20] Tardieu agreed that the *député-avocat* was the chief agent of corruption.[21] *Le Jour* campaigned to forbid deputies from pleading in the Paris Bar.[22] For the royalist Léon Daudet, Chautemps was surrounded in the Chamber by "the worst scum of the bar, magistracy, police and press, capable of quietly doing his adversaries in."[23]

Secondly, left-wing politicians had been educated in abstractions—Kantian idealism or worse Marxism—rather than in practical science based on experience: hence Marin's denunciation, as the scandal broke, of a "politics of demagogy ... impregnated with primary school Marxism."[24] Left-wing parliamentarians were demagogues in Le Bon's sense: they were half-educated men, capable only of flattering the materialism of the mass and flaunting utopias before its eyes. They could not genuinely "know" the people, since they were insufficiently detached from its passions and materialism and knew only abstract theories. The Stavisky scandal confirmed left-wing deputies' inherent corruption, and explained their resistance to budget cuts.

Corruption was all the more dangerous because it weakened France in the struggle between nations. Historians have underestimated the extent to which conservative politicians envisaged international relations in Darwinian terms. True, conservatives did not advocate conquest (if we forget the Empire) and they applied Lamarckian notions of organic harmony to domestic policies. Yet they regarded a strong economy and domestic order, as well as a numerous population, as essential to France's survival in a competitive international environment, in which Communists and Germans were bent on the destruction of France. Stavisky symbolized these threats. The Right saw itself as an elite, engaged in a life-and-death struggle with a demagogic counter-elite for the allegiance of the masses, the guarantee of national strength. I shall now turn my attention to the signs by which the Right recognized this counter-elite.

Anti-Southern Prejudice

Historians sometimes mention in passing that professional politicians were often depicted in literature as southerners.[25] Anti-meridional prejudice is less well known than anti-Masonism or anti-Semitism, but was more widely spread across the political spectrum. It has a long history in France and Europe, dating back to the seventeenth century, when northern civilizations displaced Mediterranean preeminence. For instance, Jules Michelet and Hippolyte Taine attributed the alleged inferiority of southerners to mongrelization of the race, or to Arab admixture.[26] Certainly the Right rarely evoked a conspiracy of southerners and no one

advocated legal discrimination against them. Yet the southern accent was a sign by which one could recognize the defects of the professional politician.

The association between political corruption and the south was well established: Marx and Ernest Renan both saw the Second Empire as dependent upon southern clientelism.[27] With the establishment of the Republic, monarchists redeployed the stereotype to signify the supposed leveling of parliamentary democracy. The southerner Léon Gambetta, as the herald of the *couches nouvelles*, was a favorite target.[28] The high point of political anti-southern prejudice followed the Radical-Socialist triumph in the elections of 1902. The religious struggles of those years took on the air of a conflict between southern anti-clericalism and northern piety, provoking Maurice Barrès to describe the Loire as a "profound fissure" in the nation.[29] Meanwhile, the Radical-Socialist campaign for income tax provoked attacks on southern materialism, while the Midi winegrower rebellion of 1907 apparently confirmed the south's desire for subsidies and the expense of northern taxpayers.

In 1911, the moderate conservative Maurice Colrat, in the review *L'Opinion*, launched an enquiry into the alleged southern preponderance in parliament. His article provoked many approving responses, some from the great names of French intellectual and political life.[30] Almost all contributors endorsed Colrat's views. They attributed southern domination of parliament to the racial predisposition of Latin types toward talkativeness and expansiveness, which prevented them from pursuing a profession but facilitated the formation of a clientele, and thus to a parliamentary system in which talk mattered more than action. Contributors also assumed that southern weaknesses were aggravated by the sun, which caused both laziness and the overheating of the brain, especially when stimulated by alcohol (just as women's brains were destabilized by anything from the vibration of the uterus to intellectual activity). Worse, southerners' selfishness made them antipatriotic: Barrès claimed, "there is no France except on the frontier of the Rhine."[31]

We may note two further points. First, the north/south antagonism dramatized the elite/mass dichotomy that was intrinsic to crowd psychology. In his *Psychologie des foules*, Le Bon described the democratic crowd as Latin and feminine; he denounced the republican elite's lack of will and practical knowledge, and its predilection for abstract constitutions. He regarded the English elite as more in touch with practical reality.[32] He contributed to the Colrat enquiry the view that "we are in the age of crowds. To be an effective agitator one must be able to speak well and think little. Southern politicians, who possess this double quality to a high degree, will govern until the day of the debacle."[33] Secondly, the south was geographically malleable: to serve his purpose, Colrat excluded Nice, Cannes, and Antibes from the south. Sometimes the south stood for a specific geographical area; sometimes for France as a whole, often in contrast to Britain; sometimes it represented rural France, or simply southern cities.

The flexibility of anti-southern prejudice and the persistence of anti-parliamentarianism accounts for its long survival. During the Great War, it was sustained by the alleged "cowardice" in 1914 of the 15th Corps of Marseille, by the belief that southerners shirked service in the northern war, and by the alleged treason of the Gascon interior minister, Louis Malvy.[34] The war also encouraged contrary tendencies, for hostility to German culture and the entry of Italy into the war provoked a movement in favor of "Latinity."

The postwar "années folles" brought new attacks on the south as a site of easy pleasure. Politically, the question of the south became more complex. Initially some were optimistic, in line with Barrès's conviction that the loss of Alsace-Lorraine had unhealthily increased southern influence in the national psyche. The deputy George Noblemaire thus felt that its recovery now permitted northern tenacity to compensate southern enthusiasm.[35] Yet the rise of autonomism in Alsace deeply worried conservatives. Some blamed the appointment of southern administrators to Alsace for the rise of autonomism.[36] This tendency to demonize southerners jostled with fear that excessive criticism would further undermine national unity. That was especially true in Brittany, where the once monarchist far Right tried to reconcile Breton regionalism with nationalism and anti-southern prejudice. In 1931, on the foundation of the nationalist newspaper *Breiz atao*, a contributor to *L'Écho de Paris* recalled Barrès' warning of the dislocation of France, and expressed concern about links between Breton and Alsatian autonomism. The writer also admitted that the government's favoritism toward the south provided autonomists with real grievances, and that when *Breiz atao* declared the unwillingness of Bretons to die for regions with low birthrates, they expressed "certain essential truths."[37]

Thus, doubts reconfigured anti-southern prejudice without eliminating it from political discourse. In 1923, the business journalist Lucien Romier described "the winegrowing Languedoc as one of the gravest factors of instability in our national life." His article was part of a sustained tirade against the south.[38] Neither was Colrat's enquiry forgotten.[39] In 1928, a journalist at the right-wing veteran newspaper *La Voix du combatant* evoked it in an article about Président du conseil Raymond Poincaré's decision to present his policies in Carcassonne and Bordeaux. The journalist promoted Colrat to the status of "eminent statistician," and remarked that if Poincaré had chosen to speak in the south "in order to prove that politics is only really interesting beyond the Loire," he had troubled himself for nothing: "even those from the deepest Midi" know that "it's a matter of professional politics, of the so-called politics of the stomach, of which the purpose is to feed some well while reserving the consequent nausea to others, the 'cash cows' [cochons payants]."[40]

Narrowing our focus to the years immediately preceding the Stavisky scandal, it is possible to see that anti-southern stereotypes persisted in popular culture, press, and political science. Detective fiction represents a good example, since

it stretched from *Détective* magazine, with a circulation of 800,000, to the more bourgeois appeal of the new wave of detective fiction, which in 1930 began its golden age. The links between elite and mass culture are evident in the contributions of eminent politicians and lawyers to the lurid *Détective*, and the magazine's success permitted Gallimard to finance the *Nouvelle revue française*—in which André Gide wrote a column on the *fait divers*. Besides illustrating the *chassé-croisé* between high and low culture, *Détective* blurred the frontier between imagination and reality.[41]

In 1929, the critic René Messac described the crime novel as essentially republican, in that the policeman uncovered the truth through an investigation of facts and applied universal standards of justice to the guilty.[42] Commissaire Maigret, the creation of the Belgian Catholic Georges Simenon, proceeded differently. Maigret reconstructed a criminal's motivations through immersion in her/his milieu and through understanding of his/her ethnic and class determinisms.[43] Maigret's method chimed with the combination of reason, science, and intuition that was essential to crowd psychology.

Indeed, Maigret's immersion in the crowd could be dangerous. In *Liberty Bar* (1932) he makes a rare trip to the south, and is nearly overcome by the ambiance of this place of laziness and pleasure. Maigret is the uneasy, apparently slow northerner, dressed in his suit and bowler hat, among the scantily clad vacationers and locals of Antibes.[44] A local commissaire who "does not like silence" annoys him; Maigret struggles with the sun, and with the constant offers of aperitifs; readers familiar with a beer-loving detective are surprised to hear him order a Vittel. Maigret felt that since the murder victim, a hard-working Protestant Australian, had surrendered to the local atmosphere, the weakness of local functionaries was understandable. Yet on a café terrace on the Place Jean Macé in Antibes, Maigret rouses himself and takes the "path of work." Simenon may have been thinking of Michelet's depiction of "the vaporous thoughts that fill a northern brain between a stove, tobacco and beer" as he conceived Maigret, a man who loved his pipe, beer, and a warm stove.[45]

Nothing illustrates the reach and pliability of anti-southern prejudice better than Gabriel Chevallier's satirical novel *Clochemerle*. It was published in March 1934, with the Affair still monopolizing the front pages, and was on its 142nd edition within a year. Half ironically, *Lyon républicain*, published in the department in which *Clochemerle* is set, reassured its readers that the story was fictional. The latest in a long line of parodies of political life, *Clochemerle* recounts a *querelle de clocher* in a Beaujolais village. A dispute about the building of a public lavatory in a passageway adjacent to the church escalates into a national political crisis, and causes the failure of a major international conference. True, the Beaujolais is not necessarily the south. However, it may be significant that the real inspiration for the novel was Burgundy, some miles to the north, where the young Chevallier had spent his summers. Whatever the reason for moving the action southward,

the novel contains all the usual anti-southern motifs—sun, alcohol, and corruption, coupled with 1930s anti-parliamentarianism. One character, the deputy Alexandre Bourdillat, left Clochemerle as a young man to work in a Parisian café, which happens to host an unnamed political group resembling the Radical-Socialist Party. One day he cries: "By God, I've helped elect deputies for so long by serving drinks that it ought to be my turn. I want to be a deputy, by God!" During the war, Clemenceau makes Bourdillat a minister because "the more fools I have around me, the more chance there is that they'll leave me the f ... alone!"[46] *Clochemerle* is sometimes read as an indulgent portrait of *la France profonde*. In fact, Chevallier's use of anti-southern stereotypes shaded into a dislike of the countryside and provinces, of the "routine agitation leading men to enact the same inexorable tasks, by the same routes, in the same perpetual monotony"—precisely the characteristics of the mass.[47]

These prejudices were not confined to popular literature. Contemporary electoral geography was based on the notion of regional *mentalités*. The discipline was founded by André Siegfried, a member of the board of the *Annales* and the son of a moderate republican deputy. Regional stereotypes were fundamental to his *Tableaux des partis en France* (1930). Siegfried depicted himself as "a heavy northerner," contrasting with the light, talkative southerners, of mobile opinion. "The Midi," he says, "is no more than a caricature of the rest of France, but the caricature is not always a bad portrait."[48] Siegfried denounced deputies who were more responsive to local clienteles than to the national interest, the *bonhomie* of parliament, in which deputies "se tutoyaient trop facilement," the weakness of the executive, empty debates about grand principles, and lack of competence. Siegfried concluded, "We are a Latin democracy, in which the individual affirms himself not only through action, but by denial. In the Anglo-Saxon democracies, practical social realisation is more important than anything else."[49]

The conservative press understood the Cartel's 1932 election victory in this light. During the campaign, *L'Écho de Paris* ridiculed southern politics. One article evoked the argumentative nature of Marseille inhabitants, which found an outlet in every bistro, where "sub-orators" adapted the party program, while activists sat and ate, as if around the "trough" [*assiette au beurre*].[50] After the election, Fernand Laudet of the Institute proclaimed that "it is to the honour of the hardworking departments, those that have suffered [in the War], that they have halted the progress of the Cartel; the latter advances more easily in the sunny regions, where empty words prevail over arguments."[51] Meanwhile, the Depression renewed attacks on southern wine producers for their excessive protectionism. These prejudices were linked to understandings of the Stavisky Affair.

Just as the scandal broke, *L'Alliance démocratique* argued that moderates' task in left-wing parliaments was to "regulate" the "excessive opinions" that resulted from Latin peoples' predilection for speculative thought and for pushing their ideas to the limits.[52] In terms of crowd psychology, the Alliance saw itself as an

elite that would channel the energies of the mass. More immediately, the racial predispositions of the French required a reversal of majorities and a disciplining of parliament through strengthening of the executive.

That Bayonne was the starting point of the Stavisky Affair stimulated anti-southern prejudice. The writer François Duhourcau remarked in *La Liberté* that it was appropriate that the name "Bayonne" meant both "country infested with brigands" and "commercial place." He described the population as a mélange of Basques, Gascons, and Spaniards, from which arose the "showiness that se-duces whoever passes through Bayonne."[53] In a similar vein, a *Figaro* journalist remarked that Parisians would be surprised that the *Bal de l'aviation* interested the inhabitants of Bayonne more than the arrest of député-maire Joseph Garat. He evoked the elegance of those received by the municipal council and the sunny and picturesque streets, thus connecting with the notion of the south as a place of frivolity.[54]

Le Jour more explicitly linked the south with the crisis of parliament. Under the headline, "Garatt, Garatt … ," it ridiculed the Bayonnais accent. The news-paper depicted Garat's crime as the culmination of minor transgressions, includ-ing the introduction of car-parking charges in the town. The portrayal of Garat is worth quoting in full:

> [Garat is] a mediocre politician, of which there are so many.... If one examines the Garat fact, one quickly understands the mechanism that permits a man of this sort to be undone by Stavisky: one begins with little exactions; one becomes a lo-cal tyrant, and thanks to the appointment of postmen and street-sweepers, thanks to doing favors in the Latin style for a fairly poor clientele—without anyone ever protesting that they are suffocated by this scattering of little scandals—one ends up believing that anything goes. One lives in contact with brilliant towns, in which the masters dine with dazzling women, and where they put on great shows. One even comes to Paris, as he [Garat] once did, in the hope of becoming a minister (it's astonishing to think that two years ago he nearly became a minister).[55]

During the Affair, the fact that three of the first four jackpot wins in the new National Lottery went to southern towns provided another opportunity for jests concerning "trop heureux Provence." One journalist evoked the negative reac-tion of northern taxpayers, and concluded "Bayonne lives now only in expecta-tion of the jackpot."[56] Conservatives had already denounced the Lottery, which the Radical-Socialists introduced a few weeks previously, as a swindle. The fact that Stavisky had been involved in fraudulent dealing in southern casinos, and had first met Garat in the Biarritz casino, added fuel to the fire. Anti-southern prejudice was shared even in the administration's reading of events: the prefect of the Haute-Loire remarked upon the local population's "snobbery" [*forfanterie*] toward national events.[57]

The relationship between anti-southern prejudice and anti-parliamentarianism was less straightforward than it had been in 1911, and in any case it was never an unthinking reflex. For one thing, as a Basque city, Bayonne puzzled the Right. Conservatives viewed the Basques positively because, like linguistic minorities in Alsace, Flanders, and Brittany, they showed a predilection for Catholic conservatism. Yet the Right also feared that Alsatian autonomism would encourage separatism in other minorities.

L'Action française found anti-southernism particularly problematic because its founder, Charles Maurras, preached that the origin of true France was to be found in the Greco-Roman tradition. It therefore depicted the Stavisky Affair as evidence of the corruption of national life by Paris, rather than by the south. It described Garat's story as "the drama of one of these politicians of the provinces who leave more or less honestly for Paris, and end up in the grip of the Parisian mafia."[58] L'Action française stressed the probity of the Bayonnais, whereas the more moderate Le Jour had depicted them as frivolous.[59] L'Action française could not, however, free itself entirely from anti-southern prejudice, for Maurras accepted that the contemporary south did not (like Greece) live up to its classical past, thanks to infiltration by "wogs," Jews and Freemasons.[60] Similarly, L'Action française saw disturbances in Marseille during the 12 February general strike as confirmation that "as in the state swindle of the Jew Stavisky, the wog element played its great role." It denounced the involvement of the non-naturalized in Marseille and suggested that the Italian consulate was the real power in the city.[61]

Even more equivocal was the pro-Action française group behind the Breton newspaper, La Province, for it defended Breton identity, but opposed separatism. It was alarmed by the stance of the nationalist Breiz Atao, which saw the Stavisky Affair as evidence of the corruption not just of the Republic, but of France. Breiz Atao was particularly antipathetic to André Dalimier, who had allegedly referred to separatists as "assholes" (cons) in a visit to Brittany. It saw the 6 February riots as a "vigorous scrap between north and south, a bit like a rugby match" (the violence of southern rugby was sometimes contrasted with the gentlemanliness of northern and English rugby[62]), and felt that "southerners had defended their finest colony [Paris] with bullets." For Breiz Atao, Jews (Stavisky), half-negroes (the scandal journalist Pierre Darius), Freemasons, and mocos (a derogatory term for southerners and more particularly for Provençal sailors) represented France.[63] In response, the editor of La Province, Eugène Delahaye, reminded readers that Brittany was not free from scandal. He added that "this is not the time to set one province against another or for advocating separatism on the grounds that Dalimier is a bastard; this is the time for the rapprochement of all honest men, from Brest to Strasbourg, and from Lille to Bayonne, precisely, Bayonne." Delahaye acknowledged that anti-southern feeling was an ingredient in the crisis,

but preferred to downplay it and to emphasize the involvement of Freemasons instead.[64]

The right-wing Parisian press crossed anti-southern prejudice with dislike of the provinces more generally. It situated the demonstrations of January and February within the tradition of Parisian national-populism, and in keeping with organicist crowd psychology, journalists described Paris as the "brain" of France. Léon Bailby, editor of Le Jour, felt that if Paris "instructed" the provinces, they would eventually understand.[65] He wrote against the background of the provincial success of the general strike of 12 February. After the strike, Kerillis at L'Écho de Paris became embroiled in a polemic with a Marseille journalist, who had claimed that the provinces would save France. Kerillis imagined his adversary concocting his article in a Marseille café "under the influence of a too-strong aperitif and electoral funds from local gangsters." He denounced the provinces that sent to Paris hordes of Radical-Socialist and Socialist deputies who fought like cats and dogs over the spoils of office.[66] Since 1924, Kerillis had been campaigning against corruption in Marseille, and we have already noted his newspaper's caricatures of southern politics in 1932.[67]

These attacks were part of Kerillis's campaign to create what he saw as a conservative party on the British model, and one of the major functions of his Centre de propagande des républicains nationaux (created in 1926–1930) was precisely to prevent electoral fraud. The identification of northern France with England (often defined in opposition to its Celtic neighbors) was an old theme in conservative thought, and Kerillis had often visited the country to learn about party organization.[68] Tardieu, the dominant figure in the new Doumergue government, also evoked the English model as a solution to the French crisis, interpreting its parliamentary system in as one in which the executive predominated over the legislature.[69] Thus, anti-southern prejudice linked the Stavisky scandal to a crisis of the parliamentary system, and via the contrast with the north and with England, it indicated the solution. I shall now explore the stereotypical association of southerners with organized crime, immigration, and communist infiltration.

Xenophobia and Anti-Semitism

In the interwar years, many immigrants had come from Eastern Europe. They included Orthodox Jews, who became a target of anti-Semitism in Paris. In the few months before the Stavisky Affair broke, some 25,000 Jewish refugees had arrived from Germany. Artisans, shopkeepers, and professionals already resented foreign competition, and there was often an anti-Semitic note to their complaints. The Stavisky Affair and the Right's complaints about the participation of foreigners in the 12 February counter-demonstration encouraged the Doumergue government to strengthen surveillance of them.[70]

Explicit prejudice was most common in the extreme-Right press, especially *L'Action française*.[71] The Catholic republican *Frontière de l'Est* also described Stavisky as a *métèque*.[72] As one moves toward the moderate Right, references to Stavisky's foreignness were fewer, without disappearing completely. During the Affair, Émile Buré, editor of the pro-Alliance démocratique *L'Ordre*, denounced Hitler's crimes against the Jews, but admitted that there was a "Jewish question," and felt that it was "obviously" a problem that the number of Jews in Paris had risen dramatically and that the international banks, which were so opposed to French interests, were "Jewified and of Asiatic origin." Buré's conviction that a strong government would have nothing to fear from the banks showed the entanglement of anti-parliamentarianism, xenophobia, anti-Semitism, Eastern European gangsterism, and the Stavisky Affair.[73]

Maigret illustrates the reach of this implicit anti-Semitism and connects it to Eastern European gangsters. The eponymous protagonist of *Petr-le-Letton* (1932) is a rootless and wandering Eastern European, linked to international crime, banks, and politicians. Much of the action takes place in the Parisian Jewish quarter, from the Rue des Rosiers to the Rue des Écouffes in the Fourth Arrondissement. Simenon portrays the district as a "ghetto," with its nauseating smells and overweight women. The commissaire remarks: "All that in the shadow of Notre Dame!"[74] Stavisky was a familiar figure to the numerous readers of Maigret and of the detective genre more generally.

Maigret's relevance is all the greater because *Paris-Soir* hired him, via Simenon, to investigate the supposed suicide of the magistrate Prince. Simenon told a friend: "Do you understand, we're swimming in a novel, so we must ask a character from a novel to lead the enquiry." Simenon gullibly gathered tips from habitués of Chez Cotti, a notorious gangster hangout. He attributed Prince's assassination to Corsican gangsters from Marseille, including the notorious Paul Carbone and François Spirito and an ex-boxer, Jo-les-cheveux blancs (re-christened Jo-le-terreur in the *Paris-Soir* articles). Under the headline "From murder to detective novel," the moderate conservative *L'Alliance démocratique* commented that there were many others who for unknown reasons walked around freely, and acted as electoral agents in their spare time.[75] After the gangsters were released without charge (having received a "Simenon-lieu," rival journalists mocked), Carbone called the house at which Simenon was dining with friends, and reassured him that since friendship was sacred for Corsicans, he would not take revenge. Carbone nevertheless advised Simenon to stick to writing his rather good novels, of which he had enjoyed reading the latest while imprisoned in the Santé. Subsequently, colorful rumors circulated about the revenge inflicted on the "snitch", Simenon.[76] Meanwhile, Carbone returned to Marseille, where his longtime ally, the fascistic Mayor Simon Sabiani, gave him a hero's welcome. Doubtless Sabiani was grateful that Carbone had allowed his thugs to intimidate the city's dockers, on strike since 12 February.

Stavisky's Jewishness also resonated with international threats to France. The connection between the Bayonne and Hungarian frauds evoked fears that the defeated of 1918 were planning revenge and manipulating French opinion. Stavisky bought unredeemed bonds that Hungarians had received in return for land lost with the collapse of the Habsburg Empire, and who lobbied at international conferences for compensation. The Right accused Stavisky of promoting the Hungarian desire for revision of the Versailles Treaty in the French press, theatre, and cinema. Buré commented that these activities depended especially on Radical-Socialist protection, for plutocracy and demagogy naturally went together.[77]

Communism represented the other aspect of the foreign danger. In 1934, the Right saw communism as an Asiatic, barbarian power bent upon the destruction of France, usually in alliance with Germany.[78] Occasionally, these conspiracies were linked explicitly to southern gangsterism. Urbain Gohier's polemics against Maurras associated anti-meridionalism with anti-Semitism. He depicted Maurras as "this Mediterranean ruffian, as fabricated by generations of thieves, gypsies and gangsters, in the cabarets and brothels of Smyrna, Salonika, Constantinople and Naples: the type of *ma'ras* or *Maurras* on whom the Saracens spat."[79] Gohier went much further than most, but we may now understand why the *Journal des Débats* believed that the Stavisky scandal exposed the submission of parliamentarians to internationalism (i.e., communism) and their feebleness before German infiltration.[80] Deputies were part of a web of demagogic conspirators, incapable of recognizing or defending the national interest.

Freemasonry

Anti-Masonic feeling represented another, familiar element of right-wing political culture, and it too was related to crowd psychology. Catholic conservatives especially were convinced that Masonic involvement in the Affair signified generalized corruption. Before the Great War, intransigent Catholics had seen Freemasonry as the enemy in the ageless struggle of good against evil. This Manichean worldview was especially strong among Legitimists, who had, since the 1870s, celebrated the popular piety of pilgrimages, local saints and prophecies as an antidote to republican rationalism. Subsequently, anti-Masonism was transmitted through the Rallié Action libérale populaire (ALP) and Action française. The latter saw Masonry, along with Jews, Protestants, and *métèques* (wogs), as one of the "four confederated estates" that sought to destroy France. At first, the AF polemicist Léon Daudet integrated Stavisky into the baffling web of conspiracies that he recounted each day on the front page of *L'Action française*. He connected Stavisky to the deaths in 1923 of the Action française veterans' leader, Marius Plateau, and of his own son, Philippe. Improbably, he declared that the

southerner Louis Malvy, the wartime interior minister and longtime *bête noire* of Action française, stood at the center of the Affair.[81]

Even the most indulgent of Daudet's readers probably retained from his articles little more than an impression of the malevolent power of the nation's enemies. They might have found greater clarity (of a sort) in *La Province*. Three days before the 6 February riots, Delahaye published an interview with the Abbé Élie Daniel, author of *Serait-ce vraiment la fin des temps?* (1927, republished 1932). Posing as a scientific critic of prophecies, Daniel insisted that they should be treated carefully, but contained an "element of truth." He maintained that the breakdown of the Disarmament Conference demonstrated the failure of the League of Nations and therefore the collapse of the Tower of Babel. Universal bankruptcy represented another "great event," which would lead to a world war in which France would be the first victim. The enemy would invade through Switzerland and the southeast, and Paris would be partially destroyed; Freemasons would attack the Church. However, divine providence would ensure that a Breton general, or perhaps Weygand, who loved Brittany, would save France, and thus prove that the province could not be separatist. Delahaye hoped for a restoration, but Daniel refused to commit himself.[82] Delahaye commented on the 6 February riots, "with God's permission there are in the world two ideas that will struggle until the last day: the just and the false." Freemasons represented the second.[83]

As in crowd psychology, good and evil battled for the soul of the mass. Delahaye claimed that the "crowd" was apparently "satisfied by the injection that the newspapers give it each morning." Yet "if the people is still capable of a reaction in the true and beautiful physiological sense of the word, it will make the revolution of the Right, impose a chief who will restore order in the house, reorganize the administration and give France the solid and normal constitution that it lacks." Delahaye saw the people as "a big child"; instead of following the "bad shepherds of the lodges," it must understand that its interests lie on the side of those who demand justice, and not with the "gilded bellies" of politics.[84] Similarly, the neo-Maurrassian *Je suis partout* saw Freemasonry as a "camaraderie and fraternity, evident in the *tutoiement* to which even deputies of the right have surrendered," and in the cult of incompetence.[85]

Anti-Masonism was not confined to the extreme Right. Louis Marin, leader of the Fédération républicaine, had expressed reservations about anti-Masonism in the 1900s,[86] but now made it an integral part of his discourse. His party saw Freemasonry, anti-clericalism, socialism, free thought, and trade unionism as "a fatal cocktail from which France will die unless we resist it."[87] The Fédération's journal published weekly denunciations of Masonic action in the administration and schools, and Marin described Stavisky as a "scandal of the lodges." He also saw Freemasonry as a dimension of the professionalization of politics: "these people, these serfs, have replaced the competences, the workers." Masons oper-

ated openly through the distribution of jobs and "demagogies designed to flatter low passions"; in obscurity, they operated through plutocracy.[88] In April 1934, a confidential circular to local committees warned them that that the "common front of Masons and the extreme Left was preparing a violent campaign against Fédération meetings."[89] Delahaye's belief in diabolical conspiracies was also present: Masonry had become even more secretive because it feared Mussolini and Hitler. Indeed, the Fédération attributed the Left's opposition to an alliance with Italy to Masonic influence.

For both extremist and parliamentary Catholics, anti-Masonism and collective psychology were integral to anti-parliamentarianism. Their critique of the Republic rested upon unproven assumptions about the relative merits of professional and amateur politicians, on belief in obscure conspiracies and a struggle between good and evil. Masons represented a counter-elite that manipulated the impressionable mass in order to win the spoils of office.

Conclusion

Whether they saw dictatorship or constitutional reform as the solution, conservatives regarded the Stavisky Affair as the sign of a crisis of the regime. In various proportions, the moderate and extreme Right used crowd psychology, anti-southern racism, xenophobia, anti-Semitism, and anti-Masonism to understand it. Southern clientelism and gangsterism connected Stavisky to an Eastern European plot, orchestrated by Communists and Freemasons. Living in a world of dichotomies and plots, conservatives vastly overestimated the power of their opponents. At stake was the very being of France, engaged in a life-and-death Darwinian struggle for survival.[90]

Of course, none of the prejudices that I have described is sufficient to explain the Stavisky Affair, the events of 6 February, or their consequences. I have discussed only *some* of the inherited assumptions that right-wingers used to identify dangers and guide their action. The worldview of the veterans, for instance, is a fertile area of research on which I have not touched.[91] Furthermore, recourse to inherited available ideas may not be the only way that protagonists respond to new circumstances.[92] My major point is that we cannot account for how people understood the Stavisky Affair and responded to it by using our own generalizations or theories about effectiveness, modernity, or the national psychology. There is no alternative to careful analysis of beliefs and political strategies. Nevertheless, anti-southern prejudice—and regional tensions more generally—have played a greater part in French history than some have allowed.

Antipathy to southerners persisted through the Occupation, and remained connected to anti-parliamentarianism. César Fauxbras, the left-wing novelist-activist, reported that one of his fellow prisoners of war blamed work-shy southern

ministers for the defeat, and would have been happy to join a new country made up of Northern France, Belgium, and Holland, if the Germans wanted that.[93] The Vichy government, based in the south, was nevertheless concerned to preserve national unity. Its 1942 Plan d'équipement nationale stated that France is at confluence of two currents: "Mediterranean thought, the daughter of leisure thanks to a gentle climate, inclined towards abstraction; northern thought, which the harshness of the climate turns towards the practical realization of useful mechanisms." The Plan regretted that French greatness had been based on the heritage of Latin and Greek civilization, but the country had fallen behind in 150 years of industrial progress, because it was too given to abstract speculation and demagogy. The result was technological weakness in agriculture and feebleness in "organization in general."[94]

As for Charles de Gaulle, he allegedly preferred the windy northern plains of the Franks to southern cushiness and superficial cordiality.[95] The constitution of 1958 was meant to ensure the predominance of will, authority, and competence over the ineffective talkativeness of parliament. Todd Shepard argues that decolonization was associated with a new emphasis on the racial purity of France.[96] Perhaps the old association between the Midi and Africa extends that insight— all the more so given that partisans of Algérie française were cast as defenders of tradition and routine against de Gaulle's embracement of France's European future.

I shall finish by returning to February 1934. The new prime minister, Doumergue, or "Gastounet," was a native of Marseille, who had chosen to retire to Tournefeuille in the Haute-Garonne.[97] For some time he had been seen as a possible recourse. During the 1932 elections, L'Écho de Paris depicted him as "the only man in the Midi uninvolved in politics," an area in which new candidates every day "felt bubbling up in themselves the temperament of a great tribune."[98] The conservative press nearly unanimously welcomed Doumergue's appointment, and frequent references to his "return from Tournefeuille" established his credentials as a man of la France profonde. Doumergue claimed to understand nothing of parliamentary language, only the langue d'oc.[99] Others could not resist contrasting a man (i.e. Doumergue) "made in the mould of the regime" with the government of "new men" that the situation allegedly demanded, and the conservative press could hardly write of Doumergue without mentioning his Marseille accent.[100] Breiz Atao remarked that Gastounet "did all that southerners knew how to do: talk."[101] Delahaye was still more negative. He claimed that Nostrodamus had prophesied the appearance of a man from the southwest whom France would mistakenly take for its savior. He predicted that Doumergue would resign in about five months, after the financial situation had been secured. German invasion and the final crisis would follow.[102]

In October 1934, Doumergue did indeed fall, the immediate cause being Radical-Socialist and moderate conservative opposition to his proposed consti-

tutional reform. Four weeks before, Foreign Minister Louis Barthou and King Alexander of Yugoslavia had been murdered in Marseille, precipitating a wave of police action against refugees and immigrants.[103] Anti-southern prejudice and xenophobia were not, of course, the principal causes of Doumergue's downfall, but it is not too fanciful to suggest that they played some part in conservative perceptions of him as a man of the system, and contributed to pessimism concerning the chances of reform within the regime.

Notes

1. Serge Berstein, *Le six février 1934* (Paris, 1975).

2. Paul Jankowski, *Stavisky: A Confidence Man in the Republic of Virtue* (Ithaca, 2002).

3. Jankowski, *Stavisky*, viii; Berstein, *Le six février 1934*, 89–94.

4. *L'Alliance démocratique*, 4 April 1934.

5. Berstein, *Le six février*, 248.

6. Michel Winock, *La fièvre hexagonale: les grandes crises politiques de 1871 a 1968* (Paris, 1984); François Monnet, *Refaire la république: André Tardieu, une dérive réactionnaire, 1876–1945* (Paris, 1993), 82, 131, 172, 307–308.

7. Winock, *La fièvre hexagonale*, 196, 237–238 (my emphasis).

8. Winock, *La fièvre hexagonale*, 196, 237–238

9. Paul Warwick, *The French Popular Front: A Legislative Analysis* (Chicago, 1977).

10. Nicholas Roussellier, *Le Parlement de l'éloquence. La souveraineté de la délibération au lendemain de la Grande Guerre* (Paris, 1997).

11. Gilles Le Béguec, "L'Entrée au Palais-Bourbon: les filières privilégiées d'accès à la fonction parlementaire 1919–1939" (Thèse pour le doctorat d'état, Paris X Nanterre, 1989).

12. Julian Jackson, *The Fall of France: The Nazi Invasion of 1940* (Oxford, 2003).

13. Peter Jackson, "Post-War Politics and the Historiography of French Strategy and Diplomacy Before the Second World War," *History Compass* 4, no. 3 (2006): 870–905.

14. Paul Jankowski, *Shades of Indignation: Political Scandals in France, Past and Present* (Oxford, 2008).

15. Michel Dobry, *Sociologie des crises politiques: la dynamique des mobilisations multisectorielles* (Paris, 1986); Michel Dobry, "Février 1934 et la découverte de l'allergie française à la révolution fasciste," *Revue française de sociologie* 30 (1989): 511–533; Michel Dobry, "On an Imaginary Fascism," in *France in the Era of Fascism: Essays on the French Authoritarian Right*, ed. Brian Jenkins (New York, 2007), 232. Bruno Goyet, "La réception du fascisme en France dans les années 20," in *Le mythe de l'allergie française du fascisme*, ed. Michel Dobry (Paris, 2003), 69–105; Brian Jenkins, "Plots and Rumors: Conspiracy Theories and the Six Février 1934," *French Historical Studies* 34, no. 4 (2011): 649–678.

16. Mark Meyers, "Feminizing Fascist Men: Crowd Psychology, Gender, and Sexuality in French Antifascism, 1929–1945," *French Historical Studies* 29, no. 1 (2006): 109–142.

17. Gustave Le Bon, *La psychologie des foules* (Paris, 1895); Benoît Marpeau, *Gustave Le Bon: parcours d'un intellectuel, 1841–1931* (Paris, 2000); Robert Nye, *The Origins of Crowd Psychology: Gustave Le Bon and the Crisis of Mass Democracy in the Third Republic* (London, 1975).

18. Herman Lebovics, *True France: The Wars Over Cultural Identity, 1900–1945* (Ithaca, 1992).

19. François de La Rocque, *Service public* (Paris, 1934), 19; *L'Alliance démocratique*, 18 November 1935, 20 March 1936; Meyers, "Fascist Men," 122–124.

20. *Journal des débats*, 23 January 1934.

21. *La Liberté*, 14 January 1934.

22. See also *L'Action française*, 7 January 1934.

23. *L'Action française*, 8 January 1934.

24. *La Nation*, 6 January 1934.

25. Le Béguec, "L'Entrée au Palais-Bourbon," 179–188.

26. Georges Liens, "L'Image du Provençal et le 'racisme' envers les méridionaux au XIXe siècle," *Congrès national des sociétés savantes 1971, Toulouse, Histoire moderne* (1976): 143–154.

27. Karl Marx, *The Eighteenth Brumaire of Louis-Napoléon Bonaparte* (Moscow, 1974); Ernest Renan, *La Réforme intellectuelle et morale* (Paris, 1990), 66–67.

28. Patrick Cabanel and Marylise Vallez, "La haine du Midi: l'antiméridionalisme dans la France de la Belle Époque," *Archives ouvertes* (2000), http://hal.archivesouvertes.fr/docs/00/17/77/53/PDF/La_haine_du_Midi_doc.pdf.

29. Maurice Barrès, *Les Lézardes sur La Maison* (Paris, 1905), 10, 19–20.

30. *L'Opinion*, 8 April 1911.

31. *L'Opinion*, 1 April 1911.

32. Le Bon, *La psychologie des foules*, 24, 41, 51, 59.

33. *L'Opinion*, 1 April 1911.

34. Liens, "L'Image du Provençal et le 'racisme' envers les méridionaux au XIXe siècle"; Charles Ridel, *Les embusqués* (Paris, 2007).

35. Georges Noblemaire, *Carnet de route au pays des parlementaires* (Paris, 1923), 9–11.

36. *La Démocratie nouvelle*, 4 October 1919.

37. *Écho de Paris*, 1 September 1931.

38. *L'Opinion*, 15 and 29 June 1923; Simenon echoes these complaints in his "Inventaire de la France."

39. *La République française*, 7 October 1922.

40. *La Voix du combattant*, 7 April 1928. See also La *République française*, 7 October 1922.

41. David H. Walker, *Outrage and Insight* (Leamington Spa, 1995), 33–50.

42. Deborah E. Hamilton, "Gender, Genre and Politics in French Detective Fiction of the 1930s: Camille Hedwige's *L'Appel de la morte*," *Forum for Modern Language Studies* 35, no. 1 (1998): 57.

43. Philippe Corcuff and Fleury Lison, "Profondeurs du social et critique politique—hypothèses comparatives sur Maigret et le néo-polar," *Mouvements* 15/16, no. mai-août (2001): 28–34.

44. Georges Simenon, *Liberty Bar (1932)*, in *Tout Maigret*, 3 vols., ed. Michel Carly (Paris, 2007). In *Maigret à Porquerolles* (1948) the commissaire recalls his visit to Antibes and admits his dislike of southern laziness. In *Le Monde*, 5 July 2007, Michel Carly described Maigret as a "man of the north," and as "un ministre de l'identité française."

45. Zeev Sternhell, "The Political Culture of Nationalism," in *Nationhood and Nationalism in France*, ed. Robert Tombs (London, 1991), 22–36.

46. Gabriel Chevallier, *Clochemerle* (Paris, 1934), 111–112.

47. Gabriel Chevallier, *L'Envers de "Clochemerle": propos d'un homme libre* (Paris, 1966), 168–169.

48. André Siegfried, *Tableau des partis en France* (Paris, 1930), 72–76.

49. Ibid., 225–234; Sean Kennedy, "André Siegfried and the complexities of French anti-Americanism," *French Politics, Culture & Society* 27, no. 2 (2009): 1–19.

50. *Echo de Paris*, 15, 20, 30 April 1932.

51. *Le Figaro*, 17 May 1932. See also *L'Ouest-Éclair*, 14 May 1932; *La Nation*, 13 May 1922.

52. *L'Alliance démocratique*, 3 January 1934.

53. *La Liberté*, 13 January 1934.

54. *Le Figaro*, 9 January 1934.

55. *Le Jour*, 7 January 1934.

56. *Le Jour*, 11 January 1934; *La Liberté*, 12 January 1934.

57. Archives Nationales, F⁷ 13206, 26 March 1934.

58. *Action française*, 9 January 1934.

59. *Action française*, 7, 11 January 1934.

60. Marcel Pagnol also depicted Marseille as a place of promiscuity and corruption and idealized the Provençal countryside. See Brett Bowles, "Politicising Pagnol: France, Film and Ideology under the Popular Front," *French History* 10, no. 1 (2005): 112–142.

61. *L'Action française*, 13 February 1934.

62. *L'Écho de Paris*, 13 November 1931.

63. *Breiz Atao*, 21 January, 18 February 1934.

64. *La Province*, 24 January 1934.

65. *Le Jour*, 11, 15 February 1934.

66. *Echo de Paris*, 12 February 1934.

67. *Echo de Paris*, 15, 20, 30 April 1932; for further attacks on southern electoral corruption see *L'Alliance démocratique*, 1 July 1928.

68. "Les préjugés antiméridionaux en France et anticeltiques en Grande Bretagne," in *À droite de la droite. Les droites radicales en France et en Grande Bretagne au XXᵉ siècle*, ed. Philippe Vervaecke (Lille, 2012), 59–86; Kevin Passmore, *The Right in France from the Third Republic to Vichy* (Oxford, 2013), 266–268.

69. André Tardieu, *La réforme de l'État* (Paris, 1934), 72.

70. Ralph Schor, *L'antisémitisme en France pendant les années trente* (Bruxelles, 1992); Ralph Schor, *Histoire de l'immigration en France de la fin du XIXe siècle à nos jours* (Paris, 1996), 130–131; Vicki Caron, *Uneasy Asylum: France and the Jewish Refugee Crisis, 1933–1942* (Stanford, 1999), 46.

71. *La Province*, 10, 13 January 1934.

72. *Frontière de l'Est*, 6 January 1934.

73. *L'Ordre*, 2 January 1934.

74. Jean-Louis Robert, "Maigret à Paris," *Sociétés et Représentations* 17, no. 1 (2004): 159–169.

75. *L'Alliance démocratique*, 4 April 1934.

76. Assouline, *Simenon: biographie* (Paris, 1993) 195–205; see *L'Ouest-Éclair*, 13 January 1934, for a satirical comparison of the legal procedures used by a Stavisky defendant to the flight of Corsican bandits into the *maquis*.

77. *L'Ordre*, 5 January 1934.

78. For example, *L'Alliance démocratique*, 25 July 1934.

79. Urbain Gohier, *Sidi ben Ma'aras ou le Maure pion* (Paris, 1926), quoted in Cabanel and Vallez, "La haine du Midi," 4.

80. *Journal des débats*, 11, 23, 31 January 1934; Jean Guiraud in *La Croix*, 30 January 1934.

81. *L'Action française*, 7 January 1934.

82. *La Province*, 3 February 1934; see also 31 December 1932.

83. *La Province*, 7 February 1934.

84. *La Province*, 10 January 1934.

85. *Je suis partout*, 13 January 1934. See also *Écho de Paris*, 3 January 1931: "le tutoiement du bagne."

86. AN 317 AP 163 Fonds Marin, Déglin to Marin, 13 and 30 September 1905.

87. *La Nation*, 6 September 1930.

88. *La Nation*, 20 January 1934.

89. AN 317 AP 75 Fonds Marin, circular, 13 April 1934.

90. *Journal des Débats*, 23, 31 January 1934.

91. Chris Millington, *From Victory to Vichy: Veterans in Interwar France* (Manchester, 2012), 52–108.

92. Dobry, *Sociologie*, 299.

93. César Fauxbras, *Sondage*, No. 170, 80–81, 17 June 1941. Thanks to Matt Perry for this reference.

94. AN F⁶⁰ 658, Plan d'Équipement national, 2e Partie (1942), 80–81.

95. Jean Lacouture, *De Gaulle*, Points (Paris, 1990), 18–19; Pierre Milza (ed). *De Gaulle et l'Italie* (Paris, 1997), 8; Paul-Marie de La Gorce, *De Gaulle entre deux mondes* (Paris, 1963), 39–40.

96. Todd Shepard, *The Invention of Decolonization: The Algerian War and the Remaking of France* (Ithaca, NY, 2006).

97. Cabanel and Vallez, "La haine du Midi," 9.

98. *Écho de Paris*, 15 April 1932.

99. *La Nation*, 17 February 1934.

100. *L'Echo de Paris*, 9, 16 February 1934.

101. *Breiz Atao*, 1 April 1934.

102. *La Province*, 14 February 1934.

103. Caron, *Uneasy asylum*, 46–47.

AVEC UNE BRUTALITÉ TOUTE PARTICULIÈRE

Fascist Sympathies, Racial Violence, and the Municipal Police and Gendarmerie in Oran, 1936–1937

Samuel Kalman

On 23 August 1937, in the Algerian department of Oran, a local police captain named Léon Nicolas wrote a letter to French Interior Minister Marx Dormoy demanding a transfer to the state police. A sympathizer with the *Section française de l'Internationale ouvrière* (SFIO), the French socialist party, Nicolas had been initially posted to Sidi-Bel-Abbès in 1932 and then Perrégaux from 1935 onward. However, from his arrival he encountered unceasing harassment from extreme-Rightist colleagues, threats of violence from fellow officers, and official reprimands from his superiors. His situation became even more perilous during a 25 February 1937 demonstration by local communists called to protest an attack by members of the fascist Parti populaire français (PPF) against left-wing newsvendors. A police captain and PPF member named Ferro led the extreme-Rightist counter-demonstration, while fellow officers who arrived on the scene beat and shot at the protestors, resulting in two civilian deaths. After filing this information in his report, Nicolas was accused of ordering troops to fire on the crowd due to worries that his account would result in prison sentences for the culprits. Fearful for his safety, Nicolas sought the protection of Oran socialist *doyen* Marius Dubois, and the transfer to a metropolitan-supervised force.[1]

The Nicolas affair exposes the sordid reality of the municipal police and gendarmerie in interwar Oran: that both officers and the rank and file were frequently fascist sympathizers and involved in violent episodes against Leftists, Jews, and

Muslims. Although historians have extensively studied the popularity of the extreme-Rightist leagues and political parties in metropolitan France, very little has been written about the tremendous popularity of such organizations in the French empire.[2] Furthermore, although scholars have investigated the recruitment of members among various segments of the French population (farmers, women, and intellectuals, among others), there has been relatively little discussion of the relationship between the extreme Right and security forces, either in the *métropole* or the colonies.[3] Authors primarily refer to the two in antagonistic terms; for example, the role of the municipal police in suppressing the 6 February riots or arresting various figures for assault, defamation, and unlawful assembly. The few links that have been established, such as the sympathies of Paris Chief of Police Jean Chiappe for the Right, are invariably discussed exclusively in the context of the metropolitan forces.[4]

Yet colonial law enforcement officials often sympathized with the extreme Right, and nowhere was this more apparent than in Algeria. Whether on the local force or in the employ of the Gendarmerie / Garde républicaine mobile (GRM) they were trained and commanded in an ultra-conservative atmosphere which often evoked anti-communist, anti-Semitic, and xenophobic themes. Jews and Muslims were portrayed as anti-European, desiring Algerian independence or revolution, a position bolstered by the violence troops encountered on active duty. Already chronically underpaid and poorly housed, and often under considerable pressure to keep order with far too few personnel in the field, police forces and gendarmerie units proved susceptible to the appeal of various local leagues and from Oran's municipal governments, many of which were firmly on the extreme Right. This was particularly true during the 1936–1937 Popular Front era, when a ministry led by Jewish socialist Léon Blum championed moderate socialism and colonial reform.

In theory, any such deviation from official policy was rendered impossible by strict governmental control of police and army units. In the *métropole*, policing was both a national and municipal affair, with the Sureté nationale's 7000 officers under the purview of the Ministry of the Interior, while municipal forces and the Police judicière composed of detectives solved crime on a local level. The Renseignements généraux (RG) provided additional support, tracking the movements of those groups and individuals deemed dangerous to the state.[5] A similar arrangement existed in Algeria, where the governor general controlled the police through the auspices of the Sûreté générale, who were supported at the departmental level by both the RG and the Police administrative in charge of public security. The Police municipale patrolled various communities, including those in the Department of Oran. However, in practice these resources proved insufficient, and the GRM were frequently needed to restore order in various municipalities in times of crises, while patrolling rural areas and *communes mixtes* at the behest of the governor general's office.[6]

Yet there existed another fundamental difference between metropolitan and Algerian security forces: the persistence of race as a vector in administrative decision making and policing. Such attitudes reflected both the institutionalized racism inherent in the colonies and a long history of violence perpetrated by the municipal authorities and the armed forces throughout the French Empire, and particularly in Algeria. As Jean-Pierre Peyroulou has noted, from an administrative perspective "the *indigène* was criminalized. Along with religion, violence became one of his defining characteristics."[7] That Muslims were primitive, violent, religious fanatics was taken for granted by the French authorities, who concluded that such a dangerous population should be rigidly controlled. In response to these fears, the colonial administration in Algeria developed a multipronged legal strategy. On one hand the government enacted the repressive *indigénat*, a series of laws that imposed a severe judicial and criminal code, empowering the prefects with broad police and disciplinary powers, including a harsh indigenous tax code. The authorities wedded this approach to the seizure of 1.75 million hectares of land through dubious legal machinations, granting direct territorial control to large-scale European landowners, those deemed "fit" to operate wineries and farms. Finally, Muslims suffered the indignity of the *Statut musulman*, which declared that citizenship and rights would be granted solely to Algerians who agreed to abandon sharī'ah / Islamic law and accept French customs and the *code civil*, a step rejected by the vast devout majority.[8] Not for nothing did Gustave de Beaumont infamously exhort that "in Africa, one needs two things: force and the law; force for the Arabs and law for the *colons*."[9]

During the period of conquest and "peaceful penetration" from 1830 onward, violence and terror tactics were commonly used to this end.[10] Yet after 1870, neither the governor general nor the prefects viewed force as the preferred mode of engagement with Algerians, seeking instead to combine military prowess, technological capacity, and community policing with efforts to preempt violence, pacifying the colonized by other means. Thus the mobilization of ethnography, for example, into what one historian terms "an empire of facts" designed to simultaneously differentiate the superior European from the inferior Muslim and provide a peaceful means to subjugate them.[11]

Yet such efforts were consistently hampered by the racism of the settlers, who rejected the subtle machinations of symbolic violence in favor of direct confrontation.[12] This was particularly true in Oran, where the municipal authorities had a long history of anti-Semitism, combined with anti-Muslim xenophobia that typified official discourse. Jews had traditionally been the target of European xenophobia in late-nineteenth-century Algeria, yet by the interwar era officials and populace alike in Alger and Constantine grew increasingly concerned with potential Muslim insurrection, and feared that anti-Semitism would further agitate a population already quite susceptible to such ideas. The Constantine riot of August 1934, during which Muslims attacked Jews and pillaged shops, seem-

ingly proved this point. Hence by 1936–1937, settlers in Alger and Constantine backed away from overt anti-Semitism, and violence against Jews was eclipsed by growing uneasiness over the increasing popularity of the Messali Hadj and the Parti populaire algérien, strike activity and Muslim labor militancy, and a mounting press campaign in favor of independence.[13]

However, Europeans in the department of Oran constituted the majority of the population, and thus were less immediately threatened by potential Muslim insurrection. Rejecting the 1870 Crémieux Decree, which granted French citizenship and political equality to Algerian Jewry, politicians and populace alike throughout the region consistently attacked the department's substantial Jewish community. As a result, Oran's Jews were victimized by rioting, assault, and a constant stream of invective in the press and electoral campaigns during the 1898 anti-Semitic wave that swept Algeria, and again after 1924 when Jules Molle and the stridently xenophobic Union latines (UL) controlled the municipal government in Oran-Ville. From 1936 onward, Gabriel Lambert and the Rassemblement national d'Action sociale (RNAS) similarly dominated local politics through anti-Semitism, while other municipalities suffered the same fate: Lucien Bellat and the local chapter of the Unions latines controlled Sidi-Bel-Abbès, for example.[14] Nor could the population completely ignore the threat posed by Muslim independence, and by the 1930s, Algerians were habitually identified with potential insurrection, portrayed variously as the followers of communist or socialist parties bent on transforming Algeria into a Soviet paradise, the nationalist aspirations of the PPA, or the supposedly fanatical Islamic societies led by Chékib Arslan or the 'ulamā.[15]

This strident xenophobia was exacerbated by the success of the extreme-Rightist leagues throughout Algeria, and particularly in Oran. Local denizens flocked to the extreme Right in far greater numbers than elsewhere in North Africa, and almost 10 percent of the department's population joined the leagues, while many more actively sympathized with their goals.[16] As a result, Molle and the UL predominated in Oran from 1924 onward, buoyed by anti-metropolitan sentiment, suspicion of the Muslim population, and overwhelming anti-Semitism. Molle and his confreres better understood the settler mentality, inspired by the notion of *algérianité* espoused by various cultural figures and populist political voices, which proffered the cultural and racial superiority of Europeans, and excluded both Muslim/Jewish "undesirables" and the French authorities (those opposed to the doctrine and plans of the settlers) in equal measure. Thus the UL flirted openly with separatist sentiment, believing that the *colons* in Algeria forged a superior society and institutions due to the fusion of various Latin peoples into a unique race, freed from French decadence and meddling.[17] Molle also identified with the hatred toward Jews that persisted among the inhabitants of Oran to a far greater degree than elsewhere in Algeria, primarily due to the presence of a large Jewish community that comprised over a fifth of the department's Euro-

pean population.[18] Unsurprisingly, given his attention to local concerns rather than metropolitan ideas, Molle remained the mayor and parliamentary deputy for Oran until his death in 1931, harnessing the support of a vast majority of electors, while the UL enjoyed a substantial membership and a successful daily newspaper.[19]

By the 1930s, a variety of metropolitan organizations began to adopt the political tactics, ardent xenophobia, and *algérianiste* mentality that characterized the UL, succeeding in the streets and at the ballot box. The Croix de Feu first appeared in Algeria in 1929, and the group emerged in Oran shortly thereafter, garnering almost 3500 members throughout the department by 1935.[20] Only two years later, in the wake of the Popular Front electoral victory, the combined membership in Oran's extreme-Rightist organizations topped 15,000, the vast majority engaged by the PPF whose mercurial leader Jacques Doriot prioritized Algerian recruitment and moved the bulk of his operations to Oran.[21] Of equal significance, both the Croix de Feu (transformed into the Parti social français in 1936[22]) and PPF, along with various smaller fascist groups, joined the RNAS, under the guidance of Oran-Ville mayor Gabriel Lambert. In the tradition established by Molle and the Unions latines, Lambert and the RNAS adopted the mantle of *algérianité* and anti-Semitism, readily lambasting French authorities and the Jewish community.[23]

Its members reserved particular ire for socialist Prime Minister Léon Blum and the Popular Front administration. Blum named Maurice Viollette as his minister of state, the ex–governor general of Algeria derided by settlers as "Viollette l'arabe" for his friendly overtures toward Muslims. He promptly unfurled an electoral law designed to grant the vote to 20,000–25,000 "Europeanized" Arabs, the so-called *évolués*, educated and favorably disposed to France. Believing that the law would actively aid Muslim separatist elements, while auguring the specter of equal rights for the numerically superior Muslim population, the *colons* openly fought the metropolitan authorities, including the mass resignation of nearly 200 mayors throughout the colony.[24] In Oran, fascist leagues became the focal point of the protest, engaging in the defense of *l'Algérie française* against its supposed enemies: the Popular Front and its communist/socialist allies, Muslim separatists, and Jews. Their opposition quite frequently turned violent, culminating in Lambert's 25 February 1937 demand that all inhabitants of the department openly defy the governor general and prefects throughout Oran and Algeria.[25]

In the midst of this atmosphere, which the metropolitan authorities equated with a civil war, the police and gendarmerie were seen as defenders of law and order, engaged in preserving the Republic's authority. Throughout the empire, the colonial state frequently called upon these auxiliaries to utilize violence against a variety of enemies. This was particularly true in Algeria, where authority often became equated with brutality. The army perpetrated multiple massacres of such severity during the process of "pacifying" Algeria that one historian has termed

the colonial state "a power that saw itself more as a purveyor of death than a regulator of life."[26] Neither was this unique to Algeria: units stationed throughout the empire were acutely aware of their brutal role, crushing insurrections in Morocco, Syria, and Indochina during the interwar era.[27] Although overwhelming physical force was used more sparingly in Algeria after the defeat of the Kabyle revolt in 1871, at least until the 1945 massacres in the department of Constantine, the Algerian authorities did not hesitate to utilize municipal police at the slightest hint of trouble, particularly from the so-called *indigènes*.[28]

The combination of official xenophobia, the Popular Front electoral victory, the increasing popularity of Algerian independence organizations, and the overwhelming popularity of fascist movements in various locales throughout Oran naturally impacted the municipal police and gendarmerie. Officers and soldiers were also affected by the social and political nature of the institutions in which they served. Neither police nor gendarmes were necessarily extreme Rightists upon recruitment, but many were selected on the basis of their political leanings, and candidates were often inculcated with such views during training and service.[29] In various municipalities, mayors and their assistants personally selected recruits to the local force, enlisting along racial and ideological lines. That a candidate was not Jewish or Muslim—or worse still, a Leftist—was paramount, even if they were highly undesirable in other respects. Hence in Sidi-Bel-Abbès, certain officers were functionally illiterate or did not fulfill their military service, while others included pimps and ex-convicts. This situation became so acute by 1937 that the governor general recommended the censure and removal of the metropolitan force in that city.[30] Similarly, in Oran-Ville Mayor Gabriel Lambert personally vetted all recruits and frequently disallowed candidates for reasons of race or political orientation, despite a shortage of qualified personnel.[31] Such attitudes reflected both the institutionalized racism inherent in the colonies and the long history of brutality and violence throughout the French Empire, and particularly in Algeria.

This xenophobia was combined with the realities of colonial policing: principally the role of officers and gendarmes in the maintenance and defense of the colonial system, and their marginal living and working conditions. For as David Killingray notes in surveying the British Empire: "the subjection and domination implicit in colonialism meant that policing could not but be political." In addition to preventing criminal activity, Algerian police officers and gendarmes were expected to function as a paramilitary unit against nationalists and Leftists, an armed response team during riots, and the defenders of colonial order, including the preservation of racial hierarchy. These duties were carried out in an often hostile environment, with limited intelligence resources and manpower.[32] Moreover, police and gendarmes performed these tasks as underpaid and poorly housed individuals, their potential loyalty challenged by the reality of disease, alcoholism, and a language barrier—most spoke little or no Arabic.[33]

These factors combined to create a culture of violence and xenophobia in the Oran police force and gendarmerie. Serious incidents occurred following the election of Blum and the Popular Front in June 1936, in the wake of increasing labor militancy and wildcat strikes in imitation of metropolitan unrest, and the promulgation of the *Projet Blum-Viollette*. Viewed as the first step toward independence, its authors purportedly in league with the Salafist 'ulamā and the banned Étoile nord-africaine, the settlers turned toward the extreme Right, attacking Leftists, Jews, and Muslims—the supposed allies of the Popular Front, themselves emboldened by the new ministry.[34]

In Oran-Ville, run by a fascist mayor, police frequently clashed with demonstrators, seeking to suppress any manifestation of support for the Popular Front. Recruiting in tandem with various officers across the city, Lambert brought a significant number of municipal policemen into the RNAS, often with the encouragement of their commissaires.[35] Thus from the foundation of the RNAS on 26 June 1936 onward, the municipal police allowed members of the Croix de Feu and other leagues to run riot throughout the city, assaulting and intimidating Jews and Leftists, and refusing aid from the gendarmerie. Officers actively suppressed any demonstrations by Popular Front organizations, and particularly those led by Jews or *indigènes*. A gathering of socialists, Jews, and left-leaning Muslims on 28 June 1936, for example, was met with extreme force from the local constabulary. Led by neo-fascist Commissaire Pancrazi, the police charged those gathered in Oran's Place d'Armes, injuring fifteen demonstrators with "extreme brutality," in the words of the Prefect of Oran.[36] They were particularly vile with Jews. As the local *Sûreté* leader noted in his report: "With each sortie, this same police force mercilessly attacks Jews, with utter contempt for the law." During the 28 June demonstration, witnesses testified that officers rounded up Jewish demonstrators with blood streaming down their faces, while one superior on the scene shouted "allez-y et frappez fort!"[37] Such incidents were frequently repeated, leading the public prosecutor in March 1937 to declare that the RNAS had successfully substituted brute force for law and government, policing Oran with a private militia. With this in mind, his office called for the immediate dissolution of extreme-Rightist organizations throughout the department.[38]

By far the worst situation occurred in Sidi-Bel-Abbès, a town of 55,000 inhabitants—two-thirds European—in the southern portion of the *département*. In typical Algerian fashion, municipal elections there were frequently decided through fraud, either the purchasing of votes for cash payments or doctoring voting lists. As a result, Lucien Bellat and the anti-Semitic Unions latines dominated local politics from 1929 onward, and the fascist mayor antagonized opponents through violence.[39] Uniting partisans of the PPF, PSF, and Amitiés latines, the UL utilized the swastika and the fascist salute, while publicly lauding Hitler, Mussolini, and Franco. Bellat further enjoyed the patronage of police officials and the local gendarmerie, often recruited from his electors and unfailingly loyal to his

administration. The former beat Leftist leaders and newsvendors in the streets and intimidated voters, or looked the other way when the town's hired thugs attacked opponents. In the mayor's employ, hoodlums pillaged stores, hoarded arms, and plotted a Spanish-style uprising against the metropolitan government. Police officers and rank and file openly supported such actions, often affiliated with the UL or Croix de Feu, including the Commissaire central and several of his assistants. Jews and socialists were strictly forbidden from serving on the police force and denied municipal employment—obtainable only with a UL or RNAS membership card.[40]

Thus gendarmes and police were permitted to engage in extreme violence at the behest of the mayor and commissaires, as on 14 June 1936, when a cortege of Popular Front supporters, including women and children, were attacked by the mayor's hired muscle alongside police wielding batons, revolvers, and tear gas, resulting in forty-six injuries.[41] Due to fascist sympathies among the local judiciary no indictments were handed down, and there was no official inquiry into police brutality despite a request to Léon Blum, the governor general, and the Sous-préfet from the local Popular Front committee. The following February, police once again openly supported the extreme Right, intervening in an armed dispute between local members of the Parti social français and Parti populaire français, and Leftist newsvendors, railway workers, and laborers. A wave of police descended upon the town center, firing first into the crowd of workers, and subsequently on a group of Muslims, killing two and wounding eight, causing general panic in the streets, and resulting in the official protest of Captain Léon Nicolas.[42]

The mayor's office frequently played a leading role in the violence, inciting protestors and ignoring police brutality. On 16 March 1937, a municipal councilor's mistreatment of unemployed workers—he urged a crowd to "go ask Blum" for bread and jobs—predictably resulted in a near riot. This was facilitated by the use of an *agent provocateur* in the crowd, urging those assembled to attack the police and gendarmes, after one of them savagely struck a demonstrator. The official response came from the Garde républicaine mobile, who proceeded to the *Village Nègre*, where they attacked protestors with truncheons, while PPF members and Bellat supporters fired on the crowd, resulting in mass hospitalizations. The restoration of order by the GRM left many injured and hospitalized, primarily Muslims.[43]

Faced with such actions from municipal authorities and the police in Sidi-Bel-Abbès and Oran, and the testimony of officers like Léon Nicolas, the governor general of Algeria requested an expansion of the state police in the Department, to ensure order and suppress fascism.[44] As early as June 1936, he noted the lack of effectiveness of the Oran police force in combating extremism, particularly in comparison to municipal authorities in Alger, and even Constantine, where the response to riots and disturbances was often tepid at best. Noting that the

police were almost entirely sympathetic to Lambert, Bellat, and extreme-Rightist organizations, Le Beau asked for platoons of state police to be stationed in all municipalities with more than 80,000 inhabitants.[45] Following the incidents in Sidi-Bel-Abbès in early 1937, the request was renewed, this time for all towns with 25,000 residents, due to fears that fascist violence would spread throughout the department. Le Beau noted that police corruption and patterns of assault had spread to Blida and Mostaganem, as well as various communities in Constantine, and appended the draft of a *décret-loi* to the request in order to speed up the process.[46] Mere months later, Blum and Minister of the Interior Marx Dormoy subsequently ushered in legislation mandating the expansion of the state police in Algeria.

The governor general's request also responded to several incidents involving the gendarmerie. Government personnel initially assumed that the Garde républicaine mobile would provide support in case of disturbances. Despite its small numbers—only hundreds of men patrolled an area the size of France—the GRM was regularly used in a support role, buttressing local police squadrons, particularly during demonstrations and riots. This was particularly true in Oran, where the political polarization created by the ascension to power of extreme Rightists like Lambert and Bellat led to continual disturbances, often initiated by the authorities themselves. However, the effectiveness of the local gendarmerie was compromised by fascist sympathies and xenophobia among the leadership and rank and file. A pre-1914 preserve for royalists and ultra-rightists, in the interwar era the GRM command in Algeria continued to demand that officers remind soldiers of their duty to the *patrie* and family values, and insisting that their families and friends "only frequent healthy places and do not profess any subversive ideas." This vague directive was made more clear by the lieutenant-colonel in charge of the Algiers gendarmerie, who arranged for each soldier to receive a copy of the pronatalist Alliance nationale's neo-fascist pamphlet *Comment nous vaincrons la dénatalité*, and ordering officers to persuade enlisted men to join the AN and uphold its values.[47] This reflected a marked partiality for any number of extreme-Rightist organizations that assailed the local Popular Front, which became so prevalent by February 1937 that the Oran section of the SFIO wrote the metropolitan leadership to complain, demanding that the government be pressured into censuring the GRM's Algerian officer corps.[48] Nor were such reactions confined to Oran. The Commissaire central in Alger noted a similar pattern, reporting that both officers and enlisted men from the local garrison supported the leagues, following an intensive propaganda campaign by various extreme-Rightist groups.[49]

A xenophobic *mentalité* was equally evident in the gendarmerie. Discussions of strategy at the highest levels invariably portrayed Algerian Muslims as religious fanatics, defenders of barbaric customs, and out to murder the European population. A 1938 memorandum prepared by the Ministry of War delineated the

need for surveillance networks and troops to combat ultra-Islamic and nationalist movements, describing the enemy as "an indigenous mob, far superior in number, and easily led into acts of savagery due to racial and religious hatred."[50] The *indigène*, one author concluded, "n'obéit que la force."[51] Neither did gendarmes shy away from anti-Semitism. In Constantine, the public prosecutor accused the GRM in Sétif of engaging in verbal and physical acts against the local Jewish community in May 1937, a charge weakly refuted by Général de Brigade Lavigne as resulting from ineffective leadership.[52]

Hence gendarmes and their superiors claimed that Muslims were anti-European zealots, a homogenous morass rather than a diverse population. True, certain reports mentioned socioeconomic conditions, hinting that poverty and exclusion might be to blame, as low salaries and unemployment had battered Algeria since the onset of the depression. Yet most authors simply saw a subversive threat to be neutralized, along with the Algerian Leftists who mobilized Muslim discontent in the service of global revolution. Naturally, nationalist and communist *agents-provocateurs* exploited the situation, transforming Muslim anger into disrespect for French authority. The Popular Front worsened things, allowing "foreign influences" to inflame opinions and thus leaving the gendarmerie in the line of fire.[53] Although commanding officers claimed that the solution to the "Algerian problem" ultimately rested with civil authorities, the GRM frequently sought to pacify Muslims through violence. As North African Commander General Baert noted: "Far too often officers and gendarmes resort to violence against the individuals that they have the duty to protect."[54]

This was certainly the case in Oran in January 1937, when the GRM intervened on behalf of local authorities during a strike, wounding eighty-seven demonstrators, many of them women and children. Almost all were Muslims, for the action occurred in the neighborhood of Eaux de Brédéah, and the beatings were particularly brutal, administered with truncheons and rifle butts.[55] Numerous witnesses, many of them seriously injured, testified against the gendarmes, and specifically accused Captains Chevalier and Didion of leading the assault. One onlooker described being hit in the head and right leg with a rifle butt as he stood in conversation with an Oran Commissaire de police, while others received similar head traumas, including a fifteen-year-old boy.[56] Neither were the victims alone in their harsh assessment: in a memo to the prefect of Oran, the head of the Sûreté départementale noted that the GRM charged into the crowd merely because they were booed by the local *indigènes*, and acted with "*une brutalité toute particulière*, against a group primarily composed of women and children." Far from calming the crowd, their actions stiffened the resolve of the strikers, most of whom had not previously displayed any hostile or violent behavior.[57]

The combination of official pressure and Muslim outrage led to an inquest at the request of the minister of national defense, conducted by the GRM's Inspector-General Lavigne, who received testimony that accused both Chevalier and

Didion of being fascist sympathizers and mingling with the local extreme Right during the demonstration. Both had allegedly revealed their sympathies in private conversations on numerous occasions, and had a history of brutality toward Jews, Muslims, and Leftists, demonized due to their association with the Popular Front and the Oran anti-fascist movement. One local commissaire on the scene backed up these claims, stating that the crowd had posed no threat to public order, neither rioting nor threatening businesses or private property. In fact, he noted that subsequent violence was the consequence of GRM brutality, a position backed by Oran's Commissaire central, and that Didion personally charged into the crowd brandishing a whip, yelling "cognez sur cette vermine" in order to encourage his men.[58]

Chevalier and Didion naturally declared their innocence on all charges, and their superiors blamed the *indigènes* as a whole for the demonstration and its aftermath. Rather than being a victim of GRM aggression, they stated, the injured child merely fell to the ground.[59] Furthermore, the Oran company commander noted the frequency of strikes and riots in Popular Front–era Algeria, including Muslim-perpetrated violence in Oran before and after January 1937. The real issue, he claimed, was "the arrogance of certain *indigènes*," who believed that they could treat gendarmes like slaves after breaking the law. Striking Muslims were probably armed with canes, just like their brethren all over the country, and sought to correct perceived injustices through violence, as the *indigènes* were prone to aggressive behavior. If anything, he concluded, the officers had shown restraint, using rifle butts rather than live ammunition, a position defended with the false allegation that Muslims throughout the country often menaced Europeans and law enforcement officials.[60]

For his part, Lavigne's report principally worked to debunk testimony against Chevalier and Didion, rejecting the notion that either was a fascist, while insisting that police eyewitnesses were Leftists looking to denigrate the gendarmerie. All those who were attacked clearly threatened security forces (including, presumably, the victimized child) and those who claimed otherwise should be transferred, as their subterfuge compromised police work and GRM operations.[61] Lavigne declared the commissaire who testified against Chevalier and Didion dangerous to the security of the department, and devoted a large portion of his official correspondence to debunking the testimony of the offending officer and an inspector who testified along similar lines.[62] He further claimed that the true author of the complaints against his men was Oran socialist leader Marius Dubois, responsible for the press campaign against the GRM's actions and the false accusations of the eyewitnesses, while the general in charge of the gendarmerie wrote the governor general demanding the immediate transfer of all officers who testified against the accused.[63] Curiously, in his final report Lavigne did not directly confront the issue of fascist sympathies in the gendarmerie, noting in response

solely that a few mistakes had been made, while claiming that the riots were simply an excuse to perpetuate racial antagonism, the product of religious zealotry, economic malaise, and extremist propaganda. Neither did he attempt to counter charges of GRM xenophobia, instead positing that where the *indigènes* had once been respectful of authority, this "insufficiently evolved race" had become prone to shootings, senseless violence, property destruction, and open revolt.[64]

For their part, GRM commanders simply tied the events of January 1937 to a larger pattern of violence in Oran, placing the lives of gendarmes in danger on multiple occasions across the department. Yet they cautioned soldiers that the use of lethal or excessive force was proscribed, and simply exacerbated the hostile attitude of the *indigènes*. Responding in an internal memorandum to public criticisms of the GRM in April, including charges of fascist sympathies and police brutality, Lavigne reminded gendarmes that pacifying Muslims required "very firm" action. Any weakness only encouraged aggression, and he claimed that the department was rife with shooting, stabbings, and property destruction caused by indigenous discontent with European status, continuing recession, and high unemployment.[65] Although its commanders successfully prevented the imposition of disciplinary action against the GRM, the governor general openly contradicted their claims, consistently insisting that the chief security threat in Algeria and Oran came from European extremism, and not Muslim violence.[66]

In a recent study of the North African GRM, Martin Thomas notes that "on the eve of Word War II the gendarmes had conflated their roles as overseers of the colonial economy and political police, paving the way for the more violent future as targets of anti-colonial opposition and perpetrators of state killing that lay ahead of them during the 1945 Sétif uprising and beyond."[67] This was precisely the reality of policing, violence, and race relations in 1930s Oran. Both municipal police and gendarmerie units there regularly brutalized Leftists, Muslims, and Jews, and particularly after the Popular Front's election in 1936, when they perceived them to be potential threats to the established European settler elite and colonial order. That Léon Blum had no desire to end the French presence in Algeria, while the Left had traditionally demonstrated considerable imperial racism in its own right, was never considered by the fascist leagues, or their sympizers in local government and law enforcement.[68] Neither were Jews or Muslims ever a genuine threat in the department of Oran of the 1930s, where Europeans enjoyed a clear demographic advantage throughout the interwar era.[69] Nonetheless, a combination of official indoctrination, a belief in the danger posed by the *indigènes* and the Algerian Left, and the prevalence of sympathy for the extreme Right among Algerian police and gendarmes inexorably led to political and racial violence. Given the subsequent history of law enforcement in the region, it is not unreasonable to suggest that such actions clearly foreshadow the xenophobia, torture, and murder that characterized security services during the Algerian War.

Acknowledgments

The author wishes to thank Raphaëlle Branche, Ruth Ginio, Sean Kennedy, and Martin Thomas for their helpful suggestions and comments.

Notes

1. Institut d'histoire sociale / Archives Charles Dumas (hereafter IHS/Dumas) I, Léon Nicolas, Commissaire de Police to Minister of the Interior Marx Dormoy, Perrégaux/23 August 1937.

2. The empire appears as a mere footnote at best in the vast majority of the works listed in the introduction to this volume.

3. See, for example, Robert O. Paxton, *French Peasant Fascism: Henry Dorgères's and the Crises of French Agriculture, 1929–1939* (New York, 1997); Kevin Passmore, "Planting the Tricolor in the Citadels of Communism: Women's Social Action in the Croix de Feu and Parti Social Français," *Journal of Modern History* 71, no. 3 (1999), 814–851; Zeev Sternhell, *Ni droite ni gauche: L'idéologie fasciste en France* (Brussels, 2000); Cheryl Koos and Daniella Sarnoff, "France," *Women, Gender and Fascism in Europe, 1919-1945*, ed. Kevin Passmore, (New Brunswick, 2003); Mark Antliff, *Avant-Garde Fascism: The Mobilization of Myth, Art, and Culture in France, 1909–1939* (Durham, 2007).

4. On the role of the police on 6 February, see Brian Jenkins, "The *Six Février* 1934 and the Survival of the French Republic," *French History* 20, no. 3 (2006): 333–351. Concerning relations between Jean Chiappe and the French extreme Right see Robert Soucy, *French Fascism: The Second Wave, 1933–1939* (New Haven, 1995), 30. The best account of the Paris police force, including relations with the extreme Right, is Clifford Rosenberg, *Policing Paris: The Origins of Modern Immigration Control Between the Wars* (Ithaca, 2006). The comparable history of the gendarmerie contains comparatively little such information: Anthony Clayton, *France, Soldiers, and Africa* (London, 1988).

5. Rosenberg, *Policing Paris*, 9.

6. Jean-Pierre Peyroulou, *Guelma 1945: Une subversion française dans l'Algérie coloniale* (Paris, 2009), 121–122.

7. Ibid., 70–71.

8. John Ruedy, *Modern Algeria: The Origins and Development of a Nation* (Bloomington, 1992), 80–86.

9. Peyroulou, *Guelma 1945*, 72.

10. On the massacres, *razzias*, and campaigns of terror waged in pre-1870 Algeria, see Benjamin Claude Brower, *A Desert Named Peace: The Violence of France's Empire in the Algerian Sahara, 1830–1902* (New York, 2009).

11. George Trumbull IV, *An Empire of Facts: Colonial Power, Cultural Knowledge, and Islam in Algeria, 1870–1914* (Cambridge, 2009), 48. As Trumbull notes: "As a system of ruthless, authoritarian policing of difference, French rule required the organization of knowledge into discrete, utilitarian facts. It created cultural 'facts' to render the processes of control simpler." See also Moshe Gershovich, *French Military Rule in Morocco: Colonialism and its Consequences* (London, 2000), 19.

12. On symbolic violence as a means of domination, see Pierre Bourdieu, *Masculine Domination* (Stanford, 2001) and *Language and Symbolic Power* (Cambridge, 1991).

13. Increasing Muslim radicalization in interwar Algeria is discussed in Martin Thomas, "European Crisis, Colonial Crisis? Signs of Fracture in the French Empire From Munich to the Outbreak of War," *International History Review* 32, no. 3 (2010), 397–399; Mahfoud Kaddache, *Histoire du nationalisme algérien* (Paris, 2003), chapters 6–18; Benjamin Stora, *Mesali Hadj (1898–1974): pionnier du nationalisme algérien* (Paris, 1986), chapters 4–6.

14. Geneviève Dermenjian, *La Crise anti-juive oranaise, 1895–1905* (Paris, 1986); Samuel Kalman, "Le Combat par tous les moyens: Colonial Violence and the Extreme Right in 1930s Oran," *French Historical Studies* 34, no. 1 (2011): 125–153. On Molle/Bellat and the Union Latines, and Lambert and the RNAS, see Docteur J. Molle, *Le Néo-antisémitisme* (Millau: Inprimérie Artières & Maury, 1933); IHS/Dumas III, Alger/30 June 1936, Governor General Le Beau to Léon Blum and Minister of the Interior Roger Salengro; Archives d'Outre-Mer (hereafter AOM) Oran/2530, Commissaire divisionnaire to Chef de la Sûreté départementale, Oran/15 November 1937; IHS/Dumas I, "Rapport sur la situation politique à Sidi-Bel-Abbès" (1937).

15. Martin Thomas, *The French Empire Between the Wars: Imperialism, Politics, and Society* (Manchester, 2005), 221–223, 246–265; Kaddache, *Histoire du nationalisme algérien*, chapters 14–18. The Left were variously portrayed as allies of Arslan, the 'ulamā, the ENA/PPA, etc., in European press organs throughout the region. Yet as scholars have recently observed, the standard European portrait—of the PPA or 'ulamā as fanatics driven by ultra-nationalism or religious fanaticism, for example—is false on numerous levels. See, for example, Rabah Aissaoui, *Immigration and National Identity: North African Political Movements in Colonial and Postcolonial France* (London, 2009), chapters 2–3, and James McDougall, *History and the Culture of Nationalism in Algeria* (Cambridge, 2006), 12–15, 64–66, 74–76, 82–86.

16. Kalman, "Le Combat par tous les moyens," 142.

17. On the *Algérianité* movement, see variously Christopher Churchill, "Neo-Traditional Fantasies: Colonialism, Modernism and Fascism in Greater France 1870–1962," PhD dissertation, Queen's University, 2010; Seth Graebner, *History's Place: Nostalgia and the City in French Algerian Literature* (Lanham, 2007), 27–101; Jonathan K. Gosnell, *The Politics of Frenchness in Colonial Algeria, 1930–1954* (Rochester, 2002), chapters 1, 6; Patricia Lorcin, *Imperial Identities: Stereotyping, Prejudice, and Race in Colonial Algeria* (London, 1995), 196–206.

18. The best exposition of the UL's anti-Semitism can be found in Molle, *Le Néo-antisémitisme*. The term *néo* refers to the large Spanish population of Oran, notoriously xenophobic and a bulwark of their support. The group's *algérianité* is discussed in various articles in their *Petit oranais* daily newspaper, for example: Jacques Roure, "Notre politique," 5 July 1925; "La Réunion de Boulanger," 27 April 1929; "L'Avenir de la latinité en afrique du nord," 24 November 1929. The 1931 government census details the size of the Jewish population in Oran/Algeria. See AOM GGA/3CAB/95, "Recensement de la population en 1931."

19. On the electoral success of Molle and the UL, see AOM Oran/95, 20 April 1931, Commissaire central de la ville d'Oran to Préfet; AOM Oran/95, n.d., "L'Union latine." Algerian elections were determined by electors representing the population at large rather than the universal suffrage of metropolitan France.

20. AOM GGA/3CAB/47, Alger, 11 July 1935, Préfet/Alger to Le Beau; AOM Oran F/92/2413, "Renseignements receullis en juin 1935 sur les Croix de Feu, Volontaires nationaux, et Briscards."

21. AOM GGA/3CAB/100, "Note sur la creation, l'activité et le developpement du Parti populaire français en Algérie"; IHS/Dumas III, Alger/30 June 1936, Le Beau to Léon Blum and Roger Salengro.

22. The change occurred after the Popular Front government banned the extreme-Rightist leagues in summer 1936.

23. AOM GGA/3CAB/95, Oran, 1 September 1936, Chef de la Sûreté départementale to Directeur Général de la Sécurité générale de l'Algérie; IHS/Dumas III, Alger, 30 June 1936, Gouverneur-Général to Léon Blum and Marx Dormoy; AOM GGA/3CAB/95, Rapport: "L'Antisémitisme et le Rassemblement national d'Action sociale, le Parti social français, les Unions latines, et le Parti populaire français," 1936; AOM Oran/424, Gouverneur Générale to Préfet (Oran), 21 February 1938, "Mouvement antisémitique."

24. On the Blum-Viollette bill, see Thomas, *The French Empire Between the Wars*, 297–303.

25. Kalman, ""Le Combat par tous les moyens," 144–152.

26. Brower, *A Desert Named Peace*, 18. As the author rightly asserts, this pattern of violence and murder deflates to a certain degree (although it does not entirely eradicate) the claims of certain historians that the French Empire provides an effective case study of what Michel Foucault termed *bio-politics*. Far from merely acting as a "bio-power," concerned with controlling/regulating the physical and biological environment of the colonized, both French and municipal authorities far too often intervened solely in a threatening manner.

27. Thomas, *The French Empire Between the Wars*, 213, 222, 234–236. Moshe Gershovich additionally notes that Algerian troops participated in the Moroccan Rif War in July 1925. In *French Military Rule in Morocco*, 136–140.

28. On the quelling of the Kabyle insurrection, see Lorcin, *Imperial Identities*, 174. On the massacres in Sétif and Guelma in May 1945, see Jean-Louis Planche, *Sétif 1945: Histoire d'un massacre annoncé* (Paris, 2006); Peyroulou, *Guelma 1945*. The latter author also discusses police action in Algeria prior to 1945.

29. On recruitment practices in 1930s Oran, see IHS/Dumas III, Alger/30 June 1936, Le Beau to Léon Blum and Roger Salengro; IHS/Dumas I, "Rapport sur la situation politique à Sidi-Bel-Abbès" (1937).

30. IHS/Dumas III, "Rapport sur la situation politique à Sidi-Bel-Abbès" (1937).

31. IHS/Dumas III, Alger/30 June 1936, Governor-General Le Beau to Léon Blum and Roger Salengro.

32. David Killingray, "Securing the British Empire: Policing and Colonial Order, 1920–1960," in *The Policing of Politics in the Twentieth Century*, ed. Mark Mazower (New York, 1997), 169; David M. Anderson and David Killingray, "Consent, Coercion, and Colonial Control," in *Policing the Empire: Government, Authority, and Control* (Manchester, 1991), 6–9; Martin Thomas, "The Gendarmerie, Information Collection, and Colonial Violence in French North Africa between the Wars," *Historical Reflections/Réflexions historiques* 36, no. 2 (2010), 76–96; and *Empires of Intelligence: Security Services and Colonial Disorder After 1914* (Berkeley, 2007), 17–18, 43.

33. Thomas, "The Gendarmerie." The living and working conditions of the colonial police and gendarmes was in no way specific to Oran or Algeria. See the articles concerning Cyprus, India, etc., in Anderson and Killingray, *Policing the Empire*.

34. Malcolm Richardson, "Algeria and the Popular Front: Radicals, Socialists, and the Blum-Viollette Project," *Proceedings of the Annual Meeting of the Western Society for French History*, 5 (1977), passim; Martin Thomas, *The French Empire Between The Wars: Imperialism, Politics, and Society* (Manchester, 2005), 297–302. The notion that the 'ulamā were revolutionaries allied with the ENA, and the idea that both worked with the Left to topple the French colonial regime, represents a complete misreading of Algerian politics. See McDougall, *History*, chapter 2.

35. GGA 3CAB/95, Oran/29 June 1936, Chef de la Sûreté départementale to Préfet.

36. GGA 3CAB/95, Oran/1 July 1936; Préfet to Le Beau.

37. GGA 3CAB/95, Oran/29 June 1936, Chef de la Sûreté départementale to Préfet, "Incidents en ville dans la journée du 28 juin."

38. IHS/Dumas III, Alger/10 March 1937, Procureur Général to the Garde des Sceaux.

39. IHS/Dumas I, "Rapport sur la situation politique à Sidi-Bel-Abbès" (1937). On electoral fraud in Algeria see David Prochaska, *Making Algeria French: Colonialism in Bône, 1870–1920* (Cambridge, 1990), 180–205.

40. On the Algerian settler perception of Jews as an enemy within, see variously Emmanuel Sivan, "Stéréotypes antijuifs dans la mentalité Pied-noir," in *Les Relations entre Juifs et musulmans en Afrique du nord, XIXe–XXe siècles: actes du Colloque international de l'institut d'histoire des pays d'outre-mer* (Paris, 1980); Dermenjian, *La Crise anti-juive oranaise*; Gosnell, *The Politics of Frenchness in Colonial Algeria*. This stereotype frequently contradicted the multifaceted reality of Jewish existence, for many members of the community were assimilated, well to do, and certainly not socialist sympathiz-

ers. See Prochaska, *Making Algeria French*, chapter 5; Joëlle Bahloul, *The Architecture of Memory: A Jewish-Muslim Household in Colonial Algeria, 1937-1962* (Cambridge, 1996).

41. IHS/Dumas I, "Rapport sur la situation politique à Sidi-Bel-Abbès" (1937). On Lambert's notorious Service de nettoiement in Oran-Ville see Oran F/92/3121, Oran/24 July 1936, Marcel Hazan to Procureur de la République.

42. IHS/Dumas I, "Rapport sur la situation politique à Sidi-Bel-Abbès" (1937).

43. IHS/Dumas I, "Rapport sur les evenements du 16 mars 1937 à Sidi-Bel-Abbès."

44. IHS/Dumas III, Paris/9 March 1937, Le Beau to Minister of the Interior Marx Dormoy.

45. IHS/Dumas III, Alger/30 June 1936, Le Beau to Roger Salengro.

46. IHS/Dumas III, Alger/27 February 1937 and Paris/9 March 1937, Le Beau to Marx Dormoy.

47. SHAT Algérie Brigade T/Mouzaiaville, Mouzaiaville/13 October 1936, Rapport du Maréchal des Logis; SHAT R/2 Algérie, Légion de Garde républicain mobile, "Programme annuel d'instruction (1939–1940)"; SHAT R/2 Algérie, Alger/25 April 1939. Lt.-Cnl. Le Bars/Commandant la 19e Légion de Garde républicain mobile to Chefs de l'Escadron. On the traditional ultra-Rightist bent of the officer corps see Clayton, *France, Soldiers, and Africa*, 9–11. For an examination of the Alliance nationale's links to fascism, see Cheryl Koos, "Gender, Anti-Individualism, and Nationalism: The Pronatalist Backlash Against the *Femme Moderne*, 1933–1940," *French Historical Studies* 19, no. 3 (1996): 699–723.

48. IHS/Dumas 1, Oran/2 February 1937, SFIO Oran to Paul Faure and Jean-Baptiste Sévérac.

49. AOM Alger 1K/26, Blida/1 July 1935, Commissaire Central to Préfet.

50. SHAT ZM 1/307/676, Perpignan/24 January 1938, Ministère de la Défense et de la Guerre, memorandum.

51. SHAT ZM 1/307/676, Ministère de la Défense et de la Guerre, 24 January 1938; SHAT ZM 1/307/676, Perpignan/20 January 1938, memo from Général de Brigade Lavigne. This point is underscored in Thomas, *Empires of Intelligence*, 26, 76–77.

52. SHAT ZM/1/307/692, Alger, 10 May 1937, Général de Brigade Lavigne to Colonel commandant la Gendarmerie et la Garde républicaine mobile en Algérie.

53. SHAT ZM 1/307/692, Alger, 14 December 1936, General Lavigne to Minister of War and National Defense; SHAT 1/307/676, Perpignan, 20 January 1938, Général de Brigade Lavigne, memorandum; Thomas, *Empires of Intelligence*, 17–18.

54. SHAT 1/307/676, Perpignan, 20 January 1938, Général de Brigade Lavigne, memorandum; SHAT ZM 1/307/666 Marseille/15 December 1934, Général Baert to Général de Division Commandant le 15e Région.

55. IHS Dumas I, Oran/2 February 1937, Secretary of Oran SFIO to Paul Faure and Jean-Baptiste Severac.

56. SHAT ZM1/307/692, "Journée du 23 janvier—Rapport no. 657"; SHAT ZM1/307/692, Oran/31 March 1937, Procureur de la République—Oran to Général de Brigade Lavigne, Inspecteur du 4e arrondissement de Gendarmerie.

57. SHAT ZM1/307/692, Oran/23 January 1937, Chef de la Sûreté départementale to Préfet.

58. SHAT ZM1/307/692, Paris/23 March 1937, Ministre de la Défense nationale et de la Guerre to Général Inspecteur du 4e arrondissement de Gendarmerie; SHAT ZM1/307/692, Oran/31 March 1937, Marceau Gitard, Commissaire de Police (Oran) to Général Lavigne/Inspecteur Générale de la Gendarmerie (Algérie). Gitard also confirmed eyewitness accounts concerning the beating of children with rifle butts. Interestingly, the Commissaire central denied that fascist sympathies played a role in the events. Nonetheless he did admit that excessive force was used in response to mere hostile language, and no disciplinary action was taken against Gitard for his (supposedly false) testimony. In SHAT ZM1/307/692, Inquest notes—interview with Commissaire Central/Oran.

59. SHAT ZM1/307/692, Oran/1 April 1937, Rapport du Capitaine Didion, commandant les 3e et 4e compagnies.

60. SHAT ZM1/307/692, Oran/4 March 1937–1 April 1937, "Rapport du Capitaine Chevalier, Commandant la Section d'Oran," "Rapport du Capitain Didion, Commandant les 3e et 4e Compagnies," and "Rapport du Chef d'Escadron Roubaud, Commandant la Compagnie d'Oran." The notion that Muslims hoarded weapons is completely false. In fact, Europeans in Algeria were deemed a serious security risk due to increased possession of firearms in the aftermath of the Popular Front electoral victory and the rise of the RNAS. See GGA 3CAB/95, "La Vente des armes en Algérie," Report prepared for Senator Roux-Freyssineng, 1937.

61. SHAT ZM1/307/692, Général Lavigne, "Conclusions et propositions," "Discussions des elements de l'enquête," and untitled memo.

62. SHAT ZM1/307/692, General Lavigne, "Conclusions et propositions" and "Discussion des éléments de l'enquête." Lavigne claimed that the testimony of Gitard and Inspector Cabet was substantially different. Yet his evidence—that one claimed that the crowd yelled "he he" while the other had them screaming "hou hou," or that Gitard exaggerated in his claim that the fifteen-year-old boy who sustained a head injury was a "child"—was clearly insubstantial.

63. SHAT ZM1/307/692, General Lavigne, "Conclusions et propositions"; SHAT ZM1/307/692, Alger/12 April 1937, Général de Division Catroux, commandant le 19e corps de l'Armée to Le Beau.

64. SHAT ZM1/307/692, Alger/7 April 1937, untitled memos by Général de Brigade Lavigne.

65. SHAT ZM1/307/692, Oran/4 March 1937, Rapport du Chef d'Escadron Roubaud, commandant la compagnie de gendarmerie d'Oran sur une manifestation à Mercier-Lacombe et l'état d'esprit des indigènes and Alger/17 April 1937, Général de Brigade Lavigne, Inspecteur du 4e arrondissement de Gendarmerie.

66. See, for example, IHS/ Dumas III, Alger, 30 June 1936, Le Beau to Léon Blum and Marx Dormoy.

67. Thomas, "The Gendarmerie," 89.

68. On the Left's rather ambiguous relationship with anti-colonialism and independence, see Claude Liauzu, *Histoire de l'anticolonialisme en France* (Paris, 2007), 139, 150.

69. SHAT ZM/1/307, Marseille/6 June 1925, Colonel Pacault, Commandant le 5e secteur de Gendarmerie to Ministre de la Guerre; Kamel Kateb, *Européens, "indigènes", et juifs en Algérie (1830–1962)* (Paris, 2001), 176. Among the large urban centers in the department, only Mostaganem contained a vast Algerian majority.

THE VETERANS AND THE EXTREME RIGHT

The Union nationale des combattants, 1927–1936

Chris Millington

In spite of the attention devoted to the study of French fascism in recent years, the French veterans' movement has largely escaped the consideration of scholars. Veterans were an important constituency for the extreme Right but histories of the period for the most part accept the benign role of the *anciens combattants* during the interwar years.[1] This is likely due in no small part to the influence of Antoine Prost's *Les anciens combattants et la société française, 1914–1939* (1977), which argued that French ex-servicemen were essentially Republican. Prost claimed that though veterans' associations were anti-parliamentarian and some "fascistic" leaders attempted to harness the movement for authoritarian ends, the veterans' true convictions lay in their ideas on a "democratic" reform of the state. They rejected the extreme Right and their associations impeded the development of fascism in France. The combatant movement was an integral part of the Republican political culture that weathered the challenges of the interwar period, only to collapse under the external pressure of defeat in 1940.[2]

This essay challenges Prost's conclusion on the veterans' rejection of the extreme Right. The extreme Right was certainly not a "foreign body," something different and otherworldly, for a broader section of the veterans' movement than Prost allows.[3] The essay therefore contributes to the debate on French fascism; yet rather than rehash the intricacies of this "dialogue of the deaf," it follows recent scholarship in moving beyond the sole issue of classification.[4] Suffice it

to say that the classification of a movement is useful for comparative purposes, yet it becomes unhelpful when used to explain a group's behavior or "essence." Thus in categorizing the veterans' movement as Republican, one can dismiss its inherent and striking anti-parliamentarianism as "incantatory" bombast. Such conclusions are predicated on the apparent ability to tell the serious from the unserious, selecting "true" intentions from "idle" threats. A group's policies and tactics did not derive from an inherent nature but were subject to myriad internal and external influences within a political, social, and cultural context, and were adapted accordingly.

With this in mind, this essay examines the Union nationale des combattants (UNC). With approximately 900,000 members, the UNC was one of the largest veterans' associations in interwar France. The primary focus of this essay is the period between the nationalist riot of 6 February 1934 and the election of the Popular Front government in 1936. During that period, France witnessed unprecedented political mobilization. In response to the violence of February 1934, the Left and Radical parties formed the Popular Front, a coalition that established a vociferous presence in the streets and proved to be a winning electoral formula in June 1936. On the right, nationalist leagues mustered their troops in preparation for an expected communist seizure of power. In spring 1934, the Jeunesses patriotes (JP), Solidarité française (SF), and Action française (AF) founded their own coalition, the National Front, to fight the Left in the street. Nationalist leagues had traditionally maintained their independence yet a pool of similar ideas was common to many groups. Their boundaries were therefore permeable, which allowed members to share or switch allegiances at will.[5] UNC members were not different in this respect. Despite the efforts of the National Front alliance, it could not compete with the success and sheer size of Colonel François de La Rocque's Croix de Feu (CF), which by June 1936 boasted half a million recruits and several ancillary formations.

This essay examines how UNC veterans reacted to and interacted with the extreme Right in this period of extraordinary politicization. It uncovers the previously ignored diversity of opinion within the association, bringing to light a complex situation in which some UNC members collaborated with political extremists while others rejected this collaboration outright. UNC policy was neither fixed nor uncontested. In reaction to the changing political climate in France and especially the success of the CF, the association adapted its tactics. It established a league-style group called Action combattante de l'UNC, which however soon became a site of conflict between factions in the parent organization. Members with an activist tendency, who favored entry into the political arena and relations with political groups, clashed with those of a more moderate inclination who shunned political involvement. These factions contested the aims, meaning, and implementation of the UNC's program.

The UNC and the Croix de Feu, 1927–1934

Founded in December 1933, Action combattante did not gain any real momentum until after the events of February 1934. The UNC's Parisian section had taken part in the riot. UNC veterans mixed with leaguers, fought with police, and smashed through barricades.[6] An undated document authored by UNC Vice-President Jean Goy, and titled "Quelques constatations," appears to mark the second phase of Action combattante's development and a veritable burst of energy. "Quelques constatations" reveals how closely the group's foundation was linked to the perceived success of the CF and its influence on the UNC. Goy asked: "Where does their [the CF's] success come from?" He responded: "From their propaganda in youthful and non-veteran milieus! From their mysterious gatherings! From their large and imposingly executed meetings! From their discipline! From their leadership mystique!"[7] Goy recommended that the UNC adopt a similar style.

In the UNC, Goy, a CF member himself, was neither alone in his admiration nor his patronage of La Rocque's league, for the CF attracted many veterans. While it is unwise to judge the whole veterans' movement on the basis of the CF alone, it is nevertheless incorrect that veterans perceived the league as a foreign body, alien to their world and something to be avoided.[8] True enough, its elitism and admiration for the military set the CF apart from the mainstream veterans' movement yet differences between the league and veterans groups have been exaggerated. Like many combatant associations, the CF's discourse condemned political figures and claimed to embody the camaraderie of the trenches. Its members participated in the events of the veteran calendar throughout France. Like the veterans' associations, the CF abhorred parliamentarians. Steeped in the mystique of the "fraternity of the trenches," both the CF and the UNC targeted the same clientele: right-wing veterans.

How did CF and UNC members themselves perceive each other's group? Some UNC members joined the CF but defections did not occur en masse. When examining the extent of cooperation and cross-membership between the UNC and the CF, one cannot be sure of the number of veterans who took this course of action. One must rely upon police reports, anecdotal evidence, and the information printed in partisan newspapers. The picture is unavoidably partial. The motivations of veterans who joined the league are unclear. Moreover, motivations could change depending on the individual and the circumstance. In order to discern a veteran's motives for joining the CF, it is necessary to look at the evolution of the league during 1927–1936, from an association exclusively for decorated veterans into a "fascist" paramilitary league.

From its foundation in 1927 to the creation of the Fils et filles des Croix de Feu (FFCF) youth section in 1932, the CF was open only to decorated veterans and men who had served at least six months on the front line, known as *Briscards*. At

this time it was a veterans' association and UNC members perceived it as such. In April 1928, Jacques Péricard, a member of the executive and policy-making committees of the UNC, wrote a short article on the new veterans' group. This apolitical, interclass organization was for "true" combatants who wished to give "a bit of splendor to their ribbons." Reprinted in the national *La Voix du combattant* the following month, the article provided details on how to join the CF.[9] Péricard's attention to the league was not disinterested; he was a founding member of the CF and would remain a president of honor.[10]

New CF sections sought a liaison with their UNC counterparts, with varying degrees of success. In February 1931, the Rhône section of the CF admitted in its press organ, *La Relève*, "Many of its members [the CF's] belong to other associations (UNC, U[nion des] M[utilés et] A[nciens] C[ombattants], *Gueules Cassées*, etc. ...) and even hold important posts in them."[11] Relations between the movements were not always harmonious, however. In May 1932, *La Voix du combattant* responded acerbically to La Rocque's accusation that the large veterans' associations were replete with "false combatants." The UNC denied the charge and invited La Rocque to come and inspect the quality of its members. Despite La Rocque's attempt to clear up the matter, the UNC remained intransigent.[12] Nevertheless, some sections were open to a form of collaboration. In January 1933, the UNC's ninth section went as far as to open the pages of its bulletin to other groups, including the CF. It claimed that the arrangement would better allow an exchange of ideas.[13] In this period of its development, the league was not so "foreign" as to dissuade UNC members from joining it. However, the CF was not yet the radical movement that it would become when its paramilitary activity increased. Though some of its members may have sympathized with the extreme Right, others joined for reasons of solidarity with veteran comrades and there were also moderate Republicans in the movement.[14]

In 1933, as successive governments struggled to find a solution to the deepening economic crisis, the CF radicalized. A new, more vociferous manifesto in October 1933 denounced the failings of French leaders. If politicians proved incapable, the movement promised to restore order by physical force. At the same time, the CF's membership criteria became less stringent. Anyone with a subscription to *Le Flambeau* could join the new Regroupement national autour des Croix de Feu. Younger men who had not fought in the war were eligible for membership in the Volontaires nationaux (VN), which went onto absorb the *Briscards* and the FFCF in mid-1934. It became the most dynamic of all the CF's affiliates.[15]

The change in the CF did not deter veterans from joining it. In late 1933, some UNC members, while still considering the CF a veterans' association, now saw something different in the league. In November 1933, Jacques Toutain, president of the UNC's Seine-Inférieure section, was invited to the first official meeting of the Rouen CF section. Though the large combatant formations concentrated solely on improving a veteran's material circumstances, Toutain reported that the

CF concerned itself with "national restoration." For him, a "particularly evocative sight" was that of the CF marching "in rhythmic step … crossing the great streets of the large town, sharply regimented." This imposing demonstration of discipline revealed the high caliber of the CF. Contained within this display, Toutain perceived the "something" that France had been waiting for since the victory of 1918. Nevertheless, though different from other combatant associations, Toutain still perceived the league as a bona fide veterans' group; in fact, it was one of the finest *groupements de combattants* one was likely ever to encounter.[16]

Relations between some UNC members and the CF continued to be warm into the following year. Members of both groups attended the same meetings. *Le Flambeau* reported that on 4 February 1934, the league's sixty-fifth section held a meeting at Choisy-le-Roi at which CF speakers outlined the "perilous terrain" that France faced. CF members, *dispos,* and veterans of the Choisy UNC attended. All were noted to have "acclaimed [the orators] with the same unanimous spirit."[17] On the night of the 6 February riot, CF members joined the UNC's march to the Place de la Concorde. They fought alongside UNC veterans in clashes with police on the Rue du Faubourg Saint-Honoré.[18]

In 1934, the force of attraction that the CF exerted on UNC members concerned Goy. He wrote that despite the fact that the UNC possessed a skilled team of propagandists and a concrete program on state, moral, and economic reform, the association's membership was stagnating. Goy acknowledged that a section of the membership also participated in the activities of other groups, notably the CF, despite the fact that La Rocque's league had "done nothing for the veterans." The only way forward for the UNC was to adopt similar tactics and undertake "a rapid and brutal reform."[19]

Action combattante de l'UNC

Action combattante would be the means to regain the initiative. Yet in spite of the importance that some members of the leadership placed on Action combattante, others on the executive committee were ignorant of its workings. Several disputes in the executive committee over the UNC's political action demonstrate a split between moderates and activists. Originally, the leadership had agreed to undertake civic action within the structures of the association, and so remain "100 percent UNC," rather than establish a separate entity, which would recruit non-veteran sympathizers. Some feared that this latter course of action would attract "political black balls" who wished to improve their reputation through membership of the UNC. It was decided that no independent group should be founded. Civic action would concern only veterans.[20]

Action combattante apparently contravened this decision. UNC executive members expressed reservations in June and July 1934 that the new association

had been founded without the express permission or the knowledge, of the committee. President of the UNC in the Ille-et-Vilaine Dr. René Patay, Francisque Gauthier, vice-president of the Lyon section, and Daniel Desroches, UNC president in the Finistère, feared losing control of Action combattante, which acted with apparent independence yet was funded largely by the UNC. Gauthier complained that the committee had not been informed from the start that the UNC was responsible for the new group. Citing the CF as an example, Vice-President Alfred Charron explained that, contrary to the earlier decision of the executive committee, it had been necessary to found a separate organization in order to take action as quickly as possible. Other executive members objected to the rumored provenance of Action combattante funding, namely from industrialist Ernest Mercier. A "ranking member" of the Paris UNC and with "numerous friends among its leaders," Mercier was not new to the combatant world. During the 1920s, his Redressement Français utilized the *esprit combattant* in an attempt to unite industrialists with right-wing veterans. It was closely associated with the national UNC and Goy collaborated with the Redressement from its creation.[21] With the founding of Action combattante, the activists in the executive committee had outmaneuvered their colleagues.

Like the CF's Regroupement National, Action combattante expanded the UNC's action into the non-veteran milieu. The association encouraged youths, women, and all "honest" people to join.[22] Yet unlike the Regroupement National, there is no evidence to suggest that women actually joined Action combattante. It would be unsurprising if women were indeed absent from the group. After all, the UNC's plan for rescuing France was gendered; it depended upon the veterans and their sons. Nevertheless, the association was now publicly prepared to welcome non-veteran members.

Despite this foray into the non-veteran milieu, local UNC veterans were closely involved with the establishment of Action combattante. UNC Vice-President Paul Galland left delegates under no illusions that it was their responsibility to help Action combattante: veterans should act as the catalyst.[23] The task of recruitment was left to local sections. It is possible that local UNC section chiefs found it hard to resist the recruitment of readymade leaguers from within the CF. Indeed, the national UNC leadership sent men, probably CF, under the auspices of Action combattante to preside over departmental UNC meetings.[24] The new association would found groups affiliated to the UNC that could then be absorbed into the organization proper.[25] Action combattante was successful to this end in departments where the UNC had not been previously established, helping to create new UNC sections in the Drôme, the Var, the Alpes-Maritimes, the Hautes-Pyrénées, the Basses-Alpes, and the Gard.[26]

Throughout France, Action combattante *chefs de région* molded public opinion, informed local newspapers of local activities, and produced posters and tracts. Each departmental section further trained orators and conference orga-

nizers. The program of Action combattante took center stage at these meetings. This program was essentially the UNC's plan for state reform: the institution of proportional representation followed by dissolution of the Chamber. A constituent assembly of "worthy" figures would then reform the state. The largest of these meetings took place at Rennes on 14 October 1934. Action combattante already had a presence in the area, at least since June 1934, when a meeting of forty men took place under the auspices of the local UNC president, Dr. Patay. At the October congress, Goy and Roger d'Avigneau, founder of the UNC's Loire-Inférieure section and secretary of the Fédération interalliée des anciens combattants addressed a reported 8000-strong attendance. Police stated that the meeting demonstrated the discipline of the group and its willingness to "enter into the struggle" if its demands were not satisfied. Later in October, a similar meeting took place in Caen that 8000 people attended.[27]

Within the UNC, the meaning of Action combattante was contested. This conflict reflected the different tendencies that coexisted in the association. In some cases, Action combattante activity was organized for street confrontation with the Left. In the Ille-et-Vilaine, the local UNC designated district and cantonal Action combattante delegates, each of whom possessed a telephone and a car. It was thanks to this organizational structure that Action combattante was able to mobilize an entire arrondissement against potential "political" (read Leftist) demonstrations.[28] This tactic was not dissimilar to CF action. Thus at Tours on 27 June 1935, La Rocque declared: "From now on we are able to affirm that thirty-six hours would suffice to muzzle the red suburbs and to take power if necessary."[29] In "Quelques constatations," Goy had demanded that future UNC tactics emulate those of the CF. In the Ille-et-Vilaine, Action combattante, like the CF, used technology to assemble members in a short space of time when left-wing action threatened.

Perhaps Action combattante could have ultimately functioned as a combat group. In September 1934, UNC President of Honor Humbert Isaac described it as an auxiliary force in which a taste for action, even combat, motivated devoted activists. Yet for Isaac and others of the more moderate trend in the UNC, street action held less appeal. The use of Action combattante in the broader campaign for state reform trumped its use in combat, for the time being at least. Even Georges Lebecq, the UNC president who had led street action on 6 February 1934, admitted that this latter tactic had proved fruitless.[30]

Action combattante was thus oriented more toward electoral participation. According to the UNC, as the veterans alone could initiate national renovation it was necessary to increase the number of *anciens combattants* in the Chamber of Deputies.[31] Yet until the national elections in 1936, the UNC had to settle for the municipal elections of May 1935. Action combattante supported the campaigns of UNC members and put up its own candidates in this election. Goy summed up this new political direction: "What it is necessary to establish are ententes with

sympathetic town councils … the constitution of [electoral] lists with youths and under the title Action combattante … [to act] purely on veterans' issues would result in failure."[32] Moreover, Action combattante's intervention on behalf of UNC candidates would preserve the apolitical image of the UNC. In preparation for the election, the UNC reported that 23 departmental delegates and 700 communal Action combattante activists had discerned the "electoral mentality" of each area.[33] In the Ille-et-Vilaine, where the UNC printed its election victories, UNC members or candidates won 53 percent of council seats (701 of 1317), with a majority share on 68 percent (63 of 93) of councils. The organization boasted a UNC mayor in 54 percent of councils (50 of 93). The UNC credited Action combattante with the electoral success of its members in this department.[34]

Despite the success of Action combattante in some areas, overall it must be judged a failure, a fact that the UNC recognized at its national Pau congress in 1936.[35] Does this prove a general distaste for political action among the veterans? In some areas this was the case.[36] In the absence of membership lists, one cannot specify the proportion that was favorable to Action combattante. Yet although the UNC's claim that Action combattante had 100,000 members is likely an exaggeration, one can argue that the veterans' rejection of militant political action was not unanimous. The desire for such action did not pervade the UNC but it was greater than historians have estimated.

The UNC and the Extreme Right, 1934–1936

Recognizing the importance of the context in which groups existed, one must look beyond the confines of the UNC in seeking the reasons for Action combattante's failure. The group failed to halt the recruitment of veterans to the CF after the riot of February 1934. The fact that these individuals were joining a movement embarking upon increasingly provocative paramilitary displays suggests a radicalization among sections of the UNC.[37] Rather than being a foreign body, therefore, some UNC veterans considered the league a viable option for political action. CF sections continued to recruit members from the veterans' movement and especially the UNC.[38] In the Parisian suburb of Meudon, UNC activists defected to the CF.[39] In May 1934, after a conference held by La Rocque in Bordeaux, the local CF section welcomed 500 new members, the majority of which came from the UNC. Police suggested that UNC members preferred the CF as this association only admitted "real veterans."[40]

The CF was not the only league to target the anciens combattants. Other leaguers sold newspapers and distributed leaflets at the doors of veterans' meetings.[41] Soon after the February 1934 riot, extreme right-wing groups founded the National Front coalition. Pierre Taittinger, head of the JP, and SF leaders Jean Renaud and Jacques Fromentin, courted the UNC in an effort to secure the association's

membership of the alliance.[42] The JP depicted UNC veterans and its own followers as the avant-garde of "national ideas," and proclaimed the similitude of the groups' programs.[43] The SF recognized too the UNC's civic action program as compatible with that of the National Front. In May 1934, Jacques Fromentin urged the UNC to enter into the Front and show the way to all other veterans. Yet while *L'Ami du peuple*, the coalition's official organ, named the affiliation of those men who attended National Front meetings it reported only *anciens combattants* as having participated. This suggests that if UNC members did attend these meetings, it was not in any official capacity.[44]

The UNC did not officially join the National Front. Police reported that Lebecq was wary of signing a pact with the organization, as it might provoke attacks from the Left and perhaps see the resignation of UNC members. Instead, Lebecq, himself a member of the JP, decided to encourage members to work with the anti-revolutionary alliance and attend its meetings without signing a public agreement. This tactic would obtain the desired collaboration without officially compromising the UNC.[45] This relatively cautious stance is interesting, given that Lebecq was not alone in his patronage of the JP. During the 1920s, some UNC veterans had attended JP meetings and joined the league. Among those members affiliated or sympathetic to the league were vice-president of the Nord section André Auguste, president of the UNC in the Aisne, André Parmentier, his comrade in the department right-wing deputy Henri Rillart de Verneuil, and national executive committee member and deputy of the Deux-Sèvres Emile Taudière. Deputy of the Seine Edouard Soulier was both a member of the UNC and president of honor of the JP. Members and section leaders of the JP, the VN, and the Centre des Républicains Nationaux were present in the leadership of the UNC's youth auxiliary, the Jeunes de l'UNC (JUNC).[46]

Though the National Front was frustrated with the UNC's apparent reluctance, local veterans did indeed pursue informal collaboration with the coalition.[47] UNC members and section presidents attended National Front meetings, alongside JP, AF, and SF activists.[48] On 23 June 1934, *Le National*, the JP's newspaper advertised a meeting of the National Front in the sixteenth arrondissement at which Pierre Plument of the UNC would speak. Entry to National Front meetings was granted upon production of either a National Front or a UNC membership card.[49] In October 1934, at a meeting of 2000 UNC veterans in Caen, police noted the presence of numerous CF and the AF's street fighters, the *camelots du roi*.[50] At Metz in October 1935, Magny, head of a sub-group of the UNC, presided over a meeting of 600 people, with the presidents of the local JP and AF. He called for the fusion of all "national" groups to "clean up the country."[51]

Collaboration with the National Front did not please all UNC veterans. In July 1934, president of the Nord section Aimé Goudaert advised his colleagues on the executive committee to avoid involvement in both the Leftist Common Front and the National Front. In the Nord, the UNC had remained neutral, a

decision which had allowed the association to hold meetings even in "the most socialist regions" without the threat of disruption. Goudaert recognized that the UNC was hostile to the Common Front but warned that if the association declared this publicly it could expect to lose a third of its members. Eugène Félix of the Eastern group, Goy and Isaac agreed.[52]

Throughout 1934, UNC cooperation with the CF had also remained on apparently informal terms, though UNC president Lebecq did not hide his personal endorsement of the CF. On 10 November 1934, he and La Rocque attended a ceremony under the Arc de Triomphe. In response to a telegram from La Rocque, which expressed the colonel's "cordial feelings" for the UNC, Lebecq wrote, "I was particularly pleased about our meeting at the Tomb of the Unknown Soldier: this gesture will be understood by our comrades and by the country."[53] What was to be understood from this meeting? At the very least, Lebecq appeared to endorse some form of alliance between the CF and the UNC.

In 1935, links between the UNC and the CF were formalized. During a single night in January, La Rocque spoke to approximately 17,000 CF across four venues in Paris. The colonel lauded cooperation with the UNC, affirmed the "common thought" of both associations, and announced that he and Lebecq were "working towards the close and united collaboration of [their] two great associations."[54] On this subject, a press communiqué was published in the following days that bore the signatures of both the UNC and the CF presidents.

Lebecq and UNC national Vice-President Charron's attendance at a CF march on 14 July 1935 appeared to confirm the alliance, though their participation caused consternation among some in the UNC. At a meeting of the executive committee the previous week, members had unanimously decided not to take part.[55] Subsequently, Lebecq protested that he had attended, "in a personal capacity ... wanting to associate [himself] with a patriotic demonstration."[56] He stated that if the UNC and CF had collaborated in the past it was because both groups acted "in a purely national mind (pensée)," and not because there was an official alliance in place.[57] Lebecq's apparent lack of forethought concerning his attendance at a CF march is unlikely to have simply been a matter of political naivety. A public association with the CF may have pleased a man who had led street action on 6 February 1934 and desired political activism from his organization. As a sop to his comrades, Lebecq offered to resign if the executive committee believed him to have sullied the good name of the organization. His offer was rejected.

The CF took great profit from the incident. Maillard of the Manche UNC complained that CF propaganda in his department had focused on Lebecq's attendance at the march.[58] Certain UNC sections interpreted his participation as evidence that the associations were "united in the same spirit."[59] In October 1935, Desroches informed the committee that a CF militant in his department had stated: "We are the moving flank, the UNC is the main body of the group."

The situation was particularly galling because this very CF supporter was also a member of the committee of the local UNC section.[60] Goy and former national President Henry Rossignol also profited from Lebecq's uncomfortable situation. Police reported that they had stirred up opposition among provincial members. If the right wing of the UNC, behind Lebecq, split from the left wing, then police expected the former would join the CF.[61]

While the importance of the veteran in CF discourse declined during 1935, La Rocque continued to encourage his followers to recruit veterans from regimental associations and the UNC. He advised his activists to march with the veterans in the coming Armistice Day parades: "if you take to the street, do not go alone, march with the UNC.... Heads of sections [must] recruit amongst members of the UNC."[62] La Rocque's plan was to entice veterans away from the UNC, a fact of which the UNC's executive committee was aware.[63] The colonel ordered that new recruits "must not come to us as UNC but as CF."[64] In spite of the movement's expanding popular base, veterans remained an important component of the membership.[65] By July 1935, perhaps one in three members was a veteran.[66] Throughout this period, the image of the Great War soldier, whether fallen or a veteran, was used to encourage the cohesion of the group.[67] André Gervais, a prolific author in the veterans' movement, noted that UNC veterans joined the CF because the league offered them something missing from the veterans' organizations—the satisfaction of their desire for action. Yet he also noted that such veterans belonged to both groups at once.[68] Goy knew of several cases in which veterans had left the UNC to join the CF, only to return to their original association.[69]

Veterans in the wider movement were aware of the CF's advances to the UNC. Henri Pichot, president of the Union fédérale veterans' association, expressed concern that the CF was infiltrating the veterans' movement through the UNC.[70] Similarly, some UNC members considered the CF a threat. President of Honor Isaac was the most prominent critic of La Rocque's league. In late 1935, he set out his views regarding the CF in two articles in the pages of the UNC's national newspaper, La Voix du combattant.[71] Admitting that their programs were similar, he wrote that if an ostensible alliance had existed between the UNC and the CF it was now time to clarify matters: this had never been the case. While he was aware that some veterans did hold sympathies for the other "camp," to leave the UNC and follow the colonel would be to betray the génération du feu and the country itself.

Isaac's opposition to the CF was due in part to his defense of Republican legality. He warned that to follow the league would lead to violence and civil war.[72] Within the UNC, Isaac was not alone in his suspicion of the CF. The size of the UNC's membership precluded political homogeneity and political action was not to the taste of everyone. While CF sympizers in the UNC may not have considered the league to be fascist, conversely its opponents may well have classified it as such. A group of veterans that resigned from the UNC in the aftermath of

the February riot accused the CF of being fascist and having plans to install a dictatorship under La Rocque.[73]

Isaac's warning to his comrades also represented an attempt to avoid a loss of members. It would be disastrous for the UNC if its activists spent their energies on CF action, rather than on the important tasks for which they were needed.[74] As president of the UNC's Lyon section, Isaac himself had experience of cross-association membership in the Rhône department. Isaac refused patronage to the CF in the Ardèche, founded by a UNC Rhône member.[75] Other provincial members feared too that an alliance with La Rocque would ultimately see the UNC absorbed into the colonel's league. In April 1934, eighteen months before the publication of Isaac's *Voix du combattant* articles, the creation of a new CF section in Amiens was met with little enthusiasm from the local UNC. Police reported that these veterans felt that to join the CF would be detrimental to the cohesion of their section.[76] In the Côtes du Nord, the UNC's campaign against Radical deputies in the wake of the February 1934 riots caused several members to resign. Some subsequently founded UF sections in the department.[77]

On 18 June 1936, Léon Blum's government announced the dissolution of the paramilitary leagues. Fears of violent resistance to the decree were unfounded; La Rocque accepted the decision and founded the Parti social français (PSF). The UNC expressed anger that the leagues should be dissolved while more threatening Leftist formations continued to exist. *La Voix du combattant* pilloried Minister of the Interior Roger Salengro for being a "frightened weakling" in his refusal to stand up to the communists and "cholera-spreading Bolshevik *métèques*."[78] UNC President Goy warned that communism was preparing to replace the Republic with a Soviet regime. With the leagues dissolved, he argued, it now fell to the UNC to "prevent the triumph of Asian barbarism" and rally all those who wanted "France to remain for the French."[79]

As hundreds of thousands of French turned to authoritarianism in the 1930s, a proportion of veterans radicalized. There can be little doubt that UNC leaders Lebecq and Goy wanted to take their association in a political direction. This view found echo among members throughout France, and the creation of Action combattante was a concrete manifestation of this desire. Other UNC veterans rejected Action combattante because of its political orientation, yet one would be mistaken to blame this failure on a wholesale rejection of political activism among UNC veterans. Some preferred to pursue political action through a more successful alternative. Not a few UNC veterans collaborated with established extreme right-wing groups. They were willing to collaborate with associations with whom they perceived to have common goals. They patronized the meetings of the CF and the National Front and in some cases even abandoned the UNC to join these groups.

One must be cautious, though, about exaggerating the scale of collaboration between UNC veterans and the extreme Right and making assumptions about their motivations for doing so. It is always difficult to discern the motives of po-

litical activists. A veteran may have joined the CF as he believed it was a genuine veterans' association. After all, even up to 1936 the CF still used the image of the heroic and selfless veteran in its rhetoric. Yet the CF's increasing paramilitary activity after October 1933 renders this explanation less plausible. The league had moved beyond solely preserving wartime camaraderie to demand the wholesale renovation of France along authoritarian lines. In the case of the National Front, veterans threw their lot in with leagues that had long been openly hostile to the parliamentary and democratic Republic.

In March 1938, the UNC joined forces with the usually moderate UF in a campaign for an authoritarian reform of the state. That both associations supported the founding of the Vichy regime in 1940 may therefore seem unremarkable. However, it would be a mistake to judge Vichy as the culmination of the veterans' authoritarian designs and discourse alone. Marshal Philippe Pétain's regime arose from the circumstances of the defeat and the armistice. Nor were the veterans unusual in their support for Vichy. In the wake of the defeat, with the Republic discredited, few in number were the French who did not lend their support to Pétain's project for national and moral renovation.[80] Though some ex-servicemen joined Vichy's Légion in 1940, this did not imply support for the Légion's later, more extreme offshoot, the Service d'ordre légionnaire. For, if some veterans were pleased with the winding up of the Third Republic, it was not yet clear what Vichy would become.

Nevertheless, since the riot of February 1934, the UNC's discourse and actions (and to a lesser extent those of the UF) had shown a marked preference for authoritarianism, and consequently helped to prepare the ground for Pétain's regime. Veterans were neither inherently predisposed toward the Republic nor were they an obstacle to the development of a French fascism. This finding forces one not only to reassess the veterans' status as a pillar of French democratic political culture but also whether such a culture existed at all.

Acknowledgments

The author thanks Caroline Campbell, Alison Carroll, Kevin Passmore, Louisa Zanoun, and the anonymous reviewers for their helpful comments and suggestions. Sections of this chapter were published in *From Victory to Vichy: Veterans in Inter-war France*. Copyright 2012. Reprinted by kind permission of the publisher, Manchester University Press.

Notes

1. The most recent work on the veterans and the extreme Right is Didier Leschi, "L'étrange cas La Rocque," in *Le mythe de l'allergie française au fascisme*, ed. Michel Dobry (Paris, 2003), 155–194.

According to Leschi, the virulent anti-parliamentarianism of the veterans was greater than a marginal phenomenon within the wider movement.

2. Antoine Prost, *Les anciens combattants et la société française, 1914–1939*, 3 vols. (Paris, 1977), 1: 164–165, 3: 219.

3. Prost, *Les anciens combattants*, 1: 173, 3: 179.

4. See Samuel Kalman, *The Extreme Right in Interwar France: The Faisceau and the Croix de Feu* (Aldershot, 2008), and Sean Kennedy, *Reconciling France Against Democracy: The Croix de Feu and the Parti Social Français, 1929–1935* (Montreal, 2007). Kennedy's study of the Croix de Feu and the Parti social français still attempts to give a political classification to the movement, although this is not its primary objective.

5. Brian Jenkins, "Introduction," in *France in the Era of Fascism*, ed. Brian Jenkins (New York, 2005), 17.

6. Chris Millington, "February 6, 1934: The veterans' riot," *French Historical Studies* 33, no. 4 (2010): 545–572.

7. Jean Goy, "Quelques constatations," n.d., Rossignol dossier, UNC archive, 18 rue Vézelay, Paris, 1.

8. Prost, *Les anciens combattants*, 1: 119, 3: 179.

9. *L'UNC de Normandie*, April 1928; *La Voix du combattant* (hereafter referred to as *La Vdc*), 6 April 1928.

10. Jean-Paul Cointet, *La Légion francaise des combattants: La tentation du fascisme* (Paris, 1995), see note, 429.

11. Archives Nationales (heareafter referred to as AN) 451 Archives Privées (hereafter referred to as AP), Fonds La Rocque 83, February 1931; AN 451 AP 81, Colonel Chevassu to La Rocque, 2 August, 16 August, and 22 August 1930.

12. *La Vdc*, 7 May, 21 May 1932.

13. *Le Combattant du IXe*, December 1932–January 1933.

14. Kennedy, *Reconciling France*, 39.

15. Kennedy, *Reconciling France*, 41; Robert Soucy, *French Fascism: The Second Wave* (New Haven, 1995), 109–110; Kevin Passmore, *From Liberalism to Fascism: The Right in a French Province, 1928–1939* (Cambridge, 1997), 220.

16. *L'UNC de Normandie*, December 1933.

17. *Le Flambeau*, 1 March 1934.

18. Police, press, and CF members reported cooperation between the CF and the UNC. See Archives de la Préfecture de Police, Paris (hereafter referred to as APP) BA 1853/B1, "Le mouvement Croix de Feu," n.d.; *Le Petit Journal*, 7 February 1934; Paul Chopine, *Six ans chez les Croix de Feu* (Paris, 1935), 115.

19. Goy, "Quelques constatations," 1.

20. Minutes of the UNC's executive committee (hereafter referred to as UNC/EC), UNC archive, 18 rue Vézelay, Paris, 9 December 1933.

21. UNC/EC, 10 May, 30 June, 28 July 1934; Richard F. Kuisel, *Ernest Mercier: French Technocrat* (Berkeley, 1967), 106–108.

22. *Le Combattant d'Ille-et-Vilaine*, September 1934; UNC/EC, 30 June 1934.

23. Report on Action combattante at the UNC's national congress in Metz, featured in *La Vdc*, 19 May 1934.

24. Prost, *Les anciens combattants*, 1: 166.

25. UNC/EC, 28 July 1934.

26. Report on Action combattante prior to the UNC's national congress at Brest, featured in *La Vdc*, 31 May 1935.

27. AN F[7] 13026, 2 July 1934; AN F[7] 13026, 28 October 1934; *La Vdc*, 17 November 1934.

28. *La Vdc*, 22 June 1935.

29. Kevin Passmore, "Boy-Scouting for Grownups? Paramilitarism in the Croix de Feu and the PSF," *French Historical Studies* 19, no. 2 (1995): 549. Paul Chopine believed that one in four CF members owned a car. See Chopine, *Six ans chez les Croix de Feu*.

30. UNC/EC, 28 July 1934.

31. UNC/EC, 28 July 1934.

32. UNC/EC, 24 November 1934.

33. *La Vdc*, 31 May 1935.

34. *Le Combattant d'Ille-et-Vilaine*, July and August 1935.

35. *La Vdc*, 6 June 1936.

36. *La Vdc*, 20 October 1934: "Yes I know, the UNC's action for a national revival (what we call Action Combattante) surprises and worries some among you."

37. Kennedy, *Reconciling France*, 94.

38. This was the case of Commandant Leclerc, who resigned from the UNC and founded the first CF section in the Finistère at Landernau. By the end of the year there were four sections with 420 members. See David Bensoussan, *Combats pour une Bretagne catholique et rurale. Les droites bretonnes dans l'entre-deux-guerres* (Paris, 2006), note 10, 608; Kennedy, *Reconciling France*, 94; Jacques Nobécourt, *Le Colonel de La Rocque (1885–1946): ou, Les pièges du nationalisme chrétien* (Paris, 1996), 286.

39. John Rymell, "Militants and Militancy in the Croix de Feu and Parti Social Français: Patterns of Political Experience on the French Far Right (1933–1939)," PhD dissertation, University of East Anglia, 1990, 12–13.

40. Centre des archives contemporaines, Fonds Moscou (hereafter referred to as FM), 19 940 500: 237, 24 May 1934.

41. See for example AN F⁷ 13317, 19 November 1933.

42. FM, 19 940 500: 237, 23 May 1934; FM, 19 940 500: 237, 3 May 1934. The UNC had reportedly already given its agreement to an "Interligues" association that was ready to act in case of trouble from the left.

43. *Le National*, 24 March, 19 May 1934.

44. *L'Ami du peuple*, 12 May, 14 November 1934.

45. FM, 19 940 500: 237, 30 May 1934.

46. The information in this paragraph on UNC members in the JP may be found in: J. Philippet, *Le Temps des Ligues: Pierre Taittinger et les Jeunesses Patriotes*, 5 vols (Lille, 2000), 4: 2020; 5: annex III-B-3, 189, 201, 210, 276; *Le National*, 24 January 1926; E. P. Fagerberg, *The "Anciens Combattants" and French Foreign Policy* (Savoie, 1966), 46, citing a report of a JP gathering in *La Voix du Poilu*, July 1925; Soucy, *French Fascism: The First Wave* (New Haven and London, 1986), 50; A. Schweitz, *Les parlementaires de la Seine sous la Troisième République*, 2 vols. (Paris, 2001), 2: 544; *La Vdc*, 7 September 1935.

47. Writing in October 1934, Jacques Fromentin could not hide his frustration at the UNC's apparent lethargy: "The UNC ... has missed a good chance! ... The UNC *must* take its place in the National Front, not tomorrow but immediately, before it's too late" (italics in original), *L'Ami du peuple*, 9 October 1934.

48. FM, 19 940 500: 237, 29 October 1935; FM, 19 940 500: 237, 29 July 1936.

49. *Le National*, 23, 30 June 1934; *L'Ami du peuple*, 5 June 1934.

50. AN F⁷ 13032, 5 November 1934.

51. FM, 19 940 500: 237, 29 October 1935.

52. UNC/EC, 28 July 1934.

53. *Le Flambeau*, 1 December 1934

54. AN F⁷ 13320, 25 January 1935.

55. UNC/EC, 5 October 1935.

56. Lebecq to UNC executive committee, Lebecq folder, UNC archive, n.d.

57. UNC/EC, 5 October 1935.

58. UNC/EC, 5 October 1935.

59. AN F[7] 13040, 18 July 1935.

60. UNC/EC, 5 October 1935; Prost, *Les anciens combattants*, 1: note 188.

61. AN F[7] 12960, 22 July 1935.

62. APP BA 1901, 31 October 1935.

63. UNC/EC, 24 November 1934.

64. APP, BA 1901, 31 October 1935.

65. Kennedy, *Reconciling France*, 93.

66. Rymell, "Militants and Militancy," 20.

67. Kennedy, *Reconciling France*, 108.

68. *La Vdc*, 10 August 1935.

69. UNC/EC, 24 November 1934.

70. *Cahiers de l'UF*, 20 December 1935.

71. *La Vdc*, 26 October, 14 December 1935.

72. *La Vdc*, 10 October, 21 November 1936.

73. F[7] 13028, 9 April 1934.

74. *La Vdc*, 14 December 1935.

75. Prost, *Les anciens combattants*, 1: 165.

76. AN F[7] 13029, 16 April 1934.

77. Bensoussan, *Combats*, note 9, 608.

78. *La Vdc*, 27 June, 4 July 1936.

79. *La Vdc*, 11 July 1936, 6 February 1937.

80. Julian Jackson, *France: The Dark Years, 1940–1944* (Oxford, 2003), 289–290.

PACIFISM, THE FASCIST TEMPTATION, AND THE LIGUE DES DROITS DE L'HOMME

Norman Ingram

Michel Dobry and others have written about the "myth" of the French allergy to fascism.[1] France also suffered for many decades from an apparent allergy to pacifism—equally mythical, and one, too, which has begun to dissipate in the past twenty years or so. The alleged allergy to pacifism is strangely linked to the myth of the allergy to fascism. Despite the fact that many First World War and interwar commentators believed in a quite incoherent way that France was a profoundly pacifist nation, nevertheless the term *pacifist* acquired a strongly negative connotation in France following the Second World War because it was assimilated in the popular, and indeed scholarly, mind with defeatism, collaborationism, and hence ultimately in some cases with fascism.[2] At the same time that the consensus school was strenuously denying that France had experienced any form of fascism in the period of the two world wars, it was also, by a kind of perverse, logical, albeit unconscious necessity, driven to conclude that there was no pacifism in interwar or Second World War France. How else to explain the almost complete silence, until recently, of French historiography on the subject? The fact, too, that the Communist Party had made the peace issue its own in the post-1945 period only served to add grist to the mill of those French historians, denizens of what might be called the "national" school of French history, who deny the existence of an independent French peace movement in the interwar period.[3]

In both cases, pacifism was a casualty of the early Cold War in the French mental universe. It was either a political perversion ostensibly linked to Vichy, or it was an integral part of the communist threat. The fact that it was neither was almost beside the point. This makes it all the stranger that when, almost twenty

years ago now, the French historical profession "discovered" pacifism as a subject worthy of historical analysis, there was a tendency to revert to the status quo ante, to a rose-colored view of the interwar period in which everybody in France was allegedly a pacifist.[4] The word was denuded of meaning, but France was try-ing to play catch-up with Anglo-American and German scholarship, which had been interested in the peace question and pacifism for almost thirty years by that point.[5] The history of French pacifism is thus doubly damned: it is suspect because of the post-1945 links with communism and it is assimilated with Vichy, collabo-ration, and fascism. The fact that the French Communist Party had an ambiguous relationship with the Resistance in the first two years of the war only serves to muddy the waters further.[6]

This apparent paradox is perhaps not so paradoxical. Many, although certainly not all, of the pacifists who became "fascists" under Vichy were of the hard Left. They were not necessarily communists, but they belonged to a Marxist tradition. Their apparent evolution toward fascism seems thus in some measure consonant with Zeev Sternhell's thesis regarding the significant contribution made by dis-sident Leftists to the genesis of fascist ideology. At the same time, however, this "evolution" needs to be historicized and understood in the context of the trauma of the Great War. It is clear that there were other factors in play—most notably pacifism, which drew deeply on the memory of the Great War for its inspira-tion—and, secondly, it seems evident that the political positions of pacifists-turned-"fascists" under Vichy owed something to a historical dissent with deep roots in an interpretation of the Robespierre of the pre-French revolutionary war period, that is to say, the period *before* the declaration of war in April 1792.[7]

To return to the aftermath of the Second World War, however, the post-1945 Republican consensus demanded that France subscribe to the Gaullist myth of the experience of the Vichy years. There was no room for an admission of the existence of a French fascism, and the same was true of pacifism—and for many of the same reasons. No less a person than Madeleine Rebérioux, the noted his-torian and first woman president of the Ligue des droits de l'homme (LDH), was quite categorical in 1991 that there was no pacifism in the LDH because the Ligue was "one hundred percent patriotic"—as if one concept necessarily pre-cluded the other.[8]

The inconvenient fact, however, is that the Ligue des droits de l'homme was not "one hundred percent patriotic"—at least not in Rebérioux's definition of the word—any more than all of France had been in 1940. The Ligue was riven with the same political dilemmas and temptations as the rest of French soci-ety, and as Simon Epstein has so ably underlined, the role of the "Dreyfusards during the Occupation" was often on the side of the Vichy regime and even of the Nazis.[9] Cylvie Claveau has shown that there was actually a strong current of anti-Semitism in the Ligue right through the 1930s.[10] And William Irvine has demonstrated how the Ligue at the local level was more often about venal,

small-town politics than it was about high-flown human rights ideals.[11] Even at the level of the largely Paris-based intellectuals who formed the majority of its Comité central (CC), there are many cases of important Ligue members who ended up on the wrong side during the Second World War. Finally, the LDH was not killed by the experience of the Second World War, but rather was already in extremis by 1937. In 1938 and 1939, for the first time in the interwar period, the Ligue was unable to publish the usual stenographic record of the debates at the national congresses held respectively in Avignon and Mulhouse. In fact, not only was it dead or dying by 1937, but some parts of the Ligue des droits de l'homme, at both the national and local levels, exhibited a strange ambivalence, passivity and quiescence in the face of the Nazi invasion of France two and a half years later in 1940. Most of the Ligue remained staunchly anti-fascist, sometimes in the face of appalling personal suffering, but the number of *ligueurs* who crossed the line during Gestapo interrogations and gave up the identities of Ligue members who were Freemasons or Jews is noteworthy and difficult to explain away.[12]

What killed the Ligue, then? A facile explanation would be that pacifism killed the Ligue des droits de l'homme.[13] This is a superficial analysis, however, and does not ask the deeper, more salient question, namely, what provoked this pacifist evolution within the Ligue. The LDH ultimately expired because of its inability to square the circle of its political position within the *Union sacrée* during the Great War with the swelling tide of protest within its own ranks about the question of unique German war guilt.[14] This historical dissent begat a strident minority that raised troubling questions about the Ligue's (and France's) position during the 1914 war, which in turn was one of the factors which led to the creation of the *pacifisme nouveau style* which emerged in France at the end of the 1920s.[15] Some of the members of this minority represented a rather vague pacifism during the Great War, but the majority of what was then a very small group were not overtly pacifist. They were, however, deeply troubled by the way in which France had been dragged into the war, and their search for answers to this conundrum led many of them toward a pacifist engagement by the end of the 1920s. It is this historical dissent that was one of the key progenitors of the new pacifism which emerged in France a decade after the war's end. What the by-now pacifist minority could not see, however, was that 1933 changed everything, and that while there might well have been good reasons for condemning France's position during the Great War, the world was a different place after the Nazi seizure of power.

It is thus inaccurate to suggest that pacifism killed the Ligue; rather it was the Great War that killed it, for reasons that were little appreciated or understood at the time. The men (and women) who appeared to travel down the fascist road into the Second World War did so in many cases not out of an instinctual philo-fascism, but rather out of a moral and political contingency that had its origins in their visceral rejection of war.

There were many interwar pacifists who did not support Vichy or collaboration with the Nazis. There are also strangely ambivalent surprises in places one would least expect them. One of these is undoubtedly Théodore Ruyssen, the president of the Association de la paix par le droit (APD) and a member of the LDH's Comité central from 1921 to 1944. The APD represented what I have called *pacifisme ancien style*. It was formed in 1887 in Nîmes and by the outbreak of the Great War was the most important voice in French pacifism. Essentially collaborative (as opposed to sectarian) in its relationship to French political society, it incarnated a liberal, bourgeois internationalist approach to pacifism which eschewed the approaches of the more radical *pacifisme nouveau style* which emerged at least partially from within its ranks by the late 1920s.[16] Many of the APD's members were professors, teachers, lawyers, and medical doctors. During the Great War, it had fulsomely supported the *Union sacrée*, and in the interwar period it was one of the strongest proponents of the League of Nations idea in France. Ruyssen, for example, was the secretary-general of the Union internationale des associations pour la Société des Nations from 1921–1939.[17]

During the Vichy era, Ruyssen wrote a small number of articles in the collaborationist newspaper *L'Effort* published in Lyons.[18] William Irvine downplays the importance of Ruyssen's publications in *L'Effort*, calling them "momentary aberrations."[19] Perhaps. They were certainly one of the factors, however, which created problems for the APD, of which Ruyssen was the long-serving president, in the immediate post–World War II period.[20]

What is more disturbing than the essentially benign collaboration of a Ruyssen is the much more hardened variety of some prominent interwar pacifists who were also, or had been, important members of the Ligue des droits de l'homme. The political trajectory of Léon Emery, the influential president of the Lyon section of the Ligue and a member of the Comité central from 1934–1937, is instructive in this regard, and can be taken as a kind of test case of the nexus between pacifism and collaboration within the LDH.

Emery is a particularly troubling example. In 1934, the section of the Ligue des droits de l'homme in the XIVe arrondissement in Paris published Emery's speech to the Ligue's Nancy Congress in May of that year as a small booklet.[21] Entitled *Contre le fascisme*, there is little in it that any convinced anti-fascist at the time would have found offensive. In fact, the Nancy Congress responded to Emery's speech with a long, standing ovation.[22] Lucien Cancouët, the president of the section in the XIVe, wrote with regard to Emery that "democracy still has defenders worthy of it."[23] Emery stated clearly that fascism was something new and dangerous; it was not a simple reincarnation of older French extreme right-wing traditions. He rejected the idea that fascism represented a crisis provoked by a "traditional Caesarism" or one similar to the Boulangist crisis of the 1880s, a position which put him at odds with the officially sanctioned resolution of the Comité central, which argued that "the fascist regime is only, in sum, a new and

aggravated form of the Caesarean regime of which France on two occasions has experienced the negative effects."[24] Ironically, the CC's position was not a little unlike that of the "consensus" school of our own times.

Instead, Emery sounded the tocsin, warning that the democratic state was perhaps in danger of succumbing to the fascist threat, because "some democrats, some socialists, even some communists are coming out in support of fascism, because they think that through it they will defend and save the State, and even better, the popular State!"[25] Fascism was anti-parliamentary, anti-capitalist, and most dangerously of all, nationalist. There was more, though. Emery presciently noted that fascism represented a form of revolution—and it was this paradox that had put the democracies on the defensive and made them conservative.[26] He underlined the "almost mystical and religious" nature of fascism, a phenomenon that was "essentially popular" in form, that rested on the very social groups that in the normal course of things ought to have been "our friends and our supporters"—namely, the lower middle class, the workers, and the peasants.[27] What is important, however, is that despite the jeremiad Emery delivered on the fortunes of democracy, he clearly saw fascism as a threat and something to be opposed.

The question remained what to do in the face of this threat, and why Emery could not support the motion presented by the Comité central to the Congress. He believed that the CC's motion was too complicated, too detailed, and hence too scattered to have the effect that was needed.[28] Instead, he declared that the Ligue needed to move beyond the sterile discussions, the platonic votes of yesteryear, and embrace action. In order to achieve this, Emery proposed a fight against fascism based on four easily understood formulas.

The first was that of a "crusade for morality." In the wake of the events of 6 February 1934, he argued that parliament had to be pure, that no one should sit as a *député* who was not "purely and simply a parliamentarian."[29] This particularly meant excluding lawyers from the Chamber since their loyalties were almost by definition divided between their constituents' political needs on the one hand, and the economic imperatives of their corporate clients on the other. Emery's plea for action contains more than a whiff of Jacobinism: he "begged" the Ligue to "run the risk of the bad taste of Jacobinism or, as some will say, of demagogy" in order to take "some brutal and immediate measures" to reform Parliament.[30]

Secondly, he argued that the banks, trusts, and the "venal" press needed to be nationalized immediately because the democratic regime was in reality nothing more than "a dictatorship of the banks and a dictatorship of the press." He called this "a life and death question for democracy." Once again, the radical Jacobin heritage was fully evident as he excoriated the election of Schneider to the Académie des Sciences morales et politiques, and the sight of de François de Wendel chairing the Congress of the Union nationale des combattants. The only remedy was "a Robespierrist intransigeance."[31]

Thirdly, he argued that the political parties were no longer a sufficient support for the democratic regime. He feared that they were in an advanced state of disintegration similar to that seen in Italy and Germany before the advent of Mussolini and Hitler. The only solution lay in the perhaps temporary establishment of an ancillary "economic Parliament with a syndicalist base." This economic parliament would essentially be corporatist in structure, reflecting the interests, social groups, and categories of producers and consumers in France. It would not dominate the political system, but rather would be subservient to the traditional parliament. In order to strengthen the new system, though, he demanded the institution of the referendum and the immediate abolition of the Senate—once again, in the latter instance certainly, an idea consonant with radical Jacobin thinking.[32] The support for a corporatist addition to the political process in France can certainly be seen as similar to Italian Fascist corporatism, but the importance of this element should not be overemphasized given the radically democratic nature of Emery's other proposals.

Finally, Emery underlined the necessity of the "intransigent maintenance" of the pacifist policies adopted by the Ligue at its Paris Congress in 1932. This rested on his "profound conviction" that nationalism had become the "essential instrument of fascist propaganda." Interestingly, this critique of fascism was conceived in purely French terms, that between the "France of Saint Joan of Arc" on the one hand, and the "anti-France of the [Communist] International" on the other. He fulminated against what he saw as the Barthou government's preparation of France for war by the cultivation of a heightened nationalism. In a foreshadowing of the seminal debate that would almost destroy the Ligue in 1937, Emery intoned that "More than ever, a resolute pacifism remains the very condition for the democratic struggle." Defending democracy would not save peace. On the contrary, it was through defending peace that democracy would be saved.[33] This, too, is entirely consonant with a reading of Robespierre that Emery's friend, Georges Michon, was to make in most explicit form in a book he published in 1937.[34]

Emery's thinking on where the fascist danger lay in France is interesting. The first face of fascism was undoubtedly the fascist leagues, and in particular the Croix de Feu, which was the most redoubtable of all. Secondly, there was the problem of the banks, and thirdly, there was the Union nationale government, which was, so he said, "nothing more than the constitutional disguise of fascism."[35] Since its formation after the events of 6 February, every single one of its acts had been censured by the Ligue's Comité central as an "intolerable partiality in favor of the right wing organizations and the fascist leagues."[36] The link here with Emery's pacifism was clear: he believed that the government of national unity had created a "nationalist and pre-war" atmosphere by its policy of alliances deemed necessary because of a supposedly inevitable future conflict and its steadfast refusal to countenance "real disarmament."[37] He called the Ligue to

resist against the fascist leagues, the government, and also against the apparatus of the state itself.

What is interesting, given the positions Emery was to take later during the Second World War, is that he envisaged a union of all of the forces of the Left—from the most tepid to the most extreme. In short, he asked for nothing less than what was to become the Popular Front: "a coalition which must bring together all of the forces of the Left and the extreme-Left, including the Communists, despite what one might think of them."[38] And, in fact, the LDH was to go on to become one of the prime movers in the creation of the Popular Front.[39] The Ligue had to take the political initiative in this, which led him to his second conclusion, namely that the LDH needed to develop an expertise in the creation and diffusion of propaganda—with trained orators at its disposal, using model speeches, and blanketing the country with propaganda tracts delivered by teams on bicycles and motorcycles. Finally, in order to deal with the problem of a venal press, he said that the Ligue needed to establish its own press, with a documentation office at its disposal.

Did Emery think that France was fascist in 1934? No, he did not: "France is not fascist; the parliamentary regime has been allowed to continue to exist, but it has been separated from that which gave it life, it has been separated from all communication with the people that it supposedly represents."[40]

That said, despite the fact that the final version of the resolution passed by the Nancy Congress incorporated some of the ideas and wording desired by Emery and his supporters, there were certain aspects that the mover of the Comité central's motion, Salomon Grumbach, could not accept. In particular, Emery's text had read that "In order to make these declarations more than just a series of platonic wishes, the Ligue will depend only on the people, not on a political class which, taken together, was incapable of foreseeing, desiring or acting."[41] Grumbach warned that this way of thinking was redolent of what he called a "fascism of the Left." In his view, "it is not fair, it is not wise to put the entire political caste of today into the same bag without any distinction whatsoever."[42] Emery agreed to remove the offending phrase on condition that Grumbach withdraw his accusation of a "fascism of the Left," something Grumbach was only too pleased to do since, as he said, he had only been warning Ligueurs against the "mirage" of a left-wing fascism, not accusing anyone of anything in particular.[43]

This long analysis of Emery's position in 1934 is necessary in order to underline even more forcefully the evolution he underwent in the following ten years. That notwithstanding, arguably the seeds of Emery's wartime positions may be seen already in this 1934 tract: above all the anti-parliamentarianism, but also the insistence on peace as an "ethic of ultimate ends," to use Max Weber's phrase.[44] In fact, Emery's pacifism is the unifying thread through the entirety of his political life. It was his pacifism that provided the justification for his harsh critiques of the foreign policy of the Third Republic after the Munich crisis, and which created

the continuity in his thinking right into the Second World War.[45] In a speech given at Bordeaux in June 1942, under the auspices of Marcel Déat's Rassemblement national populaire (RNP), he stated clearly "without demagogy" that "collaboration, the reconstruction of Europe, are and will be difficult and demanding tasks" but that this was the price France had to pay for its past mistakes.[46]

Two things seem clear from Emery's analyses of foreign policy immediately before the war and certainly under Vichy. The first is the profound antipathy with which he viewed the motives and actions of the Communist Party. Secondly, it is clear that he was deeply suspicious of Russian motives generally, in a line of criticism that can be traced back to the Great War.

Dominique Sordet, in a forward to Emery's *La Troisième République*, published in 1943, congratulated Emery for his evolution away from his left-wing origins, but regretted what he called "certain silences" in the book. The first of these was Emery's refusal to "pronounce himself on democracy," and the second, qualified as "very significant," was the lack "anywhere in his study of the role of this formidable and almost apocalyptic international power that are the Jews."[47] Emery stuck determinedly to his position, however, writing to Sordet that "I intend neither to deny past actions for which I accept complete responsibility, nor to contest some differences of itinerary and point of view which are obvious."[48] Emery defined his position as one opposed to parliamentary democracy, but insisted that he still hoped for a workers' syndicalism that would be the "origin of a new state."[49] He mentioned his support for the Frontist program, but subordinated everything to the "demands of a realistic pacifism which could only propose the reorganization of Europe, and first of all the settling of the Franco-German problem." It was because of this view of pacifism that Emery declared himself a determined adversary of a "demagogic anti-fascism, communist-inspired and transposed onto external affairs in order to bring us to a Crusade of the democracies."[50] As for Sordet's charge that Emery was ignoring the role of the Jews and Freemasons in the disintegration of the regime and the road to war, his answer was equivocal; basically he did not know the answer to this "terrible problem" and said that "in order not to be unjust or summary, I take the provisional position of leaving aside an obvious lacuna from which there is nothing to conclude but my intellectual and moral scruples."[51]

In fact, it seems clear that what some have construed as philo-fascism under Vichy was in fact something less than that. Emery's primary concern was peace. Even as late as the 26 May 1944 issue of *Germinal*, he insisted that his critique of the Third Republic in his eponymous book was above all in the foreign policy realm. That said, he argued that the regime he was still trying to help build just days before D-Day needed to be "popular and social, or it will not be at all, its failure leaving the door wide open to civil war and Bolshevism."[52] The fault lay in anti-German sentiment, a way of thinking that spanned the Third Republic from

the Action française on the Right to the most convinced Republicans on the Left. This "absurd anti-German position, fed by disgusting legends and founded on an ignorance of European realities, has been increasingly our diplomatic doctrine and the demagogic means to move the masses."[53] France needed to give up the "obsession" of Alsace-Lorraine and move beyond the Treaty of Verdun of 843. The real problem was France's "blind" alliance first to Tsarist and then to Stalinist Russia, the latter "still more imperialist" than the former.[54]

There was more, too. The problem was not just the threat of Soviet Russia, but also of an equally "barbaric empire," that of the United States. The key to the future of Europe was the need to put behind the quarrels of yesteryear that had taken on the appearance of "absurd anachronisms"; the Franco-German conflict in the Second World War was thus reduced, in Emery's thinking, to a simple quarrel of long standing between two peoples. Nothing was said about the ideological nature of the conflict, or indeed of the atrocities being committed by the Nazi regime.[55]

What is one to make of this? Is Emery's apparent philo-fascism a position of "principle" or a tactical discourse? The minority within the Ligue des droits de l'homme, of which Emery had become a leading member, had represented a stance of opposition to the Union sacrée since the earliest days of the Great War. They were convinced that France had gone to war in 1914 for the wrong reasons, that the real culprits were Tsarist Russia and a complicit French republican political establishment bent on revenge for Alsace-Lorraine. Flowing out of this analysis of French domestic and foreign politics was the belief that Article 231 of the Versailles Treaty was a lie. What the minority could not or would not see was that the advent of Hitler in 1933 changed everything. Hitler was no ordinary statesman—no ordinary German for that matter—but Emery and his colleagues in the minority could not see that.[56]

When Emery was tried for collaboration at the épuration, his erstwhile pacifist colleagues all supported him fulsomely, including those who apparently were not in the slightest suspected of collaboration, such as Georges Pioch, and above all, Michel Alexandre. Alexandre was a "comrade of the first hour" in the nascent pacifist Ligue minority during the Great War, and a Jew who had lost his position under Vichy as a philosophy teacher and been more or less on the run for the four years of the regime. Despite his ardent pacifism, he had impeccable moral credentials in the post–Second World War épuration.

Pioch wrote to Emery's wife that even though their political positions had diverged, this had not at all changed his "feelings of admiration and respect for his mind, his work and his character, and my attachment to him remains unbroken."[57] F. Ferre, a reserve captain, Croix de Guerre, and a German prisoner of war in both world wars, wrote that he had known Emery for thirty years. Emery had always been, according to Ferre, in favor of a policy of Franco-German recon-

ciliation. There was therefore nothing exceptional in his position following the French defeat. Emery had not performed a sudden about-face on the question of Franco-German relations. In Ferre's view, therefore, if Emery had committed an error it had been in good faith; Emery's "so-called collaboration," according to Ferre, implied neither "embrace nor capitulation."[58] Ferre wrote that Emery had been horrified by the brutal police measures of the war years, by the deportations, by the shootings; far from being a colloborationist informer, Emery had helped at least two "unfortunates held in concentration camps" to get out of occupied France into the southern zone.[59] Marcel Bataillon, who had been a colleague of Emery's in the Comité de vigilance des intellectuels antifascistes, wrote that "It is only through this sentiment of a duty towards peace that I can explain to myself the error in which he became engaged after 1940 ... his obsession with Franco-German peace made him less sensitive to the atrocities of the German peace which remained a war and whose prison cells dripped with blood."[60] Michel Alexandre said as much, too, writing that Emery's actions were the result of "the depths of unfathomable despair into which the war had plunged him"[61]; in another note in the same file, Alexandre writes, "thus, the purest pacifism became the source and the only source of the errors of attitude that he committed over the past three years."[62] What is disturbing in Alexandre's correspondence with Emery's lawyer is the sense that, despite the suffering of which Alexandre himself had been the object, nevertheless, out of a kind of "pacifist solidarity" Emery needed to be presented in the best light no matter what. The inference is clear: Alexandre was prepared even to edit the evidence in defense of Emery.[63]

Even Jules Isaac, despite stating forthrightly that he did not approve "in any way the ideas professed, the position taken by L. Emery during this awful four year period," nevertheless went on record as saying that "if there is one thing of which I am sure, it is the sincerity, the good faith of his absolute impartiality."[64]

What can be concluded about Emery's political trajectory and the putative link between pacifism, fascism, and the Ligue des droits de l'homme? The key is perhaps to be seen in the title of an article by Henri Jeanson published in *La Flèche* back in March 1936 at the time of the remilitarization of the Rhineland: "La paix prime le droit."[65] For many of the pacifist minority within the Ligue des droits de l'homme, pacifism had become by the end of the 1930s an "ethic of ultimate ends," an absolute philosophical and political proposition that took precedence over justice. Couple this with the increasingly firm conviction that the Third Republic was an accomplice in the outbreak of the Great War, and a view of history which owed not a little to a reinterpretation of Robespierre, and one arrives at a position that looks like fascism, but which in its fundamentals is not. It was in some cases anti-Semitic. It was often anti-parliamentary, to the extent that the Third Republic was seen as the problem. Because of its anti-Semitism and anti-parliamentarianism, it was morally distasteful. But it was not fascist.

Acknowledgments

The author wishes to thank the Social Sciences and Humanities Research Council of Canada for the provision of the research grant that facilitated the preparation of this chapter.

Notes

1. Michel Dobry, ed., *Le Mythe de l'allergie française au fascisme* (Paris, 2003).

2. See, for example, Jean Defrasne, *Le Pacifisme* (Paris, 1983), 3, wherein the author writes, "In denying the virtue of war, sanctified by tradition, pacifism upsets established ideas. It is thus equated with defeatism, cowardice, and treason."

3. For a short introduction to the post-1945 problems faced by the independent French peace movement, see Norman Ingram, "Ambivalence in the Post-World War II French Peace Movement," in *The Pacifist Impulse in Historical Perspective*, ed. Harvey L. Dyck (Toronto, 1996), 397–412.

4. In a paper delivered to a conference on "Le Pacifisme en Europe des années vingt aux années cinquante," organized by Maurice Vaïsse at the Université de Reims in 1992, François-Georges Dreyfus argued that all of France, from left to right, was profoundly pacifist. In the written version of his paper, after agreeing with the definition of *pacifist* as anyone who "wants peace at any price, who refuses war whatever the reasons for it might be," he goes on to spend the rest of his essay describing a whole array of allegedly pacifist positions in the 1930s, nearly all of which were highly contingent and not based on a primary, principled rejection of war. Perhaps that is why he writes at the beginning of his essay, "the debate on the definition of pacifism seems a trifle vain." See François-Georges Dreyfus, "Le Pacifisme en France, 1930–1940," in *Le Pacifisme en Europe des années 1920 aux années 1950*, ed. Maurice Vaïsse (Brussels, 1993), 137–144.

5. It would take too much space to list the numerous American, British, Canadian, and German scholars (to say nothing of other national historical traditions) who have been active in historical peace research since the 1960s, and sometimes earlier. Suffice it to say that in Germany an important group of historians has been busy for some forty years in the Arbeitskreis Historischer Friedensforschung, and in America the 1960s saw the creation of the Conference on Peace Research in History, which has since become the Peace History Society. It is ironical that I, at the time a Canadian graduate student studying French history in the UK, should have been the only person speaking "for" France at the 1986 "American-European Consultation on Peace Research in History" held at Stadtschlaining, Austria.

6. There is a large literature on this subject, too, but English-speaking readers can consult David Wingeate Pike, "Between the Junes: The French Communists from the Collapse of France to the Invasion of Russia," *Journal of Contemporary History* 28, no. 3 (1993): 465–485.

7. Norman Ingram, "Repressed Memory Syndrome: Interwar French Pacifism and the Attempt to Recover France's Pacifist Past," *French History* 18, no. 3 (2004): 315–330. Cf. Sergio Luzzatto, *L'Impôt du sang: la gauche française à l'épreuve de la guerre mondiale, 1900–1945* (Lyon, 1996). On the general question of the impact of the Great War on the development of interwar French pacifism, see Norman Ingram, *The Politics of Dissent: Pacifism in France, 1919–1939* (Oxford, 1991, reissued 2011), 122–133.

8. Interview with the author at the then headquarters of the Ligue des droits de l'homme, 27, rue Jean-Dolent, Paris XIVe, 19 June 1991.

9. Simon Epstein, *Les Dreyfusards sous l'occupation* (Paris, 2001).

10. Cylvie Claveau, "L'Autre dans les Cahiers des droits de l'homme, 1920–1940: une sélection universaliste de l'altérité à la Ligue des droits de l'homme et du citoyen" (PhD dissertation, McGill University, 2000).

11. William D. Irvine, *Between Justice and Politics: the Ligue des droits de l'homme, 1898–1945* (Stanford, 2007).

12. Norman Ingram, "Selbstmord or Euthanasia? Who Killed the Ligue des droits de l'homme?" *French History* 22, no. 3 (2008), 337–357. See also Ingram, "La Ligue des droits de l'homme et le problème allemand," *Revue d'histoire diplomatique* 124, no. 2 (2010): 119–131.

13. This is the analysis underpinning Epstein, *Les Dreyfusards*.

14. See Norman Ingram, "A la Recherche d'une guerre gagnée: the Ligue des droits de l'homme and the War Guilt Question (1918–1922)," *French History* 24, no. 2 (2010): 218–235.

15. On the origins of *pacifisme nouveau style* and the central place of historical dissent about the origins of the Great War, see Ingram, *Politics of Dissent*, 121–133.

16. I owe the distinction between collaborative and sectarian pacifism to Martin Ceadel's groundbreaking work, *Pacifism in Britain: the Defining of a Faith, 1914–1945* (Oxford, 1980).

17. See Ingram, "Pacifisme ancien style, or the Pacifism of the Pedagogues," *Politics of Dissent*, 4, 17–118.

18. Théodore Ruyssen, "La Justice en marche," *L'Effort* I, 37 (9 September 1940): 1; and "Révolution et Tradition," *L'Effort* I, 72 (14 October 1940): 1. I am indebted to Nicolas Offenstadt for drawing my attention to these articles in *L'Effort*. On *L'Effort*, see Yves Bongarçon, "Un Vichysme de gauche? Les débuts de *L'Effort*, quotidien socialiste lyonnais (1940)," *Cahiers d'histoire* 32, no. 2 (1987): 123–146.

19. Irvine, *Between Justice and Politics*, 214.

20. See Norman Ingram, "'*Nous allons vers les monastères*': French Pacifism and the Crisis of the Second World War," in *Crisis and Renewal in Twentieth Century France*, ed. Martin S. Alexander and Kenneth Mouré (Oxford, 2002), 137–138.

21. The question of "Defence and Adaptation of the Democratic State" was the main subject of discussion at the Ligue's 1934 Congress held in Nancy. See Ligue des droits de l'homme, *Le Congrès national de 1934. Compte-rendu sténographique (Nancy, 19–21 Mai 1934): Défense et adaptation de l'État démocratique* (Paris, 1934), 271–300, 301–328, 330–363, 365–367, 371–387, 389–399, 441–466, and 467–511. The separate, published version of the speech is available as Léon Emery, *Contre le fascisme: le devoir de la Ligue des droits de l'homme* (n.p.[Paris], n.d.[1934]).

22. *Congrès national de 1934*, 354.

23. Lucien Cancouët in Emery, *Contre*, introductory letter before Emery's text.

24. *Congrès national de 1934*, 505.

25. Emery, *Contre*, 4.

26. Ibid., 3.

27. Ibid.

28. Ibid., 5. The final amended text of the "Résolution sur la défense et l'adaptation de l'État démocratique" spans eight pages in the published proceedings of the Congress; Emery's original resolution was much shorter, slightly less than two pages in length. *Congrès national de 1934*, 504–511, and 356–358.

29. Emery, *Contre*, 6–7.

30. Ibid., 7.

31. Ibid., 7–8.

32. Ibid., 8–9.

33. Ibid., 9–10.

34. See Georges Michon, *Robespierre et la guerre révolutionnaire, 1791–1792* (Paris, 1927). The theses of Michon's book were presaged in his 1920 article "Robespierre et la guerre (1791–1792)," *Annales révolutionnaires (Organe de la société des Etudes robespierristes)*, vol. 12 (1920), 265–311. The advent of Vichy seems not to have altered Michon's views one iota. See Georges Michon, *Le Rôle de*

la presse en 1791–1792: La déclaration de Pillnitz et la guerre (Paris, 1941). This was reviewed very positively by Georges Albertini in 1941 in *L'Atelier*. See also Ingram, "Repressed Memory Syndrome."

35. Emery, *Contre*, 10.

36. Ibid., 11.

37. Ibid.

38. Ibid., 12.

39. See Irvine, *Between Justice and Politics*, 2, 160–165; and Françoise Basch, *Victor Basch: de l'affaire Dreyfus au crime de la milice* (Paris, 1994), 254–297.

40. Emery, *Contre*, 13.

41. Ibid., 15.

42. Grumbach in *Congrès national de 1934*, 488.

43. Ibid., 488–489.

44. This idea from Weber underlies Martin Ceadel's analysis of British pacifism from 1914 to 1945. French pacifism politicized this "ethic of ultimate ends" in a way that is not seen in Britain where pacifism devolved more into an ethical principle, rather than a political position as such. See Ceadel, *Pacifism in Britain*. See also Ingram, *Politics of Dissent*, esp. 1–16 and part II ("Pacifisme nouveau style, or the Politics of Dissent"), 121–245.

45. Léon Emery, *1918–1938: Panorama de vingt années. La paix qui n'est pas encore faite* (Lyon, 1938).

46. Léon Emery, "La Paix qui n'est pas encore faite: Panorama de vingt années, 1918–1938," *Bulletin Corporatif: Revue bi-mensuelle du Syndicat de l'Enseignement laïc du Rhône* 45, no. 385 (5 November 1938). Cf. Léon Emery, "De Munich à Montoire: Conférence faite à Bordeaux sous les auspices du R.N.P., le 27 Juin 1942," in I[nstitut d']H[istoire] S[ociale], Archives Léon Emery, Dossier "Ecrits de la 2e guerre mondiale."

47. Dominiqe Sordet, "Avant-Propos," in Léon Emery, *La Troisième République* (Paris, 1943), 13–14.

48. Léon Emery to Dominique Sordet, Allevard, 3 October 1943, in ibid., 207.

49. Ibid., 208.

50. Ibid.

51. Ibid., 209. William Irvine neglects to include Emery's important caveat regarding his "intellectual and moral scruples" in his discussion of the Sordet–Emery correspondence, which attenuate considerably the equivocal position Emery seemed to take on Sordet's accusation that he had not dealt with the question of the Jews in *La Troisième République*. See Irvine, *Between Justice and Politics*, 198–199.

52. Léon Emery, "Conditions de vie d'un régime," *Germinal* no. 5 (26 May 1944): 1.

53. Ibid.

54. Ibid.

55. Léon Emery, "Le socialisme et la paix," *Germinal* no. 2 (5 May 1944): 1–2. Robert Jospin took an analogous position after the Second World War, arguing that France needed to take a stance of disarmed neutrality in the nascent Cold War; in order to prevent war, it was necessary to refuse engagement in the ideological—some might say moral—debate separating the Soviet from the American side. See Ingram, "Ambivalence in the Post–World War II French Peace Movement," in *Pacifist Impulse in Historical Perspective*, ed. Dyck, 406–407.

56. See Ingram, "A la recherche."

57. Georges Pioch to Mme Emery, n.d. in IHS, Archives Emery, Dossier: "Léon Emery: Son Procès."

58. F. Ferre, Capitaine de réserve actuellement sous les drapeaux, ancien combattant de 1914–1918 et de 1939–1940, croix de guerre, Ancien prisonnier de guerre en Allemagne en 1919 et 1940, sinistré total en 1940. "Témoignage en faveur d'Emery," 12 November 1944, in IHS, Archives Emery, Dossier: "Léon Emery: Son Procès."

59. Ibid.

60. B[ibliothèque de] D[ocumentation]I[nternationale]C[ontemporaine], Dossiers Jeanne et Michel Alexandre, FΔRés 348, Marcel Bataillon to Mme Emery, 19 October 1944.

61. Michel Alexandre to "Mon cher Maître" (probably Emery's lawyer), 27 November 1944 in IHS, Archives Emery, Dossier "Emery. Sur et de lui."

62. "Témoignage de MA pour Emery: Notes justificatives," in BDIC, Dossiers Jeanne et Michel Alexandre, FΔRés. 348, n.d.

63. Michel Alexandre to "Mon cher Maître" (probably Emery's lawyer), 27 November 1944 in IHS, Archives Emery, Dossier "Emery. Sur et de lui." Alexandre writes with regard to the question of how best to use the many letters of support for Emery that he has received, "How to use these? ... Perhaps we might be obliged to produce the originals (the entire letters) and that would be troublesome on several levels; because inevitably they contain a little bit of everything. It seems to me that, without putting them in the official file, you could (with me guaranteeing their authenticity—After all, I could have copied these extracts and destroyed the rest) *use them in your oral arguments* (notably in response to truncated and untruthful citations)." Emphasis in the original.

64. L'Inspecteur Général Jules Isaac à Mr. le Juge d'Instruction, Paris, 19 February 1945 in IHS, Archives Emery, Dossier: "Léon Emery: Son Procès."

65. Henri Jeanson, "La Paix prime le droit," *La Flèche* (21 March 1936), cited in Charles Rousseau, "La Dénonciation des Traités de Locarno devant le droit international," *La Paix par le droit* 46/4 (April 1936): 198.

PART II

GENDER AND THE RIGHT

RIGHT-WING FEMINISM AND CONSERVATIVE WOMEN'S MILITANCY IN INTERWAR FRANCE

Magali Della Sudda

This chapter addresses an unacknowledged paradox during the interwar era in France: The presence of female agency within conservative movements. Since the publication of the *Les Droites en France* by René Rémond, historians have sought to provide a new understanding of the French Right, from the place of conservatism in Gallic politics to the vociferous debate concerning French fascism and the "immunity thesis."[1] Among the new insights provided, the use of gender analysis has challenged the traditional view of Rightist hostility toward women's emancipation. The pioneering work of Kevin Passmore on women's militancy analyzed female agency within the Croix de Feu and its successor the Parti social français (PSF), groups frequently compared with Italian Fascism.[2] Laura Lee Downs similarly pointed out right-wing social action involving children as a locus of political socialization.[3] Other works based upon cultural analysis demonstrate the ambivalence of gender and how masculinity and femininity have been reshaped within the leagues.[4] As Daniella Sarnoff demonstrates, support for feminine enfranchisement within the ranks of the far-Right leagues—such as the Jeunesses patriotes, the Solidarité française, and the Croix de Feu, among others—often consisted of attempts to gain women's allegiance through the prioritization of their roles as mothers within the regeneration of the nation.[5] Nevertheless, a close look at the platform of their women's sections as well as the Catholic women's leagues, suggests a continuity rather than a rupture within right-wing organizations.[6]

Yet for all of the consideration of gender and the extreme Right, moderate and conservative movements and organizations have aroused comparatively little scholarly interest.[7] Focused exclusively upon the Belle Époque, the French historiography of gender and the Catholic Right has not addressed the crucial interwar period and the transformation of conservative women's militancy. With the exception of Church-based women's organizations under the rubric of Catholic Action, almost all conservative and far-Right movements endorsed gendered activism through *sections féminines*. The main exception remained the Fédération nationale des femmes (National Federation of Women), which was based solely upon the defense of women's interests, along with strident opposition to the liberal and left-wing feminist organizations such as the Conseil national des femmes (National Council of French Women). Hence, this chapter aims to examine the interwar transformation of the Right from a women's perspective, critically challenging existing writing about female participation in the French conservative movement.

This entails a shift away from the analysis of extreme-right-wing movements in favor of a focus upon another key feature of the Right between the wars: the sexual division of political activity and the gendered dimension of political militancy. In this pursuit, the present chapter examines the women's branch of the Action libérale populaire (ALP, a conservative and liberal party born in 1901), the Ligue patriotique des Françaises (LPDF), and a right-wing political party, the Fédération nationale des femmes (FNF), founded in 1928. These groups were key proponents in a field crowded with organizations linked to the Roman Catholic Church, practicing what Paul Smith termed "Catholic and Conservative feminisms": the Fédération nationale des femmes, the Union nationale pour le vote des femmes (UNVF), the Union féminine civique et sociale (UFCS), and the Women's Catholic Action (LFF and LPDF, respectively, which merged into the Ligue féminine d'Action catholique française in 1933).[8]

In the interwar era, the prevailing definition of feminism was forged by secular organizations affiliated with the French branch of the International Council of Women and close to the Radical Party, a fervent proponent of secularization. In other words, feminism connoted left-wing doctrine and secularization. For this reason, the demand for gender equality within a secular frame was contested by Catholic organizations that simultaneously advocated for the defense of the Church and the defense of women. Accordingly, the true feminism was Christian (i.e., Roman Catholic) because it was based on the "natural" order, in which men and women acted according to divinely assigned duties within family, church, and society. In this view, masculinity and femininity were consubstantial with the familial categories of fatherhood and motherhood. Family was conceived as the primary social unit, with the link between the different family members based upon a religious commitment whose cornerstone is the sacred spousal union. The importance of what Anne Verjus defines as "conjugalism" is thus a key feature of such

movements: The concept of "family," and more specifically the couple, became the relevant political unit in the eyes of the French legislator from 1789 until the introduction of the franchise.[9] Yet the household as a political category did not disappear when the Republic was established; rather, the familial and conjugal model of citizenship prevailed in the political discourse of Catholic organizations despite the introduction of universal suffrage during the 1848 revolution.

As a result, this chapter analyzes how Catholicism (rather than republican discourse) shaped right-wing women's movements. More specifically, it explores the link between male political parties—or leagues—and female organizations. In accordance with conjugalist views, pre-1914 French conservatives founded women's associations in order to provide human and material resources to members, and to gain electoral support. The gendered distribution of political tasks between a male-dominated political party, the liberal Action libérale populaire (ALP) or the royalist Action française (AF), for example, and an allied (primarily female) association such as the LPDF and to a lesser extend the LFF, was grounded in the Catholic conception of sexual differentiation in which men and women have separate civic duties. In Catholic dogma, the vote was defined as much by male prerogative as electoral suffrage. Social institutions and philanthropic work characterized female citizenship. The repeated condemnations of clerics and Pope Pius X toward feminism and suffrage enforced this separate sphere.[10] Thus, before 1914, right-wing women were often instructed to participate in politics by canvassing or fundraising, yet the organizations in question strongly opposed the franchise.[11]

After the Great War, the institutional context within the Catholic Church and the aftermath of the conflict led to a major conceptual shift. First and foremost, in 1919, Pope Benedict XV accepted the vote for women. The shift toward democracy was interpreted as a second Ralliement, and included the acceptance of political rights for women.[12] In the eyes of the Vatican, female suffrage was no longer considered a transgression of gender roles, but an electoral opportunity to vault conservative parties into power. With this in mind, mass movements like the LPDF (which claimed 800,000 members in 1919) proposed civic training for women and campaigned for suffrage, along with new organizations such as the UNVF, founded in 1921 "to join together all Catholic women who desire the franchise," and the UFCS.[13] After the condemnation of the Action française in 1926 by Pope Pius XI, the Republic was considered a valuable arena to promote women's rights and to establish Catholic principles within a democratic framework, resulting in a shift toward political militancy for right-wing women[14] Yet another group emerged in 1928, when a Catholic woman named Aimée Bazy formed the Fédération nationale des femmes (FNF) as a counterweight to the overly moderate UNVF. How did this renewed mobilization of right-wing women reshape the "conjugal model" that prevailed before the war? In answering this question, the chapter will examine two specific organizations. The first one was the most important women's association in terms of membership:

the LPDF reached more than a million members before it merged with the LFF into the Ligue féminine d'Action catholique française in 1933.[15] The LPDF was ultimately joined by the FNF, which represented a unique attempt to establish a women's political party within a republican framework. Their efforts directly affected the second Ralliement and the emergence of a genuine women's party between 1928 and 1935.

The Second Ralliement: A Gendered Perspective

The second Ralliement has traditionally been defined by the end of the consubstantial link between the Church and the Right. From a gender perspective, the conversion of the Church to the cause of women's franchise was part of this Ralliement, and was the product of several factors: women's participation in the war effort, the bill for women's suffrage voted in the Chamber in 1919 (but rejected by the Senate a few months later), sociological and demographic changes affecting the Catholic women's leagues themselves, and the election of a pope more open to democratic government in 1914. The issue of electoral reform first appeared in Italy in 1919. Italian Catholic women petitioned for suffrage as the only way to defend women's interests which were deemed "badly known and hardly defended by men."[16] Thus the Commission for Electoral Reform determined that "the vote should be conceded to women to reach a balanced collaboration with man in the administration of public affairs."

The same year, Catholic suffragist and President of the International Suffrage Alliance Annie Christitch publicized the new papal stance regarding the franchise for women. On 15 July 1919, during a private audience, the pope officially endorsed the legitimacy of women's suffrage, and a few months later, Cardinal Raffaele Merry del Val, secretary of state of the Vatican, further justified the demand for the vote: "Today, we can say with reason that times have changed and the actual conditions have broadened the field of women's activity. For the woman, an apostolate within the world has replaced the more restrictive and intimate action she previously led in the domestic sphere."[17] Civic duty would merely supplement familial duty, the primary mission for women.

In order to justify this shift on religious grounds, the ecclesiastical authorities relied upon theology such as the writings of the Dominican theologian Antonin de Sertillanges, who called for the participation of women in elections on the basis of past religious experiences.[18] Catholic women's organizations across Europe rapidly endorsed the franchise; in France, the vote for women seemed to be an ineluctable fact after the 1919 adoption by the Assemblée nationale of the Barthou bill. The LPDF claimed that suffrage would indelibly moralize the nation while restoring the primacy of Catholic principles to the state.[19]

Yet it is important to note that the LPDF were not left-wing suffragettes. If they supported the vote, league members never considered this activity a step toward political equality, but rather a potential weapon against secularization. As LPDF President Marthe de Vélard noted during the organization's twenty-fifth anniversary celebrations:

> We are told too often that the Women's vote is perceived with incredulity, irony or indifference and that civic training is not followed with great enthusiasm. But Catholic Women must not disdain their future civic responsibilities, because if tomorrow they are to be enfranchised, they will have to use the vote. Abstention is either unconsciousness or cowardice. Women will have to use the vote to defend the Family and its rights, to defend the rights of God in the soul of their children, in their home, in the City and in the whole Fatherland.[20]

Contrary to liberal feminists, therefore, the executive of the LPDF did not consider suffrage an achievement for gender equality. If the vote was to be conceded to women, even against their will, it would necessarily be used very carefully to send politically sound (i.e., right-wing) candidates to the Chamber. This necessarily included the preparation and training of righteous female citizens who could oppose the threats of communism. Thus, throughout 1919, the year of the first postwar election, each monthly issue of the LPDF's bulletin published at least one article about women's suffrage. The vote could be considered as a reward, following the Barrèsian perspective on the female vote: "For four and a half years you have held the Rear heroically; at the Front, your sons, your husbands, your brothers, have resisted even more heroically, often until death. It is your duty (to vote), you owe it to God, you owe your Fatherland and your Children whose interests are at stake."[21]

Despite considerable pressure from Left and Right, and the clear example of women's war service, the French parliament did not grant suffrage. As the issue temporarily disappeared from the headlines, fewer articles appeared in the LPDF broadsheet between 1920 and 1923 concerning the vote. The league's leadership instead focused upon issues as diverse as the defense of war widows, the laic education controversy, and the rebuilding of French society in the aftermath of the war. This approach was further aided by the gradual detente between the Vatican and the French government, a consequence of the predominance of the right wing in the Chamber. But in 1923, the alliance of left-wing parties within the Cartel des gauches provoked fears of anti-clerical measures, including a potential revision of the status of Alsace-Lorraine, which remained under the aegis of a concordat with the Vatican. Catholic organizations mobilized to fight the Cartel, especially at the ballot box, and in 1923 the *Echo de la LPDF* published the "Idées de Marthe" to provide electoral tips and advice. During this period, the LPDF also published monthly articles concerning the law and civil rights for Catholics

in their popular press organs the *Echo de la Ligue patriotique* and the *Petit Echo de la Ligue patriotique*.

In keeping with their emphasis on the vote, in 1925 the LPDF joined the Union nationale pour le vote des femmes, a Catholic suffragist organization. This move proved to be somewhat controversial, provoking a denunciation, mere months after the alliance to the office of Cardinal Pizzardo, prefect of the Affari ecclesiastici straordinari (AES) and the Vatican's minister in charge of political matters. The president of the UNVF similarly complained about unfair competition from some provincial committees of the LPDF. The latter received the support of most of the Episcopate to train Catholic women involved in parish activities and the diocese, while the UNVF was intended to prepare non-believers or non-practicing Catholics to vote properly for right-wing candidates.[22] Yet the LPDF nonetheless continued to actively promote women's political rights, particularly after 7 April 1925, when the Chamber passed a new bill on women's suffrage. The league bulletin promptly published an article urging members to embrace Catholic suffrage:

> Let's start to convince those who are shy, those who are scared, those who are behind their times, that we do not have the right to neglect the weapon of the vote. That we must want to use it; that we need to know how to use it. Faithful to the concept of people's education, the League is ready to give all necessary instructions. We enter a new era of the national life where a woman's influence increases and moves toward new destinies. Let's open our eyes and face all our responsibilities.[23]

Furthermore, once the rank and file accepted suffrage and democratic principles, the association used a variety of modern propaganda initiatives to prepare its members for their civic duties, including leaflets, newspaper articles, conferences, a "Civic Day," training retreats, and talks given by the "*dizainières*," a cadre of the association trained to supervise ten grassroots members. Thus Miss Mouton, a member of the central office of the association, addressed the local presidents of the Seine-et-Oise district about the importance of the home visit paid by each cadre of the association to its members as an appropriate means to exert "a discrete and pressing influence."[24] For the LPDF did not believe that members were born citizens, but rather formed into them through civic education. As President Viscountess de Vélard explained in 1927, the "League has never neglected the civic training of its members," informing women about the law or their rights and duties. In a speech delivered to the twenty-fifth Congress of the League she defined the new agenda for militants: "It is high time for the League not only to form Mothers and Women but also to train future voters (*électrices*)."[25]

Once again, however, the LPDF rejected the notion of the vote as an opportunity for women to express their political preferences on individualistic grounds. As stated in a circular in 1926, "the LPDF, actually, does not demand the vote, the league prepares its members by a civic training, that always proved to be use-

ful and yet is more important than ever."[26] In keeping with Church views, clerics and the heads of the local group associations should alone determine political preferences, especially for women. Jesuits supervised every aspect of civic training for LPDF members, with Olivier Bréhier, the chaplain of the association, charged with ensuring that women received the same "electoral catechism" used to convince Catholic men to vote for "decent candidates" from 1848 onward.[27] This "patronized citizenship" was justified by the lack of electoral experience for women. Contrary to the experience of liberal or left-wing feminist suffragist organizations, the civic training of the LPDF maintained a gendered division of political activity that reproduced the gendered hierarchy within the Church. The clergy defined the norms for laywomen, maintaining a strict division between feminine and masculine duties, while Catholic associations paved the way for a collective repartition of political tasks between right-wing male political parties and women's organizations.

Becoming Catholic Citizens Without Doing Politics: The Case of the Ligue Patriotique des Françaises

In his discussion of feminism in the Third Republic, Paul Smith underlined the link between political parties and the various organizations that claimed to support women's political rights.[28] Christine Bard similarly notes that the exponents of the Conseil national des femmes françaises simultaneously belonged to the Radical Party. The case of the LPDF offers a convincing example of a competing alliance between a masculine organization and a feminine association on conjugalist grounds. In 1924, the preparation of the general and senatorial elections gave Catholic parties the opportunity to formulate electoral lists to counter left-wing *unions*.[29] While the Fédération républicaine indépendante (FRI) proposed a common right-wing front composed of Catholic candidates, the LPDF countered with the broader prewar notion of universal appeal in order to gain the support of women from diverse backgrounds. The FRI ultimately faltered, however, having failed to win support for its proposals, and this led the Ligue patriotique to set up an alliance with Général Castelnau's Fédération nationale catholique (FNC).[30] Formed in autumn 1924, the FNC initially fought the Herriot ministry's revision of the status of religious associations and the Concordat in Alsace-Lorraine, termed a persecution by right-wing Catholics.[31] Buoyed by the Fédération's successful mobilization of French conservatives, the Church hierarchy supported the shift toward a vast alliance of Catholics groups under the supervision of a bishop.[32]

To the FNC and the LPDF, it was essential to remain above the political fray. FNC leaders publicized their intention "to exert all kind of civic action, necessary or useful, in the interest of religion, the family, society and the preservation

of national heritage. We remain aloof from party politics."[33] As a consequence, although the FNC and the LPDF could generate petitions, organize support for "good Catholic candidates," or influence their clientele's votes through active propaganda, their members could not be involved in political parties or the electoral process.[34] They were to actively prepare the battleground solely for Catholic males involved in party politics. Nevertheless, at the May 1924 LPDF Congress, the league vigorously promoted the feminine vote alongside its civic training in order to "wage war against the government" alongside the FNC.[35]

What this precisely meant became evident in the aftermath of a 9 February 1925 FNC meeting in Marseille, during a period of increasing tension between right-wing Catholics and the communist and socialist Left. The gathering degenerated into a series of riots between Catholic activists and communist groups that ended with two dead and several wounded. One of the victims was the son of an LPDF militant, and the league responded forcefully in the columns of the *Echo*, depicting the death of the activist's son as the first act of a religious war: "One of the first martyrs of the religious persecution … , M. Louis Auguste Marie Vian, aged 34, foully murdered in the street in the evening of February 9th, while he was going to Général Castelnau's conference, was the son of a *ligueuse* from the parish St Barnabé in Marseille: Mme Charles Vian. We ask for prayers from all the members of the league for the heroic victim and for the mother, so painfully distressed."[36] The crime, committed by an Italian communist, was thus transformed into the first salvo of a war led by anti-clerical elements. The emphasis on the mother, an LPDF member, reminds the female reader of her duty as *mater familias* and "*ligueuse*" to pray for the cause, while FNC men engage in armed combat.

The alliance with the Fédération inaugurated a gendered collaboration of the two organizations on multiple levels. FNC adherents regularly addressed LPDF meetings and conferences, a significant component of civic training, and the League published and sold Fédération leaflets and publications. In March 1925, conservative lawyer and deputy Xavier Vallat, member of the Fédération indépendante and the FNC, presented a report on the "right for freedom of education" for Catholics.[37] Besides these public events, the alliance between the LPDF and the FNC was sealed by members of a secret society, the Société des filles du coeur de Marie. Founded during the French Revolution by a Jesuit and his penitent, its founders narrowly avoided persecution under the laws against religious orders by supplementing the three ecclesiastical vows—obedience, chastity, and poverty—with a fourth vow of secrecy, enabling the society to pursue their apostolate without incurring "religious persecution." Hence the Société des filles du coeur de Marie could offer its members the possibility of living a consecrated life outside the walls of the convent. Composed of aristocratic women, it aimed to Christianize the masses discretely through the actions of an elite few. Their missionary know-how and social standing provided a valuable means to promote Catholic

associations, gaining the endorsement of the Church hierarchy, and most LPDF leaders were SFCM members, as were leading figures in the Fédération nationale catholique. This development was not entirely welcomed by certain clerics, who perceived the SFCM as a threat to their authority. A report send to the nuncio in Paris by Gustave Desbuquois (1869–1959), a Jesuit director of the Action populaire, detailed the influence of these "secular nuns" and attempted to warn the Catholic hierarchy of the dangers caused by their influence:

> In France, at the present time, the two biggest associations are more or less run by a secret religious congregation, virtually unknown and independent from the Episcopate. Regarding the apostolate, this congregation formulates its inspirations and direction on its own. ... There we find a very conservatist [sic] mind and a lot of sympathy for the *Action française*. We are speaking here about the *Ligue Patriotique des Françaises* and the *Fédération Nationale Catholique*. The first one is completely run by the *Filles de Marie*. ... The *Fédération Nationale Catholique*, although it is re-served for men only, has entrusted the same congregation with the administration of the *Secrétariat Central*, which represents half of the board of directors. In so do-ing, the congregation exerts an influence over the FNC as real as it is veiled.[38]

Most French conservatives did not share Desbuquois's opinion, and the lead-ership of Miss Bouchemousse within the LDPF received accolades from none other than the ultramontane Xavier Vallat, who characterized her management style as efficient, methodical, and rational.[39] Nonetheless, visibly upset by the influence of these "Demoiselles," the Jesuit Desbuquois enjoined the nuncio to solicit the intervention of the Vatican. In spite of his denunciation, the cardinals did not oust the nuns. The president of the LPDF, Viscountess de Vélard, the general secretary, Miss Marie Frossard, and most of the Central Office of the as-sociation who were filles de Marie remained at their posts. They shared the same religious superior with the ladies of the FNC and were empowered to give orders to the administration of both Catholic organizations.

Increasingly acting within the rubric of missionary work, by 1925 the LPDF became a de facto secular branch of the ecclesiastical institution known as Cath-olic Action, while their original political role disappeared. Although various other Catholic women's groups flourished, none could claim a Vatican mandate through an association with Catholic Action. LPDF civic training further eroded as a result of a new church policy concerning lay Catholics, demanding that men and women's participation in civil life be conducted under the strict supervision of the episcopate. Exponents of Catholic Action were strictly forbidden from meddling in the doctrine of political responsibility, a judgment partially respon-sible for the condemnation of the Action française, equally attributable to the pagan leanings of leader Charles Maurras and the group's anti-republican po-litical campaigning ostensibly in the name of throne and altar. Not only did the condemnation provoke various conflicts within right-wing political parties and

associations, it also had genuine consequences for women's activism at a crucial moment. New associations led by lay Catholic women were placed firmly under the heel of the episcopate, though not without some difficulties.[40] This veto on political militancy was considered by some republican right-wing women as a threat to the Church and the Fatherland, since left-wing women were already involved in politics. Thus the LPDF monopoly over civic training for Catholic women was rapidly challenged by the Fédération nationale des femmes, a women's political party that claimed its independence from men's organizations, and operated independent of Church sanction.

Representing Right-Wing Women in Politics:
The Fédération Nationale des Femmes

From 1925 onward, the supremacy of the Catholic women's leagues was challenged by the creation of the Union féminine civique et sociale, founded in order to promote social action, to enforce the preservation of the family through state welfare policies, and to train women to accomplish their civic duties. Although its members and leader were openly Catholic, the UFCS did not receive a specific mandate from the episcopate; the association had the support of French bishops but was not considered a secular branch of the ecclesiastical institution. Nonetheless, although the UFCS enjoyed close ties with the Church, its goal was very different from those of the Fédération nationale des femmes (FNF). Founded in autumn 1928 by Aimée Bazy, daughter of the famous surgeon Dr. Pierre Bazy, the FNF claimed to be a feminine political party, dedicated to preparing women for the vote. The radical journal *La Nouvelle Lanterne* portrayed Aimée Bazy as "a representative of the *Grande bourgeoisie conservatrice*."[41] A graduate of the *Ecole normale diocésaine* in Paris that offered preparation for social action, she trained with Mme. Daniélou, an aristocrat, staunch Catholic, and founder of the UNVF in 1921. Initially interested in the UNVF, Bazy objected to the moderate and conciliatory politics of its president, and left in 1928 in order to form the FNF.[42]

The main goal of the FNF was to train women for suffrage, preparing them for the franchise through membership in a genuine political party. The platform of the FNF was clearly right wing, yet it also presented gendered views on political organization, attempting to raise a political "sex-consciousness" based on naturalized differences between men and women.[43] According to the federation's manifesto, *L'Organisation politique féminine:* "By joining together, women could extend their zone of attraction. A feminine organization does not raise the same objections as masculine political parties. It is logical and normal that women meet together to discuss issues that concern them as women, and the men of their family should not be offended by this." In short, the FNF made women "aware

of their own power" to formulate an agenda.[44] Such feminist rhetoric belies the personal ties of various FNF leaders to male organizations. Paul Smith emphasizes that the Fédération nationale des femmes "was created after an appeal by Paul Reynaud for conservative feminists to counter the move by Cécile Brunschvicg and other UFSF women towards the Radical Party."[45] Reynaud's wife, along with the spouses of other prominent right-wing politicians, joined the founding FNF national committee in 1928, seemingly confirming the presence of a conjugalist pattern within the movement.

Officially, the FNF did not claim any religious affiliation. As the President Mrs. Blanche Lescouvé stated during the 1933 Congress, the FNF "is a political organization, with its own doctrine, its clearly shaped program; it takes stances on all issues, it supports all political propositions that coalesce with its ideal of order, liberty, national dignity. It already goes into action, it is actually very busy."[46] Openly conservative, the FNF appealed to all right-wing women to join a female party. It was considered a right-wing political party by the Assembly of the French Cardinals in February 1932: according to a memorandum, the FNF was "1° clearly inspired by Christian principles (since it has a chaplain), 2° independent from masculine political organizations, in order to avoid partisan and personal quarrels and to favor a broader union, 3° independent from Catholic Action in order to avoid compromising the political neutrality of the Church."[47] Although the leaders of the FNF tended to embrace women's rights within the party, they eventually made clear that their actions were inspired exclusively by the defense of religion.

Thus in one early 1930 pamphlet, Aimée Bazy specifically mentioned that the FNF "addresses non-Catholic women as well as Catholic ones," due to its insistence on the foundation of a social order on moral grounds, with the Church as its guardian.[48] Moreover, in her correspondence with the nuncio, Bazy presented the foundation of the FNF as a consequence of the Catholic Action veto of political activity and overtures by the secular Union française pour le suffrage des femmes (UFSF) toward Catholic women. In a report sent to the nuncio in 1931, Bazy wrote: "The (FNF's) priority was to enable Catholic women to pursue efficient action in the political field, which was prohibited to them as members of Catholic Action. Secondly, they aimed to block the road to organizations with dubious and appalling spirit that worked to bring to power the candidates most hostile to the principles of the Catholic Church."[49] Fearing the influence of the UFSF, an anti-clerical movement close to the Radical Party, the apostolic nuncio alerted Mgr. Chollet, archbishop of Cambrai and president of the Assembly of French Cardinals, suggesting that the French episcopate draw Catholic women's attention to the danger of left-wing and "neutral" suffragism. Chollet agreed to the proposal and supported efforts to promote the cause of the Fédération nationale des femmes as an effective counterweight, observing that in some "diocese

not only has Mme Brunschvicg recruited some members, but she also received help from the female leaders of Catholic's organizations."[50]

The Fédération nationale des femmes received additional help from the Jesuits of the Action populaire and, more specifically, Jesuit Gustave Desbuquois, who enjoyed warm relations with the Curia in Rome.[51] Desbuquois frequently lobbied on behalf of the FNF, while Jesuit Gaston Vanneufville wrote of the Federation:

> [T]his organization deserves to receive the most benevolent attention. . . . It is headed by Mrs Lescouvé, wife of the magistrate who presides over the inquiry into the Stavisky Affair. The Secretary General, Mlle Aimée Bazy, is a very intelligent person and furthermore from a very wealthy background. It is the only organization that, in this matter of political training for women, is able to counter the *Union française pour le suffrage des femmes*, presided by Cécile Brunschvicg, and that is actually an annex of the Radical Party, heavily influenced by the Masonic spirit.[52]

Shortly after these letters were written, Aimée Bazy received an audience on 12 March 1934 with Cardinal Ottaviani, prefect of the *Saint Office*. Despite the entreaties, however, no evidence exists of support from the Vatican's Curia for the women's party after 1934, and the subsequent evolution of the FNF toward a feminine branch of the Fédération républicaine (FR) suggests the failure to obtain the full approval for a female political party from Church authorities after the events of February 1934, despite the FNF's sincere promotion of Catholic principles.

Whether the FNF's failure to obtain the monopoly on political training for Catholic women made it susceptible to appeals from the Fédération républicaine is open to debate. Regardless, FNF President Blanche Lescouvé supported the move, and after 1935, the organization set up the feminine branch of the Fédération républicaine with Lescouvé as president of the section while Aimée Bazy remained the leader of the FNF. In an interview with *Le Devoir des femmes*, the monthly publication of the new section, Lescouvé claimed to be motivated by the desire to raise "the eloquent voice of women," placing feminine issues firmly on the agenda.[53] This platform seconded the policies of FR leader Louis Marin, and provided common ground for the formation of a women's section of that party, potentially strengthening its ties with the FNF.[54] Although his work does not focus explicitly on gender, William D. Irvine considers that the Fédération républicaine paid significantly greater attention to women's sections than the socialist or communist parties, not to mention the strongly anti-feminist Radical Party.[55] To some extent, the evolution of the FNF into a women's section of the FR and the concomitant failure to inaugurate an exclusively feminine political party confirmed that the conjugalist pattern was deeply rooted in the political culture of the right. As spouses and as allies, right-wing women could not possibly enter the political arena without being enfranchised.

The Two Paths of Politicization for Conservative Women

Excluding the women's sections of established political parties that flourished after the Great War, two types of right-wing women's organizations emerged under the Third Republic. The first one was the heir of prewar Catholic women's organizations, such as the Ligue patriotique des françaises, who offered civic training and social action for women under the supervision of the episcopate. It took the shape of Catholic action, and eventually feminine organizations such as the UFCS and the UNVE. A second type of organization was made possible by the Ralliement and allowed conservative women to join within their own political party, the short-lived FNF—the sole example of an attempt to create a political party for women on the Right. Unsurprisingly due to the preeminence of the naturalization of sexual difference as part of conservative ideology, all-women associations were found on the Right. This development also owed its success to support provided by the Church to feminine militancy within the Catholic Action program, and to a lesser extent within Catholic suffragist groups. Yet by the mid-1930s, the conflict between Catholic Action, defined as "above and outside" political parties in order to avoid conflicts between the Vatican and the European States, and a political party based on women's membership, provoked a shift within right-wing activism. While the Ligue féminine d'Action catholique française embraced spiritual and strictly religious activities under the control of the Episcopate, the Fédération nationale des femmes became the women's section of the Fédération républicaine. Although opposition to the vote for women remained strong among ruling politicians, right-wing parties saw in women a resource for their organization, capable of delivering an electoral victory for conservative parties. From this organizational perspective, it was not very different from extreme-Right organizations, providing space for women's activism within their ranks, on the condition that their program not openly challenge the established gender hierarchy.

Notes

1. Sean Kennedy, "The End of Immunity: Recent Work on the Far Right in Interwar France," *Historical Reflections/Réflexions historiques* 34, no.1 (2008): 25–45.

2. Kevin Passmore, "Planting the Tricolor in the Citadels of Communism: Women's Social Action in the Croix de Feu and Parti social français," *The Journal of Modern History* 71, no.4 (1999): 814–851.

3. Laura Lee Downs, "Each and every one of you must become a *chef*": Towards a Social Politics of Working-Class Childhood on the Extreme Right in 1930s France," *Journal of Modern History* 81, no. 1 (2009): 1–44.

4. Mary Jean Green, "Gender, Fascism and the Croix de Feu: The 'Women's Pages' of *Le Flambeau*," *French Cultural Studies* no. 8 (1997): 229–239; Mary Jean Green, "The *Bouboule* Novels: Con-

structing a French Fascist Woman," in *Gender and Fascism in Modern France*, ed. Melanie Hawthorne and Richard J. Golsan (Hanover, 1997), 49–68.

5. Daniella Sarnoff, "Interwar Fascism and the Franchise: Women's Suffrage and the Ligues," *Historical Reflections/Réflexions historiques* 34, no. 1 (2008): 112–133.

6. See chapter 7, this volume; Magali Della Sudda, "Gender, Fascism and the Right-Wing in France between the Wars: The Catholic Matrix," *Totalitarian Movements and Political Religions* 13, no. 2 (2012): 179–195.

7. Evelyne Diebolt, "Les Femmes catholiques entre Église et société," in *Catholicism, Politics and Society in Twentieth Century France*, ed. Kay Chadwick (Liverpool, 2000), 230–232; Magali Della Sudda, "La Ligue féminine d'Action catholique et les ligues de droite radicale (1919–1939)," in *A la droite de la droite. Droites radicales en France et en Grande-Bretagne au XXe siècle*, ed. P. Vervaecke (Lille, 2012), 425–448.

8. Paul Smith, *Feminism and the Third Republic: Women's Political and Civil Rights in France, 1918–1945* (New York, 1996), 43–62. The term *feminism* was intensely discussed by the various women-based organizations in competition for a large-scale support. See Christine Bard, *Les Filles de Marianne (1914–1940)* (Paris, 1995).

9. Anne Verjus, *Le Cens de la famille: les femmes et le vote (1789–1848)* (Paris, 2002); Anne Verjus, *Le Bon mari* (Paris, 2009).

10. Susan Pedersen, "Catholicism, Feminism, and the Politics of the Family during the Late Third Republic," in *Mothers of a New World: Maternalist Politics and the Origin of the Welfare States*, ed. S. Seth Koven and Sonya Michel (New York, 1993), 246–276.

11. Magali Della Sudda, "Discours conservateurs, pratiques novatrices," *Sociétés et représentations* 24 (2007): 211–231.

12. René Rémond, *Histoire du catholicisme en France* (Paris, 1962), 579–580; Harry W. Paul, *The Second Ralliement* (Washington, 1967).

13. Report of Mrs. Levert-Chotard on the UNVF transmitted to the Cardinal Pizzardo in January 1927, Historical Archives of the Secretary of State, Affari ecclesiastici straordinari, (AA.EE.SS), IV, Vatican, Francia, 643PO, n°118/27.

14. Jacques Prévotat, *Les Catholiques et l'Action française: Histoire d'une condamnation* (Paris, 2001).

15. The rich archives of the *Action catholique des femmes* and the *Secrete Archives* of the Vatican constitute the main sources for this chapter.

16. M. Patrizi, *Report to the Commission of Electoral Reform*, 1918, Archive of the Istituto Paolo VI/ISACEM, Fondo UDCI, busta n.1, congresso UFCI, 1919: 7.

17. *Bolletino d'organizzazione dell'Unione femminile cattolica italiana*, 15 November 1919, n°7, Archivium Segretum Vaticanum (ASV), Segreteria di Stato (Seg.di Stato), anno 1926, rubr.325, fasc.3:1.

18. *Feuille d'information Union internationale des Ligues catholiques féminines*, "Quelques réflexions au sujet du Congrès de l'Alliance internationale pour le suffrage des femmes de janvier 1922," ASV, Seg.di Stato, anno 1926, rubr.325, fasc.3, n°18435: 1; "Extrait du Bulletin paroissial de Saint Honoré d'Eylau de janvier 1919," in *Petit Écho de la LPDF*, February 1919, n°227: 1.

19. Steven C. Hause, *Women's Suffrage and Social Politics in the French Third Republic* (Princeton, 1984); "Risposta alla pro-suffragio femminile (I)," ASV, Seg.di Stato, anno 1919, rubr. 12, fasc.6, n°86 083.

20. Viscountess de Vélard, *Faire face : vingt-cinq ans d'Action féminine catholique* (Paris, 1927), 91.

21. O. Bréhier, "Ligueuses songez au scrutin de 1919!" *Écho de la LPDF*, June 1919.

22. Mrs. Levert-Chotard, "Memorandum," Historical archives of the Archbishop of Paris (AHAP), Paris, 1KII7 UNVF, 1.

23. Anonymous, *Echo de la LPDF*, May 1925.

24. "Causerie," *Echo de la LPDF*, May 1925.

25. Viscountess de Vélard, *Faire face*.

26. "The Ligue patriotique," spring 1926, (AHAP), Paris, 1KII7, UNVF, 1.

27. Yves Déloye, *Les Voix de Dieu, le clergé français et le vote XIXe–XXe siècle* (Paris, 2006).

28. Smith, *Feminism and the Third Republic*, 63–103.

29. "Elezioni Politiche," AA.EE.SS., IV, Francia, 547 PO, fasc.33, 1923–1924, "Elezioni politiche," n° 20087.

30. Corrine Bonafoux-Verrax, *A la droite de Dieu: La Fédération nationale catholique 1924–1944* (Paris, 2004), 7–60.

31. Ibid., 29.

32. Letter from Segreteria di Stato to S.E. Cardinal Dubois sd (1925), AA.EE.SS, IV, Francia, 603 PO 126, n°38946.

33. Statutes, 22 November 1925, AA.EE.SS., IV, Francia, 603 PO 126, n°38 946, Fédération nationale catholique.

34. Letter from Mgr. Courbe, General-Secretary of the Catholic Action in France to His Excellency the Secretary of State, Paris, 9 December 1931, AA.EE.SS, IV, Francia, 728 I PO, fasc. 275, 1930–1934, "Action catholique française."

35. Viscountess de Vélard, "Pour une action efficace rapport de la Vesse de Vélard au congrès des catholiques du Nord," *Echo de la LPDF*, n°251, January 1925: 1.

36. "Nécrologie," *Echo de la LPDF*, March 1925.

37. "Journée d'études," *Écho de la LPDF*, March 1925.

38. Report transmitted by G. Desbuquois to the nuncio, 22 September 1927, ASV, Archivio Nunziatura Parigi (ArchNunzParigi), b.528, fasc.1364:10.

39. Vallat's sympathies for the *Action française* might explain its positive judgment on the *Filles de Marie*.

40. Magali Della Sudda, "La Ligue patriotique des Françaises et la condamnation de l'Action française, 1926–1929," in *Pie XI et la France: l'apport des archives du pontificat de Pie XI à la connaissance des rapports entre le Saint-Siège et la France*, ed. J. Prévotat (Rome, 2010), 205–244.

41. "Les Femmes voteront-elles," *La Nouvelle Lanterne*, February 1935, 98.

42. M. Junghans, letter to Chanoine Gerlier, direction des Oeuvres de l'Archevêché, 29 March 1928, AAP, Paris, 1KII7, UNVF, 2.

43. Smith, *Feminism and the Third Republic*, 52–53; Sîan Reynolds, *France between the Wars: Gender and Politics* (New York, 1996), 167.

44. Fédération nationale des femmes, *L'Organisation politique féminine* (Paris, n.d.), 25–26.

45. Smith, *Feminism and the Third Republic*, 91.

46. B. de Lescouvé, "La Participation de la Femme à la vie nationale," *La France judiciaire*, 22 June 1933.

47. "Annexe de la réunion du Comité Archiépiscopal de l'ACF lundi 22 février 1932," AA.EE. SS, 781PO, fasc.282:96.

48. Fédération nationale des femmes, *L'Organisation politique féminine* (Paris, n.d.), 15.

49. ASV, Arch. nunz. Parigi, b.454, ff.17, "Note explicative sur la constitution du dossier n°2," note dact, n.d.

50. ASV, Arch. Nunz. Parigi, n°16335, Letter of Chollet to Nuncio Maglione, 26 September 1931, ms, ff.186–187.

51. Paul Droulers, *Le Père Desbuquois et l'Action populaire* (Paris, 1981), 219.

52. Letter from G. Vanneufville, to Secretary of State, Rome, 6 March 1934, ASV, Segr. di Stato, rubr. 325, fasc.2:3.

53. Smith, *Feminism and the Third Republic*, 92.

54. William D. Irvine, *French Conservatism in Crisis: The Republican Federation of France in the 1930s* (Baton Rouge, 1979), 19–20.

55. Ibid.

Gender, the Family, and the Fascist Temptation

Visions of Masculinity in the Natalist-Familialist Movement, 1922–1940

Cheryl A. Koos

In an essay featured in the August 1940 issue of Alliance Nationale contre la dépopulation's monthly *Revue*, Paul Haury, a history educator and one of the organization's chief propagandists since the early 1920s, could hardly refrain from gloating. For almost two decades, Haury had been condemning the fruits of republicanism as manifested in not only a declining birthrate, but also in an impotent parliamentarianism and an egoistic, self-possessed society. Since 1789, France had been gradually ruined by what he viewed as the most deadly byproduct of republican political philosophy: unbridled individualism. Here, two months after France's defeat at the hands of the Germans, Haury once again attempted to expose this great evil that had brought France to its knees; "an individualist illusion and a sordid egoism" had finally revealed itself fully in the dissolution of the Third Republic and had caused death, displacement, destruction, and suffering. Haury concluded, though, that the defeat had also revealed the true *puissance* of France, the power of familial sentiment. He claimed complete trust in Maréchal Pétain's ability to implement a new constitution centered on *travail, famille, et patrie*.[1]

At the center of Haury's analysis lay an explicitly gendered critique of republicanism that he wove from the early 1920s well into the Vichy regime, in which he served as a key architect of family and educational policy. In particular, he utilized constructions of masculinity not only to define both powerful and weak

nations but also to prescribe the roles that its gendered citizens were to perform: men were to be strong, virile, and dynamic, just like the nations such qualities embodied, while women were to be passive, violable, and physically weak and in need of protection. These arguments were made often and frequently by politicians and cultural commentators who inhabited not only the *mouvement natali-ste et familial*, but also by those in the leagues and political organizations of the extreme Right. Haury, and by extension the Alliance Nationale, is of particular interest because he is a primary example the way in which these gender constructions found their way centrally into French politics and culture during the interwar period and beyond.

Moreover, Haury, along with associates in the Alliance Nationale, developed and deployed visions of masculinity that bore much resemblance to and dialogued with similar constructions of manhood within extreme-Right, fascist, and, perhaps more broadly, authoritarian political movements within France and abroad, thus developing what seemed like not just a fascist temptation but one that could be characterized as an authoritarian temptation albeit with fascist proclivities.[2] They did so in two key ways. First, they used the birthrate policies of Mussolini's Italy and then Hitler's Germany to laud these authoritarian regimes' prioritization of family issues while providing a condemnation of France's parliamentary republican system. Indeed, always shrouded in their campaign to raise the French birthrate was a scathing critique of republican masculinity and the republican state.[3] Second, Haury, a secondary school history teacher, analyzed and compared the youth policies of these governments as well as that of the Soviet Union, particularly those directed toward the civic education of young men. Haury's and his colleagues' call for a virile, disciplined cadre of young men, the future of the nation, to replace the sterile, cerebral, and selfish young men whom they accused of dominating interwar France, was consonant with similar pronouncements emanating from the fascist and *fascisant* leagues following the election of the Cartel des gauches in 1924 and the fascist intellectuals of the 1930s. These constructions of masculinity were markedly different than those on the non-fascist, non-authoritarian Right, formulations that historian Geoff Read has identified and analyzed.[4] Antoine Rédier, Pierre Taittinger, Georges Valois, Jean Renaud, and François de La Rocque, among others in the leagues, along with Robert Brasillach, Maurice Bardèche, Thierry Maulnier, and Pierre Drieu La Rochelle, among others in the circle of more overtly fascist and later collaborationist intellectuals, all yearned for an authoritarian dictatorship of one form or another that would restore dynamism and a mystique to a France they believed had grown stale, withering from republican individualism and egoism.[5]

As historian Christopher Forth has demonstrated with his incisive study of the Dreyfus Affair, the practice of one side of the political spectrum attempting to demonize the other as emasculated men and/or figurative women was not the exclusive domain of the nationalist Right. Indeed, Dreyfus's champions on the Left

developed their own gendered critique of their political foes. What is instructive about this important period in both the political and gender history of France is that one can argue that political discourse prominently featured constructions of masculinity (and, by contrast, femininity) in a historical moment that obsessed about male and female gender roles.[6] I would argue that the Right, particularly the extreme nationalist Right that would develop at times into fascism and embraced authoritarianism over republicanism at the minimum, more adeptly developed a sustained gendered critique of the Third Republic and its supporters, one that culturally weakened republicanism and helped pave the way for the French public's initial embrace of Vichy and its architects. As Sean Kennedy has recently argued, the far Right, particularly in the case of the Croix de Feu / Parti social français, was part of a project to fundamentally recast France and both "reflected and contributed importantly to a sea change in interwar French political culture which ultimately—though not inevitably—manifested itself in the Vichy regime's National Revolution."[7] Paul Haury and many of his colleagues in the Alliance Nationale, though not traditional political figures, advanced similar ideological and political arguments that aided those figures across the spectrum of the Right in welding their authoritarian agenda into the public imagination and thus propelling the political culture of the waning years of the Third Republic decidedly to the right.

Paul Haury and the Fascist Temptation

Paul Haury's rise in the natalist-familialist movement in the 1920s was nothing less than meteoric. Haury burst onto the pronatalist scene in 1922 when his essay "La Vie ou la mort de la France" won the Alliance Nationale pour l'accroissement de la population française's Michelin Natality Prize of 50,000F for the best essay on the country's depopulation problem. A *normalien* and a history teacher at a *lycée* in Lyon, Haury penned his winning essay as a critique of republican political philosophy. At the core of his argument, he attempted to show that France's declining birthrate corresponded to a rise in republican and democratic political sentiment espousing individual rights. Citing French population statistics that showed a proportional decline in comparison with other countries, Haury established 1789 as the date at which France began its downfall as a world power.[8] In doing so, he implicated republicanism as one of the prime culprits for the ills that had plagued France from the fall of the Bastille to the present. Through numerous examples, he concluded that the Revolution and liberal-democratic thought, by rejecting the family in favor of egotism and individualism, had led to what he saw as the present state of decay and decline.[9] To counter this, he outlined nothing less than a plan, taken out of pronatalist orthodoxy, for "the transformation of the

general atmosphere of the country." Central to this project was a revaluation of family virtues that would become national virtues and replace what he called the *république du garçonnisme* that was given to a "withered egotism."[10]

Following the Michelin award and the public acclaim that followed, Haury moved his wife and four children to Paris, where he became increasingly involved in the Alliance Nationale and became the editor of its monthly *Revue* as well as one of its two chief propagandists. Along with the indefatigable Fernand Boverat, Haury frontally assaulted the French state's unwillingness to tackle the birthrate issue, which they collectively saw as France's greatest political, military, economic, and moral weakness. Not surprisingly, given his career as an educator, he called for the government and the nation to instill natalist-familialist values in his country's youth, thus mirroring an aspect of authoritarian political cultures in interwar Europe.[11]

Moreover, this theme was not Haury's only tie to rightward movements in European and French politics. Shortly after his emergence on the public stage in the mid 1920s, he began to laud political developments in Mussolini's Italy. Fascism, with its emphasis upon community and the state, order, and duty, prioritized and valued the family in ways that impressed Haury. Much in line with his ideological stance, the Fascist Italian state promoted traditional gender roles and hierarchies as the basis of its political system; Haury, like Mussolini, saw the family and its products—children—as the key to national demographic, economic, and military renewal. Italian Fascists and French natalist-familialists both venerated the father of large families whose virility was a sign of personal as well as national strength and spirit and revered mothers who stayed at home and did their duty to society and state by bearing many children.[12]

Haury repeatedly praised the merits and successes of Mussolini and his policies relating to both population and the family. The Alliance Nationale *Revue*, under Haury's directorship, closely followed such developments in Italy. In this manner, he attempted to stir the French to action not only by showing that natalist-familialist policies did have a place in government activities and that they were effective, but also by raising the specter that Italy's expansionist plans could very easily include French territory acquired from Italy and that its increased military capabilities, made possible through a steadily increasing birthrate, could indeed make its threats reality.[13]

One such example of Haury's and the Alliance Nationale's affinity toward Italian natalist policy appeared in the January 1927 issue in an article trumpeting Mussolini's announcement of a tax on bachelors. The article reprinted a sizeable portion of a December 1926 speech in which Mussolini pronounced the unmarried man to be "one of the most serious social maladies that could menace the development of a nation."[14] Haury and his colleagues continued to publicize and affirm the successes of Italian pronatalist activity throughout the late 1920s.

They frequently published excerpts of Mussolini's speeches as well as articles that highlighted Fascist legislation designed to reinforce the family, traditional gender roles, and the birthrate.[15]

A 1929 piece, "La Paille et la poutre," alluded to how Haury's political beliefs paralleled and even embraced elements of the Fascist political agenda. The article in question detailed a conversation between Haury and a colleague about Mussolini's population-related policies. Brandishing a leaflet from the Radical-Socialist newspaper *L'Œuvre*, Haury's associate asserted, "Well, the famous natalist policy of *your* Mussolini hasn't yielded brilliant results!" Upon reading the leaflet entitled, "The Severity of the Numbers," Haury proceeded to refute its author's contentions that, one, Mussolini's recent natalist legislation had been an abject failure, and, two, that the French should criticize Mussolini's policies in response to his frequent ridiculing of the low French birthrate. According to Haury, France deserved Mussolini's criticism of its declining birthrate and national stature since its people have refused to have more children and thought the author's conclusion that Italian strategies had failed was too premature.[16]

By the late 1920s, Haury's advocacy of Fascist Italy's family policies was commonplace in Alliance Nationale propaganda. Increasingly, however, his praise of Mussolini's activities raised questions about his support for fascism more broadly. In the midst of one such debate, a colleague asked worriedly, "Have you become a fascist?" Haury cryptically reassured his friend that he, as a historian, would "leave fascism to Italy," and concluded by warning that France was perhaps encouraging the spread of Italian Fascism by not taking stock of its feeble demographic condition and admitting its severe problems.[17]

Haury's mild-mannered and slightly evasive response to such questions is indicative of his fascination and even approval of authoritarian, even Fascist political structures. He did not forcefully take exception to being allied with fascist policies, but merely offered a mild rejoinder when his friend labeled him an Italian Fascist. Haury objected only when his Frenchness—something he saw as antithetical to Italian Fascism—was questioned; it was not the ideology per se that he eschewed, but the national identification related to the ideology.

Such comments did not appear in a vacuum but rather within a context in which Haury had repeatedly sung the praises of Mussolini's success and ideological framework that lay in opposition to France's liberal-democratic tradition. They suggest that Haury's associates recognized that perhaps his political sympathies with fascist ideology existed beyond the natalist debate. It seems that Haury endorsed aspects of Fascist and, later, Nazi family policy not only for the purported effectiveness of raising the birthrates of Italy and Germany, but also because fascism provided an agreeable authoritarian alternative form of government to the republican system he so despised. Pronatalism and familialism emerged as components of Haury's fundamental beliefs about political and social structures, not merely as noble ends.

Gender and the Future of Young Men

As the perceived military threat to France's eastern and southeastern borders grew after the Nazi seizure of power in 1933, so did the Alliance Nationale's efforts to construct an effective campaign designed to elicit children from the French on a scale never before seen in the natalist-familialist movements. After decades of failing to find a lasting and unifying collective voice for its propaganda, the organization's most active members, Haury and Fernand Boverat, carefully built its most forceful case against *dénatalité* and its causes. To do so, they combined elements from past propaganda, namely ethnocentric and racialist nationalism, and attacks upon the republican political system, and intertwined these themes with another even more arguably potent and emotionally resonant construct in this political context, gender.[18]

In the 1930s, gender became a common theme in Alliance Nationale propaganda. Masculinity and femininity, the gendered body, and naturalized traits of men and women became convenient and frequently used metaphors for France's decline and loss of world power. Boverat vilified the *femme moderne* and all that she represented as central to France's declining birthrate. Haury joined Boverat in demonizing the modern woman as the cause not only of France's low birthrate, but also as the reason for high unemployment, the current economic problems, and what he perceived as the nation's crisis of morality. Haury also presented young women with the choice of being exalted as the life-givers of the entire nation or of damning it to extinction through their vanity and selfishness.[19]

Haury also promoted a certain vision of masculinity as the key to France's national success. The men of France needed to become strong, dynamic, and virile, as evidenced by success in fathering a large brood of children. If French men did not live up to such expectations, they proved themselves effeminate, weak, and even impotent, having forfeited any claim to manliness by their unwillingness or inability to produce children. To make such an argument, Haury once again tapped into the thriving discourse about manhood and masculinity that existed within the far Right throughout Europe.[20]

Haury's formula for the remasculinization of young French men appeared in September 1933 amidst increasing political turmoil at home and abroad. "Votre avenir, jeunes gens," addressed young men who in the face of economic depression and uncertainty about the future were struggling to plan their lives.[21] This lengthy treatise comprised an entire issue of the Alliance Nationale's *Revue* and later became a popular tract that the organization reprinted and distributed to schools throughout the 1930s and well into the Vichy era.[22]

Haury feared that young French men lacked the ability and the will to compete with their more dynamic and disciplined counterparts to the east and southeast. For over a decade, the Alliance Nationale had raised the specter of a resurgent Italy as a major political threat. Hitler's rise to power in January 1933 with a plat-

form of racialist nationalism and revenge promised a belligerent and decidedly militaristic power on France's eastern frontier as well. Haury worried that sixty-plus years of rampant republican individualism and a state-run education system that promoted this philosophy had made France's young men soft.

To highlight the damaging effects of the French educational system, he contrasted what he perceived as the marked differences between the attitudes of French youth and those of authoritarian states such as the Soviet Union, Italy, and Germany. Haury concluded that a lack of direction and organized outlets with collective goals plagued France. He commended these countries with "great collective enthusiasm," "tightly-organized machines which harnessed the natural strength and power of their respective youths for the collective good."[23] Celebrating the "virtues of action" it instilled in young Soviet men, Haury described the Komsomol, the state youth organization, as an important example for France if the nation wanted to direct *jeunes energies* for its survival and good. He saluted the USSR's efforts to persuade its young men of a mission greater than themselves, which resulted in a "militarized, standardized, and passionate youth who were guided toward practical things."[24] Similarly, Haury praised Mussolini's youth-oriented Fascist government, itself relatively "young and virile," as illustrating this attitude; this effective regime targeted male adolescents because "they represent[ed] the future; only a nation of ardent, enthusiastic young men [would be] able to set right its destiny."[25] The Italian system prepared its boys to serve the nation through a rigorous training program; it educated them physically, morally, and politically in order to instill a "collective awareness of life … a veritable moral and spiritual unity." Haury saluted the centrality of sports, strength, and practicality in Fascist education, three vital components he saw as working together to transform a culture previously discredited by its impotence.[26] He also lauded young German men under Hitler, at once "evidence and source of the dynamic nature of the Nazi regime." He posited that this government consisted of the "party of youth," and successfully and admirably generated its power by contrasting its youthful dynamism with the stagnant democracy of Weimar, an "impotent parliamentarianism."[27] By investing much energy in the formal and informal training of its youth through education, extracurricular organizations, and propaganda, Haury argued, the Third Reich had secured its future. Such methods, combined with the formality of uniforms, the "Heil Hitler" salute, and national celebrations, directed youthful enthusiasm for the benefit of the collective national good.[28]

On the other hand, most young French men, Haury maintained, having "worn-out views and a critical spirit," being "in love with individual liberty," could only smile pitifully and shrug their shoulders at such ideas. They were unable to understand the force at the root of such dynamism and *élan*. Haury tried carefully not to alienate those in France who held passionately ideals similar to those found in Italy and Germany. In a gesture to the young men who took part in the leagues

and organizations of the far Right, he saluted those who indeed yearned for an authoritarian charismatic leader; he found solace in those who were disillusioned and dissatisfied with the apathetic mediocrity of their counterparts.

As for the rest, however, Haury condemned the current generation's "egocentric apathy" and its "hardness of heart." By lumping them together with their equally weak British counterparts, he contrasted them with the strong and vigorous Italians and Germans.[29] He viewed the young men of France and Britain as victims of their heritage, particularly of their respective governments and cultures. Primarily at fault was democratic liberalism with its dilapidated parliamentary regime. Though also the byproducts of this "outmoded" political system, some French and British young men—presumably those participating in authoritarian/paramilitary organizations—could readily observe how easily the ideals of liberalism, freedom, democracy, and parliamentarianism turned respectively toward license, demagogy, gossip, and impotency. In marked contrast to their democratic peers, according to Haury, these insightful young men yearned for the restoration of authority. These vigilant youths desired a more *puissant* alternative while in France the apathetic majority continued to idolize the heroes of the pre-war era who were not "men of the people" as Hitler and Mussolini were: Marcel Proust, André Gide, Anatole France, writers who merely fostered intellectualism and individualism, the "vapid basis of republican philosophy."[30]

The contrasts that Haury employed were stark. The three authoritarian regimes connoted the ultra-masculine; they emphasized virility, strength, passion, will, action, movement, dynamism, even brute force. Their young men were commissioned to create new societies. In describing French young men as "marked by mediocrity, selfish, and impotent," hence weak and ripe for conquest by these powerful adversaries, Haury marked them as feminine, as figurative women.[31] That he juxtaposed *intellectuels* Proust, Gide, and France—two known homosexuals and a socialist, respectively—with Hitler and Mussolini reinforced this point. Haury also contrasted his condemnation of a weak bourgeois parliamentary liberalism with images that recalled a pre-industrial masculine France, particularly the heritage and myth of the hardworking, virile agrarian, but at the same time promoted technocratic modernity. In attempting to redefine what it meant to be a man, he repudiated the Enlightenment vision of manliness, one that emphasized rational thinking and intellectual pursuits, in favor of a physicality and practicality built upon twentieth-century authoritarian and fascist ideals that synthesized the past and the present.[32] Intellect and reason, once cherished, needed to take a back seat in France's quest to rebuild its status as a nation; she could only do so if the body politic reestablished and reproduced itself by becoming new men, both literally and figuratively.[33]

Key to becoming a newly regenerated nation and creating "new men," Haury proposed, was the obligation to father society figuratively as the wise, yet powerful and effective patriarch who could solve the nation's ills, and literally as the

virile progenitor of a large family who sowed the seeds of future generations. He invoked strong imagery to redefine such goals as family and home life as masculine and other pursuits as corrupting, thus less than manly.[34] He proposed that the future generation of French young men arm themselves against the daily seductions of their country's permissive liberal-democratic society with powerful weapons, namely the family and moral purity. Here Haury attempted once again to redefine the family, to masculinize it, by employing military metaphors to describe it. Instead of being the domain of women (weak, violable, and penetrable by nature) that republican formulations had prescribed, the family became "armor," an "impregnable fortress." The patriarchal home would then function as a source of resistance against the temptations and solicitations of a corrupted society, inviolable protection against the evils of an "overly-intellectualized, effeminate, and prostitute-like" world. He challenged young men to organize this battle line on two fronts: with their physical health, as found in authoritarian societies with a focus on strength and virility, and with their moral health, the correct channeling of such energy into marriage and the raising of a large disciplined and obedient family.[35]

Haury concluded this lengthy treatise on family and national values by emphasizing the masculine nature of this enterprise, the restoration of the family. He again challenged young men "to be most courageous, to repudiate pusillanimous calculation ... to accept the virile responsibilities and worries of family life," to be, in other words, true men.[36] In the final paragraph, Haury revealed his ultimate goal: the restoration of the nation through the resurrection of the "flame of French life" through the renewal of the family, the very foundation of the nation. The collectivity, whether the family or the nation, triumphed over the individual in Haury's ideal society. As in the authoritarian states that he so admired, the family and its individual members became a vital part of the structure of the state. For Haury, the newly restored family, with its virile masculine character intact, would give the nation its power and potency.

Between the publication of "Votre avenir, jeunes gens" in October 1933 and its September 1934 complement, "Votre bonheur, jeunes filles," the young men of the French far Right—those whom Haury implicitly saluted as the future of France in "Votre avenir"—rocked the world of French politics.[37] Following the riots of 6 February 1934, extremist paramilitary leagues like the Croix de Feu grew at unprecedented rates.[38] Collectively, they promoted a dynamic authoritarian, anti-parliamentarian political philosophy similar to the type that Haury had yearned for in the pages of "Votre avenir." Not only was Haury's vision of an ideal state similar to that of leagues like the Croix de Feu, so was his ideal social order, one that consisted of strong, virile fathers and feminine mothers who dutifully bore and raised many children for France.

Following the upheaval of 6 February, Haury continued to highlight the gains Italy and, more recently, Germany had made in instituting natalist and family-

related legislation. In 1934, however, what had been largely Haury's and Boverat's personal preoccupations with natalist-familialist activities and policies in these two countries became official Alliance Nationale propaganda strategy. According to the minutes of an Administrative Council session in which Haury took part, the Alliance Nationale decided to emphasize the pronatalist policies of Germany and Italy nine days after the riots.[39]

As the editor of the Alliance Nationale's *Revue*, Haury closely followed this dictum. He regularly charted and lauded the success of natalist policies in Germany and Italy, all the while contrasting them with France's dismal and ineffective efforts in this area. One such 1935 article, entitled "Nécessité d'une mystique," illustrated his and the Alliance Nationale's frustration with the government's and French people's lack of will to correct what they considered to be the dire situation of *dénatalité*. Haury utilized the same stark contrasts between the rising *puissant* nations and an increasingly weak and declining France that he had deployed previously. He respected Hitler's and Mussolini's goals to instill national pride in their respective peoples, including Mussolini's invocation of Italy's Roman tradition and Mediterranean mission and Hitler's annexation of the Saar region and his promotion of Aryan nationalism.[40] Haury postulated that such devices served as effective psychological tools and were key factors in each country's resurgent birthrate.

France, on the other hand, he maintained, sorely lacked such a powerful mystique, its only point of reference being a pathetic individualism; as in "Votre avenir," he reviled this product of nearly 150 years of republicanism. Haury suggested that French men, for the most part, had forgotten how to dream of anything larger than meager economic independence, the main tenet of republican capitalism: "[they] have lived for no more than a *petit*—to acquire a *petit* house, a *petit* business, a *petit* pension … to protect a *petit* savings, the *petit* proprietor, the *petit* shopkeeper, the *petit* bureaucrat the object of [their] policies."[41] Instead, Haury yearned for the days just following the Great War, when the national mystique embodied the ideals of the veterans, ideals similar to those promoted in 1930s Germany and Italy: "the virtue of sacrifice, necessary discipline, an awareness of a hierarchy of values, the importance of molding young leaders." Hence, France needed to emulate its neighbors by redefining notions of law, justice, and integrity, and by increasing respect for all forms of courage and the family. Additionally, he called for a charismatic leader to galvanize the French, just as Hitler and Mussolini had succeeded in creating and mobilizing national sentiment for their respective goals and policies; Haury wondered "who will be permitted to make such waves of sentiment vibrate deeply" across France. [42]

Reinforcing these demands, Haury also lauded Mussolini and Hitler in a supplement to the Alliance Nationale's trimestrially published propaganda tract series *Natalité*. In a special issue titled "Au Siècle de la Natalité Dirigée," Haury compared the countries with significant birth-control movements, primarily

Great Britain and the United States, with those where natality, not denatality, was officially sanctioned, namely Germany and Italy. As in his radio broadcast, "S.O.S. Natalité Française," and other essays, he detailed the advantages of state-directed policies aimed at increasing the birthrate. Because French anti-abortion and anti-birth-control measures had proved largely ineffective, Haury promoted Mussolini's statewide crackdown on abortion and neo-Malthusian propaganda and devices, as well as his family allowance system. Hitler also rose to near-hero status for his "veritable arsenal" of natalist measures, including marriage loans—what Haury called "the most original piece of [German] legislation"—and his ministers' promotion of large families through their own examples and their propaganda.[43]

Bolstered by the purported successes of Hitler and Mussolini, Haury asserted that it was the duty of the state that wanted to survive to help parents and their children "in their struggle for life"; it must protect them, as the German and Italian experiences demonstrated was possible, against the prejudice and injustice that affected large families. Such attitudes, he admitted, shocked the French, who were "too much in love with individual freedom" to be able to understand the benefits of a totalitarian state that "took hold of its youth in order to shape it to conform to a collective ideal," one that wanted its youth "as strong as possible in number and quality."[44] By not admitting their failures, he believed, the French were pointing their youth toward a "comfortable and convenient egoism," thus leading the country, by default, to defeat through directed *dénatalité*. To reverse such defeatism, the nation needed to assert itself and correct the folly of its ways by embracing a mystique of duty and justice, as did its neighbors, in place of individualism and selfishness.[45]

In 1937, Haury was elected vice-president of the Alliance Nationale, evidencing the extent to which his work and ideas had gained favor among its membership.[46] Alongside Fernand Boverat, the organization's newly elected president, he played a significant role in the reorganization of the group. After having shared many of the same opinions over the years, the two men conjointly controlled the preparation and distribution of the Alliance's propaganda machine.[47] Together they steered the organization further to the political Right in reaction to the Popular Front government of Léon Blum. In one essay, titled "Individualisme exaspéré," for example, Haury condemned much of the labor legislation of the Blum government as the working-class manifestation of bourgeois individualism.[48] And while the Alliance Nationale asserted that it functioned solely on the terrain of ideas and never directly involved itself in politics, Haury, the editor of the *Revue* and the organization's new vice-president, publicly endorsed the pro-family platform of the fascistic Parti social français, the 1936 political incarnation of the paramilitary league, the Croix de Feu.[49]

In the fifteen years since he first burst onto the pronatalist scene after winning the Michelin Prize, Haury had carefully articulated a detailed philosophical ba-

sis for the relationship between sharply defined gender roles, authoritarian state structures, and a powerful France: for him, republican ideology in the form of abject individualism had damaged the relationship of men and women to the state and society at large. In its place, Haury envisioned was an authoritarian ideology, replete with a charismatic leader who restructured France into a patriarchal, hierarchical society in which men were "men" and women were "women."

With the support of the Alliance Nationale's propaganda network that directed its energies toward attacking feminism and the modern woman while promoting patriarchal notions of the family, Paul Haury added philosophical depth to its positions that rooted the movement even more firmly in the trenches of far-right politics. Haury's and the Alliance Nationale's fascination with authoritarianism and fascism throughout the 1920s and 1930s were no mere anomalies. Increasingly in this period, much of the natalist-familialist movement not only allied itself with solidly right-wing philosophies and critiques, it aligned with right-wing and explicitly fascist elements in the French political spectrum. In doing so, he and the organization would play a crucial part in shaking French politics and political culture to its core after June 1940.

Notes

1. Paul Haury, "Quand le voile est déchiré," *Revue de l'Alliance Nationale contre la dépopulation* 329 (May–August 1940): 75–80.

2. On masculinity and the far Right in France, see Geoff Read, "*He is Depending on You*: Militarism, Martyrdom, and the Appeal to Manliness in the Case of France's 'Croix de Feu', 1931–1940," *Journal of the Canadian Historical Association* 19 (2005): 261–292.

3. Similarly, Françoise Thébaud identifies a similar "fascination envers les régimes fascistes," in her article "Le Mouvement nataliste dans la France de l'entre-deux-guerres: L'Alliance Nationale pour l'accroissement de la population française," *Revue d'histoire moderne et contemporaine* 32, no. 2 (1985): 296–298.

4. See Geoff Read, "*Des hommes et des citoyens*: Paternalism and Masculinity on the Republican Right in Interwar France, 1919–1939," *Historical Reflections* 34, no. 2 (2008): 88–111; and "The Republic of Men: Gender and the Political Parties in Interwar France, 1918–1940," PhD dissertation, York University, 2006.

5. For the fascist leagues, see, for example, Robert Soucy, *French Fascism: The First Wave* (New Haven, 1986); Allen Douglas, *From Fascism to Libertarian Communism: Georges Valois against the Third Republic* (Berkeley, 1992); William Irvine, "The Strange Case of the Croix de Feu," *Journal of Modern History* 63, no. 2 (1991): 271–295; Robert Soucy, *French Fascism: The Second Wave, 1933–1939* (New Haven, 1995); Kevin Passmore, *From Liberalism to Fascism: The Right in a French Province, 1928–1939* (Cambridge, 1997); Samuel Goodfellow, *Between the Swastika and the Cross of Lorraine* (DeKalb, 1998); Cheryl A. Koos, "Fascism, Fatherland, and the Family in Interwar France: The Case of Antoine Rédier and the Légion," *Journal of Family History* 24, no. 3 (1999): 317–329; Daniella Sarnoff, "In the Cervix of the Nation: Women in French Fascism, 1919–1939," PhD dissertation, Boston College, 2001; Laurent Kestel, "The Emergence of Anti-Semitism within the Parti Populaire Française: Party Intellectuals, Peripheral Leaders, and National Figures," *French History* 19, no. 3 (2005): 364–384; Sean Kennedy, *Reconciling France Against Democracy: The Croix de Feu and the*

Parti Social Français (Montreal, 2007); Samuel Kalman, *The Extreme Right in France: The Faisceau and the Croix de Feu* (Burlington, 2008); and Caroline Campbell, "Women and Men in French Authoritarianism: Gender in the Croix de Feu and Parti Social Français," PhD dissertation, University of Iowa, 2009. While this essay does not explicitly deal with the much-discussed "immunity thesis," Brian Jenkins's anthology, *France in the Era of Fascism* (New York, 2005), and introductory essay is an excellent examination of the issues at stake in studying the leagues and the presence of fascism in France, as is Sean Kennedy's essay, "The End of Immunity? Recent Work on the Far Right in Interwar France," *Historical Reflections* 34, no. 2 (2008): 25–45. For studies relating to the cultural/intellectual fascism of the 1930s, see Robert Soucy, *Fascist Intellectual: Drieu La Rochelle* (Berkeley, 1979); Alice Yaeger Kaplan, *Reproductions of Banality: Fascism, Literature, and French Intellectual Life* (Minneapolis, 1986); David Carroll, *French Literary Fascism: Nationalism, Anti-Semitism, and the Ideology of Culture* (Princeton, 1995); and Paul Mazgaj, *Imagining Fascism: The Cultural Politics of the French Young Right, 1930–1945* (Newark, 2007).

6. Christopher Forth, *The Dreyfus Affair and the Crisis of French Manhood* (Baltimore, 2004). For other discussions of fin-de-siècle masculinity, see Edward Berenson, *The Trial of Madame Caillaux* (Berkeley, 1992); Robert A. Nye, *French Masculinity and Male Codes of Honor in Modern France* (New York, 1993); Annelise Maugue, *L'Identité masculine en crise au tournant du siècle* (Paris, 2001); and Judith Surkis, *Sexing the Citizen: Morality and Masculinity in France, 1870–1920* (Ithaca, 2006). For discussions of fin-de-siècle constructions of femininity, see, among others, Debora Silverman, *Art Nouveau in Fin-de-Siècle France: Politics, Psychology, and Style* (Berkeley, 1989); and "The 'New Woman,' Feminism, and the Decorative Arts in Fin-de-Siècle France," in *Eroticism and the Body Politic*, ed. Lynn Hunt (Baltimore, 1991); Mary Louise Roberts, *Disruptive Acts: The New Woman in Fin-de-Siècle France* (Chicago, 2002); Elinor Accampo, *Blessed Motherhood, Bitter Fruit: Nelly Roussel and the Politics of Female Pain in Third Republic France* (Baltimore, 2006); Patricia Tilburg, *Colette's Republic: Work, Gender, and Popular Culture in France, 1870–1914* (New York, 2010); and Andrea Mansker, *Sex, Honor, and Citizenship in Early Third Republic France* (London, 2011).

7. Kennedy, *Reconciling France*, 10.

8. Paul Haury, *La Vie ou la mort de la France* (Paris, 1923), 8. For more on Haury's prize-winning essay, see Cheryl Koos, "Engendering Reaction: The Politics of Pronatalism and the Family in France, 1914–1944," PhD dissertation, University of Southern California, 1996, chapter 3; and Stephen L. Harp, *Marketing Michelin: Advertising and Cultural Identity in Twentieth-Century France* (Baltimore, 2001), 140–143; and Mary Louise Roberts, *Civilization without Sexes: Reconstructing Gender in Postwar France, 1917–1927* (Chicago, 1994), 102–103.

9. Haury, *La Vie ou la mort*, 1, 3, 9, 10, 18–19, 24–25.

10. Ibid., 29.

11. See, for example, Paul Haury, *Pour que la France vive* (Paris: 1927).

12. See Victoria de Grazia, *How Fascism Ruled Women: Italy, 1922–1945* (Berkeley, 1992), particularly chapters 1, 3, and 4; Chiara Saraceno, "Redefining Maternity and Paternity: Gender, Pronatalism, and Social Policies in Fascist Italy," in *Maternity and Gender Politics: Women and the Rise of the Welfare States, 1880s –1950s*, ed. Gisela Bock and Pat Thane (London, 1991), 196–212; David G. Horn, *Social Bodies: Science, Reproduction, and Italian Modernity* (Princeton, 1994); and Carl Ipsen, *Dictating Demography: The Problem of Population in Fascist Italy* (Cambridge, 1996) for more specifics about Mussolini's population policy.

13. For early *Revue* articles on Mussolini's natalist-familialist philosophy and goals, see *Revue* 148 (November 1924): 336; and 158 (September 1925): 271.

14. "Impôt sur les celibataires declaré par Mussolini le 1er decembre," *Revue* 174 (January 1927): 36.

15. See "Le Gouvernement italien et le gouvernement français en face du problème de la population," *Revue* 180 (July 1927); "La Restriction de l'emigration italienne," *Revue* 183 (October 1927); "En Italie," *Revue* 184 (November 1927); "Un auxiliaire et un danger: M. Mussolini," *Revue* (Novem-

ber 1928); and "La Paille et la poutre," *Revue* 205 (July 1929). For more information on such measures passed during the Fascist regime, see Victoria de Grazia, *How Fascism Ruled Women*, 55–56, 69–71; David Horn, *Social Bodies*, 75–94, and Chiara Saraceno, "Redefining Maternity," 205–210; as well as Claudia Koonz, "The Fascist Solution to the Woman Question in Italy and Germany," *Becoming Visible: Women in European History*, in ed. Renate Bridenthal et al. (New York, 1997), 508–510.

16. "La Paille et la poutre," *Revue* 204 (July 1929): 237–239.

17. Ibid., 239.

18. See, for example, *La Race blanche en danger du mort* (Paris, 1931). For an extended analysis of the Alliance Nationale's deployment of immigration and racial themes, see Elisa Camiscioli, "Producing Citizens, Reproducing the French Race: Immigration, Demography, and Pronatalism in early Twentieth Century France," *Gender and History* 13, no. 3 (November 2001): 593–621; and *Reproducing the French Race: Immigration, Intimacy, and Embodiment in the Early Twentieth Century* (Durham, 2009), chapter 1.

19. For further analysis of Haury's and Boverat's demonization of the *femme moderne*, see Cheryl A. Koos, "Gender, Anti-individualism, and Nationalism: The Alliance Nationale and the Pronatalist Backlash against the *Femme moderne, 1933–1940*," *French Historical Studies* 19, no. 3 (1996): 699–723. For the major study of the cultural impact of the *femme moderne*, see Mary Louise Roberts, *Civilization Without Sexes*. Victoria de Grazia shows how similar female imagery is present in Italian Fascist propaganda: the crisis woman (*donna-crisi*), "cosmopolitan, urbane, skinny, hysterical, decadent and sterile," and the mother woman (*donna-madre*), "national, rural, floridly robust, tranquil, and prolific." See *How Fascism Ruled Women*, 73, as well as 214–215 for illustrations of both typologies.

20. For a discussion of masculinity in Germany during the interwar period, see George Mosse, *The Image of Man*, chapters 6 and 8. See also Mosse's *Nationalism and Sexuality: Respectability and Abnormal Sexuality in Modern Europe* (New York, 1985), 23–47. For Italy, see Barbara Spackman, *Fascist Virilities: Rhetoric, Ideology, and Social Fantasy in Italy* (Minneapolis, 1996). For a discussion of Russian masculinities, see Barbara Clements et al., *Russian Masculinities in History and Culture* (London, 2002).

21. Paul Haury, "Votre avenir, jeunes gens … ," *Revue* 255 (October 1933): 289–328.

22. According to a brochure marking the fiftieth anniversary of the Alliance Nationale, "Votre avenir," was "particularly well received in the milieu of secondary education." See *Vitalité Française* (Paris, 1946). For information on distribution in the 1940s, see "Action de l'Alliance Nationale," *Revue* 330 (September–October 1940): 117; and Procès-verbaux de l'Alliance Nationale contre la dépopulation, 4 February 1941.

23. Haury, "Votre avenir," 292

24. For analysis of the Komsomol, see James Riordan, *Soviet Youth Culture* (Bloomington, 1989), and Matthias Neumann, "Revolutionizing Mind and Soul? Soviet Youth and Cultural Campaigns during the New Economic Policy (1921–1928)," *Social History* 33, no. 3 (August 2008): 243–267.

25. Neumann, "Revolutionizing."

26. Haury, "Votre avenir," 292–293.

27. George Mosse discusses the ways in which Germany and Italy both attempted to create the intensely masculine "New Fascist Man" in *The Image of Man*, 155–180. German illustrator Eva Bauer contrasts the "impotent (Jewish) parliamentarianism" of Weimar with the Aryan masculine ideal in an illustration from a Nazi picture book. See Mosse, *The Image of Man*, 179.

28. Haury, "Votre avenir," 294.

29. Ibid., 295.

30. Ibid., 296.

31. This conquest theme is consistently echoed in the work of Fernand Boverat. One key example is his brochure, *Comment nous vaincrons la dénatalité*, (Paris, 1938). See also Mary Louise Roberts, *Civilization without Sexes*, 105, 106.

32. For the republican reinvention of gender roles during the Enlightenment, see Lynn Hunt, ed., *Eroticism and the Body Politic* (Baltimore, 1990); *Politics, Culture and Class in the French Revolution*

(Berkeley, 1984); *The Family Romance of the French Revolution* (Berkeley, 1992); and Joan Landes, *Women and the Public Sphere in the Age of the French Revolution* (Ithaca, 1988).

33. For similar formulations of the body politic in the French far Right, see Samuel Kalman, "Faisceau Visions of Physical and Moral Transformation and the Cult of Youth in Inter-war France," *European History Quarterly* 33, no. 3 (2003): 343–366. For a sustained gender analysis of this theme in the Croix de Feu, see Read, "He is Depending on You."

34. Haury, Votre avenir," 317.

35. Ibid., 320.

36. Ibid., 328.

37. Paul Haury, "Votre bonheur, jeunes filles," *Revue* 266 (September 1934). For an extensive discursive analysis of this essay, see Koos, "Gender, Anti-individualism, and Nationalism."

38. See Soucy, *French Fascism: The Second Wave*, 106–114.

39. Procès Verbaux de l'Alliance nationale, 15 February 1934.

40. Paul Haury, "Nécessité d'une mystique," *Revue* 272 (March 1935): 65.

41. Ibid., 67

42. Ibid., 68–69.

43. Haury, "Au siècle de la natalité dirigée," *Natalité* (December 1936): 10, 11. Haury mentions Goebbels (propaganda minister) and Frick (interior minister), along with the well-known statistician Dr. Burgdörfer all as being fathers of large families who never "let an occasion pass without denouncing the state of depopulation to the German people." See ibid., 9.

44. Ibid., 12.

45. Ibid., 13. For similar rhetoric about the need for a *mystique familiale*, see Haury's later "Trois conceptions de la vie: jadis—aujourd'hui—demain," *Revue* 316 (December 1938): 351–362. Haury's 1937 brochure *Justice pour la famille ou la France est perdue* develops these ideas as well. It received critical acclaim and achieved a distribution of over 48,000 copies. *Justice* also received extensive coverage in the Parisian and provincial press. See *Revue* 302 (October 1937): 298; and Procès-Verbaux de l'Alliance Nationale, 8 December 1937.

46. Procès-Verbaux de l'Alliance Nationale, 13 December 1937.

47. Ibid., 22 April 1938.

48. Haury, "L'Individualisme exaspéré," *Revue* 306 (February 1938): 37–40.

49. "Le Parti social français reclame une politique familiale," *Revue* 293 (January 1937): 26. For the claim that the Alliance ignored politics, see Fernand Boverat, *Comment nous vaincrons la dénatalité* (Paris, 1938), 48.

CHAPTER 7

WAS THERE A FASCIST FEMININITY?

Gender and French Fascism in Political Context

Geoff Read

In 1939, France's political parties were reaching out to women in the pages of their newspapers. One paper offered expectant mothers advice on stylish but healthy clothing to wear; another promoted "a family politics," including "the return of the mother to the home"; a third asserted that the proper "role of women in the nation" was to "found a home [and] have children."[1] That these newspapers were the tribunes of the Communist Party (Parti communiste français, or PCF), the Parti démocrate populaire (PDP), and the Parti populaire français (PPF), situated on the far Left, center Right, and far Right respectively, suggests considerable convergence in the gender discourse of interwar French politics. In particular, these and other parties tended to conceive of women as mothers.

This concordance appears to challenge the view that there was a uniquely "fascist femininity" in France. There is an emerging and sophisticated literature on gender and French fascism. Many scholars including Mary Jean Green, Cheryl Koos, Daniella Sarnoff, and Caroline Campbell have examined a variety of groups, ranging from relatively marginal leagues such as the Légion to the Croix de Feu/ Parti social français (CF/PSF), the largest political formation in the country in the 1930s.[2] These authors have successfully demonstrated that gender was an important element to French fascism's aesthetic, rhetoric, and appeal.[3]

Some authors have emphasized that within the far-Right movements of inter-war France women achieved a great deal of autonomy. Campbell's recent doctoral dissertation, for example, emphasizes that women in the CF/PSF were "effective sociopolitical actors."[4] Campbell focuses, in particular, on Antoinette de Préval,

one of three key lieutenants in the movement to Lieutenant-Colonel de La Rocque, its leader. She stresses that de Préval enjoyed his confidence, exercised considerable authority, and carved out a sphere of autonomous action through her direction of the feminine section.[5] Kevin Passmore largely agrees with Campbell's analysis, arguing that women enjoyed significant space for initiative within the CF, and that they were central to its project.[6] Similarly, Sarnoff's research into five far-Right movements, the Jeunesses patriotes, Faisceau, Solidarité française, Francisme, and the CF, leads her to suggest that women were "the center of fascism, not necessarily in terms of numbers but in terms of French fascist world view."[7] Campbell, Passmore, and Sarnoff thus concur implicitly or explicitly with Claudia Koonz and Julie Gottlieb who argue in their studies of Germany and Britain, respectively, that there was such a thing as "feminine fascism."[8]

Conversely, other scholars emphasize the limitations for women of fascist gender discourse. Green, for instance argues that the CF's traditionalist construction of femininity confined women to "feminine" tasks such as social welfare work.[9] Samuel Kalman takes a similar view in his analysis of the CF and Faisceau. Exploring the tensions within both groups' desire to seem to offer new opportunities for women with their goal of raising the birthrate, he concludes that women were clearly subordinated within these movements, playing what he describes in the case of the Faisceau, as a "token role" within them.[10] It would seem in Green and Kalman's analyses, then, that while the possibility for a feminine fascism existed and was desired by some women on the far Right, it was ultimately denied due to the traditionalist orientation of far-Right gender politics.

This is the tension that lies at the heart of this essay. Was there, within French fascism, a specifically fascist formulation of femininity as Gottlieb suggests in the British case? In order to answer this question, historians need to look beyond the fascist parties themselves. Kalman observes that the far Right's desires for women to return to the home and have more babies were "views which appeared across the entire French political spectrum during the interwar period."[11] Indeed, a survey of the Communist Party, the Socialist Party (Section française de l'Internationale ouvrière), the Radical and Radical-Socialist Party, the Alliance démocratique (AD), the Parti démocrate populaire (PDP), the Fédération républicaine (FR), the CF/PSF, and the PPF confirms this view. The construction of femininity in the latter two arguably fascist groups was not unique to fascism. A traditional definition of womanhood reigned in French politics from the Communist Party on the far Left to the PPF on the extreme Right. To borrow and modify sociologist R. W. Connell's term, which she uses with regard to masculinity,[12] there was a "hegemonic femininity" within French politics in the interwar period: a view of femininity that was so widely held among French political elites that challenging it within any of France's political formations was near impossible. It is true that there were contestations of this predominant feminine ideal, but at no time was it significantly destabilized within the fascist movements or

anywhere else. The innovation of the fascists, therefore, was not in creating a new vision of femininity but in their recruitment and use of women. In the CF, in particular, women could and did play crucial roles in the movement's extensive social work and thus enjoyed a certain freedom as Campbell, Passmore, and Sarnoff argue. That said, Green and Kalman are likewise absolutely correct to stress that there were limitations to this freedom marked by the boundaries of gender. Moreover, even the originality of the fascist mobilization of women should not be overstated as non-fascist political organizations were also organizing women by the 1930s. In examining the feminine ideal and the mobilization of women in the leagues and parties from Left to Right, exactly how fascist gender discourse compared to its mainstream and far-Left counterparts will be revealed.

The Parties and the Leagues

Readers should understand the organizations under examination. The Communist Party was founded in December 1920 following a split in the old Socialist Party at its congress in Tours. By October 1921, the fledgling party could boast roughly 110,000 members. This figure, however, shrunk to 80,000 by the spring of 1922 and 25,000 by 1932.[13] With the advent of the Popular Front against fascism in the mid-1930s, which saw the Communists cooperate with the Socialists and centrist Radicals, the party enjoyed a resurgence, jumping from 11 to 72 seats in the Chamber of Deputies while seeing their vote increase from 795,000 to 1,487,000. Party membership likewise expanded to 328,457 in 1937.[14]

The Socialist Party left the schism at Tours seemingly enfeebled. It exited with only 50,000 militants in tow[15] and minus L'Humanité, the paper of party founder Jean Jaurès; yet, as early as the 1924 elections, it trounced the Communist Party and returned as the party of choice for the majority of France's socialistic voters. By 1931, party membership had climbed to 135,000, and in 1936, the Socialists emerged as France's foremost party with 2,200,000 votes and 147 deputies.[16]

The centrist Radical and Radical-Socialist Party was interwar France's party of power. No one could form a government without the cooperation of at least some of its members. Unlike the Socialists and Communists, the Radicals lacked a mass-mobilizing organization and evinced little party discipline. The party's membership during the 1930s fluctuated between 70,000 and 120,000, but its electoral strength was impressive. Even after the loss of some 400,000 votes and 50 seats in the 1936 elections,[17] the Radicals remained the second largest bloc in the Chamber of Deputies with 116 representatives.[18]

The foremost party of the center-Right was the AD, reborn as a proper political party in 1933. With the relatively young and charismatic Pierre-Étienne Flandin installed as leader the party was the right-wing formation most often participating in government. Its membership was negligible but alone among the

parties of the Right it gained electorally in the 1936 elections, and produced no fewer than three *Présidents du Conseil* (the equivalent of prime ministers) in the 1930s.[19]

The FR, standing to the right of the Alliance, was a coherent political party throughout the interwar years, although its members often belonged to multiple political organizations.[20] The Fédération often found itself excluded from governing coalitions from the mid-1920s on because the Radicals viewed it as too Catholic and conservative; it remained the largest political party on the French republican Right nonetheless.

Formed by a group of Catholic politicians and intellectuals in response to the Leftist triumph in the 1924 general elections, in terms of popular vote and electoral representation, the PDP was much less significant than either the Alliance or Fédération.[21] Never boasting more than a handful of parliamentarians, the party was, however, disproportionately influential. Contemporaries recognized *Le Petit démocrate*, the party's newspaper, as a site where key debates took place on a number of issues, including women's suffrage and family policy.

The CF was a special case. It did not become a political party as the PSF until 1936, and then only under duress (it, along with the other fascistic leagues was outlawed and had to reinvent itself). That said, while it did not stand for election prior to 1936, the CF provided important support to candidates of the Right. It enjoyed truly mass support, boasting a membership of roughly 500,000 by the end of 1935 and nearly 1,000,000 by 1937. This made the organization the country's most populous political party.[22] As an anti-republican movement, therefore, the CF represented the most serious internal threat to the survival of the Third Republic in the interwar years.[23]

Finally, the PPF appeared in 1936 under former Communist Jacques Doriot's leadership and briefly attracted a good deal of support. Jean-Paul Brunet hypothesizes that it enjoyed a membership of roughly 100,000 by early 1938.[24] Thereafter, as the threat to property of the Popular Front receded, and as Doriot entered a spiral of alcoholism and dissolution, the Party's support melted away rather markedly.[25]

The Feminine Ideal

Sarnoff argues that women as mothers were crucial to the fascists' desired regeneration of the family and race.[26] This was certainly true of both the CF and the PPF. However, while the political objectives were different in other formations, the trope of woman as mother was omnipresent across the political spectrum. Women were assumed to be mothers and their role in society was defined by motherhood. Generally, all activities that the political parties believed to be suitably feminine were seen as extensions of the motherly role.

The value that the fascist Right placed on motherhood was clear when commentators praised women for abandoning other pursuits in order to raise families. One such example came when PPF writer Yves Dautun interviewed a young woman named "Claudine," and asked how French girls could best serve their country. Claudine replied that women should pursue an education not to prepare themselves for a career but to make themselves better mothers. She believed that women should set aside work outside the home in order to pursue their true "trade": motherhood.[27] Likewise, the CF produced a discourse of motherhood that was similar to that of nineteenth-century republican educational reformers. As men like Ferdinand Buisson had pushed mothers to instill republican virtues in their sons, so the CF exhorted its women "to educate the men of tomorrow, to explain to them the ideal for which they must strive, to raise them with the love of France, of their trade, and of their family."[28] The virtues to be propagated were different, but the view of the role of mothers in forming the male citizens of tomorrow was the same.

This emphasis on motherhood was in no way unique to fascism. In fact, some on the republican Right asserted that women had no other purpose than to bear children for France. As a young Alliance démocratique woman proclaimed, husbandless young women had no choice but to wait "for marriage to make us true Frenchwomen and permit us to give sons to the Fatherland."[29] As in the CF, moreover, moderate Rightists understood the importance of motherhood to inculcating young children with desirable values. An article in La Nation, for example, the tribune of the Fédération républicaine, advised mothers to shelter their children from the pernicious influence of Communist teachers.[30]

Motherhood also dominated women's prescribed identity in Radical, Socialist, and Communist circles. Radical senator Louis Martin stressed in his plea in the Senate for women's suffrage that as mothers, female voters would make the wisest choices possible for the future of their offspring and nation.[31] The Socialist Party likewise embraced the trope of woman as mother. In 1919, the Socialist newspaper Le Populaire reprinted an eight-piece essay entitled, "Advice to a Socialist Mother," and insisted that it should be read by "all proletarian women who desire to turn their sons and daughters into noble and good combatants for our great cause."[32] The Communists too sought to deploy mothers as missionaries for the faith. "It is the mother who guides the first steps in life of he who tomorrow will be a man," explained Communist militant Solange Lecoz, "and, as she gives life to his body, at the same time she must shape his brain and heart."[33] As Louise Bodin frankly admitted, the Communists intended to make, "the education of the child ... a revolutionary tool."[34]

It is worth asking what characteristics French politicos and commentators valued among women and whether these varied across the spectrum. Clearly, all felt that women would and should bear children and all hoped they would educate their children in ideologically desirable ways: what traits did the politi-

cal commentariat believe ideal mothers should possess? Here, once again, there was a conspicuous uniformity. Without exception, the parties and leagues desired women to be nurturing, selfless, and pacifistic. That a proclivity for nurturance would be seen as desirable for women among those who placed such a high value on motherhood is perhaps unsurprising. One interesting manifestation of this conviction that crossed the Left–Right divide was the parallel campaigns to send humanitarian aid to Spain during that country's civil war. Both the fascist and Leftist camps appealed to women as mothers to send foodstuffs, medical supplies, and money to Spain with piteous stories of children's suffering.[35] The PPF focused on stories of republicans mistreating or executing children to move mothers' passions. One "first-hand" account, for instance, claimed that a group of sixteen-year-old boys were executed by republican forces for refusing to take orders and "cried 'Maman!'" as they fell before the firing squad.[36] Leftists meanwhile, such as the Communist Party's Gabriel Péri, appealed to the "mothers of France" on behalf of the "mothers of Spain" to send condensed milk and other necessities to support republican families, and focused unrelentingly on the child victims of the Francoists' bombing of civilian targets.[37]

Such appeals pulled on mothers' heartstrings and assumed their readiness to sacrifice in order to help children in need. Selflessness, in fact, was a feminine trait especially prized by commentators of all stripes. The CF's Madame de Gérus, one of de Préval's key deputies, told a parable to the group's feminine section in 1934 that celebrated this idealized characteristic. According to de Gérus, there was once a town in northern France where selfishness and egotism had reigned supreme. One day, however, the town's seigneur happened upon a woman in rags, out gathering wood for the fire:

> The seigneur stopped her and asked:
>
> —Woman, what is your name?
>
> The eyes of this woman burned with a magnificent light. She responded simply,
>
> —I am maternal love.
>
> Selfishness disappeared [from the town] never to reappear.[38]

One mother's devotion and self-sacrifice thus redeemed the entire community. On the moderate Right the rhetoric was hardly less bathetic: praise for "the perpetual selflessness of mothers" was pervasive.[39] Nor did Leftists adopt a different position. The Socialist Party's tributes to exceptional women invariably praised their "self-abnegation," for example.[40]

The apparently innate feminine inclination to nurturing and selflessness translated readily into pacifism. One might expect that fascist femininity would be more warlike and aggressive than on the center-Right or Left. This was not the case. Commentators of all kinds believed that women as mothers "naturally" op-

posed war. A CF pamphlet in 1934, for instance, urged "French Women" to join the party, "So that your sons ... have a guaranteed future, with ... peace finally ensured."[41] A flysheet the feminine section produced similarly called on women to join the movement in order to fight "for your children" against the coming of war and "disorder."[42] In the PPF, meanwhile, party intellectual Pierre Drieu La Rochelle took to print to explain to a (likely fictive) mother that she need not fear that the party's foreign policy would lead to war. He assured his correspondent and all prospective female supporters by extension that once in power the PPF would be a guarantor of peace.[43] Drieu's reassurances were in keeping with his organization's sensitivity, as a fascist party, to the accusation of warmongering as well as with its growing enthusiasm for a policy of appeasement—an evolution that led to leader Jacques Doriot's endorsing the Munich agreement in 1938.[44]

This fascist rhetoric reducing all women to mothers and portraying all mothers as natural pacifists was indistinguishable from its center-Right counterpart. Alliance démocratique writer Maurice Vincent's piece in September 1939 was typical: "how French mothers were right to fear the worst from the Germans," he lamented.[45] The PDP's Marie-Thérèse Archambault explained the logic succinctly: "Women, whose physiological function is to create life slowly and painfully, consequently instinctively hate all that threatens to destroy it."[46]

The assumption that women were pacifists also predominated on the Left. Radicals Louis Martin and Cécile Brunschvicg, for example, hoped that women's suffrage would see the abolition of war.[47] Lucie Marais similarly called on women to "protect our children" by joining the Communist Party's anti-imperialist campaigns,[48] while the Socialist Party's Compère-Morel provided perhaps the best example of the gendering of pacifism on the Left when he entitled his 1930 series on the threat of world war: "Civilization in Peril: To Men and the Mothers of Men."[49]

There were divergences from this hegemonic vision of femininity in interwar French politics. Sarnoff's research, for example, illustrates that in some of the more marginal fascist leagues such as the Solidarité française, women did sometimes wear uniforms like the men.[50] Similarly, in the 1920s, there was a group of women in the Communist Party who adopted a radical gender politics, advocating sexual equality and female militancy,[51] and the Communist Party did sometimes celebrate strong, militant women as exemplars.[52] However, the militant alternative to traditional femininity in the Communist Party was eclipsed by the early 1930s and disappeared altogether from the party's publications in the era of the Popular Front. This was due first to the Communists' growing Stalinism and intolerance of deviations from the official line; second, to the shift in the Soviet Union to a traditional gender politics signaled dramatically by the conservative marriage law of 1934; and third, to the Popular Front strategy itself, which necessitated the Communist Party reaching out to mainstream republican and middle-class voters.[53] Thus, the erasure of non-traditional femininity (and subordination

of non-traditional women) in the Communist Party combined with the marginality of the aforementioned fascist leagues suggests the overwhelming hegemony of the conventional image of women as mothers and motherly.

The Mobilization of Women

Arguably, the fascist parties distinguished themselves in their mobilization of women. As Passmore stresses, the CF was the first French political movement to have a significant female membership with over 100,000 women adherents. Further, these women undertook the social outreach programs that, especially post-1936, the PSF leadership saw as key to its success.[54] These included the activities of the Joan of Arc Medico-Social Association, which provided home visits, held clinics, ran a pharmacy, and maintained the *Allées* rest home.[55] In addition, there was the party's "social services" division, which acted as a private welfare office,[56] and the feminine section, which maintained its own apparatus and ran the organization's youth camps and activities.[57] In short, there were many roles within the movement that women could and did fill. Granted, these were "properly feminine," but that does not negate the fact that the CF provided right-wing women with an opportunity to become politically involved and to have their own role in a political endeavor validated.

The PPF too had a feminine section,[58] and its women also ran its youth organization and summer camps.[59] Beyond that, however, little is known, and it must be said that the party's feminine section was nearly invisible in its publications. One area where the PPF did display some energy was in the recruitment of young women. The party had an organization devoted to this task, the Jeunes filles françaises, one of whose leaders was Dora Sabiani, the daughter of Marseille party boss Simon Sabiani.[60] The Jeunes filles françaises appear to have been organized in early 1939, reinforcing the impression that the PPF was late in mobilizing women. The group outlined its goals as fourfold: to counteract the Jeunes filles de France, the Communist group; to defend the rights of young French girls; to win back the standing of same within their families; and to apply the social action program of the party.[61]

While the CF and, to a lesser extent, the PPF did open doors for women, their actions were not without precedent. At the initiative of talented women within their ranks, the other parties also established their own feminine sections and newspapers, and ran activities designed for female recruitment. The PDP, in particular, anticipated the CF in this regard. As early as 1925, the party's founding year, *Le Petit démocrate* reported on party women's meetings in Marseille.[62] By the end of that year, the party's feminine section, calling itself "The Civil and Social Feminine Union" (UFCS), held its inaugural congress in Paris. Interestingly, the UFCS tasked itself with preparing women for the vote, while also advocating for

the maintenance of mothers in the home and the breadwinner wage; the title of the article covering this congress was "For the restoration of *le foyer*": clearly, this was not a radical feminist organization.[63] Still, the PDP was the first mainstream party on the Right to mobilize women in this way.

The Alliance démocratique and the Fédération républicaine too sought to mobilize women. The Alliance, despite the prominence of Yvonne Foinant, president of the Ardennes section of the "French Union for Women's Suffrage,"[64] seems to have been the most lackadaisical of the three republican Right parties in its approach to women. In 1935, "The League for the Civil and Civic Emancipation of the French Woman" was born, and became the de facto feminine section of the party. Foinant was elected president.[65] However, despite the fact that the league was fairly active, it was largely ignored by the Alliance; only when Foinant forced feminism onto the agenda, as she did at the 1937 party congress, did the Alliance press take notice.[66] Tellingly, despite promising in 1935 to carry a women's page, the party's masthead never did so with any regularity. Perhaps this apathy explains the occasionally frustrated tone of Foinant's correspondence to Flandin.[67]

Like the Alliance, the Fédération only formed a feminine section in 1935. However, this group did have its own paper, *Le Devoir des femmes*, and by 1936 it also boasted sections in sixty-five departments.[68] The party called on members of the feminine section to volunteer for candidates' campaigns,[69] but otherwise, what activities party women engaged in remain unclear. Lacking the mass organization of the CF, the party's efforts at recruiting women were at best modestly successful: *Le Devoir des femmes* had only 1625 subscribers in 1936.[70]

As on the Right, all the left-wing parties sought to mobilize women. Accordingly, they too established organizations for women that engaged in activities similar to their counterparts' on the Right. In the department of the Seine at least, the Communists seem to have had a feminine section from their earliest days. The section met, for example, to discuss the party's upcoming 1921 congress.[71] One suspects that they were disappointed: in four days worth of covering the congress, the only mention the party's newspaper made of women's issues was to report that Lucie Colliard had expressed her regret that more women had not participated in the proceedings.[72] Failure, in fact, characterized the Communist Party's advances to women most of the time. The feminine section reported annually at Party congresses and unfailingly lamented its insignificant membership and slow recruitment.[73]

The Socialist Party was no more successful. By 1922, the Group of Socialist Women had been founded, with Louise Saumoneau presiding.[74] As Saumoneau explained, she hoped that creating feminine sections would foster a more welcoming attitude toward women among the party's male leaders and militants.[75] That this was less than a raging success was evident from the following facts: the Women's Group did not hold a national congress until 1930, eight years

after its founding,[76] at the 1931 party congress in Bordeaux, Saumoneau still felt compelled to justify the need for a women's organization,[77] and the group's secretary-general, Suzanne Buisson, regularly chided the party's men for their failure to support efforts to recruit women.[78] As late as 1933, eleven years after the Group of Socialist Women's inauguration, Buisson was boasting of there being thirteen federations across the country. According to her own figures, this paltry total represented a dramatic increase over the previous year, a fact that highlighted the group's long-term underachievement more than its relative short-term success.[79]

The Radicals did no better. As Serge Berstein points out, until 1924–1925, the Radical Party had never even considered admitting women members. It was the party's 1924 congress that decided to permit women's entry by a thin majority. Thereafter, it housed some impressive female talents such as Suzanne Schreiber, Cécile Brunschvicg, Marcelle Kraemer-Bach, and Éliane Brault, but on the whole, its record was unremarkable. The percentage of women on the executive committee from 1922 to 1938 provides an accurate synopsis of the place of women in the party: in that time there were 6984 delegates to the committee, including exactly 53 women, or 0.75 percent of the total.[80] Moreover, the Party put forth almost no effort to mobilize women. It had a "National Mixed Committee," founded in 1925; however, the committee's activities were confined to Paris, and it performed strictly charitable work; furthermore, men held all the key positions within the organization.[81] That men dominated the committee despite the female talent available is revealing. By 1938, there was a group called "The Radical-Socialist Women," with Kraemer-Bach as president, but its activities remain obscure and one can only presume its success was limited.[82]

Conclusion

Despite the general lack of success in the Left's approaches to women, there are many interesting parallels to such efforts on the Right. Such organizations for women as did exist were rigidly segregated into "feminine" spheres, channeling women's energies into roles supposedly suited to their biological difference. This, of course, included the CF, where women found themselves in parallel but clearly subordinate auxiliary groups. Moreover, while the CF was certainly the most successful political formation in France when it came to mobilizing women, it was not unique in trying to do so. Whatever claim it has to distinctiveness in this regard lies with its succeeding where others failed.

Just as we better understand the CF's recruitment and mobilization of women in political context, we also better comprehend the fascist feminine ideal in comparison to the discourses on femininity in the other political parties. The most striking thing about such a survey of the political spectrum is the uniformity of the feminine ideal from the Communist Party to Doriot's PPF. In all the parties

examined here, women were perceived primarily as mothers and accordingly, as nurturing, selfless, and pacifistic.

Thus, there was no distinctly fascist femininity in France, at least not in the CF or PPF. Rather, fascists subscribed to the same hegemonic femininity that predominated in the non-fascist political parties. This does not mean, however, that the fascist representation of femininity was unimportant. Rather, Sarnoff makes a salient point in discussing the role of women's pages in the Solidarité française newspaper:

> One of the accomplishments of the women's section, in linking the racist language of the Solidarité française with the preoccupations of family and female life, was the domestication of fascism. The journal managed to normalize a politics of exclusion, antagonism and violence within the context of everyday life concerns. The inclusion of feminine touches in the newspaper ... diluted the violence of the other pages; however, it also served to legitimate it.[83]

By adopting a discourse of hegemonic femininity in other words, fascists presented themselves as normal, domesticated, and unthreatening. The traditionalist conception of gender relations served to mask the insidiousness of fascists' broader ideas and the danger they represented to the Republic. Put another way, fascist rhetoric on femininity was part of fascists' strategy of appealing to conservatives on the one hand and to revolutionary elements on the other; it reassured conservatives that fascists could be trusted to uphold the social order without alienating the radicals who wanted to destroy the Republic and France's supposed internal and external enemies.

Notes

1. "Conseils aux mamans," *L'Humanité*, 23 February 1939, 4; "Pour une politique familiale," *Le Petit démocrate*, 2 July 1939, 4; Jacqueline Girard, "Jeunes filles françaises," *L'Émancipation nationale*, 28 April 1939, 8.

2. There is a contentious debate about whether or not the CF should be considered fascist. Perhaps the most sensible comment has been made by Sean Kennedy, who points out that, fascist or not, the CF was certainly authoritarian, and anti-democratic. See Sean Kennedy, *Reconciling France against Democracy: The Croix de Feu and the Parti Social Français* (Montreal, 2007), 6–16. It is the author's view that searching for subtle divergences on the part of the CF from a particular model of fascism amounts to "splitting hairs." The CF was certainly part of the fascist phenomenon that witnessed the rise of far-Right, militarized, mass-mobilizing, hyper-nationalist, social Darwinian, authoritarian, anti-democratic, masculinist, and illiberal political formations in interwar Europe. For more on this view of fascism as a "phenomenon," see Robert O. Paxton, *The Anatomy of Fascism* (New York, 2004), 3–23. See also Geoff Read, "'He is Depending on You': Militarism, Martyrdom and the Appeal to Manliness in the Case of France's 'Croix de Feu', 1931–1940," *Journal of the Canadian Historical Association* 19 (2005): 261–292.

3. See, for example, Caroline Campbell, "Women and Men in French Authoritarianism: Gender in the Croix de Feu and Parti Social Français, 1927–1945" (PhD dissertation, University of Iowa,

2009); Mary Jean Green, "Gender, Fascism and the Croix de Feu: The Women's Pages of *Le Flambeau*," *French Cultural Studies* 8, no. 2 (1997): 229–239; Mary Jean Green, "The Bouboule Novels: Constructing a French Fascist Woman," in *Gender and Fascism in Modern France*, ed. Melanie Hawthorne and Richard Golsan (Hanover, 1997), 49–68; Samuel Kalman, *The Extreme Right in Interwar France: The Faisceau and the Croix de Feu* (London, 2008), 111–144; Cheryl Koos, "Engendering Reaction: The Politics of Pronatalism and the Family in France" (PhD dissertation, University of Southern California, 1996), 120–148; Cheryl Koos, "Fascism, Fatherhood, and the Family in Interwar France: The Case of Antoine Rédier and the Légion," *Journal of Family History* 24, no. 3 (1999): 317–329; Cheryl Koos and Daniella Sarnoff, "France," in *Women, Gender and the Extreme Right in Europe, 1918–1945*, ed. Kevin Passmore (Manchester, 2003), 168–188; Kevin Passmore, "'Planting the Tricolor in the Citadels of Communism': Women's Social Action in the Croix de Feu," *Journal of Modern History* 71, no. 4 (1999): 814–852; Daniella Sarnoff, "In the Cervix of the Nation: Women in French Fascism, 1919–1939" (PhD dissertation, Boston College, 2009), 1–2; Daniella Sarnoff, "Interwar Fascism and the Franchise: Women's Suffrage and the *Ligues*," *Historical Reflections/Réflexions historiques* 34, no. 2 (2008): 112–133; Paul Schue, "The Prodigal Sons of Communism: Parti Populaire Français Narratives of Communist Recruitment for the Spanish Civil War and the Everyday Functioning of Party Ideology," *French Historical Studies* 24, no. 1 (2001): 87–111.

4. Campbell, "Women and Men in French Authoritarianism," v.

5. Ibid., 88–150.

6. Passmore, "'Planting the Tricolor in the Citadels of Communism.'"

7. Sarnoff, "In the Cervix of the Nation," 1–2.

8. Claudia Koonz, *Mothers in the Fatherland: Women, the Family and Nazi Politics* (London, 1986); Julie Gottlieb, *Feminine Fascism: Women in Britain's Fascist Movement* (London, 2000).

9. Green, "The Bouboule Novels," 49–68.

10. Kalman, *The Extreme Right in Interwar France*, 119.

11. Ibid., 144.

12. R. W. Connell, *Masculinities* (Berkeley, 1995).

13. Edward Mortimer, *The Rise of the French Communist Party, 1920–1947* (London, 1984), 68, 113.

14. Ibid., 248–251.

15. Ibid., 68.

16. Jean Lacouture, *Léon Blum* (New York, 1982), 196, 243.

17. Peter J. Larmour, *The French Radical Party in the 1930s* (Stanford, 1964), 22, 202.

18. Lacouture, *Léon Blum*, 244.

19. Donald G. Wileman, "L'Alliance Républicaine Démocratique: The Dead Centre of French Politics, 1901–1947" (PhD dissertation, York University, 1988).

20. William D. Irvine, *French Conservatism in Crisis: The Republican Federation of France in the 1930s* (Baton Rouge, 1979), 27–31.

21. Jean-Claude Delbreil, *Centrisme et Démocratie-Chrétienne en France: le Parti démocrate populaire des origines au M.R.P. (1919–1944)* (Paris, 1990), 11–13.

22. Robert Soucy, *French Fascism: The Second Wave, 1933–1939* (New Haven, 1995), 36, 108.

23. Kennedy, *Reconciling France*, 83–84, 147–154.

24. Jean-Paul Brunet, *Jacques Doriot: du communisme au fascisme* (Paris, 1986), 228–229.

25. There are many other fascistic organizations that could have been examined. While some of these organizations were irrefutably significant, the CF and PPF had the greatest mass-mobilizing potential. They have also been particularly central to debates about French fascism.

26. Sarnoff, "In the Cervix of the Nation."

27. Yves Dautun, "France, qu'as-tu fait de ta jeunesse? (Suite)," *L'Émancipation nationale*, 14 April 1939, 7–8.

28. "Servir," *Pourquoi s'en faire T.V.B.: Organe de la réconciliation française chez les étudiantes* 1, no. 2 (1937): 1–2. For a discussion of the "moral partnership" between mothers and the Republic, see Judith Surkis, *Sexing the Citizen: Morality and Masculinity in France, 1870–1920* (Ithaca, 2006), 35–42.

29. J. L., "Inquiétude de la jeune fille française devant l'avenir," *L'Alliance démocratique*, 24 January 1936, 3.

30. "Aux éducatrices," *La Nation*, 6 July 1935, 503.

31. "Discussion de propositions de loi relatives à l'élection et à l'éligibilité des femmes," *Journal officiel de la République française. Débats parlementaires. Sénat*, 7 November 1922, 1298–1299.

32. Henri Schulz, "Conseils à une mère Socialiste—I," *Le Populaire de Paris*, 27 July 1919, 3.

33. Solange Lecoz, "Il faut que la femme soit une militante," *L'Ouvrière*, 23 June 1923, 2.

34. Louise Bodin, "Pour la femme, pour l'enfant!" *L'Humanité*, 27 April 1923, 1–2.

35. Paul Schue comments insightfully on the Parti populaire français campaign and Susan B. Whitney on the Communist Party's: Schue, "The Prodigal Sons"; Susan B. Whitney, "The Politics of Youth: Communists and Catholics in Interwar France" (PhD dissertation, Rutgers University, 1994), 360–364. This discussion of the Communist *Jeunes Filles de France*'s campaign in support of the Spanish republicans does not appear in the relevant section of Whitney's book based on her dissertation: Susan B. Whitney, *Mobilizing Youth: Communists and Catholics in Interwar France* (Durham, 2009), 196–208.

36. Maurice Becuwe, "'J'ai vu fusiller des gosses de 16 ans parce qu'ils avaient peur,' *L'Émancipation Nationale*, 2 January 1937, 6.

37. Gabriel Péri, "Mamans de France! Les mamans d'Espagne vous demandent du lait pour leurs petits," *L'Humanité*, 18 October 1938, 1, 3.

38. "Section féminine du regroupement national autour des Croix de Feu," *Le Flambeau*, 1 April 1934, 4.

39. Fernande Hartmann, "La famille et l'éducation des femmes," *Le Devoir des femmes*, July–August 1937, 12.

40. See, for example, "Paula Wallisch," *La Femme socialiste*, 15 May 1934, 2–3.

41. Pamphlet dated 1934, "Gala tricolore," in carton 87/88 of the François de La Rocque Papers, Archives Nationales de France, Paris [hereafter ANF AP 451/carton number].

42. ANF AP 451/82/83, flysheet, "Femmes Françaises."

43. Pierre Drieu La Rochelle, "Réponse â une femme française," *L'Émancipation nationale*, 5 December 1936, 8.

44. William D. Irvine, "Domestic Politics and the Fall of France in 1940," *Historical Reflections/ Réflexions Historiques* 22, no. 1 (1996): 83. For the party's stance—which amounted to viewing the Soviet Union rather than Germany as the real threat to peace and stability—on Munich, see Benoist-Méchin, "Le coup de poignard dans le dos," *L'Émancipation nationale*, 7 October 1938, 5.

45. Maurice Vincent, "1870-1914-1939," *Bulletin trihebdomadaire de la presse démocratique française*, 14 September 1939, 2, in carton 2 of the Alliance démocratique papers, Bibliothèque Nationale de France (hereafter BNF don 37260).

46. Marie-Thérèse Archambault, "Pour la paix," *Le Petit démocrate*, 8 March 1931, 4.

47. L.-A. Gremilly, "Les droits de la femme," *L'Ère nouvelle*, 21 June 1920, 1–2.

48. Lucie Marais, "Défendons nos enfants," *L'Ouvrière*, 20 May 1922, 1.

49. There were four in the series. See Compère-Morel, "La civilisation en péril: aux hommes et aux mères des hommes," *Le Populaire*, 16 November 1930, 1, 3.

50. Sarnoff, "In the Cervix of the Nation," 44–46.

51. The position of these women within the party was symbolized by the status of their journal, *L'Ouvrière*, which was chronically underfunded and became decidedly less radical by the late 1920s.

52. Rosa Luxembourg was celebrated in heroic terms. See L. T., "Septième anniversaire de Karl Liebknecht et Rosa Luxembourg," *L'Humanité*, 15 January 1926, 1.

53. For a thoughtful analysis of this evolution, see Christine Bard and Jean-Louis Robert, "The French Communist Party and Women, 1920–1939," in *Women and Socialism/Socialism and Women*, ed. Helmut Gruber and Pamela Graves (Providence, 1998), 321–347.

54. Passmore, "'Planting the Tricolor in the Citadels of Communism,'" 814–851. See page 817 for membership figures.

55. For the minutes from the group's constitutive meeting, see ANF AP 451/163, minutes dated 23 December 1936, "Réunion constitutive de l'Association médico-sociale 'Jeanne d'Arc.'"

56. For a series of reports to the "Service social" in 1936, see ANF AP 451/87/88.

57. "Section féminine," *Le Flambeau*, 5 October 1935, 2.

58. "Sections féminines," *L'Émancipation nationale*, 24 July 1937, 6.

59. "Au camp de vacances de la Ferté-Milon," *L'Émancipation nationale*, 27 August 1937, 8.

60. For a discussion of her father's career, see Paul Jankowski, *Communism and Collaboration: Simon Sabiani and Politics in Marseille, 1919–1944* (New Haven, 1989). For the text of a report Dora made to the party youth congress, see Dora Sabiani, "Jeunes filles françaises," *L'Émancipation nationale*, 21 April 1939, 7.

61. Jacqueline Girard, "Jeunes filles françaises," *L'Émancipation nationale*, 28 April 1939, 8.

62. "Bouches-du-Rhône: Au groupement d'action civique et sociale de Marseille," *Le Petit démocrate*, 23 August 1925, 4.

63. E.-A Baudouin, "Pour la restauration du foyer," *Le Petit démocrate*, 24 January 1926, 6.

64. "Congrès national de l'Alliance démocratique à Arras, les 2, 3 et 4 Novembre," *L'Alliance démocratique*, 31 October 1934, 2.

65. Ginette Petit, "Les buts de la 'Ligue de la femme française,'" *L'Alliance démocratique*, 22 November 1935, 5.

66. "Motion concernant les droits civils de la femme: Congrès de Bourg 1936 de l'Alliance démocratique," *L'Alliance démocratique*, 21 May 1937, 3.

67. Yvonne Foinant, "Tribune de la femme: Un appel," *L'Alliance Démocratique*, 4 October 1935, 3; BNF don 37260/7, Yvonne Foinant to Pierre-Etienne Flandin, December 1938.

68. Irvine, *French Conservatism in Crisis*, 31.

69. Le Bureau de la S.F., "Femmes de France," *Le Devoir des Femmes*, 15 March 1936, 1–2.

70. Irvine, *French Conservatism in Crisis*, 31.

71. "Fédération de la Seine (S.F.I.C.): Femmes Communistes," *L'Humanité*, 19 December 1921, 1.

72. "Le congrès de Marseille a pris fin," *L'Humanité*, 31 December 1921, 1–2.

73. See, for example, "La résolution féminine," *L'Humanité*, 12 January 1924, 4.

74. "Statuts des femmes Socialistes," *La Femme socialiste*, November 1922, 3–4.

75. Louise Saumoneau, "Pourquoi une organisation de femmes Socialistes?" *La Femme socialiste*, 15 August 1922, 3.

76. "La propagande féminine: La première assemblée générale du groupe des femmes," *Le Populaire*, 17 December 1930, 6.

77. Louise Saumoneau, "Études et documents: De l'organisation des femmes Socialistes," *La Femme socialiste*, March 1931, 2–4.

78. See, for example, "Troisième journée du 29ᵉ congrès national du parti Socialiste," *Le Populaire*, 1 June 1932, 1–2.

79. Suzanne Buisson, "Tribune des femmes Socialistes," *Le Populaire*, 16 April 1933, 4.

80. Serge Berstein, *Histoire du parti Radical: la recherche de l'âge d'or* (Paris, 1980), 235–239.

81. Maud-Puy, "Les femmes Radicales," *L'Ère nouvelle*, 16 January 1933, 3.

82. "Les femmes Radicales," *L'Ère nouvelle*, 7 November 1938, 3.

83. Sarnoff, "In the Cervix of the Nation," 67.

CHAPTER 8

AN OVERVIEW OF WOMEN AND GENDER IN FRENCH FASCISM

Daniella Sarnoff

Assembled in Reims for a 1926 meeting, the leaders of the Faisceau declared:

> There is no greater force than that which moves a man for his children; there is no greater force of civilization than that which makes a mother save for her children.
> …
> The spirit of the family is the true founder of cities, the real force of arts and crafts.
> And it is this spirit that no institution represents in the parliamentary state.
> It is this force that fascism wants to make represented in the national state.[1]

In this proclamation, and many like it, the Faisceau presented itself as the movement that would, unlike the parliamentary system, give families political power. Fascism, as understood and proclaimed by the Faisceau, was, at heart, a domestic ideology. It was a view of the nation and the world that considered economic and political issues through the family. The Faisceau advocated that the family, and not individuals or parliament, should be the basic institution of the state and nation. And the Faisceau was not alone. For the fascist leagues of the interwar years family was both an important metaphor and a real site of intervention for fascist issues.

During the 1920s and 1930s, French fascist leagues of various stripes all appealed to women and family in their pretensions to remake the nation-state at a critical moment when the end of World War I provoked efforts to reestablish prewar gender norms and when economic volatility destabilized the nation.

This chapter touches briefly on Le Faisceau, Les Jeunesses patriotes (JP), the Croix de Feu / Parti social français (CF/PSF), La Solidarité française (SF), and the Francistes, five leagues that were formed and operated between the wars, and argues that women and gender played vital roles in defining French fascist ideology. An analysis of the leagues makes clear the significance of gender and women, as well as the centrality of domestic life, to the fascist attempts to reorder the nation. Further, by playing on gender ideals, French fascism helped to legitimate and domesticate the fascist message and take advantage of larger social ambivalence about gender roles in the interwar period.

Over the past twenty-five years, there have been numerous works confirming the reality of women's participation in European fascisms. Nonetheless, most works, even those that consider gender as operational in fascist movements, continue to posit fascism as a movement and political ideology so thoroughly focused on men and masculinity that the existence of women in fascism is a paradox that needs to be explained.[2] Certainly studies of German Nazism and Italian Fascism have emphasized these groups' appeal to domesticity and women's traditional roles. The French leagues' rhetoric often glorified women—frequently as mothers having the ability to ensure France's future by reproducing citizens. Family, and therefore women, constituted, "the essential cell of the nation."[3] French fascist leagues, however, not only made overtures to women for membership in their groups; they also incorporated a certain vision of female agency that has often been overlooked. Many French fascist groups also emphasized the importance of women as political players and supported women's suffrage. The appeal to women within traditional maternal roles and the advocacy of female political action co-existed within fascist groups and suggests the complicated gender dynamics of the movements. In examining that dynamic, I reassess the masculinist approach to defining fascism and consider, for a moment, women as essential to fascism, and not marginal to it. While men may have been the more highly ranked leaders of the leagues and accounted for greater membership numbers, women were not only present in the ranks of French fascism, they were essential to the coherence of fascist ideology. While French women and mothers were held up as the great hope for the future of France it was not in an uneasy tension with the women who attended fascist rallies in uniform and employed the racist language of their male counterparts. They were the same—a woman or mother would join a league not at odds with her feminine or maternal concerns, but to express them.

In examining French fascist ideology, one is struck by French fascist leagues' many arguments about nature: the nature of politics, the nature of parliament, but also about women's nature and the nature of the family. They invoked that phrase often and the leagues argued that it was natural for women to be in fascist organizations. It was not that these groups thought so differently about women's nature than other groups. They shared the general stereotypical beliefs of the time: that women were nurturing, suited for maternal and domestic cares, that

they were more moral and sensitive than men, that they were "natural" teachers, nurses, and caregivers. The leagues believed all that. They were not asking or expecting women to overcome this nature when they put on the blue fascist uniforms and gave straight-armed salutes; they were asking them to express that nature.

As historians have shown, the role of women in the economy and society, the restoration of men's place at work and in society more generally after the Great War, and concerns over women's apparent growing independence all played into public anxieties about gender and social order in interwar France.[4] Indeed, sociologists and political leaders worried aloud about the "health" of the nation, the birthrate, and the perceived decline of France during the late Third Republic. The fascist leagues, without exception, positioned women as essential to France's national vitality in a vision that deployed competing images of female passivity and activity, public and private.

In their meetings, publications, parades, and public demonstrations, the leagues made clear that gender ideology played an important role in their understanding of the nation in interwar France. All of the fascist organizations had female members and most created women's auxiliaries early in the groups' formation and sustained sizable women's membership.

The exact number of members, either male or female, is hard to assess. To answer the question of membership statistics, one could turn to the group's self-proclaimed membership numbers, which might have been inflated out of a desire to cast themselves as a formidable opposition to parliamentary politics. On the other hand, one might accept the estimates offered by police or the Ministry of Interior in their reports. Those policing and security bodies might be inclined to minimize the membership in the groups, thereby deemphasizing the threat the leagues posed to the state, or conversely, they could inflate membership numbers in order to force the ministry to take seriously the threat of the groups (and the necessity of police work). Further, the inclination to present the groups in a particular light (including membership numbers) might correlate with the personal politics of any reporting police or ministry worker whose job was to infiltrate league meetings and file reports on the gatherings and organization. Perhaps the gender politics of the police influenced what they noticed or didn't notice, what they reported on or chose to ignore. Because of these issues, as in any historical question, the number of women in the group, or their general membership, is difficult to discern from available sources. Many observers noted that women were present at meetings or rallies and if they were speakers; however, a lack of mention of women does not necessarily mean that women were not present. It is certain that women joined all of the leagues, and, beyond their actual numbers, the work they did, the discussions by women and about women, and gender more broadly, indicates how fundamental women were to league success and how fundamental gender was to French fascist ideology.

Overview of Women in the Leagues:
The Jeunesses patriotes and The Faisceau

The earliest of the leagues, the Jeunesses patriotes (JP), founded in 1924 by Pierre Taittinger, is estimated to have had from 100,000 to 300,000 members in the twelve years between its creation and 1936 dissolution and reformation into the Parti national et social français.[5]

There is evidence of a women's section of the JP soon after the league was formed and the group proclaimed an early intention of creating a women's section (*section féminine*) in every arrondissement of Paris.[6] Beyond simply being a vehicle to recruiting greater female membership, which was considered essential work for the men as well, the women's section was tasked with work that was seen as gender specific in terms of greater likelihood of female success. JP rules and regulations asserted that women were to help develop propaganda and distribute tracts with the belief that they could be especially successful at propaganda work "among the working class."[7] The idea that women could be more successful at political propaganda work and recruitment (than men) presents us with the possibility that women could be more politically convincing than men, an interesting proposition in a country where women did not have an institutional or protected political voice. More likely this is based on the idea that members of the women's JP were middle class (as were the men) and that they would have access to the homes and concerns of the working class because of their philanthropic work with the lower classes. The appropriateness or likelihood of welcoming a woman into one's home was greater (in this gender, political, and class equation) than welcoming a man. This political intervention and interaction is conceived of within a domestic relationship: a woman, even if acting in a political role, going to help another woman in her home, seemed a "natural" state, and one that could be leveraged by the political organizations that were interested in expansive recruiting. Male propagandists would have to meet in the streets, which was a space fraught with potential violence (especially as these groups advocated violence). So while the women of the JP would not be immune from the political violence of the streets, the greater hope was that women could penetrate the threshold of working-class homes and use their "soft power" of female charity work to bring the working class to support the movement.

It should be underscored that women's work in the JP did also take place in the streets. The *sections féminines* were warned that they needed to be prepared for violence and were in charge of readying the aid stations of the arrondissement (the Jeunesses patriotes arrondissement headquarters) in case first aid became necessary—this was especially noted and important during and after the 6 February 1934 riots.[8]

While much of the JP women's work could also be described as social work, Pierre Taittinger consistently and repeatedly urged women to engage in a wide

range of work for the movement (as his wife had) and expressed his belief that women were responsible for the successes and expansion of the organization. He urged them to participate in league demonstrations and suggested that "women are able, if they want, to steer men of their families and friends towards the league" and that ability could make women more politically effective than men.[9]

In meeting after meeting (conveyed by both official JP reports as well as police reports), women were urged to take on active work on behalf of the movement. They were frequently complimented for their fine propaganda work because "they are the best agents of propaganda because they can easily spread the Jeunesse doctrine into different milieux during the course of everyday conversations." And yet the JP leadership wanted more and urged all those "inclined by profession or taste to speak at meetings and not to hesitate to do so."[10] The group boasted about the vitality and success of the women's section, especially the Parisian section. The Jeunesses patriotes publication promoted the possibilities of "French Renovation" and proudly noted:

> Our women's sections are enjoying a marvelous expansion In Paris they exceed 3,000 members and they are not token members. At the Jeanne D'Arc parade 50 percent of the registered members were present. It is now up to the women's section of the provinces to imitate their Parisian sisters who, in the month of May alone, endowed the tuberculosis sanitarium with 92,500 francs in donations.[11]

Again and again, the women of the JP were extolled as the best propagandists, a theme repeated in the rhetoric of the other leagues. In addition to the belief that women had greater access to working class environments, they were of great help because "they know how to sooth and comfort and to help brave physical and moral suffering." Women were also better at convincing potential recruits to the JP's point of view. Men, the movement noted, were "too frank and too straightforward," and many male members claimed that "if they had not taken along a female member [to help in propaganda and recruitment work] they would have had to wait a few days [to return] so as not to seem too insistent … but have a female member take up the question and nine times out of ten where we have failed she will succeed."[12]

As if anticipating that the admirable propaganda work of women would not be recognized as important and legitimate, the league publication went on to note, "These details may seem childish to you, but they are indispensable…. It [recruitment] is the most serious and difficult work which demands that one be minutely prepared … to penetrate diverse circles of people, more or less set in their beliefs, and to convince them, and, in a way, to revolutionize."[13] Certainly women and their nature, or supposedly gendered characteristics, were being essentialized (as were men with their too-direct and straightforward manner), but they were genuinely considered necessary to the revolutionary work of the JP. There were female members who were decidedly professional and career women

(and schooled in the more "straightforward" manner of men—as lawyers), but the possibility that women's domestically bounded experiences could be an asset to this political movements was an assertion to be taken seriously—possibly exploited, but also applauded and appreciated, within a movement that was decidedly political, but also interested in mixing the social work of women into a call for revolution.

While it is difficult to be exact about the number of female adherents in the JP, a December 1929 police report gives some sense of the membership. According to the report in the beginning of June 1929, the JP had 25,700 members in Paris: 17,860 men; 3400 women; 2600 Phalangeards—men or women; along with 1840 friends of the JP. In the provinces, they estimated that there were 76,325 male and female members.[14] A general tally of the numbers and percentages of men and women who attended various JP meeting from 1925 to 1930, from around the country, indicates that women made up, on average, 32 percent of the membership of the organization.

Like the JP, the Faisceau was organized in the 1920s during a period of mounting concern on the part of the Right about the Cartel des Gauches. Founded by Georges Valois in 1925, the membership numbers for the Faisceau are also difficult to discern, as is the level of female membership. It is clear that women were members from the beginning of the organization as female membership was built into the structure of the Faisceau. The four-part membership of the league included the Combattants (veterans of the Great War or colonial wars), Faisceau des Producteurs (farmers, workers, employees, business owners), Faisceau des Jeunes (under twenty years old), and Faisceau civique (non-joining men, and women). Ultimately, the Faisceau civique was comprised primarily of women.[15] The fact of female membership and interest is also made clear by the request for women to not attend certain meetings. Fear of violence, often perpetrated by the Faisceau (especially the college-age members of the Faisceau universitaire), led the Faisceau, according to police reports, to decide that the expectation of "incidents meant that the organizers decided not to allow women into the meetings."[16]

Notices of meetings closed to women were no longer evident by late 1926 and most reports indicate that women were at Faisceau gatherings. However, the number of women in attendance is vague. While police observers frequently noted that there were "beaucoup de dames," one is left to wonder what qualifies as "beaucoup." For example, a police and special commissariat report on a Faisceau meeting in Metz in 1926 noted that "the room was full: it had about 900 people ... among which there were many women."[17]

By the end of 1926, the reality of women in the Faisceau had affected the structure of the group and where women had previously appeared to be part of the general "Faisceau civique," they were now operating as a separate unit, the "Faisceau feminin." There were also increasing calls on the part of Faisceau leaders

(Jacques Arthuys, for example) for women to increase their role in the Faisceau and its propaganda work, noting (and complimenting) that they had done their work during the war.[18] Women worked at the Faisceau newspaper, *Le Nouveau Siècle*, and served in administrative capacities as secretaries or treasurers.[19]

The core work of women in the Faisceau, however, was recruitment, propaganda, and fundraising. By 1928, all members, men and women, were expected to recruit four new members within the month after their own membership had begun.[20] For women in the Faisceau (and all the leagues), their work in the social welfare programs would be vital to attracting new members and also enacting the social politics of the league.

The Croix de Feu / Parti social français

Founded in 1927 by Maurice d'Hartoy, the Croix de Feu (CF) attracted significant public attention under the leadership of Lieutenant-Colonel François de La Rocque, who led the group beginning in 1931, transforming it from a loose association of veterans to a significant league of the extreme Right, aided by the newly created Fils et filles des Croix de Feu, Volontaires nationaux, and the combatant Dispos. With the passage of the 1936 law, La Rocque dissolved the CF and created the Parti social français (PSF), which is estimated to have had close to 800,000 members before the war.[21]

While women had been members of the organization since its inception in 1927, generally under the category of the Regroupement national, by March of 1934 the CF had formed a Women's Section specifically dedicated to social work.[22] The group, eventually known as the Mouvement social français des Croix de Feu, claimed that its goal was "the defense of the moral forces of the nation, menaced by revolutionary elements."[23] The group provided visiting nurses and social work programs, distributed clothing to the unemployed, provided programs for children, served free meals, and ran vacation camps (*colonies de vacances*).[24]

The social work of the league was an area of near total female control within the CF. Madame de Gérus, Madame de Preval, and Mademoiselle Féraud, among others, were in charge of the many different programs within the social work of the group. While women's engagement in these areas may strike one as traditional areas of female work, and therefore not positions of great influence in the league, its organization speaks not only to the ongoing presence and interest of women within the league, but one of the many ways that domestic ideals, a social view, was part and parcel of CF ideology, and, indeed, inseparable from it. As Mary Jean Green argues, the social action of the league, the major undertaking of CF/PSF women, had an important political role: turning Communist workers and families into partisans of the league.[25] The same could be said of the social or charitable works of all the leagues examined here.

For the CF/PSF, the morality of women was an essential part of their party platform, as well as part of their recruiting tactics aimed at women. This sentiment is clear in the address of Charles Vallin, a vice-president and member of the Executive Committee of the PSF, to the female delegates of the social action group: "It is a certainty that history gives us: We will not save France without women, because we will not save France if we do not first create the moral climate without which one cannot do anything serious nor durable."[26] This belief and dependence on women's moral powers was something that all the leagues used and shared. As the crisis of politics in France was cast as a moral crisis women's moral strength could be the vehicle by which France could be saved from its political crisis.

Like other leagues, the CF/PSF appreciated the impact a woman's voice might lend to their organization. *Le Flambeau*, the league's journal, published a front-page article by Marcelle Tinayre on 16 March 1935. Tinayre, a novelist, nominee for the Legion of Honneur, and winner of the French Academy's prix Barthou,[27] contemplated in "Action des Femmes" what women could do to help France. She concluded that there needed to be a total reform of state institutions, particularly suffrage, "which will allow the values of all kind, masculine and feminine, to serve the country efficiently."[28] Because the PSF believed the problems of the day could be solved by "harmony," the PSF "addresses itself to women as to the men and calls upon them to collaborate in our great common work; the role played by the one, while different than the work of the other, is not inferior to it."[29] This appeal to women, that they have equal status to men in the eyes of the league, even though they are not the same, was a theme frequently repeated. It underlined the tension in the leagues over the idea of the equality of the sexes, even as they considered women's particular skills or nature essential to their work.

The Solidarité française and The Francistes

The Solidarité française (SF), founded in 1933 by François Coty and led by Jean Renaud, claimed to have 300,000 members in 1934, though historians would consider that a significant exaggeration.[30] Like the Jeunesses patriotes and the Faisceau, the SF included a women's section from its earliest days and there is evidence that women attended meetings from the very first. However, as with the other groups, the exact number or percentage of female membership is difficult to establish (as is the membership of men, of course). Women were singled out for address by the meeting's speakers and police reports consistently noted (and guessed at) the percentage of women attending, indicating a steady presence of female members and female interest. For example, a 4 November 1934 meeting (reported by the Paris Prefecture of Police) noted, "The meeting opened … with about 500 people, among them about forty women and some children."[31] Or, a report on a late September meeting of the SF in the first arrondissement

reported that "the meeting opened at 21:15 with sixty people, where "*l'élément féminine*" dominated."[32] The women's section of the SF had its own leader though the women and men of the group had the same rules and range of activities. Male and female members wore the same uniforms (though pants were generally replaced by a skirt for women), offered the same straight-armed salute at rallies and marches, and were active in a range of league activities, including the riots of 6 February 1934.[33] Like the female cohort of the JP and Faisceau, women of the SF were responsible for circulating and selling propaganda tracts and stamps, and being part of the "humanitarian" efforts of the group.

At the Maison Bleue, the SF "club-house" and site of the women's section offices, many women and men were involved in sports, social gatherings, and charity events of the league. The full spectrum of SF work was on view at the Maison Bleue where

> the nurses section, under the direction of Cheftaine Mme Camus, would develop the education of her militants. … On the other side, the women's propaganda section, under the direction of their Cheftaine, Mme Lecouvreu would have her space to pursue her charity work and get directives for action. … The two, with Mme Pommier, would run a school for drums and bugles, which the group has used to retain the echoes of its calls and batteries.[34]

The mutual aid committee was also run by SF women and the group was responsible for helping the unemployed locate work.

Women were also part of the police force of the group. As the work of the SF could often turn to violence (and, in fact, was thoroughly rooted in political violence) it was sometimes the work of female members to set up care stations to tend to those injured during rallies. Women also participated in the specialized police force of the Soldarité française, the Milice. The highly disciplined Milice and Milicienne, "impeccably turned out" in the blue-shirted uniforms of the Solidarité française and offering the fascist salute, were charged with keeping order at the meetings. A strict hierarchy was in place and the expectation of violence, if not the promotion of it, was made clear.[35]

From instruction and participation in childcare, to political violence and paramilitary action in the Milicienne, SF women participated in a wide range of activities, in many ways illustrating the spectrum of female action in French fascist leagues: combatant and maternal. In the SF worldview, this was an ideal and natural combination.

The Francistes were also founded in 1933, and, as in the Solidarité française, women were present in league activities from the beginning. Women attended the first 1933 meeting of the movement, the smallest and most extreme of the leagues, accounting for three out of eleven attendees. Francisme's women's section met regularly, twice a week by 1935, and was enough of a presence, or of strategic importance in the league, that in early 1935 Marcel Bucard, the Fran-

cistes' leader, organized the First Franciste Women's Congress. Lauded for their work in raising money for the groups as well as charitable works in clothing and food collection the women's section, and their fundraising success, was taken as "irrefutable witness to the unprecedented progress of our movement."[36]

Gender in the Leagues

The work and structure of the various leagues illustrate the relationship of women to the organizations they served. Within French fascist leagues, women could march shoulder to shoulder in uniform, collect clothing for the unemployed, and organize charity bazaars. While there is ambivalence in much of league writing on women, it is also clear that women could play simultaneous roles within the leagues. They were, in their various capacities, responsible for some of the most essential work of fascism: recruiting, propagandizing, marching, paying dues, raising money, setting up children's camps, and providing information for new mothers. Some of these may seem "more fascist" activities than others, however, they were not. And, it may be in the childcare and social work that French fascists created their ideology most clearly and consistently. It was those endeavors that stressed the all-encompassing nature of fascism, that all aspects of French life—politics, economy, society—were connected. Women played a pivotal role in connecting all areas of life through their role as mothers and their "essential" female character. Within the most practical aspects of the leagues, this meant that women could be more tactful and convincing in recruitment; it could also mean, as mothers protecting their children, they could be the most combatant.

While many of the groups advocated a traditional view of female subordination, using the women's sections to perform and promote traditionally female tasks, other groups espoused a more egalitarian view and offered women areas of considerable influence—particularly significant for a group that had yet to win suffrage. Unlike the parliamentary Right, which did not attempt to mobilize women until 1935, the fascist leagues envisioned women as key political players as early as 1924. Gender as well figured prominently in these initial conceptions of ideal authoritarian state structures. Leaders did not simply advocate a reproductive role for women, they also promoted a more public political role for women than has generally been recognized. League spokesmen argued that women ought to engage in national politics and world affairs. Some had women wear blue shirts and emphasized their active participation. In parades they extended their arms in the salute à la romain, just like their male compatriots.

The fact that women were appealed to as mothers and also urged to give fascist salutes could strike one as an indication that French fascists had a conflicted relationship with the role of women in their particularly violent form of public politics. To be clear, there may have been moments of cognitive dissonance for

league leaders and authors who advocated the various roles and ideal of women and womanhood. However, placing the filter of the interests of the French family and nation over the dual image of nurturing mother and blue-shirted marcher makes those conflicts seem less intractable. In the name of national renovation women's identities could be quite elastic for fascists, in some cases more elastic than the traditional Right, Left, or Center parties. Whatever fears there might have been about women's changing roles (suffragist, laborer, and politically engaged) could be assuaged by the belief that women were helping to strengthen the nation.

By talking about women in largely domestic and reproductive terms, French fascists were certainly essentializing "woman." Their focus on familial and domestic activities in the service of the nation, however, meant that women were not necessarily marginalized within French fascism (nor were they necessarily emancipated). They were both important active members and important symbols. Women, even unmarried or childless women, represented the family—and not just for fascists, but in the culture of interwar France, Europe, and beyond. As representatives of the family, women also were representative of the *patrie*—that extended family—and hence they were also representative of the essence of French fascist life.

It is clear in league gatherings and publications that the league and the family were also sites for establishing expectations of femininity and masculinity, as well as national belonging, for French citizens. Within the fascist project the national and the familial were connected: the family was a symbol of the nation and a new fascist nation could reinvigorate and protect the French family.

The image of and rhetoric about the family runs throughout all league publications including reports, posters, pamphlets, speeches, references, and pictures. Mothers, fathers, and children were constant topics of discussion. The league newspapers were filled with specific advice about childcare as well as articles warning about "dangers" to the family. Many of the initiatives of the league were undertaken in the name of defending the family and political opponents were attacked as enemies of the French family. While league rhetoric did often replicate the familiar gender hierarchies of traditional family, it was not simply a matter of leaving domestic cares to the women and public labor and politics to men—the family was the highest calling for men and women. In addition to committing themselves to the protection of the family, leagues presented themselves as a family. Further, the movements were based on the belief that the nation was a great family and claimed that fascism alone recognized this and would glorify the family in their proposed new French state.

To focus on the role of women in the leagues is not to assert that men were not important in French fascism. Nor is it to claim that the leagues were equal opportunity political entities or that patriarchy found no home in the leagues. In many ways, women would be simultaneously exalted and subjugated within

fascist ideology. However, not only would women find fascist leagues welcoming of their presence, but it is clear that the assertion of the importance of family and women, as well as a belief in women's superior moral character, were both ways that fascists understood their world. It is through the gender dynamics of the league that the totalizing philosophy of fascism—the utter melding of public and private, the domestic and the political—is evident.

Amidst the pages of *La Solidarité française* and the warnings that "l'Etoile de Salomon" and the "triangle maçonnique"[37] were allied against the forces of "real" France, one could also find "Chronique gastronomique" and a source for head-cheese recipes. In addition to being alerted to the dangers of Léon Blum one could find help with what to wear during the frustrating *demi-saison* of fall and spring.[38] While these different components of the fascist press seem dissonant categories—anti-Semitic fear mongering on the one hand and fashion and food on the other—they were thoroughly and logically intertwined in the world of the Solidarité française and French fascism more generally.

The column "La Maison et le monde" featured the couture and culinary advice and by its very title conveys the interconnectedness of the ostensibly female world of frocks and cuisine and the male world of suspected Judeo-Masonic plots. Certainly the paper reproduced the more traditional roles for women (just as most women's sections of papers did, no matter their political stripe); however, in mixing the most racist rhetoric with quotidian household advice the SF furthered its agenda. It could use the home section of the paper to both soften and legitimate the accusations, conspiracy theories, and racism of the other sections. How terrible could a movement be that published a recipe for classic leek preparation? Isn't a world in which women are vexed by fashion choices of changing weather exactly the charming fashion-conscious French culture that keeps "France for the French"? That conceptualization of France is precisely the one that the SF thought was worth fighting for, even violently. Clearly, domestic life was central to their reordering of the nation and "La Maison et le monde" was one of the ways that women's domestic concerns were made part and parcel of the group's ideology and organizing strategy.

In other ways, the opening quotation of this chapter conveyed the Faisceau's ardent anti-individualism and familialist idea of the nation. In fact, the Faisceau positioned itself as the group that was willing to ask difficult questions about the nature of the relationship between familial or domestic status and one's ability to lead the country toward "prosperity, grandeur, continuity and stability." The Faisceau pointed out that most do not argue that "a man would be inept at business because he is single" or that he may have greater credentials in finance or "public instruction because he is the head of a family and the father of many children. ... But that is what we are saying, that is what we affirm."[39] And so, the Faisceau was quite clear in its proclamation that men are also judged and legitimated in their public lives by their familial and private experiences and circumstances.

To the Faisceau, the family was the starting point, and the end point, for all philosophical, economic, and spiritual contemplations. As the previously cited Assembly at Reims proclaimed:

> What then is the great, the true spirit of creation?
>
> The spirit of the family.
>
> Where is the great motor of human activity, of fertile activity? It is at the heart of the father of the family.
>
> Where is the great faculty of saving, the great force that maintains the man on the land of his fathers, that makes the walls of the city rise?
>
> At the heart of the mother of the family.
>
> Where is the great spirit of sacrifice, that makes man renounces his instant gratification for the happiness that will come later, of the generation to come?
>
> In the love of the father and mother, who renounce the minutes that go by for the hour when the child could inherit the fruit of their renunciation.[40]

The Faisceau viewed all politics and public life through the ideal of the nuclear family. In the above they legitimated and sanctioned the public power of both men and women (even if they did not share identical power) through their private roles. The Reims speech also criticized both individualism and liberal capitalism. The implication is that family connections and responsibilities are what temper individual motivations and consumption—both based in selfishness. To the Faisceau, the family had been destroyed in the modern economy and the abomination of the parliamentary system was that it was incapable of recognizing the value of the family over the individual, but, in addition, the very spiritual force of familial existence was in danger of utter destruction in the Third Republic.

The Jeunesses patriotes showed their belief in these ideas as well. The "Statutes of the Jeunesses patriotes" proclaimed: "The family is the organic and fundamental cell of society, based in morality, the stability and fecundity of the domestic home, facilitating its formation, avoiding its break up, favoring the increase of natality so necessary to the country."[41] To this end, the JP wanted to severely curtail any activity, information, or behavior they believed caused harm to the family. In targeting existing laws, the JP wanted "to severely repress all propaganda tending to pervert morals," which included information on "abortion, birth control propaganda, pornography, prostitution, hidden or public, and the abandonment of family."[42]

In contrast to the Parliament of the Third Republic, as it was perceived by the league, the JP did not "tend only to the progress and well-being of the individual. It equally wants to protect and strengthen the family 'the keystone of the social

edifice' the necessary base of public morality and the grandeur of the country."[43] In this way, the JP, like other leagues, shifted focus from individualism, which they regarded as one of the great errors of the Third Republic, to the family and the collection of families in the nation.

The JP also lamented the separation and distinction between the men of government and the people, specifically the heads of *familles nombreuses*. Such was the case when M. Restelli, a JP member and leader representing business, spoke in the name of *familles nombreuses*. "The Senate," he said, "is made up in a majority by unmarried men, who disinterest themselves in the lot of *familles nombreuses*. If the senators were elected by the people, they would have an awareness of their actions and not send the fathers of *famille nombreuses* to the slaughter."[44] For the JP, the state was a society, "not of individuals, but of families," and the only member of society "justified to supervise social management was the head of the family."[45] In a 1925 brochure, which was a joint venture between the JP and the Légion (a group not examined here), both leagues made very clear the status of men in relationship to their family: "The heads of the family are, after veterans, particularly called upon to join the league, the organism of defense against communism and all the agents of destruction."[46] Time and time again the groups called upon familial experience to lend political legitimacy to individuals, arguing that those who have "built and populated their own home, are qualified to rebuild the city where their sons live." In a belief that the "familial problem today is the premier problem," the JP reiterated much of the basic familial ideology of all the leagues—an approach to politics and the nation viewed through a relational or familial existence, thereby challenging an individualistic liberal ideal that maintained a distinction between public and private (even if just a rhetorical one). The JP called upon a familial longing on the part of the young men of the leagues, noting that they "want to feel the presence of the fathers of France of tomorrow." Proclaiming that many of these young members were recently back from the war, the JP asserted that these men had "given to the *patrie* this double gesture of fighting for her and raising, to save her again, children of their blood."[47]

With these words, the league emphasized both the family concerns of their movement and argued that the role of men—and the masculine ideal—was not simply to fight or to be a veteran, but to raise children and be a father. The publication clearly prioritized the role of the male in the family (as both father and soldier) and the leagues acknowledged the patriarchal structure of their idealized family and polity. However, it is also notable that the consideration of female sacrifice for war (giving up their children and loved ones to a national cause as well as participating directly in the war effort) was given greater importance by attaching it to masculine ideals and honor. On the one hand, it positioned men as more "feminine" by promoting their reproductive and familial value, and, by extension, it strengthened women's claim to sacrifice in wartime—a feminine

patriotism evidenced by sacrifice of her loved ones. On the other hand, it took this "special" category away from women and noted that fathers too were doing their patriotic duty by reproducing for the nation. In this way, the leagues proposed that the nation could be redeemed by altering the role of men and women. Public and political men needed to be fathers (and not bachelors) and mothers needed to embrace a public and political role. For both sexes, their familial relation could be transformative for the nation. The league's idea of saving or reinvigorating the French nation clearly rested upon changing ideas of femininity and masculinity.[48]

The Francistes too considered the family the base of the nation and all other political and social considerations were to stem from that. The Franciste press often repeated that idea: "[the Franciste economic and social plan] protects and strengthens the family, the vital cell of the country, and makes the *métier* an extension of the familial home, the region a small country, and the nation the real assembly of families."[49] This rhetoric echoes, almost verbatim, earlier sentiments of the Faisceau and the Jeunesses patriotes.

The Francistes too considered the individual only in the context of his or her function within the family and nation. And, like the other leagues, the Francistes were deeply concerned about the population's decline in quantity and quality.[50] Francisme advocated aid to families with many children, including crèches, schools, and apprenticeships and called for affordable housing, which would provide work for masons and health for their children."[51] Reflecting a fear of the racial decline of France, the Francistes argued for childcare that would create stronger and healthier French citizens: "A people of athletes cannot be perverse. Make handsome and healthy men and you will have good citizens."[52]

Paternal and familial status was also emphasized by the Croix de Feu. Like the other *ligues*, the CF believed that "The family is the elementary framework of the social collectivity."[53] Seeing the transformation of the family in political terms (currently "under the tyranny of Marxist economy"), Colonel de La Rocque argued that the family needed to be secured and reinforced in order for it to adapt to new conditions in the world. The way for that to happen, for the family to be maintained, was "to consolidate the authority of parents on their young children, to do away with the interference of the state in the instruction of children."[54] La Rocque's position was that one had to reacquaint fathers with their rights and responsibilities, as well as "assure the mother an eminent position in the legal realm."[55] Here again, the rights and duties of men and women were considered in their relationship to their family with an argument that the CF took for granted: strengthen the family and the nation will be strengthened. The combining of familial and political ideals—the idea of parents having political rights and responsibilities as parents—was part of the CF's ideology and an important way in which the movement viewed the nation and the power of its own ideology to effect positive change within the stagnant Third Republic

French fascist organizations promoted a public political role for women along-side motherhood and a paternal role for men alongside their public actions. Leagues invoked female work and sacrifice during the war, as well as women's supposedly superior moral aptitude and the leagues presented themselves as the forces that truly respected women's potential political importance in the state. Many of the leagues advocated female suffrage at a time when many mainstream political groups did not. The domestic identities and concerns of women were not only compatible with fascist notions of politics, but rendered women poten-tially better fascists and citizens.

To consider women's work in the leagues as simply subordination to those of men, believing them marginalized in areas that served as extensions of the domestic sphere, does not fully take in or address the complications of gender ideology within the league. As Kevin Passmore notes, "the position of women cannot be reduced to an extension of the familial role, not least because of the uncertainties in the discourse and practices of the leadership."[56] While Passmore wrote about the Croix de Feu, it is a statement that could be applied to all the leagues examined here. All the leagues and leaders called upon the language and ideas of the social world as they formulated league ideology. Areas that may be considered purely social (and by extension more feminine than masculine) were, indeed, deeply political. Because of this, there were often contradictions within league rhetoric (and action) on women and women's work, family, and gender. Even as women's social work might be rationalized as apolitical and maternal work, certainly, as Passmore argues, "the unintended consequence of the contra-dictions in the movement's discourses was that female activists were able, within the limits represented by their own relative lack of power resources, to invest the women's sections with their own purposes."[57] Beyond that, in many groups women took on positions of leadership and power, which helped shape league ideology and practice.

French fascist ideology positioned women as the moral force of the nation. Women's "outsider" status in French politics and society was often what lent them legitimacy as the troops of national and moral regeneration. The leagues rejected the separation of the domestic and private spheres and in that way they forcefully allied the salvation of France with the salvation of the French family. Women would and could be the heroic saviors of both the nation and the family as within fascist ideology they were one and the same. Gender ideology—men and women as real or imagined—was deeply imbricated in the work of French fascism. Women's social, moral, economic, and reproductive abilities were em-phasized by the leagues, but women's work in French fascism also included don-ning blue shirts and giving the fascist salute, parading, and preparing physically for the battle against the forces of the Third Republic—taking on a role that men had not successfully played. Men, in turn, would be called upon to embrace the

importance of their familial roles. And both sexes would march in the streets in the name of *la grande famille* and *la patrie*.

Notes

1. *Le Nouveau Siècle*, 19 June 1926.

2. Roger Griffin, *The Nature of Fascism* (London, 1993); Michael Mann, *Fascists* (Cambridge, 2004); George Mosse, *The Fascist Revolution: Toward a General Theory of Fascism* (New York, 2000); Stanley G. Payne, *A History of Fascism, 1914–1945* (Madison, 1995); Robert Paxton, *The Anatomy of Fascism* (New York, 2004); Robert Soucy, *French Fascism: The First Wave, 1924–1933* (New Haven, 1986), and *French Fascism: The Second Wave, 1933–1939* (New Haven, 1995); Zeev Sternhell, *The Birth of Fascist Ideology* (Princeton, 1994), and *Neither Right Nor Left* (Berkeley, 1986); Michel Winock, *Histoire de l'extrême droite en France* (Paris, 1993), and *Nationalism, Anti-Semitism, and Fascism in France* (Stanford, 1998) all consider fascism, in France and beyond, as nearly exclusively male. In addition to Victoria de Grazia, *How Fascism Ruled Women, Italy 1922–1945* (Berkeley, 1992), and Claudia Koonz, *Mothers in the Fatherland* (New York, 1987), some works on France, and beyond, give attention to women and gender. See Caroline Campbell, "Building a Movement, Dismantling the Republic: Women, Gender, and Political Extremism in the Croix de Feu/Parti Social Français, 1927–1940," *French Historical Studies* 35, no. 4 (2012): 691–726; Martin Durham, *Women and Fascism* (London, 1998); Melanie Hawthorne and Richard Golsan, eds., *Gender and Fascism in Modern France* (Hanover, 1997), which focuses on culture; Samuel Kalman, *The Extreme Right in Interwar France: The Faisceau and the Croix de Feu* (Hampshire and Burlington, 2008); Cheryl Koos, "Fascism, Fatherhood and the Family in Interwar France: The Case of Antoine Rédier and the Légion," *Journal of Family History* 24, no. 3 (1999): 317–329; Kevin Passmore, ed., *Women, Gender, and Fascism in Europe, 1919–45* (Manchester, 2003); and Daniella Sarnoff, "Interwar Fascism and the Franchise: Women's Suffrage and the *Ligues*," *Historical Reflections* 34, no. 2 (2008): 112–133, and "Domesticating Fascism," in *Women of the Right*, ed. Kathleen M. Blee and Sandra McGee Deutsch (University Park, 2012), 163–176.

3. AN F7/13232, Statuts of Jeunesses patriotes, attached to police report, 1925.

4. Mary Louise Roberts, *Civilization Without Sexes: Reconstructing Gender in Postwar France* (Chicago, 1994); Kristen Stromberg Childers, *Fathers, Families and the State in France, 1914–1945* (Ithaca, 2003); Judith Surkis, *Sexing the Citizen: Morality and Masculinity in France, 1870–1920* (Ithaca, 2006).

5. According to Pierre Milza in "L'Ultra-droite des années trente," in *Histoire de l'extrême droite en France*, ed. Michel Winock (Paris, 1993), 164, the Jeunesses patriotes had 100,000 members by 1934. According to Gisèle and Serge Berstein in *Dictionnaire historique de la France contemporaine* (Paris, 1995), 449, the Jeunesses patriotes had a membership of 300,000 in 1929.

6. AN/F7 13233, Prefecture de Police à Ministère de L'Interieur, "Réunion organisée par les sections des Jeunesses Patriotes du 8eme arrondt," 25 June 1925.

7. AN/F7 13232, "Reglement pour l'organisation des Jeunesses patriotes section féminine," attached to police memo, 15 January 1926.

8. AN/F7 13232, "Reglement pour l'organisation des Jeunesses patriotes section féminine," attached to Police memo, 15 January 1926; *Le National*, 17 February 1934.

9. ANF7/13235, Prefet des Alpes-Maritimes à M. Le President du Conseil, Ministre de l'Interieur, 23 November 1929.

10. AN F7/13233, clipping of *L'Echo de Paris*, "Le Congrès de Jeunesses patriotes," 21 November 1926, and police report, 21 November 1926.

11. AN F7/13235, "Les Jeunesses patriotes vers la rénovation française," n.d.

12. AN F7/13232, JP "Modèles de discours," 24 February 1928.

13. Ibid.

14. AN F7 13232, report, Paris, 10 December 1929.

15. AN F7/13208, tract attached to police report, Paris, 19 November 1925.

16. AN F7/13208, Police to Ministry of Interior, Directeur of General Security, 28 January 1926.

17. AN F7/13209, "Rapport du Comissariat special Wagner, sur une reunion privé tenue par le Faisceau, Metz, 16 April 1926."

18. AN F7/13209, Le Commissaire spécial à Monsieur le Directeur de la Sûreté Générale, Bordeaux, 21 January 1926.

19. See for example AN F7/13210, police memos dated 18 November and 20 September 1926.

20. AN F7/13212, copy of Faisceau distribution attached to police report, Bordeaux, 8 March 1928.

21. See Gisèle and Serge Berstein, *Dictionnaire historique de la France contemporaine* (Paris, 1995), 209.

22. AN 451 AP 87 [Papiers La Rocque], "Oeuvres sociales Croix de Feu," n.d.

23. Ibid.

24. AN 451 AP 87, note, 8 July 1935. Also, 451 AP 82, copy of illustrated supplement of *Le Flambeau*, May 1936.

25. Mary Jean Green, "Gender, Fascism and the Croix de Feu: the Women's Pages of *Le Flambeau*," *French Cultural Studies* 8, no. 23 (1997): 229–239. Robert Soucy further acknowledges the political purposes of female work that was purported to have purely charitable motivations. Soucy, *French Fascism: The Second Wave, 1933–1939*, 110–111.

26. Charles Vallin, "Aux femmes du Parti social français," Conférence faite aux déléguées des Groupes d'Action sociale du P.S.F. (Région Parisienne), 28 July 1937.

27. Jennifer Waelti-Walters, *Feminist Novelists of the Belle-Epoque* (Bloomington, 1990), 186.

28. *Le Flambeau*, 16 March 1935.

29. Charles Vallin, "Aux femmes du Parti social français."

30. Other historians who have studied the membership of these groups derive the number from the police estimate of 180,000 members, with 80,000 in Paris (Robert Soucy) to 10,000, with 4000 to 5000 active militants (Pierre Milza). A breakdown of the numbers, and connected historians is available in Soucy's *French Fascism: The Second Wave, 1933–1939*, 61.

31. AN F7/13239, report, 4 November 1934.

32. AN F7/13239, report, 20 September 1934.

33. AN F7/13238, police reports from Prefecture of Moselle, 15 June 1934 and 9 May 1934, and Prefecture of Police report, Paris, 6 February 1934.

34. *La Solidarité française-Problèmes actuels*, October 1935.

35. "Les Milice de la Solidarité française," Paris, n.d.

36. *Le Franciste*, 9 June 1935.

37. *La Solidarité française*, 20 February 1938.

38. *La Solidarité française*, 13 and 20 October 1934.

39. *Le Nouveau Siècle*, 19 June 1926.

40. Ibid.

41. AN F7/13232, statuts of Jeunesses patriotes, attached to police report, dated 1925.

42. Ibid.

43. AN F7/13232, "Programme de Jeunesse patriotes-Politique sociale-1929," attached to police report of 22 April 1929.

44. AN F7/13235, Directeur de Police d'état (Nice) à Monsieur le Secrétaire Général de la Sûreté Générale, 22 February 1932.

45. AN F7/13232, "Le Suffrage familial," n.d.

46. AN F7/13233, pamphlet of La Légion and Jeunesses patriotes, n.d. (probably 1925).

47. AN F7/13233, pamphlet of La Légion and Jeunesses patriotes, n.d. (probably 1925).

48. AN F7/13232, "Le Suffrage familial," n.d.

49. *Le Franciste*, 19 January 1936.

50. Paul Guiraud, *Idées premières de la prochaine Révolution Française* (Paris, n.d.).

51. Marcel Bucard, *Du Sang de leurs mains* (Paris, 1938).

52. Ibid.

53. Lt. Colonel de la Rocque, *Service public* (Paris, 1934), 113.

54. Ibid., 114.

55. Ibid., 114.

56. Kevin Passmore, "'Planting the Tricolor in the Citadels of Communism': Women's Social Action in the Croix de Feu," *Journal of Modern History* 71, no. 4 (1999): 825.

57. Passmore, "Planting the Tricolor in the Citadels of Communism," 828.

.

PART III

INTELLECTUAL AND CULTURAL TRENDS

CHAPTER 9

"OUR BODY DOESN'T HAVE TO BE UGLY"

Physical Culture, Gender, and Racial Rejuvenation in the Croix de Feu / Parti social français

Caroline Campbell

"Bodily ugliness is often due to negligence.… Our body doesn't have to be ugly if we have the will to correct the imperfections."—Gaëtan Maire, CF/PSF physical culture theorist

In the aftermath of the extraordinary destruction caused by the Great War, many Europeans were faced with mourning the dead and healing millions of bodies damaged by physical and psychological trauma. In France, an unprecedented influx of immigrants from Europe and the colonies added a new dimension to debates over how best to regenerate bodies comprising what many referred to as the "French race." Women and men of the extreme Right were key players in polemical discussions over racial rejuvenation and national strength as supporters of extremist groups formed one of the most influential political blocs of the interwar period. Of them, the Croix de Feu (CF) and its successor, the Parti social français (PSF), mobilized women and men at rates that not only made it the largest political movement in French history but enabled it to galvanize anti-democratic forces that had long characterized French political culture.[1] This chapter explores why CF/PSF militants believed that transforming French physical culture was a crucial component of national rejuvenation and how the process of embodiment developed along gendered and racial lines.[2] In its efforts to transform French physical culture, or conceptions of how the bodies of women and men should

look, the best way to transform those bodies, and the implication of bodily health on national strength, the CF/PSF promoted an inconsistent yet subversive gender ideology. By developing an array of programs, the CF/PSF provided multiple opportunities for women while it solidified existing racial hierarchies by conflating ideal beauty with whiteness.

Throughout the 1930s, the CF/PSF developed a new brand of social politics to contest the Republic's developing social model.[3] Combining social and political reform, racial rejuvenation was at the heart the CF/PSF social politics, which was based upon its militants' ultra-nationalistic vision of a France comprised not of individuals but as an organic whole. In this vein, ultranationalists believed that weak, flabby, or ugly bodies threatened the nation's fate at the precise moment when its strength was critical to fight the threats of Nazism, Stalinism, anti-colonialism, and internal political division. CF/PSF leaders argued that republican politicians underestimated the urgent need for racial rejuvenation and that the state lacked the capability to mobilize large numbers of people. They accurately claimed that the CF/PSF possessed the organizational structures necessary for mass mobilization; by the late 1930s, it had one million members, a third of whom were women.[4]

CF/PSF militants joined many across the political spectrum who believed that vibrant bodies, racial regeneration, and national rejuvenation were interconnected.[5] As a Communist-affiliated sporting society explained: "We don't want the race to degenerate. We want a strong and healthy youth"; the Popular Front asserted that the practice of sports should "be considered as one of the elements of the safeguarding of the race."[6] Women were central to debates over racial rejuvenation although attitudes toward bodily improvement were framed in stereotypical terms. State-run and Catholic physical education societies designed programs for women that essentialized their bodies by viewing them as weak and best suited for childbirth.[7] The CF/PSF, however, had a distinct approach to physical culture. As an extreme-Right movement, we might expect that its militants sought to limit women to domestic duties or produce offspring for the good of the race. However, pronatalist influences, so powerful during the interwar period, were not pervasive in the movement's physical education program. While the CF/PSF embraced the status quo with regard to men's physical education, conflating masculinity with action, self-control, competition, and struggle, its approach to women's physical education broke new ground in several important ways. CF/PSF militants were inconsistent in their rhetoric, yet its theoreticians understood that gender was culturally specific and based upon social norms. This attitude shaped their organization of a physical education program that offered remarkable opportunities to women, including vigorous training to increase circulation, heart rate, and strength, and engagement in competitive team sports like basketball and soccer. However, CF/PSF militants' efforts to improve health emphasized perfection and the ideal human form, which not only reflected the

influences of eugenics and social Darwinian conceptions of hierarchy, but played a key role in contributing to a rightward shift in French political culture during the 1930s.

Physiology, Anthropology, and the CF/PSF Approach to Transforming French Physical Culture

France's defeat in the Franco-Prussian war in 1871 and a growing pan-European interest in physical culture were two factors that drove the creation of various gymnastic and sporting societies in the early Third Republic.[8] Indeed, the new Republic faced many challenges after shock of defeat and the violence of the Commune, which civic leaders met by creating a series of associations that emphasized physical challenge and sacrifice as they prepared young men to become citizen-soldiers.[9] The broadening of conscription laws in the 1880s helped bring about the integration of physical education into the curriculum of schools and the concomitant growth of physical education groups outside of schools.[10] While the first privately sponsored French sporting clubs were aimed at the bourgeoisie, Catholic parishes eventually created clubs for the needy in an attempt to recover the influence they lost after being removed from public education in 1905; the Socialist Party developed its own sporting association in 1908 for members and opened it to all French men in 1911.[11] By the interwar period, as many as four million women and men from all classes had joined various sporting associations and virtually all political groups either had their own physical education programs or supported affiliated societies. In this context, it was no surprise that many social commentators had an opinion on the state of French bodies.

Eradicating Ugliness and Conceptualizing Race

"We are odiously ugly!" Doctor Jean Edward Ruffier proclaimed in 1914, arguing that it was this supposed ugliness that embodied a weakened nation and the social body's decent into decadence.[12] Paris, he bemoaned, while at one time renowned for its elegance and beauty, had become filled with "ridiculous stomachs, flushed jowls, rounded backs, pale faces, sloping shoulders, and hunched chests."[13] Ruffier was a leading physical culture advocate who would come to influence CF/PSF technicians in developing the movement's physical education program, including the man who formulated its conceptual basis, Gaëtan Maire. Like Ruffier, Maire believed that French society was plagued by ugliness, which for him revealed one's true character. "Bodily ugliness is often due to negligence. ... Our body doesn't have to be ugly if we have the will to correct the imperfections. Not to devote oneself to these efforts is the mark of a great weakness of character," he opined.[14] This sentiment underpinned the CF/PSF's entire approach to remaking

France; will was an essential component of character, and for France to regenerate itself, it needed women and men of strong morals. Indeed, ugliness symbolized laziness and was evidence of a significant threat facing the French nation, that of racial degeneration. Maire explained it this way: "Physical degeneration is the defect of civilized people who neglect the culture of the body."[15]

Conflating the state of civilization with race thinking was pervasive in the CF/PSF, as many militants believed that they were a part of the so-called French race. There was, however, a lack of coherence in conceptualizing the nation's racial origins and traits. In the 1934 work that laid the groundwork for much of the CF's ideology, *Service Public*, the movement's leader, Colonel François de La Rocque, proposed a conception of race that enabled some militants to claim that the movement was inclusive because he rejected the nation's biological or linguistic basis. As La Rocque maintained: "The French race is a magnificent synthesis, disciplined, cultivated, and well-balanced. It forms a whole; no linguistic, no analysis of heredity can prevail against this fact."[16] In describing these traits, La Rocque conceived of cultural aspects to race, which in turn, spurred some militants to insist upon more exclusionary concepts of race, including the idea that race produced nation. The CF/PSF's chief physical culture theorist in the Rhone, M. Thevenet, for instance, understood race in rigid terms, contending, "We must make men and women solid and robust. We must give to France this physically strong race, which had been until now, distinctively French and through the centuries and great social rifts made our *patrie* what it is."[17] Participation in the CF/PSF exacerbated militants' tendencies to think in racial terms and was a key reason why their approach to physical culture was imbued with social Darwinism and eugenics. Ideologues like Maire and Thevenet were convinced that transforming physical culture held the key to strengthening the French nation. As Maire put it, "the physical perfecting of a race is indispensable to maintain [its place] in the first rank of great modern nations."[18]

In its drive toward racial perfection, the CF/PSF perpetuated a hierarchical conception of race and nation, which its physical culture theorists believed could be achieved through positive eugenics. Since an individual could be improved according to her or his environment and personal desire for change, one's life was neither genetically fixed nor predetermined. For Maire, if one man was bigger than another, it may have been "because he received more favorable genes, but also, perhaps because he benefited from better food when he was a child."[19] Indeed, Maire worked within the Lamarckian tradition of eugenics that emphasized milieu, as he stated bluntly: "Positive eugenics presents the best means of human perfection."[20] A key component of positive eugenics was the rejection of biological theories positing that class was based upon genetic makeup in favor of the stance that education could enable an individual to seek self-improvement. On this point, there was strong agreement among CF/PSF militants that the human body could be transformed regardless of ethnic, religious, or class background. In

seeking to achieve perfection, Thevenet explained it this way: "We must make men of healthy body and spirit without the consideration of blood, money, religion, or [political] party."[21]

The CF/PSF's emphasis on perfection was rife with racist undertones that conflated civilization with whiteness and primitiveness with blackness, which derived in part from how militants developed the physical education program's curriculum. They instituted the "Natural Method" techniques of France's leading expert on physical education, Georges Hébert, whose *Hébertist* societies dominated interwar programs across the political spectrum. During his time as an admiral stationed in French West Africa, Hébert was struck by what he believed was the physical prowess of French colonial subjects. Based upon his observations, Hébert contended that Europeans, or *les civilisés* as he called them, could learn from their counterparts, *les primitifs*. Hébert was one of many who believed that a negative effect of modernity was a sedentary and weak population incapable of defending itself. Europeans had simply forgotten the types of movements that were natural to the human body. Hébert was convinced that physical work could reconfigure one's basic nature, and, based upon his observations of *les primitifs*, suggested that certain movements came "naturally" to humans: walking, running, jumping, climbing, lifting, throwing, and self-defense. In explaining the rationale for the CF/PSF's use of Hébert's "Natural Method" exercises, Thevenet lamented, "these movements have been more or less abandoned by our civilization" and drew the following distinction between "primitive" Africans and "civilized" Europeans: "The primitive acts not methodically, but by instinct and need ... his living conditions require him to become strong. To develop the civilized, it is necessary to replace his instinct and need with that of steady, regular work, based ... upon his strength and general state."[22] In this way, whiteness was self-evident for most CF/PSF militants.[23] Their thinking featured racialized, binary views of primitiveness and civilization, which formed key components of the movement's exclusionary conception of Frenchness.

Beauty and Human Nature: The Influences of Jean Edward Ruffier and Margaret Mead

Like most interwar efforts to transform French physical culture, the CF/PSF's ideological approach to reform and the programs that its militants developed were not only coded with whiteness but also deeply gendered. While in some ways the CF/PSF perpetuated narrow gender stereotypes it was arguably progressive in how its theorists used the ideas of cutting-edge scholarship to break new ground with regard to physical education. Most notably, the movement rejected the rigid view of gender that was common during the interwar years and championed by the Vichy regime in terms of ideology and policy. Encapsulating the regime's rigid view of gender, the newspaper published by the elite Vichy-era school at Uriage

explained: "Woman is built not to fight—which is the privilege of man—but to procreate; nature set the boundaries of her physical possibilities, and it would be dangerous to transgress them."[24]

In contrast, CF/PSF theorists sought to transgress the status quo in terms of physical education and applied the theories of Dr. Ruffier to do so. Ruffier's studies of the physiology of muscle provided the pedagological approach for the movement's programs. An adherent of cell theory, Ruffier examined organisms at the cellular level and determined that healthy muscle depended upon movement. In his study of the amoeba, for example, Ruffier documented how it reacted to exterior stimulus such as movement, heat, or contact with another body by contracting itself, making secretions, or dividing; these reactions were nonexistent in amoebas that did not move, or what Ruffier called "inert" amoebas.[25] Ruffier argued that since the human body was an "agglomeration" of microscopic cells, human cells needed to move lest they fall into an "inert" state.[26] Informed by Ruffier's findings, Maire stated that if one were to render "the most beautiful muscle possible" immobile for two or three months, it would become soft, deprived of energy, and eventually "disintegrate."[27] Ruffier's contention that cells instinctively wanted to return to their nascent state spurred CF/PSF leaders to create a program in which movement and bodily health were intertwined. This physiological understanding of muscle formed a crucial component of the movement's program that was gender neutral, in the sense that all muscle was made from the same tissue and thus operated in a consistent manner regardless of sex. As we shall see, because Maire viewed movement as the basic way to transform muscle, he and his colleagues implemented many gender-neutral exercises that emphasized strength, coordination, and flexibility, which they believed would form a harmonious, healthy, and attractive body.

A second important influence on CF/PSF physical culture theorists was the anthropologist Margaret Mead. They were fascinated by Mead's studies demonstrating that the behavior of men and women differed according to cultural and social norms. Based upon her observation of peoples living in the Sepik region of Papua New Guinea, the Arapesh, the Mundugumor (Biwat), and Tchambuli (Chambri), Mead concluded that temperament was not fixed but that women's and men's "nature" differed according to place and time. While Mead claimed that both sexes of the Arapesh were gentle and cooperative, traits she noted were consistent with Western conceptions of femininity, she characterized the temperaments of both sexes of the Mundugumor as aggressive and violent, which, she stated, the West viewed as masculine traits; in the Tchambuli, however, Mead reported that women were dominant and emotionally distant whereas men were submissive and emotional.[28] Turning gender stereotypes on their head, these ideas underpinned key portions of the CF/PSF's program. "According to the American Mead," Maire explained, "you [can] find women who have masculine behavior and men with feminine behavior."[29]

This supposed proof that sexual difference was not innate was critical to the CF/PSF's distinct approach to physical culture. Throughout the Third Republic, numerous social commentators had defined female bodies as weak and female minds as inferior to those of men.[30] However, Mead's ideas provided Maire with a language to contest this misogyny. "Weakness is not necessarily an attribute of women [and] biological differences between the sexes do not equate to an inequality in intelligence," Maire insisted, leading him to ask:

> What [characteristics are] innate and what are acquired? What is hereditary and what is circumstantial? When one compares the man with the woman, we must remember that it is not a question of one of two natural and biological types, but two artificial and social types of which the divergence … lies in educational factors. From birth, society molds individual conformity to a certain conventional ideal.[31]

As a progressive feminist, Mead would have been concerned that right-wing militants used her ideas for their own ends, but for theorists like Maire, Mead's view of human nature reinforced the notion that it was possible to remake French temperaments.

While Ruffier's attention to movement and muscle and Mead's findings that gender norms were culturally specific provided the basis for CF/PSF theorists to create a physical education programs that afforded new opportunities for women, they applied Mead's ideas selectively. Most significantly, Maire perpetuated a long-standing focus on physical attractiveness and beauty, explaining:

> Woman is naturally graceful; she has the instinct of elegance but the blossoming of her beauty cannot be complete if she remains a stranger to all physical exercise. Slenderness and weakness are not necessarily attributes of the woman.… Without physical education, the woman has only an ephemeral beauty; she oscillates between excessive scrawniness and portliness but never possesses the pure and well defined form that only a solid skeletal structure and a harmonious muscular development can provide in setting the contours of the body.[32]

Grace, elegance, and harmony were hallmarks of interwar discourses on ideal femininity. The idea that women could change (i.e., strengthen) their bodies, however, reflected the intersection between physical education, will, and character that was pervasive in the movement. Maire warned, "All women must have the spirit of the cult of beauty.… One can momentarily give the appearance of beauty to a feeble body by deceptive means, but the woman who doesn't do physical education deprives herself of the only elements capable of maintaining her vigor and beauty."[33]

This emphasis on pursuing beauty was not unique to the CF/PSF, as a woman's body and her level of attractiveness were subject to judgment, debate, and scorn for groups across the political spectrum. The Communist women's youth group,

for instance, instructed young women how to apply makeup and achieve the perfect tan in order to become "pretty."[34] Maire, however, was hostile to what he called the façade of beauty. Underlining the vital necessity of willpower, Maire insisted, "by methodical exercise, each woman can become a healthy being of strength and beauty because congenital ugliness is not irreparable."[35] On one hand, Maire perpetuated the insidious belief that ugliness and weakness marked a deficiency in one's character. On the other, in emphasizing health, Maire created remarkable opportunities that spurred young women to flock to the movement's physical education programs.

Men too had a responsibility to work toward perfection as CF/PSF physical education theorists sought to enhance their so-called active nature. Perpetuating commonly held stereotypes that conflated masculinity with activity and femininity with passivity, Maire declared: "Man is generally more of a creator, more of a builder, and more adept at scientific studies, whereas the woman is more intuitive and more artistic. … Man is more aggressive, more proud, more nomadic, whereas woman is softer, more sensitive, more shy, more fine, more flirty."[36] In this sense, the movement affirmed the status quo by seeking to prepare young men for action. Consequently, its programs channeled youthful masculine energy into sport. Maire framed the intersections between the body, sport, and racial regeneration this way: "The body, toned and fortified at the end of puberty, longs for performance. … It's the period of Sport, of individual sport, of team sport, the sport of combat. … Sport is essential for the formation of an energetic and robust race."[37] The competitive and team-oriented aspects of sport would prepare young men for a variety challenges. According to Maire, boys and young men needed to be ready to "struggle against a definite element: a distance, a duration, an obstacle, a material difficulty, a danger, an enemy."[38] A negative consequence of this emphasis on competition and struggle was uncontrolled aggression, which Maire believed could be ameliorated by developing a sense of camaraderie, teamwork, altruism, and discipline among male youth. For Maire, these traits were crucial in reinforcing the social bonds that CF/PSF ideologues sought to foster.[39]

The CF/PSF Program to Transform French Physical Culture

It was incumbent upon CF/PSF militants to implement an effective physical education program for these ambitious ideas to have their maximum impact. The organizer of the movement's social program, Antoinette de Préval, explained the massive endeavor in a letter to a friend: "You know the evolution of ideas. You know the subtlety, the adaptation required by the modern foundations upon which we embark. Everything that reminds us of the most respected systems of the past must disappear: in a word, paternalism is totally erased."[40] In this way, Préval articulated how the movement's militants sought to undermine the

foundations of French society by emphasizing their vision of racial and gendered rejuvenation. Structural organization, effective leadership, and grassroots mobilization were three of the key factors in how the CF/PSF galvanized thousands to transform French physical culture. While France's largest women's physical education federation claimed 25,000 members in 565 affiliates and Communists mobilized roughly 30,000 youth, CF/PSF militants had created 2800 physical education societies serving 64,000 youth across Greater France, which included 1100 basketball and 750 soccer teams by 1939, making its program one of the most dynamic of the interwar period.[41]

The Women's Section and the Center for Physical Education, 1934–1936

The first step in the CF's mission of transforming French society was Préval's creation of the league's Women's Section in early 1934. By 1935, the Women's Section had created hundreds of local sections across France, most of which comprised hundreds of members, and created multiple social centers, health clinics, summer camps, and welfare services. Emphasizing the interplay between centralized leadership and grassroots action, Préval explained that her task was "the centralization of the most important and multiple works," while she would "avoid all detailed questions and let them be sorted out on location by those in charge."[42] The first step in developing a physical education program was taken when Women's Section officials created a Center for Physical Education in 1935. Préval appointed Maire as one of the Center's directors and he worked with the Women's Section to create physical education centers for youth and adults across metropolitan France and the Maghreb. In less than two years, the CF had recruited 1200 children to its Parisian centers (table 1), had opened ten provincial centers, and was in the process of creating centers in twenty more.[43]

CF/PSF militants viewed their physical education centers as the lynchpin in transforming the nation's physical culture. As the leadership repeatedly stated, physical education focused on not only physical but moral and intellectual development. Each center was around 150 square meters in size, the staff was approved by Women's Section headquarters, and the students, separated by gender, took daily lessons.[44] The physical layout of the centers reflected Women's Section

Table 1. CF Parisian Physical Education Centers, 1936

Center	Male Supervisors	Female Supervisors	Boys Aged 7–13	Girls Aged 7–13	Boys Aged 14–16	Total Children
Rosalie	6	3	100	105	110	310
Reuilly	5	3	175	160	110	445
Madrid (Perronet)	5	3	125	75	75	275
Colombes	3	0	60	60	50	170

priorities with regard to physical education, as they included space to perform exercises and a *foyer-bibliothèque* for the program's intellectual component. The Women's Section organized regular activities, talks on the French colonies, literature, and sports, a monthly film series, and annual *fêtes* celebrating gymnastics, water sports, and the empire.[45] This eclectic range of activities demonstrated that the Women's Section sought make the centers fun in order to socialize youth into the movement's conception of what constituted the best aspects of French civilization.

The Scope Broadens: The PSF and its Associations

The Popular Front dissolved the CF in June 1936 and its leaders responded by reconstituting the league as the PSF. Préval and La Rocque oversaw the creation of four affiliated organizations that collectively sought to remake French culture and society through physical education, public health, welfare, and youth development. The PSF aimed their services at their own supporters and working-class populations that tended to support the Popular Front, whom the PSF sought to "pacify" by promoting its values. The four "new" PSF organizations were simply expansions of those initiated by the Women's Section. The Women's Section was renamed Social Action and continued to offer social assistance. Youth formation continued with social centers and summer camps, which were organized by a new association officially led by Préval, Travail et Loisirs. L'Association Médico-Sociale Jeanne d'Arc (AMSJA) operated health clinics, insurance aid programs, a convalescent home, and visiting nurses, and La Société de préparation et d'éducation sportive (SPES) organized the movement's physical education program. Additionally, two bureaus were created to streamline the formation of ideology and facilitate the coordination of services. The Social Studies Bureau, which La Rocque called "the organizer and controller of the sum of our action," was attached to his cabinet and led by Jeanne Garrigoux.[46] As La Rocque's expert on social policy, Garrigoux wielded a great deal of authority over many PSF men. For instance, in implementing the movement's social programs, the male heads of PSF sections, committees, and federations reported to the Bureau. Moreover, the Bureau supervised home visits made by social workers and nurses and oversaw inspections made by women and men at social and physical education centers, summer camps, and health facilities.[47] The offshoot of the Social Studies Bureau, the SPES Study Bureau, designed the SPES program. It was this body that Maire headed as he formulated the movement's physical culture program, although the entire SPES program required the approval of Garrigoux, Préval, and La Rocque.

The PSF's efforts to regenerate French physical culture required the collective action of each of these organizations, which brought women and men together in organizing services, although it was usually Préval who had the final word in deci-

sion making. Indeed, Préval explained to a friend that she "had the honor of co-ordinating the efforts of all the past social works."[48] As the only leader who sat on the administrative council of all four organizations, Préval worked closely with Maire to formulate the SPES curriculum, appoint staff, and organize centers.[49] The coordination of services between SPES and Social Action in metropolitan France and North Africa was to be "constant and tight," according to one circular, which warned, "If we neglect this essential coordination, we run the risks of a competition in recruitment, an overloading in the employment of children's time, a dispersion in effort, and useless expenses."[50] To this end, the leaders and staff of all four groups shared membership forms and medical files, which included notes on each child's medical history, temperament, educational level, disciplinary problems, and family members for recruiting purposes.[51]

In organizing their social programs, CF/PSF militants worked with SPES to determine the level of fitness of youth in their programs and the steps necessary for them reach certain standards of health. For instance, the director of the Travail et Loisirs social center at Saint Ouen, Madame Regnault, worked with center's head nurse, Madame Horaist, to implement the SPES curriculum. One of Horaist's primary responsibilities was to create a "strength index" file on each child by using thorough medical exams to calculate each individual's fitness level; based upon the findings, she placed each child into a group labeled along social Darwinian lines as "strong, medium, or weak."[52] Staff supervisors cataloged in three-month intervals changes in each child's height and weight and charted the increases in strength of their neck, shoulders, arms, abdomen, and thighs.[53] At Saint Ouen, Regnault's children, Jacqueline and Claude, were two of roughly twenty supervisors who monitored the groups and coached the boys' and girls' basketball and soccer teams, which were open to all youth deemed healthy enough to compete in team sports.[54] The supervisors were of vital importance due to their interactions with youth, and for this reason, Maire, Préval, and other leaders spent a great deal of time looking for qualified young women and men who embodied CF/PSF values. In order to be approved by the Social Studies Bureau, the supervisors had to be French citizens, were required to pass physical exams, and ideally were under thirty years of age.[55] Once approved, Préval and others at the Bureau assigned the supervisors wherever they were needed.

The supervisors were not only intermediaries in socializing youth into CF/PSF values but were also expected to be youthful symbols of ideal Frenchness. The SPES training manual dictated: "It is vital that the supervisors always be in good muscular shape and be trained perfectly in the practice of the exercises that they require of their students."[56] In addition to being fit and having perfect knowledge of SPES exercises, the supervisors were to exude a certain attitude as well. As the training manual explained: "The supervisors must be examples and present themselves in front of their students in a manner that is always impeccable; they must demonstrate proof of absolute mastery and calm authority, and never allow

themselves to become angry or use hurtful language."[57] In this way, the supervisors embodied the CF/PSF and represented the best of French civilization.

While the exercise curriculum that the SPES study bureau created was based primarily on *Hébertist* exercises, SPES leaders adapted Hébert's natural method to suit their own ideology and clientele. Since space was at a premium, SPES, like other interwar physical education societies, altered the exercises to the limited space available in their centers and summer camps and ensured that both sexes engaged in the exercises. As an SPES instructional booklet noted: "The same type of lesson applies to everyone: men, women, or children."[58] There were around one hundred exercises that comprised the curriculum, all of which required students to combine strength, flexibility, balance, and coordination to strengthen muscles, coordinate breathing, and reduce flab. The SPES developed a diverse range of exercises based on muscle movement and contraction that ranged from simple ones, like push-ups and sit-ups, to the complex, like the "walk like a duck" exercise, which required students to squat, place their hands on their knees or haunches, and move by alternating one foot in front of the other, straightening and bending their legs while gently moving their torso in a rotating motion.[59]

One of the most important goals of these exercises was to increase participants' circulation and heart rate, which in the case of women, differed notably from other physical education programs. Women's magazines and medical studies, for instance, emphasized the necessity of developing the muscles in the pelvic region to prepare girls for childbirth. In contrast, SPES sought to strengthen their entire body to promote stronger organ function and better health.[60] Girls from the ages of seven to thirteen focused on gymnastics and games, strengthening the muscles along the entire back and thoracic cavity, with secondary emphasis on the arms, legs, and neck. Girls from thirteen to sixteen continued to develop these muscles and added their abdominal ones to coordinate strength with flexibility through walking, running, jumping, and other exercises. Young women over sixteen not only continued to develop these muscles but could join basketball and soccer teams as well, which was unusual because many women's physical education programs envisioned women as docile and thus deemphasized competition characterized by physical contact.[61] For example, the Communists promoted gymnastics and swimming and women's health guides encouraged them to play tennis and racquetball.[62] SPES leaders created the same expectations for girls and boys with regards to sprinting, medium-range running, long-jumping, and high-jumping abilities, which contested the widely held assumption that women were weak and should to avoid prolonged or intense physical activity (table 2).[63]

The SPES was not completely egalitarian, however, as its program followed the *Hébertist* belief that the female upper body was weak, which led it to exclude girls from climbing and lifting exercises.[64] Despite this restriction from the full range of exercises, the SPES offered girls many opportunities for physical education, from participating in team sports to individual exercises, some of which

Table 2. SPES Performance Expectations for Girls and Boys

		SPES Expectations (ranges vary according to age)	
Activity	Age Range	Girls	Boys
Sprinting	8–18	11–17 seconds depending on age for a 50-meter race; 100 for those 16–18	Same as girls
Medium-Distance Running	8–18	1.30–1.50 minutes depending on age for a 300-meter race; 500 for those 16–18	Same as girls
Running Long Jump	8–18	2.25–3.50 meters depending on age	Same as girls
Standing Jump (straight up in the air)	8–18	.55–.90 meters depending on age	Same as girls
Rope Climbing (with legs)	Boys only beginning at 14	N/A	4.50–5.50 meters
Rope Climbing (without legs)	Boys only beginning at 14	N/A	4–5 meters
Shot-put	Boys only beginning at 14	N/A	4.50–5.50 meters

were rare in a physical culture that conflated onerous physical activities with men's nature.

The CF/PSF's curriculum for men mirrored the one for women, emphasizing games, calisthenics, and gymnastics at earlier ages, then with the onset of puberty, developing balance and strengthening core muscles through the *Hébertist* movements. The third stage, however, differed from the women's program.[65] While women continued to focus on exercises and calisthenics with the option of engaging in team sports, young men from sixteen to twenty were expected to embrace the competitive aspect of sport.[66] In this sense, the end goal of physical education was different for girls and boys. Boys needed to be physically ready for any sort of competitive struggle, which included boxing, rugby, basketball, soccer, and, of course, combat. In this way, the CF/PSF perpetuated the status quo: if a young man happened to dislike sports or competition, not only would his masculinity be in doubt, but he would be considered a liability to the national community.

Once in power, the Vichy government rejected virtually all of the transgressive aspects of the CF/PSF physical education program and embraced only the portion of it that had reflected views of masculinity since the aftermath of the Franco-Prussian war. Criticizing interwar physical education programs that were overly egalitarian in providing opportunities for youth of both sexes, Vichy essentialized female bodies as childbearing vessels and male bodies as inclined to-

ward competition, performance, and risk taking.[67] For this reason, the regime emphasized that physical exercise needed to become distinct at the age of seven or eight, and its Commissariat General for Sports was especially critical of organizations like the SPES whose programs for children did not diverge with the onset of puberty.[68] Moreover, the CF/PSF never made physical education compulsory, unlike Vichy, which created the Chantiers de la jeunesse for all young men twenty years of age to prepare them to become soldiers by building their moral character through hands-on work and physical education.[69] Indeed, the Chantiers embodied Vichy's worldview, which championed the cult of masculine virility and emphasized that female bodies should not be "built" for national service but protected from excessive exertion in order to ready them for child rearing.[70] While the CF/PSF certainly championed the cult of beauty, it did so on a more equitable basis for both women and men that rejected the Chantier's single-minded focus on masculinity.

While inconsistent and not always progressive, the original aspects of the CF/PSF's approach to transforming physical culture were rooted in two factors. The first was the manner in which the movement broke new ground in creating innovative programs for women based on the notion that gender was not a fixed category and that movement was the crucial component to muscle development and bodily health. Second, women like Préval sought to subvert the social order by mobilizing tens of thousands for the movement's ultra-nationalistic project, which promoted will as the key to reshaping national character. Conflating whiteness and Frenchness, CF/PSF physical culture programs were inclusive only for those who were willing or able to conform to the movement's rigid conception of ideal beauty, and yet, individuals who did so found opportunities that they could not find elsewhere. This not only provides one reason why the membership of the CF/PSF exploded during the 1930s, but helps us to understand how and why the conception of French national identity narrowed as the 1930s progressed and became one of the defining aspects of the Vichy regime.

Notes

1. For the argument that the Croix de Feu/PSF was the largest political movement in French history, see Jean-Paul Thomas, "Les Effectifs du Parti Social Français," *Vingtième Siècle* 62 (1999): 61. For its anti-democratic nature, see Sean Kennedy, *Reconciling France Against Democracy: the Croix de Feu and Parti Social Français, 1927–1945* (Montreal, 2007); Samuel Kalman, *The Extreme Right in Interwar France: the Faisceau and the Croix de Feu* (Burlington, 2008).

2. For more on the concept of embodiment, see Kathleen Canning, *Gender History in Practice: Historical Perspectives on Bodies, Class, and Citizenship* (Ithaca, 2006); and Elisa Camiscioli, *Reproducing the French Race: Immigration, Intimacy, and Embodiment in the Early Twentieth Century* (Durham, 2009).

3. On the movement's "new social politics," see Kevin Passmore, "'Planting the Tricolor in the Citadels of Communism': Women's Social Action in the Croix de feu and Parti social français," *Journal of Modern History* 71, no. 4 (1999): 815–851; and Laura Lee Downs, "'Nous plantions les trois couleurs', Action sociale féminine et la recomposition des politiques de la droite française: Le mouvement Croix-de-Feu et le Parti social français, 1934–1947," *Revue d'Histoire Moderne et Contemporaine* 58, no. 3 (2011): 118–163. For the Croix de Feu/PSF's "social turn," see Albert Kéchichian, *Les Croix de Feu à l'âge des fascismes: Travail Famille Patrie, 1927–1936* (Seyssel, 2006). For the republican social model, see Laura Levine Frader, *Breadwinners and Citizens: Gender in the Making of the French Social Model* (Durham, 2008).

4. Jean-Paul Thomas, "Les Droites, Les Femmes et le Mouvement Associatif, 1902–1946," in *Associations et champs politique: la loi de 1901 à l'épreuve du siècle*, ed. Claire Andrieu, Gilles Le Béguec, and Danielle Tartakowsky (Paris, 2001), 524.

5. See for example, Susan B. Whitney, *Mobilizing Youth: Communists and Catholics in Interwar France* (Durham, 2009), 177–179; Joan Tumblety, "The Soccer World Cup of 1938: Politics, Spectacles, and *la Culture Physique* in Interwar France," *French Historical Studies* 31, no. 1 (2008): 81–82; Christopher Forth, *Masculinity in the Modern West: Gender, Civilization and the Body* (New York, 2008); George Mosse, *The Image of Man: the Creation of Modern Masculinity* (Oxford, 1996).

6. Quoted in Whitney, *Mobilizing Youth*, 178; and Tumblety, "The Soccer World Cup of 1938," 93.

7. Mary Lynn Stewart, *For Health and Beauty: Physical Culture for Frenchwomen, 1880s–1930s* (Baltimore, 2001) 1, 147–150, 158–160.

8. Rachel Chrastil, *Organizing for War: France 1870–1914* (Baton Rouge, 2010) 112–113, 125–126; Eugen Weber, "Pierre de Coubertin and the Introduction of Organised Sport in France," *Journal of Contemporary History* 5, no. 2 (1970): 7.

9. Chrastil, *Organizing for War*, 125.

10. Ibid., 113, 119.

11. Eugen Weber, "Gymnastics and Sports in Fin-de-Siècle France: Opium of the Classes," *American Historical Review* 76, no. 1 (1971): 92–93.

12. Jean Edward Ruffier, *Soyons Fort! Manuel de culture physique élémentaire* (Paris, 1914), 3. For more on conceptions of ugliness during the Third Republic, see Rae Beth Gordon, *Dances with Darwin, 1875–1910: Vernacular Modernity in France* (Burlington, 2009), 103–144.

13. Jean Edward Ruffier, *Soyons Fort! Manuel de culture physique élémentaire* (Paris, 1914), 3

14. Le Centre d'accueil et de recherche des Archives nationales, Paris (hereafter CARAN), Fonds La Rocque (hereafter 451AP) carton 153, Med. A. Bleu and Maire, "SPES Education physique féminine technique et programme," n.d.

15. CARAN 451AP 155, Maire speech, "Les SPES et leur programme," October 1938.

16. Colonel François de La Rocque, *Service public* (Paris, 1934), 157.

17. CARAN 451AP 156, Program, Thevenet, "SPES du Rhône: cours de pédagogie à l'usage des Moniteurs d'education physique," n.d.

18. CARAN 451AP 134, Maire speech at the First PSF Social Congress, "Rapport sur les SPES," May 1939.

19. CARAN 451AP 155, Maire presentation, "Biologie élémentaire: l'hérédité, l'influence du milieu," n.d.

20. CARAN 451AP 155, Maire presentation, "Biologie élémentaire: l'eugénique et la sélection humain," n.d.

21. CARAN 451AP 156, Thevenet, SPES program, "SPES du Rhône: cours de pédagogie à l'usage des Moniteurs d'éducation physique," n.d.

22. Ibid.

23. For more on conceptions of whiteness, see Frader, *Breadwinners and Citizens*, 124–125; and "From Muscles to Nerves: Gender, 'Race' and the Body at Work in France, 1919–1939," *International*

Review of Social History 44, supplement 7 (1999): 130; Elisa Camiscioli, *Reproducing the French Race*, 12–13; Tyler Stovall, "National Identity and Shifting Imperial Frontiers: Whiteness and the Exclusion of Colonial Labor after World War I," *Representations* 84, no. 1 (2003): 52–53, 65; Thomas C. Holt, "Marking: Race, Race-making, and the Writing of History," *American Historical Review* 100, no. 1 (1995): 1–20.

24. Francine Muel-Dreyfus, *Vichy and the Eternal Feminine: A Contribution to a Political Sociology of Gender*, trans. Kathleen A. Johnson (Durham, 2001), 294.

25. CARAN 451 AP 155, Maire report, "Principes élémentaires de physiologie, selon le Docteur Ruffier," n.d.

26. Ibid.

27. Ibid.

28. Margaret Mead, *Sex and Temperament in Three Primitive Societies* (New York, 1935).

29. CARAN 451AP 155, Maire presentation, "Biologie élémentaire: differenciation des sexes," n.d.

30. See, for example, Stewart, *For Health and Beauty*, 147, 156; Frader, *Breadwinners and Citizens*, 79, 126.

31. CARAN 451AP 155, Maire presentation, "Biologie élémentaire: différenciation des sexes," n.d.

32. CARAN 451AP 153, Med. A. Bleu and Maire, "SPES éducation physique féminine technique et programme," n.d.

33. Ibid.

34. Whitney, *Mobilizing Youth*, 201.

35. CARAN 451AP 153, Med. A. Bleu and Maire, "SPES éducation physique féminine technique et programme," n.d.

36. CARAN 451AP 155, Maire presentation, "Biologie élémentaire: différenciation des sexes," n.d.

37. CARAN 451AP 156, pamphlet, Maire, "SPES Un programme d'éducation physique," n.d.

38. Ibid.

39. Ibid. For more on the Croix de Feu/PSF's emphasis on team at the expense of the individual, see Kalman, *The Extreme Right in Interwar France*, 176–178.

40. CARAN 451AP 162, letter from Préval to Madame Perrineau, 29 January 1937.

41. Stewart, *For Health and Beauty*, 171; Whitney, *Mobilizing Youth*, 181; CARAN 451AP 189/5, Travail et Loisirs report, "Centres d'éducation physique," June 1939.

42. CARAN 451AP 162, letter from Préval to Madame Perrineau, 26 April 1937.

43. Centre d'histoire de Sciences Po, Paris (hereafter CHSP), Fonds La Rocque (hereafter LR) 6, report, Gaëtan Maire, "Leçons données par semaine dans chaque groupe dans les centres de Paris," 6 June 1936.

44. CHSP LR 39, Brochure, "Le Centre social Paris-Sud"; CARAN 451AP 93, Women's Section Circular, "Centres d'éducation physique avec foyer-bibliothèque," October 1935.

45. CARAN 451AP 93, Women's Section Circular, "Centres d'éducation physique avec foyer-bibliothèque," October 1935.

46. CHSP LR 29, circular from La Rocque to presidents of local committees and sections, 18 March 1937.

47. Ibid.

48. CARAN 451AP 162, letter from Préval to Madame Perrineau, 29 January 1937.

49. CARAN 451AP 174, letter from Maire to Préval, June, 1938.

50. CARAN 451AP 153, SPES statutes, "Qu'est-ce que SPES," n.d (probably late 1936).

51. CARAN 451AP 187, report by M. Danner for M. Le Tanneur, "Compte-rendu de notre entretien avec le Bureau d'études sociales, SPES, et l'Office du tourisme," 14 October 1937.

52. CARAN 451AP 172, form, "Service des examens médico-physiologiques de Travail et Loisirs." For Downs's analysis of how children's level of fitness was used to exclude them from the movement's summer camps, see "Each and Every One of You Must Become a Chef: Toward a Social Politics of Working-Class Childhood on the Extreme Right in 1930s France," *Journal of Modern History* 81, no. 1 (2009): 29–32.

53. CARAN 451AP 172, form, "Service des examens médico-physiologiques de Travail et Loisirs."

54. CARAN 451AP 155, dossier "Cartes de Moniteurs d'éducation physique."

55. CARAN 451AP 153, SPES statutes, "Qu'est-ce que SPES," n.d (probably late 1936); CARAN 451AP 154 *bis*, Maire, "Conditions d'admission, SPES de France, EP: Ecole de Moniteurs," n.d.

56. CARAN 451AP 153, SPES training manual, "Conseils aux Moniteurs et Monitrices," n.d.

57. Ibid.

58. CARAN 451AP 155, SPES Instructional Booklet, "Éducation physique," n.d.

59. Ibid.

60. On developing girls' bodies for childbirth, see Stewart, *For Health and Beauty*, 156–162.

61. CARAN 451AP 153, Med. A. Bleu and Maire, "SPES Éducation physique féminine technique et programme," n.d.

62. Whitney, *Mobilizing Youth*, 200; Stewart, *For Health and Beauty*, 167.

63. CARAN 451AP 155, report, Maire, at the "Réunion des responsables féminines PSF," 8 March 1939; Stewart, *For Health and Beauty*, 168.

64. Ibid.

65. CARAN 451AP 156, pamphlet, Maire, "SPES Un programme d'Éducation physique," n.d.

66. Ibid.

67. Miranda Pollard, *Reign of Virtue: Mobilizing Gender in Vichy France* (Chicago, 1998); Muel-Dreyfus, *Vichy and the Eternal Feminine*, 294.

68. Muel-Dreyfus, *Vichy and the Eternal Feminine*, 294–295.

69. Debbie Lackerstein, *National Regeneration in Vichy France: Ideas and Policies, 1930–1944* (Burlington, 2012), 194.

70. Kristen Stromberg Childers, *Fathers, Families, and the State in France, 1914–1945* (Ithaca, 2003), 113–118; Muel-Dreyfus, *Vichy and the Eternal Feminine*, 251–254; Pollard, *Reign of Virtue*, 86–97.

CHAPTER 10

DEFENDING CHRISTIAN CIVILIZATION

The Evolving Message of the Parti social français, 1936–1939

Sean Kennedy

Writing in *Le Flambeau* in August 1936, Lieutenant-Colonel François de La Rocque, leader of the newly formed Parti social français (PSF), declared that there would be "no national reconciliation if it does not fall within the scope of our traditional civilization," which was "specifically, historically Christian."[1] As leader of the Croix de Feu (CF), La Rocque had long stressed the theme of national reconciliation, the process whereby the French people would reject both the class warfare of the Left and sterile elitism of the traditional Right and turn to his movement, which would ensure the regeneration of France. In the years leading up to the outbreak of the Second World War, the PSF continued to embrace this message but, as La Rocque's words suggest, combined it with an invocation of France as a "Christian civilization." The incorporation of this concept, I argue, sheds light on the evolution of the PSF's doctrine, its views on the crucial question of national identity, and its stance on foreign affairs after 1936.

That La Rocque took his own faith very seriously is well known. He was raised in a religious family—his father had participated in the Catholic organization Justice-Égalité at the turn of the twentieth century—and was influenced by the ideas of Social Catholic thinkers like Frédéric Le Play and René de La Tour du Pin. During his own military service in North Africa, he was inspired by the views of the profoundly Catholic Marshal Lyautey concerning leadership and social pacification, and participated in retreats organized by the soldier-turned-missionary Charles de Foucauld.[2] Moving from these biographical details to as-

sessing the significance of Christian values to the evolution of the CF and PSF, however, has proven far more difficult. Scholars such as René Rémond, Philippe Machefer, Jacques Nobécourt, Albert Kéchichian, and Jean-Paul Thomas all note that Social Catholic values influenced the CF and PSF. While they sometimes concede that these values had authoritarian features, they share the view that the PSF was a non-sectarian party that reached other constituencies and gradually integrated into the democratic republic. Machefer, Nobécourt, and Kéchichian, in particular, contrast the CF and PSF's commitment to Christian values with what they contend is the more secular outlook of fascism.[3] Conversely, scholars such as Robert Soucy, Kevin Passmore, and Samuel Kalman stress that while there were diverse currents of interwar French Catholicism, the CF and PSF identified with its authoritarian, right-wing elements. For Soucy, this illustrates how denials that the CF and PSF were fascist are problematic; Passmore and Kalman focus upon the ideological divisions within, and evolution of, the organizations.[4] The present essay acknowledges the diversity of French Catholicism and the varying outlooks of La Rocque's followers. However, it contends that after the creation of the PSF in 1936 the concept of Christian civilization, though not used in sectarian terms, was deployed in order to articulate an exclusionary vision of the French national community, and to signal support for authoritarian politics in international affairs. This in turn raises questions about the PSF's commitment to republican democracy.

Before examining the PSF's appeal to France's Christian heritage, the political and civic status of interwar Catholicism must be considered. After the First World War, a host of new Catholic groups were formed, including the Christian Democratic Parti démocrate populaire (PDP), created in 1924, which established a lasting though limited presence in the Chamber of Deputies. More numerous, however, were non-party organizations formed with the goal of dispelling class conflict and encouraging social harmony between workers and bourgeoisie. These included the Confédération française des travailleurs chrétiens (established in 1919) and the Équipes sociales (established in 1920); they were soon followed by Catholic Action movements aimed at encouraging spiritual engagement among young workers, farmers, and students. These organizations emphasized their civic, as opposed to political, goals and their acceptance of republican institutions. However, the election of the left-wing Cartel des Gauches in 1924 reawakened Catholic fears of anti-clericalism. For instance, the Radical Prime Minister Édouard Herriot threatened to proceed with the separation of church and state in newly regained, and hitherto exempt, Alsace-Lorraine, among other measures. This in turn gave rise to the formation of yet another organization, the Fédération nationale catholique (FNC) in 1924. More strident in its outlook, the FNC combined a fierce defense of Catholic interests with nationalist fervor and attracted as many as two million supporters at its peak. After the fall of the Cartel, and the Vatican's condemnation of the integral nationalist Action française

(AF) in 1926, tensions relaxed somewhat, but the success of the FNC served as a reminder of the complex and often troubled relationship between the Church and the Republic.[5]

La Rocque, it seems, avoided formal involvement in Catholic organizations during his time in the army. After leaving the service, however, he hoped to create an organization aimed at uniting social classes and different generations in the cause of national renewal, a goal for which he sought support from Catholic clergy and laity. In 1930, he contacted the secretary general of the French branch of Catholic Action concerning the creation of a Groupement de défense sociale et civique.[6] This initiative did not bear fruit, but as leader of the CF—which he joined in 1929 and became president of two years later—La Rocque deepened his contacts with his former patron Lyautey. In the years to come, he invoked the latter's belief, dating back to his 1891 article, "The Social Role of the Officer," in the duty of the French officer class to see to the needs of their men, and to more generally promote social peace and disciplined harmony within a divided nation. La Rocque also became friends with another "disciple" of Lyautey, Robert Garric, a fellow veteran who had founded the Équipes sociales in the hope of recreating in peacetime, through the good example and patient work of moral elites, the social concord that he believed had existed at the front in 1914–1918. As Nobécourt points out, elements of this outlook were present in La Rocque's thinking as well, though the CF leader had a nationalist focus and a military approach, which Garric did not.[7]

As the CF experienced a rapid growth in support following the 6 February 1934 riots, the fact that it was influenced by certain Social Catholic values, and that it sought to appeal to Catholics, was clear enough. La Rocque was frank about his religious convictions, declaring in an interview with the Dominican paper *Sept* in 1934, "I have done nothing which is contrary to the orthodoxy of my personal religion."[8] The movement's burgeoning ancillary organizations, such as its Section féminine and *colonies de vacances* for children, bore the influence of Catholic predecessors, although they were distinct in their intense valorization of the "front generation."[9] The organization's message of national reconciliation, whereby the French people would set aside their differences and unite in the cause of regenerating the state, bore traces of Pope Leo XIII's encyclical *Rerum Novarum*, as well as the paternalism of Lyautey and the nationalist ideas of Maurice Barrès. The fact that the CF identified itself as a civic rather than a political organization made it acceptable for a number of clergy, including several bishops, to endorse this patriotic yet supposedly apolitical movement. It may have also made the organization more appealing to some Catholic Action supporters.[10]

As for the FNC, its leader Édouard de Castelnau and La Rocque were both military men who emphasized the ideal of "service" and embraced mass mobilization, though the FNC steered away from overt anti-parliamentarism. There

were limited contacts between the two in 1934, although they do not seem to have amounted to much, and de Castelnau generally refused to attend patriotic celebrations involving the CF. Nevertheless, it seems likely that more than a few people joined both organizations, though specific numbers remain elusive and FNC cadres were advised against holding leadership positions in other groups.[11]

Despite these influences and connections, it would be inaccurate to characterize the CF as a Catholic movement. Some members of the clergy supported it enthusiastically, but others were suspicious.[12] Jean Verdier, the cardinal archbishop of Paris, evidently admired the CF but emphasized to his fellow archbishops that it was not a Catholic movement and that the church and the CF occupied separate spheres; the leaders of Catholic Action adopted a similar line.[13] For their part, La Rocque and his colleagues stressed that people of all faiths and none were welcome to join in its mission of French regeneration. They held up Marshal Lyautey as an example of how a devout Catholic could be both professional and non-sectarian when it came to vital tasks such as ensuring the moral regeneration of youth.[14] The CF underscored its ecumenism by having sections attend veteran memorial services for Protestants and Jews as well as Catholics, and hear addresses from clergy of different faiths.[15] And while La Rocque and his supporters professed the need to reassert spiritual values in public life, they did not associate this call with any one faith. A key example of this was the manifesto the CF distributed during the spring 1936 elections, which attacked the Left for its repeated "blasphemy" against religion, and suggested the need for "spiritual" education in the schools, but otherwise emphasized the CF support for patriots of all stripes.[16] This calibrated propaganda campaign seems to have had the desired effect. While committed Catholics like the young François Mitterrand saw the CF as a potential vehicle for their aspirations, the authorities reported that people of diverse backgrounds joined.[17]

However, following the victory of the Popular Front, the CF was dissolved, though La Rocque had foreseen this possibility and had already made preparations to establish a political party. As the Popular Front assumed power, he and his colleagues within the newly formed PSF stressed the need to defend France against the threat of revolution, but also to uphold its identity as part of Christian civilization. As noted in the introduction to this essay, as early as August 1936, La Rocque had made clear that the PSF would continue the CF's work of achieving national reconciliation, but added that this could only be possible by simultaneously honoring France's religious heritage. The new party reaffirmed this goal in the months that followed. At the closing of its first national congress in December, the PSF pronounced its supporters "the great defenders of this Christian civilization, the adoption of which is the actual mark of French acceptance."[18] In a second interview given to *Sept* in February 1937, La Rocque went beyond affirming the personal importance of his faith, as he had done in 1934,

and now identified it with his party's mission, noting that its platform embodied "the exact transposition of pontifical precepts into our laic domain."[19] Compared to the era of the CF, the PSF leader was noticeably more explicit in identifying with Christian values.

To be sure, the party highlighted other themes, including those that had been of central importance to the CF, notably its fidelity to the memory of the veterans of the Great War. But the defense of Christian civilization became an increasingly overt goal of the PSF, with a number of key party figures working this theme into their speeches. Jean Ybarnégaray had been an FNC orator during the 1920s, and continued to make religious references as a vice-president of, and prominent orator for, La Rocque's party. At a 1938 meeting held in Nantes, for example, he declared, "'the fiery cross' [i.e, the CF] and 'the cross of Christ' must merge."[20] Stanislas Devaud, a PSF deputy from Constantine, also promoted Catholic ideals; in 1939, he rejoiced at the victory of Franco's Nationalists in the Spanish Civil War, praising "the swift setting aright of nationalist Spain, which the Catholic faith again animates."[21] Other leading figures came from a Catholic milieu as well. Charles Vallin, a PSF vice-president who was also elected a deputy for the party in 1938, had previously supported the AF, though he had respected the papal condemnation of 1926. Christian Melchior-Bonnet, the editor of the PSF-owned daily *Le Petit journal* from 1937, and Antoinette de Préval, a driving force behind many of the CF's and then PSF's social initiatives, both appear to have been influenced by a paternalist brand of Social Catholicism.[22] It is true that some party notables had other priorities: Edmond Barrachin, the PSF's chief political strategist, avoided appeals to religious rhetoric and instead focused upon attracting disaffected supporters of the traditionally anti-clerical Radical Party.[23] However, neither Barrachin nor any other PSF notable seems to have dissented from the party's more explicit identification with Christian values.

La Rocque continued to emphasize the avowedly non-sectarian but nevertheless firm commitment of his party to promoting France's Christian heritage in the final years before the outbreak of the Second World War. In 1938, he declared, "nothing will check [our] effort until Christian civilization has once again opened the French route to complete social progress in a strong and regenerated country."[24] Commenting upon the election of Pope Pius XII in 1939, he asserted that "believers of all sorts, sincere unbelievers, all fervent with French loyalty, the men and women of the Croix de Feu freely and respectfully bow before the most illustrious apostle of our national vocation."[25] In his analysis of the French Revolution written for the sesquicentennial of 1789 that following July, La Rocque acknowledged France's republican institutions but again stressed the country's status as an "essential pillar of Christian civilization."[26] The PSF leader's commitment to identifying with Christian values was thus firm and consistent. Though he made room for other faiths and political traditions, and even non-believers, he also demanded that they respect these values.

PSF propagandists generally tried to follow this balancing act, reaching out to the faithful but disdaining religious currents that the party deemed unsuitable, all the while affirming its openness to different confessions and even non-believers. Writers such as François Veuillot, nephew of the renowned Catholic author Louis Veuillot, called upon Catholics who had not yet embraced the PSF to take note of how its message of reconciliation paralleled Church teachings.[27] However, La Rocque and his colleagues also made clear that any Christian group that embraced elements of socialism or communism was unacceptable. After an early edition of the PSF's official program made a favorable reference to "Christian socialism," the party issued a clarification. Noting that socialism had been condemned by Rome, the PSF stressed that it instead identified with the "admirable social teachings of the Church."[28]

Relations with Catholic organizations and the clergy were also complex. Some members of Catholic Action groups and the CFTC were also devoted PSF militants, and in some cases the CFTC cooperated with the PSF-inspired trade union movement, the Syndicats professionnels français (SPF). But there were also tensions between the two union organizations as they competed for supporters, with the CFTC accusing the SPF of being too deferential to employers, and the SPF denouncing Christian trade unionists for sometimes cooperating with the Leftist Confédération générale du travail (CGT). As for the Christian Democratic PDP, while some of its supporters believed that the PSF had positive qualities, others questioned its commitment to democracy, and there was friction between the two as they vied for members and votes.[29] PSF supporters also had to tread carefully when dealing with some clergy, it seems. For instance, *Réalité*, the party's regional paper for the Marne, sought to assuage the concerns that some clerics apparently had regarding its goals, declaring, "The PSF is too respectful of spiritual forces to cause [priests] the slightest worry. ... If there are unbelievers among us, very sincere unbelievers, we are all partisans of Christian civilization, and we do not want Communism or Hitlerism."[30]

Evidently, appealing to the notion of "Christian civilization" entailed various difficulties. Beyond the challenges of dealing with Catholic clergy and organizations, there was the matter of how the PSF could continue to invoke this ideal while insisting that it was not a confessional movement. The problem only intensified as the party gained mass support; with its membership nearing the 1 million mark by 1938, it had obviously attracted people of diverse views and religious backgrounds—the authorities noted, for instance, that both the editor of *Réalité* and the Marne's regional president were Protestants.[31] Clearly, the PSF could not afford to be sectarian; indeed, La Rocque and his colleagues never wanted it to be, sincere though their own personal religious convictions may have been. Rather, their notion of a Christian civilization, as advanced in their public discourse, was primarily cultural and political, a weapon of ideological and rhetorical combat. Characterizing bedrock French values in these terms allowed them to define the

national community in ways broad enough to accept a wide variety of supporters, but restrictive enough to justify the exclusion of certain individuals and groups, in some cases more explicitly than the CF had.

One example of this was the PSF's position on the political and civil rights of Algerian Muslims, a very controversial issue during the 1930s. Before the dissolution of 1936, the Algerian CF was completely dominated by Europeans who sought to protect their privileged status. The movement did make some efforts to attract Muslim supporters but had very limited success, though some alliances with Muslim elites were formed, with anti-Semitism becoming one important common cause.[32] The most prominent non-European member of the Algerian CF, it seems, was Augustin Iba-Zizen, a convert to Catholicism, French citizen, and lawyer who headed the CF and later PSF section in Tizi-Ouzou. Iba-Zizen claimed he was attracted to the CF because it recreated the harmonious spirit of 1914–1918, and therefore "ably represent[ed] the radiance of the French spirit, which alone can win the *indigène* to the French cause."[33] Such words reflected the appeal of the message of national reconciliation, as well as the Algerian CF's commitment to lasting European domination.

The volatile Algerian situation grew more complicated in 1936, when the newly elected Blum government proposed that some 25,000 individuals from the Algerian elite be enfranchised without having to renounce their personal statute and thus their legal status as Muslims, a restriction which had been a significant barrier to their participation in public life in the past.[34] Many Europeans regarded this Blum-Viollette reform, as it was called, as a threat to their interests; the newly established PSF figured prominently in the strong opposition that emerged.[35] In the process, the party articulated a very restrictive stance regarding political rights for the indigenous population.

On the surface, PSF orators in general and Iba-Zizen in particular promoted the party to Muslims as a vehicle for reform. At a meeting held in Constantine in August 1936, Iba-Zizen seemed to call for the further integration of elements of the local elite, declaring that, "at the present time, you must not, you cannot, refuse the flower of Arab or Kabyle society the right to sit at the banquet of the French family."[36] He was applauded, but the party soon clarified that political rights were not on the table. Several weeks later, Alfred Debay, at the time the head of the Algerian PSF, challenged the idea of expanding electoral rights, arguing that since "everyone recognizes that our electoral system [is] defective, is now the time to extend it to the natives?"[37] The PSF went beyond criticism by presenting its own counter-proposal for reform. Though Iba-Zizen, who was involved in the drafting process, later claimed that this proposal was more progressive than what the Popular Front offered, in fact it continued to require the renunciation of Koranic law, which in turn made it unlikely to achieve mass appeal among Muslims and more likely to cement European domination.[38]

In short, the PSF demanded a level of integration that relatively few Algerians were likely to attain, or even to desire. Comments by leading party officials at a departmental congress held in Constantine in 1938 suggest that their conception of French national identity, which afforded little room for incorporating non-Christian traditions, was at the heart of the matter. Devaud implied his refusal to see observant Muslims incorporated into the French body politic, declaring that if the PSF, "a French, Christian and Republican party" consented "to [Muslim] admission into the French family, that will be an occasion for them to make the final sacrifice; that of their personal statute." For his part, La Rocque claimed, "There is a single remedy, assimilation. Those [Muslims] who believe themselves to be sufficiently advanced must come to us and incorporate themselves totally into the great French family"—which, he had repeatedly declared, was one that abided by Christian norms. In any case, he continued, it was social reform, not political rights, which most Muslims needed: "Above all, what must be given to the natives is a better existence."[39] Disdain for the electoral institutions of the Third Republic, a belief that France was at heart a Christian civilization, and a prioritizing of the PSF's Catholic-inspired "social" mission over political reform, all figured in the movement's participation in the ultimately successful campaign against the Blum-Viollette reform.

The defense of France's religious heritage was also significant in shaping the PSF's stance on "the Jewish question," particularly with respect to La Rocque himself. As historians such as Laurent Joly have pointed out, anti-Semitic discourse was generally on the rise in France from 1936 onward, and it was not restricted to the political Right.[40] Within that context, as Richard Millman and Samuel Kalman have shown, anti-Jewish views within the PSF grew increasingly apparent.[41] They were notably strident in Algeria, long a hotbed of anti-Semitism. Stanislas Devaud's wife came from a Jewish family but this did not stop him from calling upon PSF supporters to "unite against Jewry, against the Jew Blum, to ensure the triumph of our ideal of justice, liberty and fraternity throughout this country."[42] Similar comments emanated from various elements of the party in France itself. Among the leadership, Charles Vallin slurred Blum by suggesting that his ancestors had sold trinkets to the army of emigration in the 1790s; regional PSF papers such as *La Volonté bretonne* and *La Flamme du Midi* invoked long-extant tropes of Jewish economic exploitation and political subversion.[43] Despite this, the PSF denied claims that it was anti-Jewish and on occasion denounced racial anti-Semitism. In particular, its *Bulletin d'informations* reacted to the 9 November 1938 pogrom in Germany by condemning Nazi racism as counter to "Christian civilization and to French tradition and nature."[44]

It has been argued that when it came to the PSF leader himself, La Rocque, as a devout Catholic, rejected biological racism and as such his views must be distinguished from those of his anti-Jewish colleagues and supporters. For example,

while conceding that La Rocque was not immune to the general xenophobia that characterized much of the French Right during the 1930s, Michel Winock is nevertheless impressed by the extent to which he refused to conform to the anti-Semitic "wave" of the era. Winock also points out that extreme anti-Semites such as Henry Coston even accused La Rocque of being beholden to Jewish interests, and that in 1938, La Rocque did not shrink from provoking a crisis within the PSF's Moselle organization over the issue of anti-Semitism, which apparently led to the departure of as many as 1500 militants.[45]

It does appear that La Rocque rejected biological anti-Semitism and believed that some Jews could integrate into the French nation. Nevertheless, he insisted that the onus was upon them to demonstrate their commitment by showing that they did not support revolutionary doctrines. Revealingly, in the very same August 1936 editorial where he declared the centrality of Christianity to French identity he noted how foreign propaganda depicted France's new government as a "Jewish team"; under the circumstances, he concluded, "it is incumbent upon the countless patriotic Jews to demonstrate their aversion for Marxism."[46] The implication was that La Rocque had no patience for Jews who, he perceived, were unwilling to show their respect for the precepts of Christian civilization; he soon made this particularly clear as far as Léon Blum was concerned.

Although he avoided explicitly anti-Semitic attacks, La Rocque repeatedly depicted the Socialist leader and his government as the antithesis of the Christian-inspired orderly, patriotic, and moral community that the PSF strove to uphold. At the very least this involved mockery, such as when he referred to Blum as the "qualified representative of the winegrowers of the Aude," the implication being that a "cosmopolitan" intellectual was ill-suited to speak for French farmers.[47] At times, the PSF leader went further. Commenting upon the Popular Front government's commemoration of the 11 November 1918 armistice in 1936, La Rocque scorned the prime minister's decision to feature children in the ceremonies, asserting that "the French family, whatever its origins, its religion, its condition, merits another example of traditional virtues than that of M. Blum, the disciple of free love."[48] This was a none-too-subtle reference to the Socialist leader's controversial 1907 book, *Du mariage*, which advocated greater premarital sexual freedom for women as well as men. As Pierre Birnbaum notes, accusations of sexual perversion were a common theme within French anti-Semitic discourse.[49] While La Rocque did not make the connection explicitly, it would not have been difficult for PSF supporters to do so.

Similarly, at times La Rocque cast Blum as a revolutionary whose government was a stalking horse for Soviet interests and a prelude to revolutionary terror. In the first months of the Popular Front government, he referred to Blum as a "Kerensky" who would pave the way for bloody extremists; later he went so far as to suggest that the Popular Front leader was more akin to Robespierre.[50] Again, the connection between Jews and revolution was a common theme in anti-Semitic

rhetoric; La Rocque did not refer specifically to Blum's Jewishness in this context, but it seems unlikely that he was ignorant of what he was inferring. To be sure, the PSF leader's rhetoric was never virulent like that of the AF, and he did not fixate upon the issue to the extent that certain far-Right politicians like Xavier Vallat did.[51] But by implying that Blum did not respect France's spiritual traditions, by associating him with sexual libertinism, and by playing upon fears of revolutionary terror, La Rocque invoked familiar themes of French anti-Semitic discourse, even if he did so in a relatively muted fashion.

The notion of a Christian civilization thus helped La Rocque and his colleagues to define the limits and norms of who was properly "French"; it also proved critical to orienting their views on international affairs. The formation of the PSF coincided with the outbreak of the Spanish Civil War, and the new party soon emphasized that it saw the Spanish Nationalists as kindred spirits. La Rocque declared that he hoped Franco would win "not for himself, but for us; his failure would mark a fearsome defeat of Western civilization." In North Africa, some former CF and current PSF supporters expressed solidarity by volunteering to fight for Franco.[52] The religious dimension of the conflict—notably the anti-clerical violence that took place—was an important part of this dynamic, with some Catholic clergy publicly stating that supporting the PSF was the only way to ensure that the French Church was not the victim of the kind of outrages which its Spanish counterpart was suffering.[53] Franco's victory in 1939 was cheered enthusiastically by Stanislas Devaud, as we have already seen; it was also welcomed by Jean Ybarnégaray.[54]

Although its enthusiasm for Franco was consistent, in other ways the PSF had to adjust its foreign policy stance between 1936 and 1939. So long as the Popular Front was in power, La Rocque and his colleagues, like much of the French Right, downplayed their traditional anti-German sentiment. Instead, they attacked the foreign policy of the Blum government, arguing that it recklessly sought confrontation with Hitler; this in turn, they argued, would lead to a devastating war which would facilitate revolution and Soviet expansion across Europe. But as the Popular Front coalition fragmented, the supposed threat of domestic revolution dissipated, and the Nazi threat loomed larger in 1938–1939, the PSF gradually adopted a tougher line, stressing the need to stand up to Germany, though it continued to hope that war could be avoided. For allies, La Rocque and his colleagues looked to Britain; they also hoped that Italy could be weaned away from Hitler, but were frustrated by Mussolini's deepening alignment with the Third Reich. The Soviet Union posed especially acute challenges in this regard; traditionally anathema to the PSF, it was now a potential strategic partner for France. In 1939, La Rocque uneasily tried to square the circle by raising the possibility of an economic agreement between the two nations, though he balked at going further.[55]

As it adopted a tougher line against Nazi Germany, the PSF compared it unfavorably to the Catholic authoritarian states of Europe. Here it was being con-

sistent, for it had previously indicated its admiration for such regimes. Alongside Franco's Nationalists, the Catholic-inspired authoritarian government of Austria was seen as a positive model; in 1937, the PSF deputy Paul Creyssel paid a visit and praised the "very supple discipline" of the regime.[56] By 1939, La Rocque and other contributors to Le Petit journal were also praising Salazar's Portugal as an example of how national renovation could be carried out according to humane, Christian principles while avoiding the demagogy of Hitler, or Mussolini for that matter.[57] By contrast, the Nazi leader was increasingly cast as a pagan despot who threatened not only the geopolitical stability but also the spiritual values of Europe. Marcel Gatuing, the head of the PSF's Oran federation, illustrated his party's attitude when, following the German occupation of Bohemia and Moravia in the spring of 1939, he blustered: "Ah! Let them come now, the fanatics of the swastika! After twenty years of lethargy, the Christian West is reawakening."[58]

When Nazi Germany and the Soviet Union announced that they had signed a pact in August 1939, La Rocque did not appear to be especially troubled; in fact, he seemed relieved that the situation had been clarified. Though only weeks before, he had broached the possibility of an accord with the Soviets in the name of hardheaded realism, he still felt that "Russia, an Asiatic empire in the hands of the avowed enemies of the Christian tradition, forms the antithesis of our civilization."[59] Now that the atheist Soviet Union had made common cause with the Third Reich, and with the threat of war looming, La Rocque could present the international situation in terms of a showdown between religious values on one side and the forces of paganism and atheism on the other. "Let us make clear to France each day," he wrote on 28 August 1939, "that the salvation of peace, like that of the homeland, depends and will depend upon the triumph of Christianity over barbarism."[60] He had thus pointedly emphasized religious themes, rather than characterize the confrontation as a clash between one-party and parliamentary states. Indeed, he had earlier disdained the "slogan of a struggle between 'democracies' and 'dictatorships.'"[61]

In conclusion, the promotion by key figures within the PSF—above all its leader—of the vision of France as a Christian civilization sheds light on its evolving discourse and objectives. This theme was never its sole focus; it coexisted with other emphases, including the invocation of the patriotic unity of the First World War, appeals to specific socioeconomic groups, and the idea that the PSF would defend "republican" liberties against the threat of Marxism. Nor did the PSF have a monopoly on the notion of defending Christian values. Though space precludes detailed comparisons, it should be noted that older formations like the Fédération républicaine vigorously supported Catholic interests; moreover, even newer movements of the far Right with seemingly incongruous political roots made moves in this direction. Jacques Doriot, leader of the Parti populaire français, conspicuously broke with his Communist past, even undertaking a pilgrimage to Lourdes in 1939.[62] That said, La Rocque's and other PSF notables' commitment

to the Christian ideal—as they defined it—and the implications of that commitment were clear enough. They demanded the fidelity of religious minorities and non-believers to France's Christian heritage in ways that hindered even cautious colonial reform and sanctioned xenophobic attitudes. They cast their opposition to Nazism and Communism as inspired by Christian rather than democratic values, and expressed their admiration for Catholic-inspired authoritarian regimes. All of this suggests that while the party might have been playing by the formal rules of the democratic game between 1936 and 1939, it had not yet embraced the spirit of democracy.

Acknowledgments

I would like to thank Sam Kalman for comments and suggestions on an earlier version of this chapter. Some of this material previously appeared, in a different form, in my book *Reconciling France against Democracy: The Croix de Feu and the Parti Social Francais, 1927–1945*.

Notes

1. *Le Flambeau*, 22 August 1936. Unless otherwise noted all translations from French are my own.

2. Édith de La Rocque and Gilles de La Rocque, *La Rocque tel qu'il était* (Paris, 1962), 20; on La Rocque's father, see Jacques Nobécourt, "Une 'Affaire La Rocque' en 1899: Avant le PSF, Justice-Égalité?" *Revue d'histoire moderne et contemporaine* 47, no. 3 (2000): 505–524.

3. René Rémond, *Les droites en France*, revised edition (Paris, 1982), 213–214; Philippe Machefer, "Les Croix de Feu (1927–1936)," *L'Information historique* 34, no. 1 (1972): 32; Machefer, "Le Parti Social Français en 1936–1937," *L'Information historique* 34, no. 2 (1972): 80; Jacques Nobécourt, *Le Colonel de La Rocque 1885–1946, ou les pièges du nationalisme chrétien* (Paris, 1996), 346–350, 666–668; Albert Kéchichian, *Les Croix-de-Feu à l'âge des fascismes: travail-famille-patrie* (Seyssel, 2006), 36–41, 370–381; Jean-Paul Thomas, "Le Parti social français, élément majeur d'une refonte du système du contrôle politique des droites à la fin des années trente?" in *Les deux France du Front populaire*. ed. Gilles Morin and Gilles Richard, (Paris, 2008), 134–136.

4. See Robert Soucy, "Fascism in France: Problematising the Immunity Thesis," in *France in the Era of Fascism: Essays on the French Authoritarian Right*, ed. Brian Jenkins (New York, 2005), 69–71; Kevin Passmore, *From Liberalism to Fascism: The Right in a French Province, 1928–1939* (Cambridge, 1997), 241–243, 268–270; and Samuel Kalman, *The Extreme Right in Interwar France: The Faisceau and the Croix de Feu* (Aldershot, 2008), 86, 101–102.

5. For overviews of interwar French Catholicism, see Philip Nord, "Catholic Culture in Interwar France," *French Politics, Culture & Society* 21, no. 3 (2003): 1–20; James F. McMillan, "France," in *Political Catholicism in Europe, 1918–1965*, ed. Tom Buchanan and Martin Conway (Oxford, 1996), 40–54; and Robert O. Paxton, "France: The Church, the Republic, and the Fascist Temptation, 1922–1945," in *Catholics, the State, and the European Radical Right, 1919–1945*, ed. Richard J. Wolff and Jörg K. Hoensch (Boulder, 1987), 67–81.

6. Jean-Louis Clément, "L'Épiscopat, les démocrates-chrétiens et les Croix de Feu, 1930–1936," *Revue historique* 603 (1997): 106–107.

7. Nobécourt, *Colonel de La Rocque*, 242; see also Kéchichian, *Croix-de-Feu*, 107. On Lyautey's influence during the interwar years, see also Daniel Lindenberg, *Les années souterraines 1937–1947* (Paris, 1990), 194–202; and Kathryn Amdur, "Paternalism, Productivism, Collaborationism: Employers and Society in Interwar and Vichy France," *International Labor and Working-Class History* 53, no. 1 (1998): 139, 142.

8. La Rocque, interview in *Sept*, 28 December 1934.

9. For an analysis of the continuities between Catholic movements and the interwar nationalist leagues regarding the role of women, see Magali Della Sudda, "Gender, Fascism and the Right-Wing in France between the Wars: The Catholic Matrix," *Politics, Religion & Ideology* 13, no. 2 (2012): 179–195; for an overview of women and youth in the CF, see Sean Kennedy, *Reconciling France against Democracy: The Croix de Feu and the Parti Social Français, 1927–1945* (Montreal, 2007), 96–106; for the distinctions between CF/PSF *colonies de vacances* and their Catholic counterparts, see Laura Lee Downs, "'Each and Every One of You Must Become a *Chef*': Toward a Social Politics of Working-Class Childhood on the Extreme Right in 1930s France," *Journal of Modern History* 81, no. 1 (2009):, 21–23, 29–32.

10. Kéchichian, *Croix-de-Feu*, 40–41, 105–8; Clément, "Épiscopat," 106–109.

11. See Corinne Bonafoux-Verrax, *À la droite de Dieu: la Fédération nationale catholique 1924–1944* (Paris, 2004), 271–273, 541n.176.

12. For an example of a favorable view, see the pamphlet by the Abbé Ritz, *Réflexions d'un lorrain sur le Mouvement social français des Croix de Feu* (Metz, 1935); for an example of a hostile attitude on the part of the local bishop, see A[rchives] D[épartementales] Vendée 4M 413, commissaire de police (Luçon), 1 April 1936.

13. Bonafoux-Verrax, *À la droite de Dieu*, 272.

14. *Le Flambeau*, 1 September 1934.

15. Clément, "Épiscopat," 106–109.

16. *Manifeste Croix de Feu: pour le peuple, par le peuple* (supplement to *Le Flambeau*, 11 April 1936), 13, 15.

17. Clément, "Épiscopat," 109–10; Pierre Péan, *Une jeunesse française: François Mitterrand 1934–1947* (Paris, 1994), 35, 40–41; A[rchives] N[ationales] F7 13033, commissaire spécial (Brest), 1 August 1934, commissaire spécial (Quimper), 5 July 1934, 7 December 1935.

18. *Le Flambeau*, 26 December 1936.

19. *Sept*, 26 February 1937. Nobécourt, *Colonel de La Rocque*, 347–348, suggests that the interview was "ghosted" by a PSF journalist, but believes that it still captured La Rocque's views.

20. On Ybarnégaray and the FNC, see Bonafoux-Verrax, *À la droite de Dieu*, 126–127; his speech is reported in AD Loire-Atlantique 1M 470, prefect to minister of interior, 25 May 1938.

21. See A[rchives] N[ationales d']O[utre-]M[er] Constantine B3 635, commissaire de police (Saint-Arnaud), 19 April 1939.

22. Nobécourt, *Colonel de La Rocque*, 628–629, 633–637; on links between Catholic and CF/PSF social action see Kevin Passmore, "'Planting the Tricolor in the Citadels of Communism': Women's Social Action in the Croix de Feu and Parti social français," *Journal of Modern History* 71, no.4 (1999): 830–831, 850–851; and Caroline Campbell, "Building a Movement, Dismantling the Republic: Women, Gender, and Political Extremism in the Croix de Feu/Parti Social Français, 1927–1940," *French Historical Studies* 35, no.4 (2012): 698–700.

23. I discuss the PSF's efforts to win over Radical supporters in *Reconciling France against Democracy*, 172–180; on Barrachin's strategy, see Archives de Paris 212/69/1, article 152, Edmond Barrachin, "Point de vue personnel sur la position politique du parti à ce jour," n.d., but probably fall 1936.

24. *Le Petit journal*, 6 March 1938.

25. *Le Petit journal*, 5 March 1939; see also *Le Petit journal*, 10 August 1939.

26. *Le Petit journal*, 14 July 1939.

27. François Veuillot, *La Rocque et son parti* (Paris, 1938), 86–93.

28. *Le Flambeau*, 21 November 1936.

29. On links between the PSF and Catholic organizations, see Jean-Paul Thomas, "Le Parti social français dans le Nord (1936–1945)," *Revue du Nord* 89, no. 370 (2007): 350, 352; On PSF and SPF competition with Catholic organizations, see Kennedy, *Reconciling France against Democracy*, 149, 168, 214.

30. *Réalité*, 19 February 1938.

31. AD Marne 30M146, sub-prefect (Epernay) to prefect of the Marne, 10 February 1938.

32. On this issue, see Samuel Kalman, "Fascism and Algérianité: The Croix de Feu and the Indigenous Question in 1930s Algeria," in *The French Colonial Mind*, 2 vols., ed. Martin Thomas (Lincoln, 2011), vol. 2, 112–139.

33. On Algerians in the CF/PSF, see Jacques Cantier, *L'Algérie sous le regime de Vichy* (Paris, 2002), 230; on Iba-Zizen, see AOM Alger 1K26, sûreté départementale (Algiers), 11 January 1935, prefect, July 1935, commissaire central (Algiers), 12 January 1936. He also published a memoir: Augustin Ibazizen, *Le testament d'un berbère: un itinéraire spiritual et politique* (Paris, 1984).

34. Martin Thomas, *The French Empire between the Wars: Imperialism, Politics and Society* (Manchester, 2005), 297–303.

35. Philippe Machefer, "Autour du problème algérien en 1936–1938: la doctrine algérienne du PSF—Le PSF et le projet Blum-Violette," *Revue d'histoire moderne et contemporaine* 10 (1963), 147–156.

36. AOM Constantine B3 635, sûreté (Constantine), 14 August 1936.

37. AOM Alger F405, commissaire de police (Affreville), 20 October 1936.

38. Ibazizen, *Testament d'un berbère*, 106–111; Kalman, "Fascism and Algérianité," 129–130; see also Machefer, "Autour du problème algérienne," 151–152, 155–156.

39. AOM Constantine B3 635, police spéciale (Constantine), 23 October 1938.

40. Laurent Joly, *Vichy dans la "Solution Finale": histoire du Commissariat-général aux Questions juives (1941–1944)* (Paris, 2006), 50–58.

41. Richard Millman, "Les Croix de Feu et l'antisemitisme," *Vingtième Siècle* 38 (1993): 48–54; Samuel Kalman, "'Parasites from all Civilizations': The Croix de Feu/Parti Social Français Confronts French Jewry, 1931–1939," *Historical Reflections* 34, no. 2 (2008): 46–65.

42. Kéchichian, *Croix-de-Feu*, 220; AOM Constantine B3 635, sûreté départementale (Constantine), 14 August 1936.

43. AN 451AP [Fonds La Rocque, carton] 108, "Parti social français—réunion du 15 septembre 1936 (Lyon): discours de M. Vallin"; Kalman, "Parasites from All Civilizations," 50–56; *La Flamme du Midi*, 14 May 1937.

44. "L'agitation antisémite," *Parti social français: Bulletin d'informations* no. 90 (22 November 1938).

45. Michel Winock, "Retour sur le fascisme français : La Rocque et les Croix-de-Feu," *Vingtième siècle* 90 (2006): 14–17; see also Jean-Paul Thomas, "Facisme français: faut-il rouvrir un débat?" in *Un professeur en République : mélanges en l'honneur de Serge Berstein*, ed. Rémi Badouï et al. (Paris, 2006), 296.

46. *Le Flambeau*, 22 August 1936.

47. *Le Petit journal*, 5 October 1937.

48. *Le Flambeau*, 14 November 1936.

49. Pierre Birnbaum, *Un mythe politique: la "république juive"* (Paris, 1988), 209–224.

50. *Le Flambeau*, 10 April 1937.

51. On Vallat's denunciation of Blum and its aftermath, see Tal Bruttmann and Laurent Joly, eds., *La France antijuive de 1936: l'agression de Léon Blum à la Chambre des députés* (Sainte-Marguerite sur Mer, 2006).

52. AOM Oran 70, commissaire divisionnaire (Oran), 25 April 1939; AOM Constantine B3 635, commissaire de police (Saint-Arnaud), 19 April 1939.

53. *Le Flambeau*, 22 August 1936; AN F7 14817, inspecteur de police mobile (Saint-Brieuc), 23 October 1936.

54. For Ybarnégaray's views, see his article in *Le Petit journal*, 15 February 1939.

55. Kennedy, *Reconciling France against Democracy*, 182–188.

56. *Le Petit journal*, 31 August 1937.

57. *Le Petit journal*, 10 February, 13 August 1939.

58. *La Flamme*, 31 March 1939.

59. *Le Petit journal*, 30 July 1939.

60. *Le Petit journal*, 28 August 1939.

61. *Le Petit journal*, 5 February 1939.

62. See Kevin Passmore, "Catholicism and Nationalism: the Fédération républicaine, 1927–1939," in *Catholicism, Politics and Society in Twentieth-Century France*, ed. Kay Chadwick (Liverpool, 2000), 47–72; Irvine, *French Conservatism in Crisis*, 1–26; Philippe Burrin, *La dérive fasciste: Doriot, Déat, Bergery 1933–1945* (Paris, 1986), 306–307.

WERE FRENCH ELITES ALLERGIC TO FASCISM?

A Study of the Reception of the 1930s Dictatorships in Three French Periodicals

Laurent Kestel

Translated by Samuel Kalman

One of the central problems tackled in French political histories of the interwar era has traditionally been—and certainly remains—the question of whether or not France succumbed to "fascism." Specialists acknowledge its existence; there is no need for any further discussion. Similarly, there is no need to stimulate debate when, following the appearance of Zeev Sternhell's *Neither Right Nor Left*, various French historians spoke of an "allergy" and an "impermeability of French culture" to fascism,[1] in keeping with the classic thesis of René Rémond. Over the last thirty years, this has been continuously and staunchly contested by numerous works[2] that have brought to light the rejection, indeed the aversion, of a number of right-wing political parties (whether termed authoritarian, nationalist, or radical) toward parliamentarism, democracy, or "electoralism"—to use the term employed by Croix de Feu leader Colonel de La Rocque in *Service Public*. To this list must be added, if this is even necessary, their espousal of a particularly explicit anti-Semitism.[3]

However, a mere analysis of the discourse of the parties of the radical Right, in the sense of the term used in this chapter, will not permit the formulation of a proper response to the immunity thesis expounded by the French school of political historians. To focus on the ideology of such groups and intellectuals indirectly

validates the notion that other political and social groups were "authentic repub-licans." In other words, it fully supports the thesis that France proved "immune" to fascism, with the exception of various marginal figures. The application of this methodology toward the study of interwar French politics and society is deeply problematic, not least because the "outsiders"[4] often appeared among the most fervent critics of the "system" that they wished to vanquish, yet such groups were usually more concerned with self-preservation than with the subversion of the es-tablished order. Thus this line of inquiry does not constitute a heuristic advance of paramount importance, so to speak. There is relatively little to gain by evoking the anti-Semitism of the leaders of Action française, for example, with the excep-tion of contesting the least tenable aspects of the immunity thesis, or once again insisting upon the fact that "non-conformist" groups called for the destruction of parliamentary democracy and the establishment of an authoritarian regime in order to reduce universal suffrage to a mere footnote. Or perhaps, once more, to demonstrate that their programs concerned anything but a simple attempt to regenerate political thought in France. It seems clear, then, that one cannot directly address the question of the impermeability of French political culture to fascism without taking into consideration the opinion of *established* social elites.

Before beginning such inquiries, it is necessary to construct the necessary ana-lytical framework. We must first abandon the premise that the historiography in France of French fascism must be carried out according to hitherto accepted methodology. It is not my intention to produce yet another definition of fascism in order to determine whether or not the individuals under consideration merit such labels. Without simply restating various methodological critiques previously expressed toward the classificatory approach,[5] it is clear that any resumption in extenso of the political ordering of historical actors inevitably transforms the his-torian into a judge, dispensing "good" and "bad" labels (one group or individual is republican, another fascist, etc.). A more effective modus operandi operates according to an analysis of tendencies, a study of the reception of fascism in its generic sense—the regimes, parties, and individuals that can be classified as fascist (Franco, Salazar's Estado Nuovo, the NSDAP, etc.). In other words, the fascism considered here is less an analytical concept than a social word, subject to a wide variety of meanings and interpretations.

To the best of my knowledge, only two authors have examined the reception of Fascist Italy in interwar France. In his study of the French press, Pierre Milza arrived at the conclusion that "until September 1938, French views towards Mus-solini's Italy remained more or less unchanged: hostility from supporters of the Popular Front and *démocratie chrétienne*; a wait-and-see attitude and moderate stance among centrists and conservatives; sympathy and hope for Franco-Ital-ian reconciliation from the extreme Right."[6] Bruno Goyet has revised this as-sessment, demonstrating that numerous leaders of the conservative Right went beyond mere *attentisme* and moderation, and that, *a contrario*, in the case of the

Action française they were genuinely wary of the new fascism.[7] This chapter will not focus specifically upon the French reception of the Italian Fascist regime, however, but on the ambiguity of the term *fascism* itself. Nor does it engage in the construction of an all-encompassing response to the thesis of the French school of political history, whose problematic is badly construed, for it incorporates overly general and inaccessible concepts ("France," "The French"). Rather, I seek to reformulate the terms of the debate while providing the broad outline of a resolution.

It would no doubt be erroneous to attempt to find a comprehensive set of opinions concerning a group—the established elites—whose homogeneity was illusory, and whose viewpoints mirrored the rationale inherent in each component of the various fields of power (economic, academic, cultural, political, etc.).[8] For this reason, it is preferable to limit the scope of the present research effort, undertaking an examination of three important journals from the interwar era: the *Revue politique et parlementaire* (RPP), *Revue du droit public et de la science politique* (RDP), and *Sciences politiques* (SP). All three accurately reflect the worldview of the social milieu of publicists, lecturers at the l'Ecole libre des sciences politiques, and conservative political figures. Of the three, the RDP and SP are seemingly the most interesting, because they do not belong to the traditional domain of the history of (political) ideas. Their value lies in the fact that they tended to shy away from political discussion, instead adopting the form of exotopic discourse,[9] social engineering, or even supposedly impartial descriptions of society. When used by historical actors, these modes of perception reveal less about the mindset of the author than about the workings of everyday life. The works of Norbert Elias are of particular importance here. Elias sought to explain the tensions provoked by the transformation of the noble and seigniorial warrior caste into an ecclesiastical aristocracy weakened by royal power, drawing upon d'Honoré d'Urfé's *L'Astrée*, which had a significant impact upon court society, rather than various satirical works denouncing royal omnipotence. He regarded the novel as much more than a simple literary work, "the testimony of human beings that reveals, in a given choice, the inclinations, experiences, and behavior that [pave] the way for a better understanding of humanity."[10]

This chapter takes into account articles that address, in one way or another (whether resulting from the study of social achievements, the analysis of laws, etc.), Fascist Italy, Nazi Germany, Salazar's Portugal, Spain, and, in order provide a useful point of comparison, French political, economic, and social conditions.[11] It may seem unsound to compare a periodical that offered a political reading of social affairs (the *Revue politique et parlementaire*) to two journals that provided a scientific analysis of political and social events. However, the selection is justified because the RPP enjoyed close links not only with the legal profession, but also the l'Ecole Libre des Sciences politiques and the world of politics, notably in terms of social recruitment, the circulation of elites, and simply the training of

political personnel and the civil service.[12] Moreover, this chapter does not consider ultra-conservative periodicals—*La Revue des deux mondes*, for example—as their editorial content was often quite close to that of *L'Action française*.[13] Thus it does not pay excessive attention to the *élites déclassées*, or those threatened by a loss of social standing.

For those who wish to consult a biographical dictionary, it is easy to contextualize the authors cited below and, consequently, to remove the persistent question of their responsibility (political, moral, etc.). As it is not my intention to take this into consideration, I have studiously avoided any analysis of the social class of the author. Only very occasionally does the chapter evoke social rank, in order to focus exclusively on a grammatological analysis of the discourse under examination.[14]

When Scientific Neutrality Emphasized "Positive" Fascist Action

It is almost impossible to understand the meaning and impact of the following statements, while avoiding the temptation to pass judgment, without a brief reminder of certain facts concerning academics during the first half of the twentieth century, and jurists in particular. Given the role entrusted to them by Republican governments, as arbitrators between the state and the people, in the fashion of saints who mediated between the faithful and the divine in Catholic dogma, university professors occupied a central position in the field of power via their positions in the *grandes écoles* of the Parisian elite, administrative commissions, ad hoc assignments on the government's behalf, etc. Among jurists, the possession of a monopoly on certification in other legal professions, stable recruitment patterns, and criteria for professional advancement unchanged since the mid-nineteenth century encouraged a certain *esprit de corps*.[15] But this did imply homogeneity: squabbles between Parisian professors and those in the provinces led to the emergence among the latter of alternative theoretical systems that seriously questioned the juridical models of the Republican state.[16]

Nonetheless, juridical positivism, the unifying paradigm of these approaches, operated according to a specific modality of perception concerning the "real." Declared the sole source of law, the state was most often envisioned as disconnected from the social milieu or interest groups that formed it and made up its "reality." As Georges Gurvitch notes, this legal practice led jurists to theorize "within the formalist space of the public sphere, with the legislative texts and the verdicts of the *tribunaux officiels* preventing any contact with daily life and society at large."[17] This approach produced severe consequences during the fall of the Third Republic, particularly in the appearance of anti-Semitic legislation under Vichy.[18] As Danièle Lochak has demonstrated, the commentary in Vichy's anti-Semitic laws, written by professors of public law, contributed to the trivialization of this legisla-

tion, "through the effects of euphemism and de-realization which enabled the conversion of anti-Semitic rationale into legal rationale. Perceived through the abstract veil of juridical concepts, for commentators and readers alike the anti-Semitic measures lost any concrete meaning, their tragic impact obscured by the purely formal treatment of the problems that they caused."[19]

In analyses of the Fascist and Nazi dictatorships, this manner of perceiving truth resulted in an omission of their ultimate aims and a restriction of scholarly interest to the methods and means used in both regimes. Hence this juridical positivism found an echo in the productivist arguments of economists. In a study of leisure policies under the Third Reich, one author writes: "Our intention is not to analyze the *motives* of German politics. We wish to limit ourselves to a study of the *organization* and *mechanics* of physical education, sport, and leisure; that will satisfy our curiosity."[20] This consisted, more generally, of a reading in terms of economic assessment: "More than nine hundred thousand hectares of unculti-vated and unhealthy land will shortly be sown or planted, after heroic efforts of 'improvement.' *A new order and a new spirit* today invigorate Italy."[21] As for the social assistance campaigns run in Germany, they appeared much more convinc-ing in the eyes of the auditor of the council of state than "those individuals who failed to adopt the welfare mentality."[22]

A number of editors from the *Revue politique et parlementaire* used the same methodology, combined with statements that were undeniably value judgments: "far too often, fascism is perceived solely as a proponent of order which has *com-mendably disciplined* a previously anarchic country. Yet this is only one aspect of a fascist revolution that, while reinstituting the primacy of hierarchy, also radically transformed the political, social, and economic organization of the nation."[23] What are the essential merits of Italian Fascism according to this author? "The suppression of strikes and, in a way, the severity with which they have quelled all acts of insubordination. ... [The Fascists] have restored the leadership prin-ciple, previously so enfeebled, in private life and matters of state alike."[24] The author further deplored "the frequent comparisons made between Fascism and Bolshevism, two movements that [are] so resolutely opposed to one another," as Fascism had effectuated social "pacification" and economic recovery, unlike Bolshevism.[25]

On the political spectrum, the Italian and German fascist parties (PNF and NSDAP) occupied a completely unique position. Yet what did this singularity entail, precisely: the activity of the SA or Blackshirts? The ideology propagated by their leadership? Or their stranglehold over the political machinery? None of them, claims the author in question. Their common uniqueness—and once again, their value—is to have overcome political divisions and partisan quarrels. Having emphasized that "everywhere electoral politics jeopardizes governmental stability, often in alarming fashion," the author is impelled "to note that [the PNF] is not a political party; it is in fact the opposite of a political party.... The

PNF more than any other legal entity is an ethical body; *it is not an expression of social class, but of a religious faith.*"[26] An analogous view appears in a remark by a professor of law from Strasbourg who, on the subject of the NSDAP, wrote about "the Hitlerian movement—which transcends the limits of a simple political party."[27]

To be sure, there was no shortage of warnings in the press, most notably the exceptionally lucid commentary by René Capitant concerning the Nuremberg racial laws.[28] Another author forcefully emphasized the fact that "the fascists repealed many of the guarantees contained in the old legal code that prevented errors and arbitrary decision-making."[29] Yet on the other hand, the *Revue du droit public* published the analysis of a German professor who, despite his best efforts, presented the NSDAP's racial theories in a rather unattractive fashion: "far too often … National Socialist doctrine is considered exclusively on the basis of anti-Semitism. National Socialist theory has a far greater foundation.… Racist doctrine certainly confirms racial inequality, but without actually proclaiming the superiority of any one race in particular."[30] Another author reminded his readers that racism was not a Nazi "invention," but a French one, personified by the Count Arthur de Gobineau, "one of the most profound and original thinkers of his era" who "wanted to resolve the *racial question* that others had already advanced. His knowledge was remarkably extensive; he possessed a profound knowledge of such matters."[31]

The crux of the issue can be found in the meaning that various authors ascribed to the concept of "neutrality" in the social sciences. The ambiguity born of a twin imperative, to produce studies shorn of political advocacy while examining "fascism" through the lens of models that emphasized evaluations and growth, often resulted in attempts to transform the concept of "neutrality" into "balanced and unbiased opinion," thus reconciling conflicting views on a given subject. For example, one author wrote: "In spite of the uncompromising beliefs to the contrary supported by a tempestuous press campaign, Italian racism consists of a quite moderate final solution to the Jewish question." His argument concerned the conventional distinction between Jewish citizens and Jewish foreigners.[32] This is a perfect example of the neutralization of political issues (or sentiments) through the "neutrality" of scientific discourse.

The demands of neutrality, which involves a distancing of the individual or group from contemporary political issues, no doubt facilitated the location of Nazism within the time-honored tradition of German nationalism: "Do you remember Imperial Germany? The facade of parliamentarism, sure. But on every street corner, there was a cop or soldier to quickly remind you that the German Constitution was just a forgery."[33] Nazi anti-Semitism could be explained by a supposed German atavism: "Neither anti-Semitism nor racial theory was invented by Hitler. Pan-Germanism has always been violently anti-Semitic."[34] An even more conclusive analysis of Hitler can be found in the following statement: "Let's not

fool ourselves. This man is neither a *condotierri* nor a corrupt politician foisted on the German people by foreigners; he represents the life blood of today's Germany and therein lies the tremendous, genuine danger that we must never take for granted."[35] Hence the "Germans" or Germany were less frequently criticized as a result of the peculiarity of their leadership or the ideology that they propagated, but rather due to the regression of the "German soul."

Portugal and Spain: Between the Excellence of the Leader and the Hatred of the Masses

Of all the countries that experienced dictatorships, Fascist Italy and Nazi Germany roused the greatest interest, the subjects of the vast majority of articles reviewed for this study. Contrary to what has been written by certain historians, Salazar's *Estado Novo* sparked little enthusiasm: only one article was written about him in the three periodicals examined here. To be sure, the title pulled no punches, as it evoked nothing less than "the financial and economic renaissance of Portugal."[36] The contents were a panegyric, with a laudatory portrait painted by a Portuguese academic depicting a man "without personal ambition ... motivated solely by a *sense of patriotic duty*."[37] Such unflinching praise forces one to ask whether the author is explicitly campaigning in favor of a French version of Salazar, in which case the article can be read less as a scientific article, and more as a declaration of constituency.

On the other hand, political developments in Spain stirred up far greater interest. In this regard, the Spanish Civil War produced preconceptions in almost every article concerning that country. The recurring theme of these tragic events can be summarized as follows: the civil war was the fruit of the "Spanish soul," which produced certain unique character traits, notably the absence of any understanding of the common good. The statements below are thus marred by anthropological pessimism, in addition to a rather sullen social racism toward the Spanish "masses." One author notes,

> the vast majority have never demonstrated anything but complete indifference towards the *res publica*; whether this is due to their quasi-oriental passivity and lack of political education—or any education at all, for that matter—is hard to say. The persistence of 'idiosyncratic' tendencies, in spite of advances in communications technology, and the glorification of self-sufficiency and individualism (which can be found in the Hispano-American people and lead easily to backwardness) tend to prevent the Spanish from developing a sufficiently practical sense of the concepts of the nation and state.[38]

The same author further states, "the Spaniard is above all a *passionate* man. His awakenings are brusque, even violent; the people move rapidly from one extreme

to another, but generally only for a brief time, after which they quickly relapse into their customary apathy. One must also take into account another Iberian characteristic, a messiah complex, that is to say the exaggerated hope that Spain will be forced to effectuate institutional change, whatever that may entail."[39]

André Siegfried's "racial geography"[40] serves as a theoretical model for social behavior in another article: "If we find certain representatives of the blond haired and blue eyed sort [in Spain], there are mostly brown-skinned Iberians of African origin.... This brown racial type, the most dolichocephalic in Europe ... is a Spanish people unchanged since the Stone Age. It is they who form the provincial caste among the population, altered only by a slight racial mixture."[41] The author further proclaims that "Spain is completely permeated with this African and Oriental character," and that "hard and dry like the soil, the race bred passionate characteristics, rebelling against any sense of discipline. Don Quixote was the first anarchist and it was his individualism that enabled this anarchy; he followed his own path."[42] In the final analysis, this distinctive racial identity explained the absence of genuine civilization in Spain: "in the end, despite his unshakable faith, the Spaniard has remained a primitive. He has not become the slightest bit Christian, any more than he has become altogether European."[43] Furthermore, "rational republicanism is insufficient for the average Spaniard, who is violent by nature, impatient, and incapable of initiating reform through reason and common sense."[44]

Regarding the civil war itself, some writers attempted to unmask the hidden agenda of the Spanish Republicans: "As they endeavored to find out if Soviet Russia would successfully impose its harsh dictatorship, or if an authoritarian regime, inspired by those in Italy and Germany, would come to dominate the Iberian Peninsula, the Left hoodwinked the public by claiming that we were witnessing a conflict between fascism and liberal republicanism." Between the absolutist dictatorship of the Soviets and the mere autocracy of Franco, the public did not have much choice. Moreover who, precisely, were the Republicans? "Veritable gangs, recruited among political and workers' organizations, and also—since the prison doors had been opened—among the dregs of society."[45] Thus the articles did not discuss the relative "merits" of Franco, but rather painted an apocalyptic portrait of the Republican camp (a seething herd of savage and violent yokels, unfit for civilization, etc.).

Another Constant: Le désordre français

Having completed a general overview of those European dictatorships that left an impression upon the French mindset in the 1930s, it would seem useful in concluding this chapter to examine the judgments passed on the French political situation itself. It almost goes without saying that if it is certainly possible to

find equally positive assessments of Republican institutions, their impact appears greatly diminished. In reality, these appraisals were not really that positive, for France was only ever understood in light of the disarray produced by its institutions. Moreover, comparisons between the social policies of Italy and Germany and those of France never favored the latter. In describing German athletic programs, one author noted with dismay that "the French authorities appear to have become lethargic, no longer willing to support the crusade undertaken by the apostles of reform."[46]

A government policy subjected to such commentary was often assessed in order to find tangible solutions to the problem of French "disorder." As has been shown, descriptions of "totalitarian" or "authoritarian" regimes enabled the sketching out (in broad outlines at least) of the outline of an ideal(ized) institutional order, but also—and this constitutes the final point in this study—the theoretical framework for examining economic questions or capital-labor relations.

French politics was consumed with the question of institutional reforms for the Third Republic, particularly following the events of 6 February 1934, and the formation of the Doumergue commission.[47] The prevailing slogan of the day was "parliamentary government, there is the enemy!" which perfectly summarized the collective opinion gleaned from the articles in all three periodicals. The mere mention of governmental crisis allowed authors to fire both barrels at Léon Blum's Popular Front ministry: "The government of Mr. Léon Blum has cheated. Chosen by a diverse array of voices through universal suffrage, in support of a vague program of republican defense, he [i.e., Léon Blum] consolidated his majority only to very possibly hand it over to the rioters."[48] The author then launched into an analysis wholly consistent with elitist theoreticians of democracy: "It would be completely false to claim that the country has spoken with any real understanding of the Popular Front's economic and fiscal platform."[49] The root of the problem, according to the author, lay in the fact that "the political formula of the Popular Front government *is not a French idea*. It was instead presented in minute detail by Dimitrov at the seventh Congress of the Communist International in 1935 with an eye towards coordinating the fight against fascism."[50] Basic rights and freedoms were no longer respected after the ascension of the Popular Front:

> On the pretext of defending the Republic, the rights of Parliament, and the wishes of the electorate, since June 1936 we have lived under a regime chiefly characterized by the fact that at every conceivable opportunity the government has taken the advice of extra-parliamentary groups with reckless abandon and without due parliamentary representation, and they hide behind these opinions.[51]

Thus the Popular Front ignored the fundamental principles of the Republic, proving that the nation's institutions themselves facilitated corruption and divisiveness.

Criticisms of the Popular Front also opened up the Pandora's box of anti-communism. As one author noted: "There are two main reasons for the need to take special measures against the representatives of a doctrine as dangerous as communism. The first is the complete dependence of all communist parties on the USSR, a foreign state. The second is the clearly revolutionary character of the actions of such parties."[52] The author lamented that nothing had been done on this account, despite the existence "in our legal code of the means to confront these revolutionary disturbances. Measures in the penal code concerning crimes and misdemeanors against national security, the statute concerning the leagues, certain measures within the 1881 law on freedom of the press, the law of 7 June 1848 on public disturbances, and the law of 28 July 1894 regarding anarchist leaders will provide sufficient ammunition for the government."[53] Worse still, bemoans the author, political authorities (i.e., the Chautemps government) and the judiciary have proven completely indifferent to the problem: "The absence of laws for the defense of France against communism is far too often accompanied by the failings of the police, the prosecutors, and the courts."[54] Yet beyond this "basic" critique of the laxness of the authorities, the author denounced the absence of fairness among those in power: "Everyone always remembers when it is a question of pursuing that so-called criminal organization called the Cagoulards or treating a war hero [an allusion to General Duseigneur] like the worst type of criminal. Why have we forgotten that the Communist Party's stated goal is the destruction of the current regime by violence and revolution?"[55]

When they were not providing a detailed denunciation of the supposed weakness and bias of the executive branch, various authors subjected republican institutions themselves to public ridicule. This was certainly the point that elicited the greatest agreement, a commonly shared view even among the staunchest defenders of parliamentarism:

> Three necessary measures are vital: the legislative branch must be sanitized, the authority stolen from the executive branch must be restored, and the judiciary must be protected in the most efficient manner possible. To sanitize the legislative branch, the composition of parliament must be changed, altering its work methods and limiting its power. To strengthen the executive branch, the President must be given the right to dissolve the Chamber without the approval of the Senate, the number of ministers must be limited, and the majority among them must be chosen from outside parliament. Departments must be safeguarded against the introduction of parasites [sic] into their ranks and, on the other hand, managers protected against the improper demands of government officials, notably against strikes, which are incompatible with the concept of public service. To ensure the independence of the legal system, it would be best for the justices of the Supreme Courts (appeals court, Council of State, and Court of Auditors) … to elect a leader.[56]

Such proposals largely reflected the widespread opinions of the time. The abhorrence of the parliamentary "game" was a regular topic for discussion in press,

political, and legal circles, particularly after the fall of the Daladier ministry in February 1934.[57] At that time, there were very few conservative politicians or jurists who did not regularly engage in anti-parliamentary talk. This viewpoint was so commonly expressed that even those least likely to be accused of anti-democratic tendencies employed it. Even René Capitant, while a professor at the Faculty of Law of the University of Strasbourg, described the Chamber as "a carnival sideshow where the deputies shred ministerial portraits."[58] Capitant's expression was echoed by Jacques Bardoux, for whom the "country is condemned to suffer from a regime of cabinets without specialists or stability. And the Republic is in the process of dying."[59] André Tardieu set the tone in the political milieu, demanding the "restoration in France of a minimum of executive authority, a minimum of parliamentary freedom, a minimum of financial order, a minimum of electoral etiquette, and a minimum of civic morality."[60] Tardieu campaigned for the abolition of Senatorial control over the *droit de dissolution*, strict parliamentary spending limits, the use of consultative referenda, and the institution of a *statut des fonctionnaires*. It was this plan that inspired Gaston Doumergue's program. Despite the fact that representatives quickly quashed it, jurists nonetheless warmly welcomed the proposals, to the point that some abandoned their traditional role of impartial criticism. Hence Joseph Bathélemy could write, "On the whole, the *Constitution Doumergue* tends to strengthen state authority. With all my heart and great enthusiasm, and without hesitation, I endorse this excellent, fruitful idea."[61]

The section of the *projet Tardieu* devoted to the civil service became the centerpiece of various articles in favor of institutional reform, usually viewed through the prism of modernization: "We must shake off administrative apathy, alerting the public to the perils of purchasing the enthusiasm and efficiency of our officials abroad with promotions and favoritism, along with those compatriots marshaled and guided by our diplomats in the common defense of our endangered country. … Must we borrow our motto from Germany, expressed in French terms: 'France Awaken!'"[62] Germany once again predominated. The oft proclaimed need for a strong executive in France was frequently tendered in the name of Franco-German relations:

> An accord with Germany? YES. It will be a great help. It will further be essential if France and Germany do not wish to vanish underneath the ruins of Europe.… But to find the solution to the problems at hand, there must be talks with Germany. And we know today and have always known that Germany respects only force, and has made peace only with the strong.… They despise the weak.… Their mentality has always been thus.… So we must be strong and unified, with national discipline, knowing how to sacrifice personal interest, whether in the case of political parties or churches.[63]

Calls for such harmony were even more pronounced as the nation's English ally was viewed with great suspicion: "In the course of our history, hasn't England

always been the most unceasing and unrelenting enemy of France? ... Didn't they start the Hundred Years' War? Didn't they burn Joan of Arc? Weren't they Napoleon's jailers? Haven't we long called them 'perfidious Albion?'"[64]

A broad consensus thus emerged concerning the issue of institutional reform, and particularly its political component, centered upon the strengthening of executive power and the (at times, radical) weakening of parliamentary power. Neither were reformist wishes limited to the political realm alone, also incorporating the economic and social spheres. For many, corporatism seemed to provide the answer to those problems, even a miracle cure. The reorganization of worker-ownership relations was a constant concern. If there existed a pressing need to revamp labor relations in the workplace, it was the result of "disorder" caused by unionized workers, guilty of having "betrayed" their cause: "the French syndicalism that its creators envisioned exclusively as an act of justice towards the working class has, through the natural course of events, become a revolutionary movement and the cause of social warfare."[65] Corporatism, and particularly its Italian variant, became one of the solutions most frequently proposed to put a stop to the disorder: "The corporations prepared since 1926, constituted in December 1934, and put in motion in 1935, have in eighteen months successfully regulated production and operated as skilled and capable vocational parliaments."[66]

Conclusion

Given the rather unsympathetic portraits of French politics and society on one hand and the approving, if not laudatory, depictions of the German, Italian, and even Portuguese regimes on the other, it is quite impossible to speak of the impermeability of French political culture to "fascism." Numerous works had shown that this was true of the *syndicats de cadres* that constantly referenced Italian Fascism,[67] along with the economists and corporatist theorists who ceaselessly boasted of its "merits,"[68] not to mention the ambiguity of certain leaders of the parliamentary Right or certain "non-conformist" groups. Yet beyond this observation, the validity of the results produced by an ideological analysis of political positions must be called into question. It would be absurd to claim that the economists, commentators, and any other intellectuals who, in the course of their research, expounded upon the relative merits of Italian Fascism (or any other type) were "fascist." Such stances reflect the perception schemes embedded in the specific logic of a given field rather than purely political considerations. In the final analysis, only the use of broad legal or political categorizations enabled the perception of fascist regimes in principally evaluative, yet sometimes laudatory terms. That they contributed to the development of a prevailing ideology, in the sense of a circular construction of "problems," legitimate questions, and as many suitable "answers," is undeniable.

Acknowledgments

I would like to thank Chico Villano for his help and, above all, Samuel Kalman for the translation and also for all his good advice.

Notes

1. Serge Berstein, "La France des années trente allergique au fascisme. A propos d'un livre de Zeev Sternhell," *Vingtième siècle* 2 (1984): 83–94. If Berstein articulated the most advanced thesis concerning the immunity of France to fascism, others have provided an equally notable contribution to the construction of this thesis, principally through their critiques of Zeev Sternhell's *Neither Right Nor Left*: Michel Winock, "Fascisme à la française ou fascisme introuvable?" *Le Débat* 25 (1983): 35–44; Jacques Julliard, "Un fascisme imaginaire: à propos du livre de Zeev Sternhell," *Annales ESC* 4 (1984): 849–859; Philippe Burrin, "Poings levés et bras tendus: La contagion des symboles au temps du Front populaire," *Vingtième siècle* 11 (1986): 5–20.

2. Among various references, see particularly Zeev Sternhell, *Ni droite ni gauche. L'idéologie fasciste en France*, 3rd edition (Brussels, 2000); Robert Soucy, *Fascismes français? Mouvements antidémocratiques, 1933–1933*, trans. Francine Chase and Jennifer Phillips (Paris, 2004); Kevin Passmore, *From Liberalism to Fascism: The Right in French Province* (Cambridge, 1997); William Irvine, "French Fascism in France and the Strange Case of The Croix-de-Feu," *Journal of Modern History* 63, no. 2 (1991): 271–295; Brian Jenkins, ed., *France in the Era of Fascism: Essays on the French Authoritarian Right* (New York, 2006).

3. Ralph Schor, *L'antisémitisme en France pendant les années trente* (Brussels, 1992); Paul J. Kingston, *Anti-Semitism in France during the 1930s: Organisations, Personalities and Propaganda* (London, 1983).

4. The classic distinction between "outsiders" and "establishment" is here taken from Norbert Elias and John L. Scotson, *The Established and the Outsiders: A Sociological Enquiry into Community Problems* (London, 1994).

5. For a critique of the classificatory approach, see the major contribution of Michel Dobry, "La thèse immunitaire face aux fascismes: Pour une critique de la logique classificatoire," in *Le mythe de l'allergie française au fascisme*, ed. Michel Dobry (Paris, 2003), 17–67.

6. Pierre Milza, *Le fascisme italien et la presse française, 1920–1940* (Bruxelles, 1987), 236–237.

7. Bruno Goyet, "La 'Marche sur Rome': version originale sous-titrée. La réception du fascisme en France dans les années 1920," in *Mythe de l'allergie français*, ed. Dobry 69–106.

8. I here use Bourdieu's concept of fields (see *Le sens pratique* [Paris, 1980]).

9. I have here borrowed the concept defined by Marc Angenot in *La parole pamphlétaire* (Paris, 1982), 41. Angenot describes a discrepancy between *l'être* and *le devoir-être*.

10. Norbert Elias, *La société de cour* (Paris, 1985), 279–280.

11. One article simultaneously examines Fascist Italy and Nazi Germany.

12. On these points, see especially Christophe Charle, *Les élites de la République, 1880–1900* (Paris, 1987), *La République des universitaires, 1870–1940* (Paris, 1994), and "Les parlementaires: avant-garde ou arrière-garde d'une société en mouvement? Vue d'ensemble," in *Les parlementaires de la Troisième République*, ed. Jean-Marie Mayeur, Jean-Pierre Chaline, and Alain Corbin (Paris, 2003), 45–65; Mattéi Dogan, "Les filières de la carrière politique en France," *Revue française de sociologie* 8 (1967): 468–492.

13. For example, questions concerning education. One need only compare the discussion of the fear of coeducation in the *Revue des deux mondes* examined by Antoine Prost in *Histoire de l'enseignement, 1880–1968* (Paris, 1968) with the Action française perspective described in Francine

Muel-Dreyfus, *Vichy et l'éternel féminin. Contribution à une sociologie politique de l'ordre des corps* (Paris, 1999). It is clear that there is essentially no difference between the two.

14. In the manner of Luc Boltanski, *De la justification. Les économies de la grandeur* (Paris, 1991).

15. Christophe Charle, "L'ordre des juristes," in *La République des universitaires, 1870–1940* (Paris, 1994), 243–287.

16. Guillaume Sacriste, *Le droit dans la République (1870–1914). Légitimation(s) de l'Etat et construction du rôle de professeur de droit constitutionnel au début de la Troisième République*, thèse de science de politique, Paris-I, 2002.

17. Georges Gurvitch, "Eléments de sociologie juridique (extraits)," *Droit et Société* 4 (1986): 425.

18. Dominique Gros, ed., "Le droit antisémite de Vichy," *Le genre humain* 30–31 (1996).

19. Danièle Lochak, "La doctrine sous Vichy ou les mésaventures du positivisme," in *Les usages sociaux du droit*, ed. Danièle Lochak (Paris, 1989), 255.

20. Hubert D'Hérouville, "L'organisation de la culture physique et des loisirs dans le IIIᵉ Reich," *RSP*, June 1938, 230 (emphasis by the author).

21. E. D. B., "La situation économique de l'Italie," *RSP*, July–September 1931, 461 (emphasis by the author).

22. Jacques Doublet, "L'assistance dans le IIIᵉ Reich", *RSP*, December 1937, 474.

23. André Nicolas, "L'Italie fasciste à la recherche de l'équilibre social," *RPP*, April 1933, 127 (emphasis by the author).

24. Ibid., 129.

25. Ibid., 135.

26. Jean Huszar, "Du parti à l'Etat. Etude sur le fascisme," *RSP*, October–December 1934, 517 (emphasis by the author).

27. Henry Laufenberger, "Classes moyennes et national-socialisme en Allemagne," *RPP*, April 1933, 47 (emphasis by the author).

28. René Capitant, "Les Lois de Nuremberg," *RPP*, May 1936, to which can be added Marcel Prelot's work *L'empire fasciste: les origines, les tendances et les institutions de la dictature et du corporatisme italiens* (Paris, 1936).

29. Morris Ploscowe, "La procédure criminelle dans l'Italie Fasciste," *RSP*, October–December 1932, 522.

30. Ulrich Scheuner, "Peuple, Etat, droit et doctrine nationale-socialiste," *RDP*, January–March 1937, 47.

31. René Laurent, "Les origines idéologiques du mouvement national-socialiste allemand," *RSP*, January–March 1932, 112 (emphasis by the author).

32. Jean Meynaud, "Présentation du racisme italien," *RSP* December 1938, 522 (emphasis by the author).

33. Boris Mirkine-Guetzévitch, "L'Etat Allemand," *RPP*, December 1939, 292.

34. Ibid., 295–296.

35. R. Carmille, "Sur le Germanisme," *RPP*, September–October 1939, 40 (emphasis by the author).

36. Paul Lavagne, "La renaissance financière et économique du Portugal," *RSP*, July–September 1935.

37. Ibid., 369.

38. Angel Marvaud, "La seconde République Espagnole: La genèse de la Révolution du 14 avril, le gouvernement provisoire et les élections aux Cortès constituantes," *RSP*, October–December 1931, 494.

39. Ibid., 495.

40. For a description of Siegfried's racial theory, see Pierre Birnbaum, "André Siegfried: la géographie des races," in *"La France aux Français!" Histoire des haines nationalistes* (Paris, 1993), 145–186.

41. Jean Baumel, "Psychologie politique du peuple espagnol," *RPP*, June 1939, 483.

42. Ibid., 484–485.

43. Ibid., 485–486.

44. Ibid., 492.

45. Ibid., 494.

46. Hubert D'Hérouville, "L'organisation de la culture physique et des loisirs dans le IIIe Reich," 228.

47. Jean Gicquel and Lucien Sfez, *Problèmes de la réforme de l'Etat en France depuis 1934* (Paris, 1965).

48. Jean Compeyrot, "Entre le rouge et le noir," *RPP*, May 1937, 188.

49. On this point, see Daniel Gaxie, *Le cens caché. Inégalités culturelles et ségrégations politiques* (Paris, 1979). Quoted in Jean Compeyrot, "Entre le rouge et le noir," 189.

50. Ibid., 200 (emphasis by the author).

51. Ibid., 201.

52. Frédéric Eccard, "La législation anticommuniste dans le monde," *RPP*, July 1938, 3. The author was an ex-senator from the Bas-Rhin. In addition, he wrote two articles in the *Revue des deux mondes*: "Moscou à Paris," September 1936, and "Le bolchevisme paralyse la France," May 1938.

53. Ibid., 31.

54. Ibid., 30.

55. Ibid., 31–32.

56. H. Barthélemy, "Pour une concorde nationale … S.O.S!" *RPP*, June 1934, 423–424. It is difficult to resist the temptation to link these recommendations with the contents—for the most part—of the constitution of the Fifth Republic. This confirms, if such proof is even necessary, that the debates of the 1930s finally found an (institutional) response thirty years later. See Delphine Dulong, *Moderniser la politique: Aux origines de la Ve République* (Paris, 1997).

57. Marc Simard, "Doumergue et la réforme de l'Etat en 1934: la dernière chance de la IIIe République?" *French Historical Studies* 16, no. 3 (1990): 576–596.

58. *La réforme du parlementarisme*, cited in Simard, 580.

59. Jacques Bardoux, *Le drame français*, cited in Simard, 583.

60. André Tardieu, *L'heure de la décision*, cited in Simard, 584.

61. Joseph Barthelémy, "La constitution Doumergue," *RPP*, November 1934, 225–248.

62. Rober-Reynaud, "La propagande allemande," *RPP*, April 1933, 98.

63. Colonel Grasset, "Une entente est-elle possible entre la France et l'Allemagne?" *RPP*, January 1936, 33–34.

64. Ibid., 16.

65. Maurice Ajam, "La position présente du corporatisme," *RPP*, October 1936, 40.

66. A.-E. Guillaume, "Italie et Allemagne," *RPP*, October 1936, 26.

67. Luc Boltanski, *Les cadres: La formation d'un groupe social* (Paris, 1982); Steven Kaplan, Philippe Minard, eds., *La France, malade du corporatisme ? XVIIIe–XXe siècles* (Paris, 2004).

68. See particularly Alain Chatriot, "Les nouvelles relèves et le corporatisme: Visions françaises des expériences européennes," in *Les relèves en Europe d'un après-guerre à l'autre. Racines, réseaux, projets et postérités*, ed. Olivier Dard and Etienne Deschamps (Brussels, 2005), 162.

CHAPTER 12

SALVATION, SATIRE, AND SOLIDARITY
Right-Wing Culture in Interwar France

Jessica Wardhaugh

The creative relationship between left-wing politics and culture has been justly emphasized in studies of interwar France. Many histories of the Popular Front describe the lively performances of the *October* group in the occupied factories of spring 1936, or the state-funded production of Romain Rolland's *Quatorze Juillet* in celebration of political victory, with actors and audience joining triumphantly in *La Marseillaise* and *L'Internationale*.[1] Studies of political engagement in film have drawn attention to Jean Renoir's collaboration with the French Communist Party for the creation of electoral propaganda, and to the documentaries of the socialist Marceau Pivert, testament to the transient exuberance of left-wing demonstrations of the period. The demonstration has also received close analysis as a form of political and cultural expression.[2] But what of right-wing culture in the interwar years? Certainly, the Right was similarly endeavoring to appeal to and organize the masses, not only in political formations but also in sporting associations, theatrical and cinematic societies, musical groups, and holiday camps. This was particularly true of some of the newer movements and parties of the extreme Right.[3] Right-wing films, plays, social and cultural associations have not, however, received the same attention as their left-wing counterparts. It is unusual to find reference to the plays produced by the Francistes or by Action française (AF),[4] the cultural associations of the Parti populaire français (PPF), or the theatrical and film evenings of the Croix de Feu / Parti social français (CF/PSF), other than that preceding the notorious riot in Clichy in March 1937.[5] Yet if the cultural ventures of the Right were less prominent than those of the Left—and

certainly than those of a left-wing government—they were nonetheless important to the political aspirations and experience of these formations. How, then, did these groups and parties conceive of the political role of culture, whether the latter was conceived as artistic representation or as forms of association? Is it possible to detect the influence of the Italian or German Right on the cultural theories and practices of their French counterparts? And what was the significance of this expanding role of culture in mass politics?

This chapter offers a preliminary examination of the meanings and role of culture for some of the more radical right-wing movements and parties of interwar France. It seeks first to situate the French Right in its European context, and to consider French responses to the political uses of culture in Italy and Germany for the dissemination of ideology and the forceful creation of communities on national or local levels (the response of the French Right to left-wing cultural initiatives in France I have considered more fully elsewhere).[6] It then focuses on two case studies—Action française (AF) and the Croix de Feu / Parti social français (CF/PSF)—in order to suggest the importance of cultural theories and practices in interwar French politics.[7]

Art and Power in Interwar Europe

The interwar years were characterized by an extraordinarily intense relationship between culture and politics on a European level. New regimes established in the wake of radical upheaval or revolution required in turn new sources and representations of legitimacy, and culture offered the potential for the refinement of ideology, the dissemination of propaganda, and the development of a sense of belonging (reinforced, of course, by strict policies of exclusion).[8] It was important, therefore, not only to continue state patronage of the arts, but also to establish control over all forms of expression reaching a wide audience, particularly the cinema. In Russia, state control over the cinema was established through the creation of Goskino in 1922; in Italy, Mussolini's particular interest in cinema and especially newsreel gave powerful impetus to the productions of *Cinecittà*, while the simultaneous development of the Opera Nazionale Dopolavoro strengthened state control over a wide range of leisure activities, from *bocce* groups to mass theater.[9] In Germany, the Nazi seizure of power was closely followed by the establishment of the Reich Ministry of Popular Enlightenment and Propaganda under Joseph Goebbels. By 1934, new film legislation had already extended the role of the censor and laid the foundations for the Nazification of the film industry. Meanwhile, party-approved films documented and idealized their mass meetings, most notoriously in the case of Leni Riefenstahl's *Triumph of the Will*.[10] Riefenstahl's film epitomized the theatricality of a form of politics that aimed to impress and enthrall its supporters through a heady mix of rites, symbols, and

mass fervor.[11] This was a combination also favored in Nazi theater, which drew inspiration from the *völkisch*, the expressionist, and the neoclassical to achieve its ends.[12]

This "fascination of fascism," as it is sometimes termed,[13] has captured the imagination of a number of historians in the last twenty years.[14] Two themes, closely if paradoxically linked, dominate their studies and can also be usefully applied to the French context: firstly, the aestheticization of politics through culture; and secondly, the use of culture to draw politics more closely into everyday life. On the one hand, artistic representation (films, plays, even paintings or architecture) could develop a political vision—the image of a utopian society, or the denunciation of its enemies—while at the same time aestheticizing the political experience by endowing the sense of belonging with a mystic or mythic dimension.[15] Riefenstahl's *Triumph of the Will,* for example, uses the Nuremberg rallies of 1934 to glorify the powerful relationship between the providential leader and his disciplined followers, including not only documentary footage of the mass meetings but also a heroic musical accompaniment and a series of symbolic images, notably that of the mountain.[16] Even in more consciously escapist films, political messages were not necessarily far beneath the surface.[17] Among Italian Fascist films, *The Old Guard* (1935) explicitly glorified the moment of conversion to fascism by representing a group of peasants joining in the march on Rome, whereas *Scipio the African* (1937) offered a more oblique—though no less forceful—legitimization of the regime's political aspirations through its depiction of the Roman Empire. On the other hand, the contexts in which such cultural productions were experienced by the wider population represented a political conquest of banal and everyday activities, potentially normalizing the regime through its infiltration of the comfortably familiar. As Victoria de Grazia argued in *The Culture of Consent* (1981), Fascist occupation of daily life through the control of sporting, theatrical, cinematic, and other leisure associations offered a means of anchoring the regime in the experience of its citizens, whether or not they were ideologically disposed to be its supporters. While this did not necessarily represent a complete success for Mussolini's conception of "everything in the state, nothing outside of the state," and although Italy remained characterized by a greater pluralism than Germany in cultural terms, the political organization of artistic and associative life, from football groups to peripatetic theater, certainly increased state presence in the social and cultural lives of its citizens: men, women, and children alike.

Culture and the Right in France

The differences between the French Right and its Italian and German counterparts were, of course, considerable. First and foremost, the more radical right-

wing groups and parties under consideration here were not in power during the interwar years: groups such as AF, the Francistes, the CF/PSF, and the PPF simply did not have at their disposal the material or financial means available to ruling parties in Italy or Germany, or to the left-wing Popular Front governments in France. But this did not deprive them of a cultural vision or production, albeit on a narrower scale. The cultural and intellectual influence exercised by the Right in this period has already been widely acknowledged,[18] and is clearly evident in studies of such certain right-wing theater and film critics as Lucien Rebatet, Robert Brasillach, and Maurice Bardèche.[19] In the case of Brasillach and Bardèche, nationalistic preoccupations influenced both the form and content of their analysis: films were classified according to national origin, and particular attention was paid to the collective experience of the crowd at the cinema, not least when this audience was presented with the visual and aural impression of leadership through newsreels and documentary films. Brasillach was careful to underscore the potential of the newsreel, and regretted that censorship so often suppressed images of leadership in favor of showing "anodyne boxing or tennis matches, bicycle races in France or Italy, viticulture in California, harvest-time in Denmark, regional festivals the whole world over, beauty contests on every beach, dog shows on every pavement, and truth nowhere at all."[20]

The strongly politicized reflections on culture offered by Brasillach and Bardèche are well known; other right-wing commentators have received less attention but held similar concerns. Newspapers of political groups or parties—the CF's *Le Flambeau,* for example, or the PPF's *L'Émancipation nationale*—employed their own regular theater and film critics: Lucien Romans wrote for the PPF on theater and film, while Gabriel Boissy described in *Le Flambeau* his utopian visions for the mass theater of the future: "vast amphitheaters, as welcoming as luxurious cinemas," where citizens would gather to be inspired by heroic and patriotic spectacles.[21]

On a more prosaic level, the cultural production of right-wing groups and parties was also making progress.[22] The Francistes, who quite probably received subsidies from Fascist Italy, also showed Italian films to their members: 700 gathered to watch *The Old Guard* in the Parisian Salle Pleyel in July 1935.[23] They produced their own plays on related themes, concluding a holiday camp in summer 1935 with a gymnastic display and a drama in which a young revolutionary and internationalist was converted to fascism.[24] The PPF created Cercles populaires français where workers and writers could meet (an explicit imitation of the PCF's Maisons de Culture); Action française continued to develop its satirical theater; and the CF and PSF produced documentary films of their activities, organized plays and festivals for their children's summer camps, and planned grandiose mass spectacles to celebrate their expanding influence. These last two initiatives are explored in more detail below.

The "New Laugh" of Action française

In order to appreciate the significance of Action française's interwar theater, we need to return to its creation in 1907. It was in the October of that year that Maurice Pujo, better known as leader of the movement's young street fighters or Camelots du Roi, first proposed the establishment of a theater that would complement the work of the existing Ligue, Institut, and Revue d'Action française, attracting an attentive public for the diverse purposes of pleasure, study, and political activism.[25] Pujo intended to establish firm foundations for counter-revolutionary culture, which would in turn act as "a powerful factor in the work of French Restoration." As he underlined, "the program of Action française is not solely political and social. It also encompasses the restoration of French order in the moral and aesthetic domains." The theater of AF was thus to counter romanticism in literature and republicanism in politics,[26] with the same force that the Camelots employed against their republican opponents in the streets of Paris. Pujo also made clear that this would not be an ordinary theater with regular performances in a fixed location, but a flexible enterprise offering a limited number of private performances each season. The private character he envisaged would, moreover, permit greater freedom in the eventual selection and treatment of topical subject matter. Pujo hoped for an outpouring of counter-revolutionary drama in the neoclassical style, finding its inspiration in Aristophanes but equally in Molière and Racine. While he denigrated contemporary naturalist plays for neglecting the distinction between the dramatic and didactic, he anticipated comedies and tragedies that would move away from propaganda to the depiction of timeless human emotions and foibles. Indeed, he hoped the new drama would favor a rebirth of a "freer, more audacious" comedy, pitiless in its dissection of contemporary behavior, social types, and notorious personalities. "We will attempt to recreate for our French democracy," he explained, "the ancient comedy with which Aristophanes, at the close of the fifth century BC, castigated Athenian democracy. We will bring to the stage a satire that is direct, biting (going as far as naming its objects, and even further!), insolent and comical in its treatment of contemporary men and ideas."[27]

In essence, therefore, Maurice Pujo intended this counter-revolutionary and neoclassical drama to provoke a "new laugh" at republican failings, while also offering to AF supporters further opportunities for entertainment and conviviality. Boosted by Pujo's own enthusiasm and by the collaboration of his fellow Camelots, the theater of Action française soon became an established feature of the movement's cultural life, even if it failed to achieve his initial, rather grandiose expectations. He himself composed its first play, a comic homage to Aristophanes appropriately entitled Les Nuées (The Clouds). If the plot owed much to its classical counterpart, the characters were nonetheless contemporary (though this, too, was faithful to the spirit of Aristophanes).[28] Among them were a Jewish writer,

an opportunistic aristocrat rallied to the Republic, a self-made bourgeois businessman, and a left-wing intellectual whose complex and insubstantial theories formed the clouds of the play's title. Performances of the play were held privately, but a number of critics nonetheless attended, relaying their experiences (and in some cases admiration) in such periodicals as *Gil Blas, Comœdia, Le Figaro,* and *Le Gaulois.* Pujo had intended to follow this success with a dramatic depiction of Joan of Arc, an extremely popular subject in plays of the time, but the call of the street and his motto of "politics first" led him to abandon this particular project, and pursue his counter-revolutionary ambitions by other means.[29]

Action française's "new laugh" at the Republic continued to reverberate in the cultural activities of the movement, not only in the street politics of the Camelots du Roi but also in their theatrical sketches, and most particularly in the revues that often featured in their celebrations. The satirical style of such revues changed little between the prewar and interwar years. Some of the targets also remained the same, including the once socialist premier (and many times government minister) Aristide Briand, served up as a mackerel at an AF banquet of 1909,[30] and represented in the company of "Léonie" Blum in 1930.[31]

While cultural events offered opportunities for shared laughter at the expense of the Republic, they also fostered loyalty to France's royal family and to the current Orleanist pretender. In April 1935, an Action française meeting at the Maison de la Mutualité in the fifth arrondissement of Paris featured *La Croisière de Campana,* a documentary film depicting the recent voyage of the Comte de Paris. In the film, the pretender appears as a dynamic modern prince, an excellent swimmer and sportsman, with a keen interest in the life of his crew and a generous hospitality to visitors (supposedly of all classes) on board his ship. The same evening also included another documentary film of royalist interest: *Le Sentiment populaire en monarchie.* This film portrayed Hitler's reception of a delegation of workers (which the Action française audience greeted derisively), the funeral of King Alexander of Yugoslavia, the coronation of Leopold III of Belgium, and the wedding of the Duke of Kent. As the title of the film suggests, it was the people's fervent acclamation of royal—and by implication natural—leaders that was the principal focus.[32] Other films on similar themes included *Versailles, œuvre royale* and *La Maison de France* (an overview of forty monarchs and 1000 years of French history).[33]

The "Counter-Society" of the Croix de Feu / Parti social français

The Croix de Feu movement and its successor, the Parti social français, certainly devoted less attention than Action française to the theoretical bases of a politicized culture,[34] but their projects were no less ambitious in scale. The grandest of them remained unrealized, but provide a fascinating and indeed surprising insight

into the party's cultural ambitions in the late 1930s. Among the private papers of Colonel de La Rocque are a series of anonymous designs and draft budgets for mass spectacles, intended for performance in theaters, sports stadiums, and amphitheaters across France.[35] Some of the later plans, particularly those of 1939, provide detailed insights into the content of the spectacles. One, for example, depicts the struggle of the "Croix de Feu spirit" in the years 1914–1939. While the first act charts the emergence of wartime fraternity through sacrifice and victory, the second portrays the foundation of the Croix de Feu veterans' movement, with its defense of *Travail, Famille, Patrie* explicitly contrasted with "class struggle," "free unions," and "the Internationale." The third act then focuses on the dissolution of the CF and its rebirth as the PSF in 1936.[36] There were also plans for a more abstract depiction of this struggle and victory, notably proposals for a festival of darkness and light intended for summer 1939. Here, the battle between the elements of earth, air, fire, and water was to give way to light, harmony, and collaboration, the bright and colorful finale including tricolor illuminations and a 30-meter French flag.

Several of these projects envisage not only the participation of young musicians and dancers from local sections of the PSF but also—and this represented a large proportion of the proposed expenditure—the participation of the Paris-based *Ballets fantastiques Loie Fuller*. Fuller (1862–1928) was an American dancer who had taken Paris by storm in 1892 with the premiere of her "Serpentine Dance" at the Folies-Bergère.[37] An eccentric character in her own right (she knew the Curies and had a laboratory in her garden that she once succeeded in blowing up), she impressed audiences and critics alike with her innovative use of flowing material and electric light, the latter still a rarity in the theater. Her most notorious spectacle was probably the "Fire Dance" performed to Wagner's *Ride of the Valkyries*, with Fuller dancing on a glass platform while dramatically illuminated from below with red light. No wonder that the symbolists of the 1890s rhapsodized about her intoxicating combination of light, color, and movement, or that she should prove so widely influential, even attracting praise from the Italian futurist Filippo Tommaso Marinetti, whose ideas on dance were ostensibly concerned more with the beauty of machines than with human creativity.[38] Perhaps Marinetti's interest in Fuller provides some clue as to why a French right-wing movement with its origins in a veterans' association should have considered the Loie Fuller ballet company for its political spectacles. Marinetti seems to have been moved less by Fuller's dexterity than by the dazzling effects she achieved. Such innovative use of light, color, and stage mechanics must also have suited the aspirations of this new party of the 1930s, concerned both to further its membership and prominence and also to encompass the cultural lives of its members through events and activities of mass appeal.

While these spectacular designs remained at the planning stages, smaller-scale plays did feature in the life of the CF and PSF.[39] The movement and party pro-

duced their own musical and dramatic evenings, even inviting professional actors and singers from the Comédie française and the Opéra,[40] and the Croix de Feu were in 1936 offered a special discount to performances of *H-Hour* at the Théâtre de l'Humour in Paris.[41] Plays were also performed at the Travail et loisirs holiday camps that were closely linked (though not explicitly affiliated) to the party.[42] Usually the plays were held at the concluding festival around the campfire, and were not overtly political in nature, seeking rather to integrate the working-class children attending the camps into French literary culture, for example through the enactment of some of La Fontaine's fables.[43]

The most coherent and extensive cultural production of the CF/PSF was, however, a series of silent documentary films, twenty-four of which are now preserved in the collections of the Centre National de la Cinématographie at Bois d'Arcy.[44] The films were produced by what was known as the "Groupe photo-ciné," or *Cinémalik*,[45] part of the propaganda section of the CF/PSF whose activities were praised by Charles Vallin, director of propaganda, at the National Congress of the PSF in Lyons in November 1937. Vallin explained that the films could be hired by local sections for a small fee, and promised to make available "a certain number of films representing several of our parades, our impressive participation in the festival of Joan of Arc in Paris, the charitable sale of the French royal family, and the children's holiday camps."[46] The making of one of the films is also briefly documented in a police report of 1936, which records that a hundred Volontaires nationaux (the youth section of the Croix de Feu) assembled in Neuilly to sing *La Marseillaise,* shout "Vive la Rocque!" and also mime attendance at a speaker meeting for the benefit of the attendant film crew.[47]

The collection of films that remains to us has a broadly documentary feel, recording regular events in the Croix de Feu/PSF calendar, such as the Armistice or the commemoration of Joan of Arc, as well as aspects of the wider life of the movement: mass meetings, family outings, and so on. Despite the fact that these are silent films, they rarely employ intertitles to explain or emphasize the action depicted, and only one includes flashback. The overall impression is that these have been produced with a CF/PSF audience in mind, and were designed to complement the depiction of regular and exceptional activities in photographs and articles of *Le Flambeau* or *Le Petit journal,* or in the recording of La Rocque's speeches.[48]

Yet the documentary character of the films, and their relative lack of technical sophistication, should not cause us to forget that they were produced by the propaganda section and were intended for more than entertainment. As police reports suggest, the meetings recorded in the films were sometimes staged rather than spontaneous. And if they provide a fascinating and perhaps unwitting insight into the social constitution of the CF/PSF, the films also offer a more conscious depiction of leadership, as well as satirical portraits of their adversaries, and an impression of solidarity in backstage political life that was key to both movement

and party. Unsurprisingly, many of the films follow the photographic conventions of the time for the representation of a providential leader, who is customarily shown from below in attitudes of resolution. But there is also an evident concern to project a more informal image, to move away from La Rocque's associations as leader of a veteran soldiers' movement to his role as father figure in the self-styled "great reconciled family" of the PSF. Central in both cases is the relationship between the leader and his people, vital also to the Croix de Feu/PSF's conception of political salvation. *Les Croix de Feu se déplacent* (1935–1936) and *Une réunion du PSF* (1937) are good examples of this. Although the films present different phases in the development of the movement and party, they both combine the depiction of La Rocque as the inspired leader, speaking energetically from the platform to a calm, disciplined crowd below, with images of his passage through the crowd, greeting adults and children alike, laughing and at ease.[49] His attire is formal, but non-military. Clearly he is intended to appear as a leader in direct contact with his people, far removed from the "house without windows" that was the Chamber of Deputies.[50]

The satire in these films is less pronounced than in Action française's theatrical productions, but aims at some of the same targets. These films concentrate on CF/PSF meetings rather than on moments of political opposition, whether in the streets or elsewhere, yet underlying rivalry is nonetheless evident. One of the earliest films depicts Croix de Feu members forcefully ejecting a troublemaker intent on sowing disorder among the crowd.[51] In 1935, the coincidence of rival political commemorations on 19 May—that of the Commune at the Mur des Fédérés; that of Joan of Arc on the Rue de Rivoli—offered a pretext for representing the Croix de Feu's enemies as partisans of revolution and civil unrest. The directors of *La Fête de Jeanne d'Arc, 1935* thus included newspapers headlines such as "Long live Stalin, leader of international Revolution!" to contrast with images of their own disciplined crowds acclaiming La Rocque and singing *La Marseillaise*. In 1938, *Des Croix de Feu au Parti social français* continued this diatribe against the "foreignness" of the Left in its criticism of Léon Blum for his part in dissolving the Croix de Feu. First he is represented ironically as "a true Frenchman"[52]; later, we see a rifle range at a PSF fair where the targets include not only Léon Blum, but also Communist Jacques Duclos, trade-union leader Léon Jouhaux, Mussolini, and Hitler.

Images of CF/PSF parades and family gatherings provide a valuable insight into the membership of movement and party. As in caricatures in Leftist newspapers such as *Le Populaire*, male participants in the CF parades appear well dressed and in their characteristic berets. But we also see families at the *Vente de charité*, young girls at a local PSF section in Montrouge, and women in regional costume as part of the procession in honor of Joan of Arc.[53] As well as providing images of heroic or providential leadership, these films thus offer—as they are surely intended to do—a glimpse of the banal, everyday, and familial activities of a movement and

party seeking legitimacy and acceptance, and to dispel the widespread association of La Rocque's CF with militarism and extremism. As Jean-Paul Thomas has argued, the PSF encompassed "an extraordinary range of social activities: sporting societies, working-class centers, holiday camps, university centers,"[54] so much so that its members could potentially spend most of their lives, at work or at leisure, surrounded by PSF companions in a sort of "counter-society."[55] For La Rocque, this ever-expanding network of supporters at various social levels was intended to reinforce the strength of the new party, justifying its claims to represent the masses and the "true French." "The social movement of the Croix de Feu," he insisted in March 1936, "must create … a network gathering all the true French together, for France will be strong only through the union of the French."[56] In his view, the social and cultural life of the party did not develop alongside its political aspirations; it was in fact vital to their fulfillment.

Conclusion

This desire to create "counter-societies"—political parties that would also encompass the social and cultural lives of their members—was a powerful characteristic of the interwar years, and one clearly visible in France as elsewhere in Europe. In Germany and Italy, right-wing culture was intended to render political experience at once more aesthetic and more banal, more sublime and more everyday. In France, Left and Right alike (and in deliberate rivalry) similarly turned to culture as a means of advancing and consolidating their mobilization of the masses. Though French right-wing movements had more limited means at their disposal than right-wing governments in Germany or Italy, or than Popular Front governments in France, they too employed artistic representation and associative life both to develop aspects of their ideology (such as concepts of leadership) and also to build up the common life and the fidelity of their supporters. The production of plays and films in particular offered a means to develop images of political salvation, to satirize political enemies, and finally to promote an associative life which was, for these self-consciously anti-political movements, a desirable and even essential goal.

Notes

1. See, for example, Pascal Ory, *La Belle illusion: culture et politique sous le signe du Front populaire* (Paris, 1994), and Julian Jackson, *Defending Democracy: The Popular Front in France, 1934–38* (Cambridge, 1988).

2. On the films of Pivert and Renoir, see Philippe Burrin, "Poings levés et bras tendus: la contagion des symboles au temps du Front populaire," *Vingtième siècle* 11 (1986): 14–15. Danielle Tartakowsky's work on the demonstration is indispensable. See in particular *La Manifestation de rue en*

France, 1918–1968 (Paris, 1997); *Le Front populaire: la vie est à nous* (Paris, 1996); and Tartakowsky and Michel Margairaz, *L'Avenir nous appartient: histoire du Front populaire* (Paris, 2006).

3. See Jessica Wardhaugh, *In Pursuit of the People: Political Culture in France, 1934–39* (Basingstoke, 2009), 56–93.

4. The theatre of Action française is not mentioned in Eugen Weber's *Action française* (Paris, 1982), in François Huguenin's *À l'École de l'Action française. Un siècle de vie intellectuelle* (Paris, 1998), or in Paul Renard's *L'Action française et la vie littéraire, 1931–1944* (Lille, 2003). For an overview of this theater, see Jessica Wardhaugh, "Un Rire nouveau: Action française and the art of political satire," *French History* 22, no. 1 (2008): 74–93.

5. Alan Williams, for example, suggests that the French Right did not produce any films in the 1930s (*Republic of Images: A History of French Film Making* [Cambridge, 1992]), 215; Jean-Pierre Jeancolas similarly considers only left-wing groups in his article on the "Cinéma des années trente: la crise et l'image de la crise," *Le Mouvement social* 154 (1991): 173–95. Jacques Nobécourt mentions but does not analyze the silent films of the Croix de Feu/PSF in his biography of La Rocque: *Le Colonel de la Rocque, 1885–1946, ou les pièges du nationalisme chrétien* (Paris, 1996); and the films are not discussed in Sean Kennedy's valuable study of the movement and party: *Reconciling France against Democracy: The Croix de Feu and the Parti Social Français 1929–1945* (Montréal-Kingston, 2007).

6. See Wardhaugh, *In Pursuit of the People*, especially chapter 5.

7. This chapter is drawn from a wider study of theater and politics during the Third Republic. For other examples, see Wardhaugh, *In Pursuit of the People*, chapter 5; Wardhaugh, "Popular Theatre and Revolutionary Identity: Anarchist and Communist Culture in Paris, 1900–1934," in *Entertainment, Leisure, and Identities*, ed. Roger Spalding and Alyson Brown (Newcastle, 2007), 96–111; and Wardhaugh, "Parisian Stars under a Provençal Sky: The Théâtre Antique d'Orange and the Making of Mediterranean Culture," *Nottingham French Studies* 50, no. 1 (2011): 7–18.

8. On this theme, see Mary Vincent and Erica Carter's chapter on "Culture and Legitimacy," in *The War for Legitimacy in Politics and Culture, 1936–46*, ed. Martin Conway and Peter Romijn (Oxford, 2008), 147–175.

9. Victoria de Grazia, *The Culture of Consent: Mass Organization of Leisure in Fascist Italy* (Cambridge, 1981); Jeffrey Schnapp, *Staging Fascism: 18BL and the Theatre of Masses for Masses* (Stanford, 1996); and Simonetta Falasca-Zamponi, *Fascist Spectacle: The Aesthetics of Power in Mussolini's Italy* (Berkeley, 1997).

10. Robert Brasillach and Maurice Bardèche considered the most important aspect of this film to be its depiction of "the union of the people with their leader." In *Histoire du cinéma* (Paris, 1948 [1936]), 418. David Welch offers a broader overview of contemporary German film in his *Propaganda and the German Cinema* (Oxford, 1983).

11. See Eric Hobsbawm's introduction to Dawn Ades, ed., *Art and Power: Europe under the Dictators, 1930–1945* (London, 1995), especially page 15.

12. An excellent overview of German theatrical production in this period is provided by Gerwin Strobl, *The Swastika and the Stage: German Theatre and Society, 1933–45* (Cambridge, 2007).

13. For example, Günter Berghaus, ed., *Fascism and Theatre: Comparative Studies on the Aesthetics and Politics of Performance in Europe, 1925–1945* (Oxford, 1995), 1.

14. Formerly, there was a tendency to underline the fundamental opposition between fascism and culture—an argument with strong foundations, for Nazi and Fascist regimes did not of course conceal their rejection of certain artistic forms or exponents. An important reassessment of the relationship between fascism and the artistic avant-garde is offered by Mark Antliff in his *Avant-Garde Fascism: The Mobilization of Myth, Art, and Culture in France, 1909–1939* (Durham, 2007). See also Kimberley Jannarone, *Artaud and his Doubles* (Michigan, 2010).

15. Falasca-Zamponi, *Fascist Spectacle*, 2–5. See also the work of Alice Yaeger Kaplan, who describes Brasillach and Bardèche as "professional esthetizisers of politics" in "Fascist Film Esthetics: Brasillach and Bardèche's *Histoire du cinema*," *MLN* 95, no. 4 (1980): 864.

16. Some historians have therefore followed in the footsteps of Siegfried Kracauer, who argued in his influential 1947 work that the Nazi themes of national unity and authoritarian leadership had been foreshadowed in a series of postwar German films. Siegfried Kracauer, *From Caligari to Hitler: A Psychological History of the German Film* (London, 1947), especially chapter 21, "National Epic." David Welch accepts this argument for thematic continuity (albeit with reservations) in his *Propaganda and the German Cinema.*

17. French film critics Robert Brasillach and Maurice Bardèche, discussing Nazi film production in their renowned *Histoire du cinéma*, suggested that a cinematic eulogy of health and nature might be as fervent a defense of racial superiority as a more overtly political counterpart, such as *Hitler Youth Quex*. See *Histoire du Cinéma*, 417–418.

18. One might also point to the existence of right-wing "intellectuals," even if they were often explicitly anti-intellectual in outlook. See Pascal Balmand, "Anti-intellectualisme dans la culture politique française," *Vingtième siècle* 36 (1992): 31–42.

19. On Rebatet's film criticism, see Christopher Faulkner, "Theory and Practice of Film Reviewing in France in the 1930s: Eyes Right (Lucien Rebatet and Action française, 1936–39)," *French Cultural Studies* 3, no. 8 (1992): 133–155; and on Brasillach, see Kaplan, "Fascist Film Esthetics." Some thirty Parisian newspapers (with a combined total of 8 million readers) offered weekly reflections on the latest films, and after the electoral victory of the Popular Front in 1936, it was often the right-wing papers that boasted the highest sales. *Gringoire* claimed, with a circulation of 700,000, to be the most widely read of the French weeklies. See Faulkner, "Theory and practice of film reviewing," 136.

20. Brasillach and Bardèche, *Histoire du cinéma*, 284. They suspected that the censors preferred to exclude images of leadership from the cinema for fear of unruly crowd reactions. If this was the case, then the censors' fears were not unfounded, for French police reports occasionally note the violent and conflicting reactions provoked by the depiction of political events and leaders on screen. In July 1935, for example, documentary films on the recent demonstrations prompted cries of "Vive la Rocque!" and "La Rocque au poteau!" in the cinemas, as in the street. In Archives nationales, Paris (hereafter AN), F7 13305, "P.P. 18 juillet 1935."

21. Gabriel Boissy, *Le Flambeau*, 15 February 1936. Boissy was also editor of the theatrical review *Comœdia*.

22. The Franciste leader Marcel Bucard also attended the only international fascist conference, held in the Swiss town of Montreux in 1934.

23. The film was preceded by a speech from Marcel Bucard in praise of Italian Fascism. See AN F7 13241, "P.P. 12 juillet 1935."

24. AN F7 13241, "P.P. 2 septembre 1935."

25. Maurice Pujo, "Le Théâtre d'Action française" (Reproduced in *Action française, revue bimensuelle*, 1 October 1907), Bibliothèque nationale, Paris, Département des Arts du Spectacle (hereafter DAS), Rt 3794.

26. Pujo's theories related closely to the work of Pierre Lasserre, whose widely read attack on romanticism (*Le Romantisme français*) had appeared in 1907. Charles Maurras was also influenced by Lasserre's theories.

27. Pujo, "Le Théâtre d'Action française."

28. Maurice Pujo, *Les Nuées, comédie contemporaine en trois actes et en prose, imitée d'Aristophane* (Paris, 1908). See also Aristophanes, "The Clouds," in *The Complete Plays*, trans. Paul Roche (New York and London, 2005), 129–200. For a fuller description of the plot and characters, see Wardhaugh, "Un Rire nouveau," 81–84.

29. The theatrical group did perform one further play, Jules Lemaître's *Princesse de Clèves*, at the Théâtre des Arts in June 1908.

30. AN F7 12864, "P.P. 30 septembre 1909." His detractors described him as a *maquereau* or pimp for the Republic.

31. "Ohé! Les Locarno … frageurs … ," *La Revue des Camelots du Roi*, 27 June 1930; *Action Française*, 30 June 1930, DAS Rt 3794. Briand was by this point an influential presence in the League of Nations.

32. Archives de la Préfecture de Police, Paris (hereafter APP), Ba 1895, "P.P. 4 avril 1935."

33. APP Ba 1893, "P.P. 21 décembre 1935."

34. Although critics such as Gabriel Boissy offered their reflections on theater and cinema in newspapers like *Le Flambeau* and *Le Petit journal*, there was no exact equivalent to Maurice Pujo.

35. 451 AP 187 (Archives Nationales, Fonds François de la Rocque). I am grateful for the permission granted by the La Rocque family to consult their private archives.

36. 451 AP 187, "1914–1939: 25 ans de lutte de l'esprit Croix de Feu."

37. On her life and influence, see Sally R. Sommer, "Loie Fuller's art of music and light," *Dance Chronicle* 4, no. 4 (1981): 389–401; and on the resurgence of interest in her work, see Martha Ullman West, "New light on Loie Fuller," *Dance Chronicle* 21, no. 3 (1998): 485–487.

38. Ted Merwin, "Loie Fuller's influence on FT Marinetti's Futurist Dance," *Dance Chronicle* 21, no. 1 (1998): 79.

39. As well as creating drama, the CF/PSF also inspired bonapartist poetry in praise of its leader (Gérard Jaussaud, *Aurores Croix de Feu*, Paris, 1935), and marching songs. Gabriel Boissy wrote the lyrics for the *Chanson des Croix de Feu et des Volontaires nationaux*.

40. E.g. APP Ba 1901, "P.P. 1 mars 1936" and "P.P. 14 mars 1939." Professional artists were regular contributors to partisan political events, as police archives (especially for the PCF) demonstrate.

41. APP Ba 1902, "P.P. 9 janvier 1936." In the popular imagination, Colonel de la Rocque was closely associated with such militaristic rhetoric.

42. Antoinette de Préval, director of the Travail et loisirs association and a devoted member of the PSF, was careful to emphasize the distinction between the two. For her work with the camps, see 451 AP 180.

43. 451 AP 178, Anonymous diary (20 July—20 August 1938). The double educational role of these camps encompassed not only the children but also the young *moniteurs* who looked after them, and is discussed in Laura Lee Downs, "Each and Every One of You Must Become a *Chef*': Towards a Social Politics of Working-Class Childhood on the Extreme Right in 1930s France," *Journal of Modern History* 81, no. 1 (2009): 1–44. I am grateful to Laura Lee Downs for alerting me to the existence of these plays.

44. I am grateful to the Centre National de la Cinématographie (CNC) for having allowed me to view this collection in its entirety.

45. The films name a variety of directors: Couffin (1935), Louis Carrot (1935–1936), and Jean-Paul Guittard (1945).

46. Vallin's report to the congress was subsequently published as *L'Activité du PSF* (Paris, 1937). Not all of these are among the films now preserved at the CNC, and it is hard to be certain what proportion of the overall output this collection represents.

47. APP Ba 1901, "P.P. 10 février 1936."

48. In 1937, both Colonel de la Rocque and Jacques Doriot signed a contract with "Technisonor" to produce audio recordings of their speeches (the company had recently recorded the PSF's national congress). In APP Ba 1945, "P.P. le 7 janvier 1937."

49. Comparable images appear in *Une Réunion du PSF en plein air à Lille* and *Un meeting du PSF en plein air, 1938* (CNC).

50. Michel Winock describes this conscious anti-politicism as one of the most striking characteristics of the movement. See "Populismes français," *Vingtième siècle* 65 (1997): 85.

51. *La Messe des morts* (CNC).

52. When founding his new party, La Rocque criticized Blum's leadership of the Popular Front government with the observation that "his commanding action was not taken from the front lines of trench warfare." APP Ba 1952, "P.P. 12 juillet 1936, réunion du PSF."

53. *La Vente de charité, La Section PSF de Montrouge, 1938,* and *Paris, le 14 mai 1939.*

54. Jean-Paul Thomas, "Les Effectifs du PSF," *Vingtième siècle* 62 (1999): 74.

55. William Irvine makes this point in "Fascism in France and the strange case of the Croix de Feu," *Journal of Modern History* 63, no. 2 (1991): 283. The term *counter-society* comes, however, from an article on one of the PSF's rivals, the Parti communiste Français. Marc Lazar, "Le Parti et le don de soi," *Vingtième siècle* 60 (1998): 37.

56. APP Ba 1901, "P.P. 31 mars 1936."

HISTORIOGRAPHY

CHAPTER 13

BEYOND LEFT AND RIGHT
Rethinking Political Boundaries in 1930s France

William D. Irvine

When in 1983, the Israeli historian, Zeev Sternhell, published a book on French interwar fascism, entitled *Ni droite, ni gauche*, he provoked a major controversy. To some degree, the uproar was a response to his principles of inclusion and exclusion. Bertrand de Jouvenel was not at all happy to find himself included among the ranks of French fascists; others were troubled by a definition of fascism that excluded the huge but also incontestably right-wing Croix de Feu. But lurking behind much of the unhappiness with Sternhell, I suspect, was a widespread uneasiness that any political formation in France could somehow be "neither right nor left." This violated the cherished conceptions of French historians, weaned on François Goguel's classic dichotomy of the forces of "movement" and those of the "established order": in short, the political Left and the political Right.[1] There had been, many seasoned historians of France believed, a Right and a Left and the twain simply could not meet. Pretending otherwise was perverse; it risked scrapping a conceptual framework that had long made it possible to grasp the bewildering political universe of Third Republic France.

To be sure, this framework was not always as clear to contemporary political actors as it was to their subsequent historians. Granted, Radicals and Socialists were usually comfortable enough with the label *Left*. Witness the Bloc des Gauches or the Cartels des Gauches. Socialists did, of course, periodically wonder what, apart from anti-clericalism, qualified Radicals as being a party of the Left, given their penchant, more often than not, for sitting in governments of the Right, or more accurately the center-Right. In light of how much separated them

from the Communists, not a few Socialists expressed reservations about including the latter on the Left, at least as they understood it—anticipating, as it were, Guy Mollet's later celebrated line to the effect that Communists were not left but east. Still they did believe that there was a Right, beginning at some (necessarily) ill-defined point to *their* right.

The problem was that those to their right did not see it that way. As a self-identifying label, the word *Right* lost all political currency after about 1885. It was replaced briefly and plausibly enough by *conservative*, which soon gave way, and rather less plausibly, to *liberal*. And by the early twentieth century, the preferred label for those on the right side of the political spectrum was *left!* The conservative Republicans who sat to the right of the Radicals baptized themselves "centre-gauche," apparently undeterred by the fact that in any meaningful sense they were on the Center-Right. Their spiritual descendants in the interwar years sat in a parliamentary formation called the "républicains de gauche." Right-wing Radicals in the interwar years, distressed by the promiscuous contacts of more mainstream Radicals with the Socialists, sat independently as the *Gauche Radicale*. Indeed, just about any formation that could spot anyone to their right insisted on being designated as left. Only the extreme Right, bereft of neighbors to their right, had to eschew any claim to be on the Left and had to settle for being "moderates." In due course, paramilitary, extra-, and anti-parliamentary formations did emerge with a plausible claim to being to the right of the moderates but like the Croix de Feu they persisted in designating themselves as "neither right nor left."

The French Revolutionary tradition was not much more useful in providing a political taxonomy, if only because it was invoked by almost everyone, with the notable exception of the Action française. In 1889, the Royalists attempted to spoil the centenary celebrations by pointedly wondering why the Republicans were so enthusiastically feasting off what had been a monarchist achievement, the creation of a constitutional monarchy, akin to the one the Royalists wanted to restore. The Radicals, they spitefully observed, might have the common decency to wait four years, at which time they could celebrate their own historic contribution to French history: the Terror. The Jacobin label apparently fit the Radicals and the Socialists but also, after 1935, the Communists, who in the words of historian Daniel Brower had become the "new Jacobins."[2] The pacifist Radical Gaston Bergery comes across as a Jacobin in 1940; much like the arch reactionary (and momentarily pro-war) Philippe Henriot in 1939. The Croix de Feu peppered its periodicals with Jacobin imagery much like the Jeunesses patriotes, forever calling for a Committee of Public Safety to rescue France. The famous Jacobin dictum to the effect that when the government violates the rights of the people, insurrection is both the most sacred of rights and the most indispensable of duties, was invoked with equal enthusiasm by both the Left and the Right.

Undeterred by these label-mongering antics, most historians persist in believing that Left and Right are meaningful categories because by and large they described two mutually distinct camps subscribing to mutually incompatible principles. Those on the Right identified, with various degrees of conviction and intensity, with some or all of the following: clericalism, nationalism, militarism, racism of one form or another, unabashed defense of the existing social order, and a suspicion of, or even intense hostility toward, parliamentary democracy. The political principles of the Left were in general the negation of those of the Right: anti-clericalism, internationalism and pacifism, anti-militarism, profound or even revolutionary changes to the social order, an unconditional defense of parliamentary democracy, and unqualified hostility to racism in any form. These were, as scholars often admitted, sweeping generalities. Not all members of the Left or the Right embraced these positions with equal consistency or equal conviction. Nonetheless, these broad definitions of Left and Right appeared to have a general heuristic value. And they did so for the very good reason that at certain times in the history of the Third Republic these broad-stroke categorizations did seem to conform to observable reality.

This said, though, it was equally and uncomfortably the case that at any given moment in the seventy years of the Republic, the above-listed taxonomy could do some considerable violence to political reality. Nationalism is a place to start. For at least the first two decades of the Third Republic, nationalism—or at least a super-heated patriotism seeking *revanche* against Germany—was rather more characteristic of the Radical Left than of anyone on the Right. The Right, be it the *droite capitularde* of the early 1870s, the irenic Opportunists of the 1880s, or the Royalists at any point in this period, were profoundly uneasy at the prospect of war. Mindful of the experience of 1870–1871 (not to mention that of 1792–1793), they identified war with revolution. They, or at least the more paranoid among them, were not beyond claiming that the only reason that the Radical Left sought *revanche* was to obtain the necessary preconditions for a new version of the Commune or indeed the Terror. Such fears dissipated by the later 1890s, not least because it became apparent that the current repository of revolutionary zeal, the Socialists, were increasingly dead set against war.

The obsession of the Right with the war-revolution nexus went into hibernation for a generation but did not die. It emerged in even more virulent form by the mid-1930s when the Right was confronted with a resurgent Left, some fraction of which appeared to call for war or, more accurately, a firm diplomatic posture with respect to Germany that threatened to lead to war. The clearest statement of this obsession came from the erstwhile Germano-phobic nationalist Louis Marin. At the height of the Munich crisis, he unblushingly declared that "an international clan wished diabolically to unleash a world war, at any price and at every opportunity … the weight of the war would have been supported by the French they are attempting to Bolshevize. The unquestionable purpose of war was the

triumph of the brutal revolution of Moscow."[3] But Marin was in good—or more accurately unaccustomed—company. At more or less the same time, the principled and impeccably left-wing pacifist from the Ardèche Elie Reynier was also fulminating against those on the Left who were "ready to begin yet again ... the crime of 1914" by virtue of being under the sway of "the Stalinist warmongers."[4] Marin's conversion to the cause of peace, like most of his colleagues on the Right, was of recent date, unlike his anti-communism, which was not. Reynier's pacifism went back nearly a quarter century, unlike his anti-communism, which was about three years old. Pacifists of the Left and neo-pacifists of the Right differed in one critical respect. In the late 1930s, the bulk of the Right became pacifist (although this was a label they deliberately eschewed) because they were and always had been anti-communist. A significant element of the Left became anti-communist because they were and always had been pacifist. For all that, in 1938, their positions effectively converged. By 1939, both Left and Right were returning to a neo-Jacobin diplomatic firmness, albeit for different reasons. For the Right, it was the collapse of the Popular Front and the concomitant disappearance of their fear of war-inspired revolution; for the Left, it was the German dismantling of Bohemia and Moravia, disabusing most pacifists of the illusion that Hitler's ambitions were limited to undoing the iniquitous Treaty of Versailles.

The issue of militarism poses comparable complexities. The Dreyfus affair casts a giant shadow over the whole subject. In its wake, it is hard not to envisage the French officer corps as a band of Jesuit trained *Postards,* monarchist by inclination, anti-Semitic by temperament, openly contemptuous of civilian authority, of parliamentary democracy and the elementary values of legal due process. Informed contemporaries usually knew better. A quarter century before, a war minister, General Louis André, thought it prudent to engage Freemasons in an (illegal) inquiry into the religious and political persuasion of the French officer corps, Léon Gambetta was making discreet inquiries on the same subject—much like his conservative predecessors in previous regimes, who did not assume that all army officers were archly reliable supporters of whatever political regime was currently in power. Not surprisingly, Gambetta discovered that many of the generals and colonels, having come of age under monarchies, were less than ardent supporters of the fledgling Republican regime. Equally unsurprising was the discovery that most of the up-and-coming ranks of colonels and captains did indeed favor the latter. After all, even the most obtuse middle-rank officer could grasp the elementary fact that open conformity with the current regime was a career-enhancing move. The Republic was only halfway through its second decade when it had a general and minister of war who openly and ostentatiously catered to the demands of the more militant Left. In the last years of the Republic, by far and away the most popular general in the French Army was declared, by no less an authority than Léon Blum, to be "the most republican general in France." Granted, given that the generals in question were Georges Boulanger and Philippe Pétain,

the Republican *imprimatur* probably says more about their political savvy than about their basic values. Still, for every reactionary general like Louis Lyautey, Maxime Weygand, or "the booted monk" Edouard-Noel Castelnau one can cite impeccably Republican ones like Maurice Gamelin or Maurice Sarrail. And for every general who could be found frequenting the salons of the political Right, there were rather more pacing the antechambers of Radical politicians.[5]

Still, there was the matter of military justice of which the Dreyfus affair was but the most egregious example (and made no less egregious by the fact that most Radicals, from Léon Bourgeois to Fernand Buisson, were exceptionally slow to recognize the problem). The anti-militarist Left of the early twentieth century would understandably believe, even after the post-Dreyfus reforms, to cite a later *bon mot*, that military justice is to justice roughly what military music is to music. But this was to simplify matters somewhat, since, as John Cerullo perceptively reminds us, military justice, much like military music, operated in different contexts and was designed to achieve different things than their civilian counterparts.[6] Equally worth asking is whether French military justice, disgraceful though it often was, was actually worse than French civilian justice. After all, the features of French military justice that preoccupy students of the Dreyfus affair and troubled contemporary anti-militarists—incompetent preliminary investigations, overt political pressure on judges and juries, officers of the court more concerned with career advancement than with justice—were also abundantly present in civil justice as well. As Benjamin Martin has noted, next to the "appallingly incompetent" police investigations in civil criminal matters, the French army's investigation of Captain Dreyfus, egregiously flawed though it in fact was, "appears almost professional in comparison."[7] Moreover, the overt abuses of the civilian judicial system were hardly the exclusive province of the political Right. That a rogue and scoundrel like Serge Alexandre Stavisky was able to delay his richly deserved appointment with the justice system for so long owed everything to a succession of Radical deputies, senators and ministers—all but one, ironically, members of the impeccably (not to say piously) left-wing *Ligue des droits de l'homme*.

The gender question is a relative newcomer to the political history of the Third Republic. Given some idealized version of the Left and the Right, attitudes to women ought to have clearly distinguished the two camps. The reality was rather more complex. While no political party in the Third Republic remotely met the late-twentieth-century standards of sensitivity to women, it was, by and large, the parties of the Right, and not the Left, who supported women's political rights. The Socialists and, above all, the Radicals were at best equivocal on the matter, at times conceding the legitimacy of women's suffrage in the abstract but forever finding practical reasons for postponing its implementation more or less indefinitely. At the root of this reluctance was the clerical peril, or more accurately the seemingly ineradicable belief that women were to a far greater degree than men under the influence of the clergy and would therefore cast their

votes overwhelmingly for the political Right. The same (unexamined) assumption helps to explain the active support for women's suffrage by the parties and movements of the Right and even the extreme Right. Daniella Sarnoff makes it abundantly clear that the extreme Right thought that giving women the vote would somehow free France from "the rule of egotistical and corrupt politicians, freemasons and Jews." And Geoff Read effectively demonstrates that being a suffragist was entirely consistent with a masculinist view of the world and a very traditional and paternalist view of the position of women.[8] But there was a lot of that going around, on the Left as much as on the Right. Witness the delegate to the 1923 congress of the Ligue des droits de l'homme, who unblushingly declared: "I am an old feminist and I believe that our role is to defend women and their role is to charm us."[9] Granted, it would be hard to imagine any politician of the Right, suffragist or not, authoring anything like Léon Blum's 1907 *Du mariage*. Still, as Read has recently demonstrated, with respect to women's place in society, not so terribly much separated the Right from the Left. Yes there were nuances, not always unimportant ones, but at the end of the day and most of the time, from Right to Left, this was very much the "Republic of Men."[10]

As the gender question so clearly demonstrates, the clerical question was one of the few issues that reliably separated Right from Left in the Third Republic. The Left was unwaveringly anti-clerical. Certainly by any time after 1906, it was never clear what else besides anti-clericalism situated the Radicals on the Left. The Right was in general either clerical or, as it were, "anti-anti-clerical." It encompassed politicians who ranged from those who sought to restore the role of religion in French society to those who simply thought the time had come to stop harassing an increasingly benign church establishment. By and large, the Roman Catholic Church supported the political Right, albeit with less intensity and decreasing conviction as the years went by as it became more and more obvious that close identification with the Right was not an unalloyed asset. One of the great ironies in the relations between the Church and politics is that until 1905, the concordatory regime, so decried by the anti-clerical Left, gave the ruling Republicans a wonderful weapon with which to temper the right-wing political influence of the clergy. As anyone who has been immersed in the archives of the Ministry of Cults will know, a vigilant (not to say vengeful) Republican administration could ensure that an incautious political observation by a village priest would yield a year's suspension of salary. After the 1905 separation of Church and state, the Church wavered. Uneasy with liberal Catholics who sought, by way of the social gospel, to move the church in a politically progressive direction, it was equally unsettled by archly clerical defenders of the Church like Charles Maurras, who was inconveniently an atheist (for which he was subsequently, albeit not permanently, excommunicated).

Moreover, political Catholicism and the classic political Right did not always see eye to eye. The Parti démocrate populaire that emerged after 1924 was, and

still is, classed as a party of the Right, but it always insisted that it was a party of the Center, equidistant, a point it made insistently, from the Socialist Léon Blum and the conservative Louis Marin. It did not much care for Blum's anti-clericalism or his threats to private property. But it was no more enamored of Marin's extreme nationalism. Indeed, the parliamentary representative of the PDP assured Blum when he presented his Popular Front government before the Chamber of Deputies in 1936 that "our votes will often be mixed with yours." None of this pleased Marin's Fédération républicaine. The "eternally revolutionary ferment of the gospels" that the PDP took such pride in citing, struck the Fédération as little more than "the blasphemous rapprochement between the gospels and Revolution," which no less an authority than Pope Pius X had recently condemned. Correspondingly, the Fédération was fond of suggesting that PDP really stood for "*Parti des poires*" (in French slang, "the party of morons"). Worse, it would at times imitate the Action française and refer to the PDP as "*les pédés*" (a homophobic reference which would have escaped no contemporaries).[11]

One theme that would appear to definitively separate the Right and the Left was racism, and more particularly anti-Semitism. Once again, the Dreyfus affair seems to have delineated the respective camps, leaving the Left as articulate opponents of anti-Semitism and the Right all too often attracted to it. On closer examination, though, the issue becomes more complex. In the first two decades of the Republic, the socialist Left was often explicitly hostile to Jews—or at least to the economic power allegedly wielded by Jews. Whether it be a youthful Jules Guesde, fulminating against *le juif de Francfort*, that is, Alphonse de Rothschild, or the repeated attacks on Jewish wealth in Benôit Malon's *Revue socialiste*, anti-Semitism seemed as congenial to the far Left as to the far Right. To be sure, ultramontane Catholics could at times match the anti-Jewish vituperations of the Left, but this very fact was a source of dismay for hard-nosed Orleanist leaders. The secretary-general of the royalist party, Eugène Dufeuille, a Protestant, despaired of the "narrowly clerical" anti-Semitism of arch Catholics within the party's ranks because it seemed to serve no useful purpose beyond driving French Jews, an increasingly influential community, into the ranks of the Republicans. He was properly indignant about Edouard Drumont's *La France juive*, while also noting that the book was "perhaps not absolutely regrettable from our perspective" because it might alert French Jews to the perils of anti-Semitism under the republican regime. Implicit here was the possibility that French Jews might recognize that a restored monarchy, with rather tighter controls over what could get published, might better ensure their safety.

The royalist pretender, the Count of Paris, heavily dependent on Jewish financiers and whose political tracts were frequently published by Calmann-Lévy, was also acutely alert to the fact that, for a party given to lamenting the religious persecution of Catholics, there was nothing very clever about embracing a movement that persecuted a different religion. Moreover, as he repeatedly reminded

his more earnest militants, whatever the populist attraction of denouncing Jewish wealth, it was inevitably the case that a war on Jewish capital would degenerate into "a war on capital in general." It was only under his successor, the Duc d'Orléans, that royalists embraced anti-Semitism. He was apparently persuaded by his advisors that were he to focus on Jews as a race, rather than as a distinct religion or as an economic elite, he might avoid the spillover effect that so worried his father. By the time he got around to making his views on this clear, few Frenchmen were interested in the declarations of a frivolous and dissolute head of a moribund political movement. There was, however, one notable exception: Charles Maurras, who later claimed that this is what galvanized him into an active political career.[12]

There can be no doubt that by the beginning of the twentieth century, the socialist Left had largely abandoned its anti-Semitic baggage, alert, in the words of a German counterpart, August Bebel, that anti-Semitism was "the socialism of the imbecile."[13] And for much of the remaining life of the Republic, anti-Semitism was a far more prominent feature of the extreme Right, be it the Action française, or the vituperations of right-wing *torchons* like *Je suis partout* or *Gringoire* in the late 1930s. The more traditional Right was usually, but not always, rather more circumspect when it came to anti-Semitism. Xavier Vallat, the deputy from the Ardèche and, to the point, vice-president of the Fédération républicaine, did feel the need to remind the Chamber of Deputies in the summer of 1936 that for the first time in its history, the great Gallo Roman nation of France would be governed by a Jew. But Vallat was not entirely typical of the Right, moderate or otherwise. It is of some significance that the Croix de Feu went to great lengths to deny any anti-Semitism within its ranks and to stress its (in reality, marginal) association with French Jews. To be sure, this claim (taken seriously by some of the movement's subsequent historians) has been nicely debunked by Samuel Kalman, who, with his gimlet eye for the sources, skillfully demonstrates the prevalence of anti-Semitism among the Croix de Feu's rank and file (and not merely, as other scholars have assumed, those in Algeria.)[14]

This said, though, it is also the case that by the 1930s, anti-Semitic discourse was once again finding its voice on the Left, or at least on the pacifist Left. When the aforementioned Elie Reynier denounced the politicians "linked … with the Stalinist warmongers," he took some pains to identify Jews among them. His list included Victor Basch, Emile Kahn, Salomon Grumbach, Georges Gombault, Jacques Kaiser, Georges Mandel, Jean Zay, Léon Blum, Jules Moch, and Jean Zyromski. These were Jews, all left-wing stalwarts, with the exception of Mandel, and characterized as irresponsibly pushing France into war with Germany for no better reason than a preoccupation with their coreligionists on the other side of the Rhine. In Reynier's mind, of course, his obsession with Jews was very different from that of the *fin de siècle* Right. The latter accused international Jewry of being in league with France's hereditary enemy; he, by contrast, accused them of

wanting to go to war with Germany. A distinction, to be sure, but a fairly fine one. Granted, his anti-Semitism—or at least his anti-Jewish animus—was instrumental rather than visceral as might have been the case with Vallat. Among the "Jews" he targeted were Jean Zay and Jules Moch, both in fact Protestants and the latter a notoriously devout one. Reynier, a Protestant himself, was almost certainly not unaware of this fact. But an anti-Jewish discourse—cast as widely and as sloppily as possible—seemed worth it in defense of the peace. Granted, these were the *private* ruminations of a dedicated pacifist, in most other contexts a dedicated civil libertarian. But they were entirely apiece with the *public* assertions of many of his ideological confreres in the late years of the Republic.

Jews were hardly the only targets of French racists. So too were France's colonized subjects. Here too, the French Right had no monopoly on racist diatribes and at times it was very difficult to tell the players without a program. A case in point would be the following two assertions about the native populations of French Algeria. The first regretted that the "education given to the natives will soon permit them to struggle on an equal basis and in advantageous conditions against us. If we are not careful the natives will rise in revolt and kick us out of here." The second asserted that even the "educated Arab aspires to only one thing: to dominate because he is ... fanatical, prideful and full of himself.... He is forever on the outlook for our weaknesses in order to exploit them."[15] The substantive message is the same in both cases. The first emanated from a local leader of the Algerian Parti social français; the second represented the collective wisdom of a local section of the Ligue des droits de l'homme. The first was public, made at a political rally; the second were private reflections (which, understandably, the Ligue chose not to publish.) But the first was also articulated in the Algerian context where racist diatribes were often the norm; the second reflected the sentiments of notionally left-wing elements in the Parisian suburb of Antony.

Dianne Labrosse's work on Gaston Bergery beautifully illustrates the artificiality of the left–right dichotomy, especially with respect to the Vichy period.[16] The Bergery Declaration of 10 July 1940 was the closest thing the Vichy regime had to a foundational statement. And its author was hardly a man of the Right. He began his political career as the rising star in the Radical Party. He therefore knew better than did most about the legendary corruption and governmental incompetence of the Radicals. This knowledge would inform his increasingly dyspeptic attacks on the regime itself, attacks that did not differ so dramatically from those emanating from the Right. Significantly, in the last years of the Republic he was opening the pages of his newspaper *La Flèche* to the virulent right-wing deputy from Paris, Georges Scapini. Bergery's single greatest obsession was with the peace and the insufficient commitment of his erstwhile allies on the Left in preserving it. He too sprinkled his articles with malevolent reflections on the pernicious influence of the Jews, diatribes that might not have been out of place in publications like *Gringoire*.[17]

The Bergery declaration, signed by deputies from across the political spectrum (including one Xavier Vallat), was, among other things, a passionate argument for abandoning the increasingly irrelevant categories of right and left.[18] Those on the Right who had decried the corruption of Radical governments in the early 1930s and who had descended into the streets on 6 February 1934 to topple the Daladier government actually shared much in common with those on the Left who had welcomed the Popular Front government of Léon Blum in the summer of 1936. Both groups had hoped to see profound changes and both had been utterly disappointed. The former had had to settle for Gaston Doumergue's irresolute government of National Reconciliation, which had reconciled no one and changed precisely nothing. The latter obtained only a ministry dominated by the union bosses, more interested in catering to the dictates of Moscow than the aspirations of the working masses. No government, right or left, conducted a competent foreign policy, proved able to stay out of an utterly unnecessary war, or win that war when it began.

In proposing a "national revolution," Bergery clearly hoped to paper over the artificial political divide that separated Frenchmen. But the "national" part was a bit tricky since, as Bergery was aware, that word had been for decades exclusively part of the lexicon of the political Right. This, Bergery frankly admitted, had been an error on the part of the Left, which too often underestimated the importance of the phenomenon of the nation. As if to comfort former Leftists who might feel ill at ease with the newly discovered importance of the nation, he hastened to add that embracing the idea of the nation manifestly did not entail any attempt to "consolidate the plutocracy." This concession with respect to the "plutocracy" was not calculated to discomfit the political Right, for whom vague denunciations of some nebulous plutocracy had long been a cottage industry. As for the classic division between proponents of "authority" and defenders of "liberty," this too was an outmoded distinction. Both liberty and authority lost any real meaning as concepts if they degenerated, as they usually did, into anarchy or tyranny. The trick, and the task of the new government, was to find "a synthesis of authority and liberty," which apparently meant losing the form of the latter but somehow preserving its substance. The new regime would be both national and social and yet in no way a docile imitation of the German National Socialist regime. There were any number of variations of national socialism to choose from, the more so because, apart from Great Britain, no major nation was any longer clinging to old-fashioned capitalist liberal democracy. Everywhere else, "a national form of socialism" prevailed, be it in Germany and Italy, Spain and Portugal, the Soviet Union or, apparently, New Deal America.

On its merits, this was a manifesto that ought to have been more comforting for the erstwhile Right than the Left. But many on the Left did not, certainly initially, see Vichy as somehow the "revenge of the anti-Dreyfusards." Pierre Laval was no clerical reactionary. His desire for loyal collaboration with the Germans,

something the Bergery manifesto also explicitly demanded, was entirely consistent with the prewar demands of the pacifist Left. Most on the Vichy Left were in fact outraged by Laval's marginalization from power for a year and a half and sniped petulantly from the flanks, lobbying for Laval's return in the apparent belief that back in power he might implement the brave new world articulated by Bergery in 1940. Return Laval did, but France got no closer to what Bergery had envisioned. Left-wing collaborators continued to decry the pervasive clericalism of Vichy, although the old slogan, "clericalism there is the enemy," was replaced by the more moderate formulation "neither clericalism nor anticlericalism." *Sotto voce*, they noted that of Bergery's key adjectives, "authoritarian," "social," and "national," Vichy seemed to be delivering only on the first, not at all on the second and less and less on the third. They gamely extolled the progressive features of Nazi Germany, lauded economic collaboration as the key to (an increasingly distant) future European peace, and routinely excoriated French Jews whose bellicosity had brought France to her knees.

The Vichy experience inevitably raises the question of fascism, what it was, whether it really existed in France and if so, whether it was it on the Left or the Right. French fascists, or those some scholars deem to be so, emerge from all points of the political spectrum: the Left, extreme or otherwise, if one counts Doriot, Marcel Déat, or Charles Péguy; the Right, extreme or otherwise, if one counts Maurras, Pierre Taittinger, or La Rocque. Jacques Doriot's Parti populaire français was perfectly eclectic. Only two of its principal leaders came from the classic Right (if the Croix de Feu counts as such); about half came out of the French Communist Party; the rest had cut their political teeth in either the Radical or the Socialist parties.[19] Some fascists were quite literally all over the map: Georges Valois managed to go from anarchism to the Action française to the more or less authentic fascism of his ephemeral Faisceau, then back to the anti-Munichois Left, and finally into the wartime resistance. Fascist movements incontestably shared certain features with the classical political Left: a populist dynamism, skill at mass mobilization and a related radical rhetoric, at times fairly crackling with denunciations of the established order, be it political, social, or economic. Yet none of this deterred significant elements of that very established order from demonstrating a degree of sympathy for, and at times, an overt complicity with, fascist movements. However uncomfortable they might have been with the radical language of fascist movements, many conservatives believed (more or less correctly) that they would be useful and effective auxiliaries against their enemies on the political Left.

The definitional anarchy surrounding fascism—no one can quite agree which traits define fascists and only fascists—poses problems for historians of France given that no movement of much consequence ever claimed to be fascist. For some—the proponents of the "immunity thesis" so skillfully analyzed by Sean Kennedy, for example—it follows that France was effectively free of fascism. For

others, notably Sternhell, fascists were all over the place and typically in hereto-fore unexpected places.[20] Almost every historian has to wrestle with the question of what to make of movements like Doriot's Parti populaire français and, above all, La Rocque's Croix de Feu and its successor, the Parti social français. Both were explicitly hostile to the Left, but neither reassembled the classic formations of the Right either. The issue matters most with the PSF, because it enjoyed for a year or two by far the largest membership of any political formation of the Third Republic. Some have argued, mischievously, that if, following Sternhell, being neither Right nor Left is a defining feature of fascism, then the CF/PSF, which always and strenuously made that claim, ought to qualify. Even Sternhell, once categorical in his exclusion of the CF/PSF from the fascist ranks, has made some modest concessions to this argument.[21] To be sure, the debate about the CF/PSF is not really about whether they were left or right (their claim to have been neither notwithstanding), but about whether they were fascist or traditionally conserva-tive. Their skill at mass mobilization and their (related) populist, pseudo-radical, and demagogic rhetoric persuade some scholars that they belong in the fascist camp. Others, still the majority, insist that the movement was either merely a particularly energetic formation of the traditional Right or, and less plausibly, a deeply Catholic and democratic movement dedicated to the spiritual renewal of France. Sean Kennedy, whose book on the subject[22] is by far the most authorita-tive yet, places the CF/PSF squarely in the ranks of the authoritarian nationalist Right, neither fascist in any meaningful sense of the word, nor a benign version of Gaullism *avant la lettre*.

It will be objected that none of the preceding gymnastics can quite conjure away the fact that there were (and are) two Frances—one seeking to preserve, or restore, the established social and economic order, the other seeking to reform, or overthrow it. In the broadest terms, this is probably true. The groups that called themselves the *nationaux* believed themselves to be in the former camp. But who was the true nationalist in September of 1938: the Communist who wanted to fight to save (among other things) French national honor or Kennedy's authori-tarian nationalists who by and large thought this was one fight France should stay out of? Who was more wedded to the preservation of the established order: Sarnoff's figures who wanted women to vote, or the Radicals and Socialists who, for the most part, thought they ought not to? Questions about the frankly am-biguous political signposts of Third Republic France admit no definitive answer. But they should certainly prompt further debate.

Notes

1. François Goguel, *La Politique des partis sous la IIIe République* (Paris, 1946).
2. Daniel Brower, *The New Jacobins* (Ithaca, 1968).
3. William D. Irvine, *French Conservatism in Crisis* (Baton Rouge, 1979), 187.

4. William D. Irvine, *Between Justice and Politics: The Ligue des Droits de l'Homme, 1898–1945* (Stanford, 2007), 184.

5. Douglas Porch, *The March to the Rhine: The French Army, 1871–1914* (Cambridge, 1981), 100–104.

6. John Cerullo, "The Aernoult-Rousset Affair: Military Justice on Trial in *Belle Époque* France," *Historical Reflections/Réflexions historiques* 34, no. 2 (2008): 4–24.

7. Benjamin F. Martin, *Crime and Criminal Justice under the Third Republic* (Baton Rouge, 1990).

8. Geoff Read, "He Is Depending on You: Militarism, Martyrdom and the Appeal to Manliness in the Case of France's Croix de Feu, 1931–1940," *Journal of the Canadian Historical Association* 19 (2005): 261–292; and "Des hommes et des citoyens: Paternalism and Masculinity on the Republican Right in Interwar France, 1919–1939," *Historical Reflections/Réflexions historiques* 34, no. 2 (2008): 88–111.

9. Irvine, *Between Justice and Politics*, 87.

10. Geoff Read, "The Republic of Men: Gender and the Political Parties in Interwar France, 1918–1940" (PhD dissertation, York University, 2006).

11. Irvine, *French Conservatism*, 57, 88

12. William D. Irvine, *The Boulanger Affair Reconsidered* (New York, 1989), 167–174.

13. However, it is of some significance that he felt the need to describe it as the "socialism" as opposed, say, to the "conservatism" of the imbecile.

14. See Kalman's *The Extreme Right in Interwar France: The Faisceau and the Croix de Feu* (Burlington and Aldershot, 2008).

15. The source for the first quote is Commissaire de Police de l'Arba to Prefect of Algiers, Algiers 1K/26, kindly drawn to my attention by Samuel Kalman; for the second, Irvine, *Between Justice and Politics*, 144–145.

16. Diane N. Labrosse, "*La derive Bergery*/The Bergery Drift: Gaston Bergery and the Politics of Late Thirde Republic France and the Early Vichy State," *Historical Reflections/Réflexions historiques* 34, no. 2 (2008): 66–87.

17. Irvine, *Between Justice and Politics*, 188.

18. For the text of the Bergery declaration, see Jacques de Launay, ed., *Le Dossier de Vichy* (Paris, 1967), 263–267, 291–299.

19. See in particular, Laurent Kestel, "De la conversion en politique. Genèse et institutionalisation du Parti populaire français, 1936–1940" (Thèse pour le doctorat de science politique, Université Paris-I, 2006).

20. Zeev Sternhell, *Neither Right Nor Left, Fascist Ideology in France* (Princeton, 1986); Sean Kennedy, "The End of Immunity? Recent Work on the Far Right in Interwar France," *Historical Reflections/Réfexions historiques* 34, no. 2 (2008): 25–45.

21. See his preface to the 2000 French re-edition of *Neither Right Nor Left*, *Ni droite ni gauche: L'idéologie fasciste en France*, 3rd ed. (Brussels, 2000); an abridged English-language version is also available as Zeev Sternhell, "Morphology of Fascism in France," in *France in the Era of Fascism: Essays on the French Authoritarian Right*, ed. Brian Jenkins (New York, 2005), 22–64.

22. Sean Kennedy, *Reconciling France against Democracy: The Croix de Feu and the Parti Social Français 1927–1945* (Montreal and Kingston, 2007).

Contributors

Caroline Campbell is assistant professor of history at the University of North Dakota. Her research interests focus on the intersections between women, gender, and extremist politics. She is working on a book entitled *Fascism and the Extreme Right in Greater France: Gender, Empire, and the Feminization of the Croix de Feu and Parti Social Français, 1927–1947*, the first full-length study of women in the French far Right during the interwar period.

Magali Della Sudda is a tenured researcher at the Centre Emile Durkheim in Bordeaux (CNRS, France). She has edited (with Frédérique Matonti and Lucie Bargel) the "(En)quêtes de genre" special issue of *Soctétés et representations* (2007) and a special issue of *Travail, Genre et Sociétés* with Guillaume Malochet on "Pouvoirs, genre et religions" (2012). She recently published an article entitled "Gender, Fascism and Catholicism: A New Perspective on Catholic Women's Militancy (France 1919–1939)," in Julie V. Gottlieb, ed., *Gender and Fascism: Totalitarian Movements and Political Religion*. Her main research interests concern politicization, gender, and Catholicism from a comparative perspective.

Norman Ingram is professor of modern French history at Concordia University in Montreal. He has published widely on the topics of French pacifism and the Ligue des droits de l'homme, most notably *The Politics of Dissent: Pacifism in France, 1919–1939* (Clarendon Press, 1991, republished 2011). He is presently completing a book entitled *Eyes Across the Rhine: the Ligue des droits de l'homme and the German Problem, 1914–1944*.

William Irvine is professor of history (emeritus) at York University in Toronto. His major publications include *French Conservatism in Crisis* (Louisiana State University Press, 1979), *The Boulanger Affair Reconsidered* (Oxford University Press, 1989) and *Between Justice and Politics: The Ligue des Droits de l'Homme, 1898–1945* (Stanford University Press, 2007).

Samuel Kalman is associate professor of history at St. Francis Xavier University in Antigonish, Nova Scotia. He has previously published *French Colonial Fascism: The Extreme Right in Algeria, 1919-1939* (Palgrave, 2013) and *The Extreme Right in Interwar France: The Faisceau and the Croix de Feu* (Ashgate, 2008). He is currently working on a study of crime and criminal justice in French Algeria.

Sean Kennedy is professor of history at the University of New Brunswick. He is the author of *Reconciling France Against Democracy: The Croix de Feu and the Parti Social Français, 1927–1945* (McGill-Queen's University Press, 2007), *The Shock of War: Civilian Experiences, 1937–1945* (Canadian Historical Association / University of Toronto Press, 2011), and several scholarly articles. He is currently researching the career of the intellectual André Siegfried.

Laurent Kestel received his PhD in political science from Université Paris-I Sorbonne (Centre européen de sociologie et de science politique de la Sorbonne). He has recently published *La conversion politique: Doriot, le PPF et la question du fascisme français* (Raisons d'Agir, 2012), along with articles in *French Historical Studies* and *French History*.

Cheryl A. Koos is professor of history at California State University, Los Angeles. She has co-edited the anthology, *The Human Tradition in Modern Europe* (Rowman and Littlefield, 2008), and has published essays and articles on the intersection of gender, the family, and right-wing politics in interwar France.

Chris Millington is lecturer in twentieth-century history at Swansea University, UK. He has published articles in *French Historical Studies* and *European History Quarterly*. His monograph, *From Victory to Vichy: Veterans in Interwar France* (Manchester University Press, 2012), explores the political culture and mobilization of the two largest French veterans' associations during the interwar years, the Union fédérale and the Union nationale des combattants. His current work concerns political violence in France during 1918–1940.

Kevin Passmore is reader in history at the University of Cardiff. He has published a number of works on the Right and extreme Right in France, including *From Liberalism to Fascism: The Right in a French Province, 1928–1939* (Cambridge University Press, 1997) and The *Right in France from the Third Republic to Vichy* (Oxford University Press, 2012). He also publishes on the history of historical writing and on its relationship with the social sciences.

Geoff Read is assistant professor of history at Huron University College, Western University, in London, Ontario, Canada. He has published articles on race and gender in interwar France and has co-authored others on the portrayal and

perception of Louis Riel and the Métis resistance in western Canada in the trans-Atlantic press.

Daniella Sarnoff is a director at the Social Science Research Council and a historian of Modern Europe. Sarnoff holds a PhD in European history and has taught at Xavier University, Fordham University, and New York University. She has published in journals and edited volumes on the topics of women's suffrage, gender, and fascism. Her most recent piece is "Domesticating French Fascism," in *Women of the Right: Comparisons and Exchanges Across National Borders* (Pennsylvania State University Press, 2012).

Jessica Wardhaugh is an assistant professor in French history at the University of Warwick. Her research explores the relationship between politics and culture in modern France, focusing particularly on street politics, popular theater, and imagined communities. She has published a monograph on the 1930s, *In Pursuit of the People: Political Culture in France, 1934–39* (Palgrave Macmillan, 2009), an edited volume on *Paris and the Right in the Twentieth Century* (CSP, 2007), and is currently completing a history of popular theater in the Third Republic.

SELECTED BIBLIOGRAPHY

Amdur, Kathryn. "Paternalism, Productivism, Collaborationism: Employers and Society in Interwar and Vichy France." *International Labor and Working-Class History* 53, no. 1 (1998): 137–163.

Amzalak, Nimrod. *Fascists and Honourable Men: Contingency and Choice in French Politics, 1918–1945*. Basingstoke: Palgrave Macmillan, 2011.

Andrieu, Claire, Gilles Le Béguec, and Danielle Tartakowsky, eds. *Associations et champs politiques: la loi de 1901 à l'épreuve du siècle*. Paris: Publications de la Sorbonne, 2001.

Antliff, Mark. *Avant-Garde Fascism: The Mobilization of Myth, Art, and Culture in France, 1909–1939*. Durham: Duke University Press, 2007.

Atkin, Nicholas, and Frank Tallett, eds. *The Right in France: From Revolution to Le Pen*. 2nd ed. London: I.B. Tauris, 2003.

Badouï, Rémi et al., eds. *Un professeur en République: mélanges en l'honneur de Serge Berstein*. Paris: Fayard, 2006.

Bensoussan, David. *Combats pour une Bretagne catholique et rurale: les droites bretonnes dans l'entre-deux-guerres*. Paris: Fayard, 2006.

Bernard, Mathias. *La dérive des modérés: la Fédération républicaine du Rhône sous la Troisième République*. Paris: L'Harmattan, 1998.

Berstein, Serge. "La France des années trente allergique au fascisme: à propos d'un livre de Zeev Sternhell." *Vingtième siècle* 2 (1984): 83–94.

———. *Le six février 1934*. Paris: Gallimard, 1975.

Bingham, John. "Defining French Fascism, Finding Fascists in France." *Canadian Journal of History* 29, no. 3 (1994): 525–543.

Birnbaum, Pierre. *"La France aux Français": histoire des haines nationalistes*. Paris: Seuil, 1993.

Bonafoux-Verax, Corinne. *À la droite de Dieu: la Fédération nationale catholique 1924–1944*. Paris: Fayard, 2004.

Boulic, Jean-Yves, and Anne Lavaure. *Henri de Kerillis 1889–1958: l'absolu patriote*. Rennes: Presses universitaires de Rennes, 1997.

Brunelle, Gayle, and Annette Finley-Croswhite. *Murder in the Métro: Laetitia Toureaux and the Cagoule in 1930s France*. Baton Rouge: Louisiana State University Press, 2010.

Brunet, Jean-Paul. *Jacques Doriot: du communisme au fascisme*. Paris: Balland, 1986.

Bruttmann, Tal, and Laurent Joly, eds. *La France antijuive de 1936: l'agression de Léon Blum à la Chambre des députés*. Sainte-Marguerite sur Mer: Éditions des Équateurs, 2006.

Buchanan, Tom, and Martin Conway, eds. *Political Catholicism in Europe, 1918–1965*. Oxford: Oxford University Press, 1996.

Burrin, Philippe. *La dérive fasciste: Doriot, Déat, Bergery 1933–1945*. Paris: Seuil, 1986.

———. *Fascisme, nazisme, autoritarisme*. Paris: Seuil, 2000.

———. "Poings levés et bras tendus: la contagion des symboles au temps du Front populaire." *Vingtième siècle* 11 (1986): 5–20.

Camiscioli, Elisa. "Producing Citizens, Reproducing the French Race: Immigration, Demography, and Pronatalism in early Twentieth Century France." *Gender and History* 13, no. 3 (2001): 593–621.

———. *Reproducing the French Race: Immigration, Intimacy, and Embodiment in the Early Twentieth Century.* Durham: Duke University Press, 2009.

Campbell, Caroline. "Building a Movement, Dismantling the Republic: Women, Gender, and Political Extremism in the Croix de Feu/Parti Social Français, 1927–1940." *French Historical Studies* 35, no. 4 (2012): 691–726.

———. "Women and Gender in the Croix de Feu and the Parti Social Français: Creating a Nationalist Youth Culture, 1927–1939." *Proceedings of the Western Society for French History* 36 (2008): 249–264.

———. "Women and Men in French Authoritarianism: Gender in the Croix de Feu and Parti Social Français." PhD dissertation, University of Iowa, 2009.

Caron, Vicki. *Uneasy Asylum: France and the Jewish Refugee Crisis, 1933–1942.* Stanford: Stanford University Press, 1999.

Carroll, David. *French Literary Fascism: Nationalism, Anti-Semitism, and the Ideology of Culture.* Princeton: Princeton University Press, 1995.

Chadwick, Kay, ed. *Catholicism, Politics and Society in Twentieth-Century France.* Liverpool: Liverpool University Press, 2000.

Childers, Kristen Stromberg. *Fathers, Families and the State in France, 1914–1945.* Ithaca: Cornell University Press, 2003.

Churchill, Christopher. "Neo-Traditional Fantasies: Colonialism, Modernism and Fascism in Greater France 1870–1962." PhD dissertation, Queen's University, 2010.

Clément, Jean-Louis. "L'Épiscopat, les démocrates-chrétiens et les Croix de Feu, 1930–1936." *Revue historique* 603 (1997): 103–113.

Costa Pinto, Antonio. "Fascist Ideology Revisited: Zeev Sternhell and His Critics." *European History Quarterly* 16, no. 4 (1986): 465–483.

Dard, Olivier, and Etienne Deschamps, eds. *Les relèves en Europe d'un après-guerre à l'autre: racines, réseaux, projets et postérités.* Brussels: Peter Lang, 2005.

Delbreil, Jean-Claude. *Centrisme et Démocratie-Chrétienne en France: le Parti démocrate populaire des origines au M.R.P. (1919–1944).* Paris: Publications de la Sorbonne, 1990.

Della Sudda, Magali. "Discours conservateurs, pratiques novatrices." *Sociétés et représentations* 24 (2007): 211–231.

———. "Gender, Fascism and the Right-Wing in France between the Wars: The Catholic Matrix." *Politics, Religion & Ideology* 13, no. 2 (2012): 179–195.

Dobry, Michel. "Février 1934 et la découverte de l'allergie de la société française au fascisme." *Revue française de sociologie* 30, nos. 3–4 (1989): 511–533.

———, ed. *Le mythe de l'allergie française au fascisme.* Paris: Albin Michel, 2003.

Douglas, Allen. *From Fascism to Libertarian Communism: Georges Valois against the Third Republic.* Berkeley: University of California Press, 1992.

Downs, Laura Lee. "'Each and Every One of You Must Become a *Chef*': Toward a Social Politics of Working-Class Childhood on the Extreme Right in 1930s France." *Journal of Modern History* 81, no. 1 (2009): 1–44.

———. "'Nous plantions les trois couleurs': Action sociale féminine et recomposition des politiques de la droite française: Le Mouvement Croix-de-Feu et le Parti social français, 1934–1947." *Revue d'histoire moderne et contemporaine* 58, no. 3 (2011): 118–163.

Faulkner, Christopher. "Theory and Practice of Film Reviewing in France in the 1930s: Eyes Right (Lucien Rebatet and Action française, 1936–39)." *French Cultural Studies* 3, no. 8 (1992): 133–155.

Frader, Laura Levine. *Breadwinners and Citizens: Gender in the Making of the French Social Model*. Durham: Duke University Press, 2008.

Goodfellow, Samuel. *Between the Swastika and the Cross of Lorraine: Fascisms in Interwar Alsace*. DeKalb: Northern Illinois University Press, 1999.

Gosnell, Jonathan K. *The Politics of Frenchness in Colonial Algeria, 1930–1954*. Rochester: University of Rochester Press, 2002.

Goyet, Bruno. *Charles Maurras*. Paris: Presses de Sciences Po, 2000.

Hause, Steven C. *Women's Suffrage and Social Politics in the French Third Republic*. Princeton: Princeton University Press, 1984.

Hawthorne, Melanie, and Goslan, Richard, eds. *Gender and Fascism in Modern France*. Hanover: University Press of New England, 1997.

Hellman, John. *The Communitarian Third Way: Alexandre Marc's Ordre Nouveau, 1930–2000*. Montreal: McGill-Queen's University Press, 2002.

Huguenin, François. *À l'école de l'Action française: un siècle de vie intellectuelle*. Paris: J.-C. Lattès, 1998.

Ingram, Norman. "A la recherche d'une guerre gagnée: the Ligue des droits de l'homme and the War Guilt Question (1918–1922)." *French History* 24, no. 2 (2010): 218–235.

———. "La Ligue des droits de l'homme et le problème allemande." *Revue d'histoire diplomatique* 124, no. 2 (2010): 119–131.

———. *The Politics of Dissent: Pacifism in France, 1919–1939*. Oxford: Clarendon, 1991.

———. "Repressed Memory Syndrome: Interwar French Pacifism and the Attempt to Recover France's Pacifist Past." *French History* 18, no. 3 (2004): 315–330.

———. "Selbstmord or Euthanasia? Who Killed the Ligue des droits de l'homme?" *French History* 22, no. 3 (2008): 337–357.

Irvine, William D. *Between Justice and Politics: The Ligue des droits de l'homme, 1898–1945*. Stanford: Stanford University Press, 2007.

———. "Domestic Politics and the Fall of France in 1940." *Historical Reflections/Réflexions Historiques* 22, no. 1 (1996): 76–91.

———. "Fascism in France and the Strange Case of the Croix de Feu." *Journal of Modern History* 63, no. 2 (1991): 271–295.

———. *French Conservatism in Crisis: The Republican Federation of France in the 1930s*. Baton Rouge: Louisiana State University Press, 1979.

———. "René Rémond's French Right: The Interwar Years." *Proceedings of the Western Society for French History* 5 (1977): 301–309.

Jackson, Julian. *The Fall of France: The Nazi Invasion of 1940*. Oxford: Oxford University Press, 2003.

———. *France: The Dark Years, 1940–1944*. Oxford: Oxford University Press, 2001.

———. *The Popular Front in France: Defending Democracy, 1934–38*. Cambridge: Cambridge University Press, 1988.

Jankowski, Paul. *Communism and Collaboration: Simon Sabiani and Politics in Marseille, 1919–1944*. New Haven: Yale University Press, 1989.

———. *Shades of Indignation: Political Scandals in France, Past and Present*. New York: Berghahn Books, 2008.

———. *Stavisky: A Confidence Man in the Republic of Virtue*. Ithaca: Cornell University Press, 2002.

Jenkins, Brian, ed. *France in the Era of Fascism: Essays on the French Authoritarian Right*. New York: Berghahn Books, 2005.

———. "The Paris Riots of February 1934: The Crisis of the French Third Republic." *French History* 20, no.3 (2006): 333–351.

———. "Plots and Rumors: Conspiracy Theories and the Six Février 1934." *French Historical Studies* 34, no. 4 (2011): 649–678.

———. "The Right-Wing Leagues and Electoral Politics in Interwar France." *History Compass* 5, no. 4 (2007): 1358–1381.

Joly, Laurent. *Xavier Vallat (1891–1972): Du nationalisme chrétien à l'antisémitisme d'état.* Paris: Grasset, 2001.

Julliard, Jacques. "Un fascisme imaginaire: à propos du livre de Zeev Sternhell." *Annales ESC* 4 (1984): 849–859.

Kalman, Samuel. "Le Combat par Tous les Moyens: Colonial Violence and the Extreme Right in 1930s Oran." *French Historical Studies* 34, no. 1 (2011): 125–153.

———. "Faisceau Visions of Physical and Moral Transformation and the Cult of Youth in Inter-war France." *European History Quarterly* 33, no. 3 (2003): 343–366.

———. "'Parasites from all Civilizations': The Croix de Feu/Parti Social Français Confronts French Jewry, 1931–1939." *Historical Reflections* 34, no. 2 (2008): 46–65.

———. *The Extreme Right in Interwar France: The Faisceau and the Croix de Feu.* Aldershot: Ashgate, 2008.

Kaplan, Alice Yaeger. *Reproductions of Banality: Fascism, Literature, and French Intellectual Life.* Minneapolis: University of Minnesota Press, 1986.

Kéchichian, Albert. *Les Croix-de-Feu à l'âge des fascismes.* Seyssel: Champ Vallon, 2006.

Kennedy, Sean. "The End of Immunity? Recent Work on the Far Right in Interwar France." *Historical Reflections/Réflexions historiques* 34, no.1 (2008): 25–45.

———. *Reconciling France against Democracy: The Croix de Feu and the Parti Social Français, 1927–1945.* Montreal: McGill-Queen's University Press, 2007.

Kestel, Laurent. "The Emergence of Anti-Semitism within the Parti Populaire Français: Party Intellectuals, Peripheral Leaders, and National Figures." *French History* 19, no. 3 (2005): 364–384.

———. "L'Engagement de Bertrand de Jouvenel au PPF, 1936–1938: intellectuel de parti et entrepreneur politique." *French Historical Studies* 30, no. 1 (2007): 105–125.

———. *La conversion politique: Doriot, le PPF et la question du fascisme français.* Paris: Raisons d'agir, 2012.

Kingston, Paul J. *Anti-Semitism in France during the 1930s: Organisations, Personalities and Propaganda.* Hull: University of Hull Press, 1983.

Koos, Cheryl. "Engendering Reaction: The Politics of Pronatalism and the Family in France, 1914–1944." PhD dissertation, University of Southern California, 1996.

———. "Fascism, Fatherland, and the Family in Interwar France: The Case of Antoine Rédier and the Légion." *Journal of Family History* 24, no. 3 (1999): 317–329.

———. "Gender, Anti-Individualism, and Nationalism: The Pronatalist Backlash against the Femme Moderne, 1933–1940." *French Historical Studies* 19, no. 3 (1996): 699–723.

Kuisel, Richard F. *Ernest Mercier: French Technocrat.* Berkeley: University of California Press, 1967.

Le Béguec, Gilles. "L'Entrée au Palais-Bourbon: les filières privilégiées d'accès à la function parlementaire 1919–1939." Thèse pour le doctorat d'état, Paris X Nanterre, 1989.

Lebovics, Herman. *True France: The Wars Over Cultural Identity, 1900–1945.* Ithaca: Cornell University Press, 1992.

Leymarie, Michel, and Jacques Prévotat, eds. *L'Action française: culture, société, politique.* Villeneuve d'Ascq: Presses Universitaires Septentrion, 2008.

Lindenberg, Daniel. *Les années souterraines 1937–1947.* Paris: La Découverte, 1990.

Machefer, Philippe. "Autour du problème algérien en 1936–1938: la doctrine algérienne du PSF – Le PSF et le projet Blum-Violette." *Revue d'histoire moderne et contemporaine* 10 (1963): 147–156.

———. "Les Croix de Feu (1927–1936)." *L'Information historique* 34, no. 1 (1972): 28–34.

———. "Le Parti Social Français en 1936–1937." *L'Information historique* 34, no. 2 (1972): 74–80.

Mazgaj, Paul. *Imagining Fascism: The Cultural Politics of the French Young Right, 1930–1945.* Newark: University of Delaware Press, 2007.

Meyers, Mark. "Feminizing Fascist Men: Crowd Psychology, Gender, and Sexuality in French Anti-fascism, 1929–1945." *French Historical Studies* 29, no.1 (2006): 109–142.

Millington, Chris. "February 6, 1934: The Veterans' Riot." *French Historical Studies* 33, no. 4 (2010): 545–572.

———. *From Victory to Vichy: Veterans in Interwar France*. Manchester: Manchester University Press, 2012.

Millman, Richard. "Les Croix de Feu et l'antisémitisme." *Vingtième siècle* 38 (1993): 48–54.

Milza, Pierre. *Fascisme français: Passé et present*. Paris: Flammarion, 1987.

———. *Le fascisme italien et la presse française, 1920–1940*. Bruxelles: Complexe, 1987.

Monnet, François. *Refaire la république: André Tardieu, une dérive réactionnaire, 1876–1945*. Paris: Fayard, 1993.

Morin, Gilles, and Gilles Richard, eds. *Les deux France du Front populaire*. Paris: L'Harmattan, 2008.

Nobécourt, Jacques. *Le colonel de La Rocque 1885–1946, ou les pièges du nationalisme chrétien*. Paris: Fayard, 1996.

Nord, Philip. "Catholic Culture in Interwar France." *French Politics, Culture & Society* 21, no. 3 (2003): 1–20.

Ory, Pascal. *La belle illusion: culture et politique sous le signe du Front populaire*. Paris: Plon, 1994.

Passmore, Kevin. "Boy-scouting for Grown-Ups? Paramilitarism in the Croix de Feu and the PSF." *French Historical Studies* 19, no. 2 (1995): 527–557.

———. *From Liberalism to Fascism: The Right in a French Province, 1928–1939*. Cambridge: Cambridge University Press, 1997.

———. "'Planting the Tricolor in the Citadels of Communism': Women's Social Action in the Croix de Feu and Parti Social Français." *Journal of Modern History* 71, no. 4 (1999): 814–851.

———. *The Right in France from the Third Republic to Vichy*. Oxford: Oxford University Press, 2013.

———, ed. *Women, Gender and Fascism in Europe, 1919–1945*. New Brunswick: Rutgers University Press, 2003.

Paxton, Robert. *French Peasant Fascism: Henry Dorgères's Greenshirts and the Crises of French Agriculture, 1929–1939*. New York: Oxford University Press, 1997.

Pellissier, Pierre. *6 février 1934: la république en flames*. Paris: Perrin, 2000.

Philippet, Jean. "Le temps des Ligues: Pierre Taittinger et les Jeunesses Patriotes." 5 vols. Thèse de doctorat, Institut d'Études Politiques, Paris, 2000.

Prévotat, Jacques. *Les catholiques et l'Action française: histoire d'une condemnation*. Paris: Fayard, 2001.

———, ed. *Pie XI et la France: l'apport des archives du pontificat de Pie XI à la connaissance des rapports entre le Saint-Siège et la France*. Rome: École française de Rome, 2010.

Prost, Antoine. *Les anciens combattants et la société française, 1914–1939*. 3 vols. Paris: Presses de la FNSP, 1977.

Read, Geoff. "He Is Depending on You: Militarism, Martyrdom, and the Appeal to Manliness in the Case of France's 'Croix de Feu,' 1931–1940." *Journal of the Canadian Historical Association* 16 (2005): 261–291.

———. "The Republic of Men: Gender and the Political Parties in Interwar France, 1918–1940." PhD dissertation, York University, 2006.

Rémond, René. *Les droites en France*. Paris: Aubier Montaigne, 1982.

Renard, Paul. *L'Action française et la vie littéraire, 1931–1944*. Lille: Presses universitaires du Septentrion, 2003.

Reynolds, Sîan. *France between the Wars: Gender and Politics*. New York: Routledge, 1996.

Roberts, Mary Louise. *Civilization without Sexes: Reconstructing Gender in Postwar France, 1917–1927*. Chicago: University of Chicago Press, 1994.

Rosenberg, Clifford. *Policing Paris: The Origins of Modern Immigration Control Between the Wars*. Ithaca: Cornell University Press, 2006.

Roussellier, Nicholas. *Le parlement de l'éloquence. La souveraineté de la délibération au lendemain de la Grande Guerre*. Paris: Presses de Science Po, 1997.

Rymell, John. "Militants and Militancy in the Croix de Feu and Parti Social Français: Patterns of Political Experience on the French Far Right (1933–1939)." PhD dissertation, University of East Anglia, 1990.

Sanos, Sandrine. *The Aesthetics of Hate: Far-Right Intellectuals, Antisemitism, and Gender in 1930s France*. Stanford: Stanford University Press, 2013.

———. "Fascist Fantasies of Perversion and Abjection: Race, Gender, and Sexuality in the Interwar Far-Right." *Proceedings of the Western Society for French History* 37 (2009): 249–265.

Sarnoff, Daniella. "In the Cervix of the Nation: Women in French Fascism, 1919–1939." PhD dissertation, Boston College, 2001.

———. "Interwar Fascism and the Franchise: Women's Suffrage and the Ligues." *Historical Reflections/Réflexions historiques* 34, no. 1 (2008): 112–133.

Sarti, Odile. *The Ligue Patriotique des Françaises, 1902–1933: A Feminine Response to the Secularization of French Society*. New York: Garland, 1992.

Schor, Ralph. *L'antisémitisme en France pendant les années trente*. Brussels: Complexe, 1992.

Schue, Paul. "The Prodigal Sons of Communism: Parti Populaire Français Narratives of Communist Recruitment for the Spanish Civil War and the Everyday Functioning of Party Ideology." *French Historical Studies* 24, no. 1 (2001): 87–111.

Simard, Marc. "Doumergue et la réforme de l'état en 1934: la dernière chance de la IIIe République?" *French Historical Studies* 16, no. 3 (1990): 576–596.

Sirinell, Jean-François, ed. *Histoire des droites en France*. 3 vols. Paris: Gallimard, 1992.

Smith, Paul. *Feminism and the Third Republic: Women's Political and Civil Rights in France, 1918–1945*. Oxford: Clarendon Press, 1996.

Soucy, Robert. *Fascismes français? Mouvements antidémocratiques, 1933–1939*. Trans. Francine Chase and Jennifer Phillips. Paris: Autrement, 2004.

———. *Fascist Intellectual: Drieu La Rochelle*. Berkeley: University of California Press, 1979.

———. *French Fascism: The First Wave, 1924–1933*. New Haven: Yale University Press, 1986.

———. *French Fascism: The Second Wave, 1933–1939*. New Haven: Yale University Press, 1995.

———. "The Nature of Fascism in France." *Journal of Contemporary History* 1, no. 1 (1966): 27–55.

Sternhell, Zeev. *Ni droite ni gauche: l'idéologie fasciste en France*. 3rd ed. Brussels: Complexe, 2000.

Sternhell, Zeev, with Mario Sznadjer and Maia Asheri. *The Birth of Fascist Ideology: From Cultural Rebellion to Political Revolution*. Trans. David Maisel. Princeton: Princeton University Press, 1994.

Tartakowsky, Danielle, and Michel Margairaz, eds. *L'avenir nous appartient: histoire du Front populaire*. Paris: Larousse, 2006.

———. *Le Front populaire: la vie est à nous*. Paris: Gallimard, 1996.

———. *La manifestation de rue en France, 1918–1968*. Paris: Publications de la Sorbonne, 1997.

Thébaud, Françoise. "Le mouvement nataliste dans la France de l'entre-deux-guerres: l'Alliance nationale pour l'accroissement de la population française." *Revue d'histoire moderne et contemporaine* 32, no. 2 (1985): 276–301.

Thibault, Tellier. *Paul Reynaud (1878–1966): Un indépendant en politique*. Paris: Fayard, 2005.

Thomas, Jean-Paul. "Les effectifs du Parti social français," *Vingtième siècle* 62 (1999): 61–83.

———. "Le Parti social français." *Cahiers de la Fondation Charles de Gaulle* 4 (1997): 39–77.

———. "Le Parti social français (1936–1945): Une expérience de parti des masses et la préparation d'une relève." *Annales de Bretagne et des Pays de l'Ouest* 109, no. 3 (2002): 109–119.

———. "Le Parti social français dans le Nord (1936–1945)." *Revue du Nord* 89, no. 370 (2007): 257–269.

Thomas, Martin, ed. *The French Colonial Mind*. 2 vols. Lincoln: University of Nebraska Press, 2011.

———. *The French Empire Between the Wars: Imperialism, Politics, and Society*. Manchester: Manchester University Press, 2005.

Tumblety, Joan. "Civil Wars of the Mind: The Commemoration of the 1789 Revolution in the Parisian Press of the Radical Right, 1939." *European History Quarterly* 30, no. 3 (2000): 389–429.

Verdès-Leroux, Jeannine. *Refus et violences: politique et littérature à l'extrême droite des années trente aux retombées de la Libération.* Paris: Gallimard, 1996.

Vervaecke, Philippe, ed. *À droite de la droite: les droites radicales en France et en Grande Bretagne au XXe siècle.* Lille: Presses universitaires du Septentrion, 2012.

Wardhaugh, Jessica. *In Pursuit of the People: Political Culture in France, 1934–1939.* Basingstoke: Palgrave Macmillan, 2009.

———. "Un rire nouveau: Action française and the art of political satire." *French History* 22, no. 1 (2008): 74–93.

Weber, Eugen. *Action Française: Royalism and Reaction in Twentieth-Century France.* Stanford: Stanford University Press, 1962.

Whitney, Susan B. *Mobilizing Youth: Communists and Catholics in Interwar France.* Durham: Duke University Press, 2009.

———. "The Politics of Youth: Communists and Catholics in Interwar France." PhD dissertation, Rutgers University, 1994.

Wileman, Donald G. "L'Alliance Républicaine Démocratique: The Dead Centre of French Politics, 1901–1947." PhD dissertation, York University, 1988.

———. "P.-É. Flandin and the Alliance Démocratique, 1929–1939." *French History* 4, no. 1 (1990): 139–173.

Winock, Michel. "Fascisme à la française ou fascisme introuvable?" *Le Débat* 25 (1983): 35–44.

———. *Nationalism, Anti-Semitism, and Fascism in France.* Trans. Jane Marie Todd. Stanford: Stanford University Press, 1998.

———. "Populismes français." *Vingtième siècle* 56 (1997): 77–91.

———. "Retour sur le fascisme français: La Rocque et les Croix-de-Feu." *Vingtième siècle* 90 (2006): 3–27.

Winock, Michel, ed. *Histoire de l'extrême droite en France.* Paris: Seuil, 1994.

Wohl, Robert. "French Fascism, both Right and Left: Reflections on the Sternhell Controversy." *Journal of Modern History* 63, no. 1 (1991): 91–98.

Wolff, Richard J., and Jörg K. Hoensch, eds. *Catholics, the State, and the European Radical Right, 1919–1945.* Boulder: Social Science Monographs, 1987.

INDEX

PDP	Parti démocrate populaire
PPF	Parti populaire français
PRNS	Parti républicain national et social
PSF	Parti social français
RDP	*Revue du droit public et de la science politique*
RG	Renseignements généraux
RNAS	Rassemblement national d'action sociale
RNP	Rassemblement national populaire
RPF	Rassemblement du peuple français
RPP	*Revue politique et parlementaire*
SF	Solidarité française
SFCM	Société des filles du coeur de Marie
SFIO	Section française de l'internationale ouvrière
SP	*Sciences politiques*
SPES	Société de préparation et d'education sportive
SPF	Syndicats professionnels français
UF	Union fédérale
UFCS	Union féminine civique et sociale
UFSF	Union française pour le suffrage des femmes
UL	Union latines
UNC	Union nationale des combattants
UNVF	Union nationale pour le vote des femmes
VN	Volontaires nationaux

ABBREVIATIONS

AD   Alliance démocratique
ADP   Auxiliaires de la défense passive
AF   Action française
ALP   Action libérale populaire
AMSJA   Association médico-sociale Jeanne d'Arc
APD   Association de la paix par le droit
CC   Comité central
CFTC   Confédération française des travailleurs chrétiens
CGT   Confédération générale du travail
FFCF   Fils et filles des Croix de Feu
FNC   Fédération nationale catholique
FNF   Fédération nationale des femmes
FR   Fédération républicaine
FRI   Fédération républicaine indépendante
GRM   Garde républicaine mobile
JP   Jeunesses patriotes
JUNC   Jeunes de l'Union national des combattants
LDH   Ligue des droits de l'homme
LFF   Ligue des femmes françaises
LICA   Ligue internationale contre l'antisémitisme
LPDF   Ligue patriotique des françaises
MSF   Mouvement social français
PCF   Parti communiste français

With this in mind, our collection aims to refocus scholarly energy in the pursuit of a more nuanced portrait of the French right. Its contributors do not wish to engage in the debate over the rectitude of the Immunity Thesis, or to contribute to the discussion over the existence of a unique French fascism, and what its defining characteristics might be. Rather, *The French Right Between the Wars* aims to reevaluate conservative and fascist movements and intellectuals, seeking to provide a new interpretive framework based upon the centrality of gender, imperialism, political culture, and intellectual or cultural trends to fascist discourse and action. Chapter subjects range from the cultural politics of the right in 1930s France and its twinning of physical culture and racial rejuvenation to attempts to forge a specifically fascist femininity in interwar France and the relationship between fascist movements and colonial violence in French Algeria. This volume thus provides a current snapshot of innovative trends in the study of the Gallic right and the nation's political, cultural, and social history more broadly, from a wide variety of critical perspectives.

Clearly, two people alone could not have orchestrated such an undertaking. The editors wish to thank a number of individuals whose assistance proved invaluable in the publication of this collection. Most importantly, we must thank those who contributed to the volume. Their hard work and superb scholarship alone renders this collection worthy of a readership. That they took time from very busy research and teaching schedules to provide multiple drafts deserves our sincere gratitude. We must further thank the team at Berghahn Books, and particularly Marion Berghahn, for fostering the collection in its initial stages, and Ann Przyzycki Devita, whose editorial skill greatly enhanced the final product. Thanks are also due to the three anonymous readers, whose detailed and insightful critique and suggestions improved each chapter in the volume. Finally, we are grateful to Manchester University Press for permission to reprint portions of Chris Millington's monograph *From Victory to Vichy: Veterans in Interwar France*, and to Berghahn for permission to reprint (in slightly modified form) William Irvine's chapter, which originally appeared in the journal *Historical Reflections/Réflexions Historiques* as "Beyond Left and Right, and the Politics of the Third Republic: A Conversation."

Thanks are also due to a number of colleagues whose contributions made this volume possible. Laurent Kestel, Brian Jenkins, and Bill Irvine provided encouragement, helped to sculpt the interpretive framework of the volume, and disseminated much-needed advice at key moments. In a similar vein, we thank our colleagues in the History Departments at the University of New Brunswick and St. Francis Xavier University for their unwavering support.

Most importantly, we have to thank friends and family. Samuel Kalman would particularly like to mention his wife Brenda and son Josh, whose love and understanding made the completion of this project possible: As always, I could not have done it without you both! Sean Kennedy is grateful as always to his wife Lisa, who as usual has been encouraging and good humored throughout the ups and downs of preparing this work.

ACKNOWLEDGMENTS

Those studying the extreme right in interwar France face a twin challenge. The so-called Immunity Thesis championed by a wide variety of French academics minimizes the existence of Gallic fascism, positioning such movements as miniscule and completely at odds with the vast majority of politicians and the general public alike. On the Anglo-American side, the prevailing trend seeks to define fascism as a generic political model, and particularly to underscore its success in France.

In a way, both positions reflect the established doctrines of their respective eras. The Gaullist resistancialist myth of the post–World War II period found its ultimate expression in the work of historians who, following the lead of René Rémond in the late 1950s, sought to portray France as anti-fascist, staunchly Republican, and, if anything, proponents of moderate conservatism characterized by the small-town and provincial elites of the Alliance démocratique and Fédération republicaine, their background and parliamentary liberalism not much different than the centrist Radicals. Conversely, the leading historians of French fascism from the 1970s onward, including Zeev Sternhell, William Irvine and Robert Soucy, sought to revise this portrait at the very moment when a series of scholarly and cultural voices began to challenge the prevailing narrative of France as a nation of resistance to fascism, in which the wartime Vichy regime was termed a mere blip in an otherwise unbroken republican trajectory. The result was a Manichean divide: either France was fascist or it was not, and scholarship increasingly took sides, with evidence mobilized in support of one version or the other. As for the study of the non-fascist right, it practically disappeared by the 1980s, not least because its conclusions did not easily fit into the dualist schema. This is not to deny the very real value in the research and published work that appeared during those decades. Yet by the 1990s, a number of young historians began to move beyond the traditional confines, broadening the field of inquiry to include examinations of organizations themselves (including conservative parties and groups) as individual actors, and paying increased attention to gender, culture, imperialism, and many other variables, in addition to politics.

First published in 2014 by

Berghahn Books

www.berghahnbooks.com

Library of Congress Cataloging-in-Publication Data

The French right between the wars : political and intellectual movements from conservatism to fascism / edited by Samuel Kalman and Sean Kennedy.
  pages cm
  Includes bibliographical references and index.
  ISBN 978-1-78238-240-9 (hardback) — ISBN 978-1-78533-040-7 (paperback)
  ISBN 978-1-78238-241-6 (ebook)
  1. France—Politics and government—1914–1940. 2. France—Intellectual life—20th century.
3. Fascism—France—History—20th century. 4. Conservatism—France—History—20th century.
5. Right and left (Political science)—France—History—20th century. 6. Right-wing extremists—
France—History—20th century. 7. Parti social français. I. Kalman, Samuel, 1971– author, editor of
compilation. II. Kennedy, Sean, 1969– author, editor of compilation.
  DC396.F745 2014
  320.53'30944–dc23

2013017989

British Library Cataloguing in Publication Data

A catalogue record for this book is available from the British Library

ISBN: 978-1-78238-240-9 hardback
ISBN: 978-1-78533-040-7 paperback
ISBN: 978-1-78238-241-6 ebook

THE FRENCH RIGHT BETWEEN THE WARS

Political and Intellectual Movements
From Conservatism to Fascism

Edited by
Samuel Kalman and Sean Kennedy

berghahn
NEW YORK · OXFORD
www.berghahnbooks.com

The French Right Between the Wars

CONTENTS

The long served 'Old 1961' (after its construction number 049-1961) was used as a test bed for the 3,250ehp Allison YT-56 Turboprop in 1954, which went on to power the phenomenally successful C-130 Hercules. Remarkably, both the C-130 and the T-56 are not only still in service but are also still being produced 60 years after the types made their maiden flights!

THE BURBANK MACHINE KEEPS ON RUNNING

Already geared up for mass production on a grand scale, Lockheed's fully mechanised lines at Burbank were hungry for a new aircraft to build, and the 'Connie' seamlessly took over the same lines that had been producing the P-38s from 1941.

Above: With Capt James R. Gilmore flying from the pilot's seat at left, student pilot Bill Voegeli of Athens, GA, goes up on a training 'hop' to demonstrate his skill in landings and take-offs. Voegeli has had four years of flying in Navy patrol planes but must learn the feel of the controls of the planes he will fly in his airline assignment. The tower of the Empire State building in mid-Manhattan is visible through the windshield at right. (Lockheed official caption, dated 28 May 1947)

Opposite above: AIRPLANES EN MASSE — Photo taken from overhead crane bay at Lockheed Aircraft Corporation's final assembly line in Burbank, Calif., shows big new transports and radar airplanes marching to completion in close ranks. Note the comparative size of the workman on the floor below 50ft horizontal stabilizer of the first transport and men on the tail of the second. The multimillion dollar array of airplanes above include big new Super-C- transports for Eastern Air Lines and TWA (foreground) and early warning radar sentry versions of the Super Constellation (rear). Thousands of hours of experience from both military and commercial operations — including 70,000 crossings of the Atlantic — contributed to the development of the modern aircraft above. The airliners in this photo, a small part of the 222 commercial transports in Lockheed's order books, measure 123ft from wingtip to wingtip and 116ft from nose to tail. Of Lockheed's $1,390,648,000 in production orders at midyear, about 35% was for commercial airliners of four models: the Super-G, pictured; the new propjet Electra; 1049H cargo-passenger convertible Super Constellation; and the new extra-long-range 1649A Super Constellation which will be the longest range airliner in the world. (Lockheed News Bureau original caption)

The second aircraft from the camera is TWA's L-1049G-82 Super Constellation N7121C *Star of Aberdeen*.

Opposite below: A batch of military 'Connies', under construction at Burbank, at first glance appear quite anonymous. However, the aircraft in the centre and to the rear have the numbers 4338 and 4335 on the fuselages, which are Lockheed construction numbers. The fittings of the dorsal radome confirm that both of these machines are destined to become RC-121D 52-3417 (c/n 4335) and RC-121D 52-3420 (c/n 4338), which entered USAF service in September and November 1954, respectively.

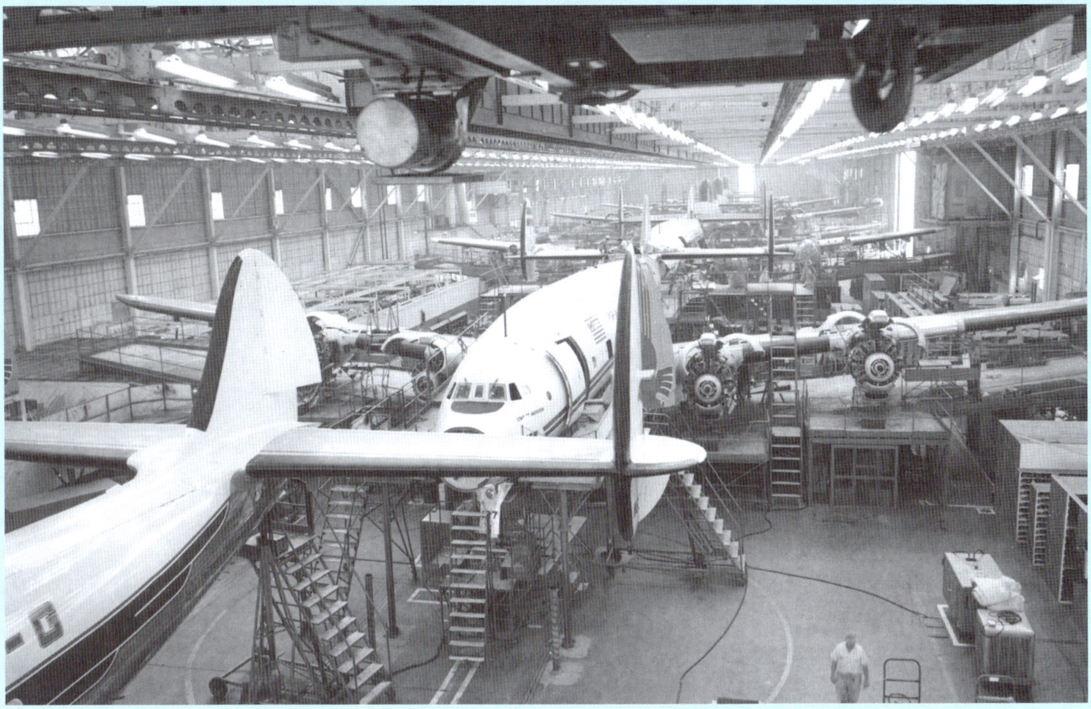

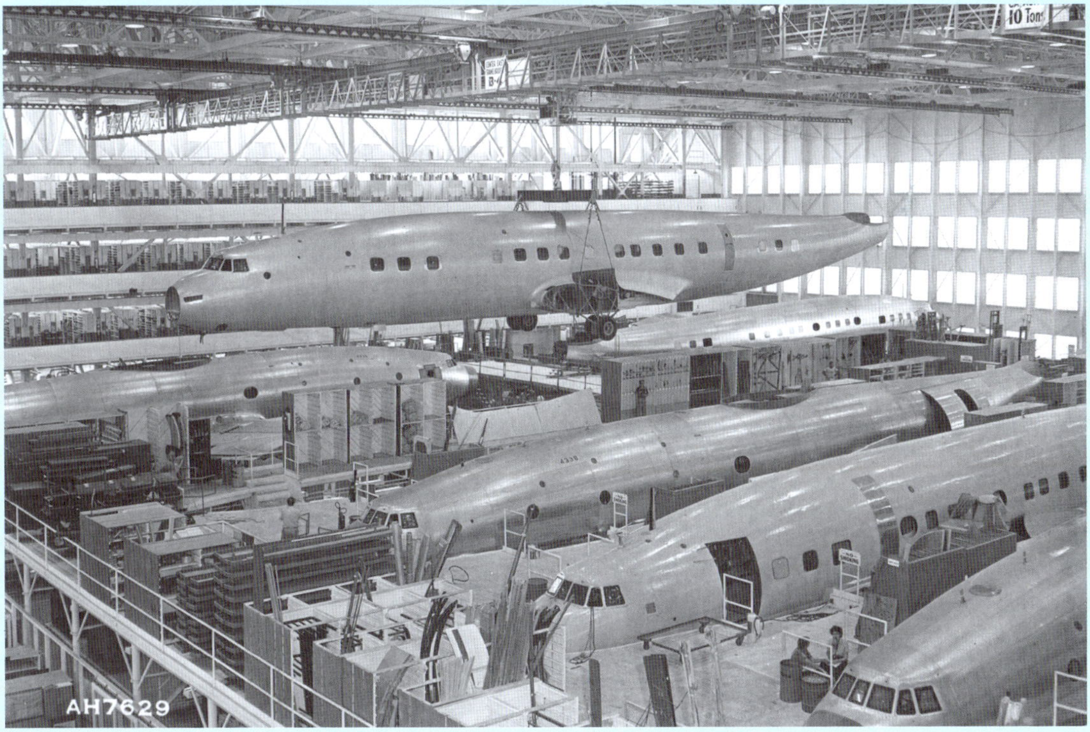
AH7629

BENDING ON THE BEAM -- Super-Constellation wing beam caps, made of new high strength 75ST6 alloy, are being shaped in the special beam bending machine developed by Lockheed Aircraft Corporation. Built by Hufford Machine Works, Inc. in accordance with Lockheed specifications, the machine can handle beams with an overall length of 60ft or more. Heat, up to 325 degrees Fahrenheit, is applied within the machine at the point of bend. As much as 50 degrees in bend can be given accurately and easily to a 5in x 3½in 75ST6 beam through the use of the new machine. (Lockheed News Bureau original caption)

NEW AIR TRAVEL TIP – The first wingtip fuel tanks ever to fly on transport aircraft are undergoing tests on Lockheed Super Constellations. This 600-gallon teardrop, being inspected by its inventor, Lockheed Chief Research Engineer Clarence A. (Kelly) Johnson, will be standard on the 450mph turbo-prop powered Super Constellations, on order for U.S. Navy. Tiptanks on each wing actually improve plane performance and provide enough extra lift to compensate for the 3,900lb weight of each Johnson reported. (Lockheed News Bureau original caption)

The serial number (131634) of this 'Connie' gives it away as a US Navy R7V-1 that was delivered on 21 September 1953. Later transferred to the USAF in June 1958 and redesignated as C-121G, the aircraft ended its days at Davis-Monthan AFB as a medical staff crew trainer until it was broken up in 1972.

Chapter 2

Developing the C-69 into a World-Beating Airliner

Capturing the post-war market

With the C-69 being a strictly limited-production aircraft, Lockheed began to think about the company's post-war business. It seemed that orders for the P-80 Shooting Star, the USA's first operational jet fighter, would remain fairly firm, despite the massive cutbacks in aircraft production at the war's end. Britain, impoverished by war, was also struggling to develop a home-grown fleet of long-range airliners, the Avro Tudor and Handley Page Hermes proving to be failures. Lockheed and local rival Douglas were, therefore, in a good position to capture a lucrative percentage of the post-war airliner market.

The original military contract specified improved C-69A, C-69B and C-69D variants. The C-69A was to be a dedicated troop-carrier with 100 seats, upgraded R-3350 engines and, in an odd continuation from the C-47, ports in the windows through which the troops could fire their M-1 rifles; one wonders what this would have done to cabin pressurisation! The C-69B, with extra tankage, was intended as a long-range troop transport, while the C-69D was to have further improvements over the 'B'.

Because of the low priority of the C-69 programme, difficulties with the R-3350 and Lockheed's numerous problems getting C-69s out of the door, military planners took a long, hard look at the programme. Douglas' C-54 Skymaster was being produced much more efficiently, and its long, tube-like fuselage was ideal for cargo hauling. Accordingly, C-69 production was cut back in stages. The Production Engineering Section of the army proposed that it be stopped after completion of the 20th airframe, but this was overruled.

This did not mean that the production line was saved, however. All the C-69As were cancelled, but work continued, and design effort focused on the C-69B. The contract was soon reduced to 210 airframes, including just three C-69Bs. In April 1944, the C-69Bs were cancelled, Lockheed being instructed to deliver the aircraft as straight C-69s. During March 1945, the contract was further trimmed to just 79 transports, and Lockheed countered with a proposal that the last 53 be completed at US$706,846 apiece, while three would be completed as C-69Bs.

Lockheed had completed licensed manufacture of Boeing B-17s, and production of the P-38 Lightning was coming to a close, so when the army requested that C-69 production be delayed to allow cargo doors and heavy-duty floors to be installed to make the aircraft as useful as the C-54, the company should have been well set to expedite this request. It was not to be. Air Materiel Command had put a maximum-priority order on the P-80, and if C-69 or P-38 production interfered, it was to be cut back or stopped. During October 1945, the last 50 C-69s on the contract were cut, leaving only 22 of the original contract for 260 aircraft.

Lockheed C-69-1-LO Constellation 43-10317 (c/n 049-1969) presents itself to the camera in this striking pose. The aircraft was sold to TWA on 30 November 1948 and was registered as N90830 *Star of Zurich*.

TWA L-049-46, NC90825, during a test flight before it was delivered to the airline on 15 May 1947. (Lockheed)

In the confusion following the war's end, Lockheed was able to broker a fairly good deal. Since the United States Army Air Force (USAAF) had accepted just 15 C-69s, Lockheed agreed to purchase the seven remaining aircraft on the production line for just over US$402,000 each. It also acquired all military-owned production tooling in the factory. As well as buying back most of the in-service C-69s at a bargain-basement rate, the Lockheed management decided to complete the aircraft on the production line as airliners, and convert the C-69s to a similar configuration, giving the company a significant lead over Douglas, whose pressurised DC-6 was still two years away.

Converting the military transports was not easy. The government had to approve the new airliner, so a C-69 was transferred to the CAA (Civil Aeronautics Administration) for flight testing to define the conversion requirements. As the C-69s had accumulated a fair amount of flying time, the CAA pilots had a known quantity, and, on 14 October 1945, the coveted Approved Type Certificate (ATC), A-763, was awarded.

Lockheed did have to make numerous changes to the C-69's interior, however. The stark military cabin gave way to a civilian interior, and since it was a long-range aircraft, an efficient galley had to be designed, and this was located behind the navigator's station and in front of the passenger cabin. For aircraft on international operations, the navigator's compartment was provided with bunks for crew members.

Because of the immense problems with the R-3350 in military service, the CAA demanded an extensive fire-extinguishing system in the cowlings, plus an upgraded fire-detection system. To make the interior as comfortable as possible, insulation was increased, and a new cabin heating and cooling system was installed. The somewhat 'homebuilt' interiors were adapted to suit different airlines.

The new designation Model 049 was applied to the converted C-69s, the aircraft on the production line, and machines newly ordered by the airlines. The first L-049 flew on 25 August 1945, and TWA took delivery of it on 14 November. Lockheed offered a number of engines, including the Pratt & Whitney R-2800 and Bristol Centaurus, but all buyers opted for the 2,200hp Wright Double Cyclone 745C-18BA-1, despite its troublesome reputation.

It was no surprise that TWA was the biggest customer, with 28 aircraft, followed by Pan Am, which had 22. American Overseas Airlines bought seven, Air France and BOAC had four apiece; KLM, having been virtually destroyed during the war, purchased six, and LAV of Venezuela rounded out the order book with two.

TWA L-049 crews underwent extensive training on the type and made numerous proving runs, including a pioneering New York–Paris flight on 25 November 1945. Oddly, Pan Am made the first revenue flight, a New York–Bermuda run on 3 February 1946. Close behind came TWA, starting a Washington DC–New York–Paris service on 6 February. As planned, TWA quickly expanded its intercontinental service by inaugurating flights to Cairo on 1 April and a New York–Lisbon–Madrid route on 1 May.

Soon after launching its intercontinental operations, TWA opened transcontinental Constellation routes between New York and Los Angeles. With such a quantum leap in performance and comfort over previous airliners, the Constellations received considerable publicity in the world's press, overshadowing the DC-4s flown by United and American and often bettering the competitors' schedules by up to 3 hours.

However, good publicity soon turned to bad when TWA Constellation NC86513 went down on fire near Reading, Pennsylvania, during a training flight, killing its crew. An investigation attributed the crash to an electrical failure. This led to a widely publicised grounding from 12 July to 23 August 1946. Lockheed made modifications, and the aircraft returned to service.

The L-649

During May 1945, design of the first purely civilian Constellation, the L-649, was started. Designers could now make the aircraft more 'passenger friendly' and introduce changes to ease maintenance. A greatly improved heating and air-conditioning system was installed (L-049

Pan Am's L-749 Constellation, *Clipper America*, is marshalled to a stop at Heathrow airport on 18 June 1947.

Originally built as a C-69-6 (42-94557), G-AHEM, named *Balmoral*, was one of the first 'Connies' to be delivered to BOAC as an L-049E-46. The aircraft is pictured during a Lockheed test flight; note the 'G' of the registration is covered over.

Only Eastern Air Lines took delivery of the L-649; the first aircraft, an L-649-79-12, was delivered on 19 March 1947. The aircraft pictured is NC101A, which was supposed to be Eastern's first L-649 but was kept by Lockheed (under an NX licence) until 10 October 1947. The Constellation was later converted to L-749A standard.

passengers often complained of baking and then freezing in just a matter of minutes), and much additional soundproofing was installed in the cabin (layers of fire-resistant fabric, glass fibre, and pockets of air), which helped dampen engine noise and vibration. Uprated 2,500hp Wright 749D-18BD-1s were fitted.

Improved seats enhanced passenger comfort, and Lockheed offered ten different interior layouts. However, Eastern Air Lines was the only operator to purchase the L-649, choosing it to fill its L-049

production slots (TWA ordered 18 L-649s but later cancelled). A 50 per cent redesign, the L-649 did offer better economy and cruising speed, greater range and an improved cabin. Propeller vibration problems were encountered, but a solution was found after extensive testing.

Eastern called its aircraft 'Gold Plate' Constellations, but this was soon dropped. Ultimately, the company flew 14 L-649s. First flown on 18 October 1946, the type had its certification tacked onto the L-049's ATC, remarkable considering the extent of the redesign. Eastern soon put the L-649 into service on its popular and profitable New York–Miami run. The carrier intended to order seven more, but then opted for the new L-749.

The L-749

Perceiving an increasing interest in long-range Constellations for overseas operations, Lockheed produced the L-749, similar to the L-649 but with extra fuel tanks in the outer wings that increased maximum capacity to 5,820 gallons. A strengthened undercarriage enabled gross weight to rise to 102,000lb, and during some nail-biting tests Lockheed test pilot Herman 'Fish' Salmon proved that the new aeroplane could stagger off the ground at a maximum weight of 133,000lb.

The L-749 was a moderate success. American Airlines bought 23 and foreign operators another 37. A few simple modifications resulted in the L-749A, with a gross weight of 107,000lb. This had a strengthened undercarriage, with tyres having a greater number of plies, and more efficient brakes. The centre section and inner wing stubs were strengthened. South African Airways (SAA) purchased four, but by this time many L-749s were already in service, and Lockheed produced kits to convert them into L-749As. American carriers purchased 32 L-749s (added to the existing ATC on 15 February 1949), and foreign operators ordered an additional 28 after SAA. The last L-749A was delivered in September 1951. Lockheed continued with improvements, offering a new floor of Plycor, an aluminium-plastic material giving increased strength. New exhausts, dubbed 'jet stacks', were claimed to add up to 15mph to maximum cruising speed by reducing exhaust back-pressure, while new Curtiss Electric Model C6345 propellers had thrust-reversing and automatic synchronisation to maintain uniform engine speeds.

Production of the 749 nearly shut down owing to cutbacks in airline orders. Only the addition of military orders kept the production line moving, and, if it were not for these, the Constellation would probably have been driven out of service by the more efficient and less troublesome DC-6 and DC-7. Lockheed also offered a freighter variant of the L-749A. A cargo door 7ft 8in wide by 6ft high was inserted in the rear fuselage and a smaller door added behind the cockpit. Although there were no takers, numerous aircraft were modified to this configuration as the L-749 entered second- and third-line service.

The L-749 was just the start of growth in the basic Constellation design. Lockheed soon developed the type into one of the world's prestige transport aircraft.

Air India's L-749A-79-44, VT-DAR *Maratha Princess,* **was one of seven L-749s operated by the airline.**

Chapter 3

The Super Constellations

Lockheed takes the lead

When Lockheed introduced the pressurised Constellation, its main competitor doggedly stuck to its DC-4/C-54 formula, which was slow and unpressurised but economic to operate and very reliable. Douglas responded to the Constellation by introducing the pressurised DC-6, which was taken one step further with the DC-6B; it was time for Lockheed to raise the bar again.

The result was the Model L-1049, aka the Super Constellation, and the prototype was the original C-69 'Old 1961', which was taken apart and rebuilt into the new aircraft. Large fuselage extensions were installed forward and aft of the wing, which raised the length of the airliner from 95ft 2in to 113ft 7in. The cabin was 56ft long, which gave the obvious advantage of higher passenger capacity. The Super Constellation's R-3350 engines became available in a turbo compound variant with improved performance and reliability.

'Old 1961', registered as N67900, made its maiden flight from Burbank with Double Cyclones installed on 13 October 1950. While the aircraft was slower than planned, the leap to a capacity of 92 passengers, rather than 69, seemed like a good trade-off.

L-1049

Eastern Air Lines placed the first order for the L-1049 Super Constellation, N6201C (f/f 14 July 1951), which entered commercial service on 15 December 1951. Eastern received 14 of the 24 L-1049s built and used them on its New York to Miami route. The remaining ten went to TWA to be used on its

'Old 1961' after modification to the prototype L-1049 Super Constellation, complete with original oval cabin windows, original cockpit windscreen and small vertical tail surfaces, all of which were modified in the production aircraft.

The first production L-1049-53-67, N6201C, made its maiden flight on 14 July 1951. It was delivered to Eastern Air Lines in March 1952. Note the rectangular panorama windows, modified cockpit windows and larger tail surfaces.

New York to Los Angeles route, starting in September 1952. The 'Super Connie' was offered, with the option of 730-US gal centre-section fuel tanks, which TWA took up. The L-1049 had been produced with the turboprop power in mind, and the airframes were stressed to handle a 3,500hp engine. Turboprops were only ever used experimentally by a few military Constellations.

At the request of TWA, a host of modifications were applied to the L-1049 in 1954, which included extended engine nacelles, modified cowlings, blanking off one of the three intakes that supplied cabin air and a number of further alterations to improve performance. The result was a mere 12mph increase at 20,000ft!

The L-1049 carried 71 first class passengers, or 95 in economy, had 728 cu/ft of cargo space and could cruise at 320mph. On overnight transcontinental flights this aircraft was equipped with eight berths and 55 first class seats. The L-1049 was powered by four 2,800hp Wright Cyclone R-3350-CA1 engines, and the airliner was sold for approximately US$1,250,000.

Maximum visibility was possible through the installation of rectangular panorama windows. The relocation of the windows in relation to the seats made for relaxed viewing comfort and increased natural light. Greater protection against frost and fog was obtained by circulating more air between the windows' double panes.

The Super Constellation prototype was the first passenger airliner with wing tip tanks. It was thought that the 600-US gal tanks would give the turbo-prop Constellations longer range, despite engines that required 50 per cent more fuel. Regardless, the airline industry had responded, and, in no time, 62 Super Constellations had been ordered by five major airlines even before the prototype had flown. By the time the first production aircraft was in the air, there were 100 aircraft in the order book.

L-1049A and B

The L-1049A and L-1049B were both military variants of the Super Constellation. The L-1049A applied to the US Navy's WV-2, WV-3 and the United States Air Force's (USAF) RC-121D. The US Navy's R7V-1, the USAF's RC-121C and the sole VC-121E *Columbine III* were designated L-1049B.

L-1049C

When the Wright Turbo-Compound engine became available, Lockheed had the chance to create the next variant of Super Constellation, the L-1049C, which could better the performance of the competition's DC-7B. The engine was complex, but Wright claimed that it could reduce fuel consumption by up to 20 per cent thanks to its ability to convert exhaust gas heat into more power. The engine, which could produce 3,250hp, was designated as 972TC-18DA-1, and, thanks to the extra horsepower, the gross take-off weight of the L-1049C was increased to 133,000lb and the landing weight to 110,000lb.

Lockheed flew the first L-1049C Super Constellation, PH-TFP, on 17 February 1953, and KLM put the aircraft into service on the Amsterdam to New York route in August. TWA followed suit with the L-1049C on 19 October 1953. Eight other airlines put the L-1049C in service to bring the total number produced to 60. The four-engine L-1049C was a significantly improved version of the original Super Constellation, the L-1049, which Eastern had first put into service only two years earlier.

The cockpit of the L-1049 was redesigned with a much larger windscreen and repositioned posts, which not only improved visibility, but also made it feel roomier. In the passenger cabin, pressurisation maintained a feel of 8,000ft when the aircraft was at 25,000ft, which meant that the L-1049C could fly 5,000ft higher than earlier models.

The Super Constellation with the new engine pushed ahead of its competitor, the DC-6, on transcontinental routes, making non-stop West to East operations possible for the first time. The L-1049C cruised at about 330mph and sold for about US$1,500,000. By the end of production, the following airlines purchased the L-1049C: Eastern (16); Air France (ten); KLM (nine); TCA (five); QANTAS (three); PIA (three) and Air India (two).

L-1049D

Very similar to the US Navy's R7V-1, thanks to the same freight doors, magnesium heavy-duty floor and the ability to mount an electric mechanical conveyor to move cargo up and down the hold, only four L-1049Ds were ordered by Seaboard & Western Airlines in 1951. The world's largest cargo aircraft when it was introduced, the airframe was stressed to 150,000lb and, with an 83ft-long hold of 5,568sq ft, a maximum payload of 38,570lb could be carried.

The interior could also be fitted out for 109 passengers, which made the L-1049D a very capable aircraft, and it was surprising that just four aircraft were ordered. Ordered at a cost of US$10 million, which included spares, the four aircraft were delivered to Seaboard & Western in August and September 1954.

L-1049E

Very similar to the L-1049C, the L-1049E offered the same, bigger operating weights of the L-1049D. Twenty-eight L-1049Es were built, some of these were originally ordered as L-1049Cs, although a number of planned L-1049Es were built as L-1049Gs instead. Eight airlines took delivery of the L-1049E, and the first aircraft, YV-C-AMS, for LAV, made its maiden flight on 6 April 1954. L-1049E allocation was as follows: QANTAS (nine); KLM (four); Avianca (three); Iberia (three); TCA (three); Air India (three); LAV (two) and Cubana (two).

L-1049F

This was the designation that applied to civilian variants of the USAF C-121C and the US Navy R7V-1 (L-1049B).

L-1049G

The definitive version of the Super Constellation was the L-1049G, nicknamed the 'Super G'. It was basically an improved version of the L-1049E, fitted with Wright's latest creation, the 3,250hp R-3350-972TC18 DA-3 turbo-compound engine. Gross weight could now be increased to 137,500lb, and maximum landing weight was now up to 113,000lb. The L-1049G had the option of 609-US gal tip tanks, increasing the 'Super Connie's' total fuel capacity to 7,750-US gal, which effectively extended the range by 700 miles. Other improvements included new propeller hubs, de-icer boots, better cabin soundproofing and the option to install a weather radar in the nose, which increased the length of the airliner to 116ft 2in.

Northwest Orient Airlines was the launch customer for the 'Super G', and the airline placed its order for six aircraft (reduced to four at a later date) on 20 April 1953. The very first L-1049G was rolled out in November 1954, and, on 17 December, made its maiden flight. The first aircraft was delivered to Northwest on 22 January 1955, and it was not long before L-1049Gs were employed in the routes from the US west coast to the Far East.

TWA placed an order for 12 L-1049Gs on 22 October 1953, followed by eight more in November 1955. All of TWA's aircraft were supplied with weather radar and tip tanks. TWA inaugurated its new 'Super G' service from New York to Los Angeles on 11 April 1955, and this was followed by the type's first transatlantic service from Washington to London on 1 November. TWA remained the dominant Super Constellation force, peaking at 50 'Super G' Atlantic crossings per week by the spring of 1956; neither Pan Am's DC-7Bs or its Stratocruisers could compete.

Air India ordered a pair of L-1049Cs in 1954, including VT-DGL (L-1049C-55). The L-1049C was the very first civilian L-1049 to actually attain its performance goals thanks to the availability of turbo-compound engines.

Originally ordered by QANTAS as VH-EAT, L-1049G-82 was delivered to Brazilian airline Varig instead on 11 December 1957 and registered as PP-VDE. The aircraft only served with Varig and was broken up at Porto Alegre in June 1967.

Northwest Airlines ordered four L-1049G-82-102s in 1955, but, within the space of two years, the airliners had been replaced by the DC-7C.

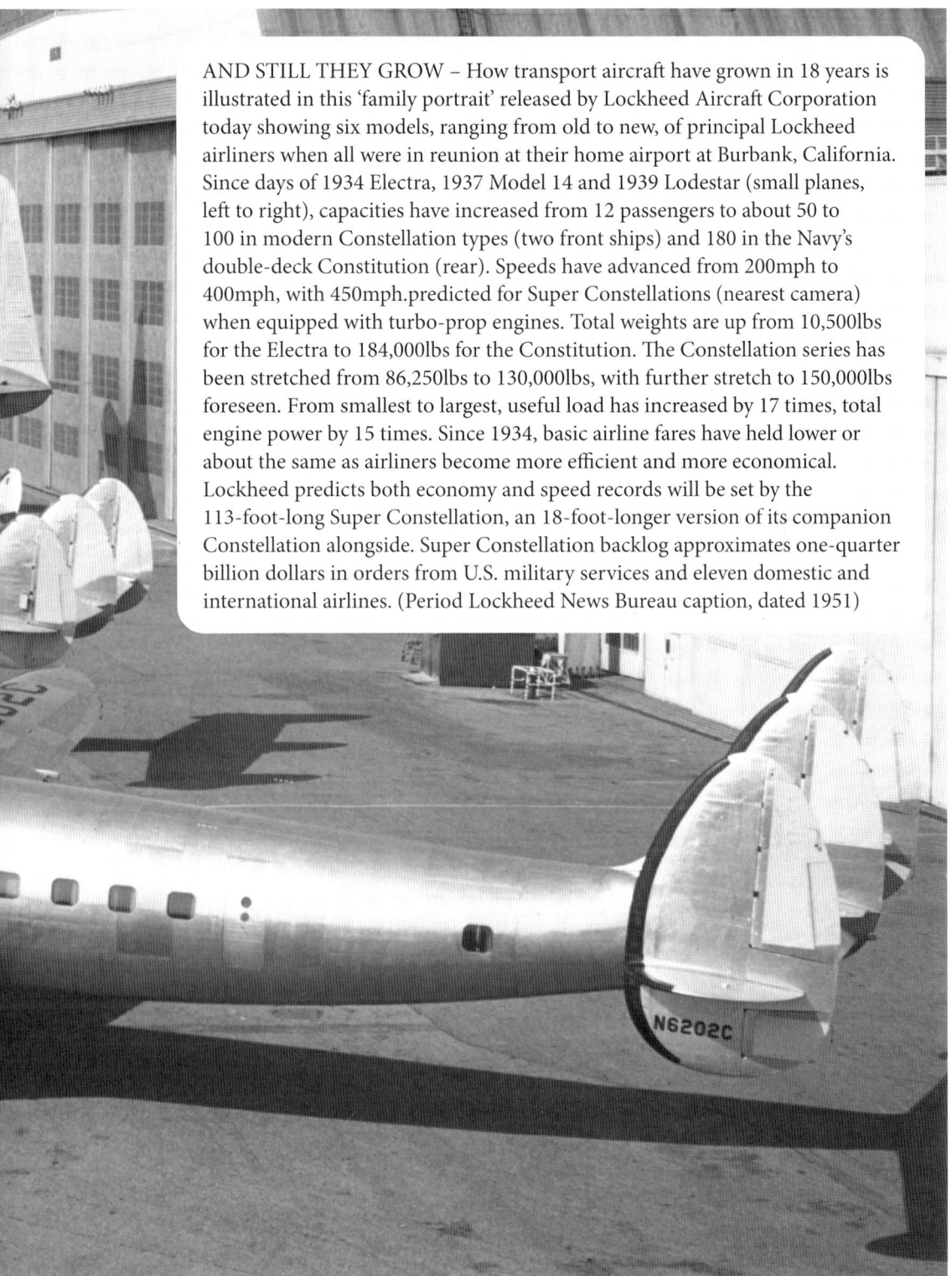

AND STILL THEY GROW – How transport aircraft have grown in 18 years is illustrated in this 'family portrait' released by Lockheed Aircraft Corporation today showing six models, ranging from old to new, of principal Lockheed airliners when all were in reunion at their home airport at Burbank, California. Since days of 1934 Electra, 1937 Model 14 and 1939 Lodestar (small planes, left to right), capacities have increased from 12 passengers to about 50 to 100 in modern Constellation types (two front ships) and 180 in the Navy's double-deck Constitution (rear). Speeds have advanced from 200mph to 400mph, with 450mph.predicted for Super Constellations (nearest camera) when equipped with turbo-prop engines. Total weights are up from 10,500lbs for the Electra to 184,000lbs for the Constitution. The Constellation series has been stretched from 86,250lbs to 130,000lbs, with further stretch to 150,000lbs foreseen. From smallest to largest, useful load has increased by 17 times, total engine power by 15 times. Since 1934, basic airline fares have held lower or about the same as airliners become more efficient and more economical. Lockheed predicts both economy and speed records will be set by the 113-foot-long Super Constellation, an 18-foot-longer version of its companion Constellation alongside. Super Constellation backlog approximates one-quarter billion dollars in orders from U.S. military services and eleven domestic and international airlines. (Period Lockheed News Bureau caption, dated 1951)

Here is one of the most unusual aerial photos ever made, a close-up so near the nose of an airliner that the smile on the pilot's face is easy to see. This Lockheed Super Constellation of Deutsche Lufthansa, the reborn German airline, seems to be flying right into the picture symbolic of the carrier's scheduled resumption of transatlantic service 8 June after 17 years of inactivity. Lufthansa has ordered eight 76-passenger Super Constellations for its overseas routes. Seldom, if ever, has an airborne transport aircraft been photographed at such close quarters, an example of the precision flying ability of both pilot and aircraft. The pilot is Paul Penrose, a Lockheed test pilot. (Period Lockheed News Bureau caption) 'This dramatic view is of L-1049G-82, D-ALAK, during a Lockheed test flight prior to its delivery to Lufthansa; one of eight purchased by the German airline'.

In total, 102 L-1049Gs were built, 42 for the US airlines and 59 for foreign airlines; they were sold new to the following customers: TWA (28); Air France (14); Eastern (ten); Lufthansa (eight); KLM (six); Varig (six); Air India (five); Northwest (four); TCA (four); Cubana (three); TAP (three); Thai Airways International (three); Iberia (two); LAV (two); QANTAS (two) and Avianca (one).

L-1049H

By the time that the final variant of the Super Constellation family, the L1049H, had arrived, airlines were already in the middle of jet fever as the Boeing 707, and the Douglas DC-8 were available. Despite the stacked odds, the L-1049H was a success, 59 of them were sold to 15 different airlines.

The L-1049H was a freighter variant of the 'Super G', which had the same over-engineered features as the L1049D. Capable of carrying up to 20 tons of freight, the fully convertible aircraft could also be reconfigured to carry up to 94 passengers, complete with cabin racks, sidewall lining and soundproofing, toilets and a galley.

The final L-1049H that was built was delivered to Flying Tiger Air Lines in November 1958, and, by December 1959, the airline's entire fleet of 13 aircraft was flying for 12 hours per day with a load factor of 84 per cent.

The 59 L-1049Hs sold new were built for the following airlines: Flying Tigers (13); California Eastern (five); Gulf-Eastern (five); Seaboard & Western (five); National (four); REAL (four); TWA (four);

One of the five L-1049H Super Constellations that were ordered by California Eastern. The L-1049H was a successful attempt at producing a 'multi-purpose' airliner, which could be quickly converted between passenger carrying and freight roles.

Air Finance Corporation (three); KLM (three); Slick (three); PIA (two); QANTAS (two); Resort (two); TCA (two); Dollar (one) and Transocean (one).

A numbers game

When the prototype Boeing 707 (367-80) made its maiden flight on 15 July 1954, the game was up for the Constellation and the world's piston-powered propliners on all passenger-carrying routes. The de Havilland Comet had already made its debut on the world scene two years earlier, but it did not have the same impact as the American-built jets, and its effectiveness diminished following several crashes.

   The long running battle between Douglas and Lockheed was only ever going one way, and it was the former, having produced 2,210 DC-4s, 5s and 6s, compared to 856 Constellations, that won the day. A large proportion of the Douglas production was for military orders as were, to a lesser extent, Lockheed's figures, but even when both are subtracted, Douglas sold 878 commercial aircraft while Lockheed sold 510. Lockheed, determined not be beaten, still had another 'Connie' derivative waiting in the wings: the Starliner.

Chapter 4

The Ultimate Propliner

Stretching the 'Connie' to meet the threat

Douglas gained the lead on Lockheed with the introduction of its DC-7C. Given the name (seldom used) of 'Seven Seas', it was a transport with prodigious range, capable of flying the Atlantic non-stop in both directions. Douglas, by hard work, had slowly overtaken the Constellation by creating a more straightforward aircraft that also reduced overall operating costs.

Lockheed was fatally late in responding to the DC-7C. Although the company decided to build an entirely new high-performance wing and mate it to a Super Constellation fuselage, it would be overtaken by advancing technology.

When TWA's management had learned that Pan Am had approached Douglas about designing a variant of the DC-7 capable of regular non-stop Atlantic operation, it went to Lockheed to see how the Connie could be stretched to meet the threat. Lockheed and TWA knew that even the extended-range L-1049G could not make non-stop crossings when winds were unfavourable, so the stretch to produce the required range would have to be in the wing.

The new wing was an elegant affair, spanning a massive 150ft, and, with a higher aspect ratio than its forebear (12:1 compared with 9.17:1) and a reduced thickness (15 per cent at the root and 11 per cent at the tip, compared with 18 per cent and 12 per cent). The wing area would be 1,850sq ft, and fuel capacity was to be a massive 9,600 US gal. The wing was to be built up of large integrally stiffened skin panels up to 37ft long and from 1¾in to ½in thick. At the time, they were the largest machined panels

JETSTREAM BEAUTY — shown in its first in-flight portrait, this new Lockheed long-range luxury airliner. This first 'grand manner' giant with its extra-long 150ft wing will be used for crew familiarization before going into commercial service. Next in line to receive Lockheed Model L649s this year are Air France, Deutsche Lufthansa and Linee Aeree Italiane. (Lockheed News Bureau caption)

for a transport aircraft. A single integrally stiffened sheet skin ran from the root to the tip between the spars on both upper and lower surfaces, and between the spars the whole wing comprised a vast torsion box used for integral fuel tankage out to the outer engine nacelles. There, full-depth tank-end wing ribs formed the ends of the four-tank fuel system.

Each half-wing was continuous from the aircraft's centreline to the tip. On the Model 1649A, the single-skin panel between the spars was replaced by five 24in panels top and bottom at the wing root, adjacent sections being joined by double rows of rivets.

The wing trailing edges and flaps were revised, the tailplane chord was slightly increased to reduce the thickness/chord ratio to a point comparable with that of the wing, and the tailplane span was increased. The wing leading edge sub-structure hinged upwards as far as the outer engines to provide access to interior equipment.

Power was to come from four 6,000shp Pratt & Whitney PT2F-1 turboprops. Consideration was also given to a variant powered by the Allison T-56, which would also power the new Lockheed Electra. The fuselages of both models were to be stretched, but the Pratt & Whitney engine was problematic, and Lockheed reasoned that an Allison-powered aircraft would be a direct competitor with the Electra. It was decided to drop turboprop power and use the new wing, combined with a standard Super Constellation fuselage, to create the Model L-1649.

Work on the L-1649 (to become L-1649A) started in May 1954. The initial name, Super Star Constellation, was changed to the shorter and more euphonious Starliner. Power was to come from four 3,400hp R-3350-988TC18EA-2 Turbo Compound engines – the ultimate production piston engine development. Metal cutting began in the first part of 1955, following an order from TWA for 25 L-1649As. Emphasis was on range rather than increased passenger load and, from the beginning, both Lockheed and TWA claimed that the Starliner would have the greatest range of any airliner and would be able to fly from Paris to New York in almost 3 hours less than its rival, the DC-7C. At ranges over 4,200 miles, Lockheed stated that the Starliner would be 70mph faster than any other transport. Moreover, every European capital would be within non-stop range from New York.

The aircraft was available with two types of propellers, both from Hamilton Standard. The Model 43H60/HA17A3-4 had hollow aluminium blades, while the Model 43H60/6993-B4 had solid blades.

TWA Lockheed L-1649A-98 Starliner, N7301C, one of 29 operated by the airline, the first of them entering service in May 1957.

TWA chose the hollow-blade units but found them troublesome in service and replaced them with the solid blades. Air France opted for Curtiss Electric props.

TWA leads again

The prototype, N1649A, was rolled out of the assembly hangar on 19 September 1956, and Roy Wimmer and Herman 'Fish' Salmon took the aircraft aloft for a 50min test flight on 11 October. The second aircraft off the line, owned by TWA, was used for the intensive test flight programme in order to achieve CAA certification as quickly as possible.

Delivery of the L-1649A progressed rapidly, and TWA received its first during April 1957 and had a total of ten by 14 June. Air France was the next major customer, originally ordering 12 but reducing the number to ten.

On July 8, 1957, Lockheed assisting general manager J. F. McBrearty issued a management memo regarding a record L-1649 flight to Paris:

Air France has notified us that it completed a non-stop flight from Lockheed Air Terminal to Orly Field Paris, in 17hr 11min with its first L-1649. The delivery flight was made with a normal-capacity fuel load of 9,785 US gal and with 33 passengers and ten crew members on board.
There were several significant things about this flight:
1. The time clipped 3hr 17min off the previous best times for a Los Angeles–Paris transport flight.
2. The 6,000-mile flight was the longest ever accomplished under standard airline operating conditions.
3. Nearly 1,000 US gal of fuel remained in the tanks after landing.
4. In addition to passengers and crew, the Starliner carried approximately 5,000lb of cargo.

The Air France aircraft took off from Lockheed Air Terminal at 0716hr, Sunday July 7, 1957, Pacific Daylight Time, and landed at Orly Field at 0827hr Paris time on July 8. The fastest previous Los Angeles-Paris flight was 20hr 28min by a DC-6B equipped with additional fuel tanks in May 1953.

The order book grew in March 1956 when Lufthansa and Linee Aeree Italiane (LAI) ordered four L-1649As each. LAI would have had the world's longest non-stop route, Rome to New York, at 4,280 miles. This flight would have taken 12hr eastbound and 15hr 30min westbound. However, in August 1957, LAI was formally liquidated and a new airline, Alitalia-LAI, was created. Alitalia had ordered DC-7Cs before the forced merger, so the four LAI aircraft were taken over by TWA.

TWA inaugurated its 'Jetstream' service on 1 July 1957, and, by the end of the month, its L-1649As were flying from New York to London, Frankfurt, and Paris. TWA also started operating the Starliner on New York–Los Angeles and San Francisco non-stop flights, soon followed by Boston–Los Angeles and Washington–San Francisco services. On 2 October 1957, TWA inaugurated an 'over-the-Pole'

The 63-passenger seating arrangement of a Lockheed L-1649 Starliner.

Starliner service between Los Angeles and London via San Francisco, but this was three weeks after Pan Am had started the same route with DC-7Cs.

A record was set during March 1959 when a TWA Starliner flew non-stop from London to San Francisco in 19hr 5min with 18 passengers and ten crew. It was not long before the luxurious first-class cabins in the L-1649As were eliminated, and, in 1959, TWA's Starliner fleet was converted to economy/coach-class.

The Comet and 707 jet airliners were now on hand, and the days of the big propliners were numbered. In 1960, six of TWA's Starliners were converted to cargo haulers with a reinforced floor, a forward cargo door 4ft 8½in wide by 6ft high, and a rear door 8ft 10½in wide by 6ft high. Both doors opened upwards, and the aircraft could now carry 37,250lb of cargo. Six more were later converted and, with the introduction of the 707 in 1959, the Starliners were relegated to other duties.

A TWA Starliner made the type's last international passenger flight (Cairo to New York) on 28 October 1961, illustrating just how short the Starliner's life was in TWA service. In 1962, TWA withdrew the type from domestic service, but cargo transatlantic flights continued until 1963, and domestic cargo flights went on until 1967. TWA made its last L-1649A cargo flight on 11 May 1967, and its last Constellation flight with L-749A N6024C, on 6 April 1967.

The L-1649A (one prototype, 43 production examples) and the Douglas DC-7C (121 built) were the ultimate propliners, but the new generation of jets quickly relegated these once-glorious sky kings to second and third-level operators. It was the end of a golden age; one that was, unfortunately, never to be repeated.

SUPERWING TRANSPORT — Setting test flight records at Lockheed Aircraft Corporation is this new L-1649A Starliner, flying on 150-ft wings increased 27ft in span over its sisterships. Pilots conducting pre-certification tests on the first 1649A reported that it is accomplishing more air time per week than any previous Lockheed transport -- more than 40 hops lasting from a few minutes up to 10 hours each since its maiden flight in October. Note the slim and slender wing shape, with engines located far out on the wing to provide quieter travel for the 58 first-class passengers it will carry. The First L-1649As will start service by next summer on TWA and Air France, later on Lufthansa, Italian Air Lines and Varig. They will fly nonstop from east coast to any European capital. (Period Lockheed News Bureau caption, dated 1956)

TWENTY-TWO YEARS OF SERVICE WITH TWA

After TWA was acquired by Howard Hughes, the business tycoon was instrumental in not only creating the Constellation, but also in introducing it into TWA service and 22 subsequent years of service.

TWA and the Constellation timeline

1925	Transcontinental & Western Air formed.
10 Jul 1939	Howard Hughes signs contract with Lockheed for the new Model L-049-16-01 Constellation.
1940	Hughes and TWA place orders for nine Constellations.
20 Sept 1940	TWA contract taken over by military, and aircraft would become C-69s for the USAAF.
17 Apr 1944	Howard Hughes and TWA President Jack Frye pilot a new Lockheed L-049 Constellation from Burbank, California, to Washington, DC in 6hr 57min, setting a new cross-country speed record.
23 Jan 1945	TWA's Intercontinental Division is contracted to introduce the C-69 into USAAF Air Transport Command service.
Dec 1945	TWA purchases the last two C-69s off the Burbank production line.
5 Feb 1946	TWA begins transatlantic service with the Constellation flying the New York–Gander–Shannon–Paris route.
15 Feb 1946	Howard Hughes pilots L-049 'Star of California' from Los Angeles to New York in 8hrs 30mins.
1 May 1946	Inauguration of TWA's international service to Lisbon and Madrid.
10 Jun 1946	C-69C-1-LO leased to TWA as NX54212.

11 Jul 1946	TWA Flight 513 crashes near Reading, Pennsylvania, killing five out of six on board.
30 Jan 1947	Inauguration of transatlantic all-cargo service. This was the first regularly scheduled direct all-cargo service ever operated over the North Atlantic.
Oct 1947	Airline strikes forces TWA to cancel an order for 18 L-649s.
Mar 1948	First of 12 L-749s enters service.
1 Oct 1948	Inauguration of all-sleeper luxury service from New York to Paris, known as the 'Paris Sky Chief' and from Paris to New York, known as the 'New York Sky Chief'.
1950	TWA's corporate name is officially changed to Trans World Airlines.
July 1951	The Missouri River floods at Kansas City, extensively damaging the TWA overhaul base at Fairfax Municipal Airport, Kansas City, Kansas. In the aftermath of the flood, TWA and Kansas City begin development of a new, flood-proof TWA overhaul base and a new international airport north of the city.
31 May 1952	The first TWA Ambassadors Club opens at Greater Pittsburgh Airport.
10 Sept 1952	L-1049 Super Constellation enters service on the New York to Los Angeles route.
19 Oct 1953	TWA begins the first non-stop eastbound scheduled transcontinental service with L-1049C Super Constellations. The flight from Los Angeles to New York took 8hrs. Because of prevailing head winds, the westbound transcontinental service continued to stop in Chicago to refuel.

Right: Howard Hughes at the controls of a TWA Constellation in 1947.

Below: L-049-36, NC90825, on a flight test out of Burbank before delivery to TWA on 15 May 1947.

One of many publicity opportunities. Here, Hughes greets actor Cary Grant on board a TWA Constellation in 1946.

1954–1958	Most TWA executive offices are relocated to New York. Training, maintenance and engineering and administrative functions remain in Kansas City.
3 Jan 1957	TWA is the first airline to offer passengers freshly brewed coffee in-flight.
1 Jun 1957	L-1649 Starliner 'Jetstream' enters service on the New York–London–Paris service.
29 Sept 1957	TWA launches its polar route service from Los Angeles to London with the 1649A Constellation.
1/2 Oct 1957	TWA inaugurates the second 'over-the-pole' from Los Angeles to London via San Francisco. The aircraft was in the air for 23hr 19min and covered a distance of 5,350 miles.
1957	TWA occupies its new $25 million maintenance and overhaul base at Mid-Continent International Airport, Kansas City. Fifteen years later, in 1972, commercial air service for the Kansas City region is relocated from TWA's long-time home at Municipal Airport to Mid-Continent, which is renamed Kansas City International Airport.
Jan 1958	The first edition of *Ambassador Magazine* is published.
20 Mar 1959	TWA initiates its jet service from San Francisco to New York using the Boeing 707-131.

TWA L-049-79-22 Constellation, which was used for publicity images before it was delivered to the airline on 10 June 1948. The aircraft began earning its keep the following day.

30 Jun 1961	TWA files a US$115 million damage suit against Howard Hughes and the Hughes Tool Company, alleging violations of the Sherman Act and Clayton anti-monopoly acts.
19 Jul 1961	TWA introduces in-flight motion pictures. The first feature *By Love Possessed*, stars Lana Turner.
1 Sept 1961	TWA Flight 529 crashes at Chicago; all 78 on board are killed.
May 1962	The Trans World Flight Center at Idlewild (later John F. Kennedy) International Airport, New York, is opened.
1 Oct 1962	TWA inaugurates the fully automated Doppler radar system of navigation on scheduled transatlantic flights. The New York to London flight is the first transatlantic flight (commercial or military) ever operated without a professional navigator aboard.
1 Jun 1964	TWA inaugurates its Boeing 727 service.
3 May 1965	Howard Hughes liquidates his TWA share holdings, selling 6,584,937 shares and netting US$546.5 million.
11 May 1967	A TWA L-749 carries out the Constellation's last scheduled passenger flight from Philadelphia to Kansas City.
1 Dec 2001	Final TWA flight by MD-80, N948TW.

TWA CONSTELLATION FLEET AT ITS PEAK IN 1959

32	L-049	28	L-1049G
12	L-749	9	L-1049H
27	L-749A	29	L-1649
10	L-1049		

THE SPEEDPAK

The Constellation had the ability to carry aloft more weight than its cabin could accommodate. This led Lockheed engineers to come up with an interesting 'add-on', which would enhance the airliner's capabilities and, they hoped, lead to more orders. The new creation was the Speedpak, a faired pod that attached to the bottom of the Constellation's fuselage. Unpressurised, the Speedpak had a thick rubber seal that ensured a tight fit against the fuselage. Fitted with four small wheels on the bottom, the unit was fairly manoeuvrable and could be loaded and unloaded away from the aircraft. It had its own integral lift system, making raising and lowering relatively easy and was fitted with its own fire-detection and firefighting systems which were linked to the cockpit via electrical connections.

The Speedpak could be fitted to the L-049 through to the L-749A series and the biggest user was Eastern Air Lines. When attached, the Speedpak, which could carry a maximum of 8,300lb of cargo, imposed a range penalty of 4 per cent and a speed penalty of 12mph. Oddly, the Speedpak was not a great success, probably because it could not take large items of cargo, and only 75 units were produced by Lockheed.

Inset: The most unique development in baggage and cargo carrying on world air routes is the Speedpak, an external carrier that can be hoisted into position against the underside of the fuselage of a Lockheed Constellation. A Speedpak is shown here, ready to be attached to a Constellation. (Lockheed News Bureau caption)

Air France ordered nine L-749 Constellations, including F-BAZB as L-749-79-22. Later upgraded to an L-749A-79-46, F-BAZB ended its days as a bar near Dijon and was broken up in 1973.

Before the C-69 was fully accepted by the United States Army Air Force (USAAF), an incredible 486 modifications had to be implemented. The workload was so high that Lockheed established an outdoor modification line at the Lockheed Air Terminal at Burbank. The aircraft in the foreground is C-69-1-LO, 43-10315, which was subsequently registered as N90828 and delivered to Intercontinental Airways. Sold to El Al in 1951 as 4X-AXB and then to a Swiss owner as HB-IEB, the aircraft later joined Universal Sky Tours as G-ARVP on 13 February 1962. Withdrawn from use, the Constellation was broken up at Luton in May 1965.

Chapter 5

The 'Connie' in Uniform

USAF interest

When the USAAF cancelled its Lockheed C-69 Constellation contracts at the end of the Second World War, 21 C-69s had been delivered, or were nearing completion, in military configuration. Amongst these were eight C-69-1s, ten C-69-5s, and two C-69-1LOs. All were 63 seat troop carriers. One machine, designated a C-69C (later ZC-69Z), was produced as a 43-seat VIP transport. Cancelled military variants of the Constellation included: 49 C-69C, VIP, high-speed, command transports, with a seating capacity of 43; a number of C-69As, with accommodation for up to 100 troops; several C-69Bs, with seating for 94 and three C-69Ds, built to carry 54 personnel. All of these models were designed to carry a crew of six.

In the early post-war years, Lockheed was wholly involved with its commercial Constellation programme. No further military interest was shown in the developing airliner until 1948, when the USAF ordered ten of the long-range L-749As for use as long-range military personnel and freighter transports. Designated C-121As (Lockheed Model 749A-79-38), the new military Constellations were powered by four 2,500hp Wright R-3350-75 radials. Heavy-duty flooring was incorporated for the

shipment of cargo, and a sizeable freight door in the rear fuselage facilitated loading and unloading. Alternatively, removable seats could be fitted as required to provide a personnel-carrying conversion, or the aircraft was also operable in an ambulance configuration with the provision of hospital stretchers.

The VIP transports

Three C-121As became VC-121A VIP transports. They were: 48-613, named *Bataan*, for the use of Gen MacArthur; 48-614, *Columbine I*; 48-610 *Columbine II,* which had a very chequered career. First, it was the personal aircraft of Gen Dwight Eisenhower, earning the nickname 'General Ike's Eagle', and, as Eisenhower was then the commander of NATO, it was stationed in Paris. It flew to most of the major Allied bases and airports in Europe, and quite a number of transatlantic flights were made. The specially chosen crew of eight, led by the pilot, Maj W.G. Draper, clocked up approximately 50 hours in the air each month.

After its replacement in 1950 by a VC-121E, *Columbine II* was allocated to Washington DC for VIP duties, returning to Europe in 1954 as Gen Gunther's personal machine. It then returned to Washington for another spell of VIP duty before finally being declared redundant by the USAF. TWA soon purchased 48-610 for its Constellation fleet but later sold it to Ethiopian Airlines, in 1957, as ET-T-35, when it became the personal aeroplane of Ethiopia's Emperor, Haile Selassie. On 10 June

Lockheed RC-121C, 51-3842, on finals. Originally ordered as a WV-2B by the US Navy, the aircraft were instead delivered to the United States Air Force (USAF) as RC-121Cs. 51-3842 crashed on test flight in poor conditions at Marysville, California, killing six of the crew on board.

'Old 1961', still in its L-1049 prototype colours, also served as the prototype for the US Navy's WV-2. The huge radomes on the spine and below the fuselage were dummies.

that year, while flying near Khartoum, this Constellation met its end when one of the engines caught fire, causing the machine to make a forced landing. Fortunately, all those on board escaped, but the Constellation (cn.2602) was burnt out.

A one-off VC-121B (cn.2600) was built as a staff transport, fitted out with a VIP interior, and equipped for possible use by the US president. It carried USAF-style national markings, the serial 48-608 and was named *Dewdrop*. Another six VC-121Bs entered service, but these were all conversions, three C-121As (48-611, -612 and -617) and the three VC-121As mentioned earlier. The remaining C-121As in USAF service flew with the Military Air Transport Service (MATS) and, for a time, were temporarily reclassified as PC-121As. During the Berlin Airlift of 1948–1949, the C-121As of the MATS played an important role in helping to convey personnel and essential supplies of food, fuel and other commodities to Tempelhof, Berlin. Indeed, in the first month of the Soviet blockade, military Constellations clocked-up over five million miles, flying a shuttle service of supplies across the North Atlantic, from the US to Germany.

Airborne Early Warning (AEW)

Meanwhile, developments in radar techniques had been making good progress, and the US Navy, wanting to try out the latest early-warning radar and intelligence-gathering electronic equipment, decided that the long-range Lockheed L-749A Constellation would provide a suitable testing platform. Consequently, the Navy ordered two of these machines from Lockheed. Initially, they were designated PO-1W (later WV-1), the first of which, BuAer No.124437 (cn.2612), made its initial flight in June 1949. The two Airborne Early Warning (AEW) pickets proved quite successful and were soon given the nickname of 'Po Ones'. Massive radomes were fitted above and below the fuselage, the upper protuberance having the appearance of a nuclear submarine's conning tower. A number of antennae were also erected along the top of the fuselage. These radomes, together with their complementary equipment, contained height-finding radar in the top dome and plan-surveillance radar in the lower, teardrop-shaped one. They were designed to seek out enemy aircraft and surface ships in time of war. The crew of 22 included aircrew, radar operators and engineers. With an extensive range, both in duration and amount of electronic gear, the PO-1W (WV-1) concept became an accepted and essential part of naval strategy. As for the two original PO-1Ws, apart from interior alterations, the only external difference, to compensate for the additional area taken up by the radome, was an increase in dimensions for the fins.

Actually, US Navy faith in the Constellation had already been proved, as initially a naval transport version of the L-049 was ordered as the R70 (Lockheed Model 049-46). No BuAer numbers were allotted, but the type did serve with Navy Squadron VPB-101. Then, with the emergence of the L-1049 Super Constellation, the Navy had invested in the R7V-1, a cargo/troop carrying variant, incorporating a revised wing structure, heavy-duty flooring, fore and aft cargo doors and the power of four 3,250hp Wright R-3350-91 Turbo Compound engines. Then, with the favourable reports on the AEW PO-1Ws to satisfy its demands, the US Navy placed a production contract for a number of flying radar stations, based on the R7V-1 design. One of these, designated the R7V1-R, was to be equipped with photographic gear and flown on reconnaissance sorties over the Antarctic area. The R7V-1 was also updated to carry a weather-warning radar, installed forward of the flight deck, necessitating an additional 3ft of nose length.

Flying radar pickets were, in fact, airborne electronic sentries, which could extend the range of surface-type radar by great distances. In the aftermath of World War Two, 23 ex-USAAF Boeing B-17G Fortresses were acquired by the US Navy for conversion to airborne radar pickets. Designated PB-1W, these B-17Gs had extra fuel tanks installed, a large 'guppy' type radome fitted into the bomb bay, and, when the APS-20 search radar was installed, defensive armament was removed. Two B-29

The First Lockheed Constellation series adapted to early-warning duties, the WV-1, was modified to carry special radar equipment in plump 'fins' above and below the fuselage mid-section. Ranging far beyond the optical horizon of ship-borne radar stations, the WV-1 extended a warning net hundreds of miles to sea from American shores. Later versions carried far more advanced electronic equipment and much more of it. (Lockheed News Bureau caption, dated 1949)

WV-3 Warning Star 137894, 3/TH, in company with a pair of McDonnell F2H-2P Banshees in 1956. The US Navy's WV-3s were redesignated as the WC-121N from 1962, and 137897 served on into the early 1970s until it was scrapped at Davis-Monthan on 21 May 1976.

Superfortresses were also transferred from the USAAF to the Navy as P2B-1 flying radar pickets, with additional fuel capacity and search radar contained in the bomb bay. The following Lockheed PO-1W trials paved the way for a diverse series of military types based on the Turbo-Compound-powered Super Constellation, which, after the 1962 US forces aircraft redesignation system, became the EC-121 with suffixes up to the letter T.

The new AEW Super Constellations entered US Navy service during the mid-1950s as PO-2Ws, later WV-2 (EC-121K in 1962) and were allotted the official name Warning Stars. Four uprated 3,400hp Wright R-3350-34 or 42 Turbo-Compound Cyclone 18s provided the power. Wing tip tanks, similar to those on the civil Super-G, allowed for a maximum possible range, with a duration of up to 30hrs. The crew of 26 included a number of radar operators who sat facing an array of consoles and radarscopes, involving nearly six tons of radar, electronics, data links and special communication systems employed in AEW operations. These ocean-going AEW aircraft included bunks among the furnishings to enable members of the crew to take a rest from duty, although about half the cabin space contained the radar and much of its complementary equipment. Even so, a galley was incorporated, allowing the off-duty crew to prepare hot meals and drinks. A good supply of spare components was carried by each WV-2/EC-121K, so that any necessary running repairs could be carried out while the aircraft was still on patrol.

Conversions were undertaken to a number of WV-2s, which were fitted out with sophisticated electronic countermeasures (ECM) equipment, direction finding (DF) systems, jamming devices and additional aerials and antennae aft. Initially designated WV-2Qs, these machines became EC-121Ms, in accordance with the revised military aircraft classification system of 1962.

One WV-2, BuAer No. 126512 (cn.4301), was equipped with a new aerial surveillance radar system known as AN/APS-82, the aircraft being redesignated as a WV-2E (later EC-121L). This equipment was housed in a large 9-ton rotating dish atop a massive pylon embodied in the aircraft's upper

NAVY PROP-JET—Powered by jet engines spinning huge propellers, this U.S. Navy R7V-2 transport flew 479mph in rapid descent tests conducted by Lockheed-California Company pilots. The propellers have 24-inch-wide blades and are 15ft in diameter to get maximum efficiency from 5700hp engines. This transport also set a Super Constellation record by flying at a weight of 166,400lbs. (Lockheed News Bureau caption, dated 1954)

FASTEST MILITARY TRANSPORT -- Capable of crossing the United States in about six hours, the Lockheed YC-12IF is powered by four Pratt & Whitney T-34 turboprop engines, developing 5700hp each. Long, slim nacelles lead exhaust gases over the wing after their power has been harnessed to the broad-bladed propellers. Two of the big prop-jet YC-12IF Super Constellations were built for the USAF and two (designated RTV-2) were built for the USN. The 600-gallon tip tanks on the ends of the wings give the aircraft capability of extended range. (Lockheed News Bureau caption, dated 1955)

MILITARY MAGIC CARPET — The triple-duty C-121C, a military version of the Super Constellation, can cruise at 335mph as a passenger, cargo, or hospital litter transport. Stronger and lighter magnesium flooring provides sturdy 'footing' for more than 14 tons of bulk cargo. Assigned to the Military Air Transport Service, the C-121C can be converted quickly to a 75-passenger version — or adapted as an aerial ambulance carrying 47 litter patients and their hospital attendants. The U.S. Navy counterpart of the C-123C is the C-121J (R7V-1). Powered by four Wright turbo-compound engines, it has a maximum takeoff weight of 133,000lbs. (Lockheed News Bureau, caption dated 1955)

fuselage. In this configuration, the WV-2E made its initial flight during 1956, but the EC-121L did not reach production status. However, a rotodome dish-scanner was fitted to a Grumman WF-2 Tracer, a combination that was accepted by the US Navy, albeit for use aboard aircraft carriers.

The Navy also received nine, special weather-reconnaissance versions of the Super Constellation, designated the WV-3 (later WC-12IN). Eight were produced, BuAer Nos 137891-137898 (cns 4378-4385). The remaining machine was a WV-2, BuAer No.141323 (cn.4447), converted to WV-3 configuration. The last two of the eight newly built machines, BuAer numbers 137895 and 137898, were later transferred to the USAF and became EC-121Rs, 67-1471 and 67-1472, respectively.

The WV-3 weather machines, although employing the same basic airframe as the WV-2, together with the large radome and ventral 'guppy' dome, contained a different internal layout, in which the plotting crew numbered only eight, while the wing tip fuel tanks were omitted. Earning the nicknames 'Storm Seeker' and 'Hurricane Hunter', the nine WV-3s used a type of radar capable of covering over 190,000 square miles of ocean in one sweep. Operating with Navy Squadron VW-4, these weather-seeking Super Constellations flew from the US Naval Air Station at Roosevelt Roads, Puerto Rico, and from Jacksonville, Florida.

The world's fastest propeller-driven transport

Meanwhile, the proposed fitting of four turboprop engines to a Super Constellation certainly interested the US Navy. It was decided, at Burbank, in 1952, to produce a Super Constellation powered by four 5,500ehp Pratt & Whitney YT34-P-12A turboprop engines, driving Hamilton Standard Turbo Hydromatic propellers, of 15ft in diameter, featuring three paddle-type blades, each 2ft wide. The Navy ordered four turboprop Super Constellations, aware that the R7V-2, as it would be designated, would emerge as perhaps the world's fastest propeller-driven transport aircraft at that time. The first R7V-2 made its initial flight on 1 September 1954. By the summer of 1955, all four machines were flying. This model featured wing tip fuel tanks, each containing 600 US gal, which complemented the main tanks to provide a maximum fuel capacity of 8,750 US gal. Gross take-off weight was 150,000lb, and the service ceiling was 35,800ft. During take-off, the Pratt & Whitney T-34s were on full power, at 11,000rpm, but, because of a very efficient gear-reduction arrangement, the large propellers rotated at only 1,000rpm.

The R7V-2 was considered to be quite a viable proposition, with great military and commercial potential, but surprisingly little interest was shown in the type and no production contract was forthcoming. The four R7V-2s built remained in the category of test aircraft and were allotted BuAer numbers 131630, 131631, 131660 and 131661 (cns 4131, 4132, 4161 and 4162, respectively). However, in 1956, the latter two machines were transferred to the USAF as YC-121Fs, with the serials 53-8157 and 53-8158. One of the two remaining Navy R7V-2s later served as a flying test bed with four, 3,750ehp, Allison 501-D13 turboprop engines and nacelles fitted, as used on Lockheed's Model L-188 Electra airliner.

Another two Navy variants were the NC-121Ks. These were converted EC-121Ks and EC-121Ps. The EC-121Ks were converted for special purpose tests and projects, including *Birdseye*, the Antisubmarine Warfare Environmental Prediction Systems (ASWEPS) programme, and *Magnet*, in which the earth's magnetic field was studied and mapped out. The EC-121PS were a batch of EC-121K conversions, equipped for anti-submarine warfare (ASW), their interiors contained ASW sensors and Navaids for operations under water. Additionally, a substantial number of US Navy R7V-1 (later C-121J) transports were transferred to the USAF, which was another major operator of military Super Constellations.

JEEPERS, WHAT PEEPERS! — The strangest and farthest looking shape in the sky is the U.S. Navy 'flying saucer' EC-121L radar research airplane. The Lockheed-built sentry 'sees' half again as far as any current radar plane, has vertical coverage from sea level to 100,000ft. Looking like a flying saucer riding piggy-back on an airplane, the big radome houses antenna for a super-vision electronic eye able to do the work of dozens of ground radar stations. Operational Super Constellation sister-ships fly extended Navy and Air Force missions spanning all the way from the mid-Pacific to the mid-Atlantic to the shadow of the Arctic Circle. (Lockheed News Bureau caption, dated 1956)

Long-range transport and Warning Stars

After the success of its C-121As, the USAF ordered the L-1049 Super Constellation during 1951, designating it the C-121C, for long-range transport duties. Seventy-five personnel, 14 tons of freight, or 47 stretcher cases could be carried, as dictated by circumstances. Four 3,500hp Wright R-3350-34 Turbo-Compound radials powered the Lockheed C-121C, which had a maximum take-off weight of 135,400lb, an increase of 28,400lb over the earlier C-121A model. Like the US Navy, the USAF saw the Super Constellation as ideal for the AEW role, and the air force initially ordered ten, designated the RC-121C. These USAF flying radar pickets carried some 15,000lb of radar equipment, including ANAPS-20 search radar and APS-42 cloud collision gear. The aircraft was similar in profile to the navy's WV-2, possessing the upper and lower radome layout. The 8ft vertical dome above the fuselage housed the height-finding antenna, while the lower 'guppy' ventral dome contained the bearing scanner. No wing tip tanks were fitted to RC-121Cs, but, with a maximum load, the endurance at a cruising speed of 335mph was 24 hours, given reasonable weather conditions. Designated EC-121C in 1962, these RC-121Cs had entered USAF Air Defence Command service during 1953. They were employed mainly on patrol duties along the western seaboard of the US.

May 1954 saw the first of 72 RC-121D Warning Stars (later EC-121D) delivered to the USAF. These updated machines featured wing tip auxiliary fuel tanks, resulting in a longer operating range, and they were fitted out with improved AEW equipment and electronics. RC-121D/EC-121D Warning Stars were employed as long-range patrol aircraft or as a flying control centre for the guidance of interceptor fighters. They were known as AEW&C (Airborne Early Warning & Control) aircraft. This variant was the basis for several other types of advanced electronics and surveillance aircraft. Its maximum take-off weight was by then an impressive 143,000lb.

With the designation EC-121D, applied in 1962, the Warning Stars had a computer and other modified electronic equipment added so that the type was able to operate with other forces committed to defending North America under the NORAD/SAGE (North American Air Defence/Semi-Automatic Ground Environment) programme. As more sophisticated radar and electronics were developed, no less than 42 EC-121DS received considerable internal modifications, in which SAGE data links, an advanced airborne computer, revised navaids and other updated electronic equipment, were installed. Distinguishable by having a small, streamlined radome located on top of the fuselage, just ahead of the main dome, this version was designated the EC-121H.

The majority of AEW&C aircraft flew with the USAF (ADC) 551st Airborne Early Warning & Control Wing, which operated out of Otis Air Force Base (AFB), Massachusetts. In their more sophisticated configuration, they were used to feed information to NORAD surface bases. Several machines were converted as TC-121C radar crew trainers, but these aircraft later reverted to their original EC-121C configuration. Two EC-121Ds (c/ns 4334 and 4410), with the USAF serials 52-3416 and 55-137, respectively, featured special, classified, electronics equipment and were designated EC-121Js. Another operator of Warning Stars was the 552nd AEW&C Wing of the USAF based at Sacramento, California. This unit took delivery of four EC-121Q aircraft, which were EC-121Ds specially adapted for AWACS (Airborne Warning & Control System) operations.

During the Vietnam War, three types of ground sensors were employed to relay information back to American forces. Two types were designed to bury themselves in the ground, leaving just the antenna above the surface, and one was attached to a parachute, intended to hang from trees. The sensors were dropped either from fast, low-flying jets, or from slow, twin-engine aircraft. Their intelligence signals were picked up by specially modified Lockheed EC-121K/EC-121P Super Constellation relay stations, designated EC-121R. Thirty of this variant were supplied for these operations, which were known as

Project *Igloo White*. Their upper and lower radomes were omitted, but wing tip fuel tanks were fitted. They were in a tactical camouflage finish.

The choice of EC-121Rs for use in Project *Igloo White* was due to the type's ability to fly low-level missions for up to 24hrs, if necessary, at the same time keeping an accurate course to stay within receiving range of the signals emitting from the ground sensors. The EC-121R crew then relayed any information received from the sensors to an Infiltration Surveillance Centre (ISC) in Thailand. If a

79th AEWS (Homestead, Florida), Lockheed EC-121T Warning Star, 54-2301 at the RAF Mildenhall Air Fete on 27 August 1978. One of the last Warning Stars in USAF service, this aircraft was originally built as a RC-121, redesignated as an EC-121D in 1962 before being converted into an EC-121T. On returning to the US from Mildenhall, the aircraft was retired and delivered to MASDC at Davis-Monthan on 19 September 1978. It was transferred to DMI Aviation, Tucson, on 15 February 1984 and then scrapped.

The cargo/personnel variant of the L-1049B Super Constellation was initially delivered to the US Navy as the R7O-1. Lockheed R7O-1, 128438, was later redesignated as an R7V-1, a C-121J from 1962 and, after being transferred to the USAF, became a C-121G, re-serialled 54-4051.

PACIFIC DIVISION

PACIFIC DIVISION

PACIFIC DIVISION

128438

U.S. NAVY

delay occurred in relation to ISC processing when a vital target was involved, the EC-121R was able to send the required information direct to the attack aircraft, which were already airborne.

The 'Connie' bows out

The US Navy and USAF received more than 220 main variants of the Super Constellation. The interiors of many were completely re-equipped with updated electronics, while others underwent a rebuilding programme. A number of the less electronically sophisticated versions of the Super Constellation continued operating with US Air Defence Command into the 1970s, several serving with the 79th Air Reserve Squadron (915th AEW&CG), flying from the AFB at Homestead, Florida, on Atlantic patrol duties. Aircraft used by this unit during the late 1970s included the EC-121T, a modified version of the EC-121D, for use as an 'Elint' electronic intelligence platform, incorporating a computerized AEW&C feedback system. The large dorsal radome and its equipment were omitted, while a cooling air intake was incorporated beneath the forward fuselage. The EC-121T was the heaviest of the Super Constellations, with a gross take-off weight of 152,000lb. At least 24 of these aircraft are believed to have been delivered. EC-121Ts were the last in the Warning Star series, some of them being deployed from Keflavik, Iceland, until 1978. A handful of EC-121Ts retained their large radomes and it was one of these, 54-2307 (cn. 4389), which had the distinction of being one of the last Warning Stars in service.

As a purely military transport vehicle, the Super Constellation served with the US Navy, USAF and the Air National Guard (ANG) in its C-121C and C-121G variants. One of the type's primary roles was as an air ambulance and casualty evacuation. A rather bizarre colour scheme was applied to

one US Navy BuAer No 135756 (cn.4323), which was attached to the US Navy Pacific Missile Range Squadron. It had a white upper fuselage and radome, orange/red (Day-Glo) front fuselage, tail unit and rear fuselage, and black rudders and nose cone. The remainder of the aircraft was in US Navy blue finish, with 'Navy' in white lettering on the fuselage sides and beneath the port wing. Another Navy Super Constellation BuAer 131642 (cn.4143), later went to the USAF as C-121G, number 54-4065, and was leased to the National Aeronautics and Space Administration (NASA) for use by the Goddard Space Flight Centre. This was in connection with the evaluation of tracking equipment concerning the Mercury, Gemini and Agena projects and flights. Based in Australia from May to October 1966, this C-121G later returned to the US and was initially registered as NASA20. It later became NASA420 before eventually transferring to the US Army for employment at a Maryland proving ground.

Super Constellations also flew with the Indian Air Force (IAF), in the form of nine L-1049 Super-G types acquired from Air India. Eight were for use in the maritime reconnaissance (MR) role and one was a military transport. The reconnaissance machines flew with No.6 (MR) Squadron of the IAF, but, despite their ability to fly long distance patrol duties, they could only provide limited information on the movement of surface ships. These IAF Super-Gs were controlled by the Indian Maritime Air Operations Directorate of 1971, which could also call in attack aircraft for interdiction duties.

The last military Constellations to remain in service, although they were not military variants, were those that saw service with the Indian Air Force. Pictured is L-1049G, which was delivered to Air India in July 1958 as VT-DJW Rani of Bijapura. Converted by Lockheed Air Service into a freighter in 1960, the aircraft joined the Indian Air Force on 2 April 1963 as BG-583. The aircraft was retired on 11 November 1983 with just 4½ flying hours left on the airframe.

RC-121D ON PATROL
(Info from Lockheed News Bureau – 1 March 1955)

FALMOUTH, Mass., March 1 – The U.S. Air Force will lift its radar warning network high above the Atlantic Ocean aboard Lockheed Super Constellation radar planes in a strategic move to 'buy time'. The first plane of the 551st Airborne Early Warning and Control Wing, which will begin patrol shortly, arrived at Otis AFB here at eleven this morning piloted by Colonel Oliver R. Cellini, Chicago, wing commander.

The Lockheed RC-121D was flown from McClellan AFB, Sacramento, California.

The remaining aircraft, flight crew and ground personnel of the 551st will begin arriving here in a few days to inaugurate round-the-clock sentinel duty off the East Coast.

Similar in appearance to Lockheed's familiar airlines Super Constellations, but with huge radar domes protruding from top, bottom and nose, the immense planes carry five and a half tons of radar and electronics gear hundreds of miles out over the Atlantic where their 30-man crews can 'see' for additional hundreds of miles any ship or aircraft approaching the North American continent.

If the 'bogey' - a blip on the radar scope - is unable to identify itself to the satisfaction of the patrol plane's crew, the control officer calls for fighter planes to come out and investigate, and, if necessary, destroy the intruder.

Described by engineers as 'the next best thing to a phone call from Moscow', the airborne early warning and control planes inaugurate a new phase of eastern air defence. Hitherto, early warning has been limited to the range of surface radar installations on the east coast. The 75-ton radar planes were put into Pacific Coast service earlier.

Otis at present bases two squadrons of Lockheed F-94C Starfires, part of the Eastern Air Defence Force. These swift fighters have been on continuous intercept duty guided by surface radar. They will continue their assignment teamed up with the new early warning aircraft.

'We are striving to buy time in the event of any possible attack by unfriendly forces,' Colonel Cellini explained. 'By pushing our warning network further out from the continental coastline, we gain precious minutes for defense.'

Dimensions of the RC-121s are basically those of the Super Constellation 123 foot wingspan, 116 foot overall length. Four 3250hp Wright turbo-compound engines produce speeds of approximately 300mph. Wingtip fuel tanks extend the range for as much as 24 hours of patrol.

Because of the extremely long endurance of early warning missions, special provisions have been made aboard for crew comfort. The cabin is sound-proofed and completely pressurized for 10,000ft altitude conditions at actual heights of 25,000ft. The temperature remains at 75 degrees despite such extremes as 60 below zero outside. Seats at observation posts and flight stations have been scientifically designed against fatigue. Bunks are installed for relief crews. The galley is designed to include grills for cooking hot meals, a refrigerator, and a sink with running water.

All medium and heavy maintenance work for the planes of the wing will be performed at New York by Lockheed Aircraft Service-International in the newest and most modern aircraft service base on the east coast.

Headquarters for all airborne early warning and control units in the Air Force is the 8th Air Division, located at McClellan AFB. The division, activated 1 May 1954, is under the command of Brigadier General Kenneth H. Gibson. Eastern Air Defence Force headquarters are at Newburgh, N. Y., under the command of Maj. Gen. Morris R. Nelson.

Originally ordered by the US Navy as R7V-1 (BuNo 131650), this Super Constellation was modified on the production line to become a special USAF VIP aircraft (L-1049B-35-97). Complete with rectangular windows rather than the oval, port-hole type, the aircraft left the factory as the sole VC-121E, serialled 53-7885, to serve as President Eisenhower's *Columbine III*. The aircraft continued to transport the president into the Kennedy administration until October 1962 when it was replaced by a Boeing VC-137C.

The aircraft had a wide range of specialist equipment, including a teletype, which could transmit and receive classified messages, a TV set and an air-to-ground telephone link. Every 1,000 hours, the aircraft was returned to Lockheed, completely stripped down and rebuilt almost like a new aircraft.

Following *Columbine III*'s retirement, the aircraft was allocated to the 89th Military Airlift Group at Andrews AFB, for further VIP duties until it was retired in the 1970s. Luckily, its significance was recognised, and the aircraft has been preserved at the Wright-Patterson AFB, Dayton, Ohio, since 1980.

USAF CONSTELLATION VARIANTS

C-121A, based on L-749; VC-121 A, VIP variant, ex-PC-121A; VC-121B with small passenger door instead of cargo door; C-121C, based on L-1049; VC-121C, VIP conversion; VC-121E, ex-R7V-1 modified into presidential aircraft; YC-121F (L-1249A), ex-R7V-2s with T-34 turboprops; C-121G, redesignated R7V-1s; TC-121G, AWAC trainer; VC-121G, VIP aircraft; RC-121C for USAF; JC-121C, avionics test bed; TC-121C, trainer; EC-121D, redesignated RC-121D; EC-121D, test bed for QRC-IFF; EC-121H, specialist equipment including Semi-Automatic Ground Environment (SAGE) for North American Air Defence Command (NORAD); EC-121J, mid-life electronic upgrade; EC-121M Rivet Top, ex-WV-Q/ EC-121K installed with cryptologic linguistics suite; EC-121Q, ECM upgrades for *Gold Digger* operations; EC-121R, ex-EC-121K and EC-121Ps modified in airborne relay stations for Air-Delivered Intrusion Devices (ADSID), which were dropped behind enemy lines; EC-121S, ex-C-121s for the Tactical Electronic Warfare Group, Pennsylvania ANG; EC-121T, ex-EC-121D and EC-121H converted for electronic reconnaissance duties.

Ordered for the US Navy as the R7V-1, it was immediately transferred to the USAF as the C-121-G-LO. This aircraft, 54-4070, belongs to the 133rd Air Transport Group of the West Virginia Air National Guard based at Shepherd Field, Martinsburg, West Virginia.

US NAVY CONSTELLATION VARIANTS

R7V-1, ex-R7O based on L-1049; R7V-1P, ex-R7V-1 installed with cameras for aerial survey of Antarctic; R7V-2, ex-R7V-1 based on L-1249A, fitted with YT-34-P-12B turboprops; C-121J, redesignated R7V-1; TC-121J, electronics test bed; NC-121J, ex-R7V-1/C-121J installed with airborne television and radio studios, transmitters and extendible antennas above and below the fuselage; VC-121J, VIP Blue Angels aircraft; WV-1, based on L-749A, originally designated PO-1W; EC-121K (WV-2) with APS-45 height-finding equipment in upper radome and APS-20B in lower radome, originally designated PO-2W; JC-121K, used by the US Army to observe and track test-firings of ground launched missiles; NC-121K, aka ENC-121K, specialist aircraft; YEC-121K, ex-NC-121K to test new service equipment; EC-121L (WV-2E), one aircraft fitted with rotating AN/APS-70 radar system; EC-121M (WV-2Q), modified WV-2 for gathering electronic intelligence; WC-121N (WV-3), weather variant modified from the WV-2; EC-121P, ex-EC-121K installed with upgraded submarine detection equipment; JEC-121P, three redesignated EC-121P for USAF; XW2V-1, a proposed USN development with T-56 turboprops, L-1649A wings and the capability to defend itself with Bomarc missiles.

Chapter 6

Every Corner of the Globe

F rom the early L-049 to the later L-1649s, the 'Connie' not only served at the sharp end on passenger carrying services with many of the world's major airlines but continued to provide a plethora of smaller and independent airlines all over the world for four decades.

The world's 'Connie' fleet

The following listing presents the country where the airline is based, the airline, the aircraft they operated, the number they operated (in brackets) and the time they served. This is not definitive and is designed to present a general overview of the colossal number of operators that operated the type from 1946 to 1985.

BOAC Lockheed C-69-5/L049 Constellation, G-AHEN *Baltimore*, which was delivered to the airline on 29 May 1946. BOAC was the first airline in Europe to operate the Constellation.

Algeria

Air Algerie (L-749 [two] and L-1049s, 1955–61).

Argentina

Aerolíneas Carreras (L-749A [one], July 1964–67); Aerotransportes Entre Ríos (AER) (L-0749A [one], L-1049G [one] and L-1049H [three], 1962–72); Aerovias Halcon SRL (L-1649 [one], leased in 1968); Trans Atlántica Argentina (L-1649A [four], 1960–5 Nov 1961); and Transcontinental S.A (L-1049H [two], Sept 1958–March 1960).

Australia

Qantas (L-749 [seven], L-1049C [four], L-1049E [six], L-1049G [three] and L-1049H [two], 1947–63).

Austria

Aero Transport Flugbetriebsgesellschaft (L-049 [two], L-749A [two], June 1961–64).

The first airline to order the new L-1049 Super Constellation was Eastern Air Lines, which ordered ten (later increased to 14) aircraft on 20 April 1950. Eastern's 'Super Connies' began commercial service on 7 December 1951. N6203C, an L-1049-53-67, was the first aircraft to be delivered and remained in Eastern Air Lines' service until 1968.

A rare glimpse of Argentinian AER (Aerotransportes Entre Ríos) L-749, LV-IGS, during a visit to Britain.

Barbados
Carib West (L-1049H [two], 1974–75).

Belgium
Sabena (L-1049 [two], leased in 1958).

Bolivia
Bolivian International Airways (L-1049H [one], leased April/May 1975); Trans Bolivian (L-749A [one], Jan 1968 [not operated by airline]); and Transportes Aeroes Benianos S.A. (TABSA) (L-1049H [two] and L-1049H [one], July 1968–May 1969).

Brazil
Panair do Brasil S.A. (L-049 and L-1049 [16 in total], 1946–65); Real Transportes Aéreos (L-1049H, 1958–61); and Varig (L-1049G [six] and L-1049H [four], 1955–67).

Burundi
Royal Air Burundi (L-049 [one], 1962–63).

Cambodia
Royal Air Cambodge (L-1049G [one], 1958–60).

Canada
Beaver Air Spray (L-749 [three], from April 1979); Canrelief Air (L-1049H [one], 1962); Conifair Aviation (L-749 [three] and C-121A [two], Jan 1980–85); Downair (L-1049H [one], Aug–30 Sept 1973); Eastern Provincial Airways (L-1049H, leased in 1968); Montreal Air Services (L-1049G [one] and L-1049H [one], June 1964–Aug 1965); Nordair (L-1049H, 1960s) and Trans Canada Airlines (TCA) (L-1049C [five], L-1049E [three], L-1049G [four] and L-1049H [two], 1954–63).

Ceylon
Air Ceylon (L-749A [four] and L1049G [six], all leased from 1956 to early 1960s).

Chile
Sociedad De Transportes Aeria LTDA (L-049 [one] and L-1049G [one], both leased between June 1957 and 1959).

Colombia
Avianca (L-749A [two], L-1049E [three] and L-1049G [one], 1951–68).

Cuba
Cubana de Aviación (L-049, L-1049, L-1049E [one] and L-1049G [three], c.1954–60s).

Panair do Brasil's L-049-46-26 Constellation, PP-CR, named *Bandeirante Domingos Barbosa Calhoun*. The aircraft remained with the airline until 3 March1962 when it was written off at Galeão Airport.

TCA introduced the Super Constellation into service in 1954 to replace the Canadair North Star on its transatlantic route, which extended to various locations in Western Europe. This TCA Super 'Connie' is at Düsseldorf.

Dominican Republic

Aeromar (L-1049H [one], leased 1977–79); Aerotours Dominicano (L-1049 [one], 1960s–78); Aerovías Quisqueyana* (L-049 [three] and L-749 [three], 1966–78); Argo S.A. (L-749 [one] and L-749A [one], April 1979–81); and Transporte Aereo Dominicano (L-049 [two] and L-749A [one], 1979–80).

*Last ever passenger flight in 1978.

France

Air France (L-049 [four], L-749 [nine], L-749A [ten], L-1049C [ten], L-1049G [14] and L-1649A [ten], 1947–68); Air Inter (L-749A [three] and L-1049G [one], April 1961–62); Catair (L-1049G [four], 1967-72); Compaigne Air Fret (L-1049G [four], 1968–76) and Societe Aeronautique Francoise D'Affretement (SAFA) (L-1049G [two], leased 1966–67).

Guatemala

Aviateca (L-1049H [one], leased in 1972).

Germany

Condor Flugdienst GmbH (L-1049G [two] and L-1649A [two], March 1960–62 and 1964–65) and Lufthansa (L-1049G [eight], L-1049H [two] and L-1649A [four], 1955–67).

Haiti
Air Haiti (L-749A [one], 1961).

India
Air India (L-749 [three], L-749A [four], (L-1049C [two], L-1049E [three] and L-1049G [five], 1948–62).

Iceland
Lofteidir (L-749A [one], 1960–June 1963).

Ireland
Aerlinte Eireann Teoranta (L-1049E [one], L-1049G [one] and L-1049H [two], leased from April 1958–60).

Israel
El Al (C-69 [three], L-049** [three], May 1951–late 1950s)

**Converted to L-149 standard with L-649 interiors.

Ivory Coast
Air Afrique (L-649 [one] and L-1649A [five], leased from Air France between 1961 and 1963).

Japan
Japan Airlines (L-1649 [one], leased 1960).

Kenya
Britair East Africa (L-049 [one], 1964–65).

Luxembourg
Interocean Airways (L-749A [one], June–Oct 1964); Luxair (L-1649A, joint operation with Trek Airways from April 1964–69) and Nittler Air Transport International (L-1649A [one], Aug 1969–May 1970).

Madagascar
Air Madagascar (L-1049G [one], leased 1965).

Malaysia
Malaysia Airways (L-1049s leased from Qantas, 1960).

Mexico
Aeronaves de México (L-049 [two] and L-049A, 1957–60) and Aerovias Guest S.A. (L-749 [four], L-749A [three] and L-1049G [three], 1947–61).

Morocco
Royal Air Maroc (L-749 [four], 1960s).

Netherlands
KLM (L-049 [six], L-749 [13], L-749A [seven], L-1049C [nine], L-1049E [four], L-1049G [six] and L-1049H [three], 1946–66).

Pakistan

Pakistan International Airlines (L-1049C [three] and L-1049H [two], 1954–69).

Panama

Aero Fletes Internacionales S.A. (L-1049H [one], 1970–72); Aerovias Paname (L-1049G [two], 1970–72) and Rutas Aereo de Panamenas S.A. (L-1049G [two], 1968–early 1970s).

Paraguay

Lloyd Aéreo Paraguayo S.A. (L-049 [one], Dec 1963–Jan 1964)

Peru

Lineas Aereas Nacionalis S.A. (L-749A [six], 1964–66); Peru International/COPISA (L-749A [five], Feb 1966–Dec 1969); Rutas Internacionales Peruanas S.A. (L-649A [one], Sept 1966–May 1968) and Trans-Peruana (L-749A [four], Oct 1967–70).

Portugal

Transportes Aéreos Portugueses (TAP) (L-1049G [six], 1953–67).

HK-163 was the second L-749A-79-74 Constellation to enter service with the Columbian airline Avianca.

Republic of China (Taiwan)
China Airlines (L-1049H [one], 1966–70).

Republic of Korea
Korean National Airlines (L-749A [one] and L-1049H [two, leased], 1959–67).

Rhodesia
Afro-Continental Airways (L-1049G [one], 1970–74) and Air Trans-Africa (L-1049G [one], 1967–70).

Senegal
Government of Senegal (L-749A [one], 1960s–70s).

South Africa
South African Airways (L-749A [four], 1950-64) and Trek Airways (L-749A [two], leased from South African Airways between 1961 and 1963, followed by a co-operative with Slick from 1964).

Ex-USAAF C-69-1, 43-10315, served with Intercontinental Airways as N90827 before it was sold to El Al in 1951 and re-registered as 4X-AKB. El Al operated three C-69/L-049s during the 1950s.

Spain
Aviaco (L-1049G, leased 1963–65); Inter-City Airways (L-1049H [one], 1958) and Iberia (L-1049E [three] and L-1049G [two], 1954–66).

Thailand
Thai Airways (L-1049G [three], Oct 1957–58).

Tunisia
Tunis Air (L-749A [one] and L-1049G [one], 1961).

United Kingdom
ACE Freighters (L-749A [eight], March 1964–66); BOAC (C-69/L-049 [eight], L-749s [18], L-1049D [three] and L-1049E [one], 1946–55); Britannia Airways (L-049, 1962–64); Euravia (L-049 [five], L-749 [four], May 1962–65); Falcon Airways (L-049 [three], 1961); Lanzair (L-749 [two] and L-1049G [one], Nov 1973–76); Skyways of London (L-749A [four], 1969); and Trans European Aviation (L-049 [three], 1961–62).

One of the largest 'Connie' fleets in Europe was operated by the Dutch airline, KLM, between 1946 and 1966. The biggest single order that was placed was for nine L-1049C-55 Super Constellations, the first of which was PH-TFR, pictured in the US during a pre-delivery air test.

United States (Including Independents)

Admiral Airways (L-749A [five] and L-1049 [one], June 1961–Oct 1962); Aeroborne Enterprises (L-1649A [three], 1980); Aerolessors (L-1049H [three], leased July 1966–70); Aero Sacasa (L-049 [one] and L-1049 [one], Nov 1976 and April 1979 [neither flown]); Air America (L-1049H [one], July 1963–March 1969); Air Cargo Support (L-1049G [one] and L-1049H [three], Sept 1973–82); Aircraft Specialties/Globe Air (L-749A [two], L-1049 [one], L-1049G [one] and L-1049H [four], Sept 1972–81); Air Fleets (L-1049 [one] and L-1049G [one], Jan 1970–71); Airlift International (L-1049H [seven], June 1966–67); Air Mid East (L-1049H [one], July 1968); Alaska Airlines (L-1649A [two], 1962–68); American Flyers Airlines (L-049 [four] and L-1049G [four], April 1960–68); American Overseas Airlines (L-049 [seven], 1946–50 [merged with Pan Am]); ASA International (L-049 [three], leased 1962–53); Associated Air Transport (L-749A [four], 1961–62); Aviation Corporation of America (L-1049 [11] and L-1049 [two], 1968–69); Bal Trade (L-1049H [two], 1968–70); Belezean Airlines (L-049 [one], March 1967–June 1969); Blue Bell (L-1049H [two], 1969–73); Braniff International Airways (L-049 [two], 1955–59); Burns Aviation (L-1649 [two], 1976); California Central Airlines (L-049 [one], 1947–54); California Hawaiian Airlines (L-049 [one], L-749A [four] and L-1049 [three], 1952–Oct 1953 and Dec 1960–62); Capital Airlines (L-049 [12] and L-749 [seven], 1950–60); Capitol Airways (L-049A [four], L-749A [one], L-1049E [five], L-1049G [two] and L-1049H [11], 1957–68); Carib Airways (L-749A [one], 1979); Central American Airlines (L-749A, L-1049H, 1960s–70s); Central American Airways Flying Service (L-749A [one] and L-1049H [one], Oct 1973–Oct 1978); Chicago and Southern Air Lines (L-649A [six], 1950–53 [merged with Delta]); Christler Flying Service (C-121A [five], July 1970–April 1979); CJS Aircargo (L-749A [one] and L-1649A [one], Dec 1970–72); Coastal Air Lines (L-1049 [four], 1958–62); Colonial Airlines (L-749As, leased 1954–56); Dellair (L-049 [three], 1964); Delta Air Lines (L-049 [four] and L-649A [six], 1953–58); Eastern Air Lines (L-749 [nine], L-1049C [16] and L-1049G [10 (76 operated in total)], 1951–68); Edde Airlines (L-049 [two] Sept 1962–66); FandB Livestock (L-1049H [one], 1971–May 1976); Federal Aviation Administration (L-1649 [one] and WV-1 [two], 1964–early 1970s); Florida State Tours (L-1049 [six], June 1963–64); Flying Tiger Line (L-1049H [21], 1957–67); Flying W Airways (L-1649A [two] and L-1049H [two], Nov 1968 and 1969–71); Futura Airlines (L-049 [two] 1962); General Airways (L-1049 [one], leased Nov 1960); Great Lakes Airlines

(L-749A [eight], 1961–Jan 1962); Hawthorne Nevada Airlines (L-049 [one], Jun 1968–Sept 1969); The Hughes Tool Co. (L-049 [four], L-749A [one], L-1049G [one] and L-1649A [one], 1946–60); Imperial Airlines (L-049 [three], 1960–61); Intercontinental Airways (L-1049E, 1960s); Intercontinental U.S. (L-1049H [two], May 1962–March 1964); Interior Airways (L-1049H [four], leased 1966 and 1969); International Caribbean Corp. (L-049 [one], Aug/Sept 1965); Lake Havasu City Airlines (L-049 [five], Feb 1964–70); Las Vegas Hacienda Hotel (L-049 [five] and L-749 [one], Aug 1959–March 1962); Lloyd Airlines (L-049 [two], 1961); Magic City Airways (L-049 [two], Jan 1962–65); Mercury General American Corp. (L-1049H [five], March 1966–67); Miami Airlines (L-749A [four], leased 1960–61); Midair (L-1049G [one] and L-1049H [six], April 1973); Modern Air Transport (L-049 [five], L-749A [one] and L-1049 [two], Aug 1962–65); Moral Rearmament Corp. (L-1649A [one], June 1965–66); NASA (C-121A [one], C-121G [two] and WV-2 [one], 1965–early 1970s); National Airlines (L-1049H [four], 1957–early 1960s); North Slope Supply Co. (L-1049H [seven], 1969); Northwest Orient Airlines (L-1049G [four], 1955–57); Pacific Air Transport (L-049 [one] and L-749A [one], March 1961–62); Pacific Northern Airlines (L-749 [11], 1967–70s); Pan American World Airways (L-049 [29], L-749 [four] and L-1049 [one], 1946–57); Paradise Airlines (L-049, 1960s); Paramount Airlines (L-749A [three] and L-1049 [one], March 1961–62); Passaat Airlines (L-1049 [one] and L-1649 [one], 1965–67); Produce Custom Air Freight (L-049 [one], July 1972–March 1974); Prudhoe Bay Oil Distributing Co. (L-1649 [three], Dec 1968–69); Raitron Inc. (L-1049A [one], June 1970–Sept 1973); Resort Airlines (L-1049H [two], 1957–59); Seaboard and Western Airlines (L-1049D [four], L-1049E [one], L-1049G [one] and L-1049H [five], 1950s–61); Seaboard World Airlines (L-1049D [four], L-1049E [one], L-1049H [five] and L-1049G [one], 1954–62); Sky Truck International (L-1049H [two], Sept 1972–75); Slick Airways (L-1049H [ten], 1959–65); South Pacific Airlines (L-1049 [two], March 1962–64); S. S. and T. Aerial Contracting (L-049 [one], Dec 1972–77); Standard Airways (L-049 [three], L-749A [five], L-1049 [one], L-1049G [three] and L-1049H [one], 1962–Feb 1964); Starflite (L-1649A [one], 1965–66); Transair Cargo (L-1049H [one], 1972–Nov 1977); Trans American Leasing (L-1049 [one] and L-1649A [three], May 1968–73); Trans California Airlines (L-749A [six], July 1963–64); Trans International Airlines (L-049 [one], L-749A [one], L-1049E [one], L-1049G [three] and L-1049H [nine], Dec 1960–67); Transocean Airlines (L-1049H [two] and L-749A [five], July 1957–July 1960); Trans World Airlines (see Chapter 4); Twentieth Century Airlines (L-1049G [six], 1959–60); Unlimited Leasing (L-749A [one], Nov 1970–Jan 1979); U.S. Airlines (L-049 [one], 1951–52); United States Airways (L-1049, 1960s); Vortex (L-1049H [three], Oct 1971–April 1973); Western Airlines (L-749, 1960s); Wien Air Alaska (L-749, 1960s); Wien Air Inc. (L-1649 [two], June 1973–Nov 1975); Willair International (L-1649A [two], Aug 1968–70); World Airways (L-1049H [seven] and L-1649A [four], leased 1961–64) and World Wide Airlines (L-049 [four], L-749A [two] and L-1049 [two], July 1960–Oct 1962).

Uruguay
Aerolíneas Uruguayas (L-749A [one], 1968); Compañía Aeronáutica Uruguaya S.A. (CAUSA) (L-749 [three] and L-1049H [one], 1962–May 1967) and Rymar (L-049 [one], June–Sept 1965).

Venezuela
LEBCA (L-1049H [three], 1965–66); Linea Aeropostal Venezolana (LAV) (L-049 [two], L-749 [two], L-1049E [two] and L-1049G [seven], 1947–62) and Venezolana Internacional de Aviacion S.A. (L-1049G [three], April–Dec 1961).

Vietnam
Air Vietnam (L-749s and L-1049s, leased in 1957).

One of eight L-749As to serve with ACE Freighters was G-ALAL, which served first with BOAC, and was named *Banbury*.

Delta's N88868 pictured at Atlanta on 1 January 1956 was originally built as an L-049 but was later upgraded to L-149 standard complete with long-range tanks in the outer wing sections. Delta sold off its remaining 'Connie' fleet in 1960 and N8868, after having a number of owners, was scrapped at Galveston in 1974.

Lockheed L-049 Constellation, N88837 Clipper Challenge was delivered to Pan Am on 12 January 1946. Later converted to L-149 specifications, on 11 January 1954 the aircraft was sold to Panair do Brasil and registered as PP-PDG *Joao Amaro Maciel Parente*. Withdrawn from use in 1965, the 'Connie' was purchased by ASL Arruda Industria on 28 April 1969 but was lost on 29 May 1972, when it crashed in the jungle of northern Brazil after all four engines failed.

'CONNIE' SPECIFICATIONS

Crunching the technical numbers for eight civilian Constellation variants and six military variants.
 * Radar installed
** Wing tip tanks installed

L-049, 649 and 749A

Engines	(049) Four 2,200hp Wright R-3350-745C18BA-1; (649) Four 2,500hp Wright R-3350-749C18BD; (749) Four 2,500hp Wright R-3350-749C18BD-1
Span	123ft
Length	(049 and 649) 95ft 3in; (749A) 97ft 4in*
Height	(049 and 649) 23ft 8in; (749A) 22ft 5in
Wing area	1,650sq ft
Cabin length	64ft 9in
Cabin height	10ft 8.6in
Empty weight	(049) 49,392lb; (649) 55,000lb; (749A) 55,590lb
Max take-off weight	(049) 86,250lb; (649) 94,000lb; (749A) 107,000lb
Max landing weight	(049) 75,000lb; (649) 84,500lb; (749A) 89,500lb
Max payload	(049) 18,423lb; (649 and 749A) 20,276lb
Max speed	(049) 339mph; (649) 352mph; (749A) 345mph
Cruising speed	(049) 313mph; (649) 327mph
Take-off distance	(C) 5,400ft
Range (maximum fuel)	(049 and 649) 3,995 miles; (749A) 4,845 miles
Range (max payload)	(049) 2,290 miles; (749A) 2,600 miles
Ceiling	(049) 25,300ft; (649) 25,700ft; (749A) 24,100ft
Crew and passengers	6–8 and 60–8, respectively.

L-1049, 1049C/G and H

Engines	(1049C) Four 3,250hp Wright R-3350 972-TC-18DA-1; (G) Four 3,400hp Wright R-3350-972TC-18DA-3
Span	(1049 and C) 123ft; (G and H) 123ft 5in**
Length	(1049 and C) 113ft 7in; (G and H) 116ft 2in*
Height	24ft 9.4in
Wing area	(G) 1,654sq ft
Cabin length	83ft 2in
Cabin height	10ft 8.6in
Empty weight	(1049) 69,000lb; (C) 70,083lb; (G) 73,016lb; (H) 69,326lb
Max take-off weight	(1049) 120,000lb; (C) 133,000lb; (G and H) 137,500lb
Max landing weight	(1049) 101,500lb; (C) 110,000lb; (G and H) 113,000lb
Max payload	(1049) 19,335lb; (C) 26,400lb; (G) 24,293lb; (H) 40,203lb
Max speed	(C) 374mph; (G and H) 366mph
Cruising speed	(C) 314mph; (G and H) 311mph
Take-off distance	(C) 5,780ft
Range (maximum fuel)	(C) 4,760 miles; (G) 4,815 miles; (H) 3,463 miles
Range (max payload)	(1049) 2,610 miles; (C) 2,880 miles; (G) 4,165 miles; (H) 1,890 miles
Ceiling	(1049) 25,700ft; (C) 23,200ft; (G and H) 22,800ft
Crew and Passengers	(1049C) 4 and 47–106, respectively.

L-1649A

Engines	Four 3,400hp Wright R-3350 988 TC18-EA-2
Span	150ft

Length	116ft 2in*
Height	23ft 4.8in
Wing area	1,850sq ft
Cabin length	83ft 2in
Cabin height	10ft 8.6in
Empty weight	85,262lb
Max take-off weight	156,000lb
Max landing weight	123,000lb
Max payload	24,355lb
Max speed	376mph
Cruising speed	342mph
Range (maximum fuel)	6,885 miles
Range (max payload)	5,410 miles
Ceiling	23,700ft
Crew and Passengers	4 and 99, respectively.

Military variants
C-69, C-121A, R7V-1, C-121C and RC-121D/WV-2

Engines	(C-69) Four 2,200hp Wright R-3350-35; (C-121A) Four 2,500hp Wright R-3350-75; (R7V-1) Four 3,250hp Wright R-3350-34; (RC-121D/WV-2) Four 3,400hp Wright R-3350-34 Turbo-Compound
Span	123ft
Length	(C-69 and C-121A) 95ft 3in; (all others) 116ft 2in
Height	(C-121A and R7V-1) 23ft 9in; (all others) 27ft
Wing area	1,650sq ft
Empty weight	(C-69) 50,000lb; (C-121A) 61,324lb; (R7V-1) 70,000lb; (C-121C) 72,815lb; (RC-121D/WV-2) 80,611lb
Max take-off weight	(C-69) 72,000lb; (C-121A) 100,520lb; (R7V-1) 135,400lb; (C-121C) 137,500lb; (RC-121D/WV-2) 143,600lb
Max speed	(C-69) 347mph at 20,000ft; (C-121A) 334mph; (R7V-1 and C-121C) 368mph; (RC-121D/WV-2) 321mph
Cruising speed	(C-69) 275mph; (C-121A) 324mph; (R7V-1 and C-121C) 355mph; (RC-121D/WV-2) 301mph
Climb rate	(C-69) 1,620ft/min
Combat radius	1,150 miles
Ceiling	(C-121A) 24,400ft; (R7V-1 and C-121C) 22,300ft; (RC-121D/WV-2) 20,600ft
Crew	(C-121A) 5 crew and 44 passengers; (R7V-1) 4 crew and 97–107 passengers; (WV-2) 6 flight crew and 11–25 radar operators.

TWA's L-749 Constellation, *Star of West Virginia*, taxiing for take-off at New York International Airport on 8 August 1956.

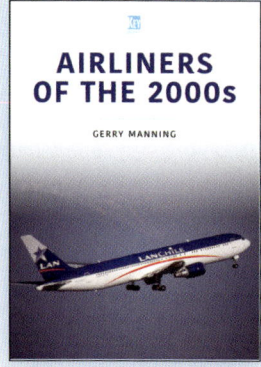
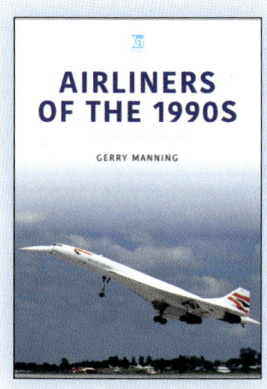
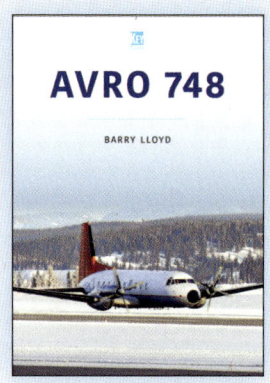
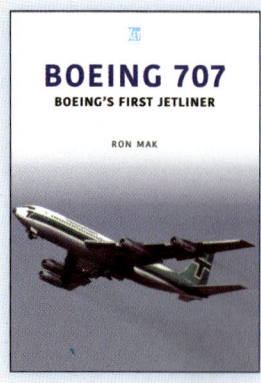